The UN and Development

UNITED NATIONS INTELLECTUAL HISTORY PROJECT

THE
UN AND
DEVELOPMENT
FROM AID TO COOPERATION

OLAV STOKKE

Indiana University Press
Bloomington and Indianapolis

This book is a publication of

Indiana University Press
601 North Morton Street
Bloomington, IN 47404-3797 USA

www.iupress.indiana.edu

Telephone orders	800-842-6796
Fax orders	812-855-7931
Orders by e-mail	iuporder@indiana.edu

⊗ The paper used in this publication meets the minimum requirements of the American
National Standard for Information Sciences—Permanence of Paper for Printed Library
Materials, ANSI Z39.48-1992.

Manufactured in the United States of America

Library of Congress Cataloging-in-Publication Data

Stokke, Olav, date
    The UN and development : from aid to cooperation / Olav Stokke.
      p. cm. — (United Nations intellectual history project)
    Includes bibliographical references and index.
    ISBN 978-0-253-35314-6 (cloth : alk. paper) —
    ISBN 978-0-253-22081-3 (pbk. : alk. paper)
    1. United Nations—Economic assistance. 2. United Nations—Technical
assistance. I. Title.
    JZ4972.S76   2009
    338.91—dc22
                                   2009001071

1 2 3 4 5   14 13 12 11 10 09

CONTENTS

BOXES AND TABLES

BOXES

TABLES

FOREWORD

Surprisingly, no comprehensive history exists of the United Nations family of organizations. True, in the last few years, histories of the UN Development Programme[1] and the World Food Programme[2] have been completed, to add to the two histories of UNICEF (UN Children's Fund) produced in the 1980s and 1990s.[3] And there is a new series of short and readable books about "global institutions" that is being edited by one of us.[4] Moreover, the UN Educational, Scientific and Cultural Organization, the World Health Organization, the UN Conference on Trade and Development, and the International Labour Organization are preparing internal volumes that bring together different perspectives about the evolution of these organizations.

But these are still patchy and incomplete, all the more so because more than six decades have passed since the founding of the current generation of international organizations. More serious and complete accounts of UN activities and contributions should be required of all intergovernmental organizations, along with enhanced efforts to organize their archives so that independent researchers can document and analyze their efforts, achievements, and shortcomings. These are essential parts of compiling the record of global governance during the last half of the twentieth century and the beginning of the current millennium.

Faced with such major omissions—which have substantial implications for the academic and policy literatures—we decided to undertake the task of writing an *intellectual* history—that is, a history of the ideas launched or nurtured by the United Nations. Observers should not be put off by what may strike them as a puffed-up billing. The working assumption behind our undertaking is straightforward: ideas and concepts are a main driving force in human progress, and they arguably have been one of the most important contributions of the world organization. As the various volumes of our project have been completed, our early assumptions about the importance of ideas among the UN's various contributions have been confirmed by the actual archival and personal records.

The United Nations Intellectual History Project (UNIHP) was launched in 1999 as an independent research effort based at the Ralph Bunche Institute for International Studies at The Graduate Center of The City University of New York. We are extremely grateful for the enthusiastic backing from the seventh Secretary-General, Kofi Annan, and other staff, as well as from scholars and analysts and governments. We are also extremely appreciative of the generosity and understanding of the governments of the Netherlands, the United Kingdom, Sweden, Canada, Norway, Switzerland, Finland, and the Republic and Canton of Geneva, as well as of the Ford, Rockefeller, and MacArthur Foundations; the Carnegie Corporation of New York; and the UN Foundation. This support ensures total intellectual and financial independence. Details of this and other aspects of the project can be found at: www.unhistory.org.

The work of the UN can be divided into two broad categories: economic and social development, on the one hand, and peace and security, on the other. UNIHP is committed to produce fifteen volumes on major themes, mainly in the first arena, but we also cover the second. These volumes are being published by Indiana University Press. Oxford University Press has published a sixteenth and related volume, *The Oxford Handbook on the United Nations*.[5]

In addition, UNIHP has completed an oral history collection of some seventy-nine lengthy interviews of persons who have played major roles in launching and nurturing UN ideas—and sometimes in hindering them! Extracts from these interviews were published in 2005 as *UN Voices: The Struggle for Development and Social Justice*. Authors of the project's various volumes, including this one, have drawn on these interviews to highlight substantive points made in the complete texts. Full transcripts of the oral histories with user-friendly indices are now available on CD-ROM (essentially a searchable electronic book) to facilitate work by researchers and other interested persons worldwide.[6]

There is no single way to organize research, and certainly not for such an ambitious project as this one. We have structured this historical effort by topics—ranging from trade and finance to human rights, from transnational corporations to development assistance, from regional perspectives to sustainability. We have commissioned world-class experts for each topic, and the argument in all of the volumes is the responsibility of the authors whose names appear on the covers. All have been given freedom and responsibility to organize their own digging, analyses, and presentations. Guidance from us as the project directors as well as from peer review groups has helped ensure accuracy and fairness in depicting where the ideas came from, how they were developed and disseminated within the UN system, and what happened with them. We are hoping that future analyses will build upon our series, and indeed go well beyond. Our intellectual history project is the first, not the last, installment in depicting the history of the UN's contributions to ideas. We trust that these publications will be of help to the eighth Secretary-General, Ban Ki-moon, and his successors.

The present volume, the twelfth in the series, is about international development cooperation. The author of *The UN and Development: From Aid to Cooperation* is Olav Stokke, who is based at the Norwegian Institute of International Affairs, where previously he was research director, deputy director, and acting director. He is also the founder and long-time editor of the journal *Forum for Development Studies*. He is a well-known specialist on European development assistance and cooperation. The present study is his first foray into global development assistance through the United Nations. We are happy to note that he has applied the same precision and creativity here as in his seminal studies about the European experience. He has produced a fascinating and deeply researched study using innumerable primary sources that does the UNIHP series pride.

The story starts with a search for the antecedents of international development assistance such as the long-standing traditions of humanitarian relief, international solidarity, missionary outreach, and human rights. But clearly the colonial tradition was the most powerful pre-aid influence, at least for the former colonial powers. Development assistance, therefore, did not fall from a blue sky, although it got defined and redefined after World War II. In terms of ideas, the focus of development assistance during the 1940s and 1950s was on economic growth, how to start it, and how to maintain it. Underdeveloped countries, as they were then called, were assumed to have low savings rates and a need for high rates of investment. This gap (which was supposed to be temporary) between national savings and investment needs could only be bridged by an inflow of *international* savings. The rationale for development aid, as it was then called, was therefore clear and simple. But over time the priorities of development theory shifted, from filling the savings gap to alleviating poverty, which involved a range of more complex issues—employment, income distribution, population, gender, human resources, and so forth.

Development aid followed these priorities and thus became the repository of the accumulated ideas of development theory of the last six decades. In the multifarious layers and branches of the tree of development aid, one can discover not only its age but the successive priorities of development theory, reflecting the "wisdom of the day." Development aid was supposed to be temporary; but through its forward movement (moving from one priority to the next without solving the preceding one), it has turned into a permanent feature of international economic and financial relations.

In this volume, one can see this evolution reflected—almost day by day—in the development assistance of the United Nations: from the Expanded Programme of Technical Assistance, the aborted attempt to create a Special UN Fund for Economic Development, the successive development decades (initiated by U.S. president John F. Kennedy in 1961), the creation of the United Nations Development Programme and the World Food Programme, to the activities of the UN specialized agencies and funds, such as the World Health Organization and UNICEF.

Olav Stokke underlines the revival of the UN economic and social activities after the "lost decade" of the 1980s with the Human Development Reports and approach and the launching of the Millennium Development Goals during the 1990s. The UN, initially on the defensive, stood firm to defend a broader concept of development, integrating economic and social development, human rights, and human security.

The question now is whether this will be enough to face the situation as we approach the second decade of the twenty-first century with a rapidly changing world. More and more countries of the South no longer have any need for development assistance. They can find the capital they need on international markets without having to jump through all kinds of conditionality loops. Countries like China are now giving development assistance themselves, albeit often linked to access to raw materials. International and national development assistance will have to increasingly concentrate on the least-developed countries and the planet's poorest one billion people.[7] And the United Nations must take the lead.

This poses the problem of the relation between the UN and international financial institutions, including the World Bank, the International Monetary Fund, the World Trade Organization, and the regional development banks. These international financial institutions are losing steam since their most important clients, such as China, India, and Brazil, need them less and less. However, these countries have an interest in working more closely with the UN to assist the bottom billion. This is also needed because, as this volume and previous ones in the UNIHP series indicate, the UN has proven to be right more frequently than the international financial institutions when it comes to development theory and practice.[8]

The present volume on international development assistance—past, present, and future—presents a unique picture of the UN in action in a crucial field for the future of an important part of the world population. It illustrates clearly how perfectly obvious objectives can be stimulated and frequently hindered by powerful member states of the UN. Or, to put it in terms we have used in this series, how the first UN (of governments) can stimulate or hinder ideas put forward by the second UN (of international secretariats) and how the third UN (of nongovernmental organizations and consultants) can come to the rescue or not.[9]

This book will interest multiple audiences: from the proverbial person in the street to the specialized researcher who wants to know what exactly happened in any given time period with respect to development aid initiatives within the United Nations. Our friend and colleague Olav Stokke has done a remarkable job of weaving together this complex story. We could not have found a better collaborator for what may be the most complicated and dense of our stories.

We are convinced that the UN story in general deserves to be better documented if it is to be better understood and appreciated. As Secretary-General Kofi Annan wrote in the foreword to the first publication in this book series, *Ahead of the Curve? UN Ideas and Global Challenges:* "With the publication of this first volume in the United Nations Intellectual History Project, a significant lacuna in twentieth-century scholarship and international relations begins to be filled."[10] The present volume is another important step in closing this gap in the historical record.

We hope that readers will feel engaged, confronted, and perhaps provoked by this account, at once a journey through both time and ideas. As always, we welcome comments from our readers.

Louis Emmerij
Richard Jolly
Thomas G. Weiss
New York, January 2009

PREFACE AND ACKNOWLEDGMENTS

The promotion of international peace and security and the promotion of social and economic development—traditionally the two main pillars of the United Nations system—are closely interlinked. Emerging in the wake of World War II, the UN's primary objective was to secure peace and build security. However, creating justice and contributing to economic and social development were also central to the UN project from the very beginning. Already in the late 1940s, the challenge of creating economic and social development in the "underdeveloped" world came to the fore and became increasingly important during the next two decades. This development took place at a time when the world organization was becoming more truly global: new independent states more than doubled the original membership. As a result, political independence, human rights and justice, and economic and social development ascended on the world body's agenda. On the other hand, the Cold War made the world insecure and triggered a resource-demanding arms race between the blocs, which in turn underscored the link between peace and development.

This work on the United Nations and international development cooperation is part of the United Nations Intellectual History Project. It follows that the prime focus will be on the development of ideas—how the UN system itself has generated ideas of development and development assistance and how it has captured, transformed, and modified ideas generated elsewhere.

Ideas are forerunners of action—they may inspire action. This volume devotes considerable space to the UN system's first major efforts in this field, the Expanded Programme of Technical Assistance and the United Nations Special Fund, which set the stage and circumscribed the space. That also explains why priority is given to exploring developments during the formative years, involving, in the first place, the UN's strategies for the first and second development decades and the first fifteen years of the United Nations Development Programme (UNDP). The emergence and development of the World Food Programme (WFP) also merit special attention because the WFP originated from a different rationale. The full histories of these institutions will not be related here, as they have been chronicled by others.[1] The focus in this volume is on those parts of their history that are particularly relevant to this project.

In an environment of the kind studied here, ideas are usually generated and adjusted within groups composed of experts, senior officials and bureaucrats, representatives of governments, and heads of administrative units (such as the UN Secretary-General or the administrator of the UNDP), or by intergovernmental bodies. Such ideas, formulated as recommendations, are then filtered through administrative (in secretariats) and political (in intergovernmental bodies) processes before they eventually become institutionalized in the form of norms, objectives, procedures, and institutions. At times, however, individuals privileged by extraordinary talent or power—or both—may turn the tide. A few examples are given of such individuals who have managed to make a difference within the UN system in the policy field of development.

The history will be told in the language of these participants. The setting is usually that of committees composed of prominent international civil servants, experienced diplomats, and experts who meet to prepare a common ground for a specific or general problem where positions are divergent. The language is often bureaucratic, detailed, balanced, and guarded. It is the language used in reports, resolutions, and statements that constitute the original sources used in this study. Robert Jackson referred to this language as "UN-ese" and took pains to avoid it in his report, striving instead for a plain, clear language that would not admit more than one interpretation.[2] The decision to adhere to this type of language has its strengths as well as its obvious weaknesses.

The history of the United Nations and international development assistance, how the world body generated ideas within this policy field and how such ideas have been implemented can be told in many different ways. It is, for instance, possible to take a bird's-eye view of developments and focus on overall ideas and large achievements, using statistical evidence as an important tool. It would also be possible to relate the history from a smaller perspective, although this would be more difficult since so many histories would necessarily have to be left out. Whatever the perspective, only a small part of a rich reality can be included.

This effort to tell the story has been undertaken by a political scientist, not by a historian, with the perspective and toolbox of that craftsmanship. Perspectives and toolboxes will vary with trades. No one author will be able to tell the full history, if indeed any such thing exists. As a political scientist oriented toward international relations, I am a captive of perspectives related to that trade. The focus will be on the institutionalization of development assistance within the UN system in terms of stated aspirations, major objectives, norms guiding implementation, the institutional setup, and ways and means of providing development assistance. I also look at the power aspects involved, including identification of the major actors, aid providers, and recipients.

During the long process of researching and writing this book, I have received invaluable help from many people and institutions. Being an "outsider" to the UN system—for years, my research has focused on the development cooperation of European donors—I feel honored at having been invited to take on this task. I am grateful to UNIHP's co-directors for the opportunity to look systematically into the policy and performance of the UN system within this policy field. I am also indebted to these co-directors—Louis Emmerij, Richard Jolly, and Thomas G. Weiss—for their valuable help throughout the process. They have provided encouragement and intellectual stimulus, generously shared their rich insights and networks with me, and given detailed comments on earlier drafts, as has Dame Margaret Anstee. I am particularly indebted to Louis Emmerij, the "guardian angel" of this volume—a role he has lived up to in more ways than one, particularly with sound editorial advice.

This project has been situated within the extended UNIHP family. The first outline was presented in mid-2000 to a meeting in Geneva consisting of members of the International Advisory Council and authors of related volumes in the UNIHP book series. A midterm review took place in Uppsala in June 2003, hosted by the Dag Hammarskjöld Foundation. I am grateful to participants at these meetings, in particular Yves Berthelot, Dame Margaret, and Leelanada de Silva, and to participants at a similar review held in December 2005, hosted by the Norwegian Institute of International Affairs (NUPI).

The project has all along been based at NUPI in Oslo as an integral part of its research program. It has been funded in part by the Research Council of Norway as part of its program The Multilateral System in the Field of Development. The project outline and some chapter drafts have benefited from the scrutiny of workshops organized by that program. I am grateful for valuable advice and comments by participants, in particular to Astrid Surkhe and Henrik Secher-Marcussen. It is with pleasure and deep appreciation that I acknowledge the research grant from the Research Council of Norway and the support provided by NUPI, which have made this project possible.

It would hardly have been possible for me to write this volume without the many years of research cooperation within the European Association of Development Research and Training Institutes, where I had the privilege of serving as the convener of the working group on aid policy and performance (1979–2002). I am deeply indebted to many colleagues and friends within this setting who have generously shared their insights about and experiences with development and development cooperation in general, the policies and performances of European governments in particular, and within more specific policy areas involving development cooperation as well.[3] Particularly warm thanks go to Edward J. Clay for his valuable comments on earlier versions of the two chapters on food aid (the WFP) included in this volume.

I am grateful and indebted to those mentioned above and to many more left unmentioned—colleagues and friends, including colleagues at NUPI. It goes without saying that I am the only one responsible for the analyses as well as for the accounts given—including any misjudgments, misrepresentations, and omissions.

During these many years, I have enjoyed the hospitality and services of the Norwegian Nobel Institute, depository library for United Nations documents in Norway. Its chief librarian, Anne Kjelling, has been of invaluable help. I would not have managed without her assistance, for which I am deeply grateful. This applies also to the librarians at NUPI, Dagfrid Hermansen, Tore Gustavsson, and Hazel Henriksen—always helpful, also in fending off overdue notices from their colleagues in other libraries. During all these years, Liv Høivik has been helpful in putting tables in order over and again. Warm thanks also go to Susan Høivik for language revision—removing language frivolities and unorthodoxies and making the language simple—a norm strived for but not always easily achieved. I am also grateful to Danielle Zach Kalbacher of The City University of New York's Graduate Center, who in the concluding phase of the project put the manuscript in style and order.

ABBREVIATIONS

ACC	Administrative Committee on Coordination
CCA	Common Country Assessment
CFA	Committee on Food Aid Policies and Programmes
CMEA	Council for Mutual Economic Assistance
DAC	Development Assistance Committee
DAG	Development Assistance Group
DD1	First United Nations Development Decade
DD2	Second United Nations Development Decade
DD3	Third United Nations Development Decade
DD4	Fourth United Nations Development Decade
DIEC	development and international economic cooperation
EADI	European Association of Development Research and Training Institutes
ECLA	Economic Commission for Latin America
ECOSOC	Economic and Social Council
EEC	European Economic Community
EPTA	Expanded Programme of Technical Assistance
EU	European Union
FAO	Food and Agriculture Organization
G-77	Group of 77
GATT	General Agreement on Tariffs and Trade
GNI	gross national income
GNP	gross national product
HDRs	Human Development Reports
HIPC	heavily indebted poor countries
HIV / AIDS	human immunodeficiency virus / acquired immune deficiency syndrome
IAEA	International Atomic Energy Agency
IBRD	International Bank for Reconstruction and Development (World Bank)
ICAO	International Civil Aviation Organization
ICRC	International Committee of the Red Cross

IDA	International Development Association
IEFR	International Emergency Food Reserve
IFAD	International Fund for Agriculture and Development
IFC	International Finance Corporation
ILO	International Labour Organization
IMCO	Intergovernmental Maritime Consultative Organization
IMF	International Monetary Fund
IPFs	indicative planning figures
ITO	International Trade Organization
ITU	International Telecommunication Union
LDCs	least-developed countries
MDGs	Millennium Development Goals
MYFF	multiyear funding framework
NATO	North Atlantic Treaty Organization
NGOs	nongovernmental organizations
NIEO	New International Economic Order
OAU	Organization of African Unity
ODA	official development assistance
OECD	Organisation for Economic Co-Operation and Development
OEEC	Organisation of European Economic Cooperation
OPEC	Organization of the Oil Exporting Countries
PRSPs	poverty reduction strategy papers
SMF/LDCs	Special Measures Fund for the Least Developed Countries
SSR	Soviet Socialist Republic
SUNFED	Special United Nations Fund for Economic Development
TAB	Technical Assistance Board
TAC	Technical Assistance Committee
TRAC	target for resource assignment from the core
UK	United Kingdom
UNCDF	United Nations Capital Development Fund
UNCED	United Nations Conference on Environment and Development
UNCTAD	United Nations Conference on Trade and Development

UNDAF	United Nations Development Assistance Framework
UNDG	United Nations Development Group
UNDP	United Nations Development Programme
UNEDA	United Nations Economic Development Administration
UNEP	United Nations Environment Programme
UNESCO	United Nations Educational, Scientific and Cultural Organization
UNFPA	United Nations Fund for Population Activities
UNHCR	United Nations High Commissioner for Refugees
UNICEF	United Nations Children's Fund
UNIDO	United Nations Industrial Development Organization
UNIFEM	United Nations Development Fund for Women
UNITAR	United Nations Institute for Training and Research
UNV	United Nations Volunteers
UPU	Universal Postal Union
USSR	Union of Soviet Socialist Republics
WFP	World Food Programme
WHO	World Health Organization
WMO	World Meteorological Organization

The UN and Development

Introduction

- **A Bird's-Eye View of More than Five Decades of Development Assistance**
- **In Search of the Core of the UN as a Development Organization: Approach, Conceptual Framework, and Main Questions**
- **About This Book**

International development cooperation became an important public concern in the second half of the twentieth century in response to changes in the political and economic international environment. It emerged at a time when Europe was recovering from more than five years of warfare. A new bipolar international system was in the making as the victorious allies divided most of Europe and the industrial North into two blocs, both of which aspired to global hegemony. In the South, an even more radical system transformation was under way: former colonies were in the process of becoming or had already become independent states.

This volume tells the story of international development assistance from its beginnings in late 1940s. The focus is on the roles the United Nations and its specialized agencies played in generating and implementing ideas in this policy area. It explores the central institutions of the UN system that deal with development assistance as well as the UN General Assembly, the Economic and Social Council (ECOSOC), and the intergovernmental and administrative bodies involved in development assistance under these major UN organs. These include the United Nations Development Programme (UNDP) and its forerunners, the Expanded Programme of Technical Assistance (EPTA) and the United Nations Special Fund.

These institutions were not the only UN actors on the scene. The World Bank and several UN specialized agencies, particularly the Food and Agriculture Organization (FAO), the International Labour Organization (ILO), the UN Children's Fund (UNICEF), and the World Health Organization (WHO) have greatly influenced international discourse on development assistance since the world body was established in 1945. UN member governments have also exerted influence on both the philosophy that guides development assistance and its practice. Nongovernmental organizations (NGOs) have also made an impact.

This story—or rather this collection of stories, because for more than half a century so many different actors have been involved—cannot be told or interpreted in isolation from political, economic, and institutional contexts. Although a large degree of continuity has prevailed, the contextual frameworks have changed over time, most often gradually but sometimes dramatically. Let us begin with a brief tour of UN development assistance through these years, focusing on the raison d'être and major objectives, strategies, and means characteristic of this policy area.

A Bird's-Eye View of More than Five Decades of Development Assistance

The international and conceptual environments of international development cooperation have changed over the years, and these changes have profoundly affected discourse and practice alike.[1] On the whole, most of the changes have been gradual and evolving trends have been characterized more by continuity than by change.

When international development assistance was first initiated in the late 1940s and early 1950s, the main patterns of the postwar bipolar international system were in the making or had already been established. That postwar political structure remained for more than four decades. During those years, an increasing number of new actors entered the scene, and the power relations between the major international players changed somewhat. Changes that took place at the conceptual level during these years are more clear. Nevertheless, the main elements of the modernization paradigm of the late 1940s and 1950s, which conceived development as a process by which a society would move from one state of development to another, higher stage, continued to exert influence in subsequent decades, although it was contested by competing ideologies.

The 1940s and 1950s

The first phase of development assistance—the 1940s and 1950s—was characterized by two major concerns: the needs (as perceived by the major international players) that surfaced in connection with the decolonization process, and the needs that were the result of the emerging Cold War. The beginning of official development assistance (ODA) can be traced to two major sources: the development activities of the colonial powers within their colonial territories and the first stumbling steps taken by international organizations established after World War II.

In the early days of development assistance, creating endogenous economic and social development in their dependencies was hardly the primary concern of the colonial powers. Some of them contributed by creating environments conducive to economic and social growth (by providing security and establishing infrastructures and institutions), but this was driven primarily by the imperial project and was aimed at serving the interests of the imperial powers, particularly their security and economic interests. The infrastructure colonial powers created for the imperial project (communications, power plants, and administrative and social institutions) was skewed in ways that created problems for the independent regimes that took over from colonial rule. Nevertheless, building up and improving a similar kind of infrastructure became a priority task to be pursued with development assistance.

In the wake of colonial administrations, private-sector and civil society "developers" from the imperial powers appeared on the scene, each with an agenda of their own, usually exploiting resources, making a profit (in the case of private-sector actors), or spreading the Gospel (in the case of nongovernmental missionary organizations). As these actors pursued their primary interests, however, they facilitated the transmission of new technologies, capital (mainly private-sector enterprises), and social services such as health and education (mainly the missionaries). At times, missionaries also voiced their concerns about living conditions prevailing in the countries concerned to the colonial government, locally and in the home country.

After World War II, the demand for self-rule in many countries made it increasingly clear that the colonial era was coming to an end. The two superpowers brought pressure to bear on the colonial powers to accelerate the decolonization process. The influence of the U.S. administration on its European allies was particularly strong. In some colonial powers, this brought new challenges to the fore, such as how to conduct postindependence relations with their colonies and how to secure their vested interests. Development assistance became instrumental in achieving these goals. Thus, in 1945, Britain reorganized its development assistance through the Colonial Development and Welfare Act; three years later, the Colonial Development Corporation was established. In 1946, France

established the Fonds d'investissement économique et social des territoires d'outre-mer. Such concerns were the driving force behind much
development assistance during the initial period.

Meanwhile, the signatories of the United Nations Charter committed themselves to promoting social progress and better standards of living in greater freedom, although not many developing countries were
among the world body's founding members. Institutions with an operational role in this regard were established about the same time, including
the International Bank for Reconstruction and Development (IBRD, the
World Bank) and the International Monetary Fund (IMF) in Washington,
D.C. The Food and Agriculture Organization was established in Rome in
1945. The International Labour Organization, founded in 1919 and head-
quartered in Geneva, became the first specialized agency associated with
the UN in 1946. In 1948 the World Health Organization was established in
Geneva. These institutions were oriented primarily toward the problems
of the "old" world, but their attention gradually extended to the needs of
developing countries as well. The 1948 Universal Declaration of Human
Rights both inspired the developed world and committed the UN to assist
beyond the confines of the old world.

In 1947, the Marshall Plan was launched, providing massive aid for
a European recovery program. It was in operation from 1948 through
1951. Even though it focused on the old world, where basic conditions
were fundamentally different from those in developing countries at that
time, it became a model for development assistance to what were called
"underdeveloped" countries at that time.

Toward the end of the 1940s, the commitment to assist "underdeveloped" countries and territories in their development was expressed
more clearly. The focus was on technical assistance. The first institution
of this kind—the Expanded Programme of Technical Assistance—was
established in 1949, entering into operation the following year. This focus
was anchored in the modernization paradigm, and experts recruited from
industrial countries were seen as crucial in assisting the governments of
developing countries in their efforts to modernize.

A major constraint was lack of capital, particularly risk capital that
could enable economic development to take place and could fund a public
administration capable of planning and implementing development plans
and providing communications, social services, and other public goods.
From the very beginning, most governments of developing countries gave

first priority to establishing a mechanism for raising risk capital within the UN system, but it took almost a decade before the Special Fund was established and put into operation. This fund supplemented the EPTA by facilitating capital investments in productive activities. The World Bank established a soft window, the International Development Association (IDA), in 1959; it went into operation the following year. In 1956, the International Finance Corporation (IFC) was created as an affiliate of the World Bank with the purpose of facilitating the growth of productive private enterprise in member countries, particularly in less-developed areas. The U.S. administration, in cooperation with other major western governments, was the main architect of these new institutions.

The 1960s and the 1970s

In the 1960s, the colonial era came to an end almost everywhere, though there were some important exceptions, especially countries in Southern Africa under Portuguese colonial rule or under white minority rule. Major colonial countries based their aid policies in the 1960s on their desires to secure the infrastructures they had built up within their dependencies and maintain relations with the new nations that had acquired independence or would soon do so. In addition, the East-West rivalry played an important role in motivating and forming the aid policy of the two superpowers until the end of the Cold War.

In the 1960s and 1970s, the hegemonic powers continued as the major players, the United States in particular. Within the Organisation of European Economic Cooperation (OEEC), which was established in part to distribute Marshall Plan aid, a Development Assistance Group (DAG) was formed in early 1960 to facilitate consultation among the major western donors about assistance to developing countries.[2] Later that year, the OEEC was reorganized into the Organisation for Economic Co-Operation and Development (OECD) and the DAG became the Development Assistance Committee (DAC) of the OECD. The DAG recommended to member countries that they make it their common objective to expand the aggregate volume of resources made available to "less-developed" countries and ensure that development assistance was effective. While the DAG encouraged private and public finance extended on commercial terms, it found that the needs of some less-developed countries required expanded assistance in the form of grants or loans on favorable terms, including long maturities where they were justified to prevent the burden of external debt from becoming too heavy. The initiative came from the Kennedy administration in the United States. At that point, about 40 percent of total ODA was provided by the United States alone, with about one-third coming from France and the United Kingdom.[3]

However, in the 1960s and 1970s, development assistance began to live a life of its own. New players, both industrially advanced countries and newly independent states, entered the scene, with both vested interests and idealist concerns related to aid, particularly involving the UN. This changed the institutional environment. The fate of emerging states and their peoples became a major issue at the UN.

In 1961, the UN General Assembly declared the 1960s as the UN Development Decade. The strategy for the decade set targets for economic growth (an annual economic growth rate of developing countries of 5 percent by the end of the decade) and development assistance (an annual flow of private capital and official assistance to developing countries of 1 percent of the combined national incomes of developed countries).[4] Previously, sources of development assistance had been largely confined to past and present colonial powers and the competing superpowers. Now it became an international obligation for other industrialized states as well, and several countries established agencies for development assistance.

BOX 0.1. Institutionalization of Aid Programs in the Early 1960s

During the early 1960s, many bilateral aid agencies were established or gained a stronger legal and institutional basis.

▪ As early as 1957, the *European Economic Community* had established the European Development Fund for Overseas Countries and Territories as part of the Treaty of Rome.

▪ In 1963, *Austria* established an interministerial committee for development cooperation that placed thirteen ministries under the chairmanship of the chancellery.

▪ In 1962, *Belgium* established an office for development cooperation. This was replaced nine years later by the General Administration for Development Cooperation.

▪ In 1960, *Canada* established an office for external aid that eight years later became the Canadian International Development Agency.

- In 1962, the *Danish* Parliament approved an act on technical cooperation with developing countries and a program for technical and financial assistance was established with a secretariat in the Ministry of Foreign Affairs. Nine years later, this secretariat was transformed into a department within the ministry, the Danish International Development Agency.

- In 1961, *Finland* established a State Committee for International Development Aid.

- In 1961, *France* established a separate ministry for development cooperation—the first of its kind.

- In 1961, the *Federal Republic of Germany* increased its allocations for development assistance, set up the Kreditanstalt für Wiederaufbau as the institution for development finance, and established a separate ministry for development cooperation.

- In 1961, *Japan* established its Overseas Economic Cooperation Fund to provide loans to developing countries; in the following year, it established an agency for technical cooperation that twelve years later was incorporated in the Japanese International Cooperation Agency.

- In 1963, a deputy minister in the Ministry of Foreign Affairs began coordinating the development cooperation of *the Netherlands*. In 1966, a minister for development cooperation took over this work.

- In 1962, *Norway* established an administration for development assistance that six years later was reorganized as the Norwegian Agency for International Development.

- In 1961, *Sweden* established an administration for technical assistance that in 1965 was reorganized as the Swedish International Development Authority.

- In 1961, *Switzerland's* Parliament allocated the first credit program for cooperation with developing countries and a service for technical cooperation was created in the Ministry of Foreign Affairs.

- In the *United Kingdom,* the Labour Government in 1964 established the Overseas Development Administration as an autonomous department with a minister in the cabinet; however, it was soon downgraded to a ministry represented in the cabinet by the Foreign Secretary.

- In the *United States,* the Kennedy Administration replaced earlier legislation in this field with the Foreign Assistance Act (1961), established the Agency for Development Assistance and the Peace Corps, and launched a ten-year program for cooperation with Latin America, the Alliance for Progress.

The early 1960s were also the time when new international institutions were established and important institutional reforms took place. In 1961, the FAO and the UN jointly established the World Food Programme (WFP) with the purpose of using food aid to generate economic and social development. In 1965, the institutions that had previously been established to deal with technical assistance and pre-investment studies, the EPTA and the Special Fund, were merged into the UN Development Programme. A tacitly agreed division of labor emerged by which the World Bank provided development finance and the United Nations provided technical assistance.

In 1970, the strategy for the second development decade continued the policies established in the first decade but in even more committed terms. A separate target was set for official development assistance from industrialized countries of 0.7 percent of gross national product (GNP) by the middle of the decade.

The 1970s were characterized by stronger, more determined, and more self-confident postures by Third World governments, manifest in their demand for a New International Economic Order (NIEO) and in their efforts to escape the Cold War trap. They built alliances, notably the Group of 77 (G-77) and the alliance of nonaligned countries. These two alliances included governments that had widely different, even conflicting, interests.

The new alliances were able to broaden the development agenda to include the unequal distribution of power between the industrial North and the new and old nations of the South, including the North-South division of labor and conditions regulating trade and investment. This approach focused on ways of improving conditions for developing countries, particularly by changing the structures that facilitated inequality. Developing countries wanted to create a new economic order, and the UN General Assembly, and several arms of the world organization, the UN Conference on Trade and Development (UNCTAD) in particular, played an important role and became the main arena of these efforts.

The first generation of pro-poor policy through aid remained mostly rhetorical. To the extent it was operationalized, the focus was on giving priority to poor countries, as exemplified in setting separate volume targets (as a percentage of GNP) for low-income countries. In the mid-1970s, it was translated into the basic human needs strategy. The various arms of the UN system were active also in forming this strategy, with its emphasis on public services. Development assistance was accorded a prominent role in this strategy—in improving public social services, particularly in education and health.

The 1980s and 1990s

Most developing countries faced harsh realities in the 1980s. Growing debt, acquired at a time when credit was easily available on favorable terms, soared out of control. Stagflation and a changed ideological current in some major western countries led to increasing protectionism and scarce resources for aid. In most developing countries, low and declining productivity made it extremely difficult to service the debts. At the same time, interest rates rose and industrialized countries began restricting imports of goods from developing countries. The economic crisis turned into a development crisis.

The result was balance-of-payments deficits that led the IMF to institute a policy of economic restructuring in developing countries. It offered structural adjustment credits that were contingent on IMF-dictated economic reforms. Development assistance became a major policy instrument, and the Bretton Woods institutions were in the driver's seat.

In order to obtain development loans, governments of developing countries had to agree to a structural adjustment program involving their total economic policy: more market, less state intervention. This first-generation aid conditionality applied not only to the structural adjustment credits provided by the World Bank in tandem with the IMF; the major bilateral aid agencies set such an agreement with the IMF as a condition for providing state-to-state development assistance.

This was a fundamental reorientation in development assistance. In the 1980s, the main purpose of ODA was to facilitate economic policy reform in recipient countries in order to create an "enabling environment" for development. ODA was increasingly provided as capital assistance and took the form of program aid rather than project aid. Its function became to provide assistance for crisis management: balance-of-payments support to help recipient governments import commodities needed to keep production up and enable them to service their foreign debts. This new policy direction became known as the Washington consensus.

During the 1980s, there was little resistance from major bilateral aid providers or other multilateral institutions to the Washington consensus. The criticism came from elsewhere, from the academic world, from NGOs in the South and North alike, from the East, and from some governments of the South.[5] Structural adjustment policies focused one-sidedly on the macroeconomics of debt-ridden developing countries. They carried a huge social deficit: budgetary cuts hit soft sectors like health and education first. When these signs became clear, UN organizations that worked with the social groups most adversely affected were first to sound the alarm, although their critique came from within the mainstream approach, as exemplified by the 1987 UNICEF study *Adjustment with a Human Face*.[6]

The 1980s also brought the concept of sustainable development to the fore. The Brundtland Commission, appointed by the UN, was instrumental in putting the environmental dimension of development on the agenda in 1987.[7] Development assistance was given a role in this regard, but the magnitude of this challenge at the national and global level far exceeded what could be achieved by modest ODA resources. The issue remained high on the international agenda throughout the 1990s as well.

In the late 1980s and the early 1990s, the transformation of the international system that ended the Cold War brought a fundamental reorientation in development assistance. First-generation conditionality geared toward reforming the economic policy of developing countries (economic liberalism) continued, but structural adjustment lending was modified to attempt to avoid the negative social consequences. The idea that a strong state was important for development was revived, and institution-building became an important objective for development assistance.

New objectives were added to the old ones and gained preeminence in rhetoric: aid should be instrumental in promoting political liberalism—democracy, human rights, and good governance—along with ecological sustainability. In the early 1990s, a commitment to such policy reforms was set as a condition for receiving development assistance (second-generation conditionality), although these objectives were increasingly sought also through so-called positive measures.[8]

The 1990s were characterized by other developments as well. The UN system played an important role in reviving the social dimension of development. A new set of indicators of development that was presented in the first issue of the *Human Development Report* was instrumental in turning the tide. Through a series of global conferences, other arms of the UN system pursued the social and human dimensions of development. The 1995 Social Summit in Copenhagen placed the social dimension firmly on the agenda: fighting poverty became the overall theme. The summit singled out education and health as strategically important for achieving development and fighting poverty. The Social Summit produced what became known as the 20:20 agreement: developing countries were to allocate 20 percent of their public expenditure for basic social programs and donors were to allocate 20 percent of their ODA for these same purposes. Other global summits in the 1990s focused on related aspects—particularly the summits on children and on women.

The 1990s were also characterized by a series of violent conflicts in the core of Europe (the former Yugoslavia) as well as in various parts of Africa (among them, the Horn of Africa, Sudan, and the Great Lakes region) and the former Soviet Union. These conflicts within states, which often had a cultural (ethnic or religious) dimension and extended throughout a region, differed from the classical pattern of interstate conflicts. They caused immense human suffering, waves of refugees, and wanton destruction of national infrastructure.

These conflicts affected development assistance in various ways. First of all, resources were turned into relief assistance, particularly for refugees streaming into donor countries and those who became refugees in neighboring countries or internally displaced persons. This changed the pattern of aid distribution away from the traditional objective of promoting economic and social development. Increasingly, security became a priority. Since development is dependent on the absence of violent conflict, the surge of intrastate wars led to a greater focus on conflict resolution and conflict prevention. Development assistance was assigned a role in both, mainly as humanitarian aid. Interventions in these conflicts, whether in the form of rescue operations or military operations, with or without UN peacekeepers, were extremely expensive and affected ODA budgets both directly and indirectly. Costly efforts to rehabilitate war-torn countries also had an impact.

The development agenda was also broadened by a strong emphasis on policy coherence that came to the fore in the early 1990s. All policies of the industrially developed states toward developing countries, whether they involved macroeconomics, trade, finance, or whatever, should be attuned to each other—or at least not contradict each other. The primary objective was to ensure the effective participation of developing countries in the global economy and their cooperation in confronting global challenges and solving regional security issues. The DAC of the OECD was the driving force behind this new focus.[9]

2000 and Beyond: The Challenges Ahead

The UN Millennium Declaration and the Millennium Development Goals (MDGs) are special for several reasons. The UN Millennium Summit in September 2000 attracted the participation of representatives of 191 nations, including 147 heads of state and government; it was the largest-ever gathering of world leaders. Reaffirming their faith in the UN and its Charter, participants recognized that "in addition to our separate responsibilities in our individual societies, we have a collective responsibility to uphold the principles of human dignity, equality and equity at the global level. As leaders we have a duty therefore to all the world's people, especially the most vulnerable and, in particular, the children of the world, to whom the future belongs."[10] Among the fundamental values deemed essential to international relations in the twenty-first century were freedom, equity, solidarity, tolerance, respect for nature, and a shared responsibility.

The Millennium Development Goals were special for other reasons as well. They had emerged from the conclusions of a series of global summits held on more specific themes during the previous decade. The strategy document adopted four years earlier by the high-level meeting of the DAC, *Shaping the 21st Century: The Contribution of Development Co-operation,* had focused on essentially the same goals. At that meeting, all governments of the major donor countries had been represented, along with other major aid-providing institutions, including the World Bank. This strategy document drew to a considerable extent on the conclusions of earlier global conferences, turning them into operational and measurable (quantified) goals that could be regularly monitored, in line with the DAC tradition.[11]

The MDGs, which were formulated on the basis of the Millennium Declaration during the following year, were not conceived of as a task to be solved by development assistance alone, although increased aid was to be part of the solution. Nor did they represent a challenge solely for the governments of well-off countries. In fact, the governments of the countries concerned were meant to carry the heaviest burden. The specific millennium goals relating to development and poverty eradication were integral parts of a broader perspective that included peace and security, protection of the environment, human rights, democracy and good governance, and protection of vulnerable groups, with a particular focus on those who were the worst off, especially in Africa. Some commitments were general, indicating the general direction of joint efforts; others were stated in quantitative terms, with fixed deadlines.

The declaration and its goals focused solely on outcomes: the input side and strategies were scarcely mentioned. The strategy for the First Development Decade (the 1960s) also placed the main focus on outcomes, particularly an annual growth of GNP in developing countries. But it included an input target: 1 percent of the developed countries' gross national income (GNI) in assistance as well. In the twenty-first century, development assistance was only one of the ways to achieve MDG targets, but it was far from the most important one. At the summit, a general commitment to raise the volume of aid was made; and several governments pledged, on an individual basis, to increase their ODA. However, these commitments did not signal a revolutionary change.

Ambitious development goals are not fulfilled by good intentions alone. Ideas and visions are important, but so are traditional inputs involving capital and technology, either generated domestically or facilitated from the outside. The brunt of the burden will have to be carried by the governments of the countries concerned. This they had to do in the mid-twentieth century when development assistance was initiated, and this will also be the case in the first decades of the new century. However, it must also be recognized that governments of the poorest countries do not have much to contribute in terms of inputs to stimulate economic and social development, and they have few resources to redistribute. When poverty eradication is the primary goal, this poses a problem that cannot be solved through general mechanisms like reliance on market mechanisms or improved terms of trade, particularly within the time horizon set for achieving the MDGs. For other countries that are struggling with poverty, however, improved terms of trade and better access to the markets of major industrial powers can be part of the answer, if judiciously combined with a policy of redistribution. Debt waiver could also be a relevant instrument.

The commitments made in the United Nations Millennium Declaration are the world's biggest promise, and attaining the results contained in the MDGs is the world's biggest challenge. However, with no agreed-upon strategy for attaining the MDGs, no agreed-upon financial framework for the costs involved in reaching the targets, and no commitments about inputs, the realism of the solemn declaration that united world leaders in September 2000 was open to question.

Follow-up on the MDGs had a slow start. In the hoary tradition of the UN, Secretary-General Kofi Annan called on outstanding experts for guidance. An independent body was commissioned to provide advice on how the MDGs might be attained. In sharp contrast to the Millennium Summit, the UN Millennium Project focused on inputs—what kinds of policies were necessary, what kinds of resources were required (and how much), and where those resources could be mobilized. In this holistic perspective, official development assistance again emerged as a major instrument for achieving the MDGs, and heightened targets for ODA became a necessity.[12]

In Search of the Core of the UN as a Development Organization: Approach, Conceptual Framework, and Main Questions

In this volume, international development assistance will be analyzed within an international relations perspective, explicitly or implicitly drawing on the theory of international politics. Such a perspective brings power and power relations to the forefront. The major players are seen as pursuing their own national interests, their security and economic interests in particular. Development assistance is conceived of as an instrument that is part of the foreign policy of governments, whether these are acting bilaterally or within intergovernmental bodies. This perspective, which predominated throughout most of the second half of the twentieth century, has been contested. It has been argued that at least for some governments, development cooperation constitutes a special case, allowing also for altruistic motives based on idealist values and norms that transcend the borders of nation-states.

Other perspectives will also be brought into the study. From the very beginning, the stated objective of development assistance has been to assist in promoting economic and social development. Behind this objective, we may also detect more selfish political and economic interests of the kind noted above: the primary aim of an aid-providing government may in fact be to serve its own political and security interests by using aid to achieve political leverage, promote exports, and interfere politically, for example. Nevertheless, an officially declared rationale influences policies within that area. Thus, another theoretical setting guides the questions posed—namely, prevailing development paradigms. Since our main focus will be on the role of the United Nations, yet another set of theories will explicitly and implicitly guide the focus: organizational theory as adapted to international organizations.

The International Power Play

The UN system serves as an arena in which member governments pursue their foreign policy aims involving national interest in a more narrow sense related to their security and economic interests but also involving values and norms. Power constitutes a central concept in this context, particularly the relative power of the major competing (and cooperating) actors.

Within the arena framework, member governments, according to the realist paradigm that dominated analyses of politics among nation-states throughout most of the post–World War II era, seek to increase their influence and ensure their vested national interests, their security interests in particular.[13] However, since the core unit of classic realism is the nation-state and its focus is on interactions among and between states, it neglects actors at other levels.[14] This applies to actors at the subnational level and to actors at international levels (regional and global), where a multitude of organizations operate and (fragments of) international regimes have been established. Such actors may play an independent role beyond state-to-state interaction, even within areas where residual powers formally belong to the participating governments. Moreover, participation in such settings may in itself influence the policy position of a participating government vis-à-vis the issues involved.

The perspective of realism, both classical and neoclassical, has been challenged from other quarters, with particular reference to the issue area in focus in this study. Political actors do not always act with the sole intention of furthering their own individual or collective self-interest. Interests may be given a long-term perspective, with a focus on future rewards as opposed to immediate gains. Long-term interests are, of course, part of the concept as defined by realist schools, although how well they are integrated may depend on the time perspective and the kinds of interests involved. Interests may also be given a broader interpretation than the individual or collective interest of the community concerned. This, too, may be contained within a realist national-interest concept, but it will make little sense in such a context if long-term interests are not at least somehow affected, whether in a negative or a positive way.

From the very beginning, development assistance became an

instrument in the international power play of the emerging superpowers in the post–World War II bipolar world system, both of which had hegemonic aspirations. During the late 1940s and early 1950s, this was stated quite openly by western powers: the promotion of democracy and an open market economy and containment of communism in the South were used as the prime arguments for development assistance. At that time, the United States stood out as the most generous provider of development assistance in both absolute and relative terms. The Soviet Union and the East also used aid as a foreign policy instrument, targeted at strategically important governments and social structures. From the perspective of the East-West rivalry, foreign aid, including development assistance, may be best analyzed within the paradigms of realpolitik.[15]

The two superpowers and other major powers were not the only actors on the international scene during the first decades of development assistance. However, they held a hegemonic position within their security systems, and the United States in particular set the agenda of the multilateral institutions concerned with foreign aid. UN membership meant that many small- and medium-sized western powers with no colonial past found themselves confronted with the conflicts that arose when former colonies aspired to become independent states. Several came under cross-pressure between their alignment to one or more of the colonial powers through security policy arrangements like the North Atlantic Treaty Organization (NATO) and/or other loyalty bonds on the one hand and commitments to the underlying norms of the decolonization process on the other. Development assistance, especially when accompanied by a "neutral" UN stamp, became an impeccable response. Several of these countries had traditions linked to the welfare state and international humanitarian relief. This applied also to some western middle powers with a colonial past, the Netherlands in particular.

Paradigms of the realist tradition in international relations fail to capture these basically altruistic features of development assistance. From this recognition, an alternative paradigm emerged for studying the foreign policy of this group of countries, that of humane internationalism.[16] The core of humane internationalism is an acceptance of the principle that the citizens of industrial nations have moral obligations toward peoples and events beyond their borders and this, in turn, has a bearing on the duties of governments.[17] This paradigm comes in various types—liberal, reform, and radical internationalism. An ethical thrust is combined with, and considered to be instrumental to, promotion of the long-term overall interests of countries in the North.[18]

Development Paradigms and International Development Assistance

Development paradigms constitute part of the political environment when ideas of development and international development assistance are shaped and cultivated. This setting is not necessarily disconnected from international politics. Development paradigms vary over time and with the ideological setting. They may be a tool in a foreign policy strategy. Ideology may, within a realist paradigm, serve as the superstructure for the vested interests of competing powers with security concerns and economic interests at stake. Development paradigms often represent, in a condensed form, the prevailing political ideology of donors. A hegemonic development paradigm may function as a gatekeeper that determines what kinds of ideas are feasible and may be picked up and developed, and what ideas are not feasible. It may also influence the way ideas are transformed into practice.

Although one particular development paradigm may have been the predominant one within the donor community at a certain point in time, there have always been alternatives. Such alternative development philosophies (or models) reflect theories of development, or more broadly worldviews, that differ from the predominant (hegemonic) one. Their real influence may vary extensively. They carry most influence when cemented as ideologies of established power structures, such as major donor governments or multilateral agencies. Most of the hegemonic development paradigms have emerged from experiences in the North or by the North.

Development paradigms tend to have long lives. As noted before, they also live parallel lives.[19] A paradigm that may be the predominant one at a certain point in time continues to influence the minds of a generation of policymakers and administrators after its heyday. And in the period that a paradigm has a hegemonic position, alternative paradigms are present or in the making. Old paradigms are adjusted to more recent development experiences and new realities, and in this way they prolong their lives. Any sequencing, therefore, runs the risk of portraying too simplified a picture.

When development assistance emerged as an idea, the predominant development paradigms were informed primarily by European experiences and the theories and models emerging from these experiences. They varied extensively across the East-West dividing line; various (capitalist) models associated with the main western powers represented one pole, and various (socialist) models associated with the eastern powers represented the other. This dichotomy makes sense, particularly in an international relations context. However, a continuum between such poles may provide a more correct description of the actual situation, given the variety of national systems, especially in the West, with regard to the major dimensions involved. The main conflict dimension at the theoretical and ideological level concerned the role of the state. In the economic room, the ideological poles were the liberal mini-state that left "decisions" to the market and the socialist central planning state. In the political room, there were similar poles: states pursuing liberal values versus states in pursuit of authoritarian values.

During the formative years of international development assistance (the 1950s and 1960s), economists were indebted to Keynesian theory, which dominated development thinking in the West. The emphasis was on planning and the intervening state. The focus was almost exclusively on economic growth, and capital accumulation was the prime factor for creating such growth—in stages. Although trade was accorded great importance by development economists closer to the neoclassical tradition, development was seen as basically a national process, and capital accumulation from national savings was at its core. Foreign trade and investment would assist capital accumulation and promote the diffusion of new technology, skills, and capital to the benefit of latecomers. The modernization paradigm dominated western development thinking—development was conceived of as the process by which a society would move from one stage to another "higher" stage, as quantified in economic and political terms.[20] Within this paradigm, the main function of aid was to fill the gaps in capital and knowledge and to overcome bottlenecks inherent in a process of unbalanced growth so as to facilitate a takeoff of the recipient-country economy.

Two additional factors affect this picture. First, multilateral institutions are conservative bodies. Unlike democratic systems, there are no periodic elections that may lead to a shift of regime at regular intervals, although (time-bound) shifts in the top management may matter. Second, when alternative paradigms are available, politicians (and the administration) may construct their agenda à la carte, picking their chosen components from several paradigms. The focus of this study will be more on ideological and strategic patterns than on theory frameworks.

An Organization as an Arena and as an Actor

Institutional patterns do matter. International organizations differ with regard to membership and the rights and duties of their members, objectives set, and how they are organized and work.[21] Such differences also affect the kinds of ideas that are generated within an organization and its selection of ideas generated elsewhere. With particular reference to the two multilateral organizations that have mattered the most within our policy area, the Bretton Woods institutions and the UN system, different ideas can be expected to emerge from an organization basically "owned" by the industrialized countries, as is the case with the Bretton Woods institutions, and an organization with a broader global ownership, the UN system.

In the Bretton Woods institutions, capital installments determine the composition of governing structures and voting rights. This has a bearing on the relative influence of the members. In the UN system, each government has one vote when development issues are involved, whether a tiny country or a major power. Such differences affect both formal structures and objectives. Although the relative influence of governments is by no means accurately reflected in the "one country, one vote" regulation, the policy does affect the self-identity of the organization, including the loyalty of secretariats. It follows that the two systems can be expected to be receptive to and themselves generate ideas that differ when it comes to development perspectives and how developing countries may be best assisted in their development efforts. However, voting power is not the only determinant.

The United Nations and its specialized agencies serve as an important arena for the major players within this policy area. These various arms of the UN system also interact with these players. The system also performs a role as an actor in its own right, mediating between conflicting positions, supplying information, and producing ideas and suggestions for how they may be followed up. As Cohen and colleagues argue, an organization may exert influence on policy outcomes beyond that of its separate members.[22] Several features of an organization contribute to this.

For all these organs, and the administration in particular, the identity of the organization, as manifested in its constitution, influence the way it operates, in terms of decisions as well as priorities. This applies to its intergovernmental bodies, notwithstanding that their members ultimately represent their governments. It applies even more strongly to the secretariats and the groups of experts appointed to supply the basis for decisions of intergovernmental bodies, although these also usually have a debt of gratitude to their governments for their appointments and, accordingly, may have dual loyalties.

The Main Problems Posed

In what follows, the emergence of development assistance from idea to practice within the United Nations arena will be analyzed from the paradigms of realpolitik and humane internationalism. We will also look for ideological changes in the political environment and the way development assistance has been affected. Attention will also be directed to the "independent" role of UN institutions.

This leads us to the following main questions:

- What main ideas related to development have been generated or captured from elsewhere and supported by the United Nations system?

- To what extent and how has the way that international development assistance has been conceptualized and institutionalized by the UN system related to evolving development paradigms? How has the system itself contributed to these paradigms?

- To what extent and how have international politics and the relative power of the major players influenced international development assistance and how it has been conceptualized and institutionalized?

- To what extent and how have the UN system's core institutions influenced conceptualization and institutionalization of international development assistance over the years?

The main focus throughout this study will be on how the idea of development assistance has been conceptualized and institutionalized in terms of rationale, objectives, major principles and norms, and strategies and means. The specific contribution of the UN will stand out more clearly when the ideas and policies generated and implemented differ from those of other major actors, bilateral and multilateral. Therefore we will zero in on such differences of focus, objectives, norms, and ways of working. When it comes to how international power politics has influenced the ideas and practices of the UN system within this policy field, more detailed questions will have to be raised. These include:

- To what extent do the outcomes reflect expressed or tacit interests of the major actors, the superpowers in particular?
- Who were the main architects?
- In what ways and to what extent were other multilateral actors and bilateral donor governments involved?
- What was the role of Third World institutions and governments?
- Finally, no less important, in what ways and to what extent has the UN system influenced the policies of other international (multilateral) and bilateral actors within this policy area?

About This Book

This book begins—in Part 1—by exploring how international development assistance through the United Nations system started. Where did the idea come from, and how was it institutionalized? The beginning of a new activity is always important, because values and norms are created that establish a tradition for the policy area that will later provide legitimacy and influence future initiatives. This is why there is such emphasis on the first steps that were taken—the creation of the Expanded Programme of Technical Assistance and the Special Fund. In describing and analyzing these beginnings, I have added a dimension: a search for the roots of this new activity.

In chapter 1, the basis for this search for the roots is established. Some potential roots of international development assistance—traditions involving similar activities, ideas of a more general character that may have triggered and sustained the idea of international development assistance, and the institutional heritage—are identified and their main characteristics briefly described. The purpose is to trace the early footprints of these various legacies.

Chapter 2 tells the history of the first systematic efforts of the UN system to provide development assistance—the establishment of the EPTA. The chapter focuses on the main objectives set, the basic principles established to guide implementation, how activities were organized, and what the chief characteristics of the outcome were.

Chapter 3 relates the history of the efforts during the late 1940s and the 1950s to provide the United Nations with an institution that could supply developing countries with capital assistance on concessionary terms to supplement the technical assistance provided by the EPTA. A majority within the central intergovernmental bodies of the UN—composed of governments of developing countries and a growing number of governments of industrial countries (East and West)—was in favor of the establishment of such a mechanism, which became known as SUNFED. However, the UN lost out to the World Bank, where a soft window was created—the International Development Association. A bone was thrown to the UN in the form of the Special Fund, established in the late 1950s.

On the basis of the main features of the development assistance provided through the United Nations system during the 1950s, some tentative conclusions are drawn in chapter 4 with regard to the roots of international development assistance.

Part 2 starts out, in chapter 5, with an analysis of the grand idea of a United Nations Development Decade, inspired by the incoming president of the United States, John F. Kennedy. The strategy for this decade, the first of a series of four development decades, brought a change in terminology, from "underdeveloped," even "backward," to the milder "less-developed" or even "developing" countries and regions. The focus was on the main goals and targets of the strategy and its overall approach to the promotion of development. Development planning and assistance to the countries concerned featured prominently in this strategy, and there was an emphasis on human resource development and science and technology. Targets were set for overall economic growth and for development within specific sectors. For the first time, an international target was set for development assistance: as soon as possible, the combined flow of international assistance and capital to developing countries should reach approximately 1 percent of the combined national incomes of the economically advanced countries. In this first in a series of quantified volume targets, no clear distinction was made between official development assistance and private financial transfers.

In chapter 6, the main features of the strategy for the Second Development Decade are outlined—the aspirations, the major goals and objectives set for the 1970s, and the policy measures designed to realize these goals. The strategy focused on improved trade conditions for developing countries and the financial resources for development. Developing countries were expected to carry the main responsibility for financing their development by mobilizing all of their domestic financial resources and committing themselves to "sound fiscal and monetary policies." However, a target was set for industrialized countries: they should contribute 1 percent of their GNP in financial transfers, of which 0.7 percent should be official development assistance.

By the mid-1970s, attention was focused on efforts to realize the program for a New International Economic Order. The midterm review of the strategy for the Second Development Decade combined scrutiny of what had been achieved with a discussion of how to realize NIEO aspirations. These aspirations were integrated into the strategy for the second half of the decade. Chapter 6 ends by outlining the aspirations, approach, objectives, targets, and priorities set for development in the 1980s as manifested in the strategy for the Third Development Decade.

The two chapters that follow focus on the two major operational development programs of the UN system—the UNDP and the WFP —during the formative years of the 1960s and 1970s. The policies and performance of the UNDP from its start in 1966 through 1981 are outlined in chapter 7.

For the first five years, the UNDP followed more or less the paths trodden by its two predecessors. By the late 1960s, however, its attention was increasingly directed toward the challenges ahead, stimulated especially by work on a new strategy for the Second Development Decade and efforts at administrative reform intended to improve the delivery system, based on a capacity study undertaken by Sir Robert Jackson.[23] The basic design that emerged from the 1970 consensus was an integrated system of country programming that combined central responsibility for all activities in the UNDP administrator with a central role for the resident representative at the country level, based on norms originally established for the EPTA.

Chapter 8 relates the history of the World Food Programme during its first twenty years. Food aid has a *problématique* of its own since, from the beginning, it was based on surplus production. This makes this type of aid especially interesting from the perspective of this volume. The original idea was to turn food surpluses in well-off countries into economic and social development in developing countries, although relief was also part of the rationale from the very start. Nevertheless, food aid soon became part of a much broader perspective, namely that of providing food security. The chapter describes and analyzes the operations of the WFP from 1966 through 1981. As a multilateral food aid program, the WFP made a difference, as compared with larger bilateral food aid programs, and served as a forum where donor and recipient governments could discuss relevant issues in food aid policy. When the idea of food aid first appeared, it had been bilateral and supply-driven: under the WFP, multilateral food aid became demand-driven.

In chapter 9, developments in the 1960s and 1970s are summed up and analyzed against the emerging international and conceptual backdrop of a bipolar international system with competing development paradigms and Third World governments that were searching for common ground, independent of the East/West stalemate. The focus is on the targets set for development assistance, the norms established for the development relationship, and the added insights food aid might provide to the rationale for development cooperation.

Part 3 describes and analyzes major developments in the UN system's aid policy in the 1980s and 1990s. The introduction outlines some major trends in the international environment during these two decades. These include the emergence in the late 1970s and early 1980s of a new dominant development ideology, international stagflation that affected most OECD countries, and a soaring increase in the debts of most developing countries. These changes made the IMF and World Bank the masters of development policy and resulted in first-generation aid conditionality. However, by the mid-1980s alternative policy initiatives were emerging, exemplified by the Brundtland Commission's focus on sustainable development and environmental challenges. The transformation of the international system in the late 1980s and early 1990s created a fundamentally new setting for international development cooperation. The responses of aid-providing governments varied as the peace dividend failed to materialize and the focus of donor countries shifted toward second-generation conditionality, promoting liberal political values, such as democracy, human rights, and good governance. The state reemerged as an important development factor, and the focus of development policies turned increasingly to building institutions.

Chapter 10 presents the UN vision for the 1990s. After a decade of stagnation, the international strategy for the Fourth Development Decade emphasized recovery. Chapter 11 focuses on the Human Development Reports and the human development index generated within the UNDP and the thematic world conferences that spotlighted the social and human dimensions of development. The following two chapters focus on the changes under way in the established patterns of the UNDP and the WFP. For the UNDP, the major change in the 1990s was perhaps the strong emphasis on sustainable human development, triggered by the *Human Development Report* and human development index project. The priority given to human development resulted in a change of strategy: advocacy was given emphasis and the increasingly scarce resources at the UNDP's disposal were directed "upstream" by emphasizing policy reforms toward achieving human development rather than support for development projects ("downstream"), as in the past. A change of perspective also took place at the WFP regarding how operational expenditures were distributed; the main emphasis changed from development towards humanitarian assistance.

Chapter 14 describes the development aspirations for the first fifteen years of the new millennium, as formulated by the UN Millennium Summit. It presents the major Millennium Development Goals and how the UN system tried to implement these goals during the first years.

The concluding chapter directs attention to some major contributions of the UN system within the policy area of development assistance. It focuses on the UN's role in generating and maintaining norms for international development cooperation, its role with regard to development funding, and its role in shaping long-term programming and planning. The chapter analyzes the ongoing cycles of UN development system reform. The more overarching issues are discussed in this final chapter—whether we, in the new century, can see a convergence of development policy, the impact of power on politics within the UN system, and the issue of *real* aid.

In the appendix, the development assistance provided by the UN system is put into perspective. Global development assistance since 1960 through 2005 is outlined, with a focus on ODA. The major donor governments are identified and their evolving share of global ODA over the years is described, as is their performance in terms of the ODA share of GNP/GNI. Data on the shares of total ODA channeled to international institutions as multilateral assistance from major groups and individual donor countries are presented, as is the distribution of total multilateral ODA among the main multilateral institutions.

PART ONE

The Emergence of International Development Assistance

Toward the end of the 1940s, the idea of providing international assistance to promote economic and social development in "underdeveloped" countries and regions became institutionalized within the UN system.[1] Where did this idea come from, what triggered its acceptance within the UN framework, and how was it realized?

The first two questions direct attention toward pre-aid North-South relations; perceptions of development and how development is achieved; and ideas and norms that underpinned and sustained the promotion of development beyond the nation-state. The third question—how the idea was realized within the UN system—requires a description of evolving trends. Attention is therefore directed toward particular features that are relevant for answering these specific questions.

During the early years of the United Nations, knowledge and capital were identified as what "underdeveloped" countries needed most. Within the United Nations, a program for technical assistance and a fund that could provide capital for economic development on concessionary terms were the world body's main instruments for assisting countries in need. The first—the Expanded Programme of Technical Assistance—was established in 1949 and became operative the following year. The second—the Special Fund—remained on the agenda for most of the 1950s before it was established in 1958 and became operative in 1959, and then in a form far removed from the original idea of a Special UN Fund for Economic

Development (SUNFED). Thus, the emphasis during the first years of UN development assistance was on technical assistance, although the need for capital was recognized as part of the wider development project.

One other activity received considerable attention during these early years: food aid. However, this was development assistance of a different kind. It was not central to UN development discourse, it did not become institutionalized and operational within the UN system until the early 1960s, and even then it was not implemented by the system's central organs. That is why the emergence of multilateral food aid is discussed in Part 2, where the focus is on the 1960s and 1970s. However, understanding the magnitude of this aid during the initial years and the way it was motivated, institutionalized, and implemented may help broaden our understanding of why and how the idea of international development assistance emerged and was realized.

The general questions posed above can be narrowed down according to the more specific development assistance that the UN system initiated, institutionalized, and pursued in the late 1940s and 1950s. Here, attention will be directed toward the more specific features of this activity in search of "footprints" left by the traditions and ideas of the pre-aid period.

The ideas generated and selected by an international organization are also influenced by changes in the evolving international political environment. In the late 1940s and early 1950s, the international system was in transition. Two major trends characterized the period: decolonization and the emergence of a bipolar international system. During the evolving Cold War, these processes became interlinked.

This leads to another set of questions: when the UN took the first steps on the road toward international development assistance in 1948, what started the process and where did it start? Was it driven by need or by foreign policy concerns? What were the explicit and implicit purposes? How was the idea of development assistance implemented in terms of major objectives, guiding principles, and institutional frameworks? How was it to be financed? The answers to these questions may reveal the footprints of the various heritages that underpin the idea of development assistance as institutionalized by the UN during the late 1940s and 1950s.

In search of these footprints, we will also look for the emergence during these early years of patterns that may explain more recent political positions regarding the role of the UN within the policy area of international aid. What formal and informal governmental alliances might we find with regard to objectives, principles, and strategies for international development assistance? What was the role of the UN system vis-à-vis other bilateral and multilateral actors within this area, especially the World Bank? The policies pursued during the initial years may reveal patterns that have survived even such dramatic international system transformations as those following the end of the Cold War.

Chapter 1 identifies some traditions and ideas of the pre-aid period that are assumed to have a potential for generating the idea of development assistance. Chapter 2 deals with the establishment of the Expanded Programme of Technical Assistance, its purpose and objectives, the principles guiding its activities, its institutional setting, and how it developed during the first decade of operation. Chapter 3 examines the establishment of the Special Fund much in the same way. In chapter 4, we look for the footprints of the potential "roots," manifested in how the idea of international development assistance was first realized by the UN system in the EPTA and the Special Fund. Some conclusions about the major roots of the idea of development assistance will be drawn on this basis.

ONE

Pre-Aid Traditions and Ideas and the Institutional Heritage

- **The Traditions**
- **The Ideas**
- **The Institutional Heritage**

A variety of traditions—each with a primary purpose of its own, a particular mode of work, and different institutional frameworks—may have inspired the UN and its member governments to take on the new commitment of providing international development assistance. Some of these traditions shared basic values and norms; some did not. This calls for a separate discussion of the influence traditions and ideas may have exerted when the idea of development assistance was first generated and institutionalized within the UN system.

The ideas pertaining to development aid in the reports, resolutions, and declarations of the League of Nations and the early years of the United Nations are a second source of inspiration. Another source of inspiration was the Marshall Plan—the massive transfers of resources by the United States to help European countries rebuild their war-torn economies after World War II.

The various traditions, ideas, institutional heritages, and more recent experiences that will be briefly outlined in this chapter represent possible sources and inspirations of what later became international development assistance. This chapter, therefore, is meant as the first step in an effort to identify the main sources of this idea and their main characteristics. In chapter 4 we will look for footprints of these possible sources in the implementation of the idea of international aid.

The Traditions

The traditions included here cover organized activities initiated in the North that were intended to provide benefits of some kind in the South. At least a grain of altruism may have been involved in the values and norms underpinning the basic objectives of these activities. Although this may be true for most of the traditions, such activities may also have been driven by other interests.

Four traditions have often been referred to as sources of international development assistance: humanitarian relief, international solidarity, human rights, and missionary work. Several of these may be subsumed under the category of humanism. In this brief overview, a fifth tradition is added: imperialism. Colonial relations constituted a high-priority issue in the ministries of foreign affairs of the imperial powers—the powers holding center court when the idea of development assistance became institutionalized in the United Nations. The other traditions were supplements or reactions to the predominant tradition of imperialism. What are the major features of these varying traditions? What were their primary aims? What norms guided their operations and institutional setup? What was the basis of their primary values and interests?

The Imperialist Tradition

The most powerful and systematic pre-aid influence the North exerted on development in the South was created by a number of imperial powers and the companies operating under their protection or even as their agents. For some European powers, this tradition had a long history that, by the late 1940s, was still in operation with the exception of only a few cases. The form of colonial rule differed from one imperial power to another, setting different marks on colonized societies. We may distinguish between the British policy of indirect rule, which relied on traditional systems and rulers that were subordinated to a colonial superstructure, and the French policy of direct rule, which adapted its own administrative system to its colonies. And then there was the Portuguese government, which considered its colonies integral parts of the motherland. All these factors make it difficult to generalize about the tradition of imperialism.[1]

The process of colonization was, by definition, characterized by suppression and authoritarian rule. The various forms of economic development that took place were skewed to serve the needs and interests of the imperial power. This process also applied to the efforts to improve infrastructure, communications, and transportation. Still, it brought technology to the colonies as well as capital investment. Schools, especially missionary schools, followed in the wake of colonialism.

Imperial powers created a web of political, economic, and cultural relations between themselves and their colonies and dependencies. Only in exceptional cases were such ties cut at independence. Asymmetrical linkages strongly influenced the idea of providing development assistance. The way that colonial relations ended—whether gradually, through a peacefully negotiated agreement, or abruptly, through a violent liberation struggle— is another relevant factor. We can assume that these past relations have also influenced the continuation and direction of the aid of these countries.

During the 1940s, most imperial powers remained colonial powers, although some of them had begun to unlock the chains in South Asia. The Philippines gained independence from the United States in 1946. India (1945), Pakistan (1947), Sri Lanka/Ceylon (1948), and Burma (1948) gained independence from Britain in the same decade, as did Indonesia (1949) from the Netherlands.

The Tradition of Humanitarian Relief

The tradition of humanitarian relief is part of the much broader tradition of humanism. It includes a wide variety of institutions working in tandem or separately within more specialized areas. These institutions operate within local or national frameworks as well as internationally. The Red Cross movement—which includes the International Committee of the Red Cross (ICRC), the International Federation of Red Cross and Red Crescent Societies, and the many national Red Cross and Red Crescent societies—has traditionally been the prime expression of this tradition, but it is far from the only one.[2]

The main mission of this tradition is to meet immediate human needs in situations of violent conflict and (increasingly) in response to natural disasters. Its institutional patterns reflect the fact that work is directed toward providing relief in emergency situations wherever they appear. An international dimension was present from the very beginning, since victims of violent conflicts were the primary target group. It follows, therefore, that its perspective transcends that of the nation-state.

Neutrality toward belligerents became the sine qua non for the Red Cross movement, whose tradition dates back more than 140 years.[3] Other institutions that operate within the tradition of humanitarian relief have not been as strict on the norm of neutrality, and some have tended to side with the party considered to be the victim. Relief activities are not necessarily separate from politics. Some governments may use relief as an instrument to attain political or strategic goals or to prevent unwanted developments from taking place.[4] Basically, the tradition is characterized by voluntary efforts by nongovernmental organizations (NGOs), often undertaken in tandem with other governments. In practice, national governments have contributed extensively to humanitarian relief efforts, at home and beyond their borders as well.

Organizations that function within the tradition of humanitarian relief contribute to an awareness of and concern for people in need across borders. Although human-made and natural catastrophes are the primary focus of relief efforts, attention to human suffering and the empathy created by alleviating suffering may have wider consequences. It may lead to a greater awareness of and concern about need and poverty in general, whatever its causes and wherever it is found. Such attitudes may generate a willingness to initiate and sustain assistance for development as well as a continuation of relief assistance.

The Tradition of Solidarity

This tradition has been closely related to socialist and social-democratic movements and trade unions, although not exclusively so.[5] The norms on which this family of ideologies are based are largely similar to those that underpin the tradition of humanitarian relief. There may even be commonalities with those of some religious traditions. However, they also contain a dimension of self-interest: reciprocity is fundamental in solidarity relations, although it is recognized that all members may not be equally able to contribute.

The raison d'être of solidarity movements is to enhance the dignity and the economic and social conditions of their members. Historically, the nation-state emerged as the most important instrument trade unions and the political wings of solidarity movements could use to realize key objectives such as social justice, equality, and improvements in the welfare of members. Although seeking political control of state power became the primary way to attain goals, the perspective of solidarity movements also transcended national borders.

At an early stage, the socialist movement split over whether to use the ballot or force to acquire political control of the state. These differences also affected the use of state power once socialists were in control, as illustrated by the differing policies pursued by the Soviet Union and social-democratic West European states. However, socialists shared the idea of a strong, controlling, and intervening state and a large public sector. Long-term planning became a major instrument for moving development in the desired direction. Economic growth, especially industrial development, was seen as a fundamental precondition for developing and sustaining the welfare state, the core instrument for ensuring social security through income distribution (involving the instrument of taxation) and social services, including health and education.

Like the tradition of humanitarian relief (but from different perspectives), solidarity movements can hardly avoid creating general attitudes among their members that favor initiating and sustaining assistance for development in the South, as long as this is not detrimental to what are perceived as their own interests.

The Missionary Tradition

Many religions have been involved in missionary activities for centuries, within their home countries and across national borders. This makes it hazardous to attempt to identify common denominators, even from the limited perspective pursued here of norms that guide economic and social relations. However, we may note that the ethics of several religions prescribe that the fortunate ones in a society should look after and share with the less fortunate, particularly those in need. Such norms are present in the main religions, including Buddhism, Christianity, Hinduism, and Islam. Although these norms are primarily meant to govern interpersonal relations, they also govern the actions of institutions (even states) and activities that transcend the borders of nation-states.

In the Christian missionary tradition, proselytizing efforts in the South have long been combined with activities similar to the development assistance of more recent years, especially education and health care. In some cases, missionaries have contributed to economic development by introducing new techniques, especially in agriculture. While this "technical assistance" was instrumental in promoting the Gospel, it also put into practice the norms that were being preached.[6]

The ethics of the main religions, their activities to improve the lot of people in need at home, and the insights brought back by missionaries about prevailing conditions in the South all make it natural to expect that religious institutions would favor the idea of development assistance and would support sustaining such activities.

The Tradition of Human Rights

Human rights are enshrined in the UN Charter. The Preamble states: "We the peoples of the United Nations determined . . . to reaffirm faith in fundamental human rights, in the dignity and worth of the human person, in the equal rights of men and women and of nations large and small." This is followed up in Chapter I: the purpose of the UN is to "develop friendly relations among nations based on respect for the principle of equal rights and self-determination of peoples, and to take other appropriate measures to strengthen universal peace" (Article 1, paragraph 2) and to "achieve international cooperation in solving international problems of an economic, social, cultural, or humanitarian character, and in promoting and encouraging respect for human rights and fundamental freedoms for all without distinction as to race, sex, language, or religion" (Article 1, paragraph 3).

Human rights were codified in the Universal Declaration of Human Rights (which was adopted by the UN General Assembly in 1948) and in a series of subsequent international declarations and conventions that define human rights over a wide spectrum, including the most fundamental of all rights: the right to life; the right to freedom from torture and from arbitrary arrest and imprisonment; civil and political rights; and economic and social rights, including the right to employment, shelter, health, and education.[7]

The tradition of human rights as institutionalized in the UN system is almost as young as the idea of international development assistance. Given their prominence in the UN Charter, human rights could be expected to inspire and set their stamp on this new activity, especially its objectives and norms. It seems only logical that human rights and international development assistance would be mutually reinforcing.

The Ideas

The prevailing development paradigms in the late 1940s and 1950s largely reflected European experiences and the theories and models that emerged from these experiences. In the bipolar international security system that came into being after World War II, a cluster of capitalist models associated with the main western powers came to represent one pole, while various socialist models associated with the main Eastern European powers represented the other. This dichotomy, however, is too simplistic, as national systems showed considerable variation with regard to the major dimensions involved, particularly in the West, where Labour Party governments were in power in several European countries.

The main ideological and theoretical conflict between these two systems concerned the role of the state. In economic policy, the ideological poles were the liberal mini-state, where "decisions" were made by market forces, and the socialist central-planning state. In the sphere of politics, similar poles appeared: at one end of the spectrum, states pursued liberal political values and norms; at the other end of the spectrum, states pursued authoritarian political values.

The various development models emerged from different historical settings. The liberal model is associated with the industrial revolution in England. It relied on market forces, industrial growth that started with light industries, private investments resulting from high profits created by low wages, and a process of continuous technological innovation and improvement. Such a system thrived with free international trade. Latecomers, however, did not find free trade equally useful. In order to enable them to catch up, an alternative model was designed, that of state capitalism combined with protective measures, especially with regard to infant industries. In the early phase, this model was associated with Germany and Russia in particular. However, mixed economies characterized by varying degrees of state intervention and participation were evolving in the West during the first part of the past century. This mix also included labor governments that professed a socialist or social democratic ideology.

The Soviet model was qualitatively different from the predominantly liberal development strategies evolving in the West, although similarities with the state capitalism of the early phase of the industrial revolution could be traced. The authoritarian state used coercive powers to enforce capital accumulation. Its main instrument was the five-year plan, which set quantitative objectives to be attained during the plan period. The emphasis was on industrialization, with priority given to heavy industry; technologically advanced methods were applied and large-scale industries developed. Resources were transferred from agriculture to industry. In this process, the agricultural sector was collectivized.

These models influenced the development strategies of political elites in newly formed states in the South. They became instruments in the East-West conflict: during the Cold War, the superpowers used their respective models in their ideological warfare to gain influence in the Third World. The UN arena was no exception in this regard.

After World War II, the focus of economists in the West was almost exclusively on economic growth. Mainstream thinking, which drew on Keynesian theory, emphasized the intervening state. As Hettne puts it, development became the art of large-scale social engineering.[8] Capital accumulation (saving) was seen as the prime factor in the creation of economic growth. The so-called Harrod-Domar model played a prominent part in this thinking.[9] Growth was seen as a continuous process toward higher stages of development: each increase in output would provide the basis for further growth because part of the surplus would be reinvested. The ability to save (invest) would therefore increase with the level of income; once the process was started, economic growth would be self-sustaining. Although economic growth was conceived of as a national process, neoclassical economists also emphasized the importance of foreign trade. Technological innovation was considered an important part of the growth process. Foreign trade would also contribute to the diffusion of new technology, skills, and capital, to the benefit of newcomers.

The modernization paradigm was hegemonic in western development thinking during these early years. Development was seen as a process by which a society would move from one stage of development to another (higher) stage. These stages were identified (and quantified) in economic, political, and cultural terms.[10] Walt Rostow, who synthesized the main elements of development economics into an ideological platform for the West in its competition with the East, was probably the most influential western economist to shape the worldview of a generation of foreign policy actors concerned with development issues. The influence of his thinking extended beyond the 1960s.[11]

The ethnocentrism of the modernization development paradigm is explicit: the ultimate goal of developing nations is to become a western consumer society. Development, by definition, implied bridging the gap between traditional societies and industrialized states by copying the West. Capital formation in terms of savings and investment, particularly through industrialization, was the golden key to development.

To what extent can we find footprints of these various development models and theories, especially the modernization paradigm, in the UN's first efforts at development assistance?

The Institutional Heritage

We can surmise that the idea of development assistance as institutionalized by the United Nations in the mid-twentieth century was influenced most strongly by the previous reports, recommendations, or practices of the UN or its specialized agencies or those of the League of Nations. The dynamics of international cooperation may also be instrumental in this regard: from an institution-building perspective, cooperation may be extended to new areas, attracting the interest of a growing number of new member governments of the South and in this way integrating them into the fold.

It is also to be expected that the idea of international cooperation at the UN would be influenced by the most recent effort to provide aid for development: the massive transfer of resources from the United States to Europe after World War II within the framework of the Marshall Plan. It is clear, though, that the prevailing conditions for development in postwar Europe were quite different from those in most of the emerging states in the South.

The League of Nations

Both the United Nations and the League of Nations were created with the primary objective of securing and maintaining peace after wars that had originated in Europe but had come to involve most of the world, including independent countries and colonies in the South. The League of Nations had focused in part on humanitarian, social, and economic affairs, especially in its later years. Its constitution had opened up the possibility for suborganizations to undertake activities within these areas, which led to the establishment of the International Labour Organization in 1919. A few other organizations and special committees were established within the League to deal with social and economic affairs, including health.

Technical assistance was provided within the framework of the League of Nations. In 1929, an agreement with the Chinese government made it possible for outside experts to assist the government with problems that included health, education, communications, and agriculture.

At the end of the 1930s, ideas to coordinate these activities within a central organ of the League of Nations—and to integrate the United States (which was not a League member) in its work—were explored. In August 1939, the Bruce Committee (named after the committee's chairman, Stanley Melbourne Bruce of Australia) came up with a proposal for a new body that would consist of ministers of finance, trade, communications, and health of the League's member governments but would be open to participation from other governments. It proposed that the League's secretary-general report annually to the body's assembly on the work carried out in the economic and social field.[12] Because of the outbreak of World War II and the collapse of the League of Nations, the recommendations of the Bruce Committee report could not be implemented. However, the ideas survived and were brought up again when the UN was created.

Although security concerns were preeminent in the formation of the United Nations, some small and middle powers, with the active support of the United States, succeeded in including the issues of social and economic development in the UN Charter.[13] ECOSOC became the central UN organ for realizing these commitments.

We can surmise that this heritage established a foundation on which new actors, inspired by ideals other than a mere concern for institution-building within the UN system, would add new building blocks.

The Marshall Plan

The Marshall Plan, named after the U.S. secretary of state at the time, was implemented from 1948 until 1952. It involved huge financial transfers from the U.S. government to European countries—some $13.5 billion—to enable them to rebuild their economies and recover from the devastation caused by World War II.[14]

This generosity was coupled with enlightened self-interest: the United States wanted to create an external economic and political environment that coincided with the ideological aspirations and the economic and security interests of a great power aspiring to global hegemony. Relations with the Union of Soviet Socialist Republics (USSR) were getting chilly, and the United States felt that rebuilding the European economy was an instrument to bolster democracy and contain communism during these years. The assistance was provided with political conditions attached: recipient governments had to commit themselves to an open market economy and to cooperation between participating European countries and across the Atlantic. It is hardly surprising that the USSR and countries within its sphere of influence turned down the offer. Some of the governments that accepted the U.S. offer had problems with the conditions of the plan but found ways of evading them. And there was something in it for American farmers: almost one-third of the assistance consisted of food, fodder, and fertilizers.[15]

These massive transfers took place close in time to the first UN efforts to create institutions for development assistance, and, in the European setting at least, they worked. The Marshall Plan thus seemed a suitable model when the perspective was broadened to include the "underdeveloped" world and its need for economic and social development through development assistance.

The Expanded Programme of Technical Assistance

- **The Beginning: Aspirations and Guiding Principles**
- **The Creation of the EPTA: Background, Objectives, Main Principles, and Funding**
- **Implementation: Evolving Patterns**
- **Some Concluding Observations**

In the UN Charter, the founding governments committed themselves to promoting "higher standards of living, full employment, and conditions of economic and social progress and development" and "solutions of international economic, social, health, and related problems" (Chapter IX, Article 55). Article 56 reiterated this commitment: "All members pledge themselves to take joint and separate action in co-operation with the Organization for the achievement of the purposes set forth in Article 55."

Toward the end of 1946, the UN General Assembly recognized the responsibility of the United Nations to assist some member states by providing expert advice "in the various fields of economic, social and cultural development." The justification was clear: development was important for world peace and prosperity.[1] Within the UN system, the central body concerned with such matters was ECOSOC, where discussion about the developmental needs of new and emerging states took place during the early years.

The United Nations became the major forum for promoting the idea of development assistance. As might be expected, representatives of governments in the South, whose numbers were increasing, played an active role in getting this idea on the agenda. The UN Secretariat also played an active role, as did other UN bodies. The UN arena globalized the issue in a way that could not have been achieved in any other forum. Providing assistance in order to promote development in "underdeveloped countries" was made a normative issue in the sense that states were expected to honor their (ideal) commitments as members of the world organization.

This is not to imply that idealism ruled supreme: the United Nations was also a major arena for power politics and the pursuit of foreign policy interests. In the early postwar period, increasing tensions between the former allies divided Europe. For the emerging superpowers that aspired to global hegemony, the growing number of newly independent states also became important. In this context, aid became an instrument for fortifying old relations, establishing new loyalties, containing the influence of rivals, and ensuring the superpowers' economic and strategic interests and ideological concerns.

The main response to the socioeconomic expectations embedded in the UN Charter came from the United States, which was the richest country in the world. Unlike its European allies, its infrastructure and economy had not been damaged in the war. By contrast, most governments in war-torn Europe were preoccupied with rebuilding and reconstructing their economies. In these efforts, they received generous support from the U.S. government in the form of financial aid and food aid through what became known as the Marshall Plan.

By the late 1940s, however, the concept of development assistance had begun to attract greater attention, particularly within the UN system. Efforts concentrated on establishing the Expanded Programme of Technical Assistance and a Special United Nations Fund for Economic Development (see chapter 3). Although the United Nations played a crucial role in bringing onto the international agenda the need for assistance to promote economic development in less-developed countries and regions, the United States played a leading role in terms of both ideas and praxis. President Harry S. Truman's inaugural address for his second term of office, which broadcasted on radio and television on 20 January 1949, was perhaps the most important event in this regard. Truman's speech was important for setting priorities and furthering progress within the United Nations, and it decisively launched a large bilateral program of technical assistance by a U.S. administration that had a financial framework that far exceeded that of UN programs. It also inspired allied governments to develop their own bilateral development assistance programs.

Although relations with the countries of the South were not high on the agenda of the industrial countries of the North during the years immediately after World War II, they began to attract increased attention due to the East-West rivalry and the decolonization process that was under way. In the West, as in the East, attention focused on the growing tensions between the emerging blocs. Security concerns became the top priority in the 1940s, increasingly burdening the budgets of the superpowers and making it even harder to release resources for development in the South. In the early 1950s, the Korean War had a similar effect.

Within the United Nations, the main focus became technical assistance. The debate on capital assistance resulted in appeals to the International Bank for Reconstruction and Development, which was then focused on reconstruction in Europe, to increase its lending to "underdeveloped" countries.[2] In ECOSOC, views were split. While most western governments believed that foreign commercial investments should be encouraged and that obstacles should be removed, the Soviet bloc opposed these ideas, seeing such investments as instruments of exploitation and imperialism. As Sixten Heppling has observed, the few developing-country governments represented in ECOSOC sought a middle ground, insisting that external capital should not adversely affect their political independence and unrestricted control of their own natural resources.[3]

A financial heritage from the United Nations Relief and Rehabilitation Agency was instrumental in stimulating operative activities both within the Food and Agriculture Organization (see chapter 8) and in the United Nations itself, especially the Department of Economic and Social Affairs. When these funds ended, provision was made in the 1947 budget to continue some of the social services rendered to countries in need of assistance.

The Beginning: Aspirations and Guiding Principles

First Steps along the Road

Within the United Nations, a breakthrough came in 1948. It had been prepared by ECOSOC-established commissions—especially the Sub-Commission on Economic Development of the Economic and Employment Commission—in response to the mandate from the General Assembly in December 1946.

Gradually, the basic principles for the new activity were hammered out. In March 1947, ECOSOC instructed the Economic and Employment Commission that its work on technical and other assistance "should be guided by the principle that such assistance should not be used for the purpose of exploitation or of obtaining political and other advantages exclusively for countries rendering such assistance."[4] This was followed up with a resolution that shaped the institutionalization of these activities and instructed the UN Secretary-General to establish machinery within the Secretariat to assist member governments in obtaining information on expert personnel, research facilities, and other resources that the world body and its specialized agencies could make available to governments requesting such assistance.[5]

General Assembly Resolution 200 (III)

On 4 December 1948, the General Assembly adopted two resolutions with far-reaching political implications for the new policy field of international development assistance: resolutions 198 (III) and 200 (III). In resolution 198 (III), the General Assembly recommended that ECOSOC and the specialized agencies "give further and urgent consideration to the whole problem of the economic development of under-developed countries in *all* its aspects." It asked ECOSOC to report on measures already devised and on proposals for other measures designed to "promote economic development and to raise the standards of living of under-developed countries."[6] The justification is important; the resolution asserted that the low standards of living in member states had "bad economic and social effects in the countries directly concerned and on the world as a whole, and create conditions of instability which are prejudicial to the maintenance of peaceful and friendly relations among nations and to the development of economic and social progress." The UN Charter "binds Member States individually and collectively to promote higher standards of living."[7] Resolution 200 (III) dealt more specifically with the role of technical assistance in promoting economic development, with particular reference to the UN contribution in this regard.[8]

THE INITIATIVE AND THE STATED PURPOSE

Four countries from the South—Burma, Chile, Egypt, and Peru—were the driving force behind resolution 200 (III).[9] The resolution referred to the UN Charter, which asserts that the promotion of economic and social progress and development is one of the organization's principal objectives. It also noted that a lack of expert personnel as well as lack of technical organization were among the factors that "impede the economic development of the under-developed areas."

On this basis, the General Assembly decided to appropriate "the funds necessary to enable the Secretary-General to perform the following functions, where appropriate in co-operation with the specialized agencies, when requested to do so by Member Governments":

a. Arrange for the organization of international teams consisting of experts provided by or through the United Nations and the specialized agencies for the purpose of advising those Governments in connexion with their economic development programmes, the organization of such teams, of course, not to preclude the invitation of individual, or groups of, experts from the United Nations or from specialized agencies in connexion with problems in the field of those specialized agencies;

b. Arrange for facilities for the training abroad of experts of under-developed countries through the provision of fellowships for study in those countries or institutions which, in particular fields of study, have achieved an advanced level of technical competence;

c. Arrange for the training of local technicians within the under-developed countries themselves by promoting visits of experts in various aspects of economic development for the purpose of instructing local personnel and for assisting in the organization of technical institutions;

d. Provide facilities designed to assist Governments to obtain technical personnel, equipment and supplies, and to arrange for the organization of such other services as may be appropriate in the promotion of economic development, including the organization of seminars on special problems of economic development, and the exchange of current information concerning technical problems of economic development.

GUIDING PRINCIPLES FOR THE NEW ACTIVITY

The norms and guidelines established for technical assistance deserve particular attention. According to the resolution, the services rendered to countries "shall be decided by the Government concerned." Moreover, countries desiring assistance "should perform in advance as much of the work as possible in order to define the nature and the scope of the problem involved."

Moreover, it stated that technical assistance should:

a. Not be a means of foreign economic and political interference in the internal affairs of the country concerned and shall not be accompanied by any considerations of a political nature

b. Be given only to or through governments

c. Be designed to meet the needs of the country concerned

d. Be provided, as far as possible, in the form which that country desires

e. Be of high quality and technical competence

FINANCIAL SCOPE

The resolution also stated that the sums appropriated for carrying out these functions should not be expended on functions or services that were the particular responsibility of a specialized agency except in agreement with the executive head of that agency. That year, a modest amount ($288,000) was included in the regular UN budget for a program of technical assistance to promote economic development.

THE PRIMARY CONCERN:
SOVEREIGNTY OF THE RECIPIENT GOVERNMENTS

In our discussion, the space given to this resolution is justified not only because of its importance in initiating technical assistance but also because it established several principles. The recipient countries were to be in full control of requests for assistance and the kind of assistance rendered. Moreover, the assistance should meet needs of the countries concerned and reinforce efforts made by the governments themselves. There was to be no economic or political interference from outside in the internal affairs of the countries concerned.

These simple principles were anchored in the UN Charter, especially the principle of noninterference. Governments of countries that only recently had won their independence or had been vulnerable and threatened conscientiously guarded their state sovereignty.

The Clarion Call from Washington

The United States, however, had the strongest impact on international development assistance in the UN and beyond. In his 1949 inaugural address, President Truman announced a program "for peace and freedom in four major courses of action." The part of the speech that addressed the fourth action merits lengthy quotation:

> We must embark on a bold new program for making the benefits of our scientific advances and industrial progress available for the improvement and growth of underdeveloped areas.
>
> More than half the people of the world are living in conditions approaching misery. Their food is inadequate. They are victims of disease. Their economic life is primitive and stagnant. Their poverty is a handicap and a threat both to them and to more prosperous areas. For the first time in history, humanity possesses the knowledge and the skill to relieve the suffering of these people.
>
> The United States is pre-eminent among nations in the development of industrial and scientific techniques. The material resources which we can afford to use for the assistance of other peoples are limited. But our imponderable resources in technical knowledge are constantly growing and are inexhaustible. I believe that we should make available to peace-loving peoples the benefits of our store of technical knowledge in order to help them realize their aspirations for a better life. And, in cooperation with other nations, we should foster capital investments in areas needing development.
>
> Our aim should be to help the free peoples of the world, through their own efforts, to produce more food, more clothing, more materials for housing, and more mechanical power to lighten their burdens.
>
> We invite other countries to pool their technological resources in this undertaking. Their contributions will be warmly welcomed. This should be a cooperative enterprise in which all nations work together through the United Nations and its specialized agencies wherever practicable. It must be a worldwide effort for the achievement of peace, plenty, and freedom.
>
> With the cooperation of business, private capital, agriculture, and labor in this country, this program can greatly increase the industrial activity in other nations and can raise substantially their standard of living.
>
> Such new economic developments must be devised and controlled to benefit the peoples of the areas in which they are established. Guarantees to the investor must be balanced by guarantees in the interest of the people whose resources and whose labor go into these developments. The old imperialism—exploitation for foreign profit—has no place in our plans. What we envisage is a program of development based on the concepts of democratic fair-dealing.[10]

With this statement, Truman gave the green light to the U.S. Foreign Service to act. According to Heppling, members of the U.S. delegation to the 1949 sessions of ECOSOC and other relevant gatherings within the UN system "came well prepared and determined to create a basis for a proper UN response to the President's challenge. They quickly took and retained an initiative in the process that now started the creation of an Expanded Programme of Technical Assistance."[11]

The Creation of the EPTA:
Background, Objectives, Main Principles, and Funding

The ball was again in the court of ECOSOC and the Secretariat. ECOSOC asked the Secretary-General to present a report that contained a "comprehensive plan for an expanded co-operative programme of technical assistance for economic development through the United Nations and its specialized agencies"; methods of financing such a program, including a budget; and ways of coordinating the planning and execution of the program.[12]

The Secretary-General established a task force within the Secretariat, headed by David Owen, to come up with a plan. Several specialized agencies—the FAO, the ILO, the United Nations Educational, Scientific and Cultural Organization (UNESCO), the World Health Organization, and the International Civil Aviation Organization (ICAO)—were invited to participate in this work.[13] In May, this task force produced an extensive report that greatly influenced the future work of the United Nations and its specialized agencies within the field of technical assistance and economic development. The first part of this report outlined the objectives and the nature of the program, identified the fields of work and the various forms of technical assistance, and proposed organizational and financial arrangements. All heads of the organizations involved, including the Secretary-General, had agreed to the text. In the second part of the report, the United Nations and its specialized agencies presented detailed proposals for their futures and budgets for the next two years (provided extra funds were made available); these varied between $20.7 million (FAO) and $0.7 million (ICAO), with the Secretariat asking for $15.2 million.[14]

Extensive discussions on the report followed at the ninth session of ECOSOC, meeting at the Palais des Nations in Geneva. Perspectives on the U.S. initiative, reflecting President Truman's Point Four, differed extensively. The Cold War between East and West was mounting, and spokesmen of the Soviet bloc reflected this increasing tension. They placed the initiative in the context of the colonial and imperialist policies of major western powers toward their colonies and less-developed countries, strongly criticizing their past and present practice. They also presented an alternative—a socialist development model.[15]

Hernando Santa Cruz (Chile) became a key spokesman for an emerging loose group of "underdeveloped" countries, emphasizing the need for development finance and rejecting the Soviet development model, which he characterized as "based on enforcement."[16] The delegations disagreed on the financial framework and on how the proposed activities should be organized. In the end, the whole question of economic development, including technical assistance programs, was referred to the Economic Committee of ECOSOC.[17]

The Economic Committee was chaired by Ambassador Santa Cruz. After three intense weeks, the committee produced its report. The president of ECOSOC congratulated them on their "masterpiece of clear drafting."[18] Based on this report, ECOSOC and the General Assembly established patterns that guided UN development assistance for years.[19] The impact went beyond the activities of the world body and its specialized agencies: these norms also influenced the development assistance of UN member governments. A closer look is therefore justified.

Objectives and Norms

The objectives and guiding principles established were almost identical with those that had been drawn up by the General Assembly in resolution 200 (III). The primary objective was to help "underdeveloped countries" strengthen their national economies through "the development of their industries and agriculture, with a view to promoting their economic and political independence in the spirit of the Charter of the United Nations, and to ensure the attainment of higher levels of economic and social welfare for their entire populations."[20]

ECOSOC and the General Assembly also confirmed the general principles established in resolution 200 (III), emphasizing the sovereignty of the recipient governments. An important related point was added; namely, that one should avoid distinctions in aid provision based on the political structure of the country requesting assistance or from the race or religion of its population.[21]

These norms were reflected in the standards for work and personnel that were established. It was emphasized that the highest professional competence should be maintained in all services undertaken; moreover, experts should be chosen "not only for their technical competence, but also for their sympathetic understanding of the cultural backgrounds and specific needs of the countries to be assisted and for their capacity to adapt methods of work to local conditions, social and material."[22] These norms were also reflected in the guidelines established for the selection of projects.[23]

Governments requesting assistance were expected to participate in and contribute to achieving the desired results. Assistance was conceived of as "help to self-help." Requesting governments were expected to "undertake to maintain or set up . . . such governmental co-ordination machinery as may be needed to ensure that their own technical, natural and financial resources are mobilized, canalized and utilized in the interest of economic development designed to improve the standard of living of their peoples and through which the effective use of any major international technical assistance resources could be assured." They were normally "to assume responsibility for a substantial part of the costs of technical services with which they are provided, at least that part which can be paid in their own currencies" and undertake "the sustained efforts required for economic development, including support and progressive assumption of financial responsibility for the administration of projects initiated at their request under international auspices."[24]

The Division of Labor between UN Specialized Agencies and Central Bodies

To ensure a high quality of assistance, ECOSOC also recommended some solutions that aimed at regulating the internal order of the UN system. One point concerned relations between the central organization and its specialized agencies: should responsibility for the program be left to the various UN specialized agencies or should there also be a coordinating and/or operational role for the center? The issue of policy coherence was central in this connection. This *problématique* was crystallized in the interrelated issues concerning the new program's governing structure, particularly regarding financing and the distribution of funding.

From the start, the specialized agencies had been included in the process that led to the creation of the EPTA: the UN Secretary-General had brought four of the most important agencies concerned with economic and social development (the FAO, the ILO, UNESCO, and the WHO) into the task force to prepare the follow-up that ECOSOC had requested. Thus, the basic document in this context was produced in close cooperation with the specialized agencies.[25] In the extensive second part of the report, the participating agencies presented their individual program proposals. The implication was that the specialized agencies, within their specific fields of responsibility, would be responsible for technical assistance. However, this document also envisaged a role for the Secretariat as a separate operational "agency" within the program, and the Secretary-General argued for the establishment of a common fund from which the program could be financed.

INSTITUTIONAL PATTERNS

ECOSOC asked the Secretary-General to invite the Administrative Committee on Coordination (ACC) to set up a Technical Assistance Board (TAB) consisting of the UN Secretary-General as chair and the executive heads of the organizations participating in the program. The Secretary-General was authorized, after consultations with the other participating organizations, to designate the executive secretary of the TAB. The participating agencies could assign members of their staff to the secretariat of the EPTA. In addition to the TAB, a standing Technical Assistance Committee (TAC) was also to be established, consisting of ECOSOC members. This committee could sit while ECOSOC was not in session. The TAC was given controlling and conflict-solving functions vis-à-vis the TAB on behalf of ECOSOC.

A CONCERN FOR COORDINATION

A concern for cooperation and coordination is reflected in the steering structure that was established. In this three-layered system—a secretariat with an executive secretary; an interagency management committee (TAB); and an intergovernmental committee (TAC) surveying the activities—the TAB represented the main coordinating body at the horizontal level, while the TAC had a vertical coordinating function.

The Economic Committee and, in turn, ECOSOC recommended several measures to enhance interagency coordination—especially with regard to mutual information and consultations among the participating organizations. In addition to this horizontal coordination between the specialized agencies and the UN Secretariat, another mechanism combined horizontal and vertical coordination. Each participating organization was to present its proposed program for the next fiscal year to the TAB and comment on its experiences with the expanded program. The TAB was to examine the programs of these organizations in relation to each other. Norms (guidelines) were established at the project level in order to enhance cooperation and coordination among participating organizations.[26]

RELATIONS BETWEEN THE MAIN ACTORS

The main issues governing the relations between the key partners involved were crystallized in the decisions of ECOSOC and the General Assembly, as outlined above. A look at some of the concerns expressed during the process may broaden the picture somewhat.

One key issue was the perception of development. In the late 1940s and early 1950s, economic growth that emphasized industrialization was the central focus. In the plenary sessions of ECOSOC and in the Economic Committee, however, development was conceived of as a more complex process involving interdependence between agriculture and industry and between social and economic factors. The committee argued for an integrated approach to development. This, in turn, had several implications for the institutional solutions to be sought along the spectrum of centralization to decentralization.

Another prominent concern regarded the program's coherence. In ECOSOC, Belgium's representative feared that centrifugal forces within the specialized agencies might cause the program to disintegrate.[27] Such a concern is well attuned to an integrated approach to development that views efforts within several sectors as interrelated. Institutions could respond to such a problem by formulating clear and unambiguous objectives and by establishing procedures that would set up mechanisms for solving possible conflicts and that would ensure that planning, decision-making, and implementation would be coordinated among the involved agencies.

Another concern also came to the fore: that the new resources should not be used to swell the budgets of participating UN organizations. If this happened, Australia argued, member countries would be less willing to contribute to the program and might prefer a bilateral approach. A centralized administration was desirable. The program's success would depend on whether the UN established "an effective central thinking unit" and whether such an organ could exert effective influence on the activities of the specialized agencies and the United Nations itself.[28]

Some western delegations also feared that new resources that in some cases might be larger than the ordinary budgets of specialized agencies might distract them from focusing on the tasks for which they were originally established. It was argued that the activities of ongoing regular technical assistance programs would be absorbed by the EPTA and its voluntary funding. Hence, the argument went, the funding of regular development assistance activities should be removed from the regular budgets of the agencies. However, this position was strongly opposed by delegates from the South.[29]

Distribution of Financial Resources: The UN and Its Specialized Agencies

PROGRAM FUNDING AND BUDGET FRAMES

The nature of the program's funding would fundamentally influence the degree of centralization of the new administrative system. The Economic Committee deliberated how to organize the collection of funds. Should member governments make separate payments to each of the specialized agencies or should they pay a lump sum to a central fund that would be distributed among these agencies in accordance with the objectives of the program and priorities established by ECOSOC?

Direct contributions to the specialized agencies would decentralize decision making to the agencies concerned. The governments that provided aid would also be able to influence the profile of the program directly by selecting the projects they wanted to support. By the same token, lump-sum payments to a central fund would reduce the direct influence of donor governments. Overall decisions involving resource distribution would be the responsibility of a central organ that might or might not include the relevant specialized agencies. This would enable greater cooperation, coordination, and coherence.

The Economic Committee recommended that the General Assembly authorize the Secretary-General to set up a special account for technical assistance for economic development to which the voluntary contributions of countries would be credited. It also asked the Secretary-General to convene a Technical Assistance Conference at UN headquarters immediately after the fourth session of the General Assembly. All members of the UN and specialized agencies participating in the program were to be invited to this conference as well as representatives of the specialized agencies (who had no voting rights, however). The purpose was to ascertain "the total amount of contributions available from participating Governments for the execution of the expanded technical assistance programme of the United Nations and the specialized agencies" during its first period of operation.[30] The majorities in ECOSOC and the General Assembly agreed.[31]

RESOURCE DISTRIBUTION FORMULA

Varying expectations had been expressed in ECOSOC plenary sessions concerning both the financial framework needed for the program to fill its functions and the amounts that could realistically be expected. A core issue was how the resources should be distributed with regard to the UN and the various specialized agencies.

The Economic Committee had no financial framework on which to base its recommendations. Instead, it decided to seek agreement on a formula for distributing whatever resources might be made available. However, it did not completely disregard what might be realistically expected in financial support: while the formula was to be automatically applied to the first $10 million available during the fiscal year, only 70 percent of the second $10 million would automatically be distributed to the participating organizations and 30 percent would be retained for subsequent allocations. All contributions above $20 million would be retained in a similar way.[32]

Main Construct and Some Dilemmas

The financial frameworks envisaged or actually placed at the disposal of the UN and its specialized agencies in 1949–1950 to realize the objectives set for the EPTA were indeed modest, particularly when compared with the figures for total official development assistance half a century later. The program came into operation in June 1950. On 12 June, when the Technical Assistance Conference at Lake Success became a pledging gathering, $20 million was promised for the eighteen-month period ending 31 December 1951. The final act of the conference confirmed the arrangements recommended by ECOSOC, including the formula for distributing resources.

The UN Secretariat and ECOSOC were in charge of the process that led up to the establishment of the EPTA. Nevertheless, the specialized agencies were the arms with which the world organization could

BOX 2.1. EPTA Activities: The Distribution Formula for Cooperating Organizations

From its inception, the Expanded Programme of Technical Assistance relied on the established organizations of the United Nations—particularly its specialized agencies and the Secretariat—as executing agencies within their areas of specialization. The resources that the EPTA made available to these entities therefore represented an attractive possibility for them to expand their operational activities. In the documents that established the EPTA, however, no reference was made to how the resources should be distributed among the competing agencies. This distribution formula—and the way it was agreed to—represents a story within the story.

The Economic Committee of ECOSOC, chaired by Hernando Santa Cruz (Chile), was instrumental in forging the formula. The members of the committee were invited to propose the percentage of the total allocations to be distributed to each of the specialized agencies and the UN Secretariat. Suggestions from the delegations varied quite substantially. Mathematics was introduced to settle the issue: the outcome was decided, more or less, on the basis of the median value of these suggestions as slightly adjusted by the chair after consultation with the UN Secretariat.

According to this formula, the UN Secretariat was to receive 23 percent of the total amount. The FAO came out as the winner among the specialized agencies (29 percent), followed by the WHO (22 percent), UNESCO (14 percent), the ILO (11 percent), and the ICAO (1 percent).

In the Economic Committee, this proposal was adopted by twelve votes against none, with six abstentions. Interestingly, the agreed outcome was not far removed from the share of the respective budgets proposed by the involved organizations in the survey on which the decision to establish the EPTA had been based.

Sixten Heppling gives a vivid description of the discussions in the Economic Committee and the main concerns of the various delegations. He concluded that "one cannot truly state that the debate was exhaustive or very profound. Nor did it result in any generally accepted conclusions with regard to the causes and consequences of the many difficulties faced by underdeveloped countries in their quest for progress."

Sources: United Nations, *Technical Assistance for Economic Development: Plan for an Expanded Co-operative Programme through the United Nations and the Specialized Agencies* (Lake Success, N.Y.: United Nations, May 1949); ECOSOC, *Report of the Economic Committee,* ECOSOC document E/1526/Add. 1, 13 August 1949; and Sixten Heppling, *UNDP: From Agency Shares to Country Programmes, 1949–1975* (Stockholm: Ministry for Foreign Affairs, 1995), 32–37.

implement this new task. The outcome reflected the strong position of the agencies.

Beyond the primary objectives set for its operations, the EPTA—with its potential for mobilizing new resources—also became an instrument through which the UN could develop its own organization. There was great potential for conflict, particularly between the UN proper and the specialized agencies and between the specialized agencies themselves. Although modest in absolute terms, in relative terms the anticipated resources offered considerable potential for the participating organizations to expand their activities, particularly compared to the allocations for such activities in their regular budgets.

A harmony model was chosen for both these conflict dimensions. As main operators of the program, the specialized agencies were to administer the lion's share of the new resources. But the program's central organ—the UN Secretariat—would also administer some resources directly. ECOSOC had a coordinating role through the TAC. Nevertheless, the specialized agencies were given considerable influence, even with regard to coordinating activities, through their participation in the TAB. The distribution formula, which basically gave each of them a fixed resource share for the years ahead, was instrumental in securing harmony and interagency cooperation.

However, the potential for other conflicts was embedded in the established structure. One concerned the institutional development of the United Nations, especially relations between the UN and member governments requesting development assistance. The norms established for the EPTA were crystal clear about who should ultimately be in control of activities: the recipient governments. But because of the way resources were to be distributed, very little room, if any, was provided for those governments to influence general priorities except indirectly through the TAC.

There were no provisions to ensure that the UN would play a central role in negotiations with the governments requesting technical assistance. Almost four-fifths of financial resources were to be channeled through the specialized agencies. The individual agency would have responsibility for planning and for distributing its share of the program. Hence, negotiations about activities would mainly take place between agency representatives and the governments requesting assistance, not directly between the UN and these governments.

Another norm prescribed that the various activities be coherent and coordinated, which meant coordination with the individual recipient country. This ambiguity, in turn, affected the nature of the UN presence at the country level, which again affected relations between the center and the specialized agencies. Who was ultimately in control of relations between the UN and its member governments?

Some of these dilemmas were addressed when the program moved from the design phase into implementation. Other dilemmas remained for years, especially the inherent incompatibility of the aim of integration and coordination and financial arrangements that ensured separate funding for the specialized agencies according to a predetermined share.

Implementation: Evolving Patterns

Objectives, norms, and the institutional framework convey a picture of how decision-makers conceived of the new commitment to development cooperation. Ideas become further developed when they are implemented in the environment in which they operate. The focus here is on institutional development, especially regarding the program's field activities. The EPTA's extensive fellowship program for education abroad that annually accounted for between 14 and 22 percent of total expenditures is not given adequate attention here. The EPTA awarded an impressive number of fellowships—17,744 up through 1960 and another 21,005 over the following four years.[33] However, no statistics exist that can ascertain the brain-drain effects of the program. We do not know how many of these fellowship holders subsequently returned to their home countries.

The way technical assistance was organized reinforced established institutional patterns in the UN system and the division of labor within the organization. Most of the new resources were distributed to the specialized agencies that were seen as most relevant for the type of activities in focus. The UN's central political bodies discussed sector priorities, giving emphasis to industrial and agricultural development. However, the EPTA prioritized only indirectly through resource distribution. The distribution formula, once established, decreased competition for resources among specialized agencies.

At an early stage, the TAC recognized the need for coordination at the regional and country levels and initiated a process of establishing a permanent UN presence in some major recipient countries.[34] This presence developed into UN resident representative offices with responsibilities beyond that of coordinating technical assistance.

The "Forward Look" of 1956

The EPTA's financial framework, as established by voluntary contributions by member governments at Lake Success in mid-1950 and at later pledging conferences, was much lower than the optimists had hoped, particularly the governments of developing countries. During the first years of operation, pledges were also slow to be honored, and requests soon reached amounts far beyond what could be met by available financial resources. This mismatch between ambitions and expectations and actual funding created frustration and disappointment among requesting governments and within the EPTA system of cooperating organizations. However, it also gave rise to visions of what could be achieved if the resources existed. These visions were embodied in the TAB's "Forward Look" in 1956.[35]

The ideas put forward were embedded within the core perspective of the program. The idea of the "Forward Look" included more support of the kind already allowed for in the third pillar of the program—equipment. It was also geared toward including more support for systematic surveys of basic resources; developing education and training services of all kinds; creating or expanding research facilities that might improve the productive capacity of the countries concerned; initiating demonstration facilities in agriculture, livestock farming, forest production, and fishing; developing universities, teacher training institutes, and institutes and centers of basic scientific research; developing housing and buildings; controlling debilitating diseases; and providing training in public and fiscal administration. The vision reflected a holistic view of development and a more ambitious financial framework: a target of $50 million in annual commitments would finance a limited expansion. The more ambitious alternative was not given a price tag, but it "would call for resources many times the size of those now available."[36]

This initiative had been spurred by the frustrations staff members of specialized agencies had experienced in trying to operate an ambitious program that was underresourced. All along, the governments of developing countries had staunchly argued for capital assistance as a complement to technical assistance. Many of the points in the "Forward Look" derived from the discourse that took place on this issue in the UN's intergovernmental bodies and in reports prepared by the Secretariat in response to requests from these bodies. Although it met with considerable goodwill, the TAB initiative did not fare much better than the long fight for the creation of SUNFED. On the other hand, it might have facilitated the final outcome of that fight: the creation of the Special Fund two years later.

Distribution of the Central Fund: Competing Concerns

The model chosen in 1949 for distributing resources among the participating organizations served as a means to avoid conflicts within the UN system. It reflected the distribution of labor between the central organization and its specialized agencies. It can also be interpreted as reflecting the real balance of power between the center and its specialized agencies at that time. The most interesting feature of the new construct was that the central organization assumed an operational (executive) role for itself. However, it left unresolved the power relations between the UN system and the governments requesting assistance.

For several years, the formula governing financial allocations remained more or less intact. However, it was challenged from several perspectives. The central leadership was concerned about the overall coherence of the program. Another concern expressed in intergovernmental bodies was related to coordination at the national level of the recipient country. And a third issue, expressed in particular by Third World representatives, concerned the "missing link": the role of the requesting government that, according to the norms established for the program, was supposed to have major influence with regard to the priorities and the implementation of projects within its borders. These concerns were interlinked.

The formula ensured extensive autonomy for the specialized agencies in terms of planning and executing their part of the program vis-à-vis the central bodies, which were responsible for political and administrative coordination (in the first place, the TAC, the TAB, and the EPTA secretariat), and the governments requesting assistance. The major justification for changing the system was the goal of integrating recipient governments into the process. However, two other concerns were probably of equal importance in driving program reform: enhancing centralization and ensuring better coordination at the national level of the recipient country.[37]

STRENGTHENING THE CENTRAL ORGAN

In 1952, it was decided that only part of the contributions should be automatically transferred to the agencies, leaving it to the TAB to distribute, according to the agreed-upon formula, a substantial portion of the funds on a project-by-project basis.[38] The formula was also slightly adapted to include additional organizations: the International Telecommunication Union (ITU) and the World Meteorological Organization (WMO). Later, the International Atomic Energy Agency (IAEA) and the Universal Postal Union (UPU) were added in 1960 and 1963, respectively.

In response to a TAC report to ECOSOC arguing for stronger central leadership and more continuous central guidance of the EPTA, ECOSOC instructed the Secretary-General to appoint an executive chairman of the TAB on a full-time basis. This person was to have wide powers, effective control over the program's economic resources, and authority to develop integrated country programs in agreement with the governments concerned and in consultation with agencies. David Owen, chair of the TAB, was appointed executive chair; he served as the head of the TAB from mid-1952 until the end of 1965, when the EPTA merged with the Special Fund to become the United Nations Development Programme.[39]

STRENGTHENING NATIONAL-LEVEL COORDINATION

One argument prominent in the intergovernmental bodies of ECOSOC was that UN technical assistance should not be a collection of isolated projects: it should seek to meet the needs of the recipient countries in a holistic way. Such coordination would necessarily have to happen at the country level. In order to meet practical goals and adhere to the program's norms, recipient governments would have to be more involved.

Another argument was that a system of priorities should be established with stricter criteria to guide resource allocation. The logic of this argument would lead developments in the opposite direction: authority might move toward the centrally placed administrative and political bodies (the TAB, the TAC, and ultimately ECOSOC). The direction would depend on the kind of criteria established. These might relate to the distribution of assistance across sectors, but it might also concern the capability of the government requesting assistance to plan and accommodate the project or its need for assistance.[40]

The first institutional response to the call for greater coordination was the creation of resident representatives in the main recipient countries. These representatives were appointed by and were to report to the TAB. The Secretary-General appointed the first resident representatives in 1950, arguing that resident technical assistance representatives should be placed in some countries. He noted that this "could greatly contribute towards the avoidance of confusion which might otherwise arise from a multiplication of channels of technical assistance" and would also assist "those under-developed countries which do not yet have an appropriate co-ordinating machinery to view their needs for technical assistance from the standpoint of the over-all economic development needs of the country."[41]

A few offices had already been established in 1950–1951. In the beginning, such an office might consist of a mixture of representatives of specialized agencies who had operative responsibility for projects in the country concerned; these representatives might even be in charge of the office.[42]

However, resident representative offices soon developed into a more streamlined organization that reported to the executive chairman of the TAB. Projects financed under the EPTA were often integrated with assistance provided under other programs, such as UN regular programs, the participating organization projects, the Colombo Plan, and initiatives organized by the U.S. Foreign Operations Administration and the Organization of American States.[43] The TAB's annual report for 1954—the year of systemic reform of the organization—asserted that these full-time resident representatives should have broader responsibilities: "It is hoped that in future the Board's representatives will be able to assist not only in providing the maximum co-ordination of efforts between receiving Governments and the United Nations, but also in the avoidance of overlapping between this and similar assistance provided under bilateral programmes."[44] This instrument, in addition to facilitating national-level coordination, strengthened the program's central organs.

The initiation of integrated country programs was a second response to the call for stronger coordination. In the 1953 TAC meetings, the U.S. delegation raised doubts about centralizing planning at the headquarters of the UN and its specialized agencies, including the role actually played by the TAB. It argued that integrated programs should be planned at the country level in consultation with the recipient government and participating organizations. Activities should be integrated in the overall development plans of the governments concerned and be coordinated with the technical assistance provided by other donors (of which the United States the largest). Representatives of other major donor governments supported the U.S. position.

This logic, however, was not generally accepted: delegates from developing countries feared greater interference in their internal affairs. The delegate from India reminded the committee that his government had its own machinery for coordinating foreign aid.[45]

The 1955 Reform: From Agency Shares to Recipient Governments' Priorities

Placing resident representatives on the ground and coordinating development programs at the country level were begun under the old system of automatic resource distribution, although these measures were somewhat circumscribed. In ECOSOC, France initiated the final attack on this distributive system in 1954 with a resolution proposing to substitute automatic resource allocation to the agencies with a country programming system.[46] However, several delegations warned against abrupt fluctuations in agency allocations, and the Indian representative repeated his previous warning against interference with the priorities a requesting government stated in its development plan.[47]

In 1955, ECOSOC abolished the automatic allocation system and replaced it with a system premised on recipient government participation in drawing up programs in accordance with their needs and in relation to their economic development plans.[48] At the same time, the council urged governments to utilize the technical resources of the various participating organizations in the preparation, review, and approval of programs. The French-initiated resolution adopted by ECOSOC and later approved by the General Assembly introduced an important innovation: target figures were to be drawn up by the TAB for each country on the basis of the funds assumed to be available for the following year.[49]

That decision, more than anything else, marked the shift of focus from agencies to individual recipient countries (country programs). The change did not necessarily shift the main influence from the headquarters of the agencies (including the EPTA secretariat) to the governments concerned. Other aspects that were described in the operational part of the resolution ensured that the system's center remained in a strong position. The procedures regulating programming, planning, and approval and funding allocations prescribed that the programs should be drawn up at country levels by the requesting governments in consultation with the TAB's resident representative. The resident representative was responsible for coordinating consultations between governments and participating organizations. The requesting governments were expected to forward their programs, with an indication of priorities, to the TAB through the resident representative. Thus, the resident representative became the principal channel of communication and coordination between the UN system and the recipient government.

After the 1955 Reform

ENSURING THE CONTINUED PARTICIPATION OF THE AGENCIES

Patterns of an established system are not easily changed. In the 1954 reform resolution, a back door was left open for the specialized agencies. When the TAB considered which country programs to include in the overall program for the next year, it was instructed to ensure that the ratio between the programs to be implemented by the agencies did not deviate too much from the ratio of the previous year. A design to prolong the existing project portfolio was also introduced in the country planning procedure. Projects were to be divided in two main categories: ongoing field projects and projects to be implemented if resources became available under the supplementary field program. This practice did not end until 1961, when ECOSOC formally brought it to an end.

The distribution of EPTA funds is shown in table 2.1. The techniques referred to help explain why table 2.1 reads the way it does for the second half of the 1950s, despite the fact that a new system had been established.

The norms established by the 1955 reform combined the seemingly contradictory concerns of strengthening the powers of the program's central bodies and giving recipient governments greater influence over priorities and planning. The mechanisms introduced also secured the program's smooth running, although a fixed slice of the central fund was replaced with a more uncertain "trust" relationship. It was some time before the new system became institutionalized. From the TAC's perspective, one prerequisite for proper functioning was a stronger agency presence at the country level, where coordination was to take place.

THE CENTRAL ROLE OF RESIDENT REPRESENTATIVES

The two major instruments envisaged in the 1955 reform—country programs and a TAB resident representative who served as coordinator—were systematically developed in subsequent years. The number of offices of resident representatives increased, more resident representatives began to occupy full-time positions, and the positions of these field representatives were strengthened through formal mandates, particularly when country programs were negotiated.[50]

This process had its own dynamic. Although centered on activities of the EPTA and participating organizations, coordination grew to include

TABLE 2.1.

Distribution of EPTA Funds to the UN and Its Specialized Agencies, Selected Years, 1949–1965 (by percent and in millions of U.S. dollars)

AGENCY	1949	1950–1951	1955	1960	1965	1950–1965 MILLIONS OF U.S. DOLLARS	1950–1965 PER-CENT
United Nations Secretariat	23.0	16.2	21.4	22.3	19.8	107.0	21.7
International Labour Organization	11.0	5.2	10.8	9.0	10.6	50.5	10.2
Food and Agriculture Organization	29.0	32.5	31.3	25.5	24.4	128.7	26.1
UNESCO	14.0	18.4	12.7	15.6	16.4	79.0	16.0
International Civil Aviation Organization	1.0	5.7	4.0	4.6	4.5	21.3	4.3
World Health Organization	22.0	22.0	17.8	17.3	16.4	86.5	17.5
Universal Postal Union	----	----	----	----	0.8	0.8	0.2
International Telecommunication Union	----	----	1.0	1.2	2.6	6.9	1.4
World Meteorological Organization	----	----	1.0	1.6	2.7	7.5	1.5
International Atomic Energy Agency	----	----	----	2.1	1.9	5.6	1.1
TOTAL	100.0	100.0	100.0	99.2	100.0	493.8	100.0

Sources: Technical Assistance Committee, *Sixth Report of the Technical Assistance Board,* ECOSOC document E/2566 E/TAC/REP.3, 14 April 1954, 17; Technical Assistance Committee, *Seventh Report of the Technical Assistance Board,* 21; Technical Assistance Committee, *Annual Report of the Technical Assistance Board for 1956,* 7; Technical Assistance Committee, *Annual Report of the Technical Assistance Board for 1960,* 7;

regional and bilateral technical assistance programs. The network also encompassed other UN agencies. The TAC's annual report for 1960 drew attention to the increasingly close cooperation between TAB offices and UN information centers; in some instances, senior officials served in both programs.[51]

This development in the field attracted the attention of ECOSOC, which set up an ad hoc committee of eight (later ten) member states to study the question of coordinating EPTA programs with other UN programs at headquarters and in the field.[52] In 1962, ECOSOC also invited the executive secretaries of the UN regional economic commissions to participate in the planning process in cooperation with TAB resident representatives.[53] In 1963, the resident representatives took on a role as agents of the World Food Programme in addition to their ordinary duties, which were now almost equally divided between the EPTA and the Special Fund.[54]

By the end of 1964, an extensive system of field representatives was in place: TAB and the Special Fund had established seven regional offices, sixty country offices, nine suboffices and correspondents, and two liaison offices. The number of offices had more than doubled in only five years— from 35 in 1959 to 78 in 1964. The number of international staff members had also increased—by 1964 there were 232, representing 50 nationalities, as compared with 147 staff members two years earlier.[55] In 1965, ECOSOC, heeding the comments of the UN Administrative Committee on Coordination, unanimously urged resident representatives to exercise their central role of achieving coordination in the field more effectively. The council also asked participating organizations to cooperate in the realization of this aim.[56]

A development toward a UN diplomatic service, in which TAB resident representatives were increasingly given more than one hand on the wheel, was in the making. Few women served the UN in that capacity. In 1957, Margaret Joan Anstee became the first woman to be appointed resident representative. It was seven more years before another woman was appointed. At that time, there were sixty-five resident and regional representatives.

Technical Assistance Committee, *Annual Report of the Technical Assistance Board for 1961,* 5; Technical Assistance Committee, *Annual Report of the Technical Assistance Board for 1964,* table 3; UNDP, *15 Years and 150,000 Skills,* Annex II; and *Yearbook of the United Nations 1965,* 290; and calculations based on data in these sources.

NATIONAL-LEVEL PLANNING AND COORDINATION

UN governing bodies emphasized planning and coordination. It was considered important that recipient governments give high priority to EPTA-supported projects. From the outset, recipient governments contributed most of the costs of projects, often up to 80 percent and beyond.[57] But not all governments were operating with advanced development plans. The resident representative's main concern was to ensure that EPTA projects were well integrated in such plans. The issue of counterpart personnel was considered crucial from a development perspective; they could give support to international experts and could assume responsibility for the operation of a project after international experts departed. The issue of sustainability was on the agenda.

The self-evaluation of 1963–1964 by resident representatives who had served for some years in major recipient countries gives a mixed picture. Although recipient governments were increasingly looking to the resident representative office as a clearinghouse for technical assistance from all international organizations, these offices were not always well informed about projects financed by the regular programs of the participating organizations. Cooperation between the participating organizations in preparing the program varied from one country to another.[58]

COOPERATION AND COORDINATION WITH THE SPECIAL FUND

The establishment of the Special Fund in 1958 posed a challenge to cooperation and coordination. In its 1959 annual report, the TAB proudly recorded that more than half of the requests approved or considered by the Special Fund had originated in projects that had been assisted by the EPTA, including about a quarter that were direct outgrowths of EPTA projects. It reported also on close cooperation at the project level in which one agency complemented and reinforced the work of the other.[59]

The 1959 Reform: A Two-Year Planning Cycle and Country Programming

A basic problem that had plagued the EPTA from its inception was that commitments had to be restricted to the budget year. If a project needed to be prolonged for more than one year, it had to go through the entire decision process anew. The negative consequences for long-term planning, on both the donor and the recipient side, were obvious. At its summer session in 1959, the TAC decided to adopt two-year program-ming on an experimental basis, beginning with the country programs for 1961–1962.[60]

The following year, the TAB urged the TAC to implement the reform by extending planning and approval for a program's entire duration, which constituted "a logical extension of the steps already taken." The TAC was in general agreement, ECOSOC accepted the proposed system, and it was put into operation in 1963. Projects intended to last for more than two years were to be planned for their entire duration. In principle, the TAC was to approve such projects for the first four years.[61]

The first tentative self-evaluation of the country programming sys-tem appeared in the TAC's 1963–1964 report. The purpose of the reform was to meet the needs of governments that wanted to embark on schemes requiring international assistance over a period of several years and give the participating organizations the advantage of greater continuity in operations.[62]

Evaluation

During the early years, the TAB considered it almost impossible to carry out a systematic evaluation of the program because it consisted of so many different projects scattered across the globe. The EPTA's share in these projects was small in relation to the total economic and social activi-ties of recipient countries, and it was not possible to isolate its impact on economic development, it was argued.

Gradually more systematic forms of evaluation were introduced. Reporting from the second systematic appraisal on projects in thirty-eight countries (including for the first time regional and interregional projects), the TAB concluded in its 1957 annual report that the planning and coor-dinating efforts carried out by recipient governments themselves were crucial for the success of projects.[63] This conclusion has repeatedly been rediscovered in subsequent decades.

From this cautious start, more comprehensive evaluation systems were developed from 1958 onward that involved the various actors on the scene. Practice varied from one recipient government to another and from one participating organization to another, depending not least on their different cultures and traditions. Toward the end of the 1950s, the appraisal carried out by the TAB in its annual report improved some-what. This came about as a result of a decision by the TAC at its summer session in 1959 that annual reports should contain an intensive study of some important part of the program to supplement the overview provided in previous reports. The first review reported on training institutes and centers (the report for 1960) followed by reviews of the fellowship program (1961–1962) and regional and interregional projects (1963). The last review focused on resident representatives' opinions about vital aspects of the program with particular reference to the period 1963–1964. Their attention focused on organizational aspects, such as the coordination by recipient governments and participating organizations, technical assistance programming and EPTA procedures for programming, implementation, and government support and follow-up.[64]

UNESCO's role in this field deserves mention. It assumed special responsibility for improving evaluation techniques during these early years and in the late 1950s established the basis for evaluating development assistance projects and programs.[65]

In 1962, ECOSOC called upon the UN Secretary-General and the executive heads of all specialized agencies and the IAEA to pay particular attention to continuous and effective program evaluations. The council noted that it found "the present arrangements for the evaluation of the impact and effectiveness of the programmes . . . inadequate."[66]

Since the projects supported were, in principle, run by recipient governments, to what extent were these projects subjected to systematic evaluation by the governments concerned? In 1964, the resident representatives were asked to respond to this question. The breakdown of the answers of seventy of these respondents in four categories showed that 55 percent of governments did not attempt to carry out any evaluation. In ten of the seventy countries, the coordinating authorities carried out systematic evaluations; in eight more countries, individual ministries carried out such evaluations; and in thirteen countries, individual ministries occasionally carried out evaluations.[67]

Subsequently, ECOSOC brought the need for evaluation to the fore, bringing the UN's central bodies into the process.[68] However, these evaluations were internal. A basic approach can be found in the preamble to resolution 1042 (XXXVII), which asserted that "evaluation can only be effective and valid if it takes place in close co-operation with the interested Governments and the international organization concerned." This is an approach well suited to the norms established for UN development assistance, particularly the norm that emphasized the sovereignty of the recipient government's basic approach. It has its obvious weaknesses as well.

Distribution of Aid Resources

The distribution of resources within the UN aid community deserves attention. Did the available means increase or stagnate over the years? Who were the main contributors and recipients? From where were the experts recruited? For what purposes were the resources used?

The EPTA was based on voluntary contributions by member governments of the UN and its specialized agencies. The pledges at Lake Success in June 1950 reached a level below what optimists had expected, and the total amounts pledged increased only moderately over the years. Funding was given on an annual basis, an arrangement that was not feasible for long-term planning. The fact that some payments were made in nonconvertible currencies was yet another constraint.

From the starting figure for the first eighteen months of about $20 million, the annual amounts pledged from 1952 onward started at $18.8 million and increased gradually to $27.6 million in 1955, $34.2 million in 1960, and $54 million in 1965, the last year of operation. In the course of those fifteen years, $510.6 million was pledged to the program. A large number of governments (and a few semi-governments) were contributing—increasing from 54 in 1950–1951 to 85 in 1960 and reaching 107 by 1965 (table 2.2).

MAIN CONTRIBUTORS

For obvious reasons, the program was true to the principle that assistance should be help to self-help, as the governments requesting technical assistance were financing a substantial share. These contributions came on top of the contributions that these governments made to the central fund. From the development perspective chosen—self-reliance—this represented a strategy intended to ensure the effectiveness and sustainability of assistance: only activities that ranked high on the priority list of the requesting governments would obtain support.

Table 2.2 provides an overview of the funding based on the pledges of member governments during the lifetime of the EPTA, from 1950 to 1965. The patterns established show a clear picture.

During the first decade, western countries provided the bulk of the funding—89 percent of total assistance early in the period, declining slightly to 87 percent in the mid-1950s and 84 percent in 1960 but

TABLE 2.2.

Contributions Pledged to the EPTA, Selected Years and Selected Countries by Group, 1950–1965 (in thousands of U.S. dollars, by percent and by number of contributors by group)[1]

Groups/countries[2]	1950–1951			1955			1960			1965		
	$	%	N	$	%	N	$	%	N	$	%	N
Western countries	17,937.6	89.4	19	24,029.9	86.9	22	28,492.0	83.8	24	47,002.2	87.1	25
United States	12,007.5	59.8	--	15,000.0	54.2	--	14,462.9	42.5	--	22,680.0	42.0	--
United Kingdom	2,128.3	10.6	--	2,240.0	8.1	--	3,000.0	8.8	--	4,750.0	8.8	--
Canada	772.7	3.8	--	1,500.0	5.4	--	2,000.0	5.9	--	2,150.8	4.0	--
France	1,207.5	6.0	--	1,450.4	5.2	--	1,543.8	4.5	--	1,851.4	3.4	--
Netherlands	400.0	2.0	--	660.0	2.4	--	1,323.0	3.9	--	1,790.3	3.3	--
Sweden	96.5	0.5	--	579.9	2.1	--	902.8	2.7	--	2,500.0	4.6	--
Soviet-bloc countries[3]	50.0	0.2	1	1,401.9	5.1	6	1,520.4	4.5	10	2,838.4	5.3	10
USSR	0	0	--	1,000.0	3.6	--	1,000.0	2.9	--	2,000.0	3.7	--
Less-developed countries	2,091.7	10.4	35	2,232.4	8.1	41	3,979.3	11.7	49	4,149.0	7.7	70
Brazil	459.5	2.3	--	270.3	1.0	--	733.9	2.2	--	104.8	0.2	--
India	250.0	1.2	--	400.0	1.4	--	750.0	2.2	--	850.0	1.6	--
Argentina	200.0	1.0	--	83.3	0.3	--	85.0	0.3	--	108.9	0.2	--
TOTAL[4]	20,079.3	100.0	55	27,666.2	100.0	70	33,992.7	100.0	85	53,990.8	100.1	106

increasing again to 87 percent in 1965. Among these countries, the United States provided more than half of the total funding during the first decade—60 percent initially, declining to 54 percent mid-decade and 43 percent in 1960, then remaining at slightly above 40 percent. The two other major western powers, the United Kingdom and France, contributed substantially from the start, and some medium and small western powers—Canada, the Netherlands, and Sweden—increasingly emerged as major contributors. In the 1960s, the Federal Republic of Germany and others joined the group of key contributors.[69]

Soviet-bloc countries entered reluctantly into the program, which they had originally denounced as an imperialist design to exploit the resources of less-developed countries. Patterns within the bloc varied: Yugoslavia contributed to the program from its inception (as did China, which is not grouped among these countries in this overview); the Soviet Union and Poland pledged their first contributions in 1953, followed, the next year, by the Byelorussian SSR, Czechoslovakia, and the Ukrainian SSR. Although their numbers and contributions increased, their share remained at a modest level (4.5 percent in 1960 and 5.3 percent in 1965) and more than half of that share came from the Soviet Union.

Many less-developed countries contributed slightly more than 10 percent of the program's funding during the first decade; their share declined somewhat in the mid-1960s. During the 1950s, almost all of this funding came from countries in Latin America, Asia, and the Middle East, although a few African governments contributed. As we have seen, India played a leading role in influencing the norms and policies of the EPTA. It also emerged as the major contributor among this group of countries.

Sources: Technical Assistance Committee, *Fifth Report of the Technical Assistance Board,* Annex VI; Technical Assistance Committee, *Annual Report of the Technical Assistance Board for 1956,* Annex I; and Technical Assistance Committee, *Annual Report of the Technical Assistance Board for 1964,* Annex I. Note that some minor differences exist in the statistics reported by the TAB over the years.

1. Not all pledges were honored immediately, but most were. By 1965, when the UNDP continued where the EPTA had pioneered, the unpaid balance amounted to $4,882,470, of which most was from 1963 and 1964. Technical Assistance Committee, *Annual Report of the Technical Assistance Board for 1964,* Annex II.

2. The countries included are the top contributors in their categories.

3. Does not include China, which is included among the less-developed countries.

4. From 1955, includes Liechtenstein and the Holy See (not included in the groups listed).

MAIN RECIPIENTS

The EPTA supported projects around the less-developed world and in Europe, spreading its assistance thinly over a large number of countries. Table 2.3 shows the regional distribution of project costs over time. Many of the resources were focused on Asia, the Far East, and Latin America, although the share of Latin America declined over the 1960s, as did aid to the Middle East. During the early years, less than 10 percent of EPTA resources were channeled to Africa, but the pattern changed as the wave of emerging independent states began in the early 1960s. By 1965, 35 percent of technical assistance was being directed to Africa.

REGIONAL ORIGINS OF EXPERTS

From the very start, experts were recruited from all over the world. Few, however, came from Africa, where most countries were still under colonial rule in the 1950s.[70] Almost three-quarters of all experts were recruited from Western Europe and North America during most of the 1950s; this proportion declined to about two-thirds in the early 1960s.

During the whole EPTA period, more than 55 percent of experts were recruited from Western Europe.[71] Colonial powers—the United Kingdom (in particular), France, and the Netherlands—were primary recruiting grounds. They remained prominent over the years, providing about one-third of recruited experts, more than twice the share they contributed to the funding. Nordic countries represented another important recruiting ground, supplying almost one-tenth of the experts during the 1950s. The Eastern European countries were late in supporting the program, politically and financially, and their contributions were modest. From the mid-1950s onwards, their share of experts was more or less identical to the share they provided to the funding.

What may seem surprising is the relative modest share of experts recruited from the United States, about 17 percent in 1953, a proportion that declined to 12 percent in 1960 and less than 10 percent in 1964.[72] During the 1950s, this represented less than one-third of what the U.S. would have provided if financial contributions to the program had served as a formal or informal key to recruitment.

Nationals from less-developed countries were also recruited under the program. A significant share of these came from some major countries in Latin America and Asia, from India in particular.

TABLE 2.3.

Cost of Technical Assistance Provided by Participating Organizations by Region, 1950–1965 (in thousands of U.S. dollars and by percent)

	1950–1951 $	%	1953 $	%	1956 $	%	1960[1] $	%	1964[1] $	%	1965 $	%
Africa	442	9.8	1,682	9.4	2,244	8.9	2,883	18.6	10,552	32.0	14,814	35.1
Americas[2]	1,183	26.2	4,616	25.9	7,298	28.8	2,372	15.3	5,059	15.3	9,065	21.5
Asia and the Far East	1,436	31.8	5,474	30.7	8,240	32.5	5,510	35.5	9,032	27.4	10,480	24.8
Europe	167	3.7	1,522	8.5	1,726	6.8	1,872	12.1	2,376	7.2	1,665	3.9
Middle East	939	20.8	3,189	17.9	4,958	19.6	1,953	12.6	2,523	7.6	2,444	5.8
Interregional and unspecified	348	7.7	1,334	7.5	856	3.4	931	6.0	3,475	10.5	3,784	9.0
TOTAL[3]	4,515	100.0	17,817	99.9	25,322	100.0	15,521	100.1	33,017	100.0	42,252	100.1

Sources: Data in and calculations based on data in these sources: Technical Assistance Committee, *Fifth Report of the Technical Assistance Board*, Annex II; Technical Assistance Committee, *Annual Report of the Technical Assistance Board for 1956*, Annex IV; Technical Assistance Committee, *Annual Report of the Technical Assistance Board for 1960*, Annex VII; Technical Assistance Committee, *Annual Report of the Technical Assistance Board for 1964*, Annex VII; and *Yearbook of the United Nations 1965, 296–300.*

1. Under regular and other programs.

2. The regional heading was "Latin America" for the years up to 1956. It was changed in 1960 to account for some minor costs incurred in Canada ($13,000 in 1960, $25,500 in 1964) and the United States ($35,000 in 1956, $41,000 in 1964).

3. Percentages do not always add up to exactly 100 because figures are rounded in the data on which the calculations are based.

MAIN PURPOSES OF ASSISTANCE

The discourse on development during the 1950s and early 1960s focused on two pillars: industrial development and modernization of agriculture. Technical assistance was considered a vital instrument in the modernization process.

Table 2.4 indicates the distribution of resources among various sectors and activities for the period 1955 to 1964. The priorities that emerge are interesting. Assistance for agricultural production accounts for the largest share. Agriculture and community development combined accounted for just over 30 percent of total assistance, followed by health services. Then follows support for development planning and implementation, a priority congruent with both the predominant development philosophy of the time and the concerns expressed in the UN system. However, industrial production was not given high priority, as measured on this parameter, in stark contrast to priorities expressed in the development discourse at the time, which were advocated strongly by representatives of developing countries and Eastern Europe.

Also interesting is the relative stability over time. The system that was established when the program was initiated whereby resources were distributed to the executing agencies according to an established formula was probably instrumental here. As argued above, this formula seemed to survive, even though it was formally discarded in the mid-1950s.

Some Concluding Observations

The EPTA was not established in a political vacuum. As we have seen, the UN arena was used as an ideological battlefield between the East and West. The main beneficiaries of UN development assistance during this period were those who took a middle position. Several years were to pass before Soviet-bloc countries fully identified themselves with development assistance activities and contributed financially to them. From the beginning, the political initiative belonged to the United States, which also provided the main funding for activities. The story told in box 2.2 illustrates that this ownership had several sides.

Nevertheless, thanks to the norms established for the new activity the EPTA represented, assistance took the form of cooperation and was provided on the premise of help to self-help. The recipient government was the one to request the assistance and set the priorities. It was also expected to contribute, not only by facilitating implementation but also

TABLE 2.4.

EPTA Field Program Costs by Major Fields of Activity, 1955–1964
(in thousands of U.S. dollars and by percent)

	1955–1959		1960–1964		TOTALS	
	$	%	$	%	$	%
Agricultural production	30,977	23.8	40,699	20.9	71,676	22.0
Health services	22,060	16.8	32,339	16.6	54,399	16.8
Assisting governments[1]	17,354	13.3	30,535	15.7	47,889	14.7
Education	12,697	9.7	26,372	13.6	39,069	12.0
Industrial production	11,700	9.1	12,103	6.2	23,803	7.3
Auxiliary services to industry and agriculture[2]	11,109	8.5	13,626	7.0	24,735	7.7
Development of public utilities[3]	10,747	8.1	16,007	8.2	26,754	8.3
Community development[4]	9,188	7.0	10,441	5.4	19,629	6.0
Other social services[5]	4,483	3.4	8,828	4.5	13,311	4.1
Atomic energy	----[6]	----	3,471	1.8	3,471	1.1
TOTALS[7]	130,315	99.7	194,421	99.9	324,736	100.0

Source: UNDP, *15 Years and 150,000 Skills,* Annex III.

1. Includes basic surveys of resources and building up of administrative services.
2. Includes promoting trade, promoting cooperatives, providing technical education and training and vocational training.
3. Power, transportation, and communications.
4. Basic education, education through agricultural extension, education in home economics and nutrition.
5. Includes contributions for construction and housing; town and rural planning; industrial relations; labor legislation; and social welfare, social security.
6. Four dashes indicate zero allocations.
7. Percentages do not always add up to exactly 100 because figures are rounded in the data on which the calculations are based.

by contributing funds. In this way, a precedent for this policy area was established at an early stage. Not only was this important for multilateral development assistance at the time, it also influenced the norms that guided similar efforts in the future, as may be seen in the aid rhetoric and the discourse on development and development cooperation more than

BOX 2.2. Big Brother Kept a Close Eye on Even Small Steps

In Bolivia in the early 1960s, the EPTA was helping the government find the first natural gas outlets by recruiting experts to work for the state oil company. When she returned from a field visit, Margaret Joan Anstee, resident representative of the EPTA in Bolivia, was informed by her (French) deputy that while she had been away, the office had received a list of candidates for the project, one of them a Russian:

> On those occasions we wrote a standard letter saying, "Here are [*sic*] a list of experts, which one would you like? Here are their c.v.'s, you choose." He [the deputy] said, "I hadn't even sent the letter to the government, when the counselor of the American embassy, a very nice man, phoned to say, 'We understand you are putting forward a Russian candidate. We want his name removed from the list.'" I said, "Well, what did you do?" He said, "I sent the letter." I said, "With the Russian included?" He said, "Yes." I said, "You did quite right. Don't worry. That's absolutely right."
>
> About a day later, there was a very small dinner given by the minister of defense, for the president, most of the cabinet, the German ambassador, the U.S. ambassador, Ben Stephansky and myself. We were the only foreigners. After coffee—it was not a very large house—Ben Stephansky descended upon me and tore me apart about this. It was very embarrassing because the German ambassador wanted to talk about mining issues. I said, "Ben, what do you mean? This has nothing to do with you. The U.S.S.R. (Union of Soviet Socialist Republics), whether you like it or not, is a UN member state and they have always put forward extremely highly qualified people." Anyway, we went hammer and tongs at the issue, while the other guests (all ministers) looked on. The president was having a whale of time. He was really enjoying himself. I was not. Stephansky said, "Will you withdraw the name?" I said, "Of course I won't withdraw it. I can't. I have made an oath as an international civil servant. I can't do that." And I added, "The British would never have asked me to do that. But even if they did, I wouldn't do that. That's it."

The "private" conversation found its way to the weekly communist newspaper, *El Pueblo*. It did not harm the popularity of the first and, at the time, only woman resident representative of the EPTA.

Source: Oral History Interview of Dame Margaret Anstee, 14 December 2000, 54–56, in the Oral History Collection of the United Nations Intellectual History Project, The Graduate Center, The City University of New York.

half a century later. The norms that were established carried influence beyond the program. As guidelines for the first and major multilateral development assistance program, they tended to become universal and impacted bilateral development assistance as well.

It was no small achievement to establish norms that emphasized the sovereignty of the recipient government and its primacy within a policy area where power relations among the parties have been characterized by extreme asymmetry. The United Nations can rightfully claim the credit: it is difficult to imagine that this could have been achieved in a different systemic setting. From the beginning, however, the United Nations emphasized using assistance to bring the necessity of development planning strongly to the attention of recipient governments and to improve their planning capacity. Economic planning was by no means an invention of the UN system. It was a sine qua non for the young development economists in the Keynesian tradition who inhabited the UN Secretariat during these early years. The program offered an opportunity to transfer this approach to developing countries along with technical assistance. Although the main emphasis in these early years was on industrial and agricultural development, a more holistic perspective on development was part of the package.

The multilateral setting nourished a concern for national-level coordination. In the mid-1950s, a system of country planning emerged and coordination was primarily associated with the country and regional EPTA offices of resident representatives. A main justification for establishing these offices was to bring program activities closer to host-country authorities, making it easier for them to influence the composition and priorities of work. Given the way the program was organized, it was some time before this aspiration could be realized. Nevertheless, the country planning system pioneered by the EPTA set standards that influenced practices developed further by the UNDP. In the late 1960s and early 1970s, they also influenced aid planning and the implementation systems of some bilateral donor countries, particularly those of the Netherlands and the Scandinavian countries.

The program also fulfilled an important role in the internal coordination of UN technical assistance activities and those of its specialized agencies and associated organizations.

Initially activities financed from the regular budgets of cooperating organizations represented only a tiny share compared with the activities of these organizations that were financed by the EPTA. This made EPTA projects attractive because they provided an opportunity for agencies to expand their operational activities and their staff.[73] However, increasingly these agencies also received funding from elsewhere for specific activities within their area of competence.

This development may be illustrated by taking the technical assistance provided by the UN Secretariat as an example. In addition to projects funded by the EPTA, the Secretariat provided technical assistance financed from its regular budget to promote economic development, social welfare, and public administration in the form of advisory services in human rights and the provision of operational, executive, and administrative personnel. Also, governments (and NGOs) increasingly provided funding for the UN Secretariat's extra-budgetary activities in this field. In 1959, its total expenditure amounted to $8.6 million, of which $6.3 million came from the EPTA, $1.9 million from its regular budget, and $0.5 million from governments for extra-budgetary activities. Of a total expenditure of $34 million six years later, $9.1 million was used for EPTA projects, $14.1 million for Special Fund projects, $4.4 million for extra-budgetary operations, and $6.5 million came from its regular budget. In 1959, the UN Secretariat funded 28 percent of its technical assistance activities from its regular budget and from contributions provided by governments for extra-budgetary operations, while the EPTA funded the remaining 72 percent. By 1965, this balance (excluding Special Fund projects) had turned around: EPTA-funded projects represented 44.5 percent and means drawn from the Secretariat's ordinary budget and extra-budgetary contributions 54.5 percent.[74]

The material outputs of the program were quite impressive. During some fifteen years of operation, the EPTA received and used $494 million in voluntary contributions from a large number of governments (106 in 1965), many of which were themselves developing countries. The amount actually spent on EPTA-supported projects was even larger, as sizeable contributions from host countries are not included in these figures.

Box 2.3 gives an overall picture of performance. The program became increasingly globalized in terms of participating governments. Available contributions increased gradually and a growing share of these resources was channeled to Africa, especially in the 1960s.

The specialized agencies were given a strong position as executing agencies when the EPTA was established. During its first decade of operation and beyond, this position was secured through various formal

BOX 2.3. 15 Years and 150,000 Skills

In an anniversary review prepared by the UN Technical Assistance Board, covering the period from mid-1950, when the EPTA started its activities, and up to the beginning of 1965, the overall results of the Expanded Programme was summarized as follows (omitting much of the performance during its last year of operation):

Financial support. The equivalent of $456.6 million pledged by a total of 109 countries, plus 26 million in local cost contributions by recipient governments and substantial further amounts in supporting services, facilities and capital investment.

Total expenditures. The equivalent of $457 million, consisting of 376 in project costs and 81 million in administrative and operational services costs.

Geographical distribution. 180 countries and territories in five main regions: Africa, where 20.3 percent of direct project costs were spent; Asia and the Far East (32.6 percent); Europe (6.3 percent); Latin America (24.1 percent); and the Middle East (13.6 percent); to which may be added inter-regional projects, which absorbed 2.9 percent.

Country and regional. Country projects, $323 million, or 85.8 percent of total project costs; regional and inter-regional projects, 53 million, or 14.2 percent.

Categories of expenditure. $278 million (60 percent) on expert assistance; 36 million (8 percent) on equipment; 64 million (14 percent) on fellowships; administrative and operational costs, 81 million (18 percent).

Number of expert man-years. 32,000, involving 13,500 men and women of 90 different nationalities.

Number of fellowship awards. 32,000, granted to trainees from 168 different countries and territories and taken in 128 different host countries.

Source: UNDP, *15 Years and 150,000 Skills,* 31.

and tacit mechanisms. The agencies' strong position vis-à-vis the governments requesting assistance was challenged, particularly in UN political bodies (ECOSOC, the TAC). However, even when a system based on a fundamentally different philosophy was introduced in the mid-1950s that emphasized the priorities of the governments requesting assistance, the UN's interests prevailed. The interest of the specialized agencies in maintaining their share was clearly an overriding concern during these years.

This priority of UN concerns stands in stark contrast to the guidelines that placed the aid-requesting governments in the driver's seat and the philosophy behind the reform of the mid-1950s. According to the prevailing common wisdom, the efforts of agencies to maintain their share of UN resources might negatively affect the ownership and, accordingly, the effectiveness of the assistance. From an instrumental perspective, however, some legitimate reasons for this priority may still be found. It contributed, first of all, to maintaining harmonious relations among agencies within the UN system. It also ensured some continuity in the activities of the various executive agencies involved in technical assistance: a stop-and-go activity might have affected the recruitment of administrative staff and experts negatively, which would have affected the quality of services rendered and the program's effectiveness.

The structure that was established when the EPTA was created came close to a revolution. The center was given a coordinating role, as reflected both in the institutional arrangements and in the establishment of a common fund. This structure was engineered by the center of the UN, with David Owen playing a crucial role. The specialized agencies retained a strong position through their representation on the Technical Assistance Board, but there the position of the executive chairman was strengthened. The system of resident representatives in the countries concerned further strengthened the EPTA vis-à-vis the operative agencies and the intergovernmental bodies of the program.

Political considerations were behind the idea of giving recipient countries the power to plan and prioritize their own aid, and France was the leader in the push for this reform in 1954. The idea was in tune with the norms established for the EPTA, although the main arguments were instrumental: it would be most practical to coordinate an integrated program at the country level.

During the 1950s and early 1960s, the intergovernmental bodies of the EPTA (ECOSOC and the TAC) made large strides in moving the major responsibility for technical assistance from the implementing agencies to the host governments. However, while the norms that were established assumed that these governments would play a decisive role in forming the country programs, the interests of the aid-implementing agencies were a stumbling block when it came to implementing these norms. It took another decade to create a better balance between norms and actual practices (see chapter 7).

THREE

A UN Fund for Economic Development

- ▪ **Capital: A Scarce Development Resource**
- ▪ **The Lost Cause: The Special UN Fund for Economic Development (SUNFED)**
- ▪ **The United Nations Special Fund**

In the 1950s, the UN system's efforts in support of economic development in less-developed countries were confined to providing governments with technical assistance and urging the IBRD system to switch a larger part of its dcvclopment lending from "developed" to "underdeveloped" countries. Although the combination of expanded technological insight and capital was widely recognized as necessary, the UN system did not combine technical assistance and financial assistance.

In the late 1940s and early 1950s, however, an ambitious idea was launched and discussed in both ECOSOC and the General Assembly: a Special UN Fund for Economic Development. The intention was to provide soft loans, even grants, to less-developed countries to finance projects to develop their economies, especially infrastructure. The Marshall Plan was the model, although differences in the settings were recognized.

The idea stayed on the UN's agenda during the first half of the 1950s. However, it met with heavy resistance from the major industrial countries, especially the United States and the United Kingdom. In 1957, a compromise proposal on a special fund was agreed on. This fund had more limited functions and a smaller financial frame than the original idea. It was initiated and driven by the United States as an alternative to SUNFED. This more limited idea won the day, and the UN General Assembly formally established the UN Special Fund on 14 October 1958.

Although the Special Fund was slimmed down in both ambition and scope, the long fight for and against SUNFED is part of the early history of the UN's contribution to the idea of international development assistance. It illustrates, better than the story of the EPTA's emergence, that ideas are not enough, however innovative they might be. Power and interests also play an important part in international relations. In the late 1940s and the

1950s, governments of new and emerging states perceived needs and priorities differently from governments of the hegemonic industrialized powers of the North that had the final say in the establishment of the fund.

Since capital is considered so important for economic development, this chapter starts with a brief survey of the predominant thinking about the role of capital during the late 1940s and 1950s at the UN.

Capital: A Scarce Development Resource

In the late 1940s and early 1950s, the United Nations attracted a number of economists who later earned reputations as pioneers in development; a few of them became Nobel laureates in economics. They served in an organization that had come to define poverty and economic underdevelopment as major international problems that demanded solutions. These economists combined theories related to the underdevelopment of new and emerging states with ideas that they hoped would solve problems. They sat down with stakeholders who represented different and often conflicting perceptions and interests to assess their analyses and to decide on the follow-up. They combined theoretical work with political and economic entrepreneurship.[1]

Most of these economists had been molded in the Keynesian tradition that emphasized the crucial role of the state in economic development. This view of economics held that planning and state intervention were important preconditions for development. On this issue, they were confronted with strong opposition from neoclassical economists.[2]

The predominant view within the United Nations was that "underdeveloped" countries were responsible for their own development. Any assistance from outside should be help to self-help and should be provided on the premises that governments of these countries set. During the early years, UN policy documents and reports took a broad perspective on economic development. Most of them reflected the view that the countries concerned should work toward diversifying their economies, diversifying their export base, industrializing, diversifying their technology, and developing their agriculture.[3] However, the theme in these documents is that industrialization was what really mattered and the first step in industrialization was the accumulation of physical capital and modern technologies.

In this view of economics, there were basically four ways of ensuring capital for development: trade (export earnings), domestic savings and investments, private financial transfers, and foreign investment and government loans on commercial conditions and loans from abroad on concessionary terms or as grants-in-aid.

Exports as the Capital Winner

Traditionally, trade was largely conceived of as the most effective instrument in capital formation. The prevailing view was that trade would have to be expanded, especially exports. Export earnings were considered to be all important also because foreign currency was needed to import capital goods from industrialized countries that were seen as essential, at least during the initial phase of industrialization. In the trade patterns of the early postwar years, exports from less-developed countries were largely primary commodities. In the development thinking of the time, developing countries needed to modernize agricultural production so they could produce more effectively for export. The same applied to other primary products and raw materials.

In the early 1950s, the UN system challenged the prevailing view on trade with primary commodities. Studies showed that trade was proving to be a tricky source of capital formation in less-developed countries. Over the long term, the price of raw materials and primary products had been falling compared to the prices of manufactured products. In addition, these prices had been volatile, which made it difficult for governments to plan, and planning was essential if development was to take place.[4] In 1951, a group of experts appointed by the UN Secretary-General came to the same conclusion.[5] The analyses and recommendations in their brief report exerted considerable influence on perceptions in the UN system about how to attain economic development in less-developed countries.[6]

Raúl Prebisch and the Economic Commission for Latin America (ECLA) offered an even more fundamental criticism of the role of trade for economic development in developing countries with particular reference to Latin America. This criticism was based on evidence of declining prices for raw materials and primary products compared to prices for industrial products.[7] Prebisch identified what he found to be the major problem and its solution in the first few sentences of his introduction to the 1950 ECLA report:

> In Latin America, reality is undermining the out-dated schema of the international division of labour, which achieved great importance in the nineteenth century and, as a theoretical concept, continued to exert considerable influence until very recently. Under that schema,

the specific task that fell to Latin America, as part of the periphery of the world economic system, was that of producing food and raw materials for the great industrial centres. There was no place within it for the industrialization of the new countries. It is nevertheless been forced upon them by events. Two world wars in a single generation and a great economic crisis between them have shown the Latin American countries their opportunities, clearly pointing the way to industrial activity.[8]

In the long run, integrating Latin American economies into the North American capitalist system as suppliers of primary commodities had negative effects for Latin American countries in terms of their ability to save. The dynamics of the established division of labor and international trade acted to increase rather than reduce inequality between the center (North America) and the periphery (Latin America).

Although Prebisch's analysis was based on data from Latin America, it influenced thinking about the relations between industrialized and the so-called underdeveloped countries both inside the UN system and beyond for more than a decade. It created the foundation of the structuralist approach to development, which confronted mainstream development theory that saw trade (exports) as the engine of capital formation and economic development. The trademark of this school was industrialization over a broad spectrum oriented toward import substitution combined with trade policies adapted to this strategy (for example, protecting infant industries). Others, mainly outside the UN system, carried this analysis further, arguing that the best way for underdeveloped countries to achieve development was to delink themselves from the industrialized world.[9]

These observations caused concern in UN bodies that dealt with economic and social development, especially ECOSOC and the General Assembly. They generated the idea of "just" trade relations and a search for mechanisms to achieve "just" prices in trade between industrialized countries and producers of raw materials and primary products, much along the lines of those that emerged, far more forcefully, some twenty years later with the proposal for a New International Economic Order.[10] Typical of the way the UN system and its denizens (development economists were given a prominent role to play) worked during these years, when a serious problem was identified, core questions would be asked. What were the empirical evidence and the theoretical challenges and implications and what could be done to resolve the problem or overcome some of its most negative effects? The intergovernmental bodies asked the UN Secretariat to provide the answers, relying on the best experts it could hire.

Although the resulting reports brought nuances to the predominant perception of trade as the engine of capital accumulation for less-developed countries, their authors recognized that the revenue that would result from trade (exports) was still the most important source of capital available to these countries. Moreover, exports provided foreign exchange as well.

Domestic Savings and Investment

For a tradition accustomed to viewing development as a process that took place within the confines of nation-states, domestic savings and investment were the most important source of capital formation. This view was well attuned to the predominant ideology in the UN's political bodies: governments of the countries concerned were responsible for development and should generate it primarily with the resources of those countries and the efforts of their people.

However, a more pessimistic outlook prevailed in UN reports that analyzed the actual performance of the countries concerned, involving private and public sectors alike, and examined future prospects based on that information. In 1951, the UN group of experts concluded that underdeveloped countries would not be able to expand their agricultural production and industrialize using domestic savings as the engine of growth: the level of domestic savings was far too low. The gap would have to be filled by other means. At the same time, analysts searched for ways to stimulate domestic savings and investment.[11]

During this initial period, the predominant view within the UN system was that the state was expected to play an active role in mobilizing domestic capital and channeling it into economic development; the market would not be able to do this job. However, the states concerned had few tools with which to do this; they were largely limited to levying export taxes on limited resources.

Private Transfers and Foreign Investment

Capital transfers from abroad was another resource available to these countries. In classical as well as neoclassical economic theory, private investment was considered to be the "normal" way of transferring capital from industrial to underdeveloped countries.

The general problem with private transfers from abroad was how to reconcile the conflicting interests of less-developed countries seeking economic development with those of the potential foreign investors, whether individuals, business enterprises, or governments. From a developmental perspective, the major concern was identifying what conditions were necessary for foreign capital to be most effective. Potential foreign investors tended to focus on profit and security rather than on development. For the governments concerned, the major questions related to the conditions necessary to stimulate a larger capital inflow, including the conditions regulating outflow. These different concerns often conflicted. Competing development ideologies added fuel to such conflicts.

The "normal" way had its limitations. A group of experts appointed by the Secretary-General to study the international flow of private capital concluded that the number of private investors was small and was not likely to increase.[12] These investments tended to concentrate on exploiting natural resources and producing primary products. In addition, a study by Hans Singer had concluded that this kind of foreign investment did not serve the best interests of less-developed countries: most of the economic development effects of such investments were exported along with the raw materials and primary products.[13] Ambivalence about the role of foreign capital in promoting development in less-developed countries was expressed in the UN system, especially by the Sub-Commission on Economic Development.[14]

Financial transfers for investment might also take the form of commercial loans to individuals or businesses in the private sector or to a government. However, the creditworthiness of governments in less-developed countries was not considered to be strong; the financial returns on public investments were not easily collected and at best belonged to the future. This was particularly the case for investments to improve the public goods—communications, education, health—that were necessary preconditions for economic development and growth.

Financial Transfers on Concessionary Terms

To start and sustain the development process, less-developed countries needed capital transfers from industrial countries. UN reports on economic development were clear on this point. This applied, in the first place, to basic investments in communication and transportation systems, power systems, health services, education systems, and so forth. In most industrialized countries, such systems had been gradually established, developed, and maintained by governments and public authorities.

Investments in such public goods had some common features: they were considered necessary for development in a limited economic sense as well as in a broader development perspective. The capital requirements were high for both the initial costs of establishing them and the recurrent costs of maintaining them. The payoffs were not easily identifiable and belonged to a distant future, being dependent on a system of revenue collection. In less-developed countries, such systems were weakly established in the 1950s, and there were few resources to collect. (More than fifty years later, establishing effective systems for revenue collection still is a major challenge, particularly in the poorest countries, where the need for income to improve public goods is the most pressing.)[15]

From the very beginning, ECOSOC's Sub-Commission on Economic Development of the Economic and Employment Commission maintained that foreign financing was important for starting and maintaining a process toward economic development.[16] The need for grants from the industrialized world was recognized, indirectly and even directly, through the establishment of the EPTA. However, when it came to involving the UN, the leading industrial countries of the West distinguished between technical assistance and capital assistance. They preferred to work through the World Bank, where they found themselves more firmly in control, when they provided multilateral capital assistance.

In the early 1950s, development finance for less-developed countries was scarce. In its 1951 report, the group of experts recommended that the World Bank set a target of no less than $1 billion annually to underdeveloped countries within the next five years.[17] At that time, such credits were provided on commercial terms and would not meet the need of less-developed countries for development funding on softer conditions with regard to interest rates and repayment periods. Foreign aid was seen as necessary to fill the gap between investment needs and the resources available. The aid supplied for technical assistance (EPTA) was not intended to meet such needs for financial aid. Besides, the financial framework was so small as to make it totally unrealistic for the EPTA to fill this function. In 1950, the UN General Assembly adopted a resolution that expressed the conviction that the volume of private capital flowing into less-developed countries could not meet the needs of these countries for economic development: these needs could not be met without an increased flow of international public funds.[18]

During the first part of the 1950s, the idea of establishing grants-in-aid to supply capital assistance to underdeveloped countries as a supplement to the technical assistance the EPTA provided was repeatedly brought up within the UN system. In 1951, the UN group of experts pressed this idea, insisting that a mechanism should be established within the UN to provide grants for less-developed countries.[19] Almost as a by-product, an idea was born that has dominated aid discourse ever since: a target of 1 percent of GNP/GNI in development assistance from nations that are economically well off.

The main objective of the proposed fund was to assist less-developed countries in their efforts to industrialize their economies. From most perspectives, this was what economic development was all about. This meant that resources, including labor, would have to be shifted from agriculture to industry. However, the agricultural sector also had to be modernized to increase the export of primary products and earn the foreign currency needed to import capital goods for industrialization, at least for an initial period. A series of UN reports and resolutions from those early years maintained that industrial diversification was the single most important way for less-developed countries to modernize.[20]

An Enabling Environment for Development

In 1951, the UN group of experts started their report by stressing the important role of the social, political, and economic environments in making it possible for development to take place. The perspective developed in the introduction to Part 2 of their report is worth quoting extensively because of the insights it gives into the prevailing perceptions of development at the time. The main cultural, social, and economic constraints to economic development, as identified by the group, are shown in box 3.1.

The group advocated social reforms in the name of progress:[21]

- ■ In any society inequalities of wealth may deny equality of opportunity to the greater part of the population, and keep ignorant many persons who, given the opportunity, would contribute to raising the national income. This is at its worst where the society is stratified by caste, colour, or creed, and where whole sections of the population are deprived of opportunity by law, by custom, or by chicanery. Rapid economic progress is seldom found in societies which do not have vertical mobility or where a section of society is seeking to maintain special privileges to itself.

- In some societies, the social system may deny enterprises the resources needed—it might, for instance, not be able to recruit labor because it is tied to the soil by law or because of caste restrictions. Or land may be concentrated in the hands of a small number of persons unwilling to sell it outside their group. Potential enterprisers might also be excluded by a monopolistic organization of production.

Rapid economic progress was impossible without painful readjustments, the experts maintained:

> Ancient philosophies have to be scrapped; old social institutions have to disintegrate; bonds of caste, creed and race have to be burst; and large numbers of persons who cannot keep up with progress have to have their expectations of a comfortable life frustrated. . . . There are a number of under-developed countries where the concentration of economic and political power in the hands of a small class, whose main interest is the preservation of its own wealth and privileges, rules out the prospect of much economic progress until a social revolution has effected a shift in the distribution of income and power.[22]

The group argued for radical political change as a prerequisite for economic progress:

> There cannot be rapid economic progress unless the leaders of a country at all levels—politicians, teachers, engineers, business leaders, trade unionists, priests, journalists—desire economic progress for the country, and are willing to pay its price, which is the creation of a society from which economic, political and social privileges have been eliminated. On the other hand, given leadership and the public will to advance, all problems of economic development are soluble. We wish to emphasize that the masses of the people take their cue from those who are in authority over them. If the leaders are reactionary, selfish and corrupt, the masses in turn are dispirited, and seem to lack initiative. But if the leaders win the confidence of the country, and prove themselves to be vigorous in eradicating privilege and gross inequalities, they can inspire the masses with an enthusiasm for progress which carries all before it.[23]

BOX 3.1. Cultural, Social, and Economic Constraints to Economic Development

The group of prominent economists appointed by the Secretary-General discussed the conditions necessary for economic development to take place and also identified the major constraints to development, including the following:

23. Economic progress will not occur unless the atmosphere is favourable to it. The people of a country must desire progress, and their social, economic, legal and political institutions must be favourable to it. . . .

24. Economic progress will not be desired in a community where the people do not realise that progress is possible. Progress occurs only where people believe that man can, by conscious efforts, master nature. This is a lesson which the human mind has been a long time learning. Where it has been learnt, human beings are experimental in their attitude to material techniques, to social institutions, and so on. This experimental or scientific attitude is one of the preconditions to progress. The greatest progress will occur in those countries where education is widespread and where it encourages an experimental outlook.

25. Even where people know that a greater abundance of goods and services is possible, they may not consider it to be worth the effort. Lack of interest in material things may be due to the prevalence of an other-worldly philosophy which discourages material wants. It may also be due to a relative preference for leisure. In the latter case, the amount of work people wish to perform will be small, but they will not necessarily be adverse to measures which increase the productivity of such work as they do. A high preference for leisure is not consistent with great material possessions, but it is not necessarily inconsistent with economic progress.

26. Alternatively, people may be unwilling to make the effort to produce wealth if the social prestige which they desire is more easily acquired in other ways. Thus, in feudal or aristocratic societies where power is inherited rather than earned, and where little respect is accorded to wealth which has been created in the first or second generation, the energies of ambitious men are not attracted so much to the production of wealth as to acquisition of skills which may secure entry into the strongholds of power—to the acquisition of military skill, or the skill of the hunt, or the skill of the lawyer or priest. In such societies, the production of wealth

is frequently held in contempt as a profession for well-bred young men. By contrast, economic progress is rapid in countries where the successful organizers of economic activity are among the more highly prized members of the community.

The report highlighted other constraints to development in points 28–32: "Little progress occurs in countries where governments are too weak to protect property or where civil disorder is endemic. Neither is there progress where governments act arbitrarily in requisitioning property—as happened in the past on frequent military campaigns." Family structures that involved obligations to the extended family might represent a disincentive, and private enterprise and communal property were not always consistent with each other and economic progress. Defects of the law—for example between laws governing the relations between landlord and tenants or laws or customs that prevented producers from making innovations—could be further constraints.

Source: United Nations, *Measures for the Economic Development of Underdeveloped Countries* (New York: United Nations Department of Economic Affairs, 1951), 13–16.

Needless to say, this perspective was not the only one around at the time.

The Lost Cause:
The Special UN Fund for Economic Development (SUNFED)

In the late 1940s and early 1950s, the World Bank was repeatedly criticized for not taking responsibility for development in underdeveloped countries, especially with development finance.[24] Beyond this pressure on the Bretton Woods institutions to increase lending to underdeveloped countries, the UN system achieved little with regard to providing development finance. Nevertheless, within the system an idea emerged that sought to provide development finance on concessionary terms, even on a grant basis. The governments of the South were the driving force behind this idea.

During these years, representatives of less-developed countries insisted that the focus should be on establishing a mechanism for providing technical assistance and ensuring that "underdeveloped" countries obtained financial support in various forms. They saw the lack of capital as the most critical constraint on development. The countries of the industrialized West, however, focused on establishing the Expanded Programme of

Technical Assistance, while Soviet-bloc countries, which offered their own model of development and were highly critical of the past and present performances of European colonial powers and U.S. imperialism, often stayed on the sidelines, particularly when it came to providing funds. Representatives of less-developed countries stubbornly insisted that the idea of increased financial transfers deserved equal if not greater attention than the EPTA idea and had proposed parallel resolutions to those that established the EPTA. They requested that the ground for a UN facility for financial transfers be cleared through investigations if not action.

Follow-up on General Assembly Resolution 198 (III)

In 1949, ECOSOC intensely discussed the problem of financing development, which was considered "one of the most serious and urgent that the Council had to consider."[25] However, the council decided to follow the Economic Committee's recommendation to postpone consideration of this issue until its next session.[26] This consideration was to be based on a number of studies that the Secretary-General was asked to prepare:

1. On private foreign investments in selected countries, the factors accounting for these investments, and the existing conditions governing foreign investments

2. On methods of increasing domestic savings and of ensuring their most advantageous use for the purpose of economic development

3. On the effects of economic development on the volume of savings

4. On an international clearing-house of information on investment.[27]

An International Development Authority

The Sub-Commission on Economic Development of ECOSOC's Economic and Employment Commission, which was established in October 1946, was particularly active in bringing the problems of long-term economic development to the agendas of the commission and the council. In 1949, the subcommission survived, by a narrow majority, a proposal from the United States to abolish it.[28]

In 1949, the subcommission's chairman, Mr. V. K. R. V. Rao of India, came up with a proposal for a United Nations Economic Development

Administration (UNEDA) that would finance basic economic development. UNEDA would be given five basic tasks: (1) provide technical assistance to underdeveloped countries; (2) coordinate the technical assistance
of the UN and its specialized agencies; (3) assist underdeveloped countries
in obtaining materials, equipment, personnel, and so forth for economic
development; (4) finance or help finance development schemes that could
not be financed from a country's own resources and for which loans were
not available on strict business principles; and (5) promote and if necessary direct and finance regional development projects.[29]

The Economic Committee and ECOSOC paid no attention to this proposal.[30] But the broader theme of the proposal stayed on the agenda both
of the subcommission and ECOSOC, resulting in the appointment, by the
Secretary-General, of the UN group of experts already referred to.[31] The
group of experts brought a similar idea to the table. In their 1951 report,
they asserted that the "United Nations should establish an International
Development Authority to assist the under-developed countries in preparing, co-ordinating and implementing their programmes of economic
development; to distribute to under-developed countries grant-in-aid for
specific purposes; to verify the proper utilization of such grants; and to
study and report on the progress of development programmes."[32]

In the Economic Committee and ECOSOC, this proposal was
firmly supported by the less-developed countries (including Chile, India,
Pakistan, and the Philippines) but was rejected by the majority, including
the major industrialized countries.[33] In the General Assembly as well, a
split appeared between industrialized and "underdeveloped" countries,
but now the majority was in favor of the proposal. In resolution 520 (VI),
ECOSOC was asked to submit a detailed plan "for establishing, as soon as
circumstances permit, a special fund for grant-in-aid and for low-interest,
long-term loans to under-developed countries for the purpose of helping
them, at their request, to accelerate their economic development and to
finance non-self-liquidating projects which are basic to their economic
development." This plan was to be submitted to the seventh session of
the General Assembly in 1953.[34]

Secretary-General Trygve Lie responded by outlining alternative ideas
about the fund's size and composition; ways of collecting contributions;
the character of the contributions; the policies, conditions, and methods
to be followed when grants and loans were provided; and the principles
that recipient countries should observe.[35] ECOSOC called for a committee

to draft a plan for the fund. This committee of nine members, appointed by the Secretary-General, proposed that a Special United Nations Fund for Economic Development be established.[36]

When ECOSOC considered the report, it focused on the annual amount suggested—$250 million. Those in favor of the fund (who were mostly developing countries) found the amount far too low to meet the stated objectives; they argued that it would have to be doubled. The major industrialized countries, who were expected to contribute to the fund, found the suggested amount totally unrealistic.[37]

In the spring of 1953, the new Republican administration in Washington introduced the idea that development should be linked with disarmament into the debate. In mid-April, President Eisenhower declared his willingness to join with all nations in devoting a substantial percentage of any savings achieved by real disarmament to a fund for world aid and reconstruction. His vision was that reductions in the huge investments in armaments resulting from the arms race between the East and West could come to better use by helping "to develop the underdeveloped areas of the world, to stimulate profitable and fair world trade, to assist all peoples to know the blessings of productive freedom. The monuments of this new kind of war would be these: roads and schools, hospitals and homes, food and health."[38]

This vision influenced the development debate, nourishing an idea of a peace dividend from disarmament and arms control that survived into the 1990s. In the international development strategies adopted for the first and second development decades (see chapters 5 and 6), the close interrelationship between development and disarmament was stressed.

However, the new idea can also be seen as a strategic move by one of the superpowers. The way President Eisenhower's vision was implemented in the UN gives ample support for such an interpretation. The U.S. representatives in ECOSOC immediately presented the idea as an alternative to SUNFED.[39] Contributions to the proposed fund were made conditional on the savings resulting from internationally supervised global disarmament. Given the international setting of the time, that was almost impossible. In this way, Eisenhower's new idea became one more hurdle for the idea of SUNFED to overcome. In December 1953, this condition was incorporated in General Assembly resolution 724 (VIII).[40]

However, in a parallel resolution, the General Assembly asked member governments and UN specialized agencies for comments and moral and material support for the establishment of SUNFED.[41] The member government positions, as summed up in a final report on the feasibility of SUNFED,[42] were split into three groups: the "underdeveloped" countries, who argued that the fund should be established immediately; the major western countries, who made internationally supervised disarmament a condition of their participation; and the remaining industrialized countries, who were prepared to contribute to the fund without the disarmament condition provided that the other major potential contributors also did so. In practice, therefore, the third group made their contributions contingent on the participation of the major western powers.[43]

Although SUNFED stayed on the UN agenda, the major actors did not change their positions much.[44] In ECOSOC and the General Assembly, representatives of developing countries argued strongly for it. The major industrial powers, on the other side, were at best reluctant about a large-scale UN fund for capital assistance. The U.S. position had all along been that this role should be assigned to the World Bank.[45]

In 1956, a group of forty-one developing countries filed a resolution asking an ad hoc committee that had been appointed the previous year to work on statutes for SUNFED. However, when the developing countries confronted heavy opposition, they agreed to a compromise: they asked the committee to construct different possible legal frameworks for the fund.[46] This did not solve the basic conflict; it only shifted it to the ad hoc committee.

The committee presented its final and supplementary reports to ECOSOC in May 1957.[47] The positions of the main actors had not changed. Some major western countries, particularly the United States and United Kingdom, again argued forcefully against the concept of SUNFED, repeating the argument that the proposed fund would not be able to serve its intended purposes unless it was acceptable to those who were supposed to provide the funding.[48]

However, the majority within ECOSOC was willing to press the issue and establish the proposed fund even if consensus could not be attained.[49] Those who argued most forcefully for the immediate establishment of SUNFED believed that from the perspective of less-developed countries, multilateral aid had particular advantages over bilateral aid. ECOSOC adopted a resolution that recommended that the General Assembly take immediate steps to establish the fund. The vote was 15 to 3; the United States, the United Kingdom, and Canada voted against the resolution.[50]

This vote showed that Soviet-bloc countries had come around to support international development assistance through the United Nations.[51]

Voting Power in the United Nations and Its Limits

This brief history of the unfulfilled idea of SUNFED ends here, with a vast UN majority recommending that it be established. Lack of capital was identified as a critical constraint on initiating and sustaining development in "underdeveloped" countries—particularly capital for improving economic and social infrastructure, which was necessary for effective production. Within the UN system, the issue was driven by the UN administration in tandem with less-developed countries. Experts of high reputation, drawn from outside as well as within the organization, served as their main instrument.

Ideas matter. However, the standing of their champions also matters. When the UN was created, ideas generated by John Maynard Keynes and others, which were based on lessons learned from the massive inflation of the early 1920s and the Great Depression of the early 1930s, held a high standing. They were reinforced by experiences gained during World War II with planning and cooperation among the Allied powers to maximize output, mobilize latent resources, and achieve full employment. The early post–World War II years were the heyday of the Keynesian consensus that emphasized the crucial role of governments in managing economies to generate full employment.

Transferred to the international scene, Keynesian economics implied that national policies should be supplemented (if not replaced) by an international regime of rules of conduct that could be controlled and managed by international institutions. At Bretton Woods, Lord Keynes, representing the UK government, played a crucial intellectual role in this regard. He argued that four institutional pillars would meet the economic challenges of the postwar era by promoting international trade and stabilizing commodity prices: the United Nations, the World Bank, the IMF, and an International Trade Organization (ITO).

Keynes was not completely successful. The institutions that were established were not as powerful as he had argued they should be, and the U.S. Congress rejected the proposed ITO when the resolution that created it was ready for ratification. At that time, the tide in U.S. economic and foreign policy had turned from that of the Democratic Roosevelt and Truman administrations of the 1940s and early 1950s to the Republican Eisenhower administration. During the McCarthy era, the U.S. government stood for a different approach to international cooperation, including its attitude to the UN system—to the extent of bringing the Cold War into the UN Secretariat.

Advocates of the Keynesian consensus in the UN system were found at all levels: in delegations representing governments in intergovernmental bodies, in the UN Secretariat, in the secretariats of the specialized agencies and programs, and in committees of experts entrusted with preparing the analyses and recommendations that constituted the basis for policy decisions. The experts of these committees were appointed either by intergovernmental bodies on the recommendation of the Secretary-General, by heads of special agencies, or directly by the Secretary-General or the head of the relevant agency.

Some of these actors were able to play a more important role than others. In Chapter 2, we noted the crucial role of David Owen in the creation and shaping of the EPTA. From his position in the UN Secretariat as deputy secretary-general and head of the Economic Department, he served as the prime facilitator and architect of the program. Once the EPTA had been established, he served as its head for fifteen years and continued to influence UN technical assistance in the UNDP. V. K. R. V. Rao's proposal to establish a comprehensive UN Economic Development Administration is another example of a UN actor shaping events. Rao represented the Indian government and chaired the Sub-Commission on Economic Development at ECOSOC.[52] Hans W. Singer was a third outstanding actor in the early processes of building development institutions in the UN system. He played an important role behind the scenes.[53] These men were all proponents of the Keynesian consensus.[54] In the changing political environment of the 1950s and beyond, these men and likeminded colleagues lost several battles, including the battle for SUNFED. But they carried on and could count some successes as well.

The history of SUNFED sheds light on some basic constraints within the UN system. Ideas that might seem rational from the perspective of the predominant development thinking of the day may not necessarily emerge as winners, not even with the support of a majority in the organization's political bodies. Although voting power will always be important and resolutions adopted by the major organs of the UN system will always give important signals, the power of the purse may be even greater in deciding outcomes. Yet when majority decisions on important issues are not implemented, the system runs the risk of signaling its powerlessness.

For almost as long as the organization has existed, this dilemma has caused frustrations within the UN system as well as among its member governments and beyond. It is illuminated in the case of SUNFED: the governments that were expected to provide the funding in the form of voluntary contributions could not be forced to do so. This provided these governments with greater influence than they could expect from their voting strength alone.

Developing countries and their supporters in the North lost the battle for a multilateral agency for capital finance within the framework of the United Nations. Nevertheless, their unswerving insistence that a multilateral agency that could provide development finance on favorable terms was needed was not totally wasted. In an effort to bring the strained relations with the majority back to "normalcy," the United States came up with the idea of the United Nations Special Fund.

The persistence of developing countries, working with the UN Secretariat, pushed the World Bank to expand its engagement with development finance. The first concession of this kind came in 1956 with the establishment of the International Finance Corporation as an affiliate of the IBRD. The other concession—a soft window of the World Bank, the International Development Association—came three years later and became operative in 1960. They were both established as a sort of compensation for the stubborn resistance of the major western powers to the establishment of SUNFED. At the World Bank, western powers were in full control, in stark contrast to the UN system.

The idea of an institution to facilitate private capital for investments had been around since the Bretton Woods conference. It failed to materialize for various reasons, mainly ideological reasons, including conflicting views within the U.S. polity.[55] Views also differed within the World Bank. Developing countries pursued the idea in the UN, although ambivalence could be detected even among these governments. In 1952, the idea of the International Finance Corporation obtained support from ECOSOC and the UN General Assembly.[56] However, neither the World Bank nor the governments that were expected to provide the main funding were enthusiastic, as reflected in IBRD reports to ECOSOC the following year. At this point, negotiations on SUNFED had reached a stalemate, and that probably affected the parallel process to establish the IFC. The major western governments compensated for their uncompromising stance on SUNFED with a more accommodating approach on the IFC.[57]

Developments regarding the proposed IFC during the second half of 1953 illustrate what a global multilateral organization operating at its best may be able to accomplish. In July, the World Bank completely wrote off the idea. But efforts were made in the Economic Committee and ECOSOC to keep the IFC alive. This pressure increased in the Second Committee, which established a working group to iron out a consensus. The General Assembly concurred.[58]

For years, the World Bank had opposed the notion of involving the United Nations in financial assistance. Indeed, it had even opposed the principle of providing concessionary development assistance. Its leadership had been reluctant to turn the bank into a major source of development finance for developing countries.[59] They maintained this position beyond the mid-1950s. Nevertheless, some staff members saw the advantages of affiliating a program of concessional multilateral financial transfers with the World Bank.[60] Within the U.S. government, there was ambivalence toward this idea. Democrats tended to support the establishment of a program for financial assistance with the World Bank and Republicans tended to oppose it.[61] However, the Democratic administration did not move to support the idea, and enthusiasm decreased after the Eisenhower administration began in 1953.[62]

In mid-1957, however, established positions on these matters were reconsidered in Washington, both within the U.S. administration and in the World Bank. The UN majority, which included, in addition to developing countries, some important western countries and, perhaps even more important, the Soviet bloc, signaled its willingness to establish SUNFED even without a consensus that included the United States. This got things moving within the UN and in Washington, and the United States proposed the alternative idea of establishing the Special Fund. Within the World Bank, strategic considerations about its outreach and ability to promote development came to the fore: a complementary soft window to its ordinary lending would facilitate this outreach, particularly vis-à-vis India and Pakistan.

Within the U.S. administration, several factors contributed to a reconsideration of the notion of a soft window associated with the IBRD. By the start of the 1950s, an anticommunist, pro-development alliance within the United States had translated the Cold War into an economic contest to be played out in developing countries by way of development assistance.[63] This group, which was based in the eastern U.S. establishment, was a growing counterweight to the conservative wing of the Republican Party. However, the catalyst that triggered the U.S. decision to support the IDA was a Democrat senator from Oklahoma named Mike Monroney, who in the mid-1950s "became seized with the needs of developing countries for soft loans, of the advantages of multilateral aid, and of the advantages of the World Bank as the dispenser of such aid."[64]

By mid-1959, thanks to the influence of Senator Monroney, the United States had decided to support the IDA. The U.S. secretary of the treasury sent a letter on 31 July 1959 to the World Bank's president proposing that draft articles of an agreement for an International Development Association be prepared. Shortly afterward, on 1 October, the governors of the IBRD unanimously agreed to the IDA. The new International Development Association would begin operations the following year.[65]

The integration of the IDA into the World Bank ended the dream that a major UN development agency would combine technical development assistance with financial assistance in the form of long-term, low-interest credits. Obviously, this had a negative impact on the standing of the United Nations as a development institution in general and vis-à-vis the Bank in particular. Its ability to influence the direction of development efforts was diminished along with its capacity to provide funding for these efforts. Its ability to coordinate development efforts was affected as well. And of course developing countries were the real losers. If development funding had been entrusted a UN agency, they would have been better situated to influence its general direction, norms, and priorities.

Nevertheless, the losers were not totally disappointed. Although they had fought hard for SUNFED, they were not unaware of the existing balance of power, particularly concerning resources, which affected their expectations about the possible outcome of their quest.[66] They had succeeded in breaking the barrier in the World Bank system against development funding on concessionary terms. They had won some important concessions: the establishment of the IFC and the IDA within the World Bank and the establishment of the Special Fund within the UN system. Moreover, the birth of the IDA turned the World Bank into a development finance agency, and that affected its perspective. A few years later, when Robert McNamara succeeded Eugene Black as president of the Bank, this almost revolutionary change of perspective became more clear, even though it was the same board and the same IBRD staff that was dealing with the new resources. The IDA was able to draw on radically different resources than those the IBRD had previously relied on, and those resources included official development assistance. This broadened the group of borrowers and the activities that were funded.

However the effects ran in both directions, as the historians of the

World Bank note: "The choice of the Bank as mediator for the new government-to-government concessional transfers also heavily conditioned the brand of multilateral concessional lending that followed."[67]

The United Nations Special Fund

The stalemate established within the ad hoc committee over SUNFED's statutes prompted Argentina to intervene. It suggested a mini-SUNFED to finance regional training centers and surveys of natural resources. The U.S. delegation sent out a similar trial balloon: an article by Paul Hoffman, then serving as the U.S. representative on the General Assembly's Second Committee, suggested a UN experimental fund of $100 million to be used for surveys of mineral, water, and soil resources and for a limited number of pilot projects.[68]

Before the General Assembly's twelfth session in the fall of 1957, the U.S. delegation proposed a special project fund that would be part of the EPTA instead of the far more ambitious SUNFED concept ECOSOC had recommended. After difficult negotiations, the General Assembly adopted a resolution that recommended a special fund "to provide systematic and sustained assistance in fields essential to the integrated technical, economic and social development of the less-developed countries."[69] This fund was intended to facilitate new capital investments by creating conditions that would make such investments more feasible or more effective.

Overall Objectives and Major Principles

The fund's overall objectives and major principles were set out in ECOSOC resolution 692 (XXVI) and its annex. Its activities would be geared toward enlarging the scope of UN technical assistance programs by adding special projects in strategically important areas such as the assessment and development of manpower; industry, including handicrafts and cottage industries; agriculture; transport; communications; building and housing; health; education; statistics; and public administration. This assistance would take the form of surveys; research and training; demonstration centers, plants, or works; and other appropriate means, including fellowships that were integral to a specific project financed by the fund.[70]

The fund was not intended to provide heavy capital investments but rather to facilitate such investments. The basic rationale behind the UN Special Fund was that many developing countries were not eligible for investments because they lacked the feasibility studies that would enable potential investors to make a decision about whether or not to invest. The

Special Fund was to provide investments that would increase knowledge and thereby provide a foundation for the governments themselves to go ahead, with or without foreign capital in the form of development assistance or private investments. In addition, pre-investment studies funded by the Special Fund were intended to provide information potential investors wanted.

In the fall of 1958, the UN General Assembly formally established the UN Special Fund, as recommended by ECOSOC.[71] Some major guidelines set for the fund were similar to those established for the EPTA almost a decade earlier:

- The Special Fund shall concentrate, as far as practicable, on relatively large projects and avoid allocation of its resources over a large number of small projects;

- Projects shall be undertaken which will lead to early results and have the widest possible impact in advancing the economic, social or technical development of the country or countries concerned, in particular by facilitating new capital investment;

- Due consideration shall be given to arrangements made for the integration of projects in national and development programmes and for effective co-ordination of the project with other multilateral and bilateral programmes;

- In accordance with the principles of the Charter of the United Nations, the assistance furnished by the Special Fund shall not be a means of forceful economic and political interference in the internal affairs of the country or countries concerned and should not be accompanied by any conditions of a political nature;

- Projects shall be devised in such a way as to facilitate transfer, as soon as practicable of the responsibilities of the Special Fund to assisted countries or to organizations designated by them.[72]

Such projects might be provided to a country, a group of countries, or a region. In a modest way, a long-term perspective was introduced: projects might be approved for the period of time needed for their execution, "even if more than one year."[73]

Structure

The Special Fund was administered by ECOSOC and the UN General Assembly. The annual reports of the EPTA and the Special Fund were considered in relation to each other. The intergovernmental control of the fund was exercised by a Governing Council consisting of eighteen state members elected by ECOSOC. The "economically more developed countries," with due regard to their contributions to the fund, had equal representation with "less-developed countries," with due regard to equitable geographical distribution among these members.[74] The Governing Council met twice a year. Overall responsibility for operations was vested in a managing director, who had the sole authority to recommend to the Governing Council projects submitted by governments. The managing director was also represented in the EPTA's TAB. A Consultative Board, consisting of the UN Secretary-General, the executive chairman of the TAB, and the president of the IBRD (or their representatives), advised the managing director about project requests and proposed programs.[75]

Funding Principles

The Special Fund depended on voluntary contributions by governments of countries that were members of the UN and its specialized agencies and other participating organizations. Each year, the UN Secretary-General convened an annual pledging conference for the Special Fund and the EPTA. Governments were invited to make pledges for a number of years and to indicate how they wanted to divide their contributions between the two programs. However, in order to maintain the multilateral character of the fund, "no contributing country should receive special treatment with respect to its contribution, nor should negotiations for the use of currencies take place between contributing and receiving countries."

The fund's programs were developed on a project basis. Contributing countries could not specify how they wanted funds to be used by a UN agency, nor could they earmark funds for specific recipient countries or projects. As was the case with EPTA projects, recipient governments were expected to finance part of the project's costs, at least the part payable in local currency. This condition might be waived in exceptional cases where the country was deemed financially unable to make such payments.

The First Years of Operation

EVOLVING POLICIES AND PRIORITIES

In a statement to ECOSOC soon after operations had started, the UN Special Fund's managing director, Paul G. Hoffman,[76] pointed to the great gap between the average national income per person in "underdeveloped" countries and those in more developed countries and suggested as the goal for the next decade the doubling of the net average increase of national incomes from 1 to 2 percent. To reach this goal, underdeveloped countries would have to increase their own investments and developed countries would have to double their investments in those areas. Hoffman stated that the main aim of the fund was to accelerate the capacity of underdeveloped countries to absorb investment capital.[77]

More specific policies were quickly adopted to determine the relative priority of requests received by the Special Fund. In 1959, the Special Fund's Governing Council agreed to the managing director's suggestion that the fund should focus at first on projects that would demonstrate the wealth-producing potential of natural resources in less-developed countries, training and research institutes, and surveys that could lead to early investments. The General Assembly's Second Committee agreed.[78]

The fund's activities expanded beyond the field of pre-investment studies. By 1962 its activities included: (a) financing surveys and studies on natural physical resources, fisheries industries, the feasibility of improving the use of land and water resources, and possibilities in the development of communications systems; (b) establishing or strengthening research and advisory services in agricultural, forestry, industrial, and other fields with a view to improving the use of existing resources, opening new markets and planning for a balanced industrial production; and (c) setting up or expanding institutions to provide advanced technical training and education to increase the number of skilled personnel at all levels in developing countries.[79]

Increasingly, the fund focused on industrial development, which eventually became an integral part of the Special Fund's policy. In 1961, when the general manager proposed that activities be expanded into small-scale industries, the response from both the fund's Governing Council and ECOSOC was positive. In 1964, the Governing Council accepted a proposal to increase the number of projects that contributed more directly to the process of industrialization, such as pilot factories and demonstration centers. This heightened focus on industrialization activities continued in 1965 through closer cooperation with the Centre for Industrial Development. Plans were made for joint preparatory missions consisting of representatives of the fund, the center, and appropriate specialized agencies and for placing industrial advisers in field offices.[80]

The development perspectives generated by the UN Conference on Trade and Development gradually influenced the debate on the future orientation of the Special Fund. As early as 1963, Yugoslavia's representative in ECOSOC proposed that the Secretary-General prepare a study of the practical steps required for transforming the Special Fund into a United Nations Capital Development Fund.[81]

The General Assembly's Second Committee emphasized the need to establish regional institutes for economic development and planning modeled on the one to be established for Latin America by the Economic Commission for Latin America.[82] In 1962, the fund responded by expanding its activities to include support for regional institutes and including in its program a regional institute in Santiago, Chile, to provide training, research, and advisory services in planning and programming for economic development in Latin America. In 1963, the fund supported the establishment of an Asian Institute of Economic Development in Bangkok, and in 1964, it responded to a 1961 request to include an African institute for economic development and planning in its program.[83]

The Special Fund's activities were increasingly viewed as part of the international strategy for the First United Nations Development Decade. In several General Assembly resolutions, the fund was requested to play its part in the efforts to fulfill the objectives set in the strategy and action plan for the decade.[84]

The Special Fund's main rationale, preparing the ground for additional finance for viable development projects, seemed well founded in practice.[85] In 1964, it was reported that sixteen pre-investment surveys and feasibility studies that had been carried out at a cost of $8.5 million to the fund and $2.5 million to recipient governments had already attracted some $730 million for financing the development that had been recommended and that more was on the way.[86]

As was generally the case when the UN established new programs, the administrative staff was very small: the Special Fund relied on the services of established institutions such as the EPTA and the executing agencies as much as possible. The fund entered into a series of cooperative agreements with other agencies, particularly concerning project execution. As described in chapter 2, this cooperation was especially extensive with the EPTA and involved projects as well as the services of the resident representatives in recipient countries. Resident representatives also served as directors of Special Fund activities in the country of operation.

With its growing project portfolio, however, the fund found it necessary to build up an administration that was adapted to its particular needs, particularly within recipient countries. In 1963, the fund increased the number of field offices and expanded the staff of existing offices. The justification was to strengthen its work and to maintain closer contact with recipient governments in order to work out how the fund could best assist them in their priority economic development efforts.[87]

FUNDING THE UN SPECIAL FUND

The Special Fund's activities were financed through voluntary contributions by member states of the UN or its related agencies at annual pledging conferences. The fund was given an annual financial framework of $100 million. Although spokesmen of leading governments of the South felt that this amount was disappointingly low, even this target was never achieved.[88]

From 1959 to the end of 1965, the program of the UN Special Fund grew from thirteen projects costing $31.1 million to 522 projects costing $1.1 billion. By the end of 1965, the recipient governments had contributed more than half of the total costs; the fund had contributed $478 million and recipient governments had contributed $673 million.[89]

The amounts pledged over the years are given in table 3.1. During the seven years of the Special Fund, almost 90 percent of the funding came from western countries. Of this group, the United States contributed over 41 percent of all funds to the Special Fund.[90] The United Kingdom followed next, at just over 8 percent (much in line with the pattern we have seen with regard to the funding of the EPTA), followed by Sweden (8 percent), the Federal Republic of Germany (6 percent), and the Netherlands and Canada (5 percent).

Sweden's contribution of 8 percent is remarkable in view of the relative size of its economy. However, this fits into a pattern that became even more pronounced during the years that followed: Scandinavian countries proved to become among the major supporters, politically and through

TABLE 3.1.

Contributions Pledged to the UN Special Fund by Country Groups, 1959–1965 (in thousands of U.S. dollars and by percent)

	$	%
Western countries[1]	377,745	89.6
Soviet-bloc countries[2]	11,543	2.7
Less-developed countries	32,517	7.7
TOTAL	421,805	100.0

Source: Yearbook of the United Nations 1959, 113–114; Yearbook of the United Nations 1960, 239–240; Yearbook of the United Nations 1961, 199–200; Yearbook of the United Nations 1962, 201–202; Yearbook of the United Nations 1963, 185–186; Yearbook of the United Nations 1964, 241–242; Yearbook of the United Nations 1965, 281–282; and calculations based on data in these sources.

1. This includes OECD member countries, members of NATO, and "neutral" countries such as Austria, Finland, Sweden, and Switzerland.

2. Yugoslavia is included in this group. China is included among the less-developed countries.

voluntary contributions, of UN development activities in general and the UNDP in particular. This commitment to development is reflected in their contributions to the Special Fund, which increased throughout the 1960s.

A growing number of developing countries also contributed. During the seven-year period of the Special Fund, their pledges amounted to $32.5 million, almost 8 percent of the total amount pledged. The pledges of several of these countries were of a modest, almost symbolic, nature. However, India, which had a high political profile on development funding issues, made substantial contributions to the fund—$12.5 million, or 3 percent of the total pledges.

THE REGIONAL FOCUS OF SPECIAL FUND PROJECTS

The UN Special Fund started its operations at a time when new states were beginning to emerge in great numbers in Africa, bringing development within that continent to the fore. This new focus is reflected in the regional distribution of assistance, both in the number of projects and the amounts allocated. As table 3.2 shows, after a slow start the focus was increasingly on Africa.

TABLE 3.2.

Distribution of UN Special Fund Resources by Region, 1959–1965 (by percent and in thousands of U.S. dollars)

	1959 %	1960 %	1961 %	1962 %	1963 %	1964 %	1965 %	TOTAL %	TOTAL $
Americas	31.4	27.7	28.1	26.9	27.1	16.5	29.7	26.2	125,233
Asia and the Far East	31.4	31.6	28.7	23.9	31.2	29.9	20.6	27.0	129,199
Middle East	14.9	19.6	10.0	14.3	5.9	4.6	5.7	6.7	32,225
Africa	8.0	17.4	33.2	32.4	32.5	44.7	33.8	33.0	157,586
Interregional	7.8	0.0	0.0	0.0	0.0	0.0	0.0	0.8	3,866
Eastern Europe	6.5	3.7	0.0	2.5	3.4	4.2	10.3	6.3	30,250
TOTAL[1]	100.0	100.0	100.0	100.0	100.1	99.9	100.1	100.0	478,359

Source: Yearbook of the United Nations 1959, 110; Yearbook of the United Nations 1960, 236; Yearbook of the United Nations 1961, 199; Yearbook of the United Nations 1962, 202; Yearbook of the United Nations 1963, 185; Yearbook of the United Nations 1964, 242; Yearbook of the United Nations 1965, 282; and calculations based on data in these sources.

1. Totals may not add up to 100 due to rounding of figures in the original sources.

RELATIONS BETWEEN THE SPECIAL FUND AND
THE SPECIALIZED AGENCIES

The norms that guided relations between the Special Fund and the executing agencies are described in the previous subsections. Operational activities were run by the participating organizations as executive agencies within their areas of specialization.[91] Decisions on projects were made by the Governing Council on the recommendation of the executive director, who was advised by the advisory board. The heads of the executing agencies were represented on the advisory board when projects within their areas were to be considered.

From its inception, the fund received requests far beyond what it could possibly manage within its budgetary frame.[92] This created competition among requesting governments and among executing agencies as well. As a result, stakeholders both within and outside requesting countries, including the specialized agencies, offered their services to governments. Since agencies did not receive a fixed share of the available funds, they had to compete with each other for assignments. The projects put forward were evaluated by the Special Fund on their own merits. The agencies were therefore confronted with a quite different situation than the situation during the first years of the EPTA.

The actual distribution of funds through the executing agencies is given in table 3.3. From the start, the FAO was entrusted with the largest number of projects and the greatest resources, followed by the UN Secretariat (as an executing agency), UNESCO, and the ILO. This distribution indicates the strategic priorities of Special Fund headquarters, although it does not necessarily convey the priority given to the various sectors because several of the projects combined concerns. Nevertheless, the distribution conveys the emphasis the Special Fund placed on improving agricultural production as a basis for economic development and the clear priority it gave to training, education, and research across sectors in this regard.

Other concerns may have influenced distribution. Looking back, one resident representative argued that the most common explanation for the actual distribution of projects on executing agencies was that "the Special Fund headquarters felt a need to keep some kind of balance in the distribution of new projects assignments among the participating organizations. If a particular Agency had not been awarded any new assignments

TABLE 3.3.

Distribution of Special Fund Resources among UN Executing Agencies, 1959–1965 (in thousands of U.S. dollars and by percent)

	THOUSANDS OF U.S. DOLLARS	%
FAO	181,352	37.9
UN	100,251	21.0
UNESCO	91,062	19.0
ILO	46,812	9.8
IBRD	18,164	3.8
ITU	13,928	2.9
ICAO	11,791	2.5
WHO	6,827	1.4
WMO	5,633	1.2
IAEA	2,459	0.5
Total	478,279	100.0

Sources: Yearbook of the United Nations 1959, 110; Yearbook of the United Nations 1960, 236; Yearbook of the United Nations 1961, 195; Yearbook of the United Nations 1965, 27; and calculations based on data in these sources.

for some time, the Special Fund would watch out for opportunities to remedy the situation."[93]

CENTRALIZED OR DECENTRALIZED DECISION-MAKING AND ADMINISTRATION?

Since the fund received far more requests for funding than it was able to meet, governments had to indicate their priorities. Thus, it would not seem unreasonable to expect that the priority list was followed when consideration was given to projects requested by a government. However, this was not always the case. As observed from the field: "Priority requests were brushed aside in favour of projects much farther down on the queue."[94]

This practice indicates the locus of decision-making power—the New York headquarters of the Special Fund. It is also indicative of the relative influence of recipient governments; to stand a chance, a project had to be accepted and brought forward by the government concerned. Special

Fund administrators considered the government's own priorities about projects to be advisory only.

In contrast to the emerging development within the EPTA, the Special Fund came to operate in a more centralized way. To a large extent, projects were both identified and formulated by agency representatives and the evaluation and decision-making process took place at the Special Fund's headquarters.

An Impressive Track Record

The Special Fund, like the EPTA, was designed to facilitate development by improving the knowledge base of developing countries. It clearly emphasized economic development, although it also sought to promote social development and technology. It did not aspire to fund development the way development finance institutions do (an idea that had been basic to the SUNFED idea). The fund's financial framework and available means were relatively modest. Although it hoped to obtain $100 million in annual contributions, pledges during the first years did not reach more than one-third of that amount.

Nevertheless, by the end of 1965, after seven years of operation, the Special Fund had an impressive track record: 552 projects in 130 developing countries and territories at a cost of $1.15 billion of which the fund had provided $478 million and the recipient countries the remaining $673 million. Seventy of these 552 projects had been completed, and the remaining projects were carried forward to the new UNDP. Increasingly, the approved projects were regional ones, although this still constituted a minority of about 4 percent of all projects.[95]

To a large extent, the Special Fund also succeeded in its main goal of facilitating development finance from other sources. Recipient governments, multilateral institutions, industrialized countries, bilateral donors, and private investors from the country concerned or from abroad provided resources. These resources supported development activities that had been identified through various surveys financed by the fund. The money invested by the fund had a multiplier effect. At the end of the seven-year period, total follow-up investments amounted to $1.07 billion—$751 million from outside the countries concerned and $317 million from various sources within these countries. The cost to the Special Fund of the twenty-five projects that led to these investments was estimated to be $19.2 million.[96]

These financial accomplishments aside, 107,500 persons had been trained in occupational skills through training institutes the fund had supported, and research centers had facilitated breakthroughs in a range of agricultural and industrial undertakings, from crop production to petrochemicals.[97]

Although the Special Fund and the EPTA were operating within the same arena, their mode of work differed. The EPTA was decentralized and sought to integrate projects at the country level, while the fund centralized evaluation and decision-making processes at headquarters. However, projects selected for funding were coordinated with the activities of the EPTA as much as possible. As noted in chapter 2, the resident representative who reported to the EPTA was also appointed director of Special Fund operations in countries where participating organizations were executing projects financed by the fund.

In 1961, a process started with the aim of merging the two institutions. Four years later, this resulted in the establishment of the United Nations Development Programme.

FOUR

First Steps Down the Road: What Can the Footprints Tell?

- Sources
- The International Environment:
  The Emerging Cold War and Decolonization
- Some Concluding Observations

What were the roots of the idea of international development assistance? What triggered the first steps in realizing this idea? These are the main questions to be addressed in this concluding chapter of Part 1.

Sources

Imperialism

Chapter 1 identified imperialism as one of the five most prominent traditions that might have inspired the idea of international development assistance, especially in the case of the colonial powers. In a transition period, neocolonialism might appear as a strong driving force. This was the case in the years just after World War II, when some colonies of major imperial powers became sovereign states or approached this status. Imperial powers might have seen development assistance as a useful instrument for maintaining and prolonging the cultural, economic, and political relations they had developed during the colonial era.

In the bilateral relations of colonial powers vis-à-vis their former colonies, similarities did exist, particularly with regard to British and French policies.[1] In colonies that approached independence through a political process, without violent conflicts, the imperial powers left behind their political and administrative systems. They also often left behind a portion of the staff who had been administering the country and the businesses and cultural activities (including missionaries) that had emerged and thrived in the imperial period. But these practices did not apply to the same extent for all colonial powers, as illustrated in several African colonies after independence, perhaps most glaringly in resource-rich Belgian

Congo. Can the footprints of imperialism and neocolonialism be detected in the first manifestations of the UN's development assistance?

We have seen that the United States, Great Britain, and France exerted considerable influence on decisions made at the UN in the early days. These three powers contributed most of the resources for the EPTA and the Special Fund. They used the UN arena to defend their colonial policies, and their colonial and postcolonial policies influenced their policies within the UN. However, the arena matters: concerns driving bilateral aid programs were not pursued to the same extent within the world body, particularly not at a time when the United Nations was becoming the driving force of decolonization. In stark contrast to the goals of imperialism and neo-imperialism, the main objective of UN technical assistance was to strengthen the capacity of "underdeveloped" countries to improve their own economic and social development.

Over and over again, UN bodies emphasized the sovereignty of recipient governments and the principle of noninterference as the guiding norms of UN technical assistance. Precautions were taken to prevent neocolonialism in multilateral assistance. The principles established for technical assistance took care to cut any linkages between the governments providing technical assistance through the UN and recipient governments.

The Humanitarian Relief Tradition

The international Red Cross system has traditionally been the prime champion of humanitarian relief, but it has not been alone. As briefly noted in chapter 1, for decades both state and private organizations such as Oxfam and Save the Children have been deeply involved in relief operations. However, we can look at the Red Cross as a prototype of this kind of relief. This tradition has basically been oriented toward meeting immediate needs created by violent conflicts and natural disasters.

Few, if any, footprints from this tradition can be traced in the way the United Nations organized its development assistance during the 1940s and 1950s. The primary rationale and objectives of UN development assistance were different; they were oriented toward facilitating long-term economic and social development. This applies particularly to the EPTA but also to the Special Fund.

However, footprints might well be found in the early development assistance provided by other arms of the UN system that were not explored in chapters 2 and 3. Such footprints are indeed deep and visible in the activities of other UN institutions, such as UNICEF, the WHO, and the United Nations High Commissioner for Refugees (UNHCR). They are also apparent in multilateral food aid, where such traces are very clear: emergency food aid was a major justification for establishing the World Food Programme and continued as a major goal of its work. However, these activities date from the 1960s, beyond the purview of Part 1 of this book.

The Solidarity Tradition

The footprints of the solidarity tradition are more visible. Several of the UN's founding members, particularly in Europe, had socialist or social democratic governments and strong trade unions. Values championed within this tradition at the nation-state level, such as economic growth in combination with social justice and income distribution, were extended to the international level. The state was seen as a major instrument for promoting economic growth and welfare. Development planning and development plans were integral parts of such a system.

At a high level of generalization, it may be concluded that international development assistance emerged from the solidarity tradition. The EPTA's idea of promoting economic development in "underdeveloped" countries through the transfer of technological knowledge and education fits well into this tradition. So does financial support for developing the resource base of recipient countries, including the funding of pre-investment studies to enable recipient governments to attract scarce foreign investment, as pursued somewhat later by the Special Fund. And so did the norms established for these forms of assistance and the way their activities were organized. Sovereignty and dignity were basic values when decolonization began but still had far to go. The system that facilitated this assistance worked in the same direction: contributions by donor governments to interstate organizations were transmitted to recipient governments and integrated into their development efforts according their own priorities and development plans. The "help to self-help" design made the similarity in approach even more explicit: the recipient governments were themselves expected to contribute to fulfilling the desired objectives.

Although the footprints of the solidarity tradition are easily traced, a few modifications need to be made. Although norms governing activities are important in their own right, the way they are implemented is important. There will almost always be a discrepancy between lofty norms and reality, as chapters 2 and 3 identified.

However, by the late 1940s, ideas such as sovereignty, dignity, and self-help were not exclusive to the solidarity tradition and its traditional champions. These ideas had become part of the heritage of many governments, including most western ones. The importance of state intervention in promoting economic stability and welfare was the core of Keynes's message and part of mainstream development thinking by the late 1940s and 1950s. However, other ideas were around, and the idea of state intervention was strongly contested by both influential economists and major western countries, including the United States.

The Missionary Tradition

It is less easy to arrive at clear-cut conclusions about the footprints of the religious missionary tradition in early development efforts of the UN. Spreading the Christian Gospel is the driving force behind missionary activities in the field. Associated development activities, such as providing basic education, medical help, and other technical assistance, particularly within agriculture, have been instrumental in the pursuit of this primary task.

It is difficult to trace this tradition's specific influences in the rationale and objectives set for the EPTA and the Special Fund. Clearly, there are no traces of its primary concern. Although its mantle-bearers (churches, religious organizations) may have been instrumental both in generating the idea of development assistance and giving it normative support, the primary objective of UN assistance was different from that of the missionary organizations. Also, the main instrument was different. UN assistance was channeled through state authorities. This kind of development did not involve charity as such.

The Human Rights Tradition

Basic human rights were written into the UN Charter. In 1948, human rights were codified in the Universal Declaration of Human Rights. Human rights were later defined over a broad spectrum of realms—civil, political, economic, and social—in a series of international declarations and conventions.

In looking for footprints, it makes sense to distinguish between human rights as a normative commitment and human rights as a method of achieving set objectives. Established human rights may correspond to political commitments to certain objectives, although provided in a more solemn form and therefore presumably more binding for the governments that have committed themselves to fulfill these rights. Human rights as a method, on the other hand, require instruments to ensure that commitments are fulfilled; these instruments vary from exerting moral pressure to using laws and courts to enforce human rights commitments. For some human rights, particularly civil rights, cohesive instruments have become well developed within the confines of the nation-state and to some extent even internationally. Economic and social rights have generally been difficult to codify internationally and even more difficult to implement.

When first proposed, multilateral development assistance was firmly anchored in the UN Charter. The Charter pledged to help promote higher standards of living and economic and social progress and development and to help find solutions to international economic, social, health, and related problems. In 1946, the UN General Assembly identified expert advice as a way to implement this commitment; this was the main rationale for establishing the EPTA. As we have seen in chapter 2, the objectives of the EPTA and the Special Fund were attuned to the general commitments expressed in the UN Charter. So were norms established for the way these institutions should operate: the principle of the sovereignty of the recipient countries was repeatedly asserted. The objectives set for the EPTA and the Special Fund were not formulated in terms of rights but rather as general commitments. Promotion of human rights was not set out as an explicit objective of assistance, and no enforcement procedures were established.[2]

Although they belong to the same family with regard to rationale and objectives, the ideas of international development assistance and human rights as institutionalized and implemented within the UN system lived parallel and separate lives for decades. Their specific objectives concerning development and human rights, respectively, were pursued by separate institutional systems. This is related to the political divide within the UN on the human rights issue, which followed the East-West conflict. The West, especially the United States, emphasized civil and political human rights and accused the East of gross violations of these rights. The East, especially the Soviet Union, stressed economic and social rights and accused the West of gross neglect in this regard. However, the East-West division was not so clear cut; some states in Western Europe, among them Scandinavian countries and the Netherlands, emphasized social and economic rights as well as civil and political rights.

This ideological warfare aside, during the initial period of the aid era, most development institutions saw the promotion of economic development as the primary objective of development assistance. They shied away from issues that might complicate that mission in a setting characterized by cooperation between governments (for bilateral aid) or cooperation between agencies and recipient governments (for multilateral aid). In the late 1980s and the 1990s, the development agenda changed dramatically on this point, as we will see in Part 3.

The Modernization Paradigm

Technological innovation and diffusion, the core of the modernization paradigm, were the guiding ideas of multilateral technical assistance. Through an interstate organization, assistance was provided by voluntary contributions by governments to other governments upon their request. At an early stage in the 1950s, the EPTA started a process that later became long-term planning at the country level, beginning with resident representatives in the main recipient countries. However, this coordination may at best be described as "planning light" and was far removed from the Soviet model of five-year plans. The emphasis on integrating assistance into the host countries' own development plans may be best explained as a concern for the sovereignty of recipient governments.

The antecedents of the modernization paradigm are easily traced in the way the UN institutionalized the idea of development assistance in the early 1950s. UN entities provided assistance over a wide range of sectors, including industrial and agricultural development, natural resources, communications, and social services. This structure clearly stems from the modernization paradigm.

However, one core concern of that paradigm was missing in EPTA assistance: the need for capital was not met within the UN system, although Third World governments strongly pressed for such assistance through the UN. This also applied to the Special Fund, although its focus— particularly its concern with pre-investment studies—was geared toward facilitating capital investment. The need for development finance was generally recognized, although the forms in which it should be provided (including the issue of concessional terms) were disputed. The stillbirth of SUNFED reflected the power situation at the time: the major powers of the West preferred an institution they could control. The UN's insistence on planning and coordination, although vaguely developed, was attuned to the school of development economy. At the time, development economists molded in a Keynesian tradition were much more firmly entrenched in the UN secretariats than in the government administrations of some major western capitals—Washington, D.C., in particular.

Institutional Heritage

THE MULTILATERAL HERITAGE

Chapter 1 suggested that the idea of international development assistance as it was institutionalized at the UN emerged from the process of international cooperation. Although organizations tend to build on precedents established in the past, within organizations, there is usually room for people with ideas and ambitions to do some "institutional engineering" that expands the organization's realm of activity. As new members entered the UN and brought new concerns and priorities, the secretariats of development entities looked for ways to extend cooperation to areas that interested the new members, in this way integrating them into the fold. However, there is a limit to such institutional engineering: it cannot challenge the vital interests of the major players within the organization.

The UN Secretariat housed such a person with the ideas and ambitions needed to expand the scope of activity: David Owen, who served as deputy secretary-general and chief of the Secretariat's economic department. He saw the opportunity to bring a new purpose and new financial resources to the UN system.

As we saw in chapter 2, these new financial resources were used in the institution-building of the UN system itself. Owen took care to build alliances with the main implementing arms of the system, the specialized agencies, while at the same time gradually reinforcing the major role of the center of the organization. Only gradually did the EPTA shift the focus to the main implementing level, the national level of the countries requesting technical assistance, and then in a way that ensured continued harmony within the UN family. In addition, the foundations were established for what later developed into the UN system's "foreign service"— resident representative offices in member countries.

THE MARSHALL PLAN

The Marshall Plan's main characteristics, as briefly outlined in chapter 1, were massive transfers of resources in financial terms and in kind from the United States to postwar Europe. Conditions were added to ensure an environment that was politically and economically in line with U.S. values and interests: the market economy and democracy. As noted, there was also something in it for U.S. farmers, who were a strong interest group in domestic politics. A large share of the transfers consisted of food, fodder, and fertilizers, an arrangement that helped the U.S. government handle the problem of growing agricultural surpluses.

The massive transfers of the Marshall Plan inspired many governments of the South that faced development challenges in the late 1940s and the 1950s, particularly in the debates about SUNFED. The Special Fund that was instead established was not intended to provide development finance like the Marshall Plan had, nor was it equipped for that. Its main function was to facilitate private investment from outside as well as inside the countries concerned by way of pre-investment studies.

Few traces from the Marshall Plan can therefore be found in the way UN first established multilateral development assistance. Of course, some vague similarities may be noted—after all, resources were transferred—but these resources were mostly transferred in the form of skills (experts) rather than in the form of capital. The main feature of the Marshall Plan, namely massive resource transfer, was absent. That the modest UN Capital Development Fund was established after the battle for SUNFED was lost in no way modifies this conclusion.

Some footprints of the Marshall Plan can be found in the huge U.S. bilateral food aid program of the 1950s: massive resource transfers (food in kind) were made available to recipient governments with conditions added and usually as an instrument of U.S. agricultural and foreign policy, including trade policy. However, few traces of Marshall Plan–type resource transfers can be found in the multilateral food aid of the World Food Programme that developed in the 1960s. The program was organized in a way that circumscribed such opportunities (see chapter 6).

THE HEAVY FOOTPRINTS:
THE SOLIDARITY TRADITION AND THE MODERNIZATION PARADIGM

This analysis has explicitly been limited in time to the late 1940s and 1950s and in scope to only two of the first manifestations of UN development assistance, albeit the most important ones during the early years—the EPTA and the Special Fund.

The footprints of the international solidarity tradition were particularly visible during the early formative years of UN development assistance. It may seem surprising that the humanitarian relief tradition, in many ways the sister tradition of international solidarity, has left so few traces. A closer look at agency-level activities, those administered by the WHO in particular, might disclose such traces. The focus has not been directed toward the humanitarian assistance provided by other arms of the system, such as refugee assistance (at the time, particularly to Palestine) or the activities of UNICEF. In contrast, the footprints of the hegemonic development ideology of modernization are found everywhere, which is not particularly surprising given that technical assistance was the main focus. The Keynesian approach to development that emphasized the intervening role of the state can also be traced in the way the idea of development assistance was formed during these years.

The dynamics of international cooperation has been identified as a major determinant. Technical assistance was instrumental in making the UN attractive to an increasing number of new members from the South. It was also instrumental in developing the UN as a system: the UN "family" had a stake of its own in driving international development assistance.

The International Environment: The Emerging Cold War and Decolonization

This volume's introduction assumed that the prevailing international environment would exert a decisive influence on the generation and survival of ideas. In the late 1940s and early 1950s, two major trends were identified, namely the emerging conflict between the United States and the Soviet Union and decolonization. It was assumed that both would influence the policies pursued by the main actors within the UN as well as policy outcomes.

The Impact of the Cold War

The bipolar international security system that emerged at the end of the 1940s was institutionalized through the establishment of the North Atlantic Treaty Organization in the West in 1949 and the Warsaw Pact in the East in 1955. The East-West conflict dominated international politics in the decades that followed. As we have seen in chapters 2 and 3, the Cold War influenced relations within the United Nations when development issues were discussed.

The conflict started in Europe, almost before World War II ended.

Geopolitics and security concerns were the dominant features of what became the new political map of Europe. The Red Army had driven Hitler's army off Soviet territory and out of countries in Eastern and Southeastern Europe, liberating them from Nazi forces and at the same time occupying them militarily. Western Europe was liberated by forces from the United States and the United Kingdom, which at the war's end occupied western Germany. The victorious powers divided Berlin among themselves in zones of occupation. In Western Europe, elections brought to power new national regimes, usually dominated by the political parties that had resisted Nazi occupation from exile or through internal movements. In Eastern and Southeastern Europe, Soviet-friendly national regimes emerged, even in countries that had had democratically elected regimes before the war.

This "traditional" geopolitical conflict, which was characterized by occupying and securing territory, was reinforced by ideological conflict. Arguably, ideologies of various kinds, from religions to political ideologies, will almost always be brought forward in conflicts, as was the case in World War II. In the postwar world, the development ideologies of the two regional superpowers became a primary instrument in their power play regarding emerging states. For the United States, it was a question of containing communist penetration, particularly in Asia; for the Soviet Union, the goal was winning new allies and challenging western influence in former and current colonial countries. Both superpowers wanted to achieve hegemony and used their development ideologies and models in tandem with development assistance as major instruments in their efforts to forge alliances in the South.

The literature on development assistance, with few dissenting voices, confirms this picture. Outstanding students of U.S. development assistance have concluded that security concerns drove policy.[3] Similar observations have been made about the Soviet Union.[4]

Nevertheless, in the two early manifestations of UN development assistance, the EPTA and the Special Fund, few clear footprints can be found. As has already been stressed, these two programs took care to remove direct links between the assistance provider and the recipient. Furthermore, the principles guiding development assistance set out to guard the sovereignty of the recipient government. Moreover, the independence of the UN Secretariat vis-à-vis the major contributors to UN development programs may be illustrated by the Secretariat's generating of arguments that contradicted western ideological orthodoxy involving trade and development. However, this is not to imply that the indirect and, indeed, even the direct influence of the major donor countries was totally absent.

Aside from verbal exchanges in UN intergovernmental bodies when development issues were discussed, few Cold War footprints can be identified in the rationale, objectives, and norms guiding the activities of these institutions or in the actual distribution of resources. Although Soviet-bloc countries placed greater emphasis on industrial development than did most western governments, western countries agreed that industrialization was important. Soviet-bloc countries also warned against private foreign capital assistance as an imperialist and neo-imperialist instrument. One of the main objectives of the Special Fund, in part, contradicted this warning: it sought to facilitate capital for development, from the private sector and governments, at home and abroad—and from multilateral financial institutions as well.

How can the near-absence of such influences be explained? The Cold War was real enough, and it was fought in most national and international arenas. The U.S. Federal Bureau of Investigation and Central Intelligence Agency kept close tabs on the UN system, both at UN headquarters and in the field, respectively. This surveillance intensified in the early 1950s, when McCarthyism infested U.S. political life. One explanation may well be that the rationale, objectives, norms, and main principles that guided EPTA and Special Fund activities during these years (and the way these activities were organized) are not the most appropriate places to look for such footprints. They might perhaps more easily be found in the field, as illustrated by Dame Margaret Anstee's experience in Bolivia (see box 2.2).

This is not to say that the United States did not seek to make it clear who was holding the upper hand. As we have seen, particularly in the debate and decisions involving SUNFED, it demonstrated the power of the purse. This was also illustrated by Anstee's experience. However, although such interferences demonstrated the arrogance of power, they fall under the category of petty interventions that did not affect the major course of the programs (although they were harmful and by no means innocent). During these years, the United States contributed generously to the Special Fund and the EPTA with ideas, political energy, and funding. Funding, in particular, contributed to ownership as well as influence.

Nevertheless, footprints that can be attributed to the Cold War are almost absent in the objectives set for Special Fund and EPTA activities and the norms that guided them. It is true that the Soviet Union argued against the creation of the EPTA and characterized it as a tool that served western imperialist interests. It did not start contributing to the funding of the EPTA until 1953 (after the death of Stalin) and then with relatively modest contributions that were tied to its own nonconvertible currency and its own experts, thereby undermining the multilateral character of the assistance. It also complained about being discriminated against when experts were selected for the services. Such features may be interpreted as Cold War influences, and in some instances probably rightly so. But there may be more trivial explanations.[5]

Perhaps UN programs were not considered important enough during these years and were sufficiently circumscribed that they did not pose a threat to the bilateral programs of the major powers. Their resources were quite modest by any standards. Or it might have been too complicated to run a service specifically geared to assisting one party in the Cold War, which would have meant the United States. Doing so might even have run the risk of backfiring, particularly since so many governments and so many experts were involved. Nor should altruism on the part of the western superpower be discarded as an explanation—in combination, of course, with enlightened self-interest at a time when it found the UN system useful. Bilateral aid policy probably offered better and less risky opportunities for the United States and other major western powers to pursue their Cold War objectives.

Some Concluding Observations

What overall conclusions can we draw from the first UN efforts to realize the idea of international development assistance? Previous chapters have emphasized that technical assistance and pre-investment surveys focused on "help to self-help" and that the Special Fund and the EPTA established basic principles to safeguard sovereignty. Previously in this chapter, we concluded that the main roots of the development idea as implemented by the UN are the solidarity tradition and the modernization paradigm. However, a few other elements deserve further comment.

The Decisive Role of the United States

The United States was instrumental in creating the first major manifestation of UN development assistance, the Expanded Programme of

Technical Assistance. President Truman provided the vision and invited other governments to join in the effort within the UN setting. In the UN, the ground was well prepared through UN General Assembly resolutions 198 (III) and 200 (III), which were adopted in December 1948. In addition to providing the idea, the initiative, and the push, the United States also provided more than 40 percent of the funding for development assistance activities.

Clearly, the initiative cannot be isolated from U.S. foreign policy and security concerns during a time of growing East-West tensions. Nevertheless, the U.S. push for multilateral development funding reflected ideal and social values of the Democratic Party's political tradition at a time when the U.S. isolationist tradition had been broken by a world war. At that point, the United States and its wartime allies were in almost full control of the world organization.

On the other hand, the Eisenhower administration and other major western powers effectively stopped the parallel vision of most developing countries of a UN agency that would combine technical assistance with development finance on concessionary terms. At that point, the East-West fronts had hardened and the Korean War been fought. Toward the end of the 1950s, the firm grip of the United States on the UN had weakened, primarily due to the influx of new members. This diminishing control, along with the predominant ideology of how capital transactions should be pursued, explains why the World Bank, which the United States and other western powers controlled, became the preferred channel of multilateral development finance.

The Power Paradox

The liberation of former colonies and dependencies changed the international system in a revolutionary way. The UN played a crucial role in promoting and facilitating the liberation process. As a result, it became a global organization in a more real sense and the prime foreign policy arena for new states.[6] To what extent were new states able to influence UN policy regarding areas important to them, especially economic development?

The agenda certainly changed: development issues were increasingly brought to the fore by both old and new members. However, equal voting power had its limitations. As best illustrated in the case of SUNFED, the grand idea of developing countries could not be realized even though it had majority support in the system's intergovernmental bodies, including the General Assembly. Decisions made in these bodies about the financial framework of the EPTA and the Special Fund tell the same story, as does the fact that development activities were financed through voluntary contributions by member governments, not through obligatory contributions according to an agreed-upon formula for regular contributions. The governments that were expected to fund the operations were not obliged to do so, and the power of the purse had the upper hand.

Nevertheless, numbers do carry influence, and developing countries influenced the principles that were established to guide development assistance: respect for the sovereignty of the governments requesting assistance. The assistance should not be imposed or directed from the outside and it should be integrated into national development plans. And these governments were "compensated" when they failed to achieve their preferred solution of the Special UN Fund for Economic Development.

An International Organization at Work

What about the institutional setting? To what extent has the multilateral organization as such contributed to the transformation of the development assistance idea into practice and put its distinct stamp on it—producing something over and beyond what its individual members might be able to achieve on their own? First of all, when the idea of international development assistance was first implemented within the system—in General Assembly resolutions 198 (III) and 200 (III)—it was explicitly anchored in the UN Charter. The same was true when the overall objectives and norms for development assistance were formulated.

The Secretariat played a prominent role in shaping UN development assistance, particularly through David Owen's creative handing of initiatives. Owen continued to administer the policy and activities of the program as the chair of the Technical Assistance Board, together with the heads of implementing UN agencies and recipient governments.

A similar picture emerges in the efforts to establish SUNFED. The Secretariat's economic department invested considerable energy in creating an agency that could combine technical assistance with concessionary development finance. Hans Singer played a prominent role behind the scenes in his interactions with core delegations of developing countries. The Secretariat introduced a technique in the early 1950s that came into more extensive use in later decades, namely engaging prominent experts of high international reputation to explore ideas and present proposals on how they could best be realized.

Although these intensive efforts did not achieve all of their aims, they did produce results. One idea generated as early as 1951 by a group of eminent experts appointed by the Secretary-General deserves special mention because of its prominence in the discourse on development and development assistance even today—the idea that the well-off countries of "Western Europe, Australasia, the United States and Canada" should contribute 1 percent of their national income in assistance to the under-developed countries.[7]

The Secretariat took on an independent role in its pursuit of ideas by requesting expert reports. Requests often originated from representatives of developing countries in the intergovernmental bodies dealing with development, including ECOSOC. Interacting with such representatives, key individuals in the secretariats have played a crucial role both in generating ideas and in transforming them into institutions. We have seen that secretariats sometimes consistently pursued ideas even when they were repeatedly voted down in the form initially presented.

Even the history of SUNFED's failure may illustrate the bargaining power of an international organization. Both the United States and the United Kingdom felt that their overall interests were best served by offering the compromise solution of the Special Fund, to which the United States became the largest contributor, and the consistent fight for SUNFED also opened a window for concessionary development funding with the World Bank.

There is more: the worldview and values of the person heading an organization are a dimension of explanations for the results of power plays among its members. It is therefore not without importance that the first UN Secretaries-General—Trygve Lie of Norway and Dag Hammarskjöld of Sweden—were molded in a social democratic tradition. In 1961, Hammarskjöld was followed by U Thant of Burma, a socialist and Buddhist by tradition.

PART TWO

The Formative Years

- ▪ **The International Environment**
- ▪ **The Ideological Environment**

Part 2 covers some of the most important developments during the 1960s and 1970s. The 1970s proved a turbulent decade in North-South relations. Economic stagflation characterized western economies and two oil crises developed. It was also a time where conflicting development ideologies were explored and pursued. The oil crisis of the mid-1970s was hard on the economies of both industrialized countries and Third World nonproducers of oil, and these effects were reinforced by a second oil crisis later in the decade. These crises heavily influenced the agenda for North-South relations, including development cooperation, as did evolving development paradigms.

The International Environment

During the late 1950s and early 1960s, many former colonies and dependencies became sovereign states and members of the United Nations. This obviously affected the world organization's agenda. More attention was given to the situation in less-developed countries and regions, bringing the issue of social and economic development up front. Moreover, North-South relations came increasingly to the fore.

Nevertheless, the bipolar system that evolved in the late 1940s remained the dominant feature of international politics. The Cold War continued to dominate relations between the two superpowers, including politics within the UN framework. North-South relations were also affected: increasingly, development assistance became an instrument in the Cold War. Security concerns were given primacy at a high price. Violent conflicts outside the core areas of the two security systems heightened the intensity of the power game, particularly the Vietnam War.

The East-West divide affected the South beyond matters of aid policy. While some governments of the South sought active alignment with one of the two parties, the great majority sought to keep out of the conflict, inter alia by creating and joining nonaligned groups of countries and adopting "middle-of-the road" positions in international politics. The Non-Aligned Movement gained fresh momentum in the 1960s and 1970s.

During these years, the United Nations broadened its position as a global organization with the influx of a large number of new members, mainly developing countries. Indeed, the UN gradually became the primary arena for developing countries to pursue their foreign policies.

The Ideological Environment

Ideologies about development, including discussions of development cooperation, also affected North-South relations. The modernization paradigm found itself confronted from both the "right" and the "left." Neoclassical traditionalists contested the wisdom of state intervention in the market. Scholars from disciplines other than development economics, although under the spell of the modernization paradigm, focused on other dimensions of the development process. They identified cultural, sociological, political, and psychological barriers to development, providing a more complex framework.

However, the modernization paradigm maintained a hegemonic position in the 1960s. In the real world, however, the development optimism of the 1950s and 1960s had not been matched by results: the gap between the North and South, in terms of indicators of aggregate economic was widening, and actual development in the South was skewed.

These failures nourished the emergence of the *dependencia* perspective, which confronted mainstream western perspectives: development could not be conceived within the limited framework of the nation-state. As early as the early 1950s, economists associated with the UN and the UN Economic Commission for Latin America had argued that development in the South depended on relations with the industrial North and that these structural relations led to dependency and underdevelopment in the South.[1] Structuralists argued for industrialization through import substitution. André Gunder Frank argued this perspective from a neo-Marxist point of view with special reference to Latin America.[2] The center/periphery model interpreted the core processes involved in a new way: the integration of the South into the capitalist North would further deepen its dependence and increase its underdevelopment, except for the elite (the "centers" in the South) that served as bridgeheads for exploitation from the North.[3] Implicitly, if not explicitly, this school argued that the South should delink economically from the North.

In the early 1970s, nevertheless, the South came up with answers that favored closer collaboration with the industrialized countries. However, the core message was that existing relations of economic and political power would have to be fundamentally reformed. The call for reform was, in part, based on arguments for a more just international division of labor and distribution of welfare and power. It was also based on a sense of strength that emerged from the experiences of the first oil crisis: what had been achieved within one raw-material sector (oil) might be copied in others. Although the perspective was general, involving most North-South relations, in practice the main focus was on improving trade relations with particular reference to the South's primary products.

The strategy for a New International Economic Order is an interesting case in the context of this study. The call emerged from the South.[4] It found fertile soil within the UN system, which took up the major demands, not least on normative grounds, and provided an institutional basis for the further development and promotion of the idea of an NIEO, especially through the UN Conference on Trade and Development. The two-track strategy that combined normative arguments (greater justice in North-South relations) with the implicit threat of using the power of resources backfired for a variety of reasons. Nevertheless, the basic idea lingered on beyond its heyday in the mid-1970s.

The NIEO strategy called for greater equity and justice in relations *between* countries, leaving equity and justice *within* countries aside as the responsibility of their governing structures.[5] Other strategies focused more specifically on microlevel development associated with norms that constitute the main justification for development assistance: poverty alleviation and increased welfare for the poorer segments of the population in particular. The framework of these approaches was generally the state (at the national, regional, and local levels), and they mainly emphasized the social dimensions of development. However, the framework included other social structures involving civil society.

Mainstream development theories of the 1950s and 1960s, with their emphasis on economic growth, had also been concerned with welfare, even poverty alleviation. However, as the expected increase in welfare for all failed to "trickle down" from economic growth,[6] additional mechanisms were in demand. In the mid-1970s, the basic human needs paradigm emerged as the main expression of the various approaches that focused on the social dimensions of development.[7] The paradigm was largely produced by craftsmanship within the UN system, especially the ILO, the WHO, and UNICEF.[8] In the years immediately after 1975, it became the dominant paradigm within the bilateral and multilateral donor community, particularly in development rhetoric. The basic weakness of the paradigm became increasingly clear toward the end of the 1970s when economies came under pressure: it presupposed a national economy that was able to invest in building and maintaining the appropriate structures and sustain the recurrent costs involved.

However, competing paradigms were also circulating, from the neoclassical traditionalist perspective to "utopian" approaches.[9] The main thrust of the alternative development perspective is that no universal road to development exists: each society must find its own path, based on its own needs and the conditions prevailing in its local and global environments, with due regard to the ecological imperative. As Björn Hettne has noted, alternative solutions are generally anti-statist and usually have two (not necessarily contradictory) points of reference: the local community and planet Earth. Ultimately, the core concern is to achieve the inclusion of the excluded.[10]

Development paradigms are not the only guiding stars of policymakers, not even the most decisive ones. In the 1970s, international economic and political conditions changed dramatically. The oil crises and stagflation in OECD countries affected their willingness to open their markets to imports from developing countries. This had a negative effect on developing countries: they encountered import restrictions for their products in their main markets, which in turn reduced their revenues. Many developing countries began to accumulate large debts during this period. This affected the situation of most developing countries profoundly, particularly after the conditions associated with a propelling debt burden worsened during the second part of the 1970s, turning a balance-of-payments crisis into a development crisis for most of them.

Part 1 focused on the beginnings of international development assistance within the United Nations. In the 1960s and 1970s, this start was consolidated and new steps were taken with regard to norms and institution-building. In Part 2, we will focus on much the same policy dimensions as in Part 1: how the main objectives and norms set for UN development assistance evolved as declared and practiced and as reflected in its institution-building.

The United Nations development strategy for the First Development Decade, the 1960s, is an important landmark. Although the strategy was general and vague, it played an important role: it justified providing international development assistance and established the first international objectives and targets as well as strategies and norms (guidelines) for this activity. Part 2 focuses on this development strategy and the international development strategies for the two ensuing development decades (chapters 5 and 6).

We will also explore to what extent the core objectives and principles established in the late 1940s and developed in the 1950s were maintained during the following two decades. The focus will be the UNDP, the new institution created in the mid-1960s into which the EPTA and the Special Fund were merged. In addition to its own activities, the UNDP was given a central coordinating role for all UN activities within the field of development assistance (chapter 7).

In 1961, the World Food Programme was established. Previously, food aid had been an extensive part of a few bilateral aid programs, particularly that of the United States. It had a rationale of its own based on food surpluses. As the WFP was established almost as a part of the First Development Decade, a core question is whether or not the multilateral setting made a difference (chapter 8).

At the end of the 1960s, the UN development system, especially the UNDP, became subject to a major review, a capacity study carried out by Sir Robert Jackson (see chapter 7).[11] The institutional development that followed and the policies pursued by this major organization for UN development assistance call for special attention. Earlier in 1969, a commission on international development chaired by Lester B. Pearson delivered a broad overview of international development assistance and recommended policy reforms.[12] This report became crucial when the development goals and the strategy for the Second Development Decade were adopted.

When looking into the evolving norms for international development assistance (development cooperation) in the 1960s and the 1970s—and the

institutional structures underpinning (or conflicting with) such norms—
we will ask the following questions:

- To what extent and how did changes in the political (the East-West divide in particular) and economic environments influence policies in the field of development cooperation?
- To what extent and in what ways were the perspectives of the competing development paradigms reflected in policy outcomes?

FIVE

The First Development Decade: An Instrument of Persuasion?

- **Main Goals and Targets of the UN's Development Strategy**
- **Priority Number 1: Planning**
- **Approaches to Promoting Development**
- **The Scope of UN Efforts**
- **Some Concluding Observations**

In 1949, a U.S. president provided the vision that set the first comprehensive development program under the UN umbrella into operation. Some twelve years later, another U.S. president, John F. Kennedy, delivered a speech that also made its mark in the field of development policy. Addressing the UN General Assembly on 25 September 1961, Kennedy proposed that the 1960s be declared the United Nations Decade of Development.[1]

The idea signaled the U.S. administration's increased commitment to development. But the vision did not bring in new ideas about activities or institutions beyond those already in operation. It was up to UN intergovernmental bodies, special agencies, and the Secretariat to explore unrecognized opportunities and, to the extent possible, transform them into policies and institutions that might give new dynamism to established activities and initiate new ones.

Less than three months later, on 19 December 1961, the General Assembly designated the 1960s as the United Nations Development Decade. The resolution declared that member states in both developed and developing countries would work to "intensify their efforts to mobilize and to sustain support for the measures required on the part of both developed and developing countries to accelerate progress towards self-sustaining growth of the economy of individual nations and their social advancement so as to attain in each under-developed country a substantial increase in the rate of growth, with each country setting its own target, taking as the objective a minimum annual rate of growth of aggregate national income of 5 per cent at the end of the Decade."[2]

The resolution called on UN member states to pursue policies designed to enable less-developed countries to sell more of their primary products at stable and remunerative prices in expanding markets "and thus to finance increasingly their own economic development from their earnings of foreign exchange and domestic savings." These policies would ensure "an equitable share of earnings from the extraction and marketing of their natural resources by foreign capital, in accordance with the generally accepted reasonable earnings of invested capital." The resolution also asked members to pursue policies that would "lead to an increase in the flow of development resources, public and private, to developing countries on mutually acceptable terms" and to adapt measures that would "stimulate the flow of private investment capital for the economic development of developing countries, on terms that are satisfactory both the capital-exporting countries and the capital-importing countries."[3]

Main Goals and Targets of the UN's Development Strategy

The First UN Development Decade (DD1) brought a change in terminology: gradually "underdeveloped" and "backward" countries became "less-developed" and "developing" countries. The emergence to statehood of several African countries that were suffering from colonial neglect and needed to prepare their inhabitants for life after colonial rule influenced development priorities: basic education as well as vocational and technical training became particularly important. The program for the development decade brought new intensity and priority into the field of development policy. However, with one important exception—the establishment of the World Food Programme on a three-year experimental basis—the strategy represented continuity in institutions and activities rather than new initiatives.

This is reflected in another General Assembly resolution, adopted at the same time, that called on UN member states and specialized agencies to bring their combined contributions to the EPTA and the Special Fund to $150 million in 1962. The resolution asked the Special Fund to "consider the desirability of establishing a service to provide developing countries, upon request, with information and guidance concerning the policies, rules, regulations and practices of existing and future sources of development capital and assistance necessary to enable the less developed countries to determine for themselves the most appropriate sources to which they may turn for assistance as needed."[4]

The strategy for DD1 anticipated that economic growth by itself would lead to improved social conditions. But it also emphasized inputs: the General Assembly established a target for the flow of international capital and assistance to developing countries of approximately 1 percent of the combined national incomes of the economically advanced countries as soon as possible. However, it did not set a particular goal for official development assistance.[5]

The DD1 targets and goals were to be achieved primarily by the governments and peoples of the countries concerned. The economically better-off countries would also help by adapting their policies to the needs of developing countries and through direct resource transfers, including development assistance. The DD1 strategy also included regional, international, and global organizations, both through their efforts to adapt the international rules of the game to the needs of developing countries and through direct contributions, particularly in the forms of advice, technical assistance, and funding. The multilateral organizations of the United Nations system, which included the UN's specialized agencies and the Bretton Woods institutions, were an important part of this web. It follows that any default within one of the components—a developing country, an economically advanced country, or the UN system or one of its specialized agencies—would automatically affect the possibility of attaining DD1 targets.

Obviously, on its own, the UN would not be able to realize the overall objectives and targets set for the decade. The UN will always be dependent on the willingness of various other independent actors to commit themselves to a set of objectives and targets and then fulfill their commitments.[6] Nevertheless, the UN has an important role to play by stimulating members to take on solemn commitments that may make a difference and then by reminding governments of their commitments, providing statistics on the state of affairs of developing countries, and evaluating the performances of member governments.

In May 1966, Secretary-General U Thant described the progress of development midway through the development decade.[7] Development had slowed down and some trends had even retarded, he noted. The terms of trade for developing countries had been weakened since 1960, and the total flow of external assistance to developing countries in 1964 was still below that of the decade's second year. Although many countries had made solid progress, "the hard fact remains that the output of developing countries as a whole increased more slowly in the first half of the nineteen-sixties than it had in the nineteen-fifties. The slower progress in development,

BOX 5.1. The Strategy for the UN Development Decade: Ways and Measures

UN General Assembly resolution 1710 (XVI) made particular reference to the following approaches and measures:

(a) The achievement and acceleration of sound self-sustaining economic development in the less developed countries through industrialization, diversification and the development of a highly productive agricultural sector;

(b) Measures for assisting the developing countries, at their request, to establish well-conceived and integrated country plans—including, where appropriate, land reform—which will serve to mobilize international resources and to utilize resources offered by foreign sources on both a bilateral and a multilateral basis for progress towards self-sustained growth;

(c) Measures to improve the use of international institutions and instrumentalities for furthering economic and social development;

(d) Measures to accelerate the elimination of illiteracy, hunger and disease, which seriously affect the productivity of the people of the less developed countries;

(e) The need to adopt new measures, and to improve existing measures, for further promoting education in general and vocational and technical training in the developing countries with the co-operation, where appropriate, of the specialized agencies and States which can provide assistance in these fields, and for training competent national personnel in the fields of public administration, education, engineering, health and agronomy;

(f) The intensification of research and demonstration as well as other efforts to exploit scientific and technological potentialities of high promise for accelerating economic and social development;

(g) Ways and means of finding and furthering effective solutions in the field of trade in manufactures as well as in primary commodities, bearing in mind, in particular, the need to increase the foreign exchange earnings of the under-developed countries;

(h) The need to review facilities for the collection, collation, analysis and dissemination of statistical and other information required for charting economic and social development and for providing a constant measurement of progress towards the objectives of the Decade;

(i) The utilization of resources released by disarmament for the purpose of economic and social development, in particular of the underdeveloped countries;

(j) The ways in which the United Nations can stimulate and support realization of the objectives of the Decade through the combined efforts of national and international institutions, both public and private.

Source: "United Nations Development Decade: A Programme for International Economic Co-Operation," General Assembly resolution 1710 (XVI), 19 December 1961.

moreover, has been accompanied by the emergence or aggravation of major imbalances which imperil future growth," the Secretary-General noted, referring to "the age-old scourges of famines and epidemics" that recently had "returned to haunt the minds of men."[8]

The decade had influenced political attitudes and national planning in developing countries and the planning and work of the UN and its specialized agencies, although not all to the same extent, U Thant noted.[9] Nevertheless, he was optimistic: "the corpus of ideas" embodied in the decade had "commanded growing support." The resolution that had designated the UN Development Decade was "an instrument of persuasion." And, "as the decade has advanced, the concepts expressed in the resolution have gained in influence."[10]

Priority Number 1: Planning

The UN sought to make DD1 ideas the organizing principles for all the development activities of the main actors involved, not just those of the UN system. It formulated guidelines for both national and multilateral action, taking as points of departure the general objectives and targets set out in the resolution that established the decade and the Proposal for Action.[11] The institutional machinery for the review and advancement of international policies within the field of social and economic development was gradually created, involving the whole family of UN organizations in their field of specialization, with ECOSOC playing a supervising role.

In the early 1960s, the UN Secretariat emphasized development planning and overall development plans. The Secretary-General and the ACC called for more realistic goals and targets as a basis for planning by governments and the multilateral system and as a basis for evaluating progress. This illustrates the evolving learning process within the UN system.[12]

Although planning was the order of the day, translating general objectives into more precisely defined goals and quantified targets to create a meaningful framework for policy decisions was a novel undertaking, at the global level and for many new national actors as well. As U Thant noted, at the beginning of the decade, many developing countries had barely begun to systematically analyze their future needs and possibilities, "which is the pre-condition for the construction of national plans or programmes." The absence of such data and the lack of such analysis "necessarily impaired the ability to define global or regional goals and targets which not only fully reflected the needs but were also firmly rooted in the realistic assessment of possibilities."[13]

The UN family saw it as a priority task to assist developing countries in improving their competence and capacity to plan their social and economic development. U Thant stated that the UN "has been very heavily engaged in contributing towards the enlargement of knowledge and in advancing understanding of the requirements and possibilities for development in individual developing countries."[14] He noted that the foundations for the construction of global and regional goals and targets had been considerably strengthened during the first half of the 1960s: there had been "a substantial accumulation of information about actual economic and social conditions in developing countries."[15] In this process, new insights had been gained about the complexity of economic and (in particular) social development, and UN agencies had begun to learn much more about the diversity in conditions among developing countries.[16]

The concept of policy coherence may be relatively new (the term was coined in the early 1990s), but the problem of lack of consistency among goals and targets is much older. In 1966, the Secretary-General noted that "there has been a growing awareness of the need, first, to bring global or regional goals and targets for individual sectors and components into consistent relationship with each other, and secondly, to explore the consistency between the goals and targets set by different countries." Similar issues pertained at the global and regional levels:

> First, there is the question of consistency between the macro-economic aggregates; the sum total of the productive resources required for realization of the various goals and targets has to be consistent with the total supply of these resources. Secondly, there is the ques-

tion of consistency in inter-sectoral and inter-industry relations; the requirements of each of the sectors and branches for goods and services from the other sectors and branches, and the supplies of goods and services from each of the sectors and branches from the others, have to be consistent with each other.[17]

By the 1960s, periodic reporting on progress and trends in economic and social development throughout the world was a long-established function for the UN and its specialized agencies.[18] Such reviews were designed primarily to inform the organization's governing body (and the governments concerned) of the current state of affairs, trends, and problems. What was new after the inception of the development decade was that it became normal practice for several of these reports to compare progress made against the main targets established for the decade.[19]

On the other hand, U Thant recognized that development planning by itself would not be sufficient. In many developing countries there was a need for administrative reform, improved public administration, and land reform.[20] He included the status of women as an important area of reform in this context.[21] However, he felt that it would be difficult for the UN to pursue reforms within these areas.[22]

Approaches to Promoting Development

The 1966 interim report indicated other priorities. Among these, the development and utilization of human resources through education and training was first, followed by a special focus on the younger generation, which constituted almost half of the population in many developing countries. The report also focused on promoting science and technology. All of these issues are relevant to the development of human resources.

Human Resource Development

The Secretary-General observed that one of the major recent changes in the approach to development had been "the greatly increased emphasis placed upon human resources," as reflected in several UN resolutions that had called for intensified concerted international action in the development and utilization of human resources and had asked for a major study on training national personnel.[23] These concerns were reflected in the policies and programs of the ILO and UNESCO. The ILO helped countries gain the full benefit from training and education through its work in employment, industrial relations, and labor administration, and UNESCO provided assistance in planning the development of education. In fact, within their various areas of special responsibility, most members of the UN family were actively involved in human development in one way or another.[24]

Targets and objectives for education had been formulated at both regional and national levels, and during the first half of the decade developing countries had come to recognize the vital role that education plays in economic development, the Secretary-General observed. Nevertheless, despite the expansion of school education, the number of illiterates had actually increased because of population growth. UNESCO gave priority to assisting member states in three fields: educational planning and administration; teacher training; and the eradication of illiteracy. UNESCO involved other agencies in these efforts, including UNICEF, the IBRD and IDA, the UNHCR, the ILO, and the FAO. The FAO had a special role in agricultural education, as did the ILO and the newly established UN Institute for Training and Research (UNITAR) in the area of training. Other specialized agencies were involved in promoting training and research, such as the WHO, which educated and trained health care staff.

The Younger Generation

The younger generation was singled out in the Proposal for Action as the segment of the population whose needs were greatest and whose contribution to development was especially vital. ECOSOC had recommended that the UN family focus on facilitating the contribution of younger people to development. This included ensuring that their efforts were directed to ends that were relevant and integral parts of the total development plan; strengthening their motivation to participate in and contribute to programs of self-help and mutual assistance; and protecting them from exploitation and excessive participation in development activities that might harm their health or hinder their physical or mental growth and their development as individuals and citizens.[25] In the mid-1960s, these general objectives were interpreted to mean that governments should pay particular attention to developing national policies and programs that would help young people with opportunities for employment and service to their communities and prepare them to use such opportunities.

Science and Technology

Science and technology have a particular place in most development paradigms, especially in the modernization paradigm. The Advisory Committee on the Application of Science and Technology to Development, which was appointed by ECOSOC, came to play a vital role in formulating the UN's approach and policy. In the mid-1960s, it proposed a World Plan of Action, taking note of the guidelines the ACC Sub-Committee on Science and Technology and the advisory committee had prepared regarding planning, training, and applying knowledge and mobilizing the efforts of scientists and research organizations in developed countries as well as in developing countries to find solutions to problems of developing countries. The guidelines focused on planning: a five-year plan for preparing basic structures in science and technology in developing countries; a plan of action to be spread over five to ten years for science education in developing countries; and a program aimed at improving documentation and technology transfer processes for developing countries.[26]

Although this task would involve most members of the UN family, UNESCO had a particular responsibility to help member states formulate national policies within this area, to survey and evaluate the resources available for these purposes, and to set up national institutions within the area of science and technology. It had also a special responsibility to assist in the training of administrators for national research institutions, particularly through fellowships. Training the necessary specialists (technicians, engineers, and scientists) more generally was also its special responsibility; this work was financed by, among others, the EPTA and the Special Fund and after 1965 by the UNDP. Other UN agencies played roles within their respective fields, often in cooperation with UNESCO. The FAO, for instance, was responsible for fostering the application of science and technology to the food and agricultural problems of developing countries, and the WHO was responsible for speeding up the application of science and technology in order to improve health conditions in the developing world.

Financing

Finding adequate financing for development has always been a critical barrier to the realization of aspirations and plans, both for multilateral organizations and for Third World governments. Mobilizing external resources was therefore an important part of the decade's strategy.

Actual contributions during the first part of the decade failed to meet the target of 1 percent of the GNP of industrialized countries in long-term private capital transfers and official assistance. In 1961, the net aggregate flow from western countries amounted to about $8 billion, or 0.84 percent of combined GNP. The next two years the amount decreased, but in 1964 it came close to the 1961 level ($7.88 billion, but only 0.65 percent of combined GNP). In 1965, it declined further in relative terms. A similar fluctuating trend could be seen in bilateral assistance commitments from the East European countries, which exceeded $1 billion in 1961 and 1964 but fell far below that level in 1962 and 1963. In 1966, Secretary-General U Thant was clear in his judgment: "The failure to meet this [1 percent] target has been one of the factors retarding the rate of growth of developing countries." A 50 percent increase in the net flows in the second part of the Development Decade would be necessary to meet both the 1 percent target and the IBRD estimates of the actual needs, he concluded.[27]

There was also a need to mobilize resources in developing countries. The UN and its member organizations (including the Bretton Woods institutions) were assisting developing countries in this regard in several programs, for example through improving education, developing human resources, and improving administrative structures. However, the Secretary-General stated that in "virtually every developing country the need for basic changes in the tax system is . . . well recognized." Changes in the tax system needed "to be planned and implemented as an integral part of the national planning activity." Increased resources for development would enable the United Nations to help with tax reform planning through increased research, expert assistance, training programs, and workshops.[28]

The Scope of UN Efforts

The objectives and targets set for the decade presupposed efforts from other major actors, not least the people and governments of developing countries and the governments of industrialized countries. UN contributions were only a part of the total effort. In an attempt to stimulate the resources and imaginations of the other main actors, the UN organized programs over a wide range of fields and activities.

Food and Agriculture

In the area of food and agriculture, the FAO was the prime operator. The work on an Indicative World Plan for Agricultural Development had high priority in FAO programs. This was intended to be a frame of reference within which both developed and developing countries could carry out national and international planning. The plan focused on improved methods and techniques in plant and animal production, fishery production, and fertilizers. The FAO also collaborated with the WHO and UNICEF in projects aimed at improving the nutrition of children, young people, and mothers. And since 1964, the FAO had been working with the IBRD in order to speed up investments in agricultural projects and with the IAEA on how to use atomic energy in agriculture.[29]

Trade

UNCTAD was a prime operator in the field of trade. A permanent secretariat tasked with preparing and implementing policies and measures conducive to the development of a world economy was established in accordance with the Final Act of the first session of UNCTAD in 1964. UNCTAD's activities were geared toward stimulating dynamic and steady growth in the real export earnings of developing countries and providing them with expanding resources for development. Its work focused on world trade in primary commodities, international commodity agreements, and measures for liberalizing access to markets. The FAO was also an important player here; it provided assistance in the agricultural development aspects of trade problems and initiated studies on commodity projections. UNCTAD also focused on expanding and diversifying exports of the manufactures and semi-manufactures produced by developing countries.

Trade negotiations took place within the confines of the General Agreement on Tariffs and Trade (GATT), which adopted a new Part IV in February 1965. GATT established the Committee on Trade and Development to supervise the implementation of Part IV, especially by identifying export products of developing countries on which action might be taken. The committee also coordinated the use of preferences by developed countries in favor of exports from developing countries and other arrangements that affected the trade conditions and market access of developing countries. The committee also looked at how developed countries used adjustment assistance measures to facilitate access to their markets for exports from developing countries. The Secretary-General reported that there was a growing realization within GATT that "in addition to the attack on obstacles to trade, attention should also be directed towards structural factors which may be inhibiting the growth of exports from the developing countries." He also reported that GATT negotiations (the Kennedy Round) intended to break down barriers to international trade, including both industrial and agricultural products and non-tariff as well as tariff barriers. A series of commitments to meet the export trade and development problems and needs of developing countries was built into the program of these negotiations.[30] Within the GATT framework, efforts had begun to help developing countries promote their exports, especially through the establishment of the International Trade Centre in Geneva in May 1964.

In the 1950s and far into the 1960s, economic development was considered to be synonymous with industrial development. The UN system's main contribution to industrial development up to the early 1960s was technical assistance and assistance with pre-investment surveys. It is therefore interesting to note that U Thant argued that experience had shown that pre-investment surveys had proved inappropriate: much time and money "can be wasted and much frustration can be caused by undertaking extensive and expensive feasibility studies and engineering studies if it is then found that financing sources are not interested; or that these sources insist on making their own feasibility studies all over again before being willing to consider financial commitment." In response, the UN had come up with a proposal for "special industrial services" to secure financial support for industrial projects before going too deep into detailed blueprints, financed by special voluntary contributions, and the UNDP had decided to finance industrial pilot projects.[31] U Thant pointed out quite openly that international action in the field of industrial development was especially difficult.[32]

Nevertheless, by the first half of the decade, industrial growth rates in developing countries were rising by 7 or 8 percent annually, although this is less impressive in view of the small starting point. The FAO, the ILO, and the World Bank group were particularly active in the field of industrial development. The FAO was primarily concerned with industries based on renewable raw materials derived from agriculture, forestry, and fisheries, and it assisted in the planning and operation of several such industrial projects financed mainly under the UNDP and UNICEF programs. The ILO, whose tripartite structure focused on industrial labor problems, increasingly dealt with industrial relations involving governments, employers' organizations, and trade unions. The World Bank group, which saw industrial development as a major objective, took steps to increase International Finance Corporation resources organized for this purpose. During the first half of the decade, the World Bank group committed about $1 billion to industrial development. It increasingly focused on technical and financial assistance to development finance companies that served industries and other productive enterprises and provided extensive technical assistance within this sector.[33]

Health

The WHO was the main actor in the field of health. In 1962, it launched a ten-year program for public health that sought to raise health standards and control diseases around the world. The program concentrated on providing environmental sanitation and controlling communicable diseases. The WHO also assisted with national health planning, trained health care personnel at all levels, and developed basic health service networks in developing countries.

Organizing and improving public health services was the primary way to strengthen disease control, sanitation, and health protection. The WHO and UNICEF helped governments develop rural health services by expanding health coverage and providing a certain minimum of preventive and curative services. In the fight against communicable diseases, these agencies did epidemiological surveillance and focused on eradicating major diseases at regional, national, and global levels. The worldwide malaria eradication program attracted great attention. The Secretary-General observed that a shortage of funds and lack of well-trained personnel had proved major difficulties for most developing countries as they sought to cope with the increasingly complex and difficult problems posed by changing environmental conditions.

Population Growth

In the 1960s, population growth was seen as a major threat to development.[34] In the UN's analysis, governments of developing countries lacked information about how population trends would affect their development plans and how policy measures might be implemented to alter these trends. They also lacked adequate statistics, trained technical personnel, and research programs.

The UN set out to help governments meet these needs. The second World Population Conference in Belgrade in 1965 focused on these issues. The UN's Population Commission came up with a five-year work program as part of a more general program outline. UNICEF provided assistance for family planning programs. A UN advisory mission on family planning in India, which the Indian government had requested in 1965, played an important role in future technical assistance in this field. The regional commissions were notably active when it came to developing and improving demographic statistics and analyzing the interrelationships of population change and economic and social factors. The FAO also participated in demographic studies that focused on the linkages between population trends and agricultural development. The WHO produced studies on the medical aspects of sterilization, fertility control methods, and the health aspects of population dynamics. The UN program for the second part of the decade had three main functions: fact-finding; bringing population trends and their implications to the attention of the governments concerned; and helping governments, upon request, implement policy measures in this area.[35]

National Resource Development

In the field of natural resource development, as in so many other areas, the main efforts of the UN and its specialized agencies expanded the knowledge base through research, surveys, conferences, and seminars and by making research results available to developing countries. An increasing share of the cost of EPTA and Special Fund projects was allocated to projects of this type. In the mid-1960s, the Secretary-General put forward a five-year program designed to contribute to the development of nonagricultural natural resources that consisted of nine surveys of mineral resources, water resources, energy, and electricity.[36] In addition, the UN and several specialized agencies (the FAO, the WHO, UNESCO, the WMO, the IAEA) were engaged in various aspects of water development: the FAO mainly with developing water resources for irrigation and the optimum use of water to satisfy food requirements; the WHO with the urgent need for water supply systems; UNESCO with the establishment of institutes for hydrological research; the WMO with hydrometeorological surveys, networks, and services; and the IAEA with feasibility studies of nuclear desalination plants. The Economic Commission for Asia and the Far East also surveyed fourteen of the largest international river basins to provide a basis for regional development planning.

By the mid-1960s, atomic energy was seen as an increasingly important energy source of economic development. The idea was to facilitate this form of inexpensive energy for peaceful uses in regions where conventional fuels were scarce and expensive, such as Asia, parts of Latin America, and Africa. The IAEA helped interested countries draw up long-term plans. It also studied individual nuclear power projects and found safe locations for nuclear power plants. However, surveys by the UN and the regional economic commissions were not limited to the development of atomic energy. They also produced surveys in other areas of natural resource development.

The Housing Sector

Proposals for Action emphasized the importance of the housing sector in national development. It set targets that were adapted to the specific circumstances of various regions. The stated objective was to increase the production of housing units and make significant reductions in construction costs. The targets involved building or rehabilitating ten dwelling units per 1,000 inhabitants each year in most developing countries at a cost of $1,000 per unit in urban areas and $200 in rural areas. However, Secretary-General U Thant noted that during the first half of the decade, achievements fell "far short of need. High and increasing rates of population growth, heavy migration from rural to urban areas and the attendant cost of land, labour and material, together with shortages of essential skills and poorly developed building technology, have caused progress to come virtually to a standstill. In many countries the housing situation has deteriorated."[37]

Even so, substantial domestic resources had been devoted to housing in many developing countries during this period and significant contributions had also been made available through foreign capital. International efforts within this sector had been broader and more varied than in any comparable previous period. For example, in 1962, the General Assembly appointed the Committee on Housing, Building and Planning, and in 1965, it endorsed the Centre for Housing, Building and Planning within the UN Secretariat. UN technical assistance programs for housing and environmental development concentrated on particular functional areas in each of the major regions: technological improvement and institutional machinery in Africa; formulating policies and plans for developing urban land, promoting regional development, and solving the problems of rapid urbanization (including coping with squatter settlements) in Asia and the Far East; and the institutional infrastructure needed to consolidate the considerable technical progress already achieved and improve the efficiency of overall investment in Latin America. Housing for refugees, the responsibility of the UNHCR, was a particular problem. Such housing had begun in Europe but was gradually extended to refugees in Latin America and the Middle East. By the end of 1965, some 36,000 refugees had benefited from the construction of over 10,000 housing units through the concerted efforts of governments, local authorities, and the UNHCR.[38]

Transport and Communications

Transport and communications, so important for economic development at all levels, involved several organizations within the UN family and, from the mid-1960s, the UN Secretariat as a liaison and coordinating center.[39] The secretariats of the regional economic commissions concentrated on ensuring that transportation schemes were given due weight in economic development.

At the beginning of the decade, the UN reoriented its work program in transportation. Whereas the emphasis had formerly been on facilitating international transport with regulatory and technical agreements, in the 1960s the focus shifted to the development and use of transport facilities within and between countries. Air transport grew rapidly during the decade, making it necessary for the ICAO to review regional air navigation plans; it also conducted studies of the economics of air transport. The Intergovernmental Maritime Consultancy Organization (IMCO) facilitated the operation of international shipping. The ITU made detailed plans of international telecommunication networks to facilitate the expansion and modernization of telecommunications. A world plan based on detailed regional plans was put into effect in 1963 to cover the period up to 1968. The ITU was also responsible for assigning radio-frequency allocations various telecommunications services and for ensuring that space telecommunications developed harmoniously and for the benefit of all countries without discrimination. The UPU helped developing countries improve and expand their postal services.[40]

The many and varied activities briefly outlined above were funded from many different sources, including the UN agencies involved. Several activities were funded by the EPTA, the Special Fund, and (after 1965) the UNDP. The WFP also funded programs.

Human Rights

In retrospect, it is interesting to note that the Secretary-General added a chapter on human rights in his 1966 interim report on DD1. He had also emphasized the promotion and protection of human rights in a separate section of his 1965 progress report.[41]

The General Assembly had also pointed to the need "to devote special attention on both the national and the international level to progress in the field of human rights, and to encourage the adaptation of measures designed to accelerate the promotion of respect for and observance of human rights and fundamental freedoms." After noting that despite repeated recommendations, "certain countries persist in practicing segregation, in violation of the fundamental laws of justice, freedom and respect for human rights," the assembly urged "all Governments to make special efforts during the United Nations Development Decade to promote respect for and observance of human rights and fundamental freedoms" and invited them "to include in their plans for economic and social development measures directed towards the achievement of further progress in the implementation of human rights and fundamental freedoms proclaimed in the Universal Declaration of Human Rights and in subsequent declarations and instruments in the field of human rights." The technical assistance personnel of the UN and the specialized agencies were called upon to give "all possible assistance, within the framework of their programmes during the United Nations Development Decade, with a view to achieving progress in the field of human rights."[42]

The Secretary-General responded that in a broad sense, "everything that is being done by the United Nations family of organizations during the Development Decade to promote economic and social development contributes to the implementation of the human rights and fundamental freedoms proclaimed in the Universal Declaration of Human Rights," noting that the assembly resolution did not specify "any particular programme of measures to be taken, or goals, targets or broad objectives to be achieved." However, he pointed out that the specific goals, targets, and broad objectives in the field of human rights had been given in the program for the international year of human rights; these goals were to be attained by 1968, twenty years after the proclamation of the Universal Declaration of Human Rights.[43]

Although human rights perspectives, especially with regard to social and economic rights, had always been part of the UN's development work, such activities had not been conceived of as an inherent part of development. The General Assembly's resolution 2081 (XX) brought human rights onto the agenda for economic and social development in a forceful way for the first time.[44] However, in his interim report, the Secretary-General did not state how the specific goals, targets, and overall objectives listed should be realized by means of aid policies or through the use of development assistance. He did not discuss how the UN should use development assistance to react to massive violations of human rights by member governments: the issue of ending aid to violating governments was not even raised. It might be inferred that his recommendation was to support positive measures toward human rights, not applying punishment in terms of conditionality or withdrawal of aid. This may explain why, for years, the development policy and the human rights policies of the United Nations continued to live separate lives.[45]

Some Concluding Observations

The United States was the major player at the United Nations during the first decades, as we have seen also in previous chapters. U.S. president Kennedy placed the vision of a UN development decade on the international agenda, and his administration managed to carry it through the UN decision-making system in a matter of months. This was part of several new bilateral and multilateral U.S. initiatives that included establishing the WFP as a multilateral supplement to the much larger bilateral U.S. food aid program that had been in place for years; extending the bilateral Food for Peace program; and creating the Alliance for Progress program directed toward Latin America.

All this happened at a time when the United States was losing its traditional control of the General Assembly, as was demonstrated in the fight over SUNFED. The United States and its western allies had not lived up to the high expectations of developing countries in the early 1950s, although they were by far the largest contributors to main UN development programs. In the cold East-West political climate, the time was ripe for new initiatives. As John Toye and Richard Toye have observed, President Kennedy responded to the loss of American control of the UN by assuming the role of moral leader.[46] Clearly, the vision of a development decade was conceived of in a security policy context, as were other new initiatives toward developing countries. These initiatives reflected more altruistic values as well and managed to create enthusiasm for the new policy drive within the United States as well as in partner countries, North and South.

However, the high hopes that contributions from the so-called developed world would increase were not met during the years that followed, although economic growth could be recorded in several developing countries. In his midterm report on DD1, Secretary-General U Thant made no direct references to governments or blocs. However, he blamed the slow and insufficient contributions of member governments for the "general crisis in the world's political relationships," which had worsened the atmosphere and lessened good will and confidence. Development, "which should be one of mankind's great constructive tasks, is often bedevilled with suspicion and misunderstanding, owing partly to the memories of the colonial era and the persistence in some cases of economic dependence." In this situation, the UN had an important role to play: "The paradoxical truth is that the United Nations development work can be one of the world's chief instruments in lessening political friction," U Thant maintained. He found this to be a strong argument for channeling a greater share of development assistance through international and multilateral agencies.[47]

Although the focus in UN development planning continued to be almost all-inclusive, the target set for financial transfers to developing countries came increasingly to the fore. The conditions on which such transfers were given also attracted more attention: increasingly, transfers on concessionary terms seemed to be necessary. The progress reports on the decade noted that the decade's success—or lack of success—was increasingly dependent on the willingness of industrial countries to meet these commitments.

The other major concern that came to the fore during the second half of the decade was the issue of the conditions of trade for developing countries. UNCTAD was the main arena here. In the second part of the 1960s, most of the demands for a NIEO, which came to occupy center stage in the mid-1970s, entered the international agenda.

Almost four years before the First Development Decade came to an end, planning for the second decade started.[48] That may, in part, explain why the UN did not present any comprehensive, analytical report on the achievements and shortcomings of DD1.[49] Already at that time, the first decade was seen as a stepping-stone to designing and implementing more vigorous action in the decade or perhaps the decades to follow. Assessments of the achievements in the first part of the decade, particularly its shortcomings, were to a large extent part of the planning process for the 1970s.

The most prominent feature in the Secretary-General's reports and in the debates in the intergovernmental bodies based on these reports was disappointment with the lack of progress achieved during the decade. These disappointments were also voiced in the General Assembly in late

1968 when it was debating about the strategy for the Second Development Decade and evaluating the lessons learned in the first decade.[50]

Although targets were not met and the willingness of industrial countries to contribute ODA was less than expected or needed, DD1 nevertheless served a valuable function. It identified economic and social development, particularly economic development in developing countries, as a joint responsibility of developed and developing countries, notwithstanding the ritual statement that the governments of the countries concerned carried the main responsibility for their own development. DD1 also managed to rally governments around a practical approach to fulfilling this venture that involved planning and setting overall objectives and targets, however fragile the bases for these targets (and therefore the targets themselves) appeared to be. The concept of a development decade provided a framework for a process where planning, setting targets and overall objectives, coordinating activities, and evaluating the results achieved could be improved and carried further multilaterally. This framework also encouraged a holistic perspective on development, although its main focus was economic development.

For the UN family of organizations, each of which tended to develop into a chiefdom that cautiously guarded its own territory, this perspective put additional pressure on the specialized agencies and other UN bodies to consider their planning and operational activities in the wider context of the decade. DD1 made it even more legitimate for the UN's central bodies to insist on policy coherence in the areas of planning and coordination. It began a process of coordinated, broad-based international cooperation to promote social and economic development in developing countries, however imperfect the process was. This could not have been achieved outside the United Nations framework.

SIX

The Second Development Decade

- **Main Features of the Development Strategy for the Second Development Decade**
- **Review and Appraisal of Objectives and Policies**
- **The Second Development Decade: A Bird's-Eye View**
- **Toward the Third Development Decade**

On 24 October 1970, the General Assembly proclaimed the Second UN Development Decade (DD2) and adopted an international development strategy for the decade.[1] The Committee for Development Planning, an eighteen-member group of experts appointed by the Secretary-General in 1966, played an important role in planning the decade, together with the UN Secretariat and ECOSOC. At the intergovernmental level, the Economic Committee of ECOSOC played a central role. Its membership was doubled in order to accommodate demands for placing the political responsibility for the decade's preparation with UNCTAD, and it served as the preparatory committee for the General Assembly.[2]

At an early stage in this process, the UN recognized the importance of mobilizing public opinion in developed as well as developing countries to support DD2. This meant disseminating the decade's targets, objectives, principles, and guidelines as widely as possible. People and decision-makers alike would need to be involved and feel a sense of participation. ECOSOC felt that this involvement would "contribute in large measure to the success" of the decade.[3]

Main Features of the Development Strategy for the Second Development Decade

Although the process had started early, the Preparatory Committee and ECOSOC were not able to agree on all issues before the draft strategy was presented to the General Assembly. It was left to the General Assembly's Second Committee to reach agreement on the most controversial issues.[4] This turned the Second Committee into a negotiations

committee. A draft proposal submitted by eighty-eight developing countries and Yugoslavia constituted the basis for these discussions.

After extensive negotiations in the Second Committee and in a working group of the committee, a revised text was approved without a vote.
The committee took into consideration the statements made by member governments and groups of governments both before and after it
approved the text. The same procedure was followed when the General
Assembly adopted the recommended draft resolution. This had serious
implications for the strategy: when it came to actual commitments, particularly those involving more industrialized countries, reservations were
many and strong. This weakened the spine of the strategy, the availability
of resources. As ECOSOC rightly pointed out, commitments with a fixed
time schedule are all-important for implementing objectives.

The Preamble

Ultimate aspirations are expressed more clearly in the preamble of an
international agreement than in its operative paragraphs, as it is generally the preamble that explains the over-arching motives and aims of the
more binding commitments of a treaty. In the resolution establishing the
Second Development Decade and the development strategy for the 1970s,
UN member governments dedicated themselves anew "to the fundamental objectives enshrined in the Charter of the United Nations twenty-five
years ago to create conditions of stability and well-being and to ensure
a minimum standard of living consistent with human dignity through
economic and social progress and development."[5]

The ultimate objective of development "must be to bring about sustained improvement in the well-being of the individual and bestow benefits on all." The preamble repeated that the "primary responsibility for
the development of developing countries rests upon themselves," but this
time it added: "however great their own efforts, these will not be sufficient
to enable them to achieve the desired development goals as expeditiously
as they must unless they are assisted through increased financial resources
and more favourable economic and commercial policies on the part of
developed countries." And governments pledged themselves, individually
and collectively, "to pursue policies designed to create a more just and
rational world economic and social order in which equality of opportunities should be as much a prerogative of nations as of individuals within

a nation. They subscribe to the goals and objectives of the Decade and resolve to take measures to translate them into reality."[6]

Major Goals and Objectives

Although the targets set for economic growth for DD1 had not been fully met, the ambitions of DD2 were even higher: on average, at least 6 percent annual growth in the gross national product of developing countries during the first half of the 1970s and possibly an even higher rate during the second half. It was up to the individual developing countries themselves to set their own targets, based on the situation in which they found themselves. On average, per capita income was to increase about 3.5 percent annually, based on an annual population growth of 2.5 percent. DD2 also focused on domestic savings and trade (see box 6.1).

The development strategy emphasized both qualitative and quantitative reforms in employment, education, health, nutrition, and housing. These measures were designed to improve the well-being of children, increase the participation of youth in economic development, and integrate women in development efforts.

Policy Measures

The policy measures designed to realize the goals and objectives called for "a continuing effort by all peoples and Governments to promote economic and social progress in developing countries by the formulation and implementation of a coherent set of policy measures."[7] They emphasized trade, the division of labor, and financial resources, including development assistance. However, other issues featured strongly on the development agenda, such as invisibles (including shipping), special measures that favored the least-developed countries and landlocked countries, science and technology, human development, and the expansion and diversification of production. South-South cooperation was also brought onto the agenda.

INTERNATIONAL TRADE

Much of the political energy and development demands of developing countries were channeled through UNCTAD, bringing issues related to international trade to the fore.

The strategy referred to the international agreements and

BOX 6.1. Principal Targets under the Second Development Decade

1. Growth targets

> *Total output:* "The average annual rate of growth in the gross product of developing countries as a whole should be at least 6 percent, with the possibility of attaining a higher rate in the second half of the Decade, to be specified on the basis of a comprehensive mid-term review. It should be the responsibility of each developing country to set its own target for growth in light of its own circumstances."

> *Output per head:* "The average annual rate of growth of gross product per head in developing countries as a whole during the Decade should be about 3.5 per cent, with the possibility of accelerating it during the second half of the Decade. . . . The target . . . is calculated on the basis of an average annual increase of 2.5 per cent in the population of developing countries, which is less than the average rate at present forecast for the 1970s."

> Agriculture: an annual average growth of 4 percent.

> Manufacture: an annual (average) growth of 8 percent.

2. Domestic saving and trade

"For attaining the over-all growth target of at least 6 per cent *per annum,* there should be an annual average expansion of

> (a) 0.5 per cent in the ratio of *gross domestic saving* to the gross product so that this ratio rises to around 20 per cent by 1980;

> (b) Somewhat less than 7 per cent in *imports* and somewhat higher than 7 per cent in *exports.*"

3. Integrated sectoral policies

"As the ultimate purpose of development is to provide increasing opportunities to all people for a better life, it is essential to bring about a more equitable distribution of income and wealth for promoting both social justice and efficiency of production, to raise substantially the level of employment, to achieve a greater degree of income security, to expand and improve facilities for education, health, nutrition, housing and social welfare, and to safeguard the environment. Thus, qualitative and structural changes in the society must go hand in hand with rapid economic growth, and existing disparities—regional, sectoral and social— should be substantially reduced. These objectives are both determining factors and end-results of development; they should therefore be viewed as integrated parts of the same dynamic process and would require a unified approach:

(a) Each developing country should formulate its national employment objectives so as to absorb an increasing proportion of its working population in modern-type activities and to reduce significantly unemployment and underemployment;

(b) Particular attention should be paid to achieving enrollment of all children of primary school age, improvement in the quality of education at all levels, a substantially reduction of illiteracy, the reorientation of educational programmes to serve developmental needs and, as appropriate, the establishment and expansion of scientific and technological institutions;

(c) Each developing country should formulate a coherent health programme for the prevention and treatment of diseases and for raising general levels of health and sanitation;

(d) Levels of nutrition should be improved in terms of the average caloric intake and the protein content, with special emphasis being placed on the needs of vulnerable groups of population;

(e) Housing facilities should be expanded and improved, especially for the low-income groups and with a view to remedying the ills of the unplanned urban growth and lagging rural areas;

(f) The well-being of children should be fostered;

(g) The full participation of youth in the development process should be ensured;

(h) The full integration of women in the total development efforts should be encouraged."

Source: "International Development Strategy for the Second United Nations Development Decade," General Assembly resolution 2626 (XXV), 24 October 1970.

arrangements on commodities recommended in 1968 by UNCTAD and stated that efforts would be made to secure international action before the end of 1972. New and old commodity agreements were to play a central role. Efforts would also be made to reach agreement before UNCTAD III (which took place in Santiago in April 1972) on a set of general principles on pricing policy to serve as guidelines for consultations and actions on individual commodities. These guidelines would focus on securing stable, remunerative, and equitable prices in order to increase the foreign exchange earnings of developing countries from exports of primary products.

Developing countries' access to world markets for the primary commodities and manufactured products they produced was central in the strategy. No new tariffs and non-tariff barriers would be raised or existing ones increased against imports of primary products of special importance to developing countries. Developed countries would give priority to reducing or eliminating duties and other barriers to imports of primary products, including those in processed or semi-processed form, with a view to ensuring improved access to world markets before the end of 1972.

Developed countries would give increased attention to "supplementing the resources of the developing countries in their endeavour to accelerate the diversification of their economies." In this way, developing countries would be able to expand their production and export of semi-processed and processed commodities. The strategy stated that "specific funds for diversification will be one of the features of commodity arrangements wherever considered necessary."[8] Furthermore, "appropriate action," including financial support, would be taken to initiate intensive research and development designed to improve market conditions and cost efficiency and diversify the end uses of natural products that faced competition from synthetics and substitutes.[9]

The strategy also committed the socialist countries of Eastern Europe to "take duly into consideration the trade needs of the developing countries, and in particular their production and export potential, when quantitative targets are fixed in their long-term economic plans." Like western developed countries, they were to promote diversification of industry in developing countries and seek ways to increase their imports of goods and commodities from developing countries.[10]

TRADE EXPANSION, ECONOMIC COOPERATION, AND REGIONAL INTEGRATION AMONG DEVELOPING COUNTRIES

South-South cooperation (although it was not known by that term until later in the decade) was written into the strategy: developing countries committed themselves to negotiate and put into effect "schemes for regional and subregional integration or measures of trade expansion among themselves." This included "mutually beneficial and preferential trade arrangements."[11]

Countries with developed market economies committed themselves to support such initiatives "through the extension of financial and technical assistance or through action in the field of commercial policy." Meanwhile, the socialist countries of Eastern Europe would extend their full support to these efforts by developing countries "within the framework of their socio-economic system."[12]

FINANCIAL RESOURCES FOR DEVELOPMENT

In line with earlier statements, the strategy categorically stated that developing countries "must, and do, bear the main responsibility for financing their development." They would therefore mobilize all their domestic financial resources and ensure the most effective use available resources. They pledged to pursue "sound fiscal and monetary policies" and to remove "institutional obstacles through the adoption of appropriate legislative and administrative reforms." They would "streamline and strengthen their systems of tax administration and undertake the necessary tax reform measures." They would also keep a watchful eye on public expenditures in order to "[release] maximum resources for investment." They would endeavor to mobilize private savings "through financial institutions, thrift societies, post office savings banks and other savings schemes and through expansion of opportunities for saving for specific purposes, such as education and housing." The available supply of savings would be channeled to investment projects in accordance with the development priorities of the countries concerned.[13]

Developed countries were expected to contribute. By 1972, each "economically advanced country" should provide "a minimum net amount of 1 per cent of its gross national product at market prices in terms of actual disbursements" in financial resource transfers to developing countries each year. Countries unable to achieve the target by 1972 "will endeavour to attain it not later than 1975," and those that had already reached the target "will endeavour to ensure that their net resource transfers are maintained and envisage, if possible, an increase in them."[14]

Special importance was given to official development assistance: "Each economically advanced country will progressively increase its official development assistance to the developing countries and will exert its best efforts to reach a minimum net amount of 0.7 per cent of its gross national product at market prices by the middle of the Decade."[15]

The strategy also highlighted qualitative aspects of this assistance. The member countries of the OECD's Development Assistance Committee pledged to do their best to achieve, as soon as possible and before the end of 1971, the norms agreed on by DAC in February 1969 designed to soften and harmonize the terms and conditions of assistance to developing countries and to further soften these terms and conditions. Furthermore, financial assistance would, in principle, be untied.[16]

The norm that the national sovereignty of recipient countries should be respected, which was established from the beginning for development assistance through the UN system, was embedded in the strategy for the DD2 as well. Financial and technical assistance "should be aimed exclusively at promoting the economic and social progress of developing countries and should not in any way be used by the developed countries to the detriment of the national sovereignty of recipient countries." Furthermore, developed countries were to provide an increased flow of aid on a long-term and continuing basis and simplify the procedures for granting and distribution of aid.[17]

The strategy emphasized multilateral development assistance, although the justification for moving aid through such channels was not developed. It stated that the volume of "resources made available through multilateral institutions for financial and technical assistance will be increased to the fullest extent possible and techniques will be evolved to enable them to fulfil their role in the most effective manner."[18]

The debt problem was also noted. Arrangements for forecasting and, if possible, forestalling debt crises were to be improved. Developed countries would help prevent such crises by providing assistance on appropriate terms and conditions, and developing countries would help by "undertaking sound policies and debt management." When difficulties arose, the countries concerned would deal with them, also through the relevant international institutions, including "measures such as arrangements for rescheduling and refinancing of existing debts on appropriate terms and conditions."[19]

Foreign private capital also had a place in the strategy—although somewhat circumscribed. Developing countries were to "adopt appropriate measures for inviting, stimulating and make effective use of foreign private capital, taking into account the areas in which such capital should be sought and bearing in mind the importance for its attraction of conditions conducive to sustained investment." And developed countries would consider "adopting further measures to encourage the flow of private capital to developing countries. Foreign private investment in developing countries should be undertaken in a manner consistent with the development objectives and priorities established in their national plans. Foreign private investors in developing countries should endeavour to provide for an increase in the local share in management and administration, employment and training of local labour, including personnel at the managerial and technical levels, participation of local capital and reinvestment of profits. Efforts will be made to foster better understanding of the rights and obligations of both host and capital-exporting countries, as well as of individual investors."[20]

INVISIBLES, INCLUDING SHIPPING

The strategy sought to promote the earnings of developing countries from invisible trade and to minimize the net outflow of foreign exchange from these countries arising from invisible transactions, including shipping. It recommended that governments and international organizations, where necessary, take action in several areas that involved individuals engaged in shipping, including the provision of development assistance to expand the merchant marines of developing countries and to develop the shipping and ports of the least-developed countries and to reduce their maritime transport costs.[21] The strategy also focused on the high cost of insurance and reinsurance for developing countries, especially foreign exchange costs; such costs were to be reduced "by appropriate measures." Developing countries would seek to expand their tourist industry by building a tourism infrastructure, relaxing travel restrictions, and promoting tourism.[22]

SPECIAL MEASURES THAT FAVORED LEAST-DEVELOPED COUNTRIES

The strategy identified the least-developed countries (LDCs) as a specific target group: every possible effort would be made to ensure the sustained economic and social progress of these countries "and to enhance their capacity to benefit fully and equitably from the policy measures for the Decade." Supplementary measures would be devised and implemented at the national, subregional, and international levels. UN bodies and organizations would consider initiating special programs to alleviate their critical development problems, and developed countries would assist in the implementation of these efforts. Among the measures mentioned were concerted efforts through programs of technical assistance and financial aid, including grants and exceptionally soft loans designed to enhance their absorptive capacity.[23] Special measures would also be taken early in the decade to improve the capacity of LDCs to expand

and diversify their production structure so they could participate fully in international trade, with particular reference to primary commodities.[24]

SPECIAL MEASURES THAT FAVORED LANDLOCKED DEVELOPING COUNTRIES

Landlocked developing countries were also identified as a distinct target group. National and international financial institutions were to pay attention to their special needs by providing technical and financial assistance to help them develop transportation and communication infrastructures, especially "the transport modes and facilities most convenient to them and mutually acceptable to the transit and land-locked developing countries concerned."[25]

SCIENCE AND TECHNOLOGY

Science and technology has been seen as a major key to development ever since the UN first entered the field of development assistance. It was no surprise when the strategy for DD2 stated that developing countries should make concerted efforts, with assistance from the rest of the world, to expand their capacities to use science and technology for development. This time a target was set: by the end of the decade developing countries were to spend a minimum average level equivalent to 0.5 percent of their GNP on research and development. They would endeavor "to inculcate, among their people, an appreciation of the scientific approach which will influence all their development policies. The research programme will be oriented to the development of technologies that are in line with the circumstances and requirements of individual countries and regions. They will put particular stress on applied research and seek to develop the basic infrastructure of science and technology." Full international cooperation would be extended to strengthen and promote scientific research and technological activities that "have a bearing on the expansion and modernization of the economies of developing countries."[26]

Development assistance emerged as the main instrument: developed countries pledged to substantially increase their aid for the direct support of science and technology in developing countries during the decade.[27] Ensuring the transfer of technology from developed to developing countries was part of the strategy, and a program to promote and implement such transfers was to be drawn up by developed and developing countries and competent international organizations.[28]

Human Development

The strategy touched on the population issue, albeit in guarded language: "Those developing countries which consider that their rate of population growth hampers their development will adopt measures which they deem necessary in accordance with their concept of development." And developed countries, "consistent with their national policies," would, upon request, provide support through the means of family planning and further research. International organizations would continue to assist governments requesting such assistance.[29]

Employment figured prominently in the strategy. Development assistance and policy reform were the main instruments for achieving employment-related objectives. This perspective remained anchored in the development thinking of the 1960s: economic growth was seen as the basis for social and human development. Developed countries and international organizations pledged to help developing countries reach their employment goals.

The two other main components of the human development strategy were education and health. As in earlier UN development policy documents, educational programs were to be geared toward increasing productivity in the short run. Special emphasis was to be placed on teacher training programs and the development of curricula. Technical training, vocational training, and retraining also featured prominently. Developed countries and international organizations were to help improve the education systems of developing countries, "especially by making available some of the inputs in short supply in many developing countries and by providing assistance to facilitate the flow of pedagogic resources among them."[30]

Developing countries would establish at least a minimum program of health facilities that would provide basic services to prevent and treat disease and promote health. A concerted international effort would be made to mount a worldwide campaign to eradicate one or more diseases that still afflicted people in many countries by the end of the decade. Developed countries and international organizations were to help developing countries formulate health plans and establish health institutions. Developing countries would adopt policies to meet the nutritional needs of their people, including the development and production of high-protein foods, and developed countries and international organizations would extend financial and technical assistance.[31]

The strategy also included some components that had been more strongly profiled in the strategy for the first decade, including a concern for children and youth, housing, and problems emerging from unplanned urbanization. It also expressed concern about the deterioration of the human environment. International assistance was part of the answer.[32]

DIVERSIFICATION OF PRODUCTION

The strategy emphasized the full sovereignty of developing countries: their full exercise "of permanent sovereignty over their natural resources" would play an important role in the achievement of the goals and objectives of the decade. They were to take steps to develop the full potential of their natural resources. Concerted efforts would be made, particularly through international assistance, to enable them to prepare an inventory of natural resources, to enable their more rational utilization in all productive activities.[33]

Agriculture continued to be a main focal point: early in the decade, developing countries would formulate "appropriate strategies . . . designed to secure a more adequate food supply from both the quantitative and qualitative viewpoints, to meet their nutritional and industrial requirements, to expand rural employment, and to increase export earnings." To this end, they would begin reforming land tenure systems as appropriate to promote social justice and agricultural efficiency. They would also institute a series of measures aimed at modernizing and making agricultural production more effective. Developed countries committed themselves to support these efforts through development assistance and through adapting trade policies to the special needs of developing countries.[34]

In parallel, developing countries were to promote industrial development "in order to achieve rapid expansion, modernization and diversification of their economies." They would, in particular, work to grow industries that used domestic raw materials, supplied essential inputs to both agriculture and other industries, and were helpful in increasing export earnings. Developing countries were also to expand their basic infrastructure by enlarging their transportation and communication facilities, through regional and subregional groups where appropriate. Developed countries and international organizations would assist in the industrialization of developing countries and in expanding their basic infrastructure, especially through financial and technical development assistance.[35]

FORMULATING AND IMPLEMENTING DEVELOPMENT PLANNING

In previous chapters, planning emerged as a main UN contribution. The Committee for Development Planning—chaired from 1966 to 1972 by the eminent Dutch economist Jan Tinbergen—played a key role when the strategy for DD2 was formulated. At an early stage in this process, the committee warned that planning and plans would be insufficient as long as the political will and the means necessary to implement the plans were not in place.[36]

The strategy reflected such concerns. Developing countries committed themselves to establish or strengthen their planning mechanisms, including statistical services, for formulating and implementing their national development plans. They would "ensure that their development plans are both realistic and ambitious enough to have an impact on the imagination of the people, internally consistent, and widely understood and accepted. Every effort will be made to secure the active support and participation of all segments of the population in the development process."[37]

Review and Appraisal of Objectives and Policies

Systematic scrutiny of the progress toward attaining the decade's goals and objectives—and shortcomings in this regard—was part of the strategy. Reviews of this kind were to take place at various levels, involving developed as well as developing countries. At the national level of each developing country, evaluation machinery was to be set up or strengthened. At the regional level, the UN regional economic commissions were to do this work in collaboration with regional development banks and subregional groups and with the assistance of other UN organizations. UNCTAD, the UN Industrial Development Organization (UNIDO), and the specialized agencies were expected to review progress within their respective sectors according to procedures already established. ECOSOC would undertake an overall appraisal of progress every second year.[38]

Mobilization of Public Opinion

Mobilizing public opinion to support the decade's objectives and policies, in developing and developed countries alike, was a strong component of the strategy. National bodies established by governments were responsible for garnering public support. In the longer term, such bodies were intended to provide increasing development information in educational curricula.[39]

Some Concluding Observations

The strategy for the DD2 can be read as the most representative expression of international development thinking within a global setting at the time it was adopted, some twenty years after the UN had begun to actively work in development operations through the establishment of the EPTA. Work on the strategy started in the mid-1960s and drew on the lessons learned halfway through DD1.

The main ideas, overall objectives, and targets set for DD2, as well as the ways and means of accomplishing the goals for the decade, had been promoted, even adopted, by more specialized bodies inside and outside the UN system prior to 1970. The feat was that these components were transformed into a comprehensive, overall strategy with dynamic development objectives.

When the strategy for the first decade was formulated, the idea and political initiative came from the United States. Much had changed during the 1960s. UNCTAD came to play an increasingly important role and provided an arena in which developing countries, together with the UN Secretariat, generated and coordinated a broad-based development policy. This policy was backed up in the General Assembly, where these governments comprised the majority. The achievement of the main actors was to pull these various policies together into a comprehensive strategy.

The General Assembly adopted the strategy without a vote. The resolution that established DD2 was submitted by developing countries and driven by their UN representatives. In contrast to their position at the helm of the first decade, the United States and several of its close allies now found themselves in a defensive position. Delegations from several developed countries in both the East and the West expressed reservations on many points, not least as to their willingness or ability to meet the strategy's targets for development assistance and other policy measures.[40]

The targets set for development assistance and financial resource transfers call for special attention. In ECOSOC's July 1970 session, representatives of several developed countries indicated approval of the targets set for net transfer of financial resources to developing countries—1 percent of their GNP, of which 0.75 percent would be in official development assistance. However, representatives of some other developed countries stated that their governments would not be able to meet the targets by 1972, as suggested by developing countries, or by any other specific date. Representatives of centrally planned economies maintained that the 1 percent target should not apply to that group of countries. Several developed countries expressed such reservations also in the Second Committee, before and after the adoption of the strategy.[41] However, equally important, several West European countries did not make such reservations and, by implication, took on the commitments set out in the strategy.

A debate took place on the status of the decision. Many developing-country representatives stated that although the strategy was not legally binding, it was a clear-cut expression of the highly moral and political commitment of UN member states to pursuing far-reaching policy objectives. Thus Chile, for one, interpreted the text to mean that all developed countries, including those with centrally planned economies, were under the obligation to try to ensure that the targets were fulfilled. In contrast, the developed countries tended to argue more generally that the strategy was not a legal commitment.

UNCTAD—and its Trade and Development Board—played a prominent role in the process leading up to the development strategy, particularly with regard to trade expansion, economic cooperation, and regional integration among developing countries and on special measures in favor of the LDCs and landlocked countries. These issues—especially questions related to the improvement of trade conditions—had begun to attract top priority among developing countries in the late 1960s and into the 1970s.

Prescriptions in the strategy provided guidance about the use of ODA, particularly involving the development funds established by the UN family of organizations but also for bilateral programs run by member states. Measures that contributed to increased earnings and foreign currency generated by trade, such as improved productivity in agriculture, industries that processed natural resources, or the tourist industry, came increasingly to the fore, as did the conditions for exporting such goods. The strategy emphasized the importance of domestic savings and (private) investments from abroad and the urgent need for financial assistance on soft conditions—ODA. Nevertheless, the main thrust of the strategy's message about development assistance implied a reorientation: aid should be oriented toward increasing the export revenue of developing countries.

The Second Development Decade: A Bird's-Eye View

In the strategy for the DD2, attaining of the goals set depended as much, if not more, on the achievements of the governments and people of developing countries themselves as on those of the economically better-off countries and multilateral organizations. However, they all committed themselves to contributing. To what extent did governments keep these commitments, and to what extent did they succeed in attaining the strategy's objectives?

The Secretary-General's midterm review took into account later commitments that had become an integral part of the strategy. These included the Declaration and Programme of Action on the Establishment of a New International Economic Order and other declarations and decisions from major UN conferences held after the strategy for DD2 was adopted. These declarations addressed the issues of the environment, population, food, industrialization, and integrating women into the development process.[42]

Overall Assessment

The Committee for Development Planning, which prepared a review for ECOSOC and the General Assembly, observed that the collective performance of developing countries in the first half of the decade had been good in terms of total output and exports. However, agriculture had lagged behind dramatically and no real inroads had been made in the key problems of mass poverty and unemployment. The gaps between developing and developed countries had widened alarmingly. Moreover, the gains vis-à-vis the goals of the strategy had come inadvertently rather than by design by virtue of the booming developed-country markets. In both international trade and international financial transfers, there had been little improvement in policy, especially in the leading countries.[43]

Nevertheless, the committee found the strategy urgently important: it had helped provide a conceptual framework for exploring such major transnational issues as the environment, population, and food. Its diagnosis of problems and recommendations of policies remained valid, and the committee argued that it would make little sense to change the various numerical targets set in the strategy. It found that the Programme of Action on the Establishment of a New International Order could be interpreted as a way to speed up the timetable of the strategy, although the enunciation of the NIEO principles was a historic break with the past and reflected a major realignment of power in the world. The committee observed that important issues for development remained internal to developing countries, including the difficult but often essential need for radical social transformation. It was important that advanced economies accept their continuing obligations to assist development, especially in the poorest countries, and, beyond that, see the gains for themselves from making a new international economic order work.[44]

In July 1975, ECOSOC agreed with the main assessments of the committee. However, members expressed concern that implementation had fallen short on two core quantitative targets: net ODA had not reached even half of the target of 0.7 percent of GNP, and agricultural production in developing countries had grown at only 2.0 percent annually, only half the target set.[45]

ECOSOC integrated the NIEO commitments into the international development strategy. Member states were urged to implement policy measures agreed upon at the special session in 1975, with particular reference to international trade, resource transfers for development, international monetary reform, science and technology, industrialization, food and agriculture, and cooperation among developing countries.

Meeting the Targets?

The review's introduction stated that developed countries "have not, by and large, implemented the policy measures of the International Development Strategy, and indeed there has been some retrogression." On the other hand, some aggregate targets had been met and even exceeded, "owing mainly to the developing countries' own efforts and to a certain extent to external factors such as the 'commodity boom.'"[46]

Net financial flows from developed countries were considered important in providing the critical margin of external financing over and above the financial resources that developing countries could obtain through their export earnings. The strategy's target (1 percent of their GNP) was reinforced by the Programme of Action on the Establishment of a New International Order: it was necessary to reach and even exceed this target at an accelerating pace to meet the minimum growth objectives set in the strategy. Performance was disappointing: net transfers as a percentage of GNP had decreased from a level of 0.76 percent in 1961–63 to 0.70 percent during the period 1968–70 and had remained at that level during the period from 1971 to 1973.[47]

Performance in terms of the target set for ODA (0.7 percent of GNP) was even more disappointing: DAC members' ODA had fallen from 0.53 percent of GNP in the early 1960s to about 0.39 percent during the period 1966–1969 and to 0.32 percent in 1970–1973—less than half of the target set. Consequently, "developing countries have resorted even more to borrowing on relatively harder terms. This has increased debt-servicing problems, which are now extremely acute for a number of developing countries."[48] The debt problem was only in its initial phase, but it was bluntly identified.

In the development strategy, the terms and conditions involving financial transfers in general and ODA in particular had been problematic. Such concerns were expressed in more transparent terms in the major policy documents establishing the NIEO. The midterm review found that the efforts of developed countries to soften and harmonize these conditions had not been adequate. In addition, an excessive amount of development assistance continued to be tied.[49] Another central theme in the development assistance discourse had been identified and put on the agenda.

Looking forward, the midterm review brought to the fore the expansion of mutual trade and economic and technical cooperation among developing countries, in line with the Programme of Action on the NIEO and decisions adopted by nonaligned countries and other groups of developing countries, emphasizing the need for collective self-reliance. Primary attention was given to measures to expand trade.

Many developing countries had made efforts to attract foreign (private) investment, although there was a growing concern with regard to the negative effects on state sovereignty over national resources and economic activities. The UN's establishment of the Commission on Transnational Corporations in order to formulate a code of conduct for their operations was an expression of such concerns. There was also concern regarding the corrupt practices of certain international and other corporations that violated the laws and regulations of host countries. The midterm review condemned such practices and called upon home and host governments alike to take all necessary measures to prevent them.

There had also been little progress in other areas that presupposed support from the developed countries, including development assistance. This applied to the most seriously affected countries that continued to face a critical situation despite international efforts carried out under UN emergency operations. Industrialized countries and international organizations such as the World Bank and the IMF were urged to extend immediate relief and assistance to these countries.

Toward the Third Development Decade

By the time of the midterm review, the international strategy for the second decade had already been overtaken by the NIEO strategy.

Developing countries were the most active players in the process that led to the resolutions on a New International Economic Order. Many representatives of these governments expressed great satisfaction at the end of 1975 with what had been achieved. Several members considered the Charter of Economic Rights and Duties of States a landmark in international relations.[50]

When the UN system reviewed the decade's objectives and performance a few months later, the aims and aspirations contained in the NIEO program constituted an important point of departure when future steps were discussed. Arguably, the NIEO perspectives were a superstructure in which the many components of the international development strategy for DD2 found their place. This was reflected in the UN's main focus and priorities during the second half of the decade and its preparation of the international strategy for a third development decade.

This political priority was also expressed at the institutional level. In December 1977, the General Assembly, seeking to give higher priority and more political attention to North-South issues, established a Committee of the Whole charged with monitoring progress in attaining the objectives set forth in the NIEO charter and plan of action.[51]

International negotiations on the issues included in the NIEO charter soon hit a stalemate between developing countries, organized as the Group of 77 (whose name referred to the number of countries when the group first met), and the major western industrial powers, with the United States at the forefront. A group of likeminded western countries that agreed on some policy positions and disagreed on others took a middle road; the Netherlands and Scandinavians were at the helm of this group. The real negotiations, inside and outside the UN system, took place between the G-77 and the major western countries, with the "likeminded" group— together with the UN system, particularly the UNCTAD secretariat —actively seeking compromises and keeping the dialogue going.

It was therefore no coincidence that the person selected to chair the Committee of the Whole, Thorvald Stoltenberg of the Norwegian Ministry of Foreign Affairs, was drawn from the group of likeminded countries. In December 1979, the General Assembly empowered the new committee to act as the preparatory committee for global negotiations on international economic cooperation for development in a special session in 1980.[52] The goal of the special session was to assess the progress made thus far in establishing the NIEO and break through the stalemate between the G-77 and western countries. The committee recommended that the upcoming special session should focus on two main themes: the proposed strategy for the Third UN Development Decade (DD3) and the global NIEO negotiations.

The preparatory committee was able to reach a sort of agreement on several components of a strategy for the DD3, leaving the most difficult ones to the special session of the General Assembly to decide. However, neither the committee nor the special session was able to produce agreement on an agenda, procedures, or a time frame for a round of global negotiations on economic cooperation for development.

Strategy for the Third Development Decade: Approach and Main Components

On 5 December 1980, the General Assembly proclaimed the Third United Nations Development Decade and adopted an international development strategy for the decade. Negotiations on the strategy took place in the General Assembly from 25 August to 15 September 1980.

BROAD PARTICIPATION

In the preparatory stage, input came from all major political groups of countries and many individual member governments and from various regional and international organizations and institutions. The preparatory committee was provided with formal and informal papers by member governments, sometimes acting for larger political groups such as the European Economic Community (EEC). Representatives of developing countries were especially active. Indeed, more often than not, their input formed the basis of the new strategy. This was particularly true of the comprehensive proposals agreed on by the G-77.

APPROACH

Based on the experience of DD2, the Committee for Development Planning concluded that a broader, more flexible approach was required for the Third Development Decade. The committee wanted less focus on rigid quantitative targets and more attention to a broader range of objectives, including structural and institutional change.[53] The director-general for development and international economic cooperation (DIEC), who was responsible for these issues within the UN Secretariat, issued a report on progress since 1974 that also took this broad view. The changes that had taken place were not enough as measured against the required structural reforms implicit in a new international economic order. Despite their potential economic and financial strength, developing countries still exerted only limited influence on international trade and financial and monetary policies, and no institutional framework existed to ensure just and remunerative prices for their commodity exports. The ODA record, particularly on concessional flows, had been disappointing.[54]

SPECIAL FOCUS AREAS

Since the late 1950s and early 1960s, UN development efforts had focused especially on the challenges facing Africa. The eleventh special session of the General Assembly, which dealt with the new international development strategy, was no exception. At the request of Nigeria, the secretary-general of the Organization of African Unity (OAU) was invited to address the assembly. He argued that the plight of African nations needed special attention, and he identified four interrelated areas that called for immediate action: energy, indebtedness, aid, and international monetary reform. He called on developed countries to increase their financial assistance and to adopt measures that would lead to a gradual reduction of the debt burden of the developing countries.[55]

Another theme in the debate was the growing interdependence of the countries of the North and South. Representatives from the South expressed great frustration about the lack of progress toward a new international economic order and what they saw as the continued lack of political will on the part of the developed countries. The representative of India, speaking in the capacity of G-77 chair, argued that developed countries could no longer escape the consequences of the current economic situation. It was in their own best interests to sustain and support the development of the developing world through massive transfers of real resources and a refashioning of the international economy that would enable developing countries to assume their rightful place in the structure of production and trade. He argued that there had been little evidence in developed countries of the far-sightedness necessary to take hard decisions in their long-term interest. Several other developing countries echoed this criticism, at times in somewhat less polished language.[56]

TOWARD A NEW TARGET FOR ODA AND A FOCUS ON POVERTY

In the plenary debate, several developing countries regretted that the suggested target for ODA transfers remained at its previous level (0.7

percent of GNP). El Salvador argued strongly for increasing the target to 1 percent of GNP. During the late 1970s, OECD countries were not the only providers of ODA. As pointed out in the debate, Arab oil-producing countries had been contributing aid far beyond 1 percent of their GNP in assistance, particularly to their less fortunate neighbors.[57]

A CONSENSUS TEXT

In the plenary debate, western countries did not show a united front regarding the various initiatives originating from developing countries, especially those from the G-77. They agreed that there was a need for a comprehensive far-sighted strategy based on mutual advantage and common interests. They also agreed that the LDCs deserved special attention. However, as had been stated during previous decades, they argued that ultimate responsibility for development rested with developing countries; in 1980, the new twist on this argument was that developing countries needed to create conditions that would attract private external resources.[58]

Several countries, among them France, the Netherlands, and the Nordic group, urged all industrialized countries—including the socialist countries of Eastern Europe—to meet the ODA target. Some of these countries also indicated willingness to increase the target to 1 percent of GNP, as proposed by the G-77. Sweden noted the widely diverging ODA performance among developed countries, referring particularly to the United States, whose level of aid was stagnating or diminishing, and to the centrally planned economy countries, whose aid Sweden held to be almost invisible.[59] The cold "dialogue" between East and West continued.[60]

Nevertheless, the special session managed to produce a consensus text of the strategy, which was adopted without a vote. That was also the case when the General Assembly later proclaimed the Third Development Decade and adopted the International Development Strategy for the Decade. These resolutions were also agreed upon without a vote.[61]

Vision and Major Goals

At every crossroads, new generations of politicians seem to feel the inherent need to present their most recent program as something entirely fresh and new, even though most ideas may be familiar from earlier key policy documents. The international development strategy for the Third Development Decade is no exception here. In essence, it was modeled on the strategy for DD2 regarding structure, ambitions, major objectives, targets, and policy measures for attaining these objectives. The main change was the added and systematic emphasis on political and institutional reform. In fact, these ideas had been promoted with even greater enthusiasm and determination in the mid-1970s and integrated into the strategy for the second half of DD2 at the midterm review. Nevertheless, when the strategy for DD3 was announced, the focus on political and institutional reform was perceived as a strategy for a new time with new challenges. In the following, our focus will be limited to the role and conditions of development assistance and targets set for ODA and financial transfers, including debt relief, in connection with the Third UN Development Decade.

THE PREAMBLE

In the preamble to the strategy, member governments rededicated themselves to "the fundamental objectives enshrined in the Charter of the United Nations." They also reaffirmed "solemnly their determination to establish a new international economic order," recalling the decisions to this effect in the mid-1970s.[62] However, the real battle for reforming the international economic system in accordance with the NIEO declaration and program of action took place in the parallel negotiations on the agenda for global negotiations. At the end of 1980, these negotiations were still deadlocked.

The preamble painted a gloomy picture of the existing situation. The system of international economic relations was characterized by inequities and imbalances that were "widening the gap between developed and developing countries, constitute a major obstacle to the development of the developing countries and adversely affect international relations and the promotion of world peace and security." Furthermore, "the goals and objectives of the International Development Strategy for the Second Development Decade remain largely unfulfilled. In addition, the present negative trends in the world economy have adversely affected the situation of developing countries and, as a result, impaired their growth prospects." The continuing economic crisis was hitting developing countries especially hard because of their greater vulnerability to external factors. The least-developed countries and the poorest sections within developing countries were particularly affected. "The stark reality confronting mankind today is that close to 850 million people in the developing world are living at the margin of existence, enduring hunger, sickness, homelessness and absence of meaningful employment."[63]

The new strategy sought to promote the economic and social

development of developing countries to reduce the disparity between rich and poor countries, eradicate poverty and dependency, and encourage sustained global development "on the basis of justice, equality and mutual benefit."[64] This development needed to promote human dignity, the strategy asserted. It concluded that "the ultimate aim of development is the constant improvement of the well-being of the entire population on the basis of its full participation in the process of development and a fair distribution of the benefits therefrom. In this context, a substantial improvement in the status of women will take place during the Decade. In this perspective, economic growth, productive employment and social equity are fundamental and indivisible elements of development."[65]

GOALS AND OBJECTIVES

Although its intention was focused less on quantitative targets and more on processes, structures, and institutions, the eleventh special session came up with quantitative targets in several areas, including targets for annual economic growth and for some elements of human and social development. The latter was not completely new but rather was an evolution of the integrated sectoral policy that had been drawn up in the strategy for DD2.

The strategy set a target for average annual economic growth that was 7 percent of GDP. This was optimistic, given the unfulfilled objectives of the previous decade and the harsh economic climate of the late 1970s and early 1980s.[66] They reflected more a willed development than a cold analysis of what might realistically be achieved. The developing countries, who were driving the process, displayed a scenario of what might be possible to obtain if the political will was there.

The preconditions were made clear. The most crucial one and the hardest to realize involved improved access to the markets of industrial countries and trade conditions more generally.[67] Other quantitative targets that were set for trade, domestic investment, savings, and development assistance were among the important preconditions for the growth targets set, along with a substantially greater flow of financial resources in real terms to developing countries at terms and conditions that were better attuned to the development aims and economic circumstances of these countries. Reaching the targets for economic growth was a precondition for the many other major goals and objectives set, including those regarding social and human development.

The G-77 succeeded in establishing the target of 1 percent of GNP in official development assistance, although a fixed date for achieving this target was not set. However, there were many reservations from representatives of industrialized countries—West and East alike—about this target.[68] The G-77 also argued that developing countries "in a position to do so" should continue to provide development assistance to other developing countries.[69]

The conditions of aid call for special attention, both with regard to stated objectives and recommended policy measures. Bilateral and multilateral flows "will be made on an increasingly assured, continuous and predictable basis"; a commitment for at least three years was recommended.[70] This was not a new idea; long-term commitments had been recommended in the DD2 strategy. In the early 1970s, a few European donor countries, including the so-called front-runners (the Netherlands and the Scandinavian countries), had taken up this idea in their bilateral aid programs, introducing systems of multiyear planning of their development cooperation with main partner countries. This applied to other recommendations of that strategy as well, including the quest for a larger share of ODA on concessionary terms in the form of grants for LDCs and the untying of aid. However, in the DD3 strategy these recommendations were made in more specified terms. In order to attract additional resources, the strategy also provided for a mixture of aid and trade— including so-called mixed credits.[71]

The strategy also prescribed the best use of development assistance, giving priority to poverty alleviation. Special attention should be given "to the need for accelerated development of the least developed countries, particularly those in the special categories, where the development needs and problems are greatest."[72] The special categories included the LDCs and landlocked developing countries and two new categories of countries with particular problems—developing island countries and the most seriously affected countries, the LDCs whose weak economies had made them especially vulnerable to the economic crises caused by sharp increases in the prices of their essential imports.[73] The flow of ODA toward these countries would increase in the Third Development Decade.

Food security was also singled out as particularly important in the context of aid. Hunger and malnutrition were to be eliminated as soon as possible, "certainly by the end of the century," in the first place through food self-sufficiency in developing countries and expanded agricultural production. Additional external resource transfers should help developing countries reach these goals.[74]

This approach was also applied to other areas of core importance for development, including improving physical and institutional infrastructures, strengthening scientific and technological capacities, and strengthening industrialization "as a means of independent and autonomous industrial development" and by strengthening and enlarging the UN Industrial Development Fund.[75]

Human and social development was emphasized even more strongly than in the previous two development decades. DD3's strategy identified international development assistance as a primary way to support and strengthen the efforts of developing countries to meet targets set for education and health care, especially primary education and primary health care.[76]

The general principle guiding all policy measures is repeated: that each country "will freely determine and implement appropriate policies for social development within the framework of its development plans and priorities and in accordance with its cultural identity, socio-economic structure and stage of development." The necessary financial and technical assistance is promised from the international community through "special international programmes to support the national endeavours of the developing countries in key areas of social policy." In this connection, the UN system was expected to play an important role.[77]

The strategy emphasized that nonconcessional flows were still an important source of development finance. The possibility of substantially increasing resource transfers would be explored "through new and innovative means," including co-financing with private resources.[78] Direct private investments would also be encouraged, provided that they were "compatible with the national priorities and legislation of developing countries."[79] New ways and forms of lending "should reflect the principles of universality and equity in decision-making." The specter of the debt problem was identified almost in the same breath as new mechanisms for achieving more lending: governments should seek debt-relief actions or equivalent measures in accordance with the general principles adopted by the Trade and Development Board in 1978. As the DD2 strategy had, the new strategy emphasized that the international community should work for stable international monetary conditions that sought a balanced and equitable development of the world economy and the accelerated development of developing countries.[80]

BOX 6.2. The Third Development Decade and Human Development

DD3 set ambitious targets for human development.

The target for *education:* "Eradication or considerable reduction of illiteracy, and the closest possible realization of universal primary enrolment by the year 2000."

The target for *health:* Immunization against major infectious diseases for all children as early as possible during the decade. Safe water and adequate sanitary facilities for all in rural and urban areas by 1990. "In the poorest countries, infant mortality should be reduced to less than 120 per 1,000 live births. Life expectancy in all countries should reach 60 years as a minimum, and infant mortality rates should be reduced to 50 per 1,000 live births, as a maximum, by the year 2000."

The target for *employment:* Full employment by the year 2000 (with an expected increase in the labor force of 2.5 percent per annum).

"The international community should provide adequate financial and technical resources to support the training of national personnel in all sectors of social and economic activities in the developing countries." All countries "will broaden the access to of their poorest groups in their populations to health facilities and, with the assistance of the international community, will ensure immunization against all major infectious diseases for all children as early as possible during the Decade."

These ideas and targets came close to the MDGs that were to be established twenty years later.

Source: "International Development Strategy for the Third United Nations Development Decade," General Assembly resolution A/RES/35/56, 5 December 1980, Annex, paragraphs 44, 46–48.

Technical cooperation figured prominently in the strategy for DD3, as it had in previous strategies.[81] In science and technology, the gaps between developed and developing countries were wider than in most other areas and would have to be bridged. The strategy signaled a gradual shift in emphasis. Previously, the focus had been on developed countries transferring knowledge and technology to developing countries. Now the focus was on developing countries generating such knowledge and skills themselves, in line with the ideology of self-reliance generated in the mid-1970s. It also identified the increasing problem of "large-scale outflow of skilled nationals" from many developing countries, which caused "economic disruption."[82] With regard to energy, the principle of "the full and permanent sovereignty of each country over its natural resources, the exploration and rational exploitation of energy resources, both conventional and non-conventional" was underlined once more.[83] A similar approach was taken when the importance of transport was emphasized.[84]

The strategy argued that accelerated development could enhance the capacity of developing countries to address the environmental implications of poverty and underdevelopment and the interrelationships among development, environment, population, and resources. "There is a need to ensure an economic development process which is environmentally sustainable over the long run and which protects the ecological balance. Determined efforts must be made to prevent deforestation, erosion, soil degeneration and desertification. International co-operation in environmental protection should be increased."[85] Later in the decade, the Brundtland Commission developed this important issue further.[86]

Basic NIEO principles were included in the strategy for DD3. These included collective self-reliance, "economic and technical co-operation among developing countries . . . a dynamic and vital part of an effective restructuring of international economic relations." Developing countries would determine "the main elements of economic and technical co-operation," and the international community "should accord high priority and urgency to supporting the efforts of developing countries to strengthen and implement their programmes of mutual economic and technical co-operation." These programs would help reduce the vulnerability of developing countries due to their reliance on external goods and services; would help achieve fair, balanced economic relations; and would increase developing countries' "self-reliance and autonomous growth and development."[87] This reflected the core of what developing countries hoped to attain in their fight for a new international economic order.

The Burial of a Vision

The Committee of the Whole, established by the General Assembly in 1977 to follow up on the negotiations to realize the NIEO and facilitate an exchange of views on global economic problems, was to prepare recommendations on procedures, a time frame, and a detailed agenda for the global negotiations on international economic cooperation for development.[88] However, during the committee's 1980 sessions, no agreement was reached on launching global negotiations on international economic cooperation for development. Several delegations introduced draft agendas and made suggestions for procedures and a time frame for the negotiations, but they disagreed on various issues within the five substantive areas that had been identified: raw materials, energy, trade, development, and monetary issues and finance.[89] Developing countries placed responsibility for the lack of progress on the doorsteps of the major western countries.[90]

In the debate at the General Assembly's eleventh special session, the chairman of the Committee of the Whole made a statement that largely supported the view India expressed on behalf of the G-77: developed countries were using stalling tactics.[91] The Ad Hoc Committee of the special session considered the many proposals presented to the Committee of the Whole and transmitted them to the assembly. On 13 September 1980, the Ad Hoc Committee informed the assembly that with the exception of three delegations, all members of the committee had accepted a text proposed by the G-77 as the procedural framework for the negotiations.[92] Two days later, the assembly decided to pass all relevant documents on to its 1980 regular session, which opened the following day.[93]

The General Assembly's president established an informal consultative group to come up with a solution. However, on 17 December, he reported that although some progress had been made, no text had been agreed upon. The assembly requested that he continue the consultations and report to its resumed session on 15 January 1981. He was again requested to pursue the consultations and report back to the assembly at a later, unspecified date.[94] The issue of continued international negotiations on a new international economic order remained on the General Assembly's agenda throughout most of the 1980s. In the early 1980s, it was quite intensively debated and with an apparent hope that the final small points of disagreement would be removed in the next consultations. That was never to be.[95]

SEVEN

The United Nations Development Programme, 1966–1981

- **The UNDP's Main Features**
- **The First Five Years: Business as Usual**
- **The Capacity Study and the 1970 Consensus**
- **The 1970s**
- **Some Concluding Observations**

The United Nations Development Programme was established in 1965 and became operative on 1 January 1966, sixteen years after the creation of the Expanded Programme of Technical Assistance and seven years after the UN Special Fund had begun its work.[1] In August 1962, ECOSOC asked the Secretary-General to study the advantages and disadvantages of a partial or complete merger of some or all of the UN's technical assistance programs. In his 1964 response, Secretary-General U Thant concluded that all countries contributing to and benefiting from UN technical cooperation programs would be best served if the EPTA and the Special Fund were brought together in one organization with a single governing body, a single interagency body, and unified management. The special characteristics of the two merging organizations should, however, be maintained. In the second part of his report, dealing with the regular programs of UN technical assistance, he concluded that a full merger, be it with the EPTA or the proposed UNDP, would create more problems than it would resolve.[2]

The overriding norm initially set for international development cooperation through the UN system was respect for the recipient country's sovereignty. There should be no foreign economic or political interference in the internal affairs of the country concerned. Other norms were derived from this principle. Self-determination was an important one, the idea that development should grow out of each country's needs, priorities, and potential. Assistance should be provided only at the request of the government concerned and be anchored in its development plan. The concept of help to self-help was also important; the recipient country was expected to participate in and contribute to the projects that received support. Finally, the principal of neutrality was prominent; in contrast to bilateral assistance, the flags and involvement of donor governments were to be removed.

The UNDP's Main Features

The main reason for combining the EPTA and the Special Fund into one organization was to avoid duplication of activities. The move would simplify organizational arrangements and procedures, facilitate planning and coordination of technical assistance programs, and improve overall effectiveness.

The merger of the two institutions began gradually: the resolution establishing the UNDP reaffirmed that "the principles, procedures and provisions" governing the EPTA and the Special Fund should continue to apply to relevant activities within the UNDP. As a transitional measure, the two heads of the old organizations worked together to run the new one, one as the administrator and the other as the co-administrator. Even the financing of the two activities was kept in its previous form: the two funds were retained and contributions could be pledged to the two programs separately. In addition, processes that had been initiated within the programs were continued. Proposals in ECOSOC to consider transforming the Special Fund into a capital development fund that would include both pre-investment and investment activities were not accepted.[3]

However, a new intergovernmental body, the Governing Council of the UNDP, took over the functions previously exercised by the Governing Council of the Special Fund and the Technical Assistance Committee of the EPTA. It considered and approved projects and programs and the allocation of funds and provided general policy guidance and direction for the UNDP as a whole and for UN regular programs of technical assistance. The thirty-seven members of this council were elected by ECOSOC according to regional criteria, with a slight majority of representatives from developing countries.[4] The council, which met twice a year, was responsible for generating reports and making recommendations to ECOSOC. Decisions of the council were made by a majority of the members present and voting. An advisory committee, the Inter-Agency Consultative Board of the UNDP, replaced the Technical Assistance Board of the EPTA and the Consultative Board of the Special Fund. It was chaired by the administrator (or co-administrator) and included the Secretary-General and the executive heads of the specialized agencies and of the IAEA (or their representatives).

The executive directors of UNICEF and the WFP were invited to attend board meetings as appropriate.

UNDP funding depended on voluntary contributions pledged by UN member governments. In 1961, the General Assembly set a target for 1962 of $150 million in contributions to the EPTA and the Special Fund. At the pledging conference in November 1965, several governments announced increased contributions to the two programs, and it was expected that the total would reach $155 million. In December 1965, the General Assembly set a new target of $200 million each year to support the work of the UNDP, to be reached "in the near future."[5]

The First Five Years: Business as Usual

During the UNDP's first years, activities followed the paths trodden by the EPTA and the Special Fund. The two main activities, pre-investment activities and technical assistance, were administered and reported as separate activities under the new common umbrella. However, the resources made available for these activities increased. Initiatives that had begun earlier were also developed further during the first years of the new institution.

Early Development Priorities at the UNDP

In the latter 1960s, patterns set earlier in the decade were reinforced. Africa continued to receive most assistance for pre-investment work and technical assistance (tables 7.1 and 7.2). A long-standing normative tradition was continued when the Governing Council discussed the criteria for aid. It decided that the program should continue to provide systematic and sustained assistance in fields essential to the integrated technical, economic, and social development of less-developed countries while giving priority to the assistance requested by countries whose needs were more urgent, taking into account the degree of their development. More well-off developing countries should increase their counterpart contributions, while counterpart contributions should be kept as low as possible and local cost requirements reduced or waived in appropriate cases in the poorest countries.[6]

Coordination

At an early stage, the intergovernmental bodies responsible for the EPTA and the Special Fund identified coordinating development assistance throughout the UN as a major concern. This became a central function of the UNDP. It upheld the principles established by its predecessors, especially the primary responsibility of member states for coordinating the development of their own countries. At the country level, the main instrument remained the offices of the resident representatives. However, the administrator was given a more central role to play, more in line with patterns practiced by the director of the Special Fund than with those developed by the EPTA.

FROM RESPONDING TO PROJECT PROPOSALS TO CENTRALLY DESIGNED STRATEGIES AND PRIORITIES

In 1968, the Governing Council agreed that the UNDP was passing from a phase where it had largely responded to individual requests for assistance as they came in to one where questions of strategy, priorities, and concentration were becoming increasingly important. The priorities agreed on included building training and other institutions, helping create an inventory of natural resources, carrying out feasibility studies, supporting agricultural and industrial development, integrating national communications and other networks into regional and global networks, bridging the technology gap, and playing a catalytic role in solving food, population, and health problems.[7] These priorities were well attuned to those set out in the DD1 strategy. This perspective, almost by necessity, entailed a more centralized decision-making process within the UNDP.

OFFICES OF RESIDENT REPRESENTATIVES

In August 1967, ECOSOC adopted a resolution stating that there was a need for "further clarification of the central role and responsibility of the Resident Representatives in co-ordinating the technical co-operation programmes of the United Nations system organizations at the field level." ECOSOC emphasized the need for governments to coordinate all technical assistance activities: an effective central coordinating authority was important. It reminded member states of the assistance that resident representatives could provide in the coordination of all UN development activities and stated that resident representatives should be fully informed (and keep themselves informed) of all UN development activities within their areas. UN organizations were invited "to co-operate whole-heartedly" with resident representatives and, in particular, "to consult with them upon the planning and development of projects for which they are responsible in the countries concerned."[8]

EXTRABUDGETARY OPERATIONS

Almost from the beginning, the EPTA, in contrast to the Special Fund, accepted financial contributions from outside the membership of the UN. The UNDP was also open to such contributions.[9] Gradually, it was also opened up for extra-budgetary operations when governments, bilateral agencies, and foundations donated money earmarked for specific activities beyond ordinary UN programs. Such arrangements included providing UN-organized technical assistance and projects where the recipient government reimbursed the costs involved; hiring experts from a particular industrialized country to work with senior technical experts on field assignments; and placing volunteer junior professional officers that were sponsored by governments and nongovernmental organizations of industrialized countries in the offices of resident representatives.

At its third session, the Governing Council authorized the UNDP to accept and administer trust funds, subject to specified terms and conditions, which included prior approval by the council. The UN specialized agencies also accepted such funds. The executive director of the agency concerned and the UNDP administrator jointly administered a few funds of this kind.

Over the years, such extra-budgetary contributions for a range of projects (mainly technical assistance) made up a growing share of total budgets.[10] They were attractive for the agencies involved, including UN central bodies (the UNDP in particular) because they made possible activities beyond what their ordinary financial frames allowed. In addition, the income they brought in for administrative and operational costs provided a golden opportunity for institution-building within the UN system.

Nevertheless, these developments were not unproblematic, especially regarding the centralization of UN field activities. Some forty years later, experience from administering the Oil-for-Food Programme in Iraq has shown how other problems might also appear.

INTEGRATING TRADE IN THE DEVELOPMENT PERSPECTIVE

During the latter 1960s, improving trade policies for the exports of developing countries came to the fore in development discourse. The first United Nations Conference on Trade and Development drove this perspective at the UN. UNCTAD was included as a participating organization in the UNDP.[11]

Evaluation

Earlier initiatives to establish a more coherent and effective system for evaluating the activities of the UNDP and its cooperating organizations were pursued. In August 1966, ECOSOC decided unanimously "to continue and develop its systematic evaluation of the over-all and the specific impact and effectiveness" of the UN's operational programs. It endorsed an interagency study group by the Administrative Committee on Coordination to examine the reports of the evaluation teams and to propose practical steps for making technical assistance programs more operationally effective. At the same time, ECOSOC underscored the responsibility of member states in this respect and encouraged them to make every effort to strengthen their own coordination and evaluation procedures.[12]

This issue remained high on the agenda during the following years. By 1967, the interagency study group was operational. An ECOSOC resolution welcomed UNITAR's initiation of a research project aimed at developing improved methods and techniques for the evaluation of projects, sectors, and overall impact of the combined programs of technical operations.[13] In July 1968, ECOSOC asked the Secretary-General to prepare a background paper covering the main policy issues and practical problems raised by efforts to evaluate technical cooperation projects and programs and to make recommendations for the development of a coherent evaluation program with a view to facilitating the objectives of the Second Development Decade.[14]

The UN Capital Development Fund

The gradual transformation of the Special Fund into a capital development program, which had been originally recommended by UNCTAD and was a major concern when the UNDP was created, remained on the agenda. In December 1967, the General Assembly asked the UNDP to establish a United Nations Capital Development Fund. The UNDP's Governing Council constituted the executive board of the fund.[15]

In 1968, the Governing Council dealt with the matter. The administrator noted that the available resources totaled only $1.3 million and suggested that the council limit the initial frame of the fund to $10 million. The council asked the administrator to continue his efforts to make the fund operational. However, the main western countries—including Belgium, Canada, Federal Republic of Germany, France, Japan, Switzerland, the

United Kingdom, and the United States—disassociated themselves from this decision. ECOSOC later endorsed the decision, expressing the hope that member states and agencies would take part in the pledging conference planned for October 1968, as did the General Assembly.[16]

However, with the major western governments on the sideline, the response was hardly encouraging. By the end of the year, only $2.7 million had been pledged, of which only $0.1 million had been paid. In January 1969, western governments again disassociated themselves from the Governing Council's repeated appeals to pledging countries to follow up their commitments. In January 1970, the council approved the guidelines and terms for loans for the fund proposed by the administrator and authorized him to implement future transactions by executing loan arrangements as and when they were ready.[17]

United Nations Volunteers

In December 1968, the General Assembly began the initiative to create an international corps of volunteers for development, requesting ECOSOC to study the feasibility of such a corps and provide "appropriate conclusions and recommendations" based on this study.[18] The idea was by no means new: a "peace corps" had already been part of western bilateral aid programs, first and foremost the U.S. Peace Corps. In response to the General Assembly resolution, however, ECOSOC put a distinct multilateral stamp on an idea picked up from bilateral agencies.[19]

In 1970, the Secretary-General recommended that an international group of volunteers be established within the existing UN framework that would take effect on 1 January 1971. This proposal had a smooth run through the system. The General Assembly asked the Secretary-General to designate the UNDP's administrator as the administrator of the United Nations Volunteers (UNV) and requested states, organizations, and individuals to contribute to a special fund to support the activities of the new institution.[20]

Development Planning Advisory Services

Another idea deserves highlighting because it reflects so well the main thrust of UN development philosophy during these early years: to organize interdisciplinary advisory services in development planning, plan implementation, public administration, and management. The idea emerged from the regional economic commissions. In 1970, ECOSOC considered reports by the Secretary-General and by the executive secretaries of the regional commissions on steps taken in response to a request by the General Assembly the previous year.[21] The council found that technical assistance in the form of advisory services through subregional interdisciplinary teams might be a highly useful way of assisting some developing countries to build up their own services in these fields. The Secretary-General was invited to examine different ways of financing projects of this nature in consultation with the administrator of the UNDP.[22]

Growth of Resources: Distribution, Activities, and Regions

PLEDGES

During the latter 1960s, pledging patterns largely followed those of the first years of the decade: any "UNDP effect" was modest. Nevertheless, the program continued to grow, and yearly pledges rose from $146 million in 1965 to $225 million five years later. Until the end of the decade, commitments continued to be made to the two components of the program—pre-investment activities and technical assistance.[23]

The evolving trends are shown in table 7. 1. Funding for pre-investment activities continued at a higher level than funding for technical assistance. The main contributors remained much the same as in the early 1960s. Although a large number of developing countries contributed to the program, most of the financial resources came from industrialized countries. The United States continued as the largest contributor to the program for both pre-investment activities and technical assistance. U.S. pledges continued to have the condition attached that they should not exceed 40 percent of the total amount provided by other governments. For 1966, the United States contributed 41 percent of total pledges. Sweden was the second largest contributor, with 8.5 percent of the total. Two neighboring countries, Denmark and Norway, increased their contributions, and together the three Scandinavian countries provided 14.8 percent. The United Kingdom (7.7 percent), Canada (5.7 percent), Germany (5.2 percent), and the Netherlands (3.6 percent) were also major contributors. Among developing countries, India remained the major contributor (2 percent), and the Soviet Union was the largest contributor among the Eastern European countries (2 percent). By 1970, the United States was still at the top (with 38.2 percent), followed by Sweden (9.3 percent), Denmark (6.9 percent), Canada (6.7 percent), the UK (6.3 percent), Germany (5

TABLE 7.1.

Pledges to the UNDP, 1965–1969 (in millions of U.S. dollars)

	1965	1966	1967	1968	1969
Pre-investment activities	91.6	97.9	111.8	106.8	125.8
Technical assistance	54.0	55.6	60.4	76.0	70.1
TOTALS	145.6	153.5	172.2	182.8	195.9

Source: *Yearbook of the United Nations 1965*, 281–282, 289; *Yearbook of the United Nations 1966*, 224–226; *Yearbook of the United Nations 1967*, 304–306; *Yearbook of the United Nations 1968*, 346; and *Yearbook of the United Nations 1969*, 299.

Pledges for the coming year are given at pledging conferences. However, pledges are also often given at a later stage—even within the actual year. This affects recordkeeping. Different sources may record different figures for the actual years, depending on whether latecomers are included or not. The same UN source may offer different figures in different contexts.

percent), the Netherlands (4.2 percent), Norway (2.6 percent), and Japan (2.2 percent). The three Scandinavian countries had increased their share to 18.9 percent of the total. India continued to be the major contributor among developing countries (1.6 percent), and the Soviet Union was still the leader among eastern-bloc countries (1.3 percent).[24]

DISTRIBUTION OF UNDP RESOURCES BY IMPLEMENTING AGENCIES

Although we may trace tendencies toward a more central role for the UNDP—from a funding agency to an operational one—it continued to function almost exclusively as a fund within the UN while the specialized agencies served as its implementing arms.

By the late 1960s, however, change was under way. In 1969, the Governing Council revised the procedures governing regional and interregional technical assistance programming; the new procedures began in 1971. The system of agency targets for regional and interregional projects was eliminated. The program shares allocated to regional and interregional funds were to be considered global targets that applied to the program and year instead of being allocated as target shares to the participating and executing agencies. These new procedures were endorsed by ECOSOC and approved by the General Assembly.[25]

The distribution of resources during the second part of the 1960s is given in tables 7.2 (technical assistance) and 7.3 (pre-investment activi-

TABLE 7.2.

Distribution of UNDP Technical Assistance Resources, Selected Years, 1950–1970 (by percent and in millions of U.S. dollars)

	1950–1965	1967	1968	1969	1970
FAO	26.1	24.5	22.3	26.0	23.4
UN	21.7	21.4	17.3	18.9	18.7
WHO	17.5	14.3	13.2	14.4	11.9
UNESCO	16.1	16.7	18.7	13.2	16.4
ILO	10.2	10.5	9.9	9.9	10.1
ICAO	4.3	4.3	4.0	4.5	4.3
WMO	1.5	2.6	2.8	2.6	2.9
ITU	1.4	2.9	3.4	3.3	3.9
IAEA	1.1	2.0	2.5	1.7	2.1
UPU	0.2	0.6	0.8	0.7	0.8
IMCO	0.0	0.3	0.2	0.2	0.4
UNIDO	0.0	0.0	5.6	4.3	4.5
TOTALS[1]	100.1	100.1	100.7	99.7	99.4
Millions of U.S. dollars	493.9	112.9	64.6	42.3	51.3

Source: Calculations based on data in Technical Assistance Committee, *Sixth Report of the Technical Assistance Board,* ECOSOC document E/2566 E/TAC/REP.3, 14 April 1954, 17; Technical Assistance Committee, *Seventh Report of the Technical Assistance Board,* 21; Technical Assistance Committee, *Annual Report of the Technical Assistance Board for 1956,* 7; Technical Assistance Committee, *Annual Report of the Technical Assistance Board for 1960,* 7; Technical Assistance Committee, *Annual Report of the Technical Assistance Board for 1961,* 5; Technical Assistance Committee, *Annual Report of the Technical Assistance Board for 1964,* table 3; UNDP, *15 Years and 150,000 Skills,* Annex II, and *Yearbook of the United Nations 1965,* 290; *Yearbook of the United Nations 1967,* 302; *Yearbook of the United Nations 1968,* 343; *Yearbook of the United Nations 1969,* 296; and *Yearbook of the United Nations 1970,* 340.

1. Percentages may not add up to exactly 100 because figures are rounded in the data on which the calculations are based.

ties). From the start, the FAO, the WHO, UNESCO, the ILO, and the UN Secretariat implemented almost all the technical assistance, with the FAO implementing the largest share. Although more organizations gradually became involved, the general picture remained much the same during this period: in 1970, the Secretariat and these four specialized agencies

TABLE 7.3.

Distribution of UNDP Pre-Investment Resources, 1966–1970 (by percent)

	1966	1967	1968	1969	1970
FAO	41.6	35.5	37.2	34.1	29.1
UN	17.2	22.4	19.1	21.4	12.3
UNESCO	15.6	12.0	12.4	9.1	14.6
ILO	10.7	14.1	11.5	13.3	9.5
WHO	4.7	2.1	3.9	1.7	6.5
WMO	4.5	1.7	1.3	0.9	2.0
IBRD	4.0	6.3	3.9	8.2	6.4
ITU	1.1	3.4	3.1	1.5	5.0
ICAO	0.6	0.0	0.7	2.0	4.5
IAEA	0.0	0.0	1.0	0.0	0.6
UNIDO	0.0	2.5	4.9	7.3	6.2
UPU	0.0	0.0	0.0	0.5	1.2
Inter-American Development Bank	0.0	0.0	0.7	0.0	0.0
African Development Bank	0.0	0.0	0.2	0.0	0.0
Asian Development Bank	0.0	0.0	0.0	0.0	0.8
UNDP	0.0	0.0	0.0	0.0	1.2
TOTALS[1]	100.0	100.0	99.9	100.0	99.9
Millions of U.S. dollars	167.9	127.7	141.3	136.7	139.3

Sources: Calculations based on data in Yearbook of the United Nations 1966, 220; Yearbook of the United Nations 1967, 300; Yearbook of the United Nations 1968, 341; Yearbook of the United Nations 1969, 294; and Yearbook of the United Nations 1970, 339.

1. Percentages may not add up to exactly 100 because figures are rounded in the data on which the calculations are based.

implemented more than 80 percent of UNDP technical assistance. The share of the individual agencies had been somewhat reduced, particularly that of the WHO, but their shares did not vary much from one year to the next. The most interesting change in the latter 1960s was that UNIDO emerged as a significant implementing agency; this was a response to mounting demands in intergovernmental bodies for a greater focus on industrial development.

As table 7.3 shows, three of the four agencies (the FAO, UNESCO, and the ILO) and the UN Secretariat implemented a large share of pre-investment activities as well—88 percent up to 1965, a share that was reduced to 66 percent in 1970, with the FAO by far the largest, followed by the Secretariat and UNESCO. The World Bank also implemented a significant share of these activities, and UNIDO appeared on the scene in the late 1960s at a level similar to that of the Bank.

REGIONAL DISTRIBUTION

During the early 1960s, Africa was a priority at both the EPTA and the Special Fund. As can be seen in tables 7.4 (technical assistance) and 7.5 (pre-investment activities), this region received the largest share of both UNDP aid components in the second half of the decade; its share of technical assistance even increased. These tables also show that the regional distribution of aid did not change much, although there were some variations from year to year.

DISTRIBUTION IN MAJOR ECONOMIC SECTORS

Decisions involving the distribution of assistance in economic sectors were primarily made indirectly by allocating resources to the implementing agencies, each of which had a separate primary mandate. Tables 7.6 and 7.7 show the evolving trends in the distribution of technical assistance and pre-investment resources by sector for the second half of the 1960s. Both components of the UNDP program emphasized agricultural development, especially pre-investment activities, which devoted about one-third of its funding to this sector. Support for industrial development came next, and public utilities ranked third. For the technical assistance component, support within social sectors—health and education in particular—was given high priority throughout the latter half of the 1960s; and by the late 1960s, pre-investment support for education was coming to the fore.

The Capacity Study and the 1970 Consensus

Toward the end of the 1960s, the UN increasingly looked toward the challenges ahead. Developing countries were disappointed with what had been achieved during the First UN Development Decade: results were lagging behind the stated expectations of the decade's strategy. The UN's intergovernmental bodies began to focus on a development strategy for the 1970s that included policy objectives and targets. A critical view was

TABLE 7.4.

Distribution of UNDP Technical Assistance Resources by Region,
Selected Years, 1960–1970 (by percent and in millions of U.S. dollars)

	1960	1965	1967	1968	1969	1970
Asia and the Far East	35.5	24.8	26.7	27.2	22.0	23.8
Africa	18.6	35.1	35.5	33.6	37.4	37.6
Americas	15.3	21.5	19.8	20.1	20.8	21.8
Middle East	12.6	5.8	6.4	6.0	5.7	5.7
Europe	12.1	3.9	3.8	4.2	4.3	3.9
Interregional and unspecified	6.0	9.0	8.0	9.0	10.2	7.2
TOTAL[1]	100.1	100.1	100.2	100.1	100.4	100.0
Millions of U.S. dollars	15.5	42.3	112.9	64.6	42.3	51.3

Source: Calculations based on data in Technical Assistance Committee, *Annual Report of the Technical Assistance Board for 1960,* Annex VII; *Yearbook of the United Nations 1965,* 296–300; *Yearbook of the United Nations 1967,* 202; *Yearbook of the United Nations 1968,* 343; *Yearbook of the United Nations 1969,* 296; and *Yearbook of the United Nations 1970,* 341. These data refer to allocations/earmarkings by the Governing Council provided in U.S. dollars.

1. Percentages may not add up to exactly 100 because figures are rounded in the data on which the calculations are based.

also directed toward the system's main operational development arms, particularly the UNDP and its cooperating organizations.

Such efforts followed different but parallel tracks. Work on the new international development strategy was organized within the ordinary system, with ECOSOC playing the central role (see chapters 5 and 6). The UNDP Governing Council initiated some delivery system reforms. But two important components to the process were commissioned from the outside. One, the Commission on International Development, focused on the policies and resources needed to bring economic development in developing countries up to an acceptable level within a generation. It was chaired by Lester Pearson, who had served as minister of foreign affairs and as prime minister of Canada and had won the Nobel Prize for Peace. The other, the capacity study of Sir Robert Jackson, focused more specifically on how the UN's delivery system might be improved and strengthened so

TABLE 7.5.

Distribution of UNDP Pre-Investment Resources by Region,
1966–1970 (by percent)

	1966	1967	1968	1969	1970
Africa	43.6	40.5	38.6	37.6	33.5
Americas	27.1	23.2	16.8	20.2	19.4
Asia and the Far East	20.1	20.3	31.2	27.4	31.3
Europe	6.9	8.6	7.8	6.7	7.0
Middle East	2.3	7.4	5.6	7.6	6.1
Interregional and global	0.0	0.0	0.0	0.5	2.6
TOTAL[1]	100.0	100.0	100.0	100.0	99.9
Millions of U.S. dollars	167.9	127.7	141.3	136.7	139.3

Source: Calculations based on data in *Yearbook of the United Nations 1966*, 220; *Yearbook of the United Nations 1967*, 300; *Yearbook of the United Nations 1968*, 341; *Yearbook of the United Nations 1969*, 294; and *Yearbook of the United Nations 1970*, 339. These data refer to allocations/earmarkings by the Governing Council provided in U.S. dollars.

1. Percentages may not add up to exactly 100 because figures are rounded in the data on which the calculations are based.

as to be capable of effectively running a development program that, within five years, would be at least twice the size of the existing one.

The Capacity Study

The push to undertake a capacity study came from the U.S. delegation. In 1966, it asked the administrator "to prepare a study of the realistic needs and capabilities for increased pre-investment assistance."[26] In January 1968, the administrator reported to the Governing Council that the anticipated demands for pre-investment assistance were far greater than the anticipated resources of the program. Both the UNDP and the specialized agencies needed a new approach to programming to enable them to realistically plan for high-priority projects.

To determine the best approach, the administrator commissioned a study of the UN's capacity to deliver an expanded program and appointed Sir Robert Jackson as commissioner. At its eighth session (June 1969), the Governing Council decided that Jackson's final report should be

TABLE 7.6.

Distribution of UNDP Technical Assistance Resources by Economic
Sectors, 1967–1971 (by percent)

	1967	1968	1969	1970	1971
Agriculture[1]	25.4	23.5	27.2	24.6	23.0
Education and science	15.1	16.4	12.3	16.4	15.5
Industry	14.7	14.9	11.6	12.3	12.7
Health	14.3	13.0	13.9	11.9	9.8
Public utilities	11.4	12.4	12.1	12.7	12.5
Public administration and other services	8.9	9.4	10.9	10.3	10.4
Multisector	4.9	4.5	6.4	6.8	9.5
Social welfare	3.5	3.7	4.3	3.7	5.4
Housing, building, and physical planning	1.7	2.0	1.7	1.4	1.3
TOTAL[2]	99.9	99.8	100.4	100.1	100.1
Millions of U.S. dollars	112.9	64.6	42.3	51.3	56.0

Sources: Calculations based on data in *Yearbook of the United Nations 1967,* 300, 302;
Yearbook of the United Nations 1968, 341, 343; *Yearbook of the United Nations 1969,* 294, 296;
Yearbook of the United Nations 1970, 340, 341; *Yearbook of the United Nations 1971,* 244.
These data represent allocation or earmarking by the UNDP Governing Council pro-
vided in U.S. dollars.

    1. In 1971, data for forestry and fisheries was added to agriculture.

    2. Percentages may not add up to exactly 100 because figures are rounded in the
data on which the calculations are based.

submitted to governments, the UNDP, and participating and executing
agencies simultaneously.[27]

    Jackson delivered the report at the end of September 1969.[28] He and
his team had come up with a critical diagnosis of the existing delivery
system that they transmitted in candid language.[29] The reforms they suggested captured ideas that had been languishing in the system for some
time, particularly concerning the evolution of technical assistance since
the mid-1950s and reform initiatives from the Governing Council during
the second half of the 1960s.

    The Jackson report proposed new procedures for planning and oper-
ating the program that was characterized by a UN development coopera-

TABLE 7.7.

Distribution of UNDP Pre-Investment Resources by Economic Sectors, 1966–1971 (by percent and in millions of U.S. dollars)

	1966	1967	1968	1969	1970	1971
Agriculture	37.6	37.8	46.1	36.8	31.1	36.1[1]
Industry	22.5	25.1	15.9	25.2	20.7	22.6
Public utilities	13.1	13.9	11.7	18.7	19.8	16.3
Multisector	10.6	8.8	6.9	5.4	3.8	7.7
Education	9.1	6.0	9.5	6.7	12.0	9.8
Public administration and other services	4.9	6.3	5.0	5.0	7.6	4.7
Housing, building, and physical planning	1.8	2.0	2.5	1.2	1.3	1.6
Social welfare	0.4	0.0	0.1	0.6	0.6	0.4
Health	0.0	0.0	2.3	0.4	3.1	0.9
TOTAL[2]	100.0	99.9	100.0	100.0	100.0	100.1
Millions of U.S. dollars	167.9	127.7	141.3	136.7	139.3	189

Source: Calculations based on data in *Yearbook of the United Nations 1966*, 220; *Yearbook of the United Nations 1967*, 300, 302; *Yearbook of the United Nations 1968*, 341, 343; *Yearbook of the United Nations 1969*, 294, 296; *Yearbook of the United Nations 1970*, 340, 341; *Yearbook of the United Nations 1971*, 244. These data refer to allocations/earmarkings by the Governing Council provided in U.S. dollars.

1. In 1971, data for forestry and fisheries was added to agriculture.
2. Percentages may not add up to exactly 100 because figures are rounded in the data on which the calculations are based.

tion cycle that "gathers together in one comprehensive and integrated pattern all the interdependent processes which together constitute the development co-operation activities of the UN development system." This cycle consisted of five phases: country programs and annual reviews, the formulation and appraisal of projects, implementation, evaluation, and follow-up. The proposed design was not restricted to the UNDP; it was to apply to the whole UN development system, including the major UN programs (such as UNICEF and the WFP) and programs of the specialized agencies that were active in the field of development (including activities financed from their own budgets). These various inputs should be subject to integrated programming so they would fit into the developing plans of the recipient country and relate to inputs from other sources, especially capital inputs. On this topic, the report made particular reference to the IBRD, "the arm of the UN system responsible for capital investment."[30]

Within this system, the UNDP would play the central role. The proposed new structure was designed "to secure the shortest line of authority between the Governing Council . . . and the governments of individual developing countries . . . through the medium of the Administrator and the Resident Representatives." The UNDP's primary need was to decentralize functions to the country level and strengthen the staffs of the resident representatives.[31]

At headquarters, the core of operations should be four regional bureaus that would form a direct link between the administrator and the resident representatives. The report recommended strong centralization of authority within the UN development system: the administrator should be explicitly responsible for all activities, including planning as well as implementation. This was a stark contrast to the prevailing practice whereby the agencies had performed both functions, especially those involving technical assistance.[32]

The core component of the proposed programming system was the country program. Repeatedly, Jackson underlined that the activities of the UN development system should be anchored in the specific conditions prevailing in individual Third World countries and the priorities of their governments—much in line with the norms set down for UN development assistance already in 1949 (see chapter 2).[33] Constraints were identified: the main problem of recipient governments related to their absorptive capacity. Jackson took a dynamic attitude about that problem: "Where bottlenecks to any country's ability to use more development cooperation are identified, they should not be regarded as a limiting factor. Rather, it should be a primary objective for the UN development system— always acting in conformity with the government's expressed wishes—to help break them."[34]

The country program should, accordingly, be prepared by the government concerned and the resident representative, the latter drawing on assistance from other components of the UN development system as necessary, "based on a thorough review of the economic situation, of the needs emerging from the national development plan . . . and the likely provision of assistance from other sources."[35] The report introduced an innovation that would be a useful tool for long-term development planning: the administrator would calculate indicative planning figures that allocated available resources to countries. The indicative planning figures informed each country of the magnitude of resources they could expect from the UNDP during the lifetime of the five-year development plans and were designed to help countries with planning.[36] The country program would be projected in increments of five years and would consist of agreed-upon objectives and projects to support these objectives. The Governing Council was to consider the program and approve global indicative planning figures for five years. The UNDP administrator would have the authority to approve projects, but the resident representative could approve smaller projects.

The agencies were expected to integrate activities financed from their regular budgets into this program, and the IBRD should also be closely associated with the process. However, they would not play the prominent role previously assigned to them.[37]

The capacity study took as a point of departure an expansion of the financial framework, doubling UNDP resources in a matter of five years.[38] In conformity with the general approach of the study, it recommended that all separate funds be merged into a central fund. This would apply at first to internal UNDP funds for pre-investment work and technical assistance but in time would apply to UNICEF and WFP funds as well.[39]

The study also recommended an integrated information system to enhance planning and implementing capacity.[40]

The 1970 Consensus

In 1970, both the Governing Council and ECOSOC considered the capacity study before sending it to the General Assembly. The agreement that emerged from this process followed most of the study's core recommendations: the general framework, the UN development cooperation cycle, and its basic component, country programming, based on indicative planning figures.[41] This agreement is known as the 1970 consensus.

The General Assembly resolution that expressed the 1970 consensus emphasized the decisive role of the recipient government even more strongly and in greater detail than the capacity study had.[42] Country programming was to be based on individual national development plans or, where these did not exist, on national development priorities or objectives. The resolution stressed that recipient countries each had "the exclusive responsibility for formulating its national development plan or priorities and objectives" and that the UN should assist in their planning when requested to do so. Country programs involving UN assistance—which would be based on national development plans, priorities, or objectives and on the indicative planning figures—were to "be formulated by the Government of the recipient country in co-operation, at an appropriate stage, with representatives of the United Nations system, the latter under the leadership of the resident representative of the Programme." Country programs should "support activities which are meaningfully related to the country's development objectives. This implies that the assistance provided constitutes a programme which receives its coherence and balance from its relationship to these national objectives." Efforts should be made at all levels to coordinate all sources of UN assistance. "It would be for the *Government* to take into account, while preparing the country programme, other external inputs, both multilateral and bilateral" [emphasis added].[43]

The capacity study had strongly recommended making the administrator fully responsible (and accountable to the Governing Council) for all phases and aspects of program implementation. The 1970 consensus agreed.[44] As noted, however, another principle opted for greater decentralization of responsibility for programming and implementation from headquarters to the country level—involving the government concerned and with greater authority also vested in the resident representative. This twin principle, involving full accountability of the administrator in combination with decentralization to the country level, called for a clear definition of functions and responsibilities at all levels of the administration.[45]

The consensus agreed with most of the study's recommendations about the relationship between the agencies and the UNDP. The role of UN organizations in implementing country programs "should be that of partners, under leadership of the Programme." The "appropriate organizations" of the UN would be given first priority as executing agents of the program. However, the consensus made it possible for others to compete, referring particularly to national institutions and firms within the recipient countries.[46] The General Assembly resolution emphasized the importance of recruiting well-qualified international project personnel and stressed the desirability of increasing the number of personnel from developing countries. This concern also applied to the personnel who managed projects: qualified nationals might be designated as project managers, assisted by international specialists.

Monitoring of project assistance was to be carried out at the country level by the resident representative. Evaluation of program activities by the UN, however, was to be made only with the agreement of the government concerned. A tripartite model was established whereby evaluations were to be done jointly by the government concerned, the UN agency concerned, and, where relevant, the executive agent outside the UN. With the agreement of the government concerned, the result would be communicated to the Governing Council.

Based on the capacity study's recommendations, the 1970 consensus established a new balance between participating organizations and the UN Development Programme's advisory and governing bodies and between the central and decentralized administrative bodies of the institution. The position of the central institutions was strengthened vis-à-vis the executing organizations: responsibility for all the program's activities was vested in the Governing Council and delegated, in a circumscribed way, to the administrator, who had responsibility for the full program, including planning, implementation, monitoring, and evaluation. The administrator delegated authority to the regional and national level of the recipient countries, providing the resident directors with strengthened authority in all matters involving program assistance at the country level. The 1970 consensus placed ultimate responsibility for program activities with the recipient government, underlining that the program's primary role was to assist governments in their own development efforts. The balance brought about by this consensus ruled on the ground for years to come.[47]

The 1970s

The life and focus of the UNDP in the 1970s can broadly be divided in two periods. During the first half of the 1970s, the main focus was on implementing the recommendations of the 1970 consensus: reforming the delivery system to improve its capacity and effectiveness. The goal of the changes was to stimulate increased development assistance through the UN. The capacity study, the report of the Commission on International Development, and the strategy for DD2 all provided important frames of reference. ECOSOC and especially the General Assembly (where developing countries commanded an overwhelming majority) kept reminding the UNDP administrator and the Governing Council of the aims, principles, and priorities underpinning the international strategy for DD2 as it related to UNDP activities and priorities.

Toward the middle of the 1970s, several political and economic changes took place that affected UNDP policies and priorities. In 1973–1974, the global economy found itself under pressure. Recession and inflation in western industrial countries had negative effects from a development perspective. It affected western trade policies, access to western markets for developing countries in particular, and the ability or willingness of western countries to contribute to development assistance. Shortages in vital commodities such as fuel, fertilizers, and food and droughts and floods throughout parts of Africa, South Asia, and Central America added to the crisis. Everywhere, the prospects for development were affected.

General impatience with development trends increased among Third World governments. Within the UN, the most prominent manifestation of the growing impatience was the 1974 Charter of Economic Rights and Duties of States, which the General Assembly adopted against the votes of major western governments. Spokespersons of Third World governments considered the charter a landmark in the evolution toward the full equality of nations in political and economic relations.[48]

This charter and the declaration and program of action on the establishment of an NIEO[49] brought a much broader agenda to the UN table than simply development assistance, although increased development assistance constituted part of the picture. Many aspects of economic and political North-South relations were part of the dialogue developing countries engendered. This broader perspective had a direct bearing on development assistance, but it was not confined to multilateral aid. The change of perspective was captured by a change of terminology: development *assistance* now become development *cooperation*.

In 1975, cost inflation and a shortfall in expected resources compelled the UNDP to substantially reduce its planned expenditures for the following year. This triggered rethinking. At the June 1975 session, Administrator Rudolph Peterson presented a report on the future role of the UNDP in the context of the preparations for the seventh special session of the General Assembly on a NIEO, which was planned for the upcoming September. The main thrust of Peterson's report was the shift in focus from assistance to cooperation.[50] The Governing Council responded by approving new guidelines for technical cooperation aimed at building self-reliance. Another goal of the new design was freeing program planning from the traditional project package of foreign experts, fellowships, equipment, and government personnel to enable the program to be more responsive to the varied needs of countries in diverse stages of development at less cost.[51]

First Development Cycle, 1972–1976: Implementing the 1970 Consensus

ADMINISTRATIVE RESTRUCTURING

In 1971, the Governing Council, ECOSOC, and the General Assembly began implementing the 1970 consensus. The Governing Council approved a major reorganization of the UNDP administration along the lines proposed: four regional bureaus were established (for Africa, for Asia and the Far East, for Latin America, and for Europe, the Mediterranean, and the Middle East). Each bureau was headed by an assistant administrator and was responsible for appraisal, implementation, evaluation, and follow-up of UNDP programs and projects within its region. In addition, a planning bureau was set up to do long-term planning, program analysis, research, and overall evaluation of the program. The council urged governments to increase their contributions to the program: the goal was to double financial contributions by 1975 in order to enable the UNDP to help achieve the aims of the DD2 strategy.[52]

The decentralization of the operational activities of the early 1970s was increased in 1974. Guidelines provided greater decision-making authority at the country level to the resident representatives. The Governing Council also considered decentralization through operational arrangement involving the UN regional commissions, and ECOSOC was asked to request these commissions to work together with the administrator in the planning and implementation of relevant regional and subregional projects and to ensure that their own activities were coordinated with the UNDP, particularly regarding the activities of the UN development advisory teams. The administrator was recommended to make full use of the expertise of the regional commissions by also using them as executing agencies of selected UNDP projects within their respective regions.[53]

In 1975, the Governing Council approved a request from the administrator to extend (until the end of 1976) his delegation of authority to resident representatives to approve projects, endorsing an increase from $100,000 to $150,000 as the upper limit.[54]

FINANCIAL SCOPE

The program's financial scope became a recurrent topic on the agendas of intergovernmental bodies—including those of ECOSOC and the General Assembly. Financial frames were related to the ability of the UNDP to assist in realizing the aims set for the DD2. In July 1971, ECOSOC expressed concern that the 9.6 percent per annum increase in overall resources for the period 1972–1976, on which the Governing Council had based indicative planning figures, would result in the program's stagnation at its current level in real terms. The Governing Council was asked to review the planning estimates with a view to doubling the resources during the coming five-year period, "thus imparting a real meaning to the concept of country programming on a long-term dynamic basis." Governments were urged to increase their financial contributions to the UNDP in order to enable the program to use as fully as possible its improved capacity to assist developing countries in attaining DD2 objectives.[55] In December that year, the General Assembly asserted that there was "a need for a fundamental and speedy strengthening of operational activities for development" of the UN system. It stated that by 1976, the UNDP should be enabled to carry a total program of at least $1 billion.[56]

COUNTRY PROGRAMS AND INDICATIVE PLANNING FIGURES

The new way of programming development assistance was initiated in 1972, accompanied by organizational and procedural changes aimed at decentralizing responsibility to the country level.[57] Although commitments to UNDP activities were made for only one year at annual pledging conferences, the programming system was based on indicative planning figures (IPFs) of the resources that were likely to be available for a five-year period. Country programs attempted to identify and define the priorities, phasing, and directions of UNDP assistance in terms of each country's development objectives, as defined by the recipient government. The total framework for indicative planning figures for the first cycle (1972–1976) amounted to $1.5 billion.

In 1972, fifty-eight countries developed integrated country programs. The cost of these programs amounted to $658 million. Several of these country programs were a continuation of projects already in operation. The programming process was started in most of the remaining developing countries and was also extended to intercountry activities with a view to making the programming system universal by the end of 1974. The following year, the number of country programs rose substantially: by the end of 1973, the UNDP and participating governments were sponsoring 102 country programs that collectively cost $1.1 billion. In 1974, the estimated financial framework was increased to $1.3 billion, of which some $1.2 billion had been committed for 116 country programs by the end of the year. By the end of 1975, the number of country programs had increased to 118 at a total cost of $1.2 billion in indicative planning figures. During the first planning cycle, IPF allocations to 127 countries and to UNDP-supported regional, interregional, and global programs amounted to $1.54 billion.[58]

The criteria the administrator used to calculate indicative planning figures for individual countries became crucially important for resource distribution. In 1972, the Governing Council set up a working group to recommend criteria to be used in calculating indicative planning figures for the next cycle (1977–1981). Two fundamental criteria were recommended: the degree of poverty as expressed in per capita income, and the population of the country.[59] The working group also recommended that 25 percent of the total frame for indicative planning figures be devoted to the least-developed countries. However, it struck a balance, suggesting that although the share of distributed resources for the more advanced developing countries was to be reduced, the absolute amount of their indicative planning figure should remain the same or be increased if resources increased. The Governing Council included the issue in its first 1973 session and generally agreed that during the first cycle (1972–1976), there would be no decreases in the level of indicative planning figures that had already been allocated. In 1974, the Governing Council approved the new system of resource allocation based primarily on population and per capita income criteria.[60]

The UN's development assistance system had effects beyond multilateral aid: some bilateral aid agencies, including those of the Scandinavian countries and the Netherlands, copied the model for their own bilateral development cooperation. In addition, the UNDP sought to coordinate its country programs with some bilateral programs for more effective coordination of all sources of technical assistance.

MAIN ACHIEVEMENTS OF THE FIRST DEVELOPMENT CYCLE (1972–1976)

A report summarizing the main results of the first cycle captures the program's key features. The self-presentation in the mid-1970s portrays its purpose: "assisting developing countries to build long-term self-sustained development capacities." It "work[ed] closely with Governments and over 24 international agencies in support of some 8,000 development assistance projects" throughout the world. Through its network of more than 100 country offices, it "help[ed] to co-ordinate strategic development planning and United Nations field development activities with national development endeavours and other forms of external assistance."[61]

At the end of the first cycle, the UNDP reported that the goals set had been attained, despite problems generated by reorganization and the cash-flow crisis in 1975: "A target of $1,537.5 million had been set for the country and intercountry programme expenditures, and actual expenditures at the end of 1976 coincided with that amount. During the cycle, the UNDP sent to the field an average of 10,000 experts annually, provided 28,200 fellowships, and spent nearly $238 million for project equipment and another $188 million in project subcontracts. Together these activities stimulated over $19,000 million in follow-up investment commitments between 1972 and 1976." Implicitly, if not explicitly, the report claimed that the intentions behind the new programming system had been attained, namely "to emphasize greater coherence and more responsiveness to the needs of developing countries and to establish a more integrated, forward-planning approach to development." Through the introduction, in 1974, of the "new dimensions" in technical cooperation, the program had "shifted towards a comprehensive forward-planning approach for its regional, interregional and global projects by linking them to global development priorities and integrating them at country level."[62]

The additional resources for investments generated by UNDP-supported pre-investment studies—more than $19 billion in commitments during the first cycle—were allocated to projects in the transport and communications sector (31 percent); development of natural resources, primarily hydro-electric and nuclear power development (20 percent); agriculture, forestry, and fisheries development (19 percent); industrial development (15 percent); and health projects (6 percent).[63]

The Second Development Cycle (1977–1981)

During the first cycle, the programming system established by the 1970 consensus was adapted to the evolving reality confronting the UNDP, including the political dynamics of the mid-1970s that brought new perspectives into political and economic North-South relations. Most of the patterns set in the first cycle continued when the program for the second development cycle was designed.

FINANCIAL FRAME, BASIC CRITERIA, AND SECTOR PRIORITIES

Total projected UNDP expenditures for the second cycle were estimated at US$3.5 billion, in current prices more than the double the estimate for the first cycle. An annual increase of 14 percent was set as a target for this period, as with the first cycle.

In determining the indicative planning figures for this period, emphasis was to be placed on the basic criteria of population, per-capita GNP, and the needs of the lower-income countries, particularly least-developed countries and countries most seriously affected by the global economic crisis. One-third of available resources was allocated for the needs of least-developed countries, and about two-thirds was allocated for developing countries with an annual per-capita GNP of $300 or less.

As in the previous cycle, the primary focus was on agriculture, forestry, and fisheries (about 24 percent), industry (21 percent), and transportation and communications (about 9 percent), which together represented more than half of planned expenditures for country programs. The main change was an increase in spending for general economic and social policy and planning, including statistics and public and financial administration. Here the planned expenditure increased from 10 to 17 percent.[64]

ADMINISTRATIVE REFORM

During the second cycle, a series of interlinked administrative reforms were initiated, some by the UNDP administrator and the Secretary-General and some by the Governing Council and the General Assembly. Most reforms sought to decentralize authority with regard to development assistance in order to promote greater involvement of recipient governments, thus transforming development assistance into development cooperation. Some reforms sought to coordinate the operational activities of the UN at the country and regional levels. This involved, in particular, strengthening the role of UNDP resident representatives. In addition, the regional commissions were to become more heavily involved in development cooperation. The more fundamental reform, driven by representatives of developing countries in intergovernmental bodies, involved the recipient governments more deeply in the process, not only in priority-setting but also in program implementation. These various moves were interlinked.

During its 1978 session, the Governing Council carried out a policy review of operational activities based on a report by the administrator on progress made toward restructuring UNDP activities in accordance with the instructions of the General Assembly.[65] The issue was passed on to ECOSOC, which also considered a report by the interagency ACC, endorsing the holding of a single pledging conference for all operational activities for development and also for the designation of a single official within each country, usually the UNDP resident representative, to exercise team leadership for all UN development activities. The General Assembly, in turn, requested the Secretary-General to ask the director-general for development and international cooperation to prepare a report on policy issues affecting the UN's operational activities, and provided detailed guidance as to the focus of that report.[66] The report was presented in 1980.

TRANSFERRING PROJECT IMPLEMENTATION FROM UN AGENCIES TO HOST GOVERNMENTS

In January 1977, the Governing Council adopted a program called "New Dimensions in UNDP Technical Co-Operation." In 1975, in a report to the Governing Council, the administrator had brought up the idea, which was designed to strengthen self-reliance among developing countries. It was endorsed by the General Assembly.[67] The 1977 program allowed for the execution of projects by developing countries.

The administrator subsequently approved several such arrangements, including six projects financed by the UN Sahelian Office. In addition, two regional projects in Latin America were to be administered by the Caribbean Development Bank and the Board of the Cartagena Agreement, respectively. Activities during the following year included stepped-up provision of advanced equipment for projects, initiation of high-risk projects, and greater use of local skills. The takeoff in 1979 was very modest: expenditures on projects implemented by direct government execution rose to $6.5 million, a tenfold increase from the previous year.[68]

Studies on the experience of country programming indicated, however, that realizing the intentions of the program would be an uphill job. Many governments continued to prefer to draw on the services of the specialized agencies as executing agencies because of their ability to handle the administrative procedures involved in project execution, the special advantages agencies had for procuring and importing equipment, and the lack of trained national personnel, especially in the least-developed countries.[69]

In 1979, the Governing Council reacted to a budget under strain and invited the UNDP administrator along with agencies and governments to consider alternatives to UNDP-financed, internationally recruited experts and to consider rendering more support to governments who wanted to recruit experts directly, use qualified nationals as experts in projects, use expatriate nationals for service in their home countries, and use institutional twinning arrangements and related methods proposed by the Joint Inspection Unit.[70]

However, turning over the execution of UNDP-funded projects to the recipient governments appeared a tall order for the administration. Approvals of such projects totaled $12.3 million in 1981, a tiny share of UNDP field activities.[71]

In June 1981, the Governing Council responded to this situation by asking the administrator, in cooperation with other UN organizations, to give full consideration to implementation of UNDP assistance by host governments. Furthermore, it asked him to review and analyze in detail the reasons for lack of progress in implementing government execution. In fact, this was a decision that Administrator Bradford Morse had invited.[72] ECOSOC also welcomed the decision. In the debate on operational activities in the Second Committee later that fall, several speakers spoke about the benefits likely to emerge from expanded government execution.[73]

In many ways, this represented the beginning of the end of a long tradition where UNDP-financed projects were executed by UN agencies, not by the governments concerned. The basic ideology had been there all along: that recipient governments should be in the driver's seat with regard to requests, priorities, and implementation of technical assistance. In the early and mid-1970s, the emphasis on self-reliance strengthened this ideology. Developing countries led this demand for both ideological and economic reasons.

The idea was part of an emerging recognition of the role development assistance should play. Emphasis was increasingly placed on cooperation. It came at a time when the manpower situation had improved in most developing countries, even in many of the least-developed countries: their own educational systems were at work. A report by the UNDP administrator in March 1980, which had been requested by the General Assembly two years earlier, reflected this recognition, especially its application to multilateral development cooperation.[74]

However, the report also offered advice with regard to policies to be pursued by governments. The report suggested that governments should foster links between human resource development and other economic and social objectives. They should promote complementary formal and informal education and training and use qualified national personnel in all economic areas and at all levels of skill and responsibility. While the bulk of resources would have to be mobilized internally, external resources would be increasingly necessary, the report observed. In line with the prevailing ideology of collective self-reliance, it recommended that governments make maximum use of expertise available in other developing countries. The Governing Council, ECOSOC, and the General Assembly each endorsed the report.[75] The General Assembly called on developed countries "to assist the developing countries, in particular the least developed among them, in their efforts to increase national capabilities and facilities for training qualified national personnel and strengthen their role in socio-economic development." It invited developing countries to pay special attention to achieving educational equality for all "irrespective of race, nationality, sex or religious and social status," to eliminating illiteracy, expanding the role of government in education, instituting compulsory education for all school-age children, and achieving the planned development of national educational and training systems. It encouraged recipient governments and the UNDP Governing Council to take into account the urgent need for qualified national personnel in identifying UNDP intercountry projects in the third programming cycle. It also invited the development and international economic cooperation director-general to arrange for the dissemination of information on the national experiences of countries with different socioeconomic systems in training qualified national personnel and enhancing their role in national social and economic development and to submit a progress report in 1982.[76]

INVOLVING THE REGIONAL COMMISSIONS

In January 1979, the General Assembly made a series of decisions aimed at restructuring the UN's economic and social sectors that gave the regional commissions the status of UNDP executing agencies. The General Assembly asked the Secretary-General to take the necessary steps to implement these changes as soon as possible, especially the components dealing with the decentralization to the regional commissions of appropriate research and analysis activities and technical cooperation projects and the strengthening of cooperation arrangements with the regional commissions with regard to program planning, research, and analysis.[77] In December 1979, the General Assembly underlined the need for more vigorous action that would enable the regional commissions to fully play their role as the economic and social development center within their respective regions.[78]

UN RESIDENT COORDINATORS

On 27 June 1979, the Governing Council prescribed the role and activities of the resident coordinators; these included all activities from country programming to evaluation.[79] The Administrative Committee on Coordination had already considered the General Assembly's recommendation that a single official represent all UN development activities at the country level and had approved a standard letter for the Secretary-General to use when he appointed "the resident co-ordinator of the United Nations system's operational activities for development" to be signed by the Secretary-General for the appointment of each resident coordinator, thus moving the ultimate authority from the UNDP to the Secretariat.[80] The General Assembly endorsed the recommendations, including the principles that should guide the functions of the resident coordinator. It asked the Secretary-General to begin designating resident coordinators with the consent of the governments concerned.[81]

The initial appointments involved officials who were already serving as UNDP resident representatives.[82] By the end of 1981, the Secretary-General had designated resident coordinators in most countries receiving UN development assistance. In June 1981, ECOSOC asked the organizations participating in the UN development system to strengthen coordination between their headquarters and in the field, in particular to enable resident coordinators to act as the central coordinating authorities in the field on behalf of the UN development system.[83]

OVERHEAD COSTS

The activities placed under UNDP supervision and ultimate responsibility increased annually as did total expenditures, including trust funds and contributions from bilateral and multilateral donors and from aid-recipient governments. By the late 1970s, the UNDP's administrative and operational responsibilities had expanded substantially beyond its ordinary activities and the extra-budgetary activities that had been part of its program almost from the start.[84]

The overhead costs of the agencies implementing assistance figured frequently on the agenda of intergovernmental bodies. Throughout the 1970s, the combined overhead costs of the implementing agencies reimbursed by the UNDP and the administrative and support costs of the UNDP itself remained well above one-fifth of the total resources made available for its operational activities.[85]

The major concern of the UN's intergovernmental bodies was to keep administrative costs to a minimum "to secure increased resources for direct assistance to recipient countries." However, they also kept insisting on the need for effective and timely preparation and implementation of the activities that were financed, as reflected in General Assembly resolution 2975 (XXVII). In justifying the overhead costs, it was argued that these were related not only to project administration—the many field offices performed a whole range of additional development activities.[86]

In June 1980, the Governing Council expressed deep concern about the fact that support costs remained high, stating that they should be reduced without adding to the regular budgets of the agencies. It invited ECOSOC and the General Assembly to recommend that the agencies review their operational support system, working methods, arrangements, and staffing with a view to substantially reducing costs. It asked the administrator to continue to control and reduce such costs for the UNDP and to set 12 percent of total program cost as an initial policy objective for program support and administrative services budgets.[87]

In December 1980, the General Assembly approved a new formula for determining the amounts the UNDP paid to agencies executing its projects to reimburse them for their costs in providing administrative and other support in project execution. The rate was reduced to 13 percent of total project costs, down from 14 percent, and was to apply for the period 1982 to 1991.[88] However, according to the decision of the Governing Council, this formula should be implemented in a flexible manner.[89]

The issue remained on the agenda. The Governing Council decided to reduce the UNDP administrative budget for 1982–1983 as proposed by the administrator, by $7 million, actually a symbolic cut in terms of magnitude (2.7 percent). Further, it advised the administrator to exercise extreme caution and to ensure that expenditures were closely controlled. The council urged the administrator to reduce the administrative budget in the third programming cycle (1982–1986) and decided that the budget should not rise in real terms beyond the level approved for 1982–1983; the need for additional resources tied to any increase in program delivery should be met by redeployment of staff and other facilities. In all this, the General Assembly heartily concurred.[90]

Presenting his 1981 report to the Second Committee, the development and international economic cooperation director-general made the point that the pursuit of administrative economy was not the sole component of efficiency or effectiveness: other elements included the objective of improving quality and responsiveness, links between operational activities and headquarter-based research and analysis functions, and the adequacy and predictability of resources. He cautioned the committee against dismantling services and getting rid of expertise that might be needed in the future when operational activities resumed their upward growth. However, the General Assembly emphasized the need for minimizing administrative and overhead costs with a view to increasing the proportion of resources available to meet the assistance requirements of developing countries. It welcomed the June decision of the UNDP Governing Council and urged other governing bodies, as a general guideline, to reduce such costs. It invited all UN organs, organizations, and bodies to adopt "measures leading to a greater use of the capacities of developing countries in local or regional procurement of material and equipment, in training and in services, in facilitating the increased use of local contractors, and in the recruitment of training, technical and managerial personnel." It asked the director-general to include recommendations on ways to step up the participation of developing countries in program execution in his 1983 report to the General Assembly. It invited governing bodies to reduce administrative and other support costs and improve efficiency and asked them for information on what was being done in that regard.[91]

CONCURRENT PLANNING AND IMPLEMENTATION

Following a midterm examination of the country programming experience in 1979, the UNDP concluded that effectiveness depended primarily on more concerted planning and implementing measures. It recommended that the identification and formulation of new projects should take place concurrently as program implementation moved forward with ongoing dialogue among government authorities, the UNDP field offices, and the executing agencies. These new programming methods also aimed at improving UNDP responsiveness by enhancing the involvement of developing countries in setting priorities for regional programs and in identifying and initiating regional projects. The methods were beginning to take effect with the planning of programs for the third development cycle.[92]

In June 1981, the Governing Council agreed to the administrator's recommendations for revised country programming procedures. These centered on the concept of continuous programming, designed to keep

UNDP technical cooperation relevant to evolving national objectives, needs, and priorities through a process of ongoing review and assessment. In a report setting out these proposals, Administrator Morse stated that ongoing dialogue between the UN system and governments and their ministries and central planning and coordinating authorities should be the cornerstone of continuous programming. That dialogue should serve as the basis for formulating the country program, continuing review of its implementation, and identifying new activities.[93]

INTEGRATED PROGRAMMING

Early in 1980, the UNDP administrator instructed the field office network to include the work of each of the allied funds in country programming and periodic program reviews. He singled out the activities of the United Nations Capital Development Fund, the United Nations Volunteers, the Interim Fund for Science and Technology, and the United Nations Fund for Natural Resources Exploration.[94]

EVALUATION

Evaluation of performance ranked high on the UNDP agenda during the first years of its existence. The focus was not to be restricted to projects but should include the overall impact and effectiveness of development assistance. This was an integral part of the administrative reform proposed by the capacity study and the 1970 consensus. As noted, however, the consensus stressed the responsibility of recipient governments and resident representatives for monitoring and evaluation—the tripartite model. Evaluation became circumscribed in other ways as well: it should be done on a selective basis and restricted to the minimum essentials for improvement or follow-up of the projects concerned, in line with the general approach of the reform.

Nevertheless, evaluation was not restricted to projects. In March 1981, the administrator summarized the work done on thematic evaluations of technical cooperation activities. Seven studies had been completed and reports were being prepared on rural cooperatives, innovation and reform in education, and export promotion. A study on industrial training was in progress, while two others—on national agricultural research institutes and manufactures industries—were in the planning stage.[95]

PREPARING FOR THE THIRD DEVELOPMENT CYCLE

At its meeting in Geneva in June 1980, the Governing Council agreed to place even greater focus on the needs of the poorest countries in the next development cycle (1982–1986). It decided to allocate nearly 80 percent of all country IPFs to countries with annual per capita income of $500 or less, with special treatment for those whose per-capita GNP was below $250. For the second cycle, this percentage was less than 65 percent. However, it also agreed that every effort should be made to ensure that no country with a per-capita income below $3,000 would receive less UNDP assistance than in the second cycle and that no country with a higher income would have a new IPF less than 80 percent of the current figure. On the basis of these criteria, the council approved the IPF for each country, on the understanding that all IPFs would be cut by a flat percentage if resources failed to meet expectations. The calculations were based on the assumption that the funds available would increase by the same percentage as for the two previous development cycles, 14 percent. The same basic criteria as those used for the second cycle—GNP per capita and population size—were used to determine the IPF of the individual countries.[96]

Eighty-one percent of the IPFs should be allocated to individual countries and the remaining 19 percent to regional and global activities. The Governing Council also endorsed illustrative IPFs for each region.[97]

In June 1981, the Governing Council agreed to a $226 million regional program for Asia and the Pacific for the third cycle. Activities were to concentrate on seven key sectors: in prioritized order, energy; natural resources and the environment; transport and communications; human resources development; agriculture, fisheries, and forestry; planning and administration; technology and industry; and trade and economic cooperation. In all, the regional program included 159 projects. Governments gave highest priority to energy and to food production.[98]

A March 1981 UNDP report summarized interregional activities during the second cycle and proposed activities for the third (1982–1986). During the second cycle, priority had been given to the development of ocean fisheries and aquaculture (one-third of the resources) and to international trade projects (one-quarter of the resources), with a special public works program for the least-developed countries, training and advisory services in transport and communications, and health projects following next in importance. The interregional program for the third cycle continued to give priority to international trade and fisheries. However, greater diversification was planned that continued to emphasize training and human resources development.[99]

The Governing Council established a global IPF of $114.8 million for the third cycle, more than twice the $52.9 million it had approved for the second cycle, which had focused on agriculture. The new cycle added global projects in health-related areas that were designed to provide new institutional structures that were important for future development. It added energy as the third priority area.[100]

In mid-1981, the Governing Council confronted the prospect that the resources available for the third programming cycle might fall short of the total envisaged when it decided on the allocations in 1980. The council decided nonetheless to base its forward planning on the level envisaged and confirmed the figures it had approved for country, intercountry, and unallocated IPFs as well as for special program resources, special industrial services, and sector support. It urged the administrator to reduce the administrative budget, asked host governments to significantly raise their contributions toward the local costs of UNDP field offices, and called for measures to increase contributions and make better use of nonconvertible currencies.[101]

ECOSOC and the General Assembly supported this decision, urging all governments to renew their efforts to provide the UNDP with the resources necessary for carrying out the activities planned for the third cycle. The General Assembly expressed deep concern that the likely shortfall in 1982 might adversely affect the delivery of the program and asked the administrator to continue consultations with donor countries with a view to achieving the level of resources envisaged for 1982–1986.[102]

THE 1980 POLICY REVIEW OF OPERATIONAL ACTIVITIES

In 1980, the newly appointed director-general for development and international economic cooperation presented a report on policy issues pertaining to operational activities of the UN system, prepared in consultation with the Administrative Committee on Coordination. Although the report was generally applauded, many delegations voiced reservations about specific points it recommended, to some extent reflecting the changing zeitgeist of the early 1980s.[103] The main points included achieving greater predictability in funding development assistance by moving to multiyear rather than annual commitments. Reactions varied; while the Nordic countries argued for stability and predictability in the flow of funds, which multiyear pledging would facilitate, other major donor countries pointed at the constraints the budgetary procedures of nation-states caused.[104] The General Assembly, however, endorsed most of its recommendations.[105]

ACHIEVEMENTS OF THE SECOND DEVELOPMENT CYCLE

In his 1981 report to the Governing Council, the administrator summarized the main achievements of the second development cycle and indicated development trends by comparing them to the achievements of the first cycle and the aspirations of the third cycle.

Project-related expenditures were increasingly directed toward lower-income countries, especially in Africa and Asia. Least-developed countries accounted for 32.6 percent of all allocations to individual countries in the 1977–1981 cycle. The dollar value of the programs they received had doubled over the previous cycle. The poverty orientation of operational activities was further strengthened in the third cycle: least-developed countries were to receive 40.2 percent of IPF allocations, while countries with an annual GNP per capita below $500 were projected to receive almost 80 percent of the IPF allocations to countries.

The share of total UNDP expenditures that went to support industry, transportation and communications, human settlement, and policy, and planning had risen in the second cycle as compared to the first, while the share of expenditures for agriculture, population, health, and education had declined somewhat. The proportion allocated to natural resources, international trade and development finance, employment, and science and technology remained relatively unchanged between the two first cycles.

Other quantitative indicators for the two first cycles showed a rough doubling of voluntary contributions and expenditures during the second cycle, a substantial increase in cost-sharing contributions to UNDP-supported projects by developing-country and third-party governments, a decline in the value of contributions received that was especially severe in 1981 because of exchange-rate fluctuations, and a significant decline in the share of project expenditures on international project personnel that was counterbalanced by a growth in the training and equipment components. Further, there was an across-the-board increase in the share of project inputs provided by developing countries, particularly in terms of experts and subcontracts. The total investment commitments resulting from UNDP assistance for the two cycles was $42 billion.

The UNDP continued to shift the mode of its country and inter-country assistance from projects to programs. Previously, the adminis-trator argued, programs had been constructed on the basis of a list of projects rather than a comprehensive assessment of the technical coop-eration needs of countries. The UNDP had made little effort to assess link-ages between national objectives, sectoral diagnoses, and specific projects. He pointed to recent qualitative improvements in programming that included efforts to assess technical cooperation needs more rigorously, an integrated approach to sector assistance based on broader participa-tion by project-implementing agencies, greater use of project personnel from the recipient country concerned and greater emphasis on technical cooperation among developing countries, the provision for additionality and coordination with assistance from other sources, and closer relation-ships with related intercountry activities.[106]

The UNDP as Coordinator of UN Development Activities

The 1970 consensus assigned the UNDP a central role in coordinating the UN's development activities. The major changes were the new pro-gramming system and a more decentralized organization that delegated more authority to the resident representatives. The resident representa-tives were given an explicit coordination function at the country level. This was a significant change. In actual practice, the Secretariat as an opera-tional agency and the UN specialized agencies had for years implemented the development assistance made available through the UNDP along with development projects within their specific fields of competence funded from their regular budgets.

During the early years the share financed from the regular budgets of the Secretariat and the specialized agencies was marginal; most of the funding for the operational development activities came from the EPTA and the Special Fund (and later the UNDP). In the late 1960s and increasingly in the 1970s, a larger share came from the regular budgets of the Secretariat and specialized agencies. Even more important, bilateral donor agencies increasingly provided funding directly to these agencies for specific purposes within their areas. The UN and its specialized agen-cies actively sought this type of funding and established new funds for specific activities. In 1978, the Department of Technical Cooperation for

Development was set up within the Secretariat to strengthen the coordination of its development operations. Although the UNDP remained the largest funding agency for development assistance involving technical assistance and pre-investment activities, the muscles of other arms within the UN system were growing. The World Bank also expanded its activities within these fields.

The administrator read the signals. At the June–July 1977 session of the Governing Council, he presented a report that examined the evolving role of the UNDP during the period of financial difficulties since 1975. He asked the council to clarify, in particular, the nature of the UNDP's contribution to development efforts, its coordinating role within the UN development system as a whole, and its role as a funding channel for technical cooperation.[107]

The Governing Council reconfirmed the principles established in the 1970 consensus and asked the UNDP, in cooperation with its specialized agency partners, to strive for greater coherence, especially by further developing planning, appraisal, and evaluation functions into a comprehensive system of analysis and feedback. It appealed to governments to increase their contributions to the maximum and to "contribute to the maintaining of the coherence of the United Nations system by avoiding the creation of new technical co-operation funds" and "by bringing such existing funds [wherever feasible] within the framework of the United Nations Development Programme." It also appealed to governments to "consider the possibility of giving indications of contributions over a period of several years." The council reaffirmed the validity of the 1970 consensus, which assigned to the UNDP the role of central funding body for technical cooperation at the UN. It asked the administrator to invite interested governments for informal discussions "with a view to the equitable sharing of the responsibility for providing resources for the Programme and with a view to achieving, if possible, a multiyear financial basis for the Programme for programming purposes."[108] ECOSOC endorsed the decisions taken by the Governing Council, as did the General Assembly.[109]

Nevertheless, the proliferation of funding for development within the multilateral system continued, challenging the UNDP's authority as the coordinating agency. Its role was also affected by the administrative reforms detailed above. In 1981, the UNDP's share of total development expenditures of the UN was only 11.1 percent. Total UN expenditures on operational activities for development amounted to $6 billion, of which

$2.1 billion was in grants, $1.7 billion in loans, and $2.1 billion in non-concessional assistance.[110] The World Bank (through the IDA) provided most of the loans on concessional terms and most of the nonconcessional assistance as well.[111]

Multilateral development assistance provided on a grant basis calls for special attention when assessing UNDP's relative position within the UN system. Here the UNDP maintained its position as the largest funding agency; it distributed 31 percent of development-related grants in 1981. Nevertheless, large shares were financed by other UN agencies—the WFP (25.1 percent), UNICEF (10.1 percent), and the UNFPA (5.8 percent). Increasing shares were financed from their regular budgets (9.9 percent) and from extra-budgetary resources provided to them by bilateral agencies for special purposes (14.9 percent).[112] A similar trend is evident in the UN's technical cooperation expenditures in 1981.[113] Contributions to the specialized agencies were rising, partly through the growth of their regular budgets and partly because of the continued growth in extra-budgetary contributions placed at their disposal.

The intergovernmental bodies did not approve of these trends. In a resolution in July 1981, ECOSOC reaffirmed "the central funding and co-ordinating role" of the UNDP in the field of technical cooperation at the UN and referred to the 1970 consensus and a number of later General Assembly resolutions.[114]

Emphasis on the Least-Developed Countries

The UN development strategy for the 1970s emphasized the urgent development needs of the LDCs. During subsequent years, the intergovernmental bodies responsible for the UNDP, especially the General Assembly, consistently expressed this concern.

This focus on poverty was implemented through guidelines set for distributing available resources and in the actual distribution of UNDP resources and those of its trust funds. In 1972, the Governing Council increased the share of resources to be received by the twenty-five LDCs to an eventual 20 to 25 percent of the total and authorized the administrator to work with governments to program new and supplementary activities adapted to their special needs. A special measure program was started the following year, with a target of $35 million for the period 1973–1976. These adjustments were made to create greater equity in the overall distribution. During this period, $27.9 million was actually used.[115]

In the second development cycle (1977–1981), even more attention was focused on the least-developed countries. As we have seen, one-third of the available resources for country programming was to be allocated to the needs of the LDCs and about two-thirds to developing countries with an annual GNP per capita of $300 or less. In the third cycle (1982–1986), the poverty orientation of operational activities was further strengthened: these countries were to receive 40.2 percent of IPF allocations, while all countries with an annual GNP per capita of under $500 were projected to receive almost 80 percent of country IPF allocations. In the first year of the second cycle, special measures for the LDCs were allocated $9.6 million of the field programs (2.9 percent) in addition to contributions from the Programme Reserve.[116]

In 1972, the Governing Council invited the administrator to explore the possibility of using the modest resources available to the UN Capital Development Fund to finance self-contained capital projects in the least-developed countries, primarily projects relating to industrial development. The following year it formally decided that projects in LDCs should be the primary focus of the fund. Both ECOSOC and the General Assembly welcomed this decision and asked the UNDP to report on all measures it had taken over the previous eighteen months to improve the quality and expand the quantity of technical and pre-investment assistance it had provided to this group of countries.[117]

Particular attention was also devoted to other specific groups of countries confronted with special problems, including landlocked countries, a group of island countries, and the countries hit by the international economic crisis during the second half of the 1970s and after.[118] They had already been identified as special target groups in the international strategies for the second and third UN development decades, and many of the countries belonging to these groups were also among the LDCs.

In September 1981, the United Nations Conference on the Least Developed Countries brought the situation of the LDCs to the fore on the international agenda.[119] The conference adopted a Programme of Action for the 1980s. Its main objectives were to promote structural changes to overcome the extreme economic difficulties of LDCs; to provide internationally accepted minimum standards for the poor; to identify and support major investment opportunities and priorities; and to mitigate the adverse effects of natural disasters. The Programme of Action asserted that every least-developed country should be enabled to increase its national income substantially, even double it by 1990 as compared with the late 1970s. This would require an annual growth rate of 7.2 percent. The countries themselves would set appropriate national objectives, giving a priority to agriculture that surpassed the 4 percent target set for the Third Development Decade. This, according to the Programme of Action, would increase food production and food security and eliminate hunger and malnutrition by 1990 at the latest. The conference also gave high priority to comprehensive and integrated rural development. It called on the LDCs to mobilize their human resources through education, training, and providing incentives. The conference document emphasized the indispensable role of women in development.

Only a substantial increase in ODA in real terms during the 1980s would enable the LDCs to achieve these objectives. The donor countries reaffirmed their commitment to the target of 0.7 percent of GNP in ODA; most donors would devote 0.15 percent of their GNP to the LDCs, while others would double their ODA to this group compared to the previous five years.

The Programme of Action based its analysis and recommendations on a holistic development perspective that was characteristic of the time and was expressed in the DD3 strategy. On 17 December 1981, it was endorsed by the General Assembly.[120]

The conference gave a renewed boost to the special situation of the groups of countries noted above. The UNDP Governing Council appealed to all countries to review their positions on the special fund for landlocked countries and contribute "urgently and generously." The General Assembly urged member states to give due consideration to the special constraints affecting the landlocked developing countries.[121] However, the issue was controversial with major donors and with neighboring transit states. Almost no additional funding came forward.

Cooperation between Developing Countries

In the mid-1970s, collective self-reliance emerged as a central theme in the NIEO strategy: this ideology held that developing countries should increase cooperation among themselves. In December 1972, the General Assembly asked the UNDP Governing Council to convene a working group to explore the best way for developing countries to share their capacities and experiences with each order in order to increase and improve development assistance. It also asked the council to investigate the relative possibilities and advantages of regional and interregional technical cooperation among developing countries.[122] A working group of the Governing Council was assigned these tasks.

In its report, the working group recognized the difficulties involved in achieving more effective cooperation that could add an important dimension to the existing programs of bilateral and multilateral development cooperation. It proposed creating a special unit within the UNDP secretariat to promote technical cooperation among developing countries. It also advised the UNDP and the executing agencies and regional commissions to collaborate more closely in formulating and implementing projects. In 1974, the Governing Council passed these recommendations to the General Assembly, which in turn asked the administrator and all agencies and institutions involved to implement them.[123]

In 1976, the UNDP administrator reported to the Governing Council about a series of UNDP initiatives to assist governments in initiating cooperation between themselves in various technical cooperation schemes. The UNDP had increased such cooperation in the execution of its own projects, he stated. Among the strategies it had used was an information referral service designed to provide developing countries with information on the technical assistance resources available for bilateral or multilateral cooperation with other developing countries.[124]

However, the 1978 Conference on Technical Co-operation among Developing Countries—and the planning process involved—was the UN's main effort to generate cooperation between developing countries at that time. In 1976, the UNDP, working together with the regional commissions, organized regional meetings in Bangkok (Thailand), Lima (Peru), and Addis Ababa (Ethiopia) where governments of these regions could identify each other's capabilities and specific regional problems that could be addressed through technical cooperation with other governments in the region and to consider ways and means for extending such cooperation.[125] During 1977, the UNDP formulated a draft world plan of action for the conference, which took place in August and September 1978 in Buenos Aires.[126]

The conference adopted a Plan of Action for Promoting and Implementing Technical Co-operation among Developing Countries with thirty-eight recommendations for action at the national, subregional, regional, and global levels. The plan stated that the UNDP, in particular, could support technological cooperation and prepare progress reports on implementing the plan. Developed countries could increase their voluntary contribution to the UN's operational programs and accelerate the process of untying their development assistance.[127]

The plan of action can be read as a document containing the common wisdom of the day on the topic of how cooperation between developing countries could be attained and how the various actors could contribute to this end. The General Assembly considered the conference in Buenos Aires "a major step in the strengthening of co-operation among developing countries" and felt that implementing its decisions would be a "major contribution in the evolution of international co-operation for development and in the establishment of a new international economic order." It endorsed the plan of action and invited countries to attend a high-level meeting of representatives of all states participating in the UNDP to undertake an overall intergovernmental review of the technical cooperation among developing countries within the UN system.[128]

The first high-level review conference met in Geneva in May–June 1980. One hundred sixteen states and representatives from organizations that participated in the UN development system attended. The conference adopted eight decisions by consensus on the last day of the meeting.[129] Immediately, the Governing Council followed up on several of the recommendations, including one involving a flexible use of country IPFs for technical cooperation among developing countries. However, the council added that this should be regarded only as a supplement to financing by developing countries themselves.[130]

The second session of the high-level review conference—renamed the High-level Committee on the Review of Technical Co-operation among Developing Countries by the General Assembly—was organized at UN headquarters in June 1981. In one of the ten decisions adopted, it urged action to reverse what it considered insufficient progress in implementing the Buenos Aires plan of action. It followed up on other key areas identified in the plan involving financing and exchange of information and institutional arrangements. The General Assembly passed a resolution that urged governments to implement the agreement reached by the committee.[131] As the Second Committee was preparing this resolution, the dissatisfaction with what had been achieved came into the open, especially the lack of support from developed countries for development activities.[132]

Promoting the NIEO

Several of the activities already mentioned promoted a new international economic order. The promotion of technical cooperation between developing countries is a case in point. As part of the UNDP's interregional activities to this end, a major study was completed in 1978 on balance-of-payments adjustments. In another initiative, the UNDP, in cooperation with UNCTAD, drew up a joint program on economic and technical cooperation among developing countries. In preparation for UNCTAD's fifth session, which was scheduled for May 1979, the UNDP made recommendations for action by developing countries. It also helped fifteen West African countries form the West African Rice Development Association, which helped introduce irrigation and develop high-yielding strains of rice.

The research-oriented global programs built up networks that focused on issues central to development needs with a particular emphasis on improved food and health measures. In 1979, these networks covered such fields as basic agricultural research, low-cost water sanitation technology, rice testing, nitrogen fixing in soil, animal diseases, and research on diarrhoeal diseases. Both global and interregional activities worked on anti-poverty policies. For example, a major interregional program in labor-intensive public works that was administered through the ILO involved twenty least-developed and five developing countries. This program mobilized international support for construction projects that generated an estimated 350,000 person-months of employment for 100,000 men and women, many of who were landless laborers who worked seasonally on the projects.[133]

Nevertheless, the 1980 policy review of UNDP development assistance made it clear that employment was not its first priority. UNCTAD and UNIDO were the primary UN organizations that drove policy issues regarding employment.

Attracting Additional Funding for Development

The main rationale for the UNDP's large-scale pre-investment projects was to attract and generate additional capital investments from other resources—in and out of the recipient country—to take advantage of the investment opportunities that had been uncovered. These pre-investment projects were usually joint projects between the UNDP and the recipient government, which would often cover most of the project costs. In 1972 investment commitments in UNDP-assisted projects amounted to $3.1 billion, twice the amount of the previous year.[134] In the following years, they continued at a high level, amounting to about $4 billion in 1980 and $4.8 billion in 1981, mostly from sources in the country concerned and mainly focused on the industrial sector.[135]

In order to stimulate pre-investment activities and follow-up investments, an Invest Development Office at UN headquarters in New York was established in January 1979. This office entered into cooperative arrangements with the FAO Investment Centre and began negotiating similar agreements with other executing agencies. It also strengthened special-interest arrangements with the World Bank and the International Fund for Agriculture and Development (IFAD) and the regional development banks. In 1981, the UNDP entered into new cooperative agreements with the ILO, UNESCO, UNIDO, and the UN Department of Technical Cooperation for Development. It strengthened arrangements with development finance institutions through a greater flow of project and country program information related to possible investment opportunities. In cooperation with the Economic Development Institute of the World Bank, it offered training courses in investment development for UNDP resident representatives and their deputies.[136]

In June 1981, the Governing Council asked the administrator to strengthen relationships with multilateral financial institutions and regional development banks and other sources of finance. It authorized the use of $100,000 from the 1981 special program resources, in addition to a similar amount from the 1980 budget, to implement cooperative arrangements with participating and executing agencies directed toward generating the information required to make such projects attractive to potential investors. The council invited governments to give due priority to pre-investment activities when preparing their country programs.[137]

Pre-investment activities were not the only method the UNDP used to generate support from potential donors and other sources for specific projects. It also helped prepare projects, financed action plans, and organized conferences and symposia to facilitate funding.[138]

The UNDP's efforts to involve development finance institutions more strongly in these activities, particularly the World Bank, were not uncontroversial. During the debate in the Second Committee on operational activities for development, the Soviet Union stated that it opposed control of UNDP activities by the World Bank and similar institutions.[139]

Extra-Budgetary Activities: The Special Funds

A characteristic feature of the way the UNDP organized its operational activities, especially pre-investment activities, has been that of producing additional resources for development. From the beginning, most of its field operations were to a large extent—on average about 60 percent—financed by the governments with which it was cooperating. These governments increasingly "owned" the projects, to use the rhetoric of the 1980s and 1990s. Some activities under the UNDP's responsibility were to be financed explicitly outside of the ordinary budget. During the 1970s, such activities were expanding, both in number and magnitude in terms of funding and complexity.

This applied to activities under a plan for providing operational, executive, and administrative personnel in the field of public administration. Experts were appointed as officials of recipient governments while at the same time remaining in the employ of the UN or specialized agencies participating in the scheme.[140] However, the main activity of this kind related to a growing number of trust funds and a variety of other special funds. By the end of the decade, their number had risen to sixteen, although some of them were dormant. These activities were increasingly integrated in the ordinary program of the UNDP: resources from its ordinary program were in various ways added for purposes that originally were to be financed outside the program.

After the reorganization in 1971, the administrator continued to carry the responsibility of a number of the extra-budgetary operations referred to above. A few of these related to operations within certain crisis-ridden countries: the UN fund for the development of West Irian, the Swedish-funded trust funds for Lesotho and Swaziland, and the Trust Fund for the United Nations Korean Reconstruction Agency.[141] Others had a more general orientation, such as the United Nations Capital Development Fund (UNCDF), the United Nations Fund for Population Activities (UNFPA), and the United Nations Volunteers. From a hesitant beginning in the late 1960s, these had developed into major—to some extent independent—programs by the 1970s. Other funds never got off the ground, including the fund established to address the specific development problems of landlocked countries[142] and, in the 1970s, the fund established to assist in the economic and social development of the Palestinian people.

The growing number of funds, the increase in funding, and the diversity of activities involved led the UNDP to establish the Bureau for Special Activities in 1979. Its job was to coordinate these activities with those of the regional bureaus and other UNDP units.

The number of special funds continued to grow. In 1980, two new—and increasingly important—special funds came under the responsibility of UNDP. One of these, the Interim Fund for Science and Technology for Development, emerged as a follow-up of the 1979 UN conference held in Vienna on that theme. It was to finance an ambitious program of action.[143] Late in 1980, the Secretary-General delegated to the UNDP the responsibility for managing and administering international and regional projects for the Voluntary Fund for the United Nations Decade for Women.[144] In June 1980, the Governing Council also authorized the administrator, on an interim basis, to seek and accept voluntary contributions in kind and cash to undertake specific projects in the field of energy designed to meet urgent needs for assistance, especially among the poorest developing countries.[145] Since these activities were barely in the making at the end of the decade, they are mentioned only in passing here.

The UNDP's network of regional and national offices invested time and administrative resources to assist with emergency and relief operations on behalf of the UN system.[146] Various UN programs and organizations were involved in providing disaster relief assistance. The United Nations Disaster Relief Organization remained the focal point for the coordination of such efforts, serving as a clearinghouse for assistance extended by external sources. However, some of these relief, rehabilitation, and recovery programs found themselves offering something that was in between development and relief, as exemplified by the assistance to Sudano-Sahelian populations mentioned below.[147]

In 1981, the last year of the period under review in this chapter, the UNDP administered thirteen trust funds with a total expenditure of $75 million. Here we will focus on only a few: the UN Capital Development Fund, the UN Fund for Population Activities (although it was not any longer under the UNDP), the UN Volunteers, the UN Trust Fund for Assistance to Colonial Countries and Peoples, the UN Revolving Fund for Natural Resource Exploration, and the UN Sahelian Office.

THE UNITED NATIONS CAPITAL DEVELOPMENT FUND

The United Nations Capital Development Fund was established in 1967 by representatives of developing countries against the will of the major industrialized countries. In a way, it represented a continuation of the old fight over SUNFED. With the main western powers in opposition, almost no funding was forthcoming.

The Governing Council's decisions, in 1972 and 1973, that the fund should mainly serve the least-developed countries changed this situation. At the joint UNDP/UNCDF pledging conference in October 1973, substantial pledges were received for the first time (although at the modest level of $5.4 million). The following year the UNCDF entered full-scale operation. By the end of that year, fifty-seven countries had contributed a total of $14.6 million; Denmark, Egypt, India, the Netherlands, Norway, Pakistan, and Yugoslavia were among the major donors. UNCDF projects were broadly classified into the categories of social infrastructure, productive facilities, and production credits. The LDCs and those with similar economic conditions were to receive assistance on grant terms. Projects were designed to facilitate rapid implementation, using simple technology adapted to local conditions and relying on organizations and agencies that could provide supportive local expertise for managerial and technical assistance.[148] That was a function far removed from the aspirations of those who had pressed for the fund's establishment.

In subsequent years, the UNCDF granted small loans to encourage initiative and assist small enterprises among the poorest people in the world's poorest countries. By the end of 1978, ninety-eight projects in twenty-six countries were running, at a cost of $72 million. This was a 53 percent increase over its 1977 activities. And the UNCDF kept growing: contributions pledged for 1979 rose by 39 percent to $25 million. In the years that followed, the number of projects and the amounts provided continued to increase. By the end of 1979, total commitments amounted to $112.4 million for 133 projects, and by the end of 1980 the commitments had risen to $165 million. In 1979, the Governing Council approved a change from full to partial funding (funding on a cash-flow basis). This enabled the UNCDF to increase its programming capacity beyond immediately available resources. In 1981, its operations accelerated sharply: project expenditures amounted to $48.2 million, a 150 percent increase over the previous year, while new commitments approved that year amounted to $71 million.[149]

By the end of 1981, total cumulative commitments had reached $220.1 million for 188 projects in forty-two countries, including twenty-four projects that had been completed. Of the thirty-nine recipient countries at that time, thirty-one were LDCs and the others were countries that the General Assembly had directed be accorded similar consideration. About 80 percent of the assistance continued to be channeled toward rural development. The UNCDF worked to increase cooperation with international and bilateral agencies and multilateral financing institutions and with UN regional commissions and other regional bodies, especially in such areas as desertification control, water resources management, and other priority sectors affecting less-developed countries.[150]

In December 1981, the General Assembly reaffirmed the role of the UNCDF "as a supplementary source of concessional capital assistance, first and foremost to the least developed among the developing countries." It endorsed the fund's program orientation and operational policy and stressed the importance of achieving a balance between resources allocated for meeting basic needs of low-income groups and those required for strengthening productive sectors and dealing with other bottlenecks, with a view to promoting national self-reliance and accelerated self-sustained economic growth in the LDCs. It appealed to governments to provide financial support to the fund.[151] By its seventh year of operation, the UNCDF had become a well-established development institution: it had shown that it could fulfill ambitious expectations.

THE UNITED NATIONS FUND FOR POPULATION ACTIVITIES

In 1967, the UN Fund for Population Activities was established as a trust fund of the Secretary-General. In 1969, the UNDP administrator was given responsibility for overall management of this fund. However, in December 1972, the General Assembly placed it under the authority of the assembly as a separate agency headed by an executive director. The UNDP Governing Council was to serve as the governing body also of the UNFPA, with due regard to ECOSOC's responsibilities and policy functions.[152]

The population issue had been central all along, although with varying focal points. In the UN setting, the World Population Plan of Action, the major outcome of the World Population Conference in 1974, provided direction to these efforts. At the policy level, the Population Commission of ECOSOC was instrumental in keeping the issue on the international agenda and giving it direction. The growth of the world population, especially in developing countries, and its impact on social and economic development remained the core issue, although specifics such as mortality (particularly child mortality) and the trend toward greater urbanization and migration also attracted considerable attention. Most governments saw population-related problems as critical factors for the success of their national development efforts. Nevertheless, perspectives differed.[153] As with other policy areas, the UN emphasized providing analyses of development trends and disseminating such information.[154]

On 4 August 1976, ECOSOC endorsed general principles for future resource allocations, based on a report by the UNFPA's executive director. The fund should promote population activities proposed in international strategies, especially the World Population Plan of Action; it should seek to meet the needs of developing countries, "which have the most urgent need for assistance" in population activities; it should "respect the sovereign right of each nation to formulate, promote and implement its own population policies"; it should promote the recipient countries' self-reliance; and it should "give special attention to meeting the needs of disadvantaged population groups." The General Assembly agreed, noting with satisfaction that the UNFPA had become "a most effective and viable entity" within the UN system, thanks not least to its increased resources.[155]

In June 1981, the Governing Council established more specific priorities related to the main categories of activities. The fund should concentrate on the following areas, listed in order of priority: family planning, including training of personnel about and research into contraceptive methods; educating the public and disseminating family planning information; collecting basic data; population dynamics; and population policy formulation, implementation, and evaluation. The executive director was asked to report on the possibilities of substantially expanding family planning, education, and communication activities at the expense of work on data collection and population dynamics.[156]

As was the case with the UNDP, UN organizations implemented the projects: during the initial period (1969–1972), the largest shares were implemented by the UN proper (34 percent), the WHO (26 percent), and UNICEF (10 percent), while the ILO, the FAO, and UNESCO each obtained allocations that amounted to less than 8 percent. It follows that a wide range of population projects were funded by the UNFPA.[157] The sector-wise distribution in 1973 can illustrate the profile in its initial phase (percentages in parentheses): family planning (29.4), communication and education (17.4), basic population data (16.1), multidisciplinary activities

(16.1), population dynamics (12.8), program development (5.9), and population policy (2.3).[158]

During the following years, the UNFPA developed into a major funding agency in the UN system. Allocations continued to increase, reaching $151 million in 1980 before declining in 1981. The reason for the decline was the same as in the case of the UNDP: a sharp reduction in pledges in 1980 and 1981. The reduced resource level necessitated extensive reprogramming and adjustments in the work plan for 1982–1986.[159]

The UNFPA's main features were already clear in the initial period. Within its policy area, it followed patterns similar to those of the UNDP. Most of the project assistance was executed by the UN and its specialized agencies, particularly the WHO, although the UNFPA itself implemented a large and expanding share of the resources. Increasingly, family planning became the main activity; the UNFPA devoted about 40 percent of its resources to such projects and programs. Most of the remaining resources were spent on basic population data, population dynamics, communication, and education within this field. The largest share went to Asia and the Pacific (40 percent in 1981), followed by Africa and Latin America. As was the case with UNDP programming, the UNFPA set aside resources also for interregional and global activities. Long-term commitments were introduced as well. In 1979, the UNDP Governing Council agreed that unless decided otherwise, allocations to new large-scale projects and programs would be approved for their whole duration (up to five years).[160]

THE UNITED NATIONS VOLUNTEERS

In 1970, the General Assembly decided to establish a volunteers program to provide an opportunity for young people to be actively involved in the UN system's social and economic development activities. ECOSOC reviewed the program the following year. All specialized agencies and volunteer organizations concerned were requested to coordinate all volunteer activities in UN-assisted projects with the coordinator of the UN Volunteers. The General Assembly supported the new endeavor, insisting that UN Volunteers should not be sent to any country without the explicit request and approval of the recipient government.[161]

In 1976, the UN Volunteers were given an extended mandate. The Secretary-General recommended that the UN Volunteers program be designated as the principal operational unit of the UN for executing youth programs and that the terms of reference of the Special Voluntary

Fund be expanded to include additional contributions for those purposes. ECOSOC agreed, as did the General Assembly. The terms of the Special Voluntary Fund were expanded to include any youth programs requested by developing countries.[162] In 1967, the UNDP and the UNV funded a joint regional project with eight Latin American countries. The General Assembly also asked the administrator to expand the UNV's activities in the field of domestic development services.[163] In this connection, the Asian and Pacific Forum of Domestic Development Services was established as an advisory group to the UN Volunteers; it consisted of both governmental and nongovernmental organizations. In a 1978 report to the Governing Council, the administrator wrote that the UNV had increasingly been recognized in the least-developed countries as being useful at the grassroots level in such areas as literacy, primary health care, vocational/technical training, and agricultural development.[164]

The number of volunteers was increasing annually, most of them serving in the LDCs. Moreover, an increasing share of volunteers was recruited from developing countries.[165] In 1979, the General Assembly accepted the General Council's suggestion to increase the number of volunteers to 1,000 by 1983.[166] This target was met well ahead of schedule: by the middle of 1981, 1,000 volunteers were serving in the field. However, funding was not readily forthcoming despite favorable comments and repeated appeals by intergovernmental bodies, including the General Assembly, for increased contributions to the Special Voluntary Fund.[167]

In December 1981, the General Assembly noted that it considered the program "a valuable instrument of multilateral technical co-operation in response to the needs of the developing countries, in particular the least developed and the newly independent countries" and reiterated its appeal to "governments, organizations and individuals" to contribute or raise their contributions to the Special Voluntary Fund.[168]

In creating the UN Volunteers, the UN system was not ahead of the curve. The idea of providing opportunities for idealistic and adventurous youth to take part in one of the greatest challenges of our time in a practical and meaningful way had been generated, institutionalized, and put into practice by the United States and other bilateral donors before it was taken up by the world body. However, some new elements were added that reflected the UN institutional setting. Most of the qualities of the bilateral experiments with the idea were retained. Those who were recruited were young people who combined idealism with competence of a kind that was in demand. In contrast to the forms bilateral peace corps took, however, this one recruited its members internationally, and they left their national flags behind. The emphasis was not just on where the volunteers were to serve but also on where they were recruited from. The focus of service was in the LDCs, and the volunteers were recruited from the developing countries themselves, which added a new dimension to the idea of self-reliance. And UN Volunteers had to be explicitly requested by the host countries concerned—the trademark of UNDP development efforts ever since the start.

THE UNITED NATIONS NATIONAL LIBERATION MOVEMENT TRUST FUND

At the 1973 pledging conference, the Netherlands pledged special financial resources for the benefit of colonial countries and people. On this basis, the UNDP established a trust fund for national liberation movements. Of the initial allocation of $1.5 million, one-third was channeled through UNICEF to assist in financing a joint UNDP/UNICEF/WHO health project for national liberation movements in Tanzania and Zambia. The remaining was earmarked for a series of regional projects to benefit several national liberation movements. These allocations took place in close consultation with the OAU and the host governments where the national liberation movements were based. Assistance was also provided to transitional governments.[169]

The following year, the UNDP entered into formal agreement with the OAU: assistance to various colonial peoples and liberation movements recognized by the OAU would be channeled through the OAU secretariat. The UNDP proposed to provide an indicative planning figure of $2 million for use by the Comoros, French Somaliland, and Seychelles and a separate indicative planning figure of $1 million for Namibia. It also entered into discussions with several liberation movements with a view to providing assistance.[170] Offices to assist some of these organizations had been or were being established in Gabon, Guinea-Bissau, and Zambia. It was the UNDP's policy to continue cooperation with transitional governments and the liberation movements of countries on the verge of independence and to support projects initiated outside such countries.

At its June 1975 session, the Governing Council found that limited funding was the major constraint and urged increased support for the trust fund. It approved indicative planning figures for the current period as well as for the next planning cycle (1977–1981). At its January–February 1976 session, the council requested the administrator to use Namibia's IPF to finance requests submitted by the UN Commissioner for Namibia and to continue to respond to requests for assistance from the South West Africa People's Organization. Support was planned for the Institute for Namibia, which was training a cadre of civil servants in preparation for independence. By 1977, commitments for such projects had reached nearly $12 million. Half of this amount was IPF the Governing Council had authorized for technical cooperation with national liberation movements. In 1979, assistance through the OAU and the trust fund totaled $24.7 million.[171]

The idea of providing assistance to people suffering under colonialism and white minority rule was far from new to the UN system: for years, the UN had been at the helm of efforts to end colonialism and white minority rule, including the apartheid system in South Africa. Nevertheless, support for liberation movements engaged in violent struggle represented a new dimension that, in the late 1960s and early 1970s, clashed with another sacred principle on which the UN system was founded: the sovereignty of the nation-state and the principle of nonintervention in internal affairs.

The UN system was not ahead of the curve. A few governments, including those of the Nordic countries, had taken the lead. They carefully chose the form of assistance they provided. In addition to political support, it included humanitarian assistance to the victims of colonialism and apartheid in combination with assistance that could prepare them for independence, particularly in terms of education. The amounts provided during the 1970s were modest. However, when voluntary contributions were not forthcoming to the extent expected, intergovernmental bodies stepped in with extra resources, including from the IPFs. Although the amounts remained modest, the fact that such assistance was provided had an important function: it legitimized this kind of assistance to liberation movements, especially in Southern Africa and the Portuguese colonies, by bilateral donors. This applied especially to the Nordic governments. It applied less to the East European governments that were providing the liberation movements with what they wanted and needed the most: military training and weapons.

THE UNITED NATIONS REVOLVING FUND FOR NATURAL RESOURCE EXPLORATION

In December 1973, the General Assembly established the UN Revolving Fund for Natural Resource Exploration. It was to be administered on behalf of the Secretary-General by the UNDP administrator during the first four years, with the Governing Council as governing body.[172] The rationale for the fund, and accordingly the modalities, were the risks involved in such exploration: few ventures actually led to the discovery of exploitable ore bodies. The fund was intended to assist countries in carrying out exploration projects that they were themselves unable to undertake. Although surveys were to be undertaken at the request of the government concerned, repayment obligation would be incurred only if and when the activities of the fund resulted in new mineral production. However, only modest resources were placed at the disposal of the fund.[173]

THE UNITED NATIONS SAHELIAN OFFICE

In 1976, the administrator was given responsibility for the UN Sahelian Office, established in 1973, and for the UN Trust Fund for Sudano-Sahelian Activities. It came into full operation with old and new responsibilities in 1979. The Sudano-Sahelian Office had been mandated by the General Assembly to act as the UN's central coordinating mechanism for implementing the medium- and long-term recovery and rehabilitation programs of the Permanent Inter-State Committee on Drought Control in the Sahel and its eight member states. In 1976, the original fifty-two priority projects had increased to ninety projects that cost $400 million. By the end of 1980, the number of projects had increased to 113—twenty-five regional and eighty-eight national—requiring financing of $646 million. At that point, about $368 million had become available from bilateral and multilateral sources, including more than $51 million through the UN Trust Fund.

In 1978, the General Assembly designated the office as the body responsible for helping fifteen countries in the region combat desertification. In 1980, three countries were added to the original list. This expanded operation of helping the countries of the Sudano-Sahelian and adjacent regions implement the Plan of Action to Combat Desertification, a joint UNDP/UNEP venture, was to assist the eight drought-stricken countries of the Sahel without prejudice. By the end of 1978, the program involved 110 projects at a total cost of more than $550 million. It covered a range of fields, including agriculture, irrigation, hydraulic development, livestock development, and road building. The office was responsible for raising $295 million of the total. By the end of 1980, the number of anti-desertification projects that had been identified and formulated with the governments of the region had increased to 118, with a price tag of $644 million.[174]

Pledges and Distribution of Resources

GROWTH IN VOLUNTARY CONTRIBUTIONS

During the 1970s, voluntary contributions by governments continued to grow. In current values, the contributions more than tripled from 1970 to 1980. Then, from 1981 on, an opposite trend emerged. Although many countries contributed, most funding continued to come from western countries, with the United States as the major contributor. However, the relative contribution of the United States was reduced quite drastically, from 40 percent in the 1960s to below 20 percent during the latter 1970s. Next to the United States, Sweden, Denmark, and (toward the end of the decade) the Netherlands were large contributors. The Federal Republic of Germany also emerged as a major contributor, and the United Kingdom and Canada continued in this league. Norway joined their ranks in the mid-1970s, and in the 1980s, Japan became a major contributor.

A new pattern emerged beginning in 1973, when the three Scandinavian countries (Denmark, Norway, and Sweden) together became the main contributor to the UNDP. During the 1970s and beyond, these countries, together with the other Nordic countries, operated as a group at the UN. On most issues relating to development and the promotion of a new economic order, they usually worked closely together with the Netherlands, another major contributor to the UNDP. During the second half of the 1970s, these four countries together contributed almost double the amount of the United States.[175]

REGIONAL DISTRIBUTION OF RESOURCES

Established patterns of distribution were, by and large, followed in the geographical distribution of resources. In the 1960s, special emphasis was placed on the development challenges in Africa. As can be seen from table 7.8, Africa received the most assistance during the 1970s as well, followed by Asia and the Far East, while Latin America's share began to dwindle. Also, in the new programming system instituted in 1972, a significant share was reserved for regional, interregional, and global projects.

These trends continued in the 1980s. The program for the third development cycle (1982–1986) distributed resources across the regions and among intercountry programs in roughly the same proportion as the 1977–1981 cycle.[176]

DISTRIBUTION OF ASSISTANCE ON ECONOMIC AND SOCIAL SECTORS

The 1970s started in the same vein as the 1960s ended: ECOSOC asked the UNDP Governing Council to pay special attention to requests from governments in the area of industrial development, especially requests for industrial technological development and industrial pilot projects from the least-developed countries.[177]

In 1971, the General Assembly established an ad hoc committee on cooperation between the UNDP and UNIDO.[178] In response to the committee's report, the Governing Council recognized the central role of UNIDO in coordinating UN industrial development activities and the UNDP and UNIDO committed to harmonization of their activities through periodic consultations. This understanding was later endorsed by ECOSOC and the General Assembly.[179]

In the 1970s, more than a quarter of all resources continued to be channeled into agricultural development (see table 7.9). In addition, the pressure in intergovernmental bodies for greater attention to industrial development worked: during the first eight years of the 1970s, a growing share of total resources was devoted to industrial development. Policy and planning also received a large share, well above 10 percent. The same applied to transportation and communications. Education also stayed at about the same level during the 1970s, somewhat below 10 percent, which was lower than levels of support in the late 1960s. The share allocated to health stayed around 5 percent. These were all core areas in traditional development assistance. The table reveals the modest attention given to the new sectors that the NIEO emphasized. For example, allocations for international trade remained below 3 percent throughout the decade. The explanation may be that the traditional sectors were also core sectors in the new context and were considered necessary for creating both self-reliance and a new international order. An institutional explanation can be added: UNCTAD and not the UNDP was in charge of the new policy area.

Some Concluding Observations

In the 1970s, some important changes took place in the UNDP's development role. Three interrelated changes merit particular note here.

The first change relates to the administrative reform of the system. As we have seen, the new decade started with a reform that sought to improve the UNDP's capacity to effectively deliver a greater amount of development assistance. System reform also aimed at strengthening established

TABLE 7.8.

Distribution of UNDP Field Assistance by Region,[1] Selected Years, 1971–1981 (by percent and in millions of U.S. dollars)

	1971	1973	1975	1977	1979	1981
Africa	32.0	27.2	25.8	31.2	31.4	30.2
Asia and the Far East[2]	24.5	20.6	21.3	28.3	29.3	26.0
Latin America	20.6	18.3	20.1	17.7	19.0	11.6
Europe, Mediterranean and the Middle East	20.2	20.1	16.9	18.6	----[3]	----
Arab States	----	----	----	----	12.8	11.8
Europe	----	----	----	----	4.2	2.3
Regional	----	11.6	13.2	0.0	0.0	13.3
Interregional	2.7	1.4	1.8	2.3	1.5	1.3
Global	0.0	0.7	0.9	1.9	1.8	3.3
TOTAL[4]	100.0	99.9	100.0	100.0	100.0	99.8
Millions of U.S. dollars	245.0	279.0	409.0	332.1	542.0	732.0

Source: Calculations based on data in *Yearbook of the United Nations 1971*, 244; *Yearbook of the United Nations 1973*, 328; *Yearbook of the United Nations 1975*, 407; *Yearbook of the United Nations 1977*, 449; *Yearbook of the United Nations 1979*, 536; *Yearbook of the United Nations 1981*, 437–441. These data refer to allocations/earmarkings by the Governing Council provided in U.S. dollars.

1. Data regarding the regional activities presented in this table have been adapted to the four regional offices since 1971 and may therefore differ somewhat from the presentation of data for years before 1971 in tables 7.4 and 7.5 in this volume.

2. Since 1978: Asia and the Pacific

3. Four dashes indicate that data for the variable was not presented as a separate category in the relevant year; it was categorized as part of other (nearby) regional activity.

4. Percentages may not add up to exactly 100 because figures are rounded in the data on which the calculations are based.

ideological norms by extending them to all activities of the organization, not just its technical assistance. An important part of the reform was the new programming system that introduced medium-term development planning. It encouraged developing countries to set long-term priorities and plan their own development efforts in a five-year perspective.

During the 1970s, further administrative reform in this general

TABLE 7.9.

Distribution of UNDP Resources by Economic Sectors, Selected Years, 1972–1982 (by percent)

	1972	1974	1976	1978	1982
Agriculture, forestry, and fisheries	29.3	25.9	27.8	27.8	18.0
Industry	15.8	15.7	15.7	18.3	7.4
Transport and communications	9.9	13.6	12.4	10.6	8.9
General economic and social policy planning[1]	10.4	11.8	13.1	12.5	8.3
Education	8.5	6.9	6.8	6.6	4.1
Science and technology	6.9	7.0	4.6	5.1	4.2
Health	5.3	5.7	5.8	5.0	19.4
Natural resources	4.8	5.0	4.8	4.1	9.7
Labor, management, and employment[2]	3.5	3.7	3.9	4.1	4.9
Social security and other social services[3]	2.3	1.8	2.0	1.8	0.8
International trade[4]	1.6	1.8	2.1	2.9	2.3
Cultural, social, and human sciences[5]	0.7	0.6	0.8	NA[7]	2.1
Relief activities[6]	0.3	0.6	0.3	NA	0.1
Population	0.3	0.1	0.0	NA	8.2
Political affairs	NA	NA	NA	NA	0.3
Human settlements	NA	NA	NA	NA	1.2
TOTAL[8]	99.6	100.2	100.1	98.8	99.9

Sources: Calculations based on data in *Yearbook of the United Nations 1976*, 369 (for 1972, 1974, and 1976); *Yearbook of the United Nations 1978*, 462; *Yearbook of the United Nations 1982*, 627.

    1. Category changed to "General development" in 1982.
    2. Category changed to "Employment" in 1982.
    3. Category changed to "Social conditions and equity" in 1982.
    4. Category changed to "International trade and development finance" in 1982.
    5. Category changed to "Culture" in 1982.
    6. Category changed to "Humanitarian aid and relief" in 1982.
    7. Not available.
    8. Percentages may not add up to exactly 100 because figures are rounded in the data on which the calculations are based.

direction continued, stimulated by the prevailing political ideology of self-reliance. In intergovernmental bodies, suggestions were put forward that an increasing share of UNDP-funded projects should be implemented directly by the host governments. This proved an almost impossible task for the organization: in 1981, the share of total UNDP expenditures for operational development activities implemented by host governments amounted to a mere 1.7 percent. That year, Administrator Bradford Morse suggested that all UNDP-financed projects should be implemented by host governments, provided they agreed to take on this responsibility. Given the long-established delivery system anchored in the extended UN family, this may seem like a revolutionary proposal, but for many bilateral aid agencies, it was already well-established practice.

The second change relates to a shift in thought about development. In intergovernmental bodies, there was a drive to bolster the active participation of developing countries in the UN's development efforts, the UNDP's in particular, by increasing the number of experts drawn from developing countries to serve on UNDP-financed projects, the dollar value of subcontracts awarded to institutions in developing countries, and the number of training fellowships provided by developing-country institutions. Toward the end of the 1970s, some changes became visible. This reorientation was driven partly by the ideology of collective self-reliance, which fostered cooperation between developing countries.

This reorientation took place at a time when the manpower situation was changing dramatically in most developing countries, which were producing more and more of their own experts. At the conceptual level, the UN adapted its policies to this new environment. It urged Third World governments to review their employment, investment, education, and planning policies to enhance human resource development. It also asked governments to make maximum use of the expertise available in other developing countries.

While the bulk of resources needed to be mobilized domestically, more and more external resources were also needed. The UN called on developed countries to assist developing countries, especially the least developed, in their efforts to boost national capabilities and facilities for training qualified national personnel. UN technical cooperation might assist in various ways, for example by establishing data banks of skilled personnel and by making greater use of national experts. In sum, the perspective gradually changed from providing technical assistance to cooperation with the goal of strengthening the capabilities of developing countries to tackle development challenges.

The third change relates to the UNDP's position in the UN development system. Its role as the coordinator of all operational development efforts of the UN was challenged. This challenge did not appear in the formal decisions: the UNDP's central role in coordinating technical assistance was repeatedly confirmed in the rhetoric of the resolutions of the main intergovernmental bodies. However, by the late 1970s some indications of a weakened position were becoming visible at the institutional level. A case in point is a General Assembly resolution stating that UNIDO was the coordinator of assistance involving industrial development. The tendency was also discernible in the establishment of UN resident coordinators and in decisions that made the director-general for development and international cooperation responsible for policy overviews and reform proposals. These changes moved the central coordinating function to the UN Secretariat, where, ultimately, it had belonged all along.

This change became increasingly evident during the latter 1970s. In part, this was related to the broadening of the development perspective: although technical assistance was still a focal point in development discourse, other aspects were coming to the fore, not least issues related to trade and development and industrial development. Within these policy areas, other arms of the UN system were in charge and maintained the initiative, UNCTAD and UNIDO in particular.

The greatest challenge to the UNDP came from the weakening of its relative position as a funding agency within the system. In 1981, its share of UN total development expenditures, excluding humanitarian aid, amounted to a mere 11 percent. Even more important, its relative position was also weakened regarding grants for development assistance: although the UNDP was still the leading UN agency, providing 31 percent of total funding, other agencies such as the WFP, UNICEF, and the UNFPA were increasing their shares. Increasingly more development activity was being financed from the regular budgets of these organizations and from extra-budgetary resources placed at their disposal. The World Bank (and the IDA) provided most of the development finance on concessionary terms. It was also approaching the level of the UNDP even within the area of technical assistance. Other agencies—in the first place the WHO and the FAO but also the ILO and UNESCO—became major funding agencies for technical assistance in their own capacities, beyond the funding they received from the UNDP. Their regular budgets were growing, allowing them to expand operational activities in their thematic fields, and they sought and received extra-budgetary funding for their operational activities. This development, by necessity, weakened the authority of the UNDP in its role as coordinator in its core area of technical assistance.

The dilemmas involved are obvious. The UN's intergovernmental bodies repeatedly called for coordination of the various operational activities and designed institutional mechanisms to facilitate that aspiration. The main responsibility for policy coherence and coordination of technical assistance activities was vested in the UNDP. The constructive idea was that the UNDP should work with and through the special agencies and other relevant organizations of the system, governed by the Governing Council, ECOSOC, and the General Assembly.

Few will listen to a policy organ with no money to back up its coordination. During the initial years, the UNDP was fortunate in this respect. It had a mandate to coordinate technical assistance and was in command of most of the available resources; the regular budgets of the specialized agencies were marginal in comparison. We have seen how the UNDP—like its two forerunners—combined its primary tasks with institution-building within the UN system, thereby also strengthening the executing agencies. When the balance changed in this regard, the coordinating role became more difficult.

In the UN's intergovernmental bodies, most governments argued that policies and activities should be coordinated more strongly. However, most governments wanted to have it both ways: they supported specialized agencies and programs directly through extra-budgetary contributions in order to follow up thematic priorities agreed upon nationally. In so doing, they contributed to the proliferation of development funding and weakened the UNDP's ability to coordinate UN development activities. Structural mechanisms at the national level of aid-providing countries were also at play: a government does not always speak with one voice. Representatives of a government may differ depending on the issue area. Policy positions and priorities may vary from one agency to another, the representatives becoming "captives" of the agency and policy area concerned and/or the ministry and reference group they relate to at home. Policy coordination begins at home.

A fourth point should be highlighted: the UNDP followed a systematic poverty orientation in terms of channeling aid to the least-developed countries and other low-income countries. This applied to the ordinary program in the norm set for distributing IPFs among recipient countries in the first development cycle (1972–1976), and increasingly so in the second cycle (1977–1981). In the program for the third cycle (1982–1986), 80 percent of all country IPFs was to be allocated to countries with an annual per capita income of $500 or less, with special treatment for those whose per-capita GNP was below $250.

The 1970s were characterized by serious economic crises involving both developing and developed countries. The oil crises of the mid- and late 1970s affected the economies and policies of developing and developed countries alike. The stagflation in the West resulted in protectionist measures that hit the exports of developing countries especially hard. The signs that a serious debt burden was under way for most developing countries were visible by the early 1970s. As explosive inflation affected debts and debt servicing, debts soared in the latter 1970s, resulting in a development crisis that affected most developing countries severely in the 1980s.

But the 1970s were also characterized by development optimism. Demands for structural reform in North-South economic and political relations that developing countries generated in conferences of the nonaligned countries were channeled through the UN. The Charter on the Economic Rights and Duties of States and the resolutions prescribing an NIEO were the prime manifestations of these demands. The UN—UNCTAD and UNIDO in particular but also the UNDP—was entrusted with responsibility for implementing this program. Parallel to this, UN organizations—the ILO, UNICEF, and the WHO in particular—generated the basic needs strategy, which focused on human development and needs through developing and improving social services.

The NIEO program was integrated into the DD2 strategy. The major industrialized powers were opposed to most of the core demands contained in UN resolutions. Throughout most of the 1970s, their strategy was to fend off the demands; they kept the dialogue going without committing themselves to the main demands involved. In the early 1980s, the situation changed. This was not unrelated to a shift in the ideological climate that was symbolized by regime change in two major powers, the United Kingdom (Margaret Thatcher) and the United States (Ronald Reagan). As we have noted, in 1981 the United States ended the dialogue for all practical purposes. These changes necessarily affected the UN and its development efforts.

The changes also affected the funding of UN development activities.

Funding for the UNDP's activities during the 1970s was never unproblematic, particularly during the economic crises and recession of the mid-1970s. Nevertheless, for three successive years at the end of the decade (1978–1980), UNDP field expenditures rose by more than 20 percent.[180] Even so, there were already signs of a tougher climate ahead, which was especially evident at the pledging conferences: resources stagnated and major donors even reduced their commitments. Total contributions by governments to finance UN operational development activities in 1981 amounted to $5.3 billion, down from $5.6 billion the previous year. Despite the reduced income, expenditures increased to a peak level of $6.0 billion, up from $4.8 billion the previous year. Expenditures for technical cooperation rose from $1.8 billion in 1980 to $2.0 billion in 1981.[181]

In 1981, UNDP expenditures exceeded $1 billion for the first time, up from $934 million the previous year. Measured by this criterion, the UNDP administered about 50 percent of the UN's grant-financed technical assistance. However, as noted, the relative position of the UNDP within the extended UN family can also be assessed with other criteria. At a time of rising expenses, incomes were declining and falling short of expectations.[182] The strongest signals of tougher times ahead came at the pledging conferences. During the 1970s, voluntary contributions by governments rose each year, reaching $729 million in 1980. In 1981, voluntary contributions amounted to $689 million and were further reduced the following year to $680 million.

The bleak prospects for the 1980s became evident at the pledging conference for 1982. Although a few donors (including Canada, France, and the Scandinavian countries) increased their pledges, some of the major industrialized countries (including Germany, the United Kingdom, and the United States) sent a strong warning to the UN: they announced no pledges (although they eventually came forward). The General Assembly expressed deep concern.[183]

More interesting than the repetition of appeals for more funding in a General Assembly resolution were the responses to this plea by the major groupings of countries only one year after the DD3 strategy had been adopted. A telling pattern emerged. The United States observed that it had provided nearly twice as much as the second-largest contributor to the UN development system. It argued that the most significant untapped source of additional revenue could be found among the capital-surplus developing countries and the industrialized socialist states. Australia, France, and Germany made similar points. Several developing countries called for greater resources to be devoted to operational activities. Some developed countries pointed to the strained international economy and argued that real growth of resources for operational activities would be low in the coming years because most industrialized countries were facing virtually insurmountable budgetary difficulties resulting from the continuing economic crisis.[184]

EIGHT

The World Food Programme, 1961–1981: Surplus Food for Development and Relief

- **Background**
- **The Creation of the WFP**
- **The Experimental Period**
- **A "New" Start**
- **The World Food Programme in Operation, 1966–1981**
- **Some Concluding Observations**

The world has been able to produce enough food to provide every citizen with an adequate diet to lead a healthy, active and productive life. Yet the hungry-poor (those earning less than the equivalent of one dollar a day, or who spend most of their income on food), comprising one-fifth of the developing world's population, do not have enough to eat. The co-existence of hunger with the capacity to end it is one of the gravest paradoxes of our time. It is not only morally repugnant and unacceptable but politically, economically and socially indefensible. Poverty is the underlying cause of hunger. Other factors, including political irresponsibility, corruption, civil unrest, ethnic and religious conflict, sudden natural disasters, and pro- longed and widespread drought, have compounded further the problem of poverty, and thereby hunger.

—D. JOHN SHAW[1]

When the United Nations was planned and formed in the early and mid-1940s, the primary concern was to establish an organization to secure peace and international stability. This was reflected in the authority given to the Security Council. Yet food security was soon identified as an impor- tant task for postwar international cooperation. In 1943, the Hot Springs conference, convened by U.S. president Franklin D. Roosevelt, set up an interim commission on food and agriculture to prepare for a permanent organization for cooperation within these fields—what was to become the Food and Agriculture Organization.

During the early days, there was no consensus about the role the UN and its specialized agencies should play in the field of economic and social affairs. It was not clear whether the UN should act as a clearinghouse or as an entrepreneur with operational functions. During this early period, most of the specialized agencies followed a strict budgetary practice that did not allow for operational activities such as development assistance to "underdeveloped" countries.[2] This applied to the FAO as well. Conflicts within the UN system often result in compromises. In the case of the FAO, the outcome was that its functions should be more on the advisory than operational side.[3] Although the budget clearly favored clearinghouse functions, this compromise opened up for a more active role for the FAO and, in the early 1960s, for the creation of the major multilateral program within this area, the UN World Food Programme.

Food aid has a *problématique* of its own. This makes it interesting in the context of the origins of the idea of development assistance and how the UN system has contributed to the idea and its implementation. Before it was integrated into the UN development system, food aid had a long history with a different rationale than the technical and financial assistance described in previous chapters. Bilaterally, food aid was formed and pursued by one main actor, the United States, as part of its domestic, trade, and foreign policy, especially its agricultural policy. Multilateral food aid must be discussed in the specific context of its origin in the huge bilateral food aid program of the United States, which continued to dominate this policy area. Only when this context is understood will it be possible to answer the main question related to the WFP: did multilateral food aid make a difference?

This chapter focuses on the WFP from its formative years until the early 1980s. (Chapter 13 will examine major changes in the late 1980s and beyond.) This division follows the decision to use development decades as organizers and does not reflect major policy shifts within the program. It looks at the main features of the World Food Programme: its aspirations and chief objectives, the norms that guided its activities, and how it has actually used food resources. Did the patterns established during the experimental period continue or did they change? The model established for multilateral food aid as a joint undertaking between the UN and one of the specialized agencies was unique. Its institutional development thus merits special attention: How was cooperation organized and what were the main lessons learned from this configuration?

Background

In 1961, when the WFP was established on a temporary basis, food aid was not a new international activity. For years, it had been put into extensive practice on a bilateral basis, especially by the United States. It had also been on the agenda within the UN system for years, especially in the FAO.

The UN Legacy

In the multilateral setting, food aid had been part of the broader concern for food security. The primary focus was on production and distribution —making food available where it was needed through more effective agriculture. Planning also became a trademark here. It was important to adapt agricultural output to demand in order to ensure price stability and to prevent developed countries from dumping agricultural surplus in developing countries. Dumping had negative consequences for international trade and the production of food and the health of food markets in developing countries.

Before World War II, food aid was associated with distribution of surplus food through relief operations that responded to natural or human-made catastrophes. The idea of using surplus agricultural commodities for relief therefore has long traditions. However, when a proposal to create a World Food Board was put forward at the first FAO conference in September 1946, the focus was much broader. This board was to ensure price stabilization (through buffer stocks), build up and maintain a world food reserve to meet famines, finance surplus disposal programs for people in need of food, establish links to a credit-providing institution in order to help governments develop and improve their agricultural production and processing industries, and coordinate bodies dealing with individual food commodities.[4] Although the proposal was not approved, it signaled a high level of ambition and direction at an early stage. Resistance came from the major industrial countries, the United States in particular. They were strongly opposed to the creation of a central multilateral organization to manage international trade in food.

As we have seen in other cases, especially in the fight for SUNFED, UN secretariats tend to persist once an idea with a grand vision has been launched, working in cooperation with governments that favor the idea. Three years later, in 1949, a modified proposal emerged to establish an international commodity clearinghouse within the FAO. When this idea too was rejected, the FAO secretariat persisted by commissioning studies on the broader issue of food aid that it presented to the intergovernmental bodies. One important stepping-stone was the adoption of principles for disposing of agricultural surpluses in 1954.[5] Of equal importance was a study on how agricultural surpluses might be used to finance economic development in "underdeveloped" countries in 1955.[6] A series of studies concentrated on yet another aspect raised in the 1946 World Food Board proposal: establishing an international emergency food reserve to respond to emergencies immediately and effectively.[7] Although recommended by relevant FAO bodies and passed on to ECOSOC and the General Assembly, the proposals at best resulted in calls for further studies.[8] In the international political climate of the 1950s, major western countries rejected such multilateral measures as contrary to their own bilateral initiatives and foreign policy interests.

The Frontrunner: The Food Aid Program of the United States

The policy and practice of the United States, which from the very beginning was the dominant actor within this policy field, is another important tradition on which the establishment of the WFP was based. Its prominent role can be explained by its considerable surplus in agricultural goods, especially cereals, that could not find commercial outlets in domestic or international food markets. This structural problem was an issue for several U.S. administrations. The question of what to do with agricultural surplus involved relations with the American Farm Bureau Federation, an important pressure group with strong influence on election outcomes and, accordingly, on U.S. agricultural policy.[9] Destroying food surpluses in order to maintain a balance between output and demand might send a wrong signal to producers as well as to those who were suffering from hunger and malnutrition. Such a policy would have been difficult to defend from an ethical perspective. The alternative of buying up surplus and storing it in order to stabilize prices involved huge expenses; since the problem was a permanent one, such a system might break down in time for lack of funds.

The challenge was to turn a negatively loaded problem into an asset. Using food surplus as an instrument of foreign policy opened up such an opportunity. This was not a new invention of the 1950s or early 1960s: the extensive relief aid to war-torn Eastern Europe, Russia, and Ukraine in 1921–1923 that was administered by the American Relief Administration is a prominent example of a tradition that dates back almost 200 years, starting with a relief operation to Venezuela in 1812.[10]

During the depression of the 1930s, President Franklin Delano Roosevelt established a regime that combined price stabilization support with production control. "Food aid" was part of the solution: exports of surplus agricultural products were subsidized and could be sold below the international price. The establishment of the U.S. Export-Import Bank was part of this design; it provided loans on concessionary terms to foreign buyers and used other mechanisms to transform government food stocks into "food aid" and subsidized exports. These policies were designed maintain the income of U.S. farmers through a supportive domestic agricultural policy. Needless to say, it was the farmers and food producers in the recipient countries that benefited from these various arrangements that picked up the bill for this "aid." From a development perspective that valued establishing food-security based on each country's own efforts, the effects might be negative for the recipient countries. In emergency situations, however, this aid served an important humanitarian relief function.

World War II created new opportunities for U.S. food aid to European allies. The mechanisms established in the 1930s set standards for the policies of the late 1940s and 1950s.[11] After the war, the Marshall Plan was yet another outlet for surplus food stocks: almost one-third of the $13.5 billion aid package to war-torn Europe from 1948 to 1952 consisted of food, feed, and fertilizers. This arrangement was beneficial to U.S. farmers as well. In the early 1950s, when the technological advances in U.S. agriculture led to mounting food surpluses, the Korean War provided "temporary relief."[12]

As Europe recovered, U.S. agricultural policy needed to be reformed, but no administration could stand up to the combined political strength of agriculturalists and food processors, who opposed restrictions on production. Internationally, the hardening of the Cold War was another factor: in addition to relief, food could buy political goodwill and help contain the expansion of communism. In 1954, the United States established the basis for a large-scale bilateral food aid program: the Agricultural Trade, Development and Assistance Act, also known as Public Law 480, or PL 480. In the ensuing years, bilateral U.S. food aid increased rapidly, reaching over eighteen million tons a year at a cost of $1.6 billion by 1964.[13]

This food aid program had its own rationale that combined several purposes, some of which contradicted each other. The baseline was the problem of mounting food surpluses that had to be removed in a way that would keep the farm lobby happy. On the recipient side, this might bring relief in emergency situations and reduce the prices of food for urban consumers. However, the program's explicit purpose was to create new markets for U.S. agricultural exports. As a consequence, it might also outcompete local producers of food and create new dietary patterns in recipient countries, exchanging traditional diets based on local agricultural products for new ones based on imported wheat. It might also create a disincentive for local production and create dependency on food imports. From a development perspective, this would work contrary to the declared purpose of development assistance by reducing self-sufficiency and food security. However, in the United States, the program appealed to the public's idealism by emphasizing that surplus food was being used to alleviate hunger. Moreover, it provided Washington with an effective foreign policy instrument.

The Creation of the WFP

In late October 1960, the General Assembly passed a resolution that facilitated a more active role for the UN in providing food aid. It noted with approval the Freedom from Hunger Campaign, which the FAO had launched earlier that year in cooperation with the UN and its specialized agencies and member governments. It invited the FAO to establish procedures by which "the largest practicable quantities of surplus food may be made available on mutually agreeable terms as a transitional measure against hunger, such procedures to be compatible with desirable agricultural development as a contribution to economic development in the less developed countries and without prejudice to bilateral arrangements for this purpose and compatible with the principles of the Food and Agriculture Organization."[14]

The UN recognized the dilemmas involved in food aid from the very beginning. The concluding paragraph of the resolution stressed that "any action taken and contemplated under the present resolution proceed in accordance with principles of surplus disposal and guidelines of the Food and Agriculture Organization, and, specifically, with adequate safeguards and appropriate measures against dumping of agricultural surpluses on the international markets and against adverse effects upon the economic and financial position of those countries which depend for their foreign exchange earnings primarily on the export of food commodities, and in the recognition that the avoidance of damage to normal trading in food-stuffs will be best assured by multilateral trading practices."[15]

This resolution transferred the initiative to the FAO. It invited its director-general to explore how food surplus might be provided to food-dependent peoples through the UN. The FAO director-general established a group of distinguished experts, chaired by Hans W. Singer, to present analyses and recommendations. The group's report exerted a strong influence on development thinking in the field of food aid and development within the UN and beyond for many years.[16]

The report was presented to the meeting of the Intergovernmental Advisory Committee of the FAO in Rome in early April 1961. Much of the future structure and magnitude of multilateral food aid for the coming years was designed during that meeting. The advisory body included strong personalities with direct access to executive power (see box 8.1).

The report of the Intergovernmental Advisory Committee was considered in the council of the FAO in June 1961 and by ECOSOC in June and August later that year. In June, the FAO council placed the issue of food aid in the broader context of economic development with its statement that "more rapid economic development of the developing countries should be seen as the ultimate goal of a world-wide policy aimed at the elimination of hunger and malnutrition."[17] Other major UN intergovernmental bodies, including the General Assembly's Second Committee, consistently maintained this perspective, insisting that the new program's activities should be coordinated with the efforts of other UN activities aimed at promoting economic and social development.

The joint proposal by the UN Secretary-General and the FAO director-general was the basis for the process that established the WFP later that year. The FAO Conference unanimously decided to authorize its director-general to borrow up to $100,000 from the working capital fund for the WFP while waiting for its expected cash contributions. The FAO council elected its ten members to the joint UN/FAO Intergovernmental Committee on the WFP.

The Experimental Period

The UN General Assembly established the World Food Programme on 19 December 1961, the day when the First UN Development Decade

BOX 8.1. The Quick Move from Idea to Reality

D. John Shaw has told a fascinating story of the birth of the WFP, with George McGovern—the first director of the newly established Office of Food for Peace in President John F. Kennedy's Executive Office and special assistant to the president—in the leading role. When he took office in January 1961, Kennedy asked McGovern to evaluate past operations of the Food for Peace Program and make suggestions about how it could be improved. McGovern had just lost his seat in the House of Representatives, where he had represented South Dakota and had served in the agriculture committee of the House as a leading spokesman of farmers' interests. In his report, he suggested that the FAO's role be expanded to include developing and executing a multilateral food aid program. This would not conflict with the bilateral U.S. Food for Peace Program—on the contrary, he argued.

A week later, the president asked McGovern to represent the United States at the meeting of the Intergovernmental Advisory Committee of the FAO in Rome. Here, he presented a specific proposal for "an initial program on a multilateral basis" aiming at "a fund of $100 million in commodities and cash contributions." The United States was prepared to offer $40 million in commodities with the possibility that Washington would explore a supplementary cash contribution. The report of the FAO director-general had not offered any concrete proposals for such a program, and there had been no prior discussion or agreement on any proposal before the U.S. delegation left for Rome. At that point, several ideas were under consideration in Washington. The proposal came therefore as a surprise to both the U.S. delegation and committee members, which had explicitly been granted an advisory mandate only. It emerged that McGovern had cleared the proposal with the U.S. president over the weekend. For all practical purposes, an idea had been institutionalized.

Source: D. John Shaw, *The UN World Food Programme and the Development of Food Aid* (New York: Palgrave, 2001), 6ff.

was declared and development targets were set for that decade. The WFP was a joint operation by the UN and the FAO in cooperation with other interested UN agencies and appropriate intergovernmental bodies.

The limitations associated with its establishment may be of equal interest to the tasks assigned to it; some of these limitations were established as principles to govern its activities. First of all, the WFP was established on an experimental basis for three years. In the Second Committee, several delegations (among them Australia and the United Kingdom) took care to avoid formulations that might indicate an automatic continuation of activities, whereas others (including France) wanted to facilitate such a continuation. The resolution that established the WFP specified that the program should in no way prejudice "the bilateral agreements between developed and developing countries."[18]

A limitation of a different kind was also recognized: "the ultimate solution to . . . the problem of food deficiency lies in self-sustaining economic growth of the economies of the less developed countries to the point where they find it possible to meet their food requirements from their food-producing industries or from the proceeds of their expanding export trade." However, using available surplus foodstuffs in a way that was compatible with the principles of surplus disposal that the FAO recommended provided "an important transitional means of relieving the hunger and malnutrition of food-deficient peoples, particularly in the less developed countries, and for assisting these countries in their economic development." The General Assembly resolution did not see food aid as a substitute for other types of assistance, especially not for capital assistance.[19]

Institutional Setup

From the beginning, FAO headquarters in Rome was designated the "home" of the WFP. Its first executive director, A. H. Boerma, who was appointed in June 1962, was the FAO assistant director-general; he was responsible for its program and budgeting. This close institutional relationship continued in the years to come. On leaving the WFP, Boerma became the director-general of the FAO.

A UN/FAO Intergovernmental Committee that consisted of representatives of twenty UN member states and FAO members was established "to provide guidance on policy, administration and operations." Ten members were to be elected by ECOSOC and ten by the FAO council. As early as October 1962, the FAO council recommended expanding the membership to twenty-four, equally divided between the UN and the FAO. ECOSOC approved this change in April the following year. The committee reported annually to ECOSOC and the FAO council on the WFP's administration and operation.[20]

Pilot projects were to be undertaken by a joint UN/FAO administrative unit. These projects, which used food as an aid to economic and social development, were to "be undertaken in agreement between the Secretary-General, acting on behalf of the United Nations, and the Director-General, acting on behalf of the Food and Agriculture Organization." The administrative unit was to "rely to the fullest extent possible on the existing staff and facilities" of the UN and FAO as well as those of other appropriate intergovernmental agencies.[21]

This prescription had two interrelated consequences for the administration of the new program: it was to be kept small, which made sense for an organization established on an experimental basis, and it had to rely on the administrative resources of other administrative arms of the UN family. The second point had its own rationale, which was to integrate the new activity into related UN development activities, particularly those of the EPTA and Special Fund, and the activities of the FAO.

The joint UN/FAO administrative unit during this initial period consisted of a program development and appraisal division, a program operation division, and a division of external relations and general affairs. The secretariat was kept small in order to reduce costs, in accordance with the program's general regulations. The administrative services rendered by the UN, FAO, and other specialized agencies had to be reimbursed from the WFP trust fund. Still, the staff of the program grew annually: by April 1965, when the Intergovernmental Committee concluded its third and final annual report for the experimental period, the total number of professional posts had reached thirty-six and the general service posts numbered forty-nine. In addition, twenty-two project officers had been appointed to ensure that the commodities contributed to projects were used properly, to assist the recipient government on all WFP food distribution matters, and to assist in the WFP's reporting and appraisal work. The officers covered thirty-seven countries and served as staff assistants to EPTA resident or regional representatives.[22]

We have seen from the first major UN development program that the EPTA's administrative leader was given the authority to administer a certain amount, increasing annually, at his own discretion to meet new developments and increase the flexibility of the program. The Intergovernmental Committee was meeting at long intervals—in practice only twice a year. As early as its second session, it authorized the executive director to implement certain categories of projects of which the total food-aid or feed component did not exceed $500,000 per project. This authorization was repeated, on a temporary basis, in later sessions. The executive director was also given flexibility to meet emergencies: he was authorized to borrow commodities from advantageously placed countries and replace them later by pledged commodities.[23]

Objectives

From the beginning, the WFP was to give priority to the following issues:

a. Establishing adequate and orderly procedures for meeting emergency food needs and emergencies inherent in chronic malnutrition (this could include establishing food reserves)

b. Aiding preschool feeding programs

c. Implementing pilot projects that used food as an aid to economic and social development, particularly when related to labor-intensive projects and rural welfare[24]

Main Principles

The main principles to guide the WFP's activities were adopted by the FAO Conference and, in turn, decided by the General Assembly:[25]

a. As was the case when the EPTA was established a decade earlier, it was stressed that projects "should be undertaken only in response to requests from the recipient country or countries concerned."

b. As already noted, the perhaps strongest emphasis was given to ensuring that food aid did not interfere negatively with the food market.

c. Emphasis was placed on coordinating WFP projects with other forms of assistance and country plans for economic and social assistance. Thus, it was recommended that both the governments requesting assistance under the program and the WFP's intergovernmental committee and administrative unit should keep UN resident representatives fully informed about and (within their field of competence) associated with the program's activities.

Funding

The financial framework of $100 million that George McGovern suggested (see box 8.1) in April 1961 was to be provided by member states on a voluntary basis. Contributions to the program might be pledged by countries in the form of appropriate commodities, acceptable services, and cash, aiming in the aggregate at a cash component of at least one-third of total contributions. A joint UN/FAO pledging conference was to be convened at UN headquarters in New York.[26]

This pledging conference was held on 5 October the following year. Thirty-three countries made pledges of about $86 million in the form of commodities, services, and cash. However, the cash component failed to reach the minimum target of one-third of total contributions. In December, the General Assembly appealed to "other State Members and members of the specialized agencies to give further considerations" to make pledges to the WFP in order reach the target of $100 million.[27] Although an increasing number of governments, the large majority representing developing countries, responded to this recommendation, the target was still not met.[28]

These contributions were credited to a trust fund that the FAO director-general established under FAO financial regulations. The cost of administering and operating the WFP were drawn from this fund.

Activities during the Experimental Period

According to its general regulations, the WFP was to provide food aid for three main purposes: to meet emergency food needs, to assist in preschool and school feeding programs, and to implement pilot projects using food to promote economic and social development. The priority —in budgetary terms—among these three areas was largely set at the Intergovernmental Committee's third session in May 1963.

ECONOMIC AND SOCIAL DEVELOPMENT

Projects that sought to further a county's economic and social development by means of external food supplies were the main activity of the program. During the first four months of operations, several teams were sent to a large number of developing countries to explore with government officials and EPTA resident representatives the possibility of providing this kind of assistance. This resulted in many project proposals that represented a wide range of activities. In the initial period, most projects related to agriculture and rural development.

The Intergovernmental Committee identified the problems with using food aid for economic development in its first report. One related to additional costs: even when human labor was a predominant element of projects and projects were well suited to use food aid, there were nearly always other costs that had to be met. In principle, such costs were the responsibility of recipient governments, but sometimes it proved difficult for developing nations to supply the required local and foreign currency. Another problem was related to the wish of some recipient governments to sell the commodities provided to help finance development projects. This was problematic because of the FAO's principle of surplus disposal, on which the WFP was founded. The answer was that such sales should be exceptional and accepted only after extensive consultations with the parties involved.[29]

SPECIAL FOOD AID PROGRAMS

Another main WFP activity was support for preschool and school feeding programs. The aim was to overcome nutritional deficiencies, which were seen as hampering the economic development of the country concerned in the longer term.

EMERGENCY ASSISTANCE

The Intergovernmental Committee's third session in May 1963 decided that up to $7 million was to be spent during 1963 for emergency operations. About a quarter of the commodities pledged to the program was to be set aside for emergencies during the following years. Efforts were concentrated on streamlining procedures for coordinating, procuring, shipping, and distributing emergency assistance. Almost from its inception, the WFP began to respond to emergency situations. A lesson learned from these early operations was that time was needed to prepare for providing immediate relief in emergencies, as the commodities required were not always available.[30]

An observation in the Intergovernmental Committee's first annual report merits mention, as later developments will reveal. It argued that notwithstanding the limitations, the program was well adapted to act as a source of longer-term aid to countries

> both to replace borrowed supplies and in undertaking planned reconstruction and rehabilitation activities to overcome the consequences of disasters. . . . Consultation and co-ordination with other organizations is a primary necessity. The Executive Director holds a very central position in this respect, as the Director-General of FAO has delegated to him part of his own operational responsibility in the field of famine relief and emergency food-aid programmes.[31]

A "New" Start

The way the WFP was established illustrates how the UN system generated and developed ideas and then followed up through institution-building during the first two decades of its existence. The process was slow and cautious. It involved many actors, both within and outside the UN. These included member governments and even sometimes individual players, as we have seen in the case of McGovern during the initial stages. Not all governments carried the same weight in the decision-making process; the U.S. administration was at the wheel and assumed most of the financial burden. But there were other actors as well, both at the inter-governmental level, in the headquarters of the UN and FAO, and in the headquarters of the implementing organization itself.

Preparing the New Start

As the date the WFP was to expire approached, its executive director was asked to prepare a report that evaluated the program's experiences and to present his recommendations for a future multilateral food aid program. This report was prepared in close cooperation with the "owners" of the program.[32] Extensive interagency consultations were also part of the process. Thereafter Secretary-General U Thant and the FAO director-general produced a joint report on the WFP's future that established the basis for the recommendations of relevant intergovernmental bodies at various levels.

Not many changes took place during the remaining process, which in itself indicates the strong influence of secretariats on outcomes. On the other hand, these preparations at the "civil service" level did not take place in splendid isolation from the "political" setting of intergovern-mental bodies and government delegations. At that level, the joint UN/FAO Intergovernmental Committee formed the basis for the decision (including a draft resolution to be forwarded to the General Assembly) on which the FAO council and ECOSOC made their recommendations. However, subcommittees, such as the Economic Committee in the case of ECOSOC, were also involved. Ultimately, it was the FAO Conference and the General Assembly that would make the decision.

In their report, the UN Secretary-General and the FAO director-general asserted that the program "should in its essential character and in funda-mental concepts as far as possible remain true to the General Assembly resolution which directly led to its creation." They concluded that "the results of the first experimental period of the programme have been sufficiently positive to warrant its continuation and indeed expansion" and said that they believed that the program had been "well and effectively administered by the Executive Director, Mr. A. H. Boerma, and his staff, and has added a creditable new page to the history of international co-operation. Both parent organizations may be proud of their offspring."[33]

The recommendation was loud and clear: to proceed with an expanded WFP that would be open to further experiments on ways and means. Nevertheless, the process had also brought critical analyses both of the idea of food aid as such and how it had been handled by the WFP during the experimental period—and of the food aid of bilateral donors as well. The critical voices, which emerged in expert studies that had been commissioned, were made transparent to decision makers. Several of the critical points and core problem areas identified in these analyses actually have remained high on the agenda on food aid for development into the new millennium.

Expert Studies

The expert studies on various aspects of multilateral food aid repeated old warnings. It was argued that since food aid in substantial quantities might result in a decline of local agricultural prices, it appeared prima facie that its effects were likely to be detrimental to the domestic agricultural production of developing countries and thus to economic development itself. Harmful effects might, however, be avoided if food aid was integrated in the overall plans of developing countries. One of the studies argued that food aid should be provided in overall support of development plans and programs.[34] The feasibility of food aid was questioned in another study: the comparative developmental effect of cash was greater than that of food aid in kind, it was argued.[35] This is also a core argument in the contemporary debate on food aid.

Another study identified the need to harmonize bilateral and multilateral food aid and argued that only a multilateral program could meet the growing need for coordination.[36] Indirectly, it also challenged one of the WFP's basic founding principles: since the primary purpose of multilateral food aid was to foster economic and social development, there was no reason why it should be confined to the project approach or why food aid in overall development plans should remain the monopoly of bilateral aid. Implicit in this argument was the need to transform food into cash (by selling the food in the domestic market), thereby interfering with the "normal" commercial market mechanisms involving food imports as well as locally produced agricultural products.

Several of the studies highlight another program weakness: its small size in absolute and relative terms. Most food aid had been provided bilaterally by the United States. Since 1954, it had provided food aid bilaterally at a value of about $14 billion, while other bilateral and multilateral programs (including the WFP, to which the United States was, by far, the largest contributor) combined amounted to only $300 million. The study further noted that the United States also exerted direct control with regard to how the resources it provided to the WFP were to be used, thus reducing the program's multilateral character. Several studies recommended an extension of the financial frame in order to reduce overhead costs and enable the program to serve effectively as a model system to guide all food-aid undertakings through research, experimentation, and the formulation of principles and policies.[37]

In his report, the executive director identified another fundamental weakness associated with this type of aid: food was an uncertain resource. Basically, food aid had come about because of the existence of surplus stocks in a very few countries, which had supplied most food aid and would probably continue to do so. In guarded language, he noted the tendency on the part of some donor countries "to consider food aid primarily from the viewpoint of their own need to dispose of specific surpluses," which in turn raised problems in ensuring the continuity of supply of commodities committed to food-aid projects extending over several years. There was the additional problem that for domestic political reasons, countries holding surplus stocks did not guarantee continuity to food-aid programs or projects. Instead, such commitments were subject to the availability of the surplus.[38]

The Suggested Scope and Main Purpose

The budget for an expanded WFP proposed by the executive director for the second half of the First Development Decade increased substantially year by year, reaching $205 million in commitments for the last year of the period. Nevertheless, the program continued to represent a relatively small part of total food aid. The budget had a longer time horizon than had been the case in the three-year experimental period, and it also argued for a longer time-horizon for individual projects. A pledging conference, proposed to be held in 1965 and covering the first three years, should aim at $275 million, whereas a pledging conference late in 1967 for the remaining two years should aim at $370 million. A substantial portion of these commitments (30 percent) should be provided in cash and shipping, leaving 70 percent to be provided in kind.[39]

The executive director was clear about the WFP's primary function: "to ensure that food which is wanted but cannot be paid for will be channelled to people who can be enabled, by its support, to train and work for the development of their countries." However, assistance should be continued to be given in emergencies, "especially after initial sympathy has subsided, nearby sources of succour have been exhausted and rehabilitation has to begin," thus adapting its role to the limitations of its capacity. Nevertheless, the main emphasis was on economic and social development through specific feeding programs, "especially in support of education and training and health" that could "contribute increasingly to development through improvement of productivity" and through the implementation of projects "using food as an aid to economic and social development, particularly when related to labour-intensive projects and rural welfare." A strong plea was made for using food aid in support of overall development plans and programs, starting on a modest experimental basis.[40]

The relative priority given to these activities became more clear in the budget for 1966–1970. The budget for emergencies remained at $7 million annually, and in an expanding program its share declined from more than 20 percent during the experimental period to about 4 percent. In contrast, allocations to projects were to increase gradually, to reach $120 million annually the two last years of the period, constituting almost 64 percent of the budget for the period. The "modest" start with program support, directed in particular to small countries and provided as balance-of-payment support, was growing to reach $70 million in 1970, representing about 30 percent of the budget for the five-year period. Administrative costs—these were also to increase annually and to reach $8 million in 1970—made up the rest.

This budget proposal made the aspirations crystal clear: the expanded program aimed at transforming food into economic and social development. It also aspired to add to other efforts by serving as an additional resource. Providing emergency relief was considered an unavoidable necessity, but it was not to be given first priority. Project aid should continue as the trademark, although the WFP also aspired to provide program aid in support of the development plans of recipient governments.

These were the main adjustments proposed when the WFP was to move from an experimental to a more permanent or open-ended basis—"to be maintained for as long as it can perform a useful role." The main objective and the principles established for the experimental period were retained. Food aid was to come as a response to requests from the recipient governments, and these governments were to carry the responsibility for implementation. However, the WFP assumed increased responsibility for appraisal and evaluation, a process initiated during the experimental period by the extension of the field staff associated with EPTA resident representatives.

The executive director saw no reason for modifying the basic institutional and organizational arrangements: in his view, the double allegiance —to the UN and FAO—had worked out well. Extensive cooperation with other UN development assistance activities—with specialized agencies such as the ILO, the FAO, UNESCO, and the WHO, and with the TAB, the Special Fund, UNICEF, and the UNHCR in particular—was to be continued and extended to the World Bank and the International Development Association. And the services of these organizations, the UN and FAO in particular, were to be drawn upon as before. However, it would be necessary to increase the staff of the WFP's own administrative "unit," partly because there was a limit to the extent to which the secretariats of the other organizations had capacity to service the WFP and partly because the proposed expanded program had a broader scope. A substantial part of this proposed increase would be in out-stationed officers. A new unit for evaluation and research was also proposed that would undertake work required and initiate and assist research on food aid.[41]

The UN Secretary-General and the FAO director-general agreed with these suggestions, although they emphasized the value of the project approach as a distinctive feature of a multilateral food aid program. The multilateral approach had some distinct advantages, they argued.[42] The overall development perspective that was present in General Assembly resolution 1714 (XVI) was retained, while new avenues were opened up for food aid in such a context.[43]

In 1964, another input into the process came from UNCTAD: additional contributions in cash, especially from developed countries, to an international food program would enable the purchase of a range of foodstuffs (in addition to those donated) needed for a nutritionally adequate diet. Such purchases should as far as possible be made from developing countries that were food exporters and were seeking to expand their food exports. This suggestion was followed up by a more daring proposal: the conversion of the WFP into a World Food Fund. A new North-South perspective had thereby been placed on the agenda. One decade later, it would be strongly pursued by developing countries in tandem with the UNCTAD secretariat, in connection with the demands for a new economic order. However, in the mid-1960s, little came out of it, not least because supplies of surplus food were the main rationale of the major food aid providers: the cash contributions necessary for bringing this food in kind to the end users had been the most difficult to obtain during the WFP's experimental period.

Toward the end of 1965, the FAO Conference and the UN General Assembly had a clear conclusion: the WFP was established on a more permanent basis. The outcome was more or less identical with the preparatory work mentioned above, as filtered through the joint report by the FAO director-general and the UN Secretary-General, the joint UN/FAO Intergovernmental Committee, and then the FAO council and ECOSOC.[44]

The World Food Programme in Operation, 1966–1981

The model of a joint undertaking between the UN and one of the specialized agencies was unique. The program was to work together with other institutions within the UN system and beyond and to coordinate its assistance. The question of institutional development, therefore, calls for special attention. Of equal importance are the main features of the food aid program: Who financed it, and what were the resources actually used for? Were the patterns established during the experimental period continued or did they change?

We will start by looking at the administrative model, which was designed with the dual intention of reducing administrative costs and integrating a new activity into administrative structures already in existence. The intention was to try to deal with a problem that has afflicted the UN system from the very start: how to create policy coherence and coordinate operational activities.

The Administration of Multilateral Food Aid: An Ideal Model?

For part of the program's activities (emergency assistance), the WFP executive director, assisted by the secretariat, acted on authority delegated to him by the FAO director-general. The FAO served as the home base for the program: the administrative unit was situated on the premises of the

FAO in Rome, and the special trust fund—to which voluntary contributions to the WFP were credited and from which its activities were paid—was established by the FAO director-general under the financial regulations of his organization. This did not change when the WFP became a more permanent institution.[45]

When the WFP was established, it was cast in the context of economic and social development. Coordination of its various activities with those of other UN agencies was emphasized during the experimental period and strongly heralded in the policy documents that set out the program's future course. This concern was followed up through institutionalized integration: instead of building up a separate staff, the program was to rely on the staff of other agencies as much as possible, the FAO in particular. And its various activities, especially those involving development projects, were to be integrated with those carried out by the other arms of the UN system, especially activities of the EPTA and the Special Fund and later the UNDP. The personnel engaged to ensure coordination, implementation, and appraisal of WFP activities in recipient countries became an integral part of the offices of the EPTA (and later UNDP) resident representatives. It could be said that this systematic harmonization of objectives and institutional integration involving the WFP followed the book with regard to attaining what, decades later, was to be reinvented as policy coherence.[46]

Ensuring that development activities were coordinated was instrumental in keeping administrative costs down. However, self-interest on the part of the various organizations was also involved: food aid was an additional resource for them, both in terms of their own institution-building and in terms of strengthening their ongoing development activities, directly or indirectly.

The services other agencies rendered to the WFP were not provided for free; they were to be paid for from the WFP trust fund. Such services were provided, in particular, by the host agency, the FAO. The UN administrative system was also strengthened as WFP field staff became integrated in the offices of the resident representatives.[47] In this way, food aid contributed to strengthening the institutional development of the service-providing institutions, especially the UN's presence in developing countries. Insisting that WFP activities should be integrated into ongoing development activities increased the probability that they would be successful. What is less obvious is whether this model also contributed to the efficient handling of multilateral food aid.[48]

The WFP-FAO relationship was a special problem. This chapter is not the place for an in-depth description and analysis of cooperation and conflicts in the WFP-FAO relationship. However, one conflict merits mention because it illustrates the difficulties involved in a complex relationship of this kind when one central actor tries to change the established power balance. In the end, this conflict affected the WFP's effectiveness.

During the first fifteen years, the relationship developed quite smoothly in spite of the complex constitutional setting with so much formal authority vested in the FAO director-general. Aside from his formal authority over the special trust fund, the single issue that created the most problems was that the WFP executive director had to act on a mandate that ultimately belonged to the FAO director-general in one of WFP's core areas: emergency food aid.

In 1967, the first executive director of the WFP, Addeke Boerma, became director-general of the FAO. Problems began when Boerma's term came to an end in 1976. He was replaced by Edouard Saouma, who had headed the FAO's land and water development division for more than a decade. Saouma's leadership style differed radically from that of Boerma.[49]

The Saouma regime lasted for almost two decades and negatively affected the WFP's effectiveness. Saouma used his powers to discourage the emergence of strong leadership in the WFP.[50] He got his way until James Ingram, a diplomat who also had served as director-general of the Australian Development Assistance Bureau (1975–1982), was appointed WFP executive director in 1982. Ingram served in this position until 1992.

Although formally the authority over the joint FAO-UN undertaking was equally divided between the parent organizations, much of the initiative in conceptualizing and forming the institution and its objectives originated and remained with the director-general, subcommittees, and intergovernmental bodies of the FAO and were then approved by the UN. This also applied when the executive director of the WFP was to be appointed: in practice, the FAO director-general took the initiative. That the WFP was located at the FAO premises in Rome, where almost all sessions of the Intergovernmental Advisory Committee of the WFP also took place, worked in the same direction.[51] As FAO director-general, Saouma used the formal mandates at hand to the greatest extent possible to extend his control over the WFP; he used his informal powers to that end as well. At times, this had obviously negative effects on the program.[52]

At an important stage in its development, the WFP itself contributed to increasing this dependency on the FAO. In 1975, its governing committee was reconstituted and broadened in membership as well as mandate. The new Committee on Food Aid Policies and Programmes (CFA) covered all food aid. It supervised the WFP's operational activities and was a forum for deliberations and debate on food aid policies and programs.[53] The WFP executive director was to be responsible for the secretariat functions of the new committee. However, the WFP decided to leave the new functions relating to food aid policy to the FAO and other relevant bodies of the UN system. The WFP would cooperate and pay for all services rendered by the FAO and others that serviced the CFA, but otherwise it preferred to concentrate on its operational functions.[54] This made it easier for the FAO director-general, under a later and less cooperative regime, to intervene in WFP affairs.

In the early 1980s, James Ingram challenged Saouma's systematic efforts to increase his control over the WFP.[55] The power struggle between the two directors was multilateral cooperation at its worst, illustrating how vulnerable the UN system can be and how dependent it is on the right leadership. In the words of a longstanding "participant observer," for years it was "a sapping and exhausting experience that diverted and took up a large part of the attention of WFP's governing body and executive management."[56] More important from a systemic perspective, this struggle demonstrated the UN's political weakness. Although the conflict was well known and had even been high on the agenda of the WFP's intergovernmental bodies since the early 1980s, member governments within the two parent organizations, the UN and the FAO, seemed unable or unwilling to put this flagrantly disordered house in order.

Pledges and the Distribution of Resources

For almost three decades, the WFP's basic features remained much the same as they had been when it was established during the first half of the 1960s. Nevertheless, the program increased in scope, and adjustments took place in response to circumstantial changes. Major humanitarian catastrophes triggered a process of change. The program responded first to the drought catastrophe in Sahelian Africa and Ethiopia in the early 1970s and then to the exodus of refugees from war and conflict in Afghanistan and Cambodia, who were streaming into neighboring Pakistan and Thailand, respectively, in 1979–1980. In 1983–1984, a new drought catastrophe struck Sahelian Africa and Ethiopia. New international food aid arrangements for emergencies were placed at the WFP's disposal as a response. Bilateral aid agencies expected that the WFP would respond to emergencies that involved getting food aid to refugees from conflicts. These developments contributed to strengthening the focus on relief assistance during the 1970s, when emergencies appeared.

TARGETS AND PLEDGES

The target for the experimental period 1962–1965, $100 million in voluntary commitments, was not fully met, although commitments reached almost $95 million in the end. The willingness (or ability) to meet the targets for subsequent pledging periods also varied, and countries did not always meet the commitments they made in time. This made it difficult for the WFP to plan and implement its activities, and the same was true for recipient governments. Annual contributions increased over the years, but they did not follow a linear pattern: at times, they varied considerably from one year to the next as extra resources became available to meet catastrophes.

The General Assembly set $275 million as the target for voluntary contributions for the period 1966–1968, of which not less than a third should be in cash and services. During the following biannual periods, the targets proposed by the Intergovernmental Committee and set by the intergovernmental bodies of FAO and the UN continued to rise.[57]

The wider perspective on food security continued during this process. Thus in 1970, when the General Assembly set the target for 1971–1972, it recognized that "the world food problem is an inseparable part of the broader problem of development" and that "the ultimate solution to the food problem of developing countries lies in increased production in the developing countries with a food deficit, in the context of their general economic development, with the co-operation of the developed countries." The assembly responded to the Intergovernmental Committee's report by suggesting that member states should be made aware of the advantages of channeling a larger share of their food aid through multilateral channels and that the WFP could, "without basic changes in its procedures, effectively utilize resources double or more than the $300 million agreed on as the pledging target for 1971–1972."[58]

The pledges are shown in table 8.1, which also gives an overview of the number of governments and organizations that took part in the

TABLE 8.1.

Pledges to the World Food Programme by Major Donors,[1] Selected Years, 1963–1982 (by percent and in millions of U.S. dollars)

	1963–1965	1966–1968	1969–1970	1973–1974	1977–1978	1981–1982
United States	53.2	60.0	39.0	38.2	30.6	28.5
Federal Republic of Germany	8.5	3.7	2.5	4.1	4.5	5.0
Canada	7.3	13.1	12.7	9.5	22.2	20.9
United Kingdom	6.1	2.9	0.0	1.7	1.9	----[2]
Netherlands	2.7	2.8	4.3	6.1	6.3	5.7
Denmark	2.1	3.3	3.5	7.7	4.8	4.7
Sweden	2.1	3.7	3.1	5.3	3.9	3.4
Norway	1.8	2.1	1.8	2.8	5.2	5.6
Saudi Arabia	0.0	----	----	----	8.1	7.1
EEC	0.0	0.0	27.1	17.5	6.6	4.8
Other	16.2	8.4	6.0	7.1	5.9	14.3
TOTALS	100.0	100.0	100.0	100.0	100.0	100.0
Total number of donors	70	78	76	88	80	92
Total donations in millions of U.S. dollars	94.0	216.8	256.1	356.4	613.6	770.6
Cash as a percent of total contributions	21.3	16.3	13.9	14.4	22.5	30.6

Sources: Data in and calculations based on data in *Yearbook of the United Nations 1965,* 304–305; *Yearbook of the United Nations 1967,* 329–330; *Yearbook of the United Nations 1969,* 322–323; *Yearbook of the United Nations 1972,* 268–269; *Yearbook of the United Nations 1974,* 428–430; *Yearbook of the United Nations 1975,* 429–430; *Yearbook of the United Nations 1977,* 468; *Yearbook of the United Nations 1979,* 667–668; and *Yearbook of the United Nations 1982,* 732.

1. The category "major donors" is defined here as donors that over a period of time provided 1.5 percent (or more) of total contributions (in U.S. dollar equivalents). In addition to those listed, some donors have qualified for inclusion for one or two periods: Australia (1963–1965, 1.6; 1981–1982, 1.9); Italy (1963–1965, 1.6; 1981–1982, 2.9); France (1963–1965, 3.2); Finland (1973–1974, 1.7); Japan (1981–1982, 1.6); and OPEC (1981–1982, 2.2).

2. Four dashes indicate a donation that constituted less than 1.5 percent of the total for a given period.

funding of WFP activities. The major donors are also identified. As table 8.1 shows, the United States made extensive contributions to the program, especially in the initial stage. However, a condition was added: U.S. contributions should not exceed a certain percentage of total contributions. During the first period (1966–1968) this percentage amounted to 50 percent, which resulted in cuts in the actual contribution compared with the amount the United States originally pledged. For subsequent periods, although the U.S. percentage was lowered, the United States remained the program's major donor. The other major donor during the period under review was Canada, which provided more than one-fifth of all resources from the mid-1970s. Several of the UNDP's major donors are also to be found among the major donors during these years, including the Scandinavian countries (here with Denmark on top) and the Netherlands, Germany, and the United Kingdom. At the end of the 1960s, the EEC came in as an important but highly volatile donor, and in the mid-1970s, Saudi Arabia emerged as one of the largest aid providers to the program.

The WFP needed cash for transportation, administration, and implementation of its operational activities. This is why one-third of total commitments was to be in cash or services (transportation). Several governments provided their contributions in the form of cash only and a few combined services with cash; most of those providing cash only were developing countries with relatively small contributions. Most contributions came in the form of commodities and cash. A few countries combined all forms. This applied to the United States especially. During the experimental period, it contributed almost 80 percent of all services pledged, and continued as the major contributor of services thereafter. Most of its contributions in cash and services were provided in the form of free transportation (on U.S. ships) of commodities from the United States.[59]

The cash component has been singled out in table 8.1, not only because the United States was almost alone in including services in "cash and services" but also because cash proved to be a scarce resource. Cash provided flexibility—it could be used to buy food at favorable prices on the market. After the mid-1970s, Saudi Arabia made this possible by providing extensive contributions in cash, and other members of the Organization of the Oil Exporting Countries (OPEC) later followed suit. A large number of countries, especially developing countries, provided their contributions in cash.

These voluntary pledges were not the only resources available. In 1968, several governments announced that they would channel through the WFP in whole or in part the food grains they were obliged to contribute as aid to developing countries under the Food Aid Convention, which had been concluded as part of the International Grains Arrangement of 1967 and later food aid conventions of 1980 (see table 8.2).

The WFP's main contributors through the Food Aid Convention up to the mid-1970s were Sweden, the United Kingdom, the Federal Republic of Germany, and the Netherlands, in that order; their annual contributions varied between $1.5 and $5.3 million. The EEC emerged as a major donor in the early 1970s; from 1974, it was the largest donor to the convention, contributing around $10 million annually from 1975–1976 to 1978–1979 and $15 and $20 million in 1979–1980 and 1980–1981, respectively. During the latter 1970s and beyond, Sweden, the United Kingdom, Federal Republic of Germany, and the Netherlands were the largest donor countries; their annual contributions varied between $3.2 and $12.3 million. The UK and the Federal Republic of Germany, in particular, increased their contributions considerably in the last two years of the decade. So did Australia, which contributed $12.5 and $18.5 million in those two years. Finland and Belgium contributed above the $1 million level annually from 1975–1976 onward, with contributions that varied from $1.1 to $4.3 million.

The International Emergency Food Reserve (IEFR) was another funding source for the WFP for relief projects. It was set up in 1976 at the recommendation of the 1974 World Food Conference. In June 1978, the World Food Council, another UN body established at the recommendation of World Food Conference, recommended that the IEFR be established on a continuing basis, with yearly replenishments to be determined by the CFA and placed at the disposal of the WFP. In 1976, the IEFR contributed $8 million to the WFP's relief operations. Its contributions climbed steeply over the next fifteen years, reaching $182 million in 1981.[60]

This is a picture of a program in extensive growth. However, the picture needs to be modified. Volatile prices for food commodities affected the amount of food actually provided in metric tons. In real terms, pledges to the regular program increased from 829,000 metric tons in 1969 to 846,000 metric tons in 1979, an increase of only 17,000 metric tons. During this ten-year period, the value in current prices increased from $160 million to $399 million. The increase in resources during this period, that is the quantity of commodities available, came mainly from IEFR resources

TABLE 8.2.

Food Aid Convention Contributions to the World Food Programme, 1968–1981, Selected Years (in millions of U.S. dollars)

	1968– 1969	1970– 1971	1972– 1973	1975– 1976	1978– 1979	1979– 1980[1]	1980– 1981[1]
Commodities	13.8	14.7	8.9	34.3	33.9	52.8	67.7
Cash	2.3	3.2	2.1	5.9	8.3	14.6	23.0
TOTAL	16.1	17.9	11.0	40.2	42.2	67.4	90.7

Sources: Yearbook of the United Nations 1969, 323–324; Yearbook of the United Nations 1971, 268; Yearbook of the United Nations 1976, 390; Yearbook of the United Nations 1979, 568; Yearbook of the United Nations 1980, 700; Yearbook of the United Nations 1981, 31, and calculations based on data in these sources.

1. Includes contributions to the IEFR through the WFC.

channeled through the WFP and directed toward humanitarian relief operations. Resources from regular pledges and Food Aid Convention contributions increased only marginally: indeed, they sometimes showed an absolute decrease, especially during the early 1970s.[61]

POLICIES, GUIDELINES, AND REGULATIONS

The policies, guidelines, and regulations that governed the WFP remained basically the same during the period under review. Nevertheless, although continuity rather than change characterized policies, some aspects should be highlighted.

The general guidelines that ECOSOC, the FAO council, and the World Food Council established for bilateral as well as multilateral donors of food aid were much in line with those established for other UN development activities; they emphasized that food aid should be provided in forms consistent with the long-term development objectives of recipient countries and be coordinated with financial aid and other forms of development assistance. The guidelines stated that donor countries should make every effort to ensure the continuity of food aid by implementing forward planning, preferably on a multiyear basis. They should give priority to low-income, food-deficit countries; finance transport and storage costs, particularly for the poorest countries; provide food aid through the WFP and other multilateral institutions; and finance triangular transactions, wherever possible, among donors, developing countries with food exports, and recipient countries. The guidelines also called for donor and recipient countries to give priority to emergency food requirements; activities designed to increase agricultural production, raise incomes, and stimulate self-reliance; and nutrition intervention programs, especially for vulnerable groups.[62]

During the 1970s, the poverty orientation of aid in terms of channeling a large share of resources to the LDCs and other low-income countries increasingly came to characterize policy prescriptions and aid implementation at the UNDP. This was true also of food aid for development during the 1970s, even before it was prescribed in the 1978 guidelines. Emergency aid is almost by definition directed toward vulnerable and hard-hit people, although the countries concerned may not necessarily be among the poorest when measured against traditional indicators.

In response to the scarcity of resources created by steeply rising food prices, the WFP prioritized the use of resources for the second part of 1973 and the remainder of the 1973–1974 pledging period. It imposed a moratorium on new development projects, cut back on some ongoing projects, and phased out other projects. It reserved the resources available after meeting unconditional commitments for the LDCs and other countries with acute food aid needs. In 1974, the CFA decided to give special aid to least-developed countries that had difficulty meeting the nonfood costs of WFP assistance.

The WFP's focus on the LDCs and those most seriously affected by the economic crisis continued throughout the 1970s. In 1975, eighty-seven of the 105 development projects that were approved involved countries in one or both of these categories.[63] In 1978, 77 percent of the approved projects benefited these groups of countries, and of the fifty-three new projects approved the following year, 79 percent benefited these countries. In 1981, some $452 million (83 percent) of total new commitments was allocated to low-income food-deficit countries. Assistance to the LDCs reached $190 million that year, 35 percent of total commitments to development projects.[64]

DEVELOPMENT PROJECTS AND RELIEF OPERATIONS

The increased level of pledges to the WFP was reflected in its commitments: during the experimental period, the program committed $77 million for 107 different development projects and relief operations. In the following five years of the program (1966–1970) it substantially increased the number of projects and the amount of assistance it provided: it committed $1.1 billion to 462 projects and relief operations. The early 1970s showed stagnation ($544 million for 244 projects), but from 1975 both the number of projects and the value of the commitments increased steeply: in 1975–1980, it committed $3.3 billion to 679 projects and relief operations.[65] From the beginning, these projects covered broad fields.[66]

When the WFP was first conceived of, aid for emergency operations was the principal justification and the main task. However, even before the program was established, the focus on this kind of assistance was downgraded: emergency assistance in natural and human-made disasters was deemed a necessity for an international food aid program but was not seen as its main task. Instead, the promotion of social and economic development was emphasized. This priority was reflected both in the administrative structure and the distribution of the available funds. Transforming food aid—food in kind as well as money for food—into economic and social development in developing countries became the principal challenge for the new program.

Table 8.3 shows how the WFP used its resources. From 1963 to 1976, it spent only 10 percent on emergency operations. This share had nearly tripled by 1980. The increase came as a response to both natural and (increasingly) human-made disasters. Nevertheless, the WFP presented itself mainly as a development agency that served the unique function of producing social and economic development using food—ideally surplus food—as the capital.

The WFP's development assistance falls into two main categories, agricultural and rural development and human resource development. Almost two-thirds of the resources for social and economic development were allocated for agricultural and rural development. Programs emphasized agricultural production, which alone accounted for close to 40 percent of all resources. Rural infrastructure came second and settlements third, accounting for 14 and 12 percent of all resources, respectively.

Most of the remaining resources used for economic and social development went to human resource development. From the start, this kind of assistance was prominent in justifications for establishing a multilateral food aid program. It drew especially on experiences in major donor countries with feeding preschool and school-age children in their own countries. Contributions to such development projects made up a large share—more than one-third—of the assistance provided for social and

TABLE 8.3.

Distribution of World Food Programme Resources for Development Projects and Emergency Operations, 1963–1981 (by percent and in millions of U.S. dollars)

	1963–1975	1976	1977	1978	1979	1980	1981	1963–1981
Development projects	89.7	93.1	81.1	81.2	80.1	71.4	75.3	83.7
Emergency operations	10.3	6.9	18.9	18.8	19.9	28.6	24.7	16.3
TOTALS	100.0	100.0	100.0	100.0	100.0	100.0	100.0	100.0
Millions of U.S. dollars	2,031.1	689.7	452.5	482.7	614.5	670.5	721.2	5,662.3

Source: Calculations based on data in D. John Shaw, *The UN World Food Programme and the Development of Food Aid* (New York: Palgrave, 2001), tables 5.2 and 6.1.

economic development projects. Most of this assistance went to mother and child health centers and primary schools, but some assistance was also provided to projects involving secondary schools and other educational training. Less than 1 percent of the total resources for social and economic development were spent on other activities (industry and mining).

Table 8.4 provides a comprehensive picture of WFP efforts during its first eighteen years of operation according to the major categories of activities. Within each category, a wide range of projects have been supported using food as the main instrument for achieving economic and social development. These efforts were summarized as follows in the 1980 report:

> Since its inception in 1963, WFP had, by the end of 1980, provided support valued at $4.8 billion for some 1,052 development projects and 495 emergency operations in about 122 countries. Its activities included: improving the health and nutrition of about 12.5 million malnourished mothers and children; food-for-work schemes for reclaiming land and building roads, houses, schools, health centres, bridges, dikes and irrigation systems in developing countries; feeding some 14 million schoolchildren and students; a Kampuchean emergency operation; feeding 1.5 million Afghan refugees in Pakistan, 1.3 million refugees in Somalia and 250,000 in Uganda; and, in answering emergencies, feeding victims of earthquakes, floods, volcanic eruptions and drought.[67]

TABLE 8.4.

World Food Programme Development Activities by Category, 1963–1981 (by percent and in millions of U.S. dollars)

	1963–1975	1976	1977	1978	1979	1980	1981	1963–1981
Agricultural and rural development								
Agricultural production	36	53	34	41	44	25	37	38.6
Rural infrastructure	15	15	9	8	13	12	19	13.7
Settlements	11	---[1]	15	9	9	13	24	11.9
Food reserves	3		2	---	1	1	3	1.5
Total agricultural and rural development	64	75	60	58	67	52	83	65.7
Human resource development								
Mother and child health centers and primary schools	28	21	34	36	30	45	14	28.4
Secondary and other educational training	8	4	6	6	3	3	3	5.5
Total human resource development	35	25	40	42	33	48	17	33.9
Other (industry and mining)	1	---	---	---	---	---	---	0.4
Total all categories[1]	100	100	100	100	100	99	100	100.0
Millions of U.S. dollars	1,822	642	367	392	492	479	543	4,737

Sources: Calculations based on data in D. John Shaw, *The UN World Food Programme and the Development of Food Aid* (New York: Palgrave, 2001), table 5.3.

1. Dashes indictae less than 1 persent.

2. Percentages may not add up to exactly 100 because figures are rounded in the data on which the calculations are based. Rounding also affects the sums given for the main categories (the given sums are the correct ones).

The other main activity was providing relief in emergency situations. However, during the early years, the WFP found that its organizational structure was not well suited to responding quickly to emerging crises, and it left first responses to bilateral agencies. Only a tiny share of the available resources was set aside to meet emergencies: from the start, a fixed sum of $7 million was reserved at the beginning of each year.

In the second part of 1969, a series of droughts and floods resulted in a sharp increase in requests for emergency assistance. In October 1969, the Intergovernmental Committee doubled the WFP's annual allocation from $10 million to $20 million. During the following three years, the annual amount set aside for emergencies varied between $20 million and $15 million. It did so again in the next two years and in 1973.[68] Gradually, the WFP extended its activities in this field by providing assistance that was coordinated with that of other UN organizations, especially involving UNHCR-coordinated operations in Bangladesh and India. It also served as a channel for bilateral contributions at donor request by purchasing and transporting food supplies from funds donated by bilateral donors or arranging for shipments of commodities made available by them. It provided similar services for the UNHCR and the United Nations Disaster Relief Organization. The WFP took on a coordinating role for these operations as well—free of charge.

The droughts of the early 1970s, which afflicted several countries in the Sahelian belt of Africa and Ethiopia, merit special mention. They lasted for years, affecting the very survival of the people living there and leading to widespread starvation. Despite food assistance, the crises resulted in a large number of casualties—it is estimated that 100,000 human lives were lost. A large proportion of the cattle on which the people in this region depended also died. Relief organizations, including the WFP, were unprepared for a crisis of these dimensions. The WFP provided some emergency assistance in 1972 and more during the following year. In 1974, it followed up emergency feeding operations with rehabilitation projects at a total cost of $12.8 million.[69] The crisis had an effect beyond the actual assistance: it focused attention at the UN on the issues of emergency aid and how to meet future emergencies of this magnitude.

Triggered by an increased demand for assistance to meet emergency situations, the WFP made efforts to enhance its capacity to provide speedy relief to disaster victims. This was made possible by borrowing from government stocks or from stocks already present in a country for use in WFP development projects and resorting to cash purchases of commodities in neighboring countries. The WFP made its expertise in commodity-purchasing and logistics available to other food aid donors and acted as a coordinating point for shipping information from all donors that contributed to relief in emergency situations. It cooperated closely with other UN bodies and programs, in particular with the Office of the United Nations Disaster Relief Coordinator, the UNHCR, the UNDP, and UNICEF and with other international and bilateral programs and nongovernmental organizations. It arranged for the purchase and shipment of foodstuffs financed from, inter alia, the Secretary-General's Special Account for Emergency Operations.[70] In this way, adapting to new demands, the WFP gradually became a more central actor within international food relief assistance toward the mid-1970s.

In 1975, the Intergovernmental Committee made an adjustment that reflected the increased concern for relief in emergency situations: $55 million was to be set aside for emergency operations instead of the original $7 million limit (in practice $15 million during the early 1970s). As it turned out, $58.2 million was used for food emergency operations that year; $3.6 million was drawn from funds earmarked for the emergency food reserve called for by the General Assembly at its seventh special session. Over 64 percent of the funds for emergency operations in 1975 were committed to the least-developed countries and countries most seriously affected by the economic crisis.[71] This development was driven by demand. However, institutional developments in 1975 worked in the same direction, such as the new general regulations for the WFP and the appointment of a new governing body (the Committee on Food Aid Policies and Programmes) with extended authority that was charged with coordinating international food aid, especially emergency food aid. The establishment of new institutions for emergency food aid to be channeled through the WFP, especially the IEFR, also worked in this direction.

In 1976, the Committee on Food Aid Policies and Programmes set aside $40 million for emergency food aid through the WFP; the following year this amount was increased to $45 million for both 1977 and 1978.[72] In addition, increasing amounts were made available by the IEFR: $8 million in 1976, increasing to $27.6 million in 1977 and $68.8 million in 1978. In 1979, emergency operations continued to grow in magnitude; $124.8 million was spent, of which $69.8 million came from WFP emergency allocations and nearly $55 million from the IEFR. In 1980, this amount increased further, reaching $191 million, of which most (63 percent) was for refugees and displaced persons affected by human-made disasters. It stayed at a high level in 1981 as well—$178 million.[73]

Although the resources spent on food for emergencies increased during the 1970s, the share of total resources remained moderate. By 1975, $209 million had been committed to 219 emergency operations around the world. Nevertheless, the amount spent was less than 10 percent of the total resources the WFP had committed for operational activities. During the next five years (1976–1980), the amount committed increased to $538 million.[74]

Within relief assistance, a distinction is made between sudden natural disasters, emergencies resulting from droughts and crop failures, and human-made disasters caused by violent conflicts. This distinction may well disguise the fact that many disasters categorized as sudden natural disasters or disasters caused by droughts may be human-made, the result of neglect or deliberate action on the part of political authorities and planners or private-sector actors—even through activities in the name of "development."

Naturally, allocations for sudden natural disasters are volatile and are driven by emerging needs. This is true as well for crop failures resulting from droughts. Even so, the share of resources spent on such emergencies has remained at a relatively high level. From 1979, a growing share of the increasing resources was spent on human-made emergencies (table 8.5). The conflicts in Afghanistan and Cambodia, which created an exodus of refugees to neighboring Pakistan and Thailand, respectively, explain this development. Major contributors of food aid, especially the United States, increasingly found the WFP to be an effective and convenient channel for such aid.

REGIONAL DISTRIBUTION OF RESOURCES

Allocations of resources for development may be planned on a medium-term basis, whereas resources for relief operations will normally come in response to emerging crises. This makes it natural to consider the regional distribution of resources separately for the two activities.

Table 8.6 shows the distribution of commitments for development projects for the world's four main regions for the period 1963–1981. The main trends were that assistance to Sub-Saharan Africa grew and assistance to Europe and the Middle East declined, while assistance to South

TABLE 8.5.

World Food Programme Commitments for Emergency Operations by Type, 1963–1981 (by percent and in millions of U.S. dollars)

	1963–1975	1976	1977	1978	1979	1980	1981
Drought/crop failures	41	30	50	25	33	32	22
Sudden natural disasters	35	18	31	41	10	5	4
Man-made disasters	24	52	19	34	57	62	74
TOTAL	100.0	100.0	100.0	100.0	100.0	99.0[1]	100.0
Millions of U.S. dollars	209.1	47.7	85.5	90.7	122.5	191.5	178.2

Source: D. John Shaw, *The UN World Food Programme and the Development of Food Aid* (New York: Palgrave, 2001), table 6.1 and calculations based on data therein.

1. Percentages may not add up to exactly 100 because figures are rounded in the data on which the calculations are based.

and East Asia by and large stayed at a relatively high level. Latin America and the Caribbean received a modest share of this assistance, with a declining trend that began in the mid-1970s.

The distribution of relief assistance in these regions during the same period is given in table 8.7. Here, assistance to Sub-Saharan Africa stayed at a high level; almost one-third of all relief assistance during this period was channeled to this region. However, an even larger share—about half of all relief assistance—went to South and East Asia, with a rising trend. Relief assistance to Europe and the Middle East declined sharply toward the end of the 1970s. Latin America received only a miniscule share of WFP emergency assistance. This regional distribution indicates the regions where major natural disasters and conflicts were taking place. Increasingly, these were human-made conflicts.

Some Concluding Observations

The United States is still the dominant actor in the food aid policy field. Food aid was originally designed to meet structural problems in U.S. agricultural policy, especially a surplus production of cereals. These

TABLE 8.6.

World Food Programme Commitments for Development Activities by
Region, 1963–1981 (by percent and in millions of U.S. dollars)

	1963–1975	1976	1977	1978	1979	1980	1981
Europe and the Middle East	38	36	29	25	12	27	21
South and East Asia	31	35	41	33	48	23	29
Sub-Saharan Africa	18	24	16	31	39	32	44
Latin America and the Caribbean	13	5	14	11	1	18	7
TOTAL	100	100	100	100	100	100	101[1]
Millions of U.S. dollars	1,822	642	367	392	492	479	543

Source: D. John Shaw, *The UN World Food Programme and the Development of Food Aid* (New York: Palgrave, 2001), table 5.2 and calculations based on data therein.

1. Percentages may not add up to exactly 100 because figures are rounded in the data on which the calculations are based.

surpluses became an international trade problem: in a supply-and-demand setting, the existence of large supplies has a negative influence on prices both at home and in the world market. From a U.S. policy perspective, the grand idea was to turn a problem within these policy areas into an asset without hurting U.S. trade policy or violating a fragile international regime that had been crafted by the FAO against dumping food products on the international market. A sizeable bilateral food aid program was the solution. In situations where countries suffered desperate food shortages but had no money at hand, food aid could provide relief and buy goodwill. It could also be effective as leverage for obtaining foreign policy concessions from governments in such situations. Surplus food constituted an additional resource that might create problems at home; but, deftly employed, it might bring political gains at home and abroad.

The multilateral food aid program, which was also initiated and designed in a U.S. political setting, entered this process late and was originally very small compared with the massive bilateral food program of the United States.[75] It was also circumscribed: it was not to be oriented toward

TABLE 8.7.

World Food Programme Commitments for Emergency Operations by Region, 1963–1981 (by percent and in millions of U.S. dollars)

	1963–1975	1976	1977	1978	1979	1980	1981
South and East Asia	40.4	24.3	44.6	46.9	55.1	57.1	56.3
Sub-Saharan Africa	27.4	32.3	31.6	41.3	25.5	36.3	35.2
Europe and the Middle East	25.9	42.6	21.8	9.2	11.7	5.8	6.4
Latin America and the Caribbean	6.1	0.8	2.1	2.6	7.8	0.8	2.1
TOTAL	99.8[1]	100.0	100.1	100.0	100.1	100.0	100.0
Millions of U.S. dollars	209.1	47.7	85.5	90.7	122.5	191.5	178.3

Source: D. John Shaw, *The UN World Food Programme and the Development of Food Aid* (New York: Palgrave, 2001), table 6.3 and calculations based on data therein.

1. Percentages may not add up to exactly 100 because figures are rounded in the data on which the calculations are based.

emergencies, which were considered "political," and should be confined to projects where it would not compete with U.S. food aid.

The core question has already been posed: did the WFP make a difference? To answer this question, we need to identify the main characteristics of food aid—whether provided bilaterally or multilaterally—but also the differences in this regard. This issue will be further pursued in chapter 13, based on the evolving multilateral food aid in the 1980s and beyond. We will, however, first address the main question posed in Part 1 of this volume: what can food aid—as institutionalized and implemented—tell us about the roots of the idea of international development assistance?

The basic idea with food aid was to use surplus production of food in one geographical area in order to meet the problems of hunger and undernutrition in another, whatever the cause of human suffering. Subsequently, finance for food (beyond the cash and services necessary for administering and transporting the food provided) was added to food in kind. Once this idea was adopted by the UN system, it was almost immediately transformed. While food aid had originally been synonymous with relief aid in connection with crises, a new, more complex, enemy was identified: poverty. The traditional rationale remained, but the UN system's primary concern became to prevent hunger by using food as an instrument to promote economic and social development through agricultural and rural development and human resource development projects.

In chapter 1, humane internationalism, with special reference to the humanitarian relief tradition, was identified among the potential sources of the concept of international development assistance. Food aid fits into this tradition. The main justification given for food aid, bilateral as well as multilateral, has been to meet immediate needs in times of crisis. Food aid has been part of such packages. This applies also to the WFP: when it was established in 1961, meeting emergencies through food assistance was cited as a prominent justification, although it was later down played. Food aid is therefore firmly grounded in the humane internationalism tradition, the humanitarian relief tradition in particular. Basically, assistance provided within the human relief tradition (or within the broader human internationalism concept) is motivated by altruism, by the desire to alleviate human suffering whenever and wherever it occurs, including beyond the confines of the nation-state.

As adopted by the UN system, the idea was mainly cast in an economic and social development perspective. For the period under review, food aid channeled through the WFP was primarily oriented toward promoting economic and social development. Food was transformed into development through food-for-work projects or, more indirectly, through human resource development. This type of support was ideally to be integrated into the development projects of other UN arms and those of the World Bank and NGOs. This primary purpose, and the way that food aid was organized, links WFP food aid (especially the "development" pillar) to the modernization paradigm, which held a hegemonic position in western development thinking in the 1950s and 1960s and beyond.

Instrumental motives related to national interests of various kinds were also at work on the donor side, even in emergency operations. We have noted such interests in relation to the postwar Marshall Plan. During the Cold War, bilateral food aid offered itself as a foreign policy instrument and was used in this way—to promote capitalist democracy, contain communism, and build alliances.

Multilateral food aid was not equally amenable to such purposes, given the structure of decision-making and the form it was given by the WFP, with its focus on mainly small development projects. Nevertheless, as the largest contributor of multilateral food aid, the United States used the power of the purse to influence WFP policies: as the sole donor, it insisted on having a say with regard to the purposes for which the means provided came to use—they had to be in conformity with the principles and objectives of U.S. bilateral food aid.

From this brief discussion we may conclude that the main "roots" of food aid can be found in humane internationalism and in the dominant development paradigm of the time, modernization theory. In the 1950s, when the United States established its large-scale bilateral food aid program—and in the 1960s as well, when the WFP was established—the Cold War framed international relations. Food aid became an instrument in this context. This also applied to multilateral food aid, although with modifications. In times of surplus production, food aid also helped donor governments solve a difficult problem of domestic policy: for the hegemonic power, also in a WFP setting, self-interest was perhaps the dominant driver.

This conclusion may be expanded on, or modified, by exploring the following core questions, to which we now turn:

- Why food aid?
- Why was the WFP established as an institution for multilateral food aid?
- Did multilateral food aid through the WFP make a difference and, if so, in what ways?

Each of these interrelated questions generates new ones, several of which are also interrelated.

Why Food Aid?

To answer this question, we need to identify the main characteristics of food aid, starting with what we mean by "food aid,"[76] the explicit and tacit rationale and justifications for this kind of aid, the objectives pursued, and the norms that have guided the activities subsumed under the concept. In addition, we need to explore the limitations and constraints associated with this kind of aid compared with other forms of development assistance, including the dangers associated with food aid, especially from an economic and social development perspective.

RATIONALE

The idea of providing food aid has long roots associated with humanitarian relief operations. This kind of assistance is driven by demand but also serves the foreign policy interests of major powers. By contrast, "modern" food aid, first institutionalized in the U.S. bilateral food aid programs in the mid-1950s, was driven by supply. The basic idea was to use surplus food products that created political and economic problems in the producer country to meet hunger and undernutrition, alleviate human suffering, and promote development in countries in need of food.

In the discourse on food aid, a prominent argument in favor of food aid has been that of *additionality:* food aid would result in more resources being transferred to developing countries than would have been the case without this kind of aid. However, food is an unreliable resource. Food aid is provided to meet immediate crises as well as agreed-upon commitments when no surplus exists and food has to be bought at market prices. It therefore makes sense to distinguish between food aid provided to alleviate humanitarian crises (relief aid) and food provided as aid to promote development. The basic rationale for using food in kind as aid is different for these two forms of aid.

Self-seeking motives on the donor side may also be at work, even in emergency operations. Food aid became an instrument in the Cold War and a foreign policy instrument in wider contexts. This applied in particular to the United States, which used food aid to attain foreign policy objectives like containing communism and seeking and fortifying allies, especially during the years immediately after World War II.[77]

Food aid can serve as an instrument in domestic policy as well. Major producers of food, cereals in particular, are at times faced with surpluses that create problems at home because the domestic and international markets are unable to handle them. International trade in food and food commodities has been regulated by rules that aim at keeping prices stable and avoiding dumping—rules that have served the interests of major producers well. The alternative would be for the major producer countries to regulate the production of food, but this might be offensive to farmers, with possible consequences at next election. It might even run counter to the ideology of the government. In a short-term perspective, the buildup of stockpiles might also offer itself as a solution, albeit an expensive one. However, confronted with a structural crisis—as was the case in U.S. agriculture before it established its bilateral food-for-peace program and also later when the WFP was conceived of and established—this response would not be sustainable. Food aid for emergencies was a way to circumvent these difficulties—especially food provided on a grant basis or sold at reduced prices to meet food crises in countries where the recipient government would not be able to pay the market price. Such aid would not interfere drastically with the international market for food.

Both bilateral and multilateral food aid has also been cast in a development perspective. Bilateral food aid, especially program food aid, has been provided as a form of budget support for the recipient government: it may be sold in the domestic market of the recipient country and the income from such sales used to finance development projects, whether freely or as circumscribed by the donor government or voluntary aid agency.

It should be added that food aid, like most other forms of development assistance, serves a host of other general purposes and purposes that are specific to the particular form of aid as well.

LIMITATIONS AND RELATIVE EFFECTIVENESS

Food aid provided in kind (cereals and other food products) shares some weaknesses common to most commodity aid:

- It is usually tied to deliveries from the donor county. Services such as shipping the food to the recipient country have been tied to vessels of the donor state, resulting in higher rates than what might be obtained on the market. This means that the actual value of the aid to the recipient in financial terms is reduced if compared with what might be obtained on the open market. In addition, administration may be difficult. Food aid may include commodities that are unfamiliar in the local diet and not readily accepted.

- Food aid may affect local production negatively. The commodities (like cereals and food products) may be sold by the recipient government at prices below what the local producers could offer, making it less attractive for farmers to produce and deliver to the market. In this way, food aid leads to dependency instead of self-sufficiency in agricultural production.[78]

For years, these weaknesses have been identified in the discourse on food aid.[79] As we have seen, the WFP has made efforts to reduce these negative effects of food aid. It has valued food products by taking current prices in the international market as the point of departure, thereby reducing the "loss" for the recipient somewhat. By orienting its food aid toward development (food-for-work projects in particular), the WFP has tried to reduce the negative effects of food aid on local productivity; these are mostly associated with bilateral food programs. Nevertheless, from a food security perspective, the priority would be promoting self-sufficiency in food production. Within the multilateral system, this perspective was highlighted in the discourse on food aid and food security from the very beginning.

Other negative aspects are associated with food aid in kind. Such aid is a cumbersome way of transferring resources for development, especially as compared with financial transfers. It became especially cumbersome for the WFP because of its high ambitions: the aim was to transform food in kind into economic and social development, with an emphasis on agricultural development in rural areas. Food-for-work programs had diets that met high nutrition standards and were adapted to local tastes.[80] Although such ambitions may channel assistance in the right direction from a development perspective, transmitting this kind of aid is administratively demanding and requires a high level of organizational skills. The transaction costs are high.

OPTING FOR FLEXIBILITY

Several devices have been invented in order to make in-kind food aid more flexible and effective and to reduce transaction costs. Food aid became increasingly monetized. The food provided as aid was sold in the recipient country (or elsewhere) in order to generate local currency that could be used to sustain emergency operations as well as development projects. However, for the WFP, this opportunity was strictly circumscribed from the start, although an opening was gradually made that adapted to delivery needs: sales proceeds were used for in-country costs of handling and delivering food aid. However, the revenues from such sales were also used for projects that did not involve any form of food assistance.

Other mechanisms with a similar objective were also used. Among these were triangular transactions—buying food in one developing country and shipping it to another as food aid.[81] Barter trade—exchanging a commodity provided as food aid for another commodity produced in the recipient country (that was more adapted to the local diet) to be used as food aid—was also used to make food aid more flexible.

Much of what has entered into international statistics as "food aid" comes close to what in fact may be described as normal trade in food. Donors, including the WFP, have bought food on the international market or the market of a developing country with ODA money in order to meet their international commitments (such as those to the WFP and the Food Aid Convention) or to sustain specific relief operations, whether organized bilaterally or multilaterally. Food aid has become increasingly monetized also in this way.

FOOD: AN UNRELIABLE RESOURCE

Food surpluses within the major food-producing countries, on which the idea of food aid was originally founded, are an unreliable resource. This was demonstrated in the early 1970s, when due food was scarce, leading to steeply rising prices. In spite of increased pledges, the amount of food actually provided (in metric tons) decreased. The balance between production and demand fluctuates, creating one of the most fundamental problems associated with food aid. The price of food and, accordingly, the amount of food available for a certain sum of money, is volatile as well. Such variations in the availability and price of food necessarily create problems for an agency established with the purpose of planning and implementing development projects based on precisely this resource. The relative value of food aid to recipients as compared with financial transfers is affected, particularly if the food is bought by (free) money set aside for development cooperation. Even more important, it negatively affects the possibilities of long-term planning for aid agencies and recipient countries alike. Long-term development projects cannot be planned and effectively implemented if they are based on an unreliable resource. As early as 1965, the UN Secretary-General and the FAO director-general warned against the inherent weakness of food aid.[82]

This problem was reinforced by the primary orientation of WFP food aid, which emphasized the nutritional aspects involving a balanced composition of the food provided. As noted, this aspect was especially prominent in food-for-work development projects: whereas surpluses might be available with regard to some types of food (such as U.S. wheat), they might not be available for other important components (such as dairy products or protein-rich foods).

THE ADDITIONALITY ARGUMENT REVISITED

A major argument for food aid has been that more resources would be provided to developing countries than would have been the case without this kind of aid. Given the many limitations and constraints associated with food aid, particularly food aid in kind, the argument that food aid would release additional resources for social and economic development and for humanitarian relief becomes critical for our conclusions in connection with our main question: why food aid?

When the WFP was created, massive food surpluses existed, and the additionality argument held true, especially for the United States. It also held true for the much larger bilateral food aid programs of the United States and a few other major agricultural producers (and exporters), particularly Canada and, increasingly, the European Economic Community.[83] In a way, the argument draws support from the way that donor governments responded to repeated calls by the WFP and its intergovernmental bodies and parent organizations for larger contributions in convertible currencies: cash remained a scarce resource. Further confirmation of the additionality argument may be seen in the negative response, in the mid-1960s, to Argentina's proposal for a World Food Fund.

The additionality argument is probably valid even today for some major donors, particularly the United States, especially regarding the assistance channeled through U.S. voluntary organizations. Nevertheless, as will be argued in chapter 13, the argument has since lost much of its strength in most donor countries, with the possible exception just mentioned.

A characteristic feature of food aid, especially food aid in kind, is that it is tied aid. There exists a vast literature on the negative effects of tied aid, including the reduced value in financial terms to the recipients of procurement tying. We return to that in chapter 13.

The limitations and inherent weaknesses of food aid, particularly food in kind, as a means to promote development also apply to food aid provided for relief operations, although not to the same extent: in relief operations, food in kind is in demand and may even be transmitted directly. Other challenges come to the fore in such emergencies, especially the difficulties of making food available on short notice. From the mid-1970s, the WFP took on an active role in providing food for relief in cooperation with other international and bilateral actors, including NGOs. Increasingly it also aspired to become a lead agency and coordinator of international relief assistance. One mechanism was to stimulate the building up of food reserves and stockpiles of other commodities ready for immediate deployment if and when an emergency situation exploded.

Why Was the WFP Established as an Institution for Multilateral Food Aid?

The WFP was established—along with other political initiatives involving international development—when the Kennedy administration took over in Washington in 1961. All along, the United States has found itself in the driver's seat, and for years it remained by far the largest contributor. However, the idea itself had matured within the UN system. In the 1940s and 1950s, it had consistently been pursued within the "civil service" of the FAO in tandem with its intergovernmental bodies. Many argued for a more ambitious program than what was later established, such as the creation of a World Food Board. However, this idea was not acceptable to the most powerful international actors, the western powers and the United States in particular.

In approaching this question, it therefore makes sense first to explore the U.S. rationale for creating and supporting this program. The country had for years been running its own large-scale bilateral food aid programs. These programs have histories of their own, financed and administered, in part, separately from (ordinary) development assistance activities. Most U.S. food aid is part of U.S. agricultural and trade policy, and its rationale derives from these policy areas. The basis for U.S. food aid is formed by bills for agriculture, agricultural trade, and aid negotiated and agreed on for a sequence of fixed periods.[84] Anchored in the agricultural policy of the world's largest food producer and the trade policy of the largest exporter of agricultural commodities, food aid policy has been adapted to domestic needs and interests within these policy areas. In addition, food aid became an instrument in the foreign policy of a hegemonic power in what was then a bipolar international system.

With a large bilateral food aid program well established, adapted to serve these various interests, why did the United States decide to front the creation of a multilateral food aid program? There may be several explanations, and they do not necessarily contradict each other. The idea of a multilateral food aid program had been around in the UN system for some time, not confined to the FAO setting, prompting the United States to respond in one way or another. Then in came a new president, a Democrat who, during the election campaign, had employed his rhetorical skills to turn the problem of vast agricultural surpluses into an asset ("food for peace") for both U.S. farmers and the people of the world and had also advanced the idea of "a world food agency." Immediately after Kennedy assumed office, an executive order provided for an expanded program for food distribution to needy families in the United States, while another gave dynamism to the Food for Peace Program.[85] With one stroke, food aid was turned into an instrument in both domestic and foreign policy, appealing to idealism in U.S. society as well.

Since World War II, the foreign policy of the United States has been torn between unilateralism and multilateralism, both approaches based on a realist international relations tradition, although multilateralism has been associated with idealism as well. The Kennedy administration clearly belonged to the latter camp. At this point, the U.S. administration was in almost full control within the UN in policy areas of this kind where the Security Council was not involved. Washington could be confident that the program created would be in line with U.S. preferences and would not interfere with its own important concerns. On the contrary, the program was seen as complementary to its bilateral programs, helping the administration out with its surpluses (in good years), without disrupting local markets or other U.S. exports. Its activities were circumscribed— UN member states, especially the main food producers, limited its role to that of running (small) projects and not entering the more political arena of program food aid to any significant extent, particularly where emergencies were involved. Besides, the resources at its disposal were tiny; these too were under full U.S. control when the program was established. Nevertheless, one uncertainty remained: a multilateral food aid program might develop into a competitor, representing an alternative with regard to resources and norms alike.

During the early years, the WFP did not constitute much of a threat when it came to the resources made available. Both McGovern and the intergovernmental bodies that recommended the establishment of the WFP argued that the program would not interfere negatively with existing bilateral food aid programs, meaning U.S. programs. From the beginning, the WFP was firmly linked to the principles agreed to within the FAO on the disposal of agricultural surpluses, which implied that only in exceptional cases would WFP food aid (in kind) be allowed to be sold in recipient countries in order to provide capital for development activities. The project approach further circumscribed the possibility that WFP activities might rival U.S. food aid. Among the justifications given for establishing the WFP was also the hope that the program might be able to prevent the creation and growth of other bilateral food aid programs—with particular reference to the EEC—thereby leaving most of the "bilateral" stage and trade in food for the United States.[86]

Nevertheless, a multilateral program with an international staff and intergovernmental steering organs might still represent a potential threat in the longer run, not least by creating alternative norms. The WFP tried, from the very beginning, to take on the challenge of setting norms within this policy area. Gradually, it also made efforts at placing itself in the strategic role as coordinator of food aid.

For other actors, especially some governments of developing countries (perspectives and vested interests differed among them), the qualities associated with a multilateral program, in contrast to a bilateral program run by a major power, were welcomed. To some extent this was reflected in the voluntary pledges to the WFP: most of these came from developing countries. However, as contributions these represented but a very small share of the total resources made available. As we have seen, most resources were contributed by major western powers, especially the United States.

Did the WFP Make a Difference?

During the period under review, what difference did the WFP make to food aid—if any at all? First and foremost, it added a multilateral dimension. The norms established for WFP operational activities were similar to those earlier established for the EPTA's technical assistance and the Special Fund's pre-investment activities. It was up to recipient countries to decide whether to provide food and what kind of food aid should be provided. In stark contrast to bilateral programs, in WFP programs, local authorities were also to be in charge of implementation once the aid had crossed the border.

The WFP strongly emphasized coordinating and integrating multilateral food aid with the development activities of other UN agencies and beyond (including the activities of the World Bank). The administrative model prescribed that the WFP should rely on the services of established institutions to cut administrative costs. The indirect effect of this interagency cooperation was that the WFP contributed to strengthening the system's capacity to coordinate its various activities within this policy field, with the resident representative system as the core. Gradually, however, it developed its own administration with separate missions in some recipient countries.

Most bilateral food aid programs sought to address hunger and undernutrition, especially through relief operations. The WFP, however, saw its primary task as the promotion of economic and social development by means of food aid. The setting in which the WFP was created may help us understand why. The UN General Assembly gave the green light for the establishment of the WFP on the same day that it established the First Development Decade, and the program was seen as an integral part of the new development strategy. The explicit expectation that the activities of the program should be coordinated with other activities geared toward promoting development within the UN—the EPTA and the UN Special Fund in particular—probably worked in the same direction.

Food aid is a cumbersome way of providing development assistance, especially when channeled through the WFP. On balance, WFP assistance was in fact provided directly to the recipient government. Bilateral U.S. food aid for development, in contrast, used U.S. NGOs as intermediaries who delivered, stored, and distributed the aid and supervised project activities.

The main advantage of multilateral food aid as compared to bilateral assistance, as perceived by several recipients, is that a multilateral agency acts as intermediary between the donor and recipient governments. The donor's flag is normally removed—not that this removes "politics" from aid. Conditions may still be attached to the assistance. For example, the United States insisted on having a say when its assistance was implemented.

In addition to substantial material contributions, the WFP—and the multilateral system surrounding this operational program—contributed extensively to putting the issue of food security high on the international agenda. The intellectual contribution in terms of research, education, and information on the subject matter is typical of the UN system in general. It fulfills an all-important function that generally is not sufficiently appreciated. In fulfilling this research and information function, a long series of reports and other publications have been prepared, focusing on the current state of affairs, development trends, and the problems involved with regard to food security, food aid, and related themes.[87]

The WFP, in cooperation with the FAO, took on the function of serving as a forum where member governments could discuss and consult among themselves about relevant and upcoming issues in the food aid policy arena. The program even coordinated some of this work. In this function, it was able to play a unique role, since both donor and recipient governments were represented in its governing committee, including food-exporting developing countries. Soviet-bloc countries, however, were an exception; they did not take part in multilateral food aid cooperation. From the mid-1970s, an annual review of food aid policies and programs was prepared for the CFA. During the initial years, this report aimed at monitoring the follow-up of the 1974 World Food Conference's recommendations. Later on, the perspective was broadened to report on evolving policies within this field globally as well as within donor countries.

Information of this kind produced by the multilateral system are a useful basis for policy formulation and action by the countries directly concerned, the multilateral system itself, for bilateral initiatives, and increasingly also for civil society actors. They also influence priorities at these various levels.

The program broadened participation in global food aid operations by providing a convenient outlet for countries with small food surpluses: as noted, the large majority of contributors during the early years were developing countries.

The United States, however, had the will and ability to influence both the policy and practice of the WFP, even to reduce its multilateral character, by insisting that objectives and norms set for its own food aid should also apply to the multilateral program. Moreover, it got away with it, which was quite exceptional in a multilateral setting and served to demonstrate the political power of the purse. Normally, the rationale and perspective of a multilateral program differs from those of a bilateral program, especially those that aim to serve the domestic and foreign policy interests of a superpower. Through its position as the major contributor of food, a superpower is well placed to influence both WFP policy and practice. Still, a difference remained, and this became increasingly manifest in the 1970s when the NIEO ideology inspired developing countries to coordinate their policies. In a multilateral setting, actors with competing perceptions of reality, values, and interests are on the stage, increasing the independence of the program. The major contributor was not always able to determine outcomes.[88]

Some of the strings related to food aid activities and the use of resources were relaxed over time. Changes in the reality that the program was created to respond to, especially the hunger catastrophes in the Sahel and Ethiopia in the mid-1970s and again in the early 1980s and the new international institutions for financing relief food aid, increasingly changed its focus toward meeting major emergencies. The conflicts in Asia in the late 1970s—Afghanistan and Cambodia in particular—alerted the organization to a challenge of a different kind: humanitarian crises caused by violent conflict. The program's experiences with these challenges started a process of change within the organization.

Initially, food aid was seen as driven by demand: the WFP was providing aid to meet the needs of large-scale hunger catastrophes caused by droughts and conflicts. When the idea of food aid was realized in the 1950s in the large U.S. programs, the main perspective was that food aid was driven by supply. This was the basic idea when the WFP was created—food surpluses should be used to meet hunger and malnutrition and produce development in developing countries. Then, in the late 1960s, this perspective was challenged: a UN study emerged with a demand-driven perspective. Food aid should respond to needs in developing countries and be planned on the basis of forecasts of food demands.[89] The UN system was to provide reliable information on developments within countries and regions about food production and prospective food deficits. This, in turn, prompted the FAO to prepare regular (annual) reviews on the outlook for food. The study also brought forward ideas that were later to become central in the discourse on food security, such as a system for early warning of food shortages.

NINE

The 1960s and 1970s: Perspectives on Development

- **The 1 Percent Target**
- **North-South Cooperation: An Asymmetrical Relationship**
- **Food for Development, Food for Relief: The Multilateral Contribution**
- **Summing Up**

In the 1960s and 1970s, the idea of international development assistance as it was institutionalized in terms of UN norms, aims, and activities entered a mature stage. This chapter concentrates on the main ideas that emerged and were pursued during those decades. What triggered these ideas? Who were the main actors involved in forming and institutionalizing them—or killing them? How can policy outcomes be explained?

The focus in this chapter is narrowed to a few issues. One major outcome of the first and second development decades was the establishment of a quantitative target for development assistance. We first look into the development of this target. Within the UNDP, greater emphasis came to be placed on achieving a better delivery system. The 1970 consensus came to set norms for the development relationship, to which we then turn. At this point, the focus will broaden to North-South relations during this period. And finally, we will focus on what the establishment of the World Food Programme adds to our understanding of the rationale behind development cooperation.

The 1 Percent Target

The idea that the well-off countries should contribute 1 percent of their income in development assistance has its roots back in the early 1950s. In 1951, the group of experts appointed by UN Secretary-General Trygve Lie picked up the idea of establishing a second pillar of grant in aid—capital assistance to developing countries as a supplement to the technical assistance provided by the EPTA. The group of experts insisted that a mechanism should be established within the UN system to provide capital assistance to less-developed countries. The idea that the economically well-off nations should provide 1 percent of their gross national income as development assistance emerged almost as a by-product of the expert group's work.[1] Since then, the idea has been around in one form or another.[2] Transformed into a target, this idea came to dominate the debate on aid and development for the rest of the century and was then given added life in connection with the Millennium Development Goals.

The idea of a development assistance target was first formulated in the strategy for the First Development Decade.[3] The target formulated by the General Assembly appeared in a resolution related to the DD1 declaration: the flow of capital and assistance to developing countries should reach approximately 1 percent of the combined national incomes of the economically advanced countries as soon as possible. As defined, the target included all kinds of transfers, private and public, regardless of the purposes for which they were to be used or whether conditions were attached. The assistance that was channeled through the multilateral system, the UN included, was part of the target. The target reflected the predominant view at the UN at that point: capital, in whatever form, was a scarce resource necessary for development in the less well-off countries. Not much has changed in this regard: in fulfilling the MDGs, not only ODA but also private financial flows—including private investments by transnational companies, however controversial—are also assumed to have an important role to play.

The target carried normative influence, emphasizing that a need existed to be met and an obligation to be honored. However, as a mechanism for fulfilling the commitments made by governments, its value was limited. Governments were in command of their own budgets. They could also recommend that the private sector invest in developing countries and they could even stimulate such investments. However, the decisions made by those involved in such transfers were informed by logic, especially of their own profits and the security of investments. This logic applied to state-owned corporations as well. Western aid-providing governments therefore had few opportunities to implement the private sector part of the target.[4]

In the beginning of the 1960s, western governments gave increased importance to development assistance, reflected in the establishment of the First Development Decade and the UN target for aid. The East-West divide triggered this engagement. For years, western countries had coordinated their economic policy in the OECD. In 1960, they established the Development Assistance Committee within the OECD to coordinate aid policy.[5] During the early 1960s, the DAC came to play an all-important role in operationalizing the 1 percent target adopted by the UN, although at first this applied only to the aid of its member governments. The DAC established a system of statistical measurement and performance reporting on the part of its member governments.[6] This exercise brought the 1 percent target into a more dynamic (and realistic) setting, although the target applied only to western industrialized countries. The DAC's annual scrutiny of the aid policies and performances of its member countries went beyond recording the private and public flows to developing countries: increasingly, the focus was directed toward quality, such as the conditions attached to aid, whether the aid took the form of grants or loans, and the degree of procurement tying. The norms established as the basis for such scrutiny were intended to improve aid both in quantitative and qualitative terms: more assistance on more concessionary conditions. This gave rise to work on the calculated grant element of development assistance.

The target established for DD1 was the basis for reporting financial flows to developing countries for most of the 1960s, although the DAC increasingly came to focus on the kinds of flows that governments could control: public transfers and ODA—that is, grants and loans provided with a grant element. The focus on public transfers and the financial terms of the flows was evident in the first DAC report.[7] One basic problem was that DAC member countries provided assistance to developing countries on widely differing conditions. The committee sought to harmonize and soften these conditions; thus, in 1965, the DAC's recommendation to member governments on the financial terms and conditions of their assistance came close to the ODA target adopted for the DD2.[8]

Although work on definitions and categories continued, it was not until the 1970 DAC report that separate figures were provided for official development assistance.[9] At that point, work was well under way on the international strategy for the Second UN Development Decade that involved a new target for international development assistance, as we saw in chapter 6. The work carried out by the DAC was instrumental in forming the new target. The Pearson report was also instrumental in this regard: in addition to insisting that development assistance should be provided on generous conditions, it made a clear distinction between official development assistance, where governments would be able to define both the conditions on which aid was to be provided and the amount of aid, in contrast to the mixture of private financial flows and other official flows in the target for DD1.[10] On this basis, it recommended a special target for ODA: 0.7 percent of GNP.[11]

The international target set for assistance provided to developing countries for DD2 (the 1970s) by "economically advanced" countries remained at 1 percent of their GNP. This target included both public and private transfers. Previously, the target had been set in GNI. The change after UNCTAD II (1968), which increased the amount by about 25 percent, stated that by 1972, each of these countries should provide a minimum net amount of its GNP at market prices in financial resource transfers to developing countries each year. Countries unable to achieve the target by 1972 were to do their best to do so by 1975 at the latest, and those that had already met the target should ensure that their net resource transfers were maintained and if possible increased. In contrast to the target for DD1, ODA was given particular importance and was a separate target: "Each economically advanced country will progressively increase its offi-cial development assistance to the developing countries and will exert its best efforts to reach a minimum net amount of 0.7 per cent of its gross national product at market prices by the middle of the Decade."[12]

The figure of 0.7 percent of GNP came to be *the* target for official development assistance in subsequent decades.[13] For a handful of DAC countries, it had a strong impact: in the early 1970s, the Scandinavian countries and a few others used a strategy involving stepped-up budget-ary allocations in order to reach the target by a set date. After having achieved it in the mid-1970s, these countries and the Netherlands set a more ambitious target for themselves: 1 percent of GNP in ODA, which these frontrunners also achieved for several years. In the 1990s, Denmark even aspired to a target of 1.5 percent of GNP in official assistance for a combination of development and environmental activities in developing countries. Several other countries aspired to reach the 0.7 percent target. France even managed to attain it in some years. Other countries made it a future target and set intermediate targets with fixed dates. The 0.7 percent target had some effect in increasing ODA.

For other countries, any effects were at best marginal, judged by actual performance (see Appendix 1). This applied especially to the United States, the largest provider of ODA in absolute terms throughout most decades;

its ODA showed a negative trend in the 1970s and the following decades. The 0.7 percent target was probably not what drove the OPEC countries in their heyday as aid providers, especially in the 1970s and 1980s, when they were providing assistance far beyond that target.

A technical device cannot substitute for politics: the political aspiration and will to reach a goal are absolute prerequisites. Should those conditions be present—as they were for a handful of governments in the 1970s and beyond—a device like the 0.7 percent target may be a useful instrument for fulfilling the aspiration.

North-South Cooperation: An Asymmetrical Relationship

Relations between the North and South have been asymmetrical, especially the power relationship between aid donors and recipients (whether the former is a government or a multilateral organization), and the more resources the donor controls and the more dependent the recipient is on the aid, the more asymmetrical the relationship becomes. The structural adjustment policy of the 1980s, which the Bretton Woods institutions orchestrated with the aim of promoting economic policy reform in debt-ridden developing countries, showed how extreme this power relationship can be. Acceptance of the prescribed policy reforms was a condition for obtaining structural adjustment support from these institutions (first-generation conditionality). Most bilateral donors also set as a condition for providing ODA that the recipient governments accepted IMF policy prescriptions.

The crucial question here is whether or not the United Nations made a difference. Did it generate norms and did it set an example in the way it implemented its assistance? The norms established for development cooperation within the UN system and the way these norms were institutionalized and practiced have been central issues in previous chapters. Chapter 7 emphasized the process leading to the 1970 consensus and its implementation at the UN. There is no need to repeat the discussion here, so let us simply highlight the main outcome: the norms established for development cooperation placed decisions with the recipient government. Development assistance from the UN system was to be provided according to the development policy and priorities of those governments and was to be integrated in their development plans. The basic norm—the sovereignty of the recipient state—was already in place when the EPTA was established in 1949.

How this norm was implemented during the initial period is another matter: priority was given to building up a UN presence in the countries concerned, particularly through a system of EPTA (later UNDP) resident representatives, who were to liaise with the governments concerned and coordinate the activities of the many arms of the UN system at the country level. In practice, however, much of the real decision making took place within the UN system itself—by the UNDP and its forerunners and the executing agencies, most of whom belonged to the UN system and were actively generating requests for projects within their fields of competence. The Jackson study of the UNDP system and the 1970 consensus that was informed by the recommendations of this study directed much attention to further improving coherence between the established norms and actual practice, focusing on institutional arrangements. The aspiration was to create an effective delivery system and place responsibility for activities with the governments of the countries concerned. However, the process of moving responsibility for the execution of assistance from the UNDP and the executing agencies of the UN system over to the governments concerned took many more years. This process is further described and discussed in chapter 12.

Nevertheless, the simple answer to the core question posed is that the United Nations made a difference, both with the major bilateral donors and the Bretton Woods institutions. The norms established for cooperation were crystal clear from the initial stage: the ultimate power was to be placed with the recipient governments. Gradually also implementation—procedures, institutions, and the delivery system for development cooperation—became attuned to these norms, although slowly and often in a cumbersome way. The norms and procedures established by the UN system in the early years had a catalytic effect. To some extent they were adopted by several donor countries, particularly the small and medium-sized western powers that emerged as frontrunners in providing real development assistance in the mid-1970s.[14] How can this be explained? The main explanation relates to systemic factors.

In Part 1, particularly in chapter 2, we saw how the norm established for this activity was attributed to the evolving international situation in which new nations had emerged and were keenly guarding their newly won sovereignty. National sovereignty was also anchored in the UN Charter.

Developments in the late 1950s and in the 1960s strengthened the political foundations on which the norm of sovereignty rested. Third World nations were increasingly coming to power within the UN system, at least in terms of voting power. They became more organized as a group both outside and inside the UN system in the group of nonaligned countries and the G-77, although these overlapping groups included nations with conflicting interests on specific issues.

Nevertheless, the asymmetry in North-South power relations remained during the 1960s and 1970s. Donors have always attached conditions to their aid. These conditions have involved the donors' primary objectives for providing aid, whether they were altruistic objectives related to social and economic development within the recipient countries or objectives in line with their various self-interests. Conditions related to the latter may turn the asymmetrical power relationship into a real problem in a development context.

The Cold War continued to dominate international relations during the 1960s and the 1970s, and the hot war that raged for years in Southeast Asia was a more or less permanent reminder of the conflict. The East-West divide dominated relations between the first and second worlds, and both parties succeeded in involving Third World countries as well. The new Third World grouping brought a North-South policy divide more strongly to the fore. In the 1970s, it succeeded in involving countries of the North as well: in most issues, the G-77 could count on the political support and votes (but not the financial commitment) of the East. In several issues involving a North-South divide, they could also count on political sympathy and support, and even financial commitments, from a group of "likeminded countries" of the West, even though these countries did not agree on all issues and at times came under pressure from the major powers of the West.

The new political energy and confidence of Third World countries found its way into ECOSOC and the General Assembly and their subsystems. In the 1960s, UNCTAD emerged as the central organization in this regard. As we saw in chapter 6, many Third World countries preferred UNCTAD as the preparatory organ for the new international development strategy (DD2).[15] In the 1960s, Third World countries contributed (through UNCTAD and other intergovernmental UN bodies and secretariats) to a more nuanced view of the role of foreign private capital as a development driver. In the 1970s, the critical spotlight on the practices of transnational corporations in developing countries led to efforts to establish norms (a code of conduct) for their operations. This influenced how the 1 percent target for the 1970s was defined and was an important background for the Jackson capacity study and its follow-up through the 1970 consensus.

The new self-confidence of Third World countries generated a "new" ideological paradigm based on an alternative to East and West (nonalignment) and neostructuralism. It assumed a dynamic form: self-reliance and collective self-reliance. In contrast to the implicit if not outright explicit policy recommendation of the neo-Marxist brand of the *dependencia* paradigm to withdraw from exploitive relations with the industrial countries of the North (the center-periphery theorem), the main strategy developed during the latter 1960s, which emerged in full force in the early 1970s, focused on demands for a new international economic order. This implied an expansion of North-South cooperation but on a political and economic basis that was more just. The DD2 strategy reflected the influence of this new political force, especially after its midterm review. DD2 placed great importance on the transfer of science and technology. Toward the end of the 1970s, this emphasis became stronger than ever, with an important shift of focus from the transfer to the generation of science and technology within Third World countries themselves.[16]

As we saw in chapter 6, the ideological climate changed in core western states in the 1980s. Most Third World countries acquired soaring debts that became increasingly more difficult to service. The Reagan administration in Washington effectively stopped further international negotiations on a NIEO with tacit support from other major western powers, including the United Kingdom and the Federal Republic of Germany. An epoch had ended.

During the 1960s and 1970s, the state continued to be seen as the key organizer of development. Most bilateral and multilateral ODA was channeled through the government system on the recipient side, although donor governments used part of their ODA to stimulate their private sector to engage in developing countries through investment and export guarantees. This strategy was further developed into export subsidies (ODA-financed export credits) in the 1980s. The predominant perception of the crucially important role of the state for the effectiveness and efficiency of aid had consequences for the purposes to which aid was channeled. The UN system prioritized technical assistance in a wide range of areas. Planning was accorded high priority, but so was assistance within other sectors to strengthen the development capacity of developing countries.

Toward the end of the 1970s, most developing countries had weakened governments, particularly in Africa. Most states were heavily debt-ridden and found it difficult to promote social and economic development. The very legitimacy of the state as a development agent was also weakened, and this perception of the state as corrupt, inefficient, and lacking sufficient administrative competence and capacity intensified in the 1980s. Gunnar Myrdal had identified the "soft state" in Asia in the 1960s.[17] In the 1980s, political scientists described such states in Africa as neopatrimonial states.[18] This exposure of the weaknesses of the state in Africa (and elsewhere) had dramatic consequences for development cooperation. The wide difference in approach between the Bretton Woods institutions, which took control of the ideology and practice governing the aid and development regime of the 1980s, and that of the UN system, as shown during previous decades and outlined for the 1980s in the strategy for the DD3, had never been exposed more sharply.

Food for Development, Food for Relief: The Multilateral Contribution

Traditionally, food aid has had a primary rationale of its own. It can be fully understood only in the context of the domestic and foreign policy of the United States. The food aid to Europe during and after World War II was part of a long U.S. tradition of massive transfers of food aid as humanitarian relief to victims of large-scale humanitarian catastrophes caused by war and nature. The large agricultural surpluses resulted in part from lack of political will to meet a structural agricultural problem through regulations of the production, confronted with a strong interest group consisting of producers of food and food-based products. U.S. food aid, both when provided ad hoc and after it was established on a more permanent basis in 1954 through PL 480 programs, was primarily based on the need to get rid of agricultural surpluses without directly dumping on the international market. It had a trade-promoting function as well, expanding markets for U.S. agricultural products.

This structurally based problem of large agricultural surpluses met the incoming Kennedy administration head on—the harvest in 1960 yielded sizeable surpluses. His team came prepared for it, combining efforts to reform agricultural production with using food surpluses as an asset in the foreign policy. The idea of a multilateral channel—developed during the presidential campaign—served to build the foreign policy image of the incoming president while offering an additional opportunity to get rid of food surpluses. Nevertheless, more overarching considerations, including the desire to promote longer-term approaches to world food problems, have also driven U.S. food aid policies during these years.

Changes in the U.S. policy environment might trigger changes in its food aid policies with consequences for global food aid, including multilateral assistance. The availability of food surpluses nationally or globally are an important determinant: in times of food scarcity, the price of food rises and food aid becomes expensive to the donor government. And in times with large domestic surpluses and little international demand for food on commercial conditions, food is available and inexpensive to the donor government. Large U.S. food surpluses were the normal situation up to the early 1960s, constituting the basis for the additionality argument discussed in chapter 8. In the early 1960s and increasingly toward the end of the decade, the traditionally large U.S. food surpluses came to an end. Food was not as readily available for aid, and as inexpensive, as it had been.

Changes in ideology and foreign policy involvements as well as conflicts have also influenced the availability of food and U.S. food aid policy. During the Nixon administration's second term, a free market agricultural policy resulted in a decline in the levels of grain carry-over stocks held at the government's expense. Another daring policy in the same period, the secretly negotiated purchase of U.S. wheat by the Soviet Union, contributed to make U.S. food a scarce resource for food aid.[19] It also weakened its previously totally dominant position in food aid.

When the WFP was designed as a complement to the large U.S. bilateral food aid program, the United States wanted to circumscribe its activities so that it would not compete its own program, especially within fields deemed "political," such as program food aid that could serve as budget assistance for a recipient government or relief assistance. The WFP's modest financial framework was an effective constraint in this regard, particularly since the United States was in almost full control of its resource availability for years to come. The new program created an opening for relief aid, but the emphasis was on project food aid. Transforming food into social and economic development through food-for-work and school feeding projects became its trademark.

The change in this profile came from outside developments such as major humanitarian crises, but shifts in U.S. domestic and foreign policies also affected its food aid capacity and policy. In the early 1960s, the United States insisted that other western powers should share the burden of providing food to meet humanitarian crises. In the 1967 GATT negotiations (the Kennedy Round), the United States made contributions in kind and in cash of food-importing European countries a condition for agreeing to concessions on industrial products.[20] This brought a new set of players— with different perspectives and interests—more actively into the arena of international food aid policy. Up to the early 1960s, the United States and Canada had provided almost all food aid. But in the 1970s, the balance of power changed somewhat, and this had implications for the WFP. In addition, in the late 1960s and increasingly in the 1970s, Third World governments made a stronger impact in the UN system's intergovernmental bodies, including the WFP. Together, these developments created change that affected the orientation of the World Food Programme's activities.

The drought catastrophes of the Sahelian region in Africa and the humanitarian catastrophes caused by conflicts in Asia (Afghanistan and Cambodia) set in motion a change of perspective within the WFP. Perhaps even more decisive were outside expectations—especially from the aid agencies of the new players within this arena—that the WFP should also take on a major role in humanitarian emergency operations. For food-importing donors, food aid was mainly to be financed from the ODA budget, not from accumulated food surpluses. It was up to bilateral donors to decide the use of their Food Aid Convention contributions, and most agencies came to see the WFP as a convenient agency for their funding, particularly when humanitarian crises required assistance. In the early 1980s, a new hunger crisis caused by drought developed in the Sahelian region.

During the 1970s, the WFP started to respond to major food crises not only by using new means placed to its disposal for relief operations but also by setting aside a growing share of its own core budget. Developments in its political environment had contributed to unlocking the restriction that WFP activities should be confined to development food aid projects. Even so, the WFP remained true to its basic identity: its goal was to transform food into social, economic, and human development. How can this be explained?

The main explanation is perhaps a simple one: a large organization is unlikely to change unless exposed to a crisis such as when its financial base dries up or the organization acquires a strong leadership that has solid support for a reorientation of activities. In the 1970s, none of this applied. What happened was that new resources were made available for relief food aid in emergencies but major crises tended to appear at intervals. Development projects and school feeding projects, in contrast, were of a more permanent nature and were well established within the program. The development perspective was strongly entrenched in the organization through the expertise that had been developed and in the organization's culture and identity. Besides, ultimate responsibility for emergency operations rested with the FAO.

From the very beginning, food aid for development was controversial for a variety of reasons that were identified and discussed in chapter 8. Based, as it traditionally has been, on food surpluses that may come and go, it is an unreliable resource that is attained at volatile prices, and the transaction costs may be high compared with other forms of development assistance. The most crucial criticism relates to the negative effects on development—food aid may serve as a disincentive to local food production and self-sustained food security by outcompeting local farmers and food producers. The main argument for food aid has been that it was an additional resource: food aid would come in addition to ordinary development assistance because it was readily available and inexpensive to the donor. As food aid became increasingly financed from ODA budgets, this argument became weakened, with the exception of aid from the main producers of surplus food, the United States in particular.

The crucial question remains: did the WFP make a difference? Many of the inherent problems connected with food aid in general apply to WFP development food aid as well. But a multilateral dimension was added to development food aid: the national flag was removed and the program sought to integrate food aid activities in the development plans of the countries concerned. One large caveat must be emphasized: the United States—the major provider of food aid, globally and through the WFP—could not resist the temptation of putting more than one hand on the wheel when it came to WFP food aid, thereby reducing the multilateral legitimacy of the program. Since the 1970s, the program came increasingly to be seen as a convenient channel of relief food aid, a role that was developed further in the 1980s.

Summing Up

When we consider the overall questions posed in the introduction to Part 2—the effects of the Cold War and competing development paradigms on developments during the 1960s and 1970s—it becomes necessary to distinguish between the decades. The East-West divide remained a constant factor: the two superpowers were competing for influence on policies and outcomes within the multilateral system. Security issues predominated, but the UN also became an important battlefield in terms of development issues and development ideologies.

The 1960s began with new policy initiatives by the Kennedy administration that struck a "moral" chord in a "realist" foreign policy tradition and emphasized the duty of the well-off countries to promote economic development in emerging nations. New major bilateral initiatives to bolster the "new frontier" approach were implemented by the UN development decade and the multilateral food aid program. This happened at a time when the United States was more or less in control of the UN system but new members from the developing world were joining in large numbers. These initiatives in the beginning of the 1960s had the additional aim of boosting the image of the United States at an important juncture. The 1970s ended with the incoming Reagan administration, which effectively ended the North-South dialogue on reform of the international economic order.

While the development strategy for the First UN Development Decade had been molded in the modernization paradigm, new ideological paradigms came to influence the strategy for DD2. The increasingly organized intellectual and political might of the Third World found a special home in the UN system in UNCTAD. Third World countries provided important inputs for the new strategy. These initiatives were carried further in the early 1970s, resulting in demands and a program for NIEO. The main elements of that program became an integral part of DD2 for the second half of the decade and continued into the strategy for DD3.

The 1970s was a decade bristling with ideas. The dominant idea, the demand for a new international economic order, focused on relations between states, a new North-South balance involving economic resources and political power. In addition, the perspective associated with the *dependencia* approaches to development lingered on, nourishing the NIEO approach. Also, the basic needs approach that appeared in the mid-1970s with its focus on developments within states and alternative development approaches came to inform strategies and development priorities in the second half of that decade. The increased focus on poor countries and poor and vulnerable groups within developing countries, reflects this web of ideological paradigms.

PART THREE

The Lost Decade and a New Beginning

- ■ **The 1980s: Neoliberal Counterrevolution**
- ■ **The 1990s: A New World Order—Implications for Development Policies**
- ■ **Political Liberalism Marching In**
- ■ **About Part 3**

By the late 1970s, the bleak prospects for future development had become evident to all. As we have seen, the optimism about development that characterized most of the 1970s influenced the international development strategy for the Third UN Development Decade. However, continued stagflation dominated most western economies, while soaring debts and serious balance-of-payment problems plagued most developing countries. In combination, these conditions affected the ability and willingness of the major donor countries to provide ODA as well as the form of development assistance and the conditions attached to it. For large parts of the developing world, the economic crisis turned into a development crisis, even reversing the economic and social gains of previous decades.

The 1980s: Neoliberal Counterrevolution

A change of development ideology was also under way, to some extent fueled by these developments. Neoliberalism, always an ideological force, emerged from the shadows and became the dominant ideology of the 1980s. The shift of regime in two of the leading western powers —Thatcher in the United Kingdom and Reagan in the United States— facilitated this ideological change and anchored it in the Bretton Woods institutions. Gradually, the ideological change took place in most other western countries. However, development paradigms tend to have long, overlapping lives; they also adjust to more recent experiences and new realities, thus prolonging their lives.[1] Any attempt to provide a clear-cut chronology, therefore, runs the risk of painting too simplistic a picture.

The Development Paradigms of the 1970s Fading Away

In the early 1980s, development paradigms that had their heyday in the 1960s and 1970s faded away when confronted with the harsh new ideological and economic realities. The *dependencia* paradigm lost much of its ideological influence on mainstream policy, particularly that of the western powers and the Bretton Woods institutions, although some elements survived at the general level, as reflected in the broad consensus on avoiding aid dependency. The same applied to the basic needs approach crafted by the UN system and the firm demands for a new international economic order driven by the South in tandem with the United Nations, UNCTAD in particular. Throughout the latter 1970s, the main western powers had fended off NIEO demands, keeping the dialogue open, while the Committee of the Whole had brought the ideas into the development strategy for the Third UN Development Decade. However, in 1981, the Reagan administration ended the continuation of the global negotiations. By the 1990s this approach, with its focus on improving North-South relations, was hardly visible in development discourse, although it was polished by the South Commission.[2]

The strained economic situation of most developing countries in the 1980s, in combination the structural adjustment programs of the Bretton Woods institutions, effectively brought the basic needs approach to an early end, although the idea lingered on in the UN system. The core of this approach, a concern for the social (and human) dimensions of development, was neglected by many of the largest donors during most of the 1980s. Nevertheless, as we shall see, the underlying ideology inspired the critique of the structural adjustment policy of the 1980s and beyond. Toward the end of the 1980s, it came to the fore again and played a prominent part in the aid rhetoric of the 1990s.

Although the core of the modernization paradigm continued to influence developing thinking and aid practice into the 1990s and beyond, this paradigm was also affected by the neoliberal counterrevolution. In the process, the modernization paradigm itself became "modernized," adapted to the changes that had taken place during previous decades in the South. It still emphasized capital formation and knowledge. But whereas, the focus had been on capital (savings and transfers) and technical assistance, with development assistance playing an important role in both, the emphasis shifted increasingly from technological transfers to self-generation of innovation and knowledge. That said, evolving norms and practices differed somewhat between the two major multilateral actors—the UN system and the World Bank.

In the 1990s, this shift in focus had implications for the role attributed to development assistance. Within the UN system, the emphasis was increasingly on human development, especially education and health. But the UN also paid increasing attention to institutional development, largely in reaction to the policies and priorities of the 1980s. In the mainstream policy approach of the UN system and major western powers, NGOs and civil society more generally in donor (and recipient) countries were expected to play a new and greater role. This approach was combined with the promotion of liberal political values, which increasingly became part of the development concept. As in the past, the private sector, including multinational corporations, was attributed an important role in diffusing technological innovation and knowledge.

Core Features of the Neoliberal Approach

Although weakened, the traditional brand of neoclassical economics that came to the fore in the early 1980s remained a predominant development paradigm in the 1990s. The neoliberal paradigm deemphasizes the role of the state as an agent of development and state and interstate intervention in the economic sphere. It interprets such intervention (including development assistance) as a constraint on development, if not outright detrimental to it.

The neoliberal counterrevolution[3] had many sources. The regime changes in major western governments that had never been attracted by ideas of international structural reform were important in turning the ideological tide. But developments in Third World countries also facilitated the advance of neoliberalism, particularly the economic crisis in which most developing countries found themselves at this stage, the result of events and policies in the second half of the 1970s—some within the control of these governments, others not.

The Debt Crisis and the Response of the Bretton Woods Institutions

For nonproducers of oil and gas in the South, the rising cost of energy following the oil price hikes of the 1970s added to their burdens. Their economies had become dependent on imported oil and commodities that were affected by the increase in oil prices. When commercial financial institutions with petrodollars in abundance and a relaxed attitude toward traditional banking norms had opened their purses, Third World governments had seized the opportunity to meet rising expectations at home and higher prices for the imports in demand. As a result, they had accumulated huge debts that became increasingly difficult to service in the context of the prolonged recession in industrialized countries, worsening terms of trade for raw materials, and continuous deterioration in productivity. Rising interest rates added to the debt-servicing and balance-of-payments problems. As a result, commercial financial sources dried up and banks became keen to see their loans repaid.[4]

The situation threatened the international financial system, especially the commercial financial institutions of North America and Western Europe. The International Monetary Fund came marching in, as was its obligation in a financial crisis like this. It followed much the same approach and prescriptions toward the crisis-ridden Third World governments as it had used earlier with western governments in temporary crisis: they had to observe certain conditions before the IMF would agree to assist with short-term credits. Its prescription was to insist that individual countries reform their economies as a condition for assistance through structural adjustment loans. The IMF (and the World Bank, especially during the early structural adjustment period) was criticized almost from day one for issuing a boilerplate recommendation that failed to take account of the widely varying conditions in the countries concerned.

Rediscovery of the "Soft State"

The declining legitimacy of many governments in the South, especially in Africa, also eased the advance of neoliberalism to a dominant ideology. The ineffectiveness of several governments as channels for development assistance was no new discovery to aid agencies: in the early days of development assistance and up to the mid-1980s, agencies felt that correcting this by improving the absorptive capacity of such governments was part of the challenge to be met by way of development assistance. The emergence, shortly after independence, of the patrimonial—or neopatrimonial—state in many Third World countries had a fundamental impact on development thinking in general and aid philosophy and practice in particular.[5] In previous paradigms, the state had been considered the main development agent and aid had been provided accordingly. In the 1980s, major western donor countries increasingly saw the state as a major barrier to development that aid should bypass.

Structural Adjustment and First-Generation Aid Conditionality

This chain of events changed the main thrust of international development assistance. In the course of the 1980s, aid increasingly became an instrument for promoting economic policy reform in developing countries, much in line with the tenets of neoliberal orthodoxy. The linking of development finance to a commitment by the recipient government to structural adjustment in the general direction of a liberal economic regime (aid conditionality) became the most manifest expression of this policy. The Bretton Woods institutions drove this policy with firm support from major western governments. The recipe prescribed was not restricted to the conventional wisdom of domestic and foreign housekeeping: the mechanisms prescribed reflected a neoliberal perspective and were, therefore, highly political.

The World Bank joined forces with the IMF and the major bilateral donors, and "likeminded" governments (including the Nordic ones, in 1987) fell in line in the late 1980s. The governments of developing countries had to agree to the conditions set by the IMF before they could obtain assistance from individual bilateral donors—which had set agreements with the IMF as a condition for providing assistance. With few other sources of finance available, individual debt-ridden Third World governments had little choice but to accept the conditions. During this period, development assistance, especially program aid, became increasingly focused on realizing the aims set for structural adjustment policies, with an implicit if not explicit aim of improving the ability of developing countries to service their foreign debts.[6]

In the 1980s, the focus centered on macroeconomics; the concern for social development and the environment was clearly subordinate. There was little room for a strong interventionist state in this paradigm. State intervention was considered detrimental to development: the market would do the job. However, toward the end of the decade, protests against neoliberal orthodoxy began to gain ground when the prescription failed to deliver results. On the contrary, in many developing countries, the economic crisis developed into a development crisis. Events took a negative turn: progress achieved during the 1960s and 1970s within important areas such as education and health was retarded.

As the negative societal effects of structural adjustment policies became apparent, the strength of counterarguments increased. While the Bretton Woods institutions had driven structural adjustment policies, the UN system initiated the reorientation process. A UNICEF study contributed considerably to turning the tide. Remaining within the mainstream analysis that economic reform and structural adjustment were necessary, it argued forcefully for a concern with the social dimension of development—adjustment with a human face.[7] Fifteen years later, another critique of the policy pursued in the 1980s and 1990s emerged from a source with in-depth insights and the authority of a Nobel laureate in economics.[8] In the "classic" conflict between Keynesian and neoliberal economists, the pendulum had swung back again, although the debate continued.

Beyond Structural Adjustment: Sustainable Development

Although developments in the 1980s were dominated by the development crisis and the crisis management prescribed by the Bretton Woods institutions, developing countries brought forward alternative policies than those prescribed by the World Bank and the IMF. There were also other initiatives. In the political climate of the 1980s, they stood little chance.[9] Most important were perhaps the reports published by two international commissions—the Independent Commission on International Development Issues (chaired by Willy Brandt) in the beginning of the decade and the World Commission on Environment and Development (chaired by Gro Harlem Brundtland) in the second half of the decade.[10] Both reports covered broad fields involving North-South relations and development. The Brandt report made a strong plea for change, integrating the core of the demands for a new international economic order into an even broader development perspective that included peace and disarmament. However, while the Brandt report, like the UN strategy for DD3, was overtaken by the combination of a new predominant development ideology and a harsh international economic climate, the Brundtland report contributed to setting the international development agenda beyond the 1980s by adding a new dimension to development discourse and a new priority area for development assistance: a concern for the environment. However, what was needed to meet this challenge, particularly threats to the global climate, went far beyond what could possibly be achieved by ODA.

In the 1980s, the focus was increasingly on the effectiveness of development assistance. The Development Committee—the Joint Ministerial Committee of the Boards of Governors of the World Bank and IMF—set up a task force on concessional flows with the primary task of scrutinizing the development effects of ODA; the World Bank served as the secretariat. A study was commissioned to be carried out by independent consultants. The basic finding of the report, delivered in 1986, was that in the broadest sense, "most aid does indeed 'work.' It succeeds in achieving its developmental objectives (where those are primary), contributing positively to the recipient countries' economic performance, and not substituting for activities which would have occurred anyway."[11] Although this basic conclusion was qualified, it came as a relief to the development community, given the zeitgeist of the 1980s and the institution that had commissioned the study.

The 1990s: A New World Order— Implications for Development Policies

By the end of the 1980s, the international political environment had changed dramatically. The international system was transformed with the collapse of the Soviet bloc and the disintegration of its dominant power, the USSR. For more than forty years, East and West had been competing for global hegemony in all fields—security, economy, ideology (including development paradigms), and culture in the broadest sense of the concept. What did the new international framework mean for North-South relations, including development cooperation?

Increased Globalization

The new system was characterized by the almost hegemonic position of the West with regard to economic, military, and ideological power. Another feature was the increasing globalization of the economy.

Increasing globalization under the new world order, although it had been under way for decades, was probably the change with the greatest impact on the situation of developing countries. Globalization, particularly in economic affairs, does not mean the same for all parties involved: it increases the marginalization of some countries. In the intense discourse on the benefits of globalization, which will not be dealt with here, the ideological positions were sharply divided, and they have remained so. However, most agree that less-developed poor countries are among those who benefit the least and who need protective measures, especially in the shorter term.

Within the general trend of globalization, where the emerging international trade regime institutionalized in the World Trade Organization was both a symbol and a driving force, an equally important trend toward regional integration was typical of this period. This applied particularly to economic integration, resulting in regional centers of power and creating a framework for interregional competition. In Europe, important strides were taken to extend the scope of regional cooperation toward a political union that included security and a joint foreign policy.

The United States was the sole remaining superpower, especially in terms of military power. On the other hand, in the new international setting, military capability had lost some of its value in terms of political power, although a spillover from military to political and economic power will always be manifest. In 2001, the events of 9/11 changed the situation drastically.

A New Security Situation

In the post–Cold War era, the pattern shifted from predominantly interstate to intrastate conflicts, at times involving regions. This security situation can to some extent be attributed to the end of the Cold War and the disappearing discipline exerted by the hegemonic powers. With the disintegration of the Soviet bloc, conflicts within former Soviet states that had been contained under the previous system now came out into the open. These involved competition for power within the new entities as well as conflicts rooted in a nationalism that had survived generations of Soviet rule. Multiethnic state constructions—where each nationality had a history of its own and a long-standing record of conflict with others in the region—were especially vulnerable when politicians began exploiting latent ethnic antagonisms in their struggle for power. Tensions based on such rivalries added fuel to conflicts involving resource distribution, political leadership, misgovernment, abuse of power, discrimination against particular minority groups, and a policy of social exclusion.[12] Developments in the former Yugoslavia illustrate this point. Africa also became well endowed with intrastate and regional conflicts framed in terms of ethnocultural divisions that often transcended modern state borders. The conflicts in the Horn of Africa, southern Sudan, the Great Lakes region in Central Africa, and the Congo are but a few examples. They had a strong impact on post–Cold War aid policies with regard to both the geographical distribution of and the purposes and objectives of aid.

Intrastate wars, like other forms of violent conflict, were increasingly seen as a major threat to development. As stated elsewhere, "violent conflicts may, in the course of weeks, destroy material resources that have taken generations to build, cause immense human suffering, make millions of innocent people refugees in their own or neighbouring countries, cause states to collapse and wreck societies."[13] In the 1990s, therefore, peace was increasingly seen as a precondition for development. Up to the late 1980s, the concept of security had been interpreted as security of territory from external aggression, protection of national interests in foreign policy, or global security, in the first place from the threat of nuclear holocaust. After the Cold War ended, other aspects of peace became important. An extended security concept, that of human security, as defined in the *Human Development Report 1994*, came to the fore.[14] The new security situation and the extended security concept posed new challenges to aid as well.

A Lost Rationale for Aid

During the Cold War, development assistance was an instrument in the competition for hegemonic power. Security concerns were prominent in driving the aid policies of the superpowers. When the Cold War ended, one of the main rationales for providing development assistance disappeared: it was no longer as necessary to buy allies and strategically important bases or to ensure that these did not fall into the hands of one's adversary. Yet in the case of the United States, security interests were never the only motivation behind aid; there has always been an ethical strand. Washington's interests in the Third World have also always included economic aspects, especially access to strategically important resources such as oil and gas.

Shrinking ODA

Nevertheless, in the 1990s global ODA declined, especially U.S. ODA. Although it was substantial in absolute terms, U.S. ODA had stayed at a low level in terms of its GNP share in the 1980s: slightly above 0.2 percent. In the 1990s, it declined even more. By 1995, U.S. ODA amounted to 0.10

percent of GNI, and it remained at about that level for the rest of the decade. This, naturally, affected the average performance of DAC countries, which in the 1980s had varied at around 0.35 percent of GNP. In the early 1990s, DAC contributions tended toward stagnation and decline, although the performance of individual DAC countries during the decade varied extensively. Some of them (Denmark in particular) increased their aid as a share of GNP.

The collapse of the Second World had several consequences that affected, directly or indirectly, the global resources available for development cooperation. An almost immediate effect was that Soviet development assistance and that of its allies in Central and Eastern Europe disappeared. The main losers were countries pursuing socialist development such as Cuba and Vietnam and other political structures in the South that were aligned with the Eastern bloc. The financial support they received deteriorated in the latter 1980s, dwindling to nothing in the early 1990s.

Yet another concern directly and indirectly affected the amount of ODA provided during the 1990s. For the major western powers, it became a priority to sustain the political revolution that had taken place in Central and Eastern Europe by means of economic support for the transition process. Support for this transition process was not supposed to be financed from the ODA of DAC countries and a new category of aid, official aid, was established for the purpose. But competition between the two categories of aid was unavoidable. In addition, several former members of the USSR that had received support from the center were now in the category of poor developing countries that competed with the traditional recipients of development assistance for shrinking ODA resources.

During the Cold War, there had been high hopes, even expectations, of a "peace dividend." It was widely expected that resources that had previously been spent on security would be converted to development, including development assistance. However, these hopes were not fulfilled—least of all by the two superpowers—after the end of the Cold War. On the contrary, ODA declined in both absolute and relative terms.

Political Liberalism Marching In

By the end of the 1980s, neoliberalism—especially its manifestation of first-generation aid conditionality in the field of development assistance— had been weakened, although it was still the dominant ideology when it came to economic policy. The Bretton Woods institutions' standard medicine, prescribed almost regardless of the specific conditions prevailing in the individual developing country, had been heavily criticized from many sides, including by prominent researchers in developing and developed countries alike, outspoken political leaders of the South, NGOs and churches in North and South, and the UN system, particularly UNICEF.[15] The most convincing arguments, however, came from the field: the prescribed medicine did not work and in fact was having negative results in terms of social and human development. This situation spurred multilateral institutions—especially within the UN system, but also the World Bank (albeit reluctantly)—to look for new, supplementary, even alternative policy approaches.

The transformation of the international system in the early 1990s facilitated this process. As the power of the Second World dwindled, ideas associated with political liberalism began to predominate. However, various international and multilateral organizations stressed different aspects of liberal political ideas. Most DAC members strongly emphasized promoting democratic development and human rights. The DAC focused on ensuring coherence in policies of developed countries vis-à-vis developing countries from a holistic development perspective. The UN system increasingly focused on the human dimensions of development. The World Bank, in search of what had gone wrong with the structural adjustment policies of the past decade, came up with the "good governance" approach as a supplement to market liberalism. Although good governance was phrased in technical terms and circumscribed, the new approach focused on core issues of liberal democracy, such as the rule of law and economic and political transparency. This massive turn toward political liberalism reflected the changed global balance of power after the end of the Cold War.

Democracy Promotion

In the early 1990s, leading western politicians who insisted on a positive correlation between development and liberal democracy dominated the policy discourse. In theoretical discourse, this correlation was contested. The controversy involved both the notion of democracy and how it should be implemented through international development assistance. Should democracy promotion be limited to the formal procedural aspects of government, such as free and fair elections in which two or more political parties competed for power, or should the concept be defined more broadly to include the substance of government policies?

Most analysts found the narrow definition unsatisfactory. In some cases, elections may even mask systems of personal rule without changing their authoritarian features. The broader concept of "real democracy," involving openness and participation with an emphasis on a thriving civil society—core components of the mainstream definition of the concept—was advocated.[16] Others found even this definition too narrow, arguing that the concept of democracy would be meaningless if it was not associated with policies that brought social justice and economic democracy onto the agenda at local, national, and even the international level.[17]

The argument that there was a positive correlation between democracy and development or more generally between the system of government and development was contested. In an earlier period, the World Bank had indicated that there was a negative correlation between the two. In the discourse of the early 1990s, the controversy was still unsettled.[18] However, whatever conclusion is arrived at cannot be unrelated to how development is defined—narrowly, related to indicators of economic growth, or more broadly, including human development indicators as well. In the 1990s, several donor countries included promoting democracy among the overall aims they set for development cooperation, thus making democracy part of their development concept.

Using aid as a way to promote democracy was not an invention of the early 1990s; this concern drove the development assistance of western countries when it was initiated in the late 1940s and early 1950s. During the following decades, though, it did not play an important role in aid policy (with a few exceptions). In the late 1980s and early 1990s, however, democracy promotion became an objective for development assistance in its own right. Democracy was seen as a necessary precondition if development was to take place. Most western donors expected the recipients of development assistance to move toward greater democracy, and they made a commitment to democracy a condition for providing this assistance. However, among the three main components included in second-generation aid conditionality, this was probably the one surrounded by the greatest ambiguity. Democracy was also promoted through so-called positive measures.[19]

Human Rights Promotion

Human rights constituted the second main pillar of the political liberalism that emerged in the early 1990s. Until the late 1980s, concern for human rights had been a separate foreign policy issue for most western donors that was administered by units different from those concerned with development cooperation. For some countries, a link between human rights and aid had been established in the mid-1970s: respect for human rights was considered a necessary precondition for a government to receive aid or to be included as a main partner in development.[20] The policy of the early 1990s, therefore, was a continuation of what these frontrunners had initiated fifteen years earlier, but now in a more active, systematic, and massive way. The emphasis was now much stronger, and the promotion of human rights became elevated to a set of objectives for development cooperation in its own right that was increasingly seen as a precondition for development in other areas, including social and economic development. More and more, the emphasis was on political and civil rights.

Promotion of "Good Governance"

The notion of good government, broadly interpreted, includes both liberal democracy and human rights. However, in the early 1990s, the World Bank defined the governance concept more narrowly as "the manner in which power is exercised in the management of a country's economic and social resources for development" and made "good governance" synonymous with "sound development management."[21] The focus was on those aspects of government that had to do with public administration, such as effective financial accounting and auditing systems, an appropriate legal framework, and open competition for contracts. The good governance approach to development emphasized the rule of law and accountability, transparency, and predictability on the part of politicians and civil servants. The World Bank definition excluded the more explicitly political aspects, such as political participation, open debate, and political legitimacy.[22] Others, however, broadened the concept. The DAC placed special emphasis on participatory aspects.[23]

The World Bank's narrow, technical definition of good governance can be explained by the element of its constitution that prevented it from getting involved in "politics." However, it is difficult to isolate a concept like this from its political environment, of which the neopatrimonial state was and is a part. The concept cannot avoid relating to both the public and private sector and must include both political leadership and public administration as more narrowly defined.

This third major component of post–Cold War political liberalism was pursued both through (second-generation) aid conditionality and through "positive measures"—aid provided for purposes assumed to improve good governance. In principle there was little new about this concern: donors have always considered an effectively functioning government structure to be of crucial importance, both for a country's development in general and for its ability to use development assistance effectively. They have targeted foreign aid to strengthen the recipient government's public administration, particularly its planning capacity, first through providing technical assistance and later by contributing to institution-building and management training. However, the new concern with governance in the early 1990s transcended earlier efforts both in scope and in emphasis.[24]

Most donors saw these three dimensions of political liberalism—democracy, human rights, and good governance—as interwoven values to be pursued simultaneously: together they represented what was considered good government in a western tradition. Individual governments and multilateral agencies emphasized different aspects of good governance, however. And the focus on human rights by most western governments was arguably more on political and civil rights than on economic, social, and cultural rights, if not almost exclusively so, although the outcomes of international UN conferences may convey a different picture. When it comes to democracy, the emphasis of almost all donor governments has been on the more formal side of democracy—free and fair elections.[25] The DAC's concern for participatory development may represent an exception to this generalization. The DAC found it useful to distinguish between the form of political regime, the processes by which authority is exercised in the management of a country's economic and social resources, and the capacity of government to formulate and implement policies and discharge government functions.[26]

Some ambiguous and controversial aspects of the policies that seek political liberalism have already been noted. The most controversial aspect is probably intervention in the policies of the countries concerned, particularly when pursued by means of aid conditionality. From the beginning, development assistance has represented an intervention in the domestic affairs of recipient countries: bilateral and multilateral donors have always been concerned with the effectiveness and efficiency of the administrative systems of aid recipients. In the 1980s, they even set up their own administrations in some countries to implement aid-financed activities, bypassing domestic administrative systems at the national and local levels.

As Gelese Mutahaba has observed, this may have improved efficiency, but it contributed negatively to development in terms of competence and capacity-building in the countries concerned.[27]

Even against such a background, good governance policy was a novelty in relations among sovereign states, especially because the interference the World Bank and major donors orchestrated in internal political and administrative structures and processes was such a massive advance. As argued by Martin Doornbos, the package of measures imposed through first-generation conditionality was a new phase in the processes of state formation in the countries concerned that placed them under external supervision. If measures are imposed from the outside, the effects might well be contrary to those intended, he warned at an early stage.[28] This points to an inherent conflict between first-generation aid conditionality, as implemented, and one of the core objectives of second-generation conditionality, the promotion of democracy and broad political participation.

In the 1990s, Amartya Sen carried the development discourse involving these values further through his entitlement approach, particularly in *Development as Freedom*.[29] Sen organized the discussion on how to understand and deal with such core development challenges as poverty, famine, population growth, unemployment, and gender inequality from the philosophical position that the ultimate aim of development is to expand human freedom.

About Part 3

The chapters that follow focus on how the UN system reacted to and responded to the major challenges of the 1980s and 1990s. In the 1980s, the Bretton Woods institutions were in the driver's seat, designing and, to a large extent, implementing global development policy. The focus was on macroeconomic policy reform in accordance with neoliberal ideology. The remaining chapters will therefore emphasize the struggle over the course of development in the new millennium. However, they will also detail the operational activities of the main development arms of the UN system. When describing and analyzing operational activities, the chapters will focus on major changes in the patterns that were presented in Part 2.

Chapter 10 presents the development ambitions for the 1990s, as reflected in the strategy for the Fourth UN Development Decade. Work on this strategy offered an opportunity for the UN system—involving several secretariats and intergovernmental bodies—to offer visions for the future that stood out as alternatives to the developments of the "lost decade" of the 1980s. By the late 1980s the pendulum was swinging back: social and human development, never totally absent, became prominent again. Themes related to social and human development were on the agenda of major conferences and the focus of major studies and reports emerging within the UN system, the UNDP in particular. After a decade of stagnation, the main focus of the strategy, which was to be the last in the series of four development decades, was recovery. However, previous commitments were reviewed in a new context.

Chapter 11 focuses on the follow-up during the 1990s. Work on the Human Development Reports (HDRs), the first appearing in 1990, provided the UNDP with new dynamism. The parallel work on the human development index (HDI) added to this by providing a new perspective on development, competing with the traditional one focused on economic growth performance (GNP/GNI). The HDI and HDRs explored the state of human development and development trends within a range of areas and put their mark on the agenda of UN member states, especially among developing countries. The new poverty agenda shifted attention in the same direction, as did a series of global thematic conferences.

The next two chapters follow up developments within the two major operational programs—the UNDP and the WFP. As was the case in Part 2, most attention is given to developments within the UNDP, which is covered in detail in chapter 12. Chapter 13 discusses the dramatic change in the WFP's operational activities from development assistance to humanitarian relief.

Chapter 14 describes the long road toward the Millennium Development Goals. The focus is on the outcome of the UN Millennium Summit in September 2000 and the implementation of the solemn commitments emerging from this gathering, with particular reference to the MDGs, during the first years of the new century.

TEN

Visions and Priorities for the 1990s: The United Nations Strategy for the Fourth Development Decade

■ The Setting: The Need to Revitalize Economic Growth and Social Development

The international strategy for the Third Development Decade became history almost before it was adopted. It was overtaken by the economic situation and political climate of the early 1980s. In 1987, however, the UN General Assembly began work on an international development strategy for the Fourth Development Decade (DD4), insisting that short-term adjustment problems of the world economy should not obscure the development of longer-term perspectives. By the end of the "lost decade," the United Nations had begun a process that aimed at a new start.

The process was all-inclusive.[1] When work on the strategy began, development prospects were bleak for most developing countries and the objectives set for the Third Development Decade were largely unfulfilled. The preparation of the strategy, which was driven by Third World countries and UN secretariats, was seen as an instrument to break the development stalemate of the early and mid-1980s. It was not the only initiative to this end. During the 1980s, the G-77 had tried to launch a round of global negotiations on international economic cooperation that was originally scheduled to begin in 1980. The General Assembly deferred the issue in 1987 and again in 1988. However, in 1988 it decided to include it on the provisional agenda for its 1989 session.[2] The 0.7 percent ODA target was brought to the fore again: transfers of financial resources to developing countries were important for sustained economic growth and development, and ODA was of particular importance for the poorest among them.[3]

In 1989, the General Assembly decided to convene a special session devoted to international economic cooperation the next year with a view to revitalizing economic growth and development in developing countries.[4] Preparations were also under way for the Second United Nations Conference on the Least Developed Countries, to be held the following year. Even the Charter of Rights and Duties of States—the key political document in the struggle for a new international economic order back in the mid-1970s—was dusted off and brought forward again by UN Secretary-General Javier Pérez de Cuéllar, with some hope that the time might be ripe for implementing it.[5]

The tide was turning. Work on the strategy had been initiated at a time of bleak development prospects, but in 1989 the ongoing relaxation of East-West political tensions reinvigorated the process. The collapse of the bipolar system in 1990, which also created a new setting for North-South relations, added fuel. The General Assembly repeatedly recognized growing interdependence among nations in its decisions. For example, a resolution on preparations for the upcoming 1990 special session noted that it was necessary to overcome the external debt crisis, provide adequate financial flows to developing countries, strengthen the international trading system, enlarge market access for exports of developing countries, address the problems of developing countries regarding commodities, promote regional economic cooperation and integration, and facilitate the creation, transfer, and absorption of new and emerging technologies. These were familiar issues that had featured prominently on the development agenda for years.[6] In a subsequent resolution the assembly set the agenda for the 1990s: international cooperation with the goal of eradicating poverty in developing countries. The resolution referred to major NIEO-related resolutions of the mid-1970s.[7]

In the spring of 1990, the eighteenth special session of the General Assembly served as a prologue to the new development strategy for the 1990s. Symbolically, on International Labor Day, 1 May, the Declaration on International Economic Co-Operation, in Particular the Revitalization of Economic Growth and Development of Developing Countries, was adopted. Its main message was that the major challenge of the decade was the revitalization of economic growth and social development in the developing countries. This would require sustained growth in the world economy and favorable external conditions.[8]

The Setting: The Need to Revitalize Economic Growth and Social Development

On 21 December 1990, the General Assembly proclaimed the Fourth United Nations Development Decade (1991 to 2000) and adopted the

International Development Strategy for this decade.[9] The strategy was based on the global consensus reached in the Declaration on International Economic Co-operation earlier that year. It emphasized that the interdependence of nations was increasing, far beyond trade and financial links: "The entire international community, rich and poor countries alike, has thus a vital stake in ensuring that the decade of 1990s is truly one of economic and social progress throughout the world. The prospects for the 1990s, assessed on the basis of the continuation of present policies, can and must be changed." The relaxation of international tensions opened the possibility for "the application of larger resources to the fight against world poverty."[10]

Goals and Objectives

The principal aim of the strategy for DD4 was to ensure that the decade would produce accelerated development in developing countries and stronger international cooperation. The decade "should witness a significant improvement in the human condition in the developing countries and a reduction in the gap between rich and poor countries." Ways should be found for the world community "to meet its needs without degrading the environment." Development "should enhance the participation of all men and women in economic and political life, protect cultural identities and assure to all the necessary means of survival." As in previous key statements on development, the strategy placed ultimate responsibility at the doorstep of individual governments.[11] However, it recognized that efforts by developing countries would easily be thwarted by an unsupportive external environment: many countries were captive to external debt problems, reductions in external resource flows, sharply declining terms of trade, and mounting barriers to market access. Major obligations, therefore, fell on the industrialized countries, "which influence the international economic environment and the functioning of the international economy and are partners in international co-operation for development."[12]

The role of the DD4 strategy was to "help provide an environment that supports the evolution everywhere of political systems based on consent and respect for human rights, as well as social and economic rights, and of systems of justice that protect all citizens." The strategy singled out human resources and institutional development, population, the environment, food and agriculture, and the eradication of poverty and hunger as areas of special priority. A strengthening of international development cooperation was among the integrated strategies designed to meet these fundamental aims.[13]

The strategy noted that more than marginal increases in growth rates would be needed: developing countries "must be enabled to generate progressively the resources needed to ensure productive employment for a fast-growing labour force, to overcome hunger, disease and ignorance and to raise living standards." However, this strategy was more restrained than its predecessors about setting specific growth rates; the primary task was to reverse the negative trends of the 1980s. Growth objectives would vary from country to country: for the relatively few countries where growth in the 1980s had been satisfactory, the aim would be to consolidate progress and ensure that it was sustainable. In the many countries where growth had been interrupted, the first requirement was to return to a path where economic growth surpassed population growth. In the second half of the decade, however, a sustained growth rate on the order of 7 percent "would provide the necessary conditions for a genuine transformation of the economy, with rapid increases in productive employment and poverty eradication, and would generate the resources needed for the protection of the environment."[14]

The strategy did not establish comprehensive and interrelated sector targets for developing countries as a whole. However, it referred to elements that had been addressed in various parts of the UN system, such as employment and health, women and children, industry and technology, agriculture and food, population, education, culture, shelter and settlement, telecommunications, transportation (including shipping), and the environment.

Policies and Measures

While previous strategies had been preoccupied with future opportunities, the strategy for the 1990s looked primarily for ways and means to reactivate development. The focus was on the economic policy framework, external debt, development finance, and international trade and commodities as well as on the traditional engines of growth—science and technology, industrial policies, and agriculture. A surge in development could take place only if supportive national and international economic policy frameworks were in place; for many developing countries, there could be no reactivation of development without an early and durable solution to external indebtedness. A strong supportive environment for international trade was also necessary: policies and measures needed to be directed, in the first place, toward arresting and reversing trends that eroded the multilateral trading system through unilateralism, bilateralism, and protectionism. Commodity exports would continue to play a key role in the 1990s in the economies of most developing countries. The strategy recommended that commodity agreements like those of the 1970s be negotiated or renegotiated, including support of the kind that was to be provided by the common fund established by UNCTAD in the mid-1970s. The strategy's first priority was to resolve the development deficits that had accumulated within these areas in the 1980s.

This chapter will focus on the role attributed to development finance, including development cooperation. The strategy emphasized the need of developing countries to mobilize domestic resources to the greatest extent possible and to implement policies and measures to this end. In most developing countries, domestic savings contributed by far the largest part of the resources utilized for development. However, for poor countries any scope for increased saving was limited: these efforts needed to be supplemented by external resources to raise investments to the levels adequate for economic growth. The crises of the 1980s had impeded such flows—in the mid-1980s, net transfers to developing countries on the aggregate turned negative because of debt servicing.

Reversing this situation was a major challenge, the strategy noted: with a negative flow of resources, a surge in the tempo of development was "virtually unimaginable." The strategy argued that a reduction in the burden of debt-service payments was essential. But significant improvements were also needed in development financing from the major sources: official bilateral assistance, loans from commercial banks, direct private investment, and multilateral financial institutions. The importance of net official flows was emphasized.[15] ODA had to continue as an essential source of concessional aid to developing countries, particularly to the poorest and least developed among them:

> Aid programmes of donor countries have in many cases remained at low levels and need to be substantially improved in the 1990s. Official development assistance has, on average, remained at only half of the internationally agreed target of 0.7 per cent of their gross national product. Donor countries should, in the 1990s, implement such undertakings as they have made to reach or surpass this target, as well as the targets for the least developed countries as adopted

by the Second United Nations Conference on the Least Developed Countries. There should also be a continued improvement in the quality of aid as well as in its utilization. The release of resources from any reduction in military spending and the recovery in the industrial countries should ease the budgetary constraints of donor countries, and rising concern about the environment and world poverty should provide new opportunities for development co-operation.

It is interesting to note that the strategy emphasized that foreign direct investment could play an increasingly important role as a source of development finance. It also said that multilateral financial institutions "could and should" play a major role in development financing.[16]

All the previous international strategies had emphasized that science and technology was crucial for development. The fourth strategy noted the widening knowledge gap between the developed and developing countries: "Policies and measures are needed to help narrow it in the coming decade. High priority must therefore be given by the developing countries to raising their endogenous capacities and capabilities in this area."[17] During 1980s, as we saw in chapter 7, the focus increasingly shifted from the transfer of knowledge and insights *to* developing countries to the generation of such knowledge and insights *within* developing countries. Emphasis shifted away from the foreign expert—who had been seen as the most prominent agent of change in the early decades of development cooperation—and toward human resource development and the development of institutions and relevant facilities in the countries themselves.

The DD4 strategy noted that efforts by developing countries to build scientific and technological capability needed external assistance. This was true as well in the areas of research and development, establishing and strengthening institutions, diffusing new technologies, and training scientific cadres. It also noted that developing countries should not be discriminated against with regard to commercial access to science and technology for development purposes.

Industrial development had also been given high, if not the highest, priority in previous development strategies. In the 1990s, it was considered a central element in the economic transformation of most developing countries and in the reactivation of development. In the 1980s, most developing countries experienced a chronic underutilization of existing industrial capacity as well as import constraints, lack of maintenance of industrial infrastructure, and obsolescent technology. These problems were at times compounded by mismanagement. The strategy prioritized the rehabilitation of industrial sectors of developing countries and an end to the underutilization of capacities. Although the rate of industrialization would vary from country to country, for many countries the objective was an increase of 8 to 10 percent.[18]

Industrial development would require investments and an improved and modernized infrastructure in such areas as communications, transportation, power, and banking and finance. It would also require supportive fiscal and monetary policies. Industrialization was also "crucially dependent" on managerial and technical skills and a trained and efficient work force. The strategy also called for new policy orientations regarding the relative roles of the public and private sectors ("there is considerable scope for enhancing the contribution that private enterprise can make to a dynamic process of industrialization") and industrial production for export versus production for the domestic market and import substitution ("policies based excessively on import substitution supported by highly protective barriers result in high cost and inefficiency").[19]

Production for export is a way to overcome these limitations. The goal of industrialization called for the building up of domestic ownership and national managerial and technological capabilities, but the strategy also noted that "direct foreign investment can make an important contribution to industrialization. Such investment not only provides additional resources, but it is also a means of having access to modern technologies, skills and markets. The rules and regulations of developing countries should encourage direct foreign investments in ways in which mutual interests are furthered." The progress of this industrialization was closely related to openness and nondiscrimination in international markets. It could also be enhanced through cooperation among developing countries at the global, regional, and subregional levels.[20]

Agriculture was still the principal means for revitalizing economic growth; the strategy focused on policies and measures aimed at raising agricultural output and strengthening food security and self-reliance in food. The goal was a transition from a traditional system of cultivation to modernized agriculture. An annual rate of growth in the order of 4 percent on average in food production was set as a target (this "would make a major contribution to food security and support agro-industrial development"). Science, technology, and research—and a well-informed farming population—were seen as vital requirements in this regard. Price incentives were also important; the strategy asserted that "policies that depress the prices of farm output in order to protect or subsidize living costs for the population at large are often counter-productive."[21]

A number of steps were necessary at the international level: finance for investments in the agricultural sector and technical assistance should form part of both bilateral and multilateral development assistance programs, developing countries should have assured access to advances in such fields as biotechnology and genetic engineering at appropriate costs, and existing distortions in international trade in agriculture should be removed.

Development Priorities

In contrast to earlier strategies, the DD4 strategy did not set many quantified growth targets. It saw an acceleration in the rate of economic growth as an essential objective for the 1990s and as a condition for expanding the resource base of developing countries. Nevertheless, it found that "economic growth by itself does not ensure that its benefits will be equitably distributed or that the physical environment will be protected and improved." The strategy noted that if poverty persisted or if countries neglected "human conditions," political and social strains would endanger stability in the 1990s. Development would also be threatened if environmental degradation increased to the point where it damaged the natural resource base of developing countries and compromised the welfare of populations. "The Strategy must therefore give special attention to the policies and measures needed in the areas of poverty alleviation, human resource development and the environment."[22] Accordingly, the principle themes of the strategy were ensuring "a significant improvement in the human condition everywhere" and establishing "a mutually reinforcing relationship between economic growth and human welfare."[23]

Eradicating poverty was the first priority. This called for "a style of development in which economic progress is distributed as widely as possible"[24] and required special and supplementary programs directly targeted to poor and vulnerable sections of the populations that were reached through this process. The strategy singled out employment and income generation through productive occupation as a major means of eradicating poverty. Women and children were identified as particularly vulnerable groups: special attention should be directed to maternal and child health care and to nutrition. Subsidized facilities and services should be carefully targeted at the part of the population that was most in need. The struggle against poverty is the shared responsibility of all countries, the strategy argued: "A substantial reduction in hunger and malnutrition is within reach. There is considerable scope for international food aid going beyond emergency situations."[25]

Human resource and institutional development—adapted to the national priorities, values, traditions, cultures, and the stage of development of individual countries—came next. The DD4 strategy considered education to be both a basic human need and a prerequisite for the achievement of other development objectives. It confirmed universal access to basic education and the completion of primary education by at least 80 percent of the school-age population as goals for the decade. But the strategy put an equal emphasis on higher education and the development of an institutional base for training skilled cadres and for vocational training. In the field of health services, the main focus was on primary health care and the prevention of chronic disease as well as general development objectives such as sanitation, safe drinking water, and better nutrition. DD4 referred to agreed-upon targets, such as the reduction of under-five mortality rates by one-third; decreasing malnutrition among children under five by half; and decreasing maternal mortality rates by half. There should also be a special focus on preventing the spread of epidemics and other diseases endemic in many developing countries. The strategy emphasized that developed countries had an important role to play in promoting human resource and institutional development. Human rights and human development were ends in themselves, and all human resource activities were mutually reinforcing.[26]

In the face of an anticipated population growth of well over 20 percent in developing countries in the 1990s, the DD4 strategy recommended that population programs should be integrated with economic goals and strategies. Population policy was the third priority, and assistance for such programs was to be increased substantially.[27] The fourth priority area was the environment: all countries should take effective action to protect and enhance the environment. However, the strategy also noted that "as the major sources of pollution, the developed countries have the main responsibility for taking appropriate measures urgently."[28]

The Least-Developed Countries

The strategies of the previous two development decades had given special attention to the needs of the LDCs, and the First UN Conference on the Least Developed Countries in 1981 adopted a Substantial New

Programme of Action for the 1980s to support the development process in these countries, including a target of 0.15 percent of GNP in ODA earmarked for them. The strategy for the 1990s was adopted a few months after the Second UN Conference on the LDCs and brought their situation to the fore, much in line with its strong commitment to poverty eradication. It was precisely these countries, together with others that were among the poorest and weakest, that were the hardest hit by the difficulties that had arisen in the 1980s—and their number, instead of declining, had increased from twenty-four in 1972 to forty-one in 1990. The LDCs were running the risk of becoming increasingly marginalized.

It was urgent to take measures to avoid this risk through joint efforts of the countries concerned and their development partners. According to the DD4 strategy, the program of action adopted by the UN's second LDC conference should be fully implemented, including the ODA target. Steps should be taken to give them increased access to major markets for their exports, and donors should provide further bilateral concessional debt forgiveness. Also other groups of countries with special development problems, the landlocked and the island developing countries, required attention, much along the same lines as those specified in previous strategies.[29]

The Special Role of the UN System

The strategy underlined the special responsibility of the UN system in the pursuit of the decade's goals and objectives, asserting that its unique role in bringing the issue of development to the fore needed to be strengthened and expanded in the 1990s. Virtually every aspect of the DD4 strategy could be located within the UN system's various areas of concern. In many such areas and sectors, goals and targets for the 1990s and action plans for their realization had already been agreed upon and were crucial to the strategy's implementation. The strategy provided guidelines for further work on the evolution of policies and programs and on seeking agreements for new actions. Major UN conferences were already scheduled; these were important occasions for reaching agreements that would give more specific content to the actions and commitments needed to realize the strategy's goals. The DD4 strategy emphasized that the UN system's organs, organizations, and bodies had a vital role to play in furthering analytical work on the strategy and its implementation, in promoting and securing international cooperation, and in providing technical assistance.[30]

Implementation

As had been the case with previous strategies, a process of review and appraisal was established, this time on a biannual basis. The General Assembly followed up on the implementation of the strategy at regular intervals, based on reports by the Secretary-General. In a 1996 report, the Secretary-General observed that despite the clear slowdown in the world economy in the first half of the 1990s, developing countries as a whole had made substantial progress. During the first part of the development decade, as a group they had achieved almost three times their annual average rate of growth in the 1980s (2.9 percent as compared with 1 percent per annum in 1981–1990). However, this masked great variations in individual situations. The Secretary-General pointed out that through global conferences and other activities, the UN had been a major actor in promoting a holistic approach to development by linking social, economic, and environmental considerations as the foundation for policy and action. Since the adoption of the strategy, UN global conferences had resulted in international agreements and identified a wide range of supportive measures and actions, refining and advancing the DD4 strategy.[31]

In July 2000, Secretary-General Kofi Annan reported on the implementation of the strategy. In his summary of the main achievements during the decade, he concluded that increased globalization and liberalization had borne some fruit during the 1990s. Developing countries as a whole had succeeded in improving their rate of growth beyond that of the previous decade. However, these economic improvements had not been large enough to permit many developing countries, especially the least developed, to make meaningful economic and social progress. In particular, the weakest individuals within a country—those who were unskilled or inadequately educated and some women and children—were unable to enjoy economic improvements as had been hoped; indeed, in some instances, they had become even further marginalized.[32]

Some Concluding Observations

The strategy for the Fourth Development Decade proved to be the last of its kind.[33] The United Nations Millennium Declaration and the Millennium Development Goals, which had a somewhat longer time frame, came to serve as a continuation of the development decades. The DD4 strategy differed from those of the previous decades in its primary focus. After a decade of stagnating economic and social development, the main focus was on reviving the development process. Previous commitments, especially those adopted for the 1980s, were given a new context, that of recovery. The emergence of a new international political environment with the ending of the Cold War nourished high hopes for a brighter future.

ELEVEN

The Revival of the Social and Human Dimensions of Development

- **The Human Development Reports and the Human Development Index**
- **The New Poverty Agenda**
- **The 1995 Social Summit**
- **Development and the Environment**
- **Gender and Development**

The neoliberal orthodoxy orchestrated by the Bretton Woods institutions since the early 1980s met with growing resistance as the social costs of structural adjustment policies became increasingly apparent. The pendulum was about to swing back again, and the UN system played a crucial role in this process. Credit has already been given to the importance of the 1987 UNICEF report *Adjustment with a Human Face*. The authors recognized the need for macroeconomic adjustments, but they found the human and social costs of structural adjustment policies unacceptable.[1]

The UN system played an important role in turning the tide against the harsh policies of structural adjustment by emphasizing, in various ways, the humanitarian, social, and ethical dimensions of development. The preparation and adoption of the UN strategy for the Fourth Development Decade played a part in this process by making poverty alleviation a priority. A series of global conferences also played a role in shifting attention to the social dimension of development. And so did the efforts made to redefine the very concept of development, from a concept based on indicators of economic growth to one based on indicators of human development.

The World Bank was not unaffected by the mounting criticism of structural adjustment policies. Criticisms from the UN system and from prominent researchers served a legitimizing function for governments that were hesitant about airing their views more directly. A clear indication of change can be seen in the 1989 World Development Report, which emphasized institutional development and prescribed a more active role for the state in development.[2] The subsequent World Development Report focused on poverty alleviation.[3] The World Bank's emphasis in the 1990s on good governance—in the public as well as in the private sectors, where the state was to play a crucial role—also represented a readjustment of World Bank policies away from its former one-sided emphasis on macroeconomics.[4]

This chapter focuses on the efforts made by—and through—the UN system to bring the human and social dimensions of development back to center court, especially the role played by thematic global conferences. The brief survey will be organized around a limited group of largely interlinked themes. The chapter's main conclusion is that a series of global conferences during the 1990s and beyond made major contributions to bringing development's human and social dimensions to the fore again.

The Human Development Reports and the Human Development Index

The UN system's most important contribution in directing attention away from a one-sided macroeconomic focus and back to the human and social aspects of development was perhaps the UNDP's search for alternative indicators of development. This work was first presented in the *Human Development Report 1990,* which was itself instrumental in turning the tide.[5] The effort to develop a human development index continued under the leadership of Mahbub ul Haq and was further elaborated in the ensuing annual Human Development Reports.[6] The main effect was to direct attention toward the social and human aspects of development and away from the traditional indicators of economic growth. From a conceptual point of view, this was a silent revolution, a shift of focus as to what development was all about: political attention, even efforts and priorities, tend to be directed to what is measured.

The first HDR set the stage and covered a wide range of fields. The definition of human development set the tone: "People are the real wealth of a nation. The basic objective of development is to create an enabling environment for people to enjoy long, healthy and creative lives." The expansion of output and wealth is merely a means: the end of development "must be human well-being. How to relate the means to the ultimate end should once again become the central focus of development analysis and planning." Human development was seen as a process of enlarging people's choices. The essential choices would enable people to live long and healthy lives, to acquire knowledge, and to have access to resources needed for a decent standard of living. But the HDRs argued that people should have other choices too; these ranged from political, economic, and social freedom to "opportunities for being creative and productive, and enjoying personal self-respect and guaranteed human rights."[7]

This basic philosophy was not revolutionary. Similar ideas had been around in many settings. For years, it had been recognized in the development literature as well as in declarations of global institutions that development was not dependent on economic growth alone. A holistic view prevailed in the international strategy for the 1990s as it had in the strategies for the two previous development decades. The great difference was that there now was an effort to develop a systematic index based on these ideas.[8] It helped that the timing was right, as was the setting: it was created in the center court of the United Nations.

It required an economist with experience drawn from academia as well as from national and international political and administrative arenas to confront the core measure of development that had predominated as long as development had been an issue. Ul Haq's goal was to bring the notion of development back to the social concerns in the writings of leading political economists of the past, such as Adam Smith, David Ricardo, Robert Malthus, Karl Marx, and John Stuart Mill. The core questions to be addressed were these: How could economic growth be managed in the interest of the people? What alternative policies and strategies need to be pursued if people, not commodities, are the principal focus of national attention?

The term "human development" denoted the process of widening people's choices and the level of well-being they had achieved. What gave the concept of human development such appeal was the quantification of the concept. The HDR focused on three essential elements of human life: longevity, knowledge, and "decent" standards of living. For the first component, life expectancy at birth was chosen as the indicator; for the second, literacy figures; and for the third, command over resources needed for a decent living, the logarithm of real GDP per capita. The major merit of the effort to visualize development in this new perspective was the boldness with which an outstanding economist confronted the challenges involved in constructing an entirely new development index, given the scarcity of reliable and comparable data about human development.[9]

These limitations were candidly recognized, not least the absence of quantitative measures for human freedom. Nevertheless, a bold start had been made—open to criticism from orthodoxy, but also open to future improvements.

The human development index, which covered 130 countries, showed a different ranking of countries than indices based on GNP per capita. It revealed that the disparity between countries was much greater when it was based on income data than when based on indices for human development. The main message was that no automatic link existed between the level of per capita income in a country and the level of its human development.

Analyzing the record of human development during the previous three decades (1960–1990), the report presented some central conclusions and policy messages that featured prominently on the international development agenda throughout the 1990s. They are summarized in box 11.1.

The main focus here has been on the birth of a grand idea. The refinements and follow-up to the new idea also deserve attention. It is important to note that the UNDP provided the home, freedom, and facilities necessary for Mahbub ul Haq and his small team to develop this alternative perspective on development.[10]

The 1995 HDR—the sixth and last produced under ul Haq's leadership—returned to another challenge identified in the first report, namely adapting the HDI to gender inequalities. The 1995 report focused on the situation of women and gender inequality with a view to preparing the ground for the Fourth UN World Conference on Women that was held in Beijing later that year. A gender-related development index (GDI) was designed to measure achievements in the same basic capabilities as those of the HDI. The other innovation was the gender empowerment measure (GEM), which examined whether men and women were able to participate actively in economic and political life and take part in decision-making. While the GDI focused on expansion of capabilities, the GEM was concerned with the use of such capabilities to take advantage of life's opportunities.[11]

As was the case with the HDI, recording the performance of countries along these indicators over several years made it possible to assess trends. In this way, the indices offered themselves as powerful instruments in the hands of those interested in and capable of using them.

The reports made their mark on the development agendas of UN

BOX 11.1. Major Conclusions of the First Human Development Report

1. The developing countries have made significant progress toward human development in the last three decades (1960–1990).

2. North/South gaps in basic human development have narrowed considerably in these three decades, even while income gaps have widened.

3. Averages of progress in human development conceal large disparities within developing countries—between urban and rural areas, between men and women, between rich and poor.

4. Fairly respectable levels of human development are possible even at fairly modest levels of income.

5. The link between economic growth and human progress is not automatic.

6. Social subsidies are absolutely necessary for poorer income groups.

7. Developing countries are not too poor to pay for human development *and* take care of economic growth.

8. The human costs of adjustments are often a matter of choice, not of compulsion.

9. A favorable external environment is vital for supporting human development strategies in the 1990s.

10. Some developing countries, especially in Africa, need external assistance a lot more than others.

11. Technical cooperation must be restructured if it is to help build human capabilities and national capacities in the developing countries.

12. A participatory approach—including the involvement of NGOs—is crucial to any strategy for successful human development.

13. A significant reduction in population growth rates is absolutely essential for visible improvements in human development levels.

14. The very rapid population growth in the developing world is becoming concentrated in the cities.

15. Sustainable development strategies should meet the needs of the present generation without compromising the ability of future generations to meet their needs.

Source: UNDP, *Human Development Report 1990* (New York: Oxford University Press, 1990), 1–7.

member states, particularly among developing countries. Over the years a large number of regional and national, even local, human development reports were produced and published that focused on the specific challenges of the region or country concerned. They carried a UN stamp, which facilitated critical scrutiny of the state of human development even in countries with authoritarian governments.[12] Even so, the traditional way of conceptualizing development and developmental trends continued to rule much of the ground, especially within the development finance institutions.[13]

The New Poverty Agenda

Poverty alleviation, which was increasingly expressed in the 1990s in more active terms as fighting poverty, has been central in the rhetoric of aid and development: improving the condition of the poor has always been the core of development assistance. Over time, this focus has taken various forms. In the early years, the main focus was on improving welfare in developing countries through contributing to increased economic growth, especially through industrialization and more efficient agriculture. In the strategies for the development decades—and especially from DD2 onward—the focus was on assisting particularly impoverished countries or groups of countries. Increasingly emphasis was also placed on particularly poor people or groups of people within countries. In the early 1970s, under the leadership of Robert McNamara, the World Bank took the lead in the latter approach by formulating a redistribution strategy and identifying the poorest part of the population as a target group for aid.[14]

These approaches—targeting ODA to particularly poor or vulnerable countries (with special reference to their GNP per capita) or to particularly poor groups or strata of the population—were pursued, to varying degrees, in the rhetoric of bilateral and multilateral providers of ODA, although many donor countries (not just the superpowers) in practice prioritized other, often interest-based, concerns when allocating their resources. During these early years, the poverty orientation also influenced the sector orientation of development assistance, especially in the development discourse within some donor countries, particularly the Scandinavian ones. The implication was that target groups would have to be reached indirectly by improving their environments, including providing employment opportunities and social services. Poverty alleviation constituted a central objective in the basic needs strategy crafted by several arms of the UN system in the mid-1970s and was a major concern when the social and human dimensions of development came again to the forefront in the late 1980s and early 1990s.

Poverty is a complex concept, and the processes that lead into and out of poverty are even more complex. In the early days, economic growth was the simple answer, and it remains part of the answer, although we now know that it is not enough in itself. A far more holistic development concept has emerged that involves a web of approaches that include "traditional" economic growth as well as social, institutional, political, and cultural development; the growth of freedoms; the participation of those involved in planning development; and human dignity. Human security has become part of the development concept.

The issue of fighting poverty dominated the development rhetoric of the 1990s and beyond. Not only was it a core issue in the DD4 strategy, it also ranked high on the agenda of the thematic world conferences in the 1980s and 1990s, including the 1995 Copenhagen summit. Since the World Bank has always exercised a strong influence on international development discourse, the way the Bank approached this *problématique* is of special interest. The conceptualizations and policies formulated in major World Bank publications have additional weight. Although similar analyses and recommendations had come from other quarters and were even more pointed, the *World Development Report 1990* and the Bank's response probably had the strongest signal effect.[15]

In the 1990s, the World Bank was in the advantageous position of commanding extensive in-house research capacity and the means of attracting high-quality additional research capacity from the outside, the ability to back up ideas with development finance, and political backing from important quarters. With these resources at hand, it increasingly gave additional attention to poverty alleviation. This did not happen in a political vacuum. The setbacks and mounting criticism of the structural adjustment policies of the 1980s had helped set in motion an intellectual reassessment process within the Bank. The new intellectual and political challenge emerging from the UN system from the human development camp and from the world conferences that highlighted the specific dimensions of a social and human development agenda certainly moved the Bank along in this direction.

The World Bank's 2000–2001 World Development Report, titled *Attacking Poverty,* strongly influenced both the conceptualization of the problem and the ways to tackle it.[16] The theme remained high on the agenda when the core development challenges were identified in the Bank's 2003 report, *Sustainable Development in a Dynamic World*.[17] The 2003 World Bank strategy for fighting poverty took the Millennium Development Goals as its point of departure. It outlined a complex reality as the starting point, defining poverty as comprised of more than inadequate income or inadequate human development. Poverty also included vulnerability and a lack of voice, power, and representation. The report outlined three main pillars of the strategy: promoting opportunity, facilitating empowerment, and enhancing security.

This World Bank report relied on and summarized debates that had been driven during the 1990s even more forcefully by other international and some regional and national institutions and by individual academics. The issue of poverty and demands for commitments to reduce poverty featured high on the international agenda and on the national agendas of individual countries. However, the follow-up was weak at all levels, particularly when it came to operationalizing and implementing the commitment to fight poverty. It still remains to be seen to what extent the strategy the 2003 World Development Report outlined and instruments such as the introduction of poverty reduction strategy papers (PRSPs) in the planning procedures for recipients of aid will do the trick.

The 1995 Social Summit

In the 1990s, several arms of the UN system explored the social and human dimensions of development. The UN World Summit for Social Development, held in Copenhagen in March 1995, was especially important in placing the social dimension firmly on the development agenda.

The Copenhagen summit, to an even larger extent than previous thematic world conferences, set a pattern that was followed later, not least in the September 2000 Millennium Summit. It was a spectacular gathering, attended by representatives of 187 countries (including 117 heads of state or government) and the European Community. A range of meetings, round tables, workshops, symposia, and panel discussions on themes related to the conference were held, and an NGO Forum was organized parallel to the summit. The massive presence of NGOs (2,315 delegates representing 811 organizations) both in the conference hall itself and in its immediate environs offered ideas, exerted pressure on delegates directly as well as via their constituencies at home, and offered comments on the day-to-day proceedings and policy positions. All these activities contributed to extensive media coverage and brought the main messages of the summit home.

On 12 March, the summit adopted the Copenhagen Declaration on Social Development. The declaration painted a bleak overview of the existing situation: far too many people—women and children in particular—were vulnerable to stress and deprivation even though progress had been made globally in some areas of economic and social development. In many societies, the gap between rich and poor had increased. More than one billion people in the world were living in abject poverty, most of them going hungry every day. The declaration asserted that the unsustainable pattern of consumption and production was the major cause of the global environment's continued deterioration. Continued population growth challenged the capacity of governments, social institutions, and the natural environment to adapt. The main challenges were establishing a people-centered framework for social development, building a culture of cooperation and partnership, and responding to the immediate needs of those most in distress.[18]

The heads of state government adopted ten commitments on which action was to be taken on the national and international levels. The main thematic issue of promoting social development at the national and international levels was seen in a holistic perspective that involved development efforts in many other policy fields. At the top of the list was creating an environment to enable people to achieve social development, eradicating poverty, and promoting full employment. Some issues had been on the development agenda for years, like the commitment to promoting gender equality. Others went more directly into the current debate on policy approaches, like the commitment to include social issues in structural adjustment programs.[19]

The program of action that was adopted outlined policies, actions, and measures to implement the declaration's principles and commitments. Chapter 1 focused on the need for an enabling environment for sustainable development. It referred to current efforts, especially those of the UN system, to establish an open, equitable, cooperative, and mutually beneficial economic environment. Chapter 2 took up poverty eradication with a focus that went far beyond anti-poverty programs: democratic participation, changes in economic structures, universal access to economic opportunity, and special efforts to facilitate access for the disadvantaged were needed. It said that governments should pay more attention to eradicating absolute poverty; they should establish national plans for poverty eradication and indicators to measure the state of affairs and should implement the commitments made to meet the basic needs of all, including a series of specific objectives to be achieved by the year 2000.[20]

Chapters 3 and 4 focused on increasing productive employment, decreasing unemployment, and creating a "society for all." The fifth and final chapter shifted attention from objectives and norms to implementation and follow-up. It stated that the responsibility for social development and implementation rested primarily with governments, although international cooperation and assistance were essential. Substantial new and additional resources would be needed at the national level in both the public and private sectors. Developing countries, especially in Africa and the LDCs, would need additional financial resources and more effective development cooperation and assistance: commitments had to be translated into deeds at both the national and the international levels.[21]

The program invoked the agreed-upon target of 0.7 percent of GNP in ODA, stating that donor countries should strive to fulfill this target and that an increasing share should be allocated for social development programs. It was probably in this area that the summit came up with its most innovative mechanism, which combined the efforts of recipient governments and donors: a mutual commitment was agreed upon between interested developed and developing country partners to allocate 20 percent of ODA and 20 percent of the national budget, respectively, to basic social programs. The program of action also stated that high priority should be given to ODA to eradicate poverty in developing countries. Assistance in the form of grants and loans should also be provided for social sector activities such as rehabilitation and the development of social infrastructure.[22]

The fight against poverty was the overarching theme. The program of action made development assistance a lever to increase the priority that governments of developing countries assigned to major social development programs in their budget allocations. ODA should be designed to meet the multifaceted problem of poverty: the "20:20 agreement" placed special emphasis on health and education, which were singled out as strategically important both for attaining development and for fighting poverty. This emphasis was not accidental: when governments sought to meet the conditions stipulated in structural adjustment policies, expenditures involving social services were the first to be cut, with drastic consequences. In several countries, the major advances in education and health achieved in the 1960s and 1970s—including life expectancy—not only stagnated but actually were reversed in the 1980s.

The issue of social development remained on the international agenda. Other global summits of the 1990s and beyond contributed to this by focusing on other aspects of the social and human development agenda. These included the World Summit for Children in 1990 and a series of world conferences on women, including the one in Beijing. The 1995 summit ensured a continued focus on social development by recommending that the UN General Assembly include in its agenda the follow-up to the summit, inter alia, by holding a special session in the year 2000 for an overall review and appraisal of the outcome. It also recommended that as part of the activities of the International Year for the Eradication of Poverty in 1996, the effectiveness of the summit's proposed steps with regard to poverty eradication be reviewed. It emphasized the importance of system-wide cooperation in implementing the summit's outcome in order to ensure coherence.[23]

In 1996, the General Assembly followed up on the summit by declaring the first United Nations Decade for the Eradication of Poverty: "Eradicating poverty is an ethical, social, political and economic imperative of humankind," the declaration stated.[24] ECOSOC established the approach and procedures for implementing the 1995 summit. Particularly noteworthy was the role and extended participation of NGOs in this work, triggered by the experiences at the Copenhagen summit.[25]

The first major assessment of the summit's implementation within the UN system took place, as planned, at the twenty-fourth special session of the General Assembly in 2000, also known as the Social Summit +5. This special session—the "World Summit for Social Development and Beyond: Achieving Social Development for All in a Globalizing World"—went beyond a review and appraisal of the results of the Social Summit. Like the Copenhagen conference, this meeting attracted a large gathering of participants, this time representatives of 178 governments and 500 NGOs. It adopted an extensive political declaration by UN members on how to promote social development as well as a series of recommendations for further initiatives at the local, national, and international levels. Against a five-year track record that revealed several trends that contradicted the summit's commitments—such as a continued decline in ODA and the fact that many developing countries continued to fall behind—the renewed and new commitments were even more specific and stronger than those set at Copenhagen. They were expressed with greater optimism and with language that was more resolute.[26]

The special session was held at a time when the benefits and adverse effects of globalization had been central in the discourse on development for some time. As the title of the special session indicates, the discussions were cast in this perspective with a specific focus on how intensified globalization affected social development in developing countries. Reaffirming that social development was a national responsibility, the political declaration underlined that "it cannot be successfully achieved without the collective commitment and efforts of the international community." It also pledged to give priority to the fight against "the worldwide conditions that pose severe threats to the health, safety, peace, security and people." It reiterated "our resolve to reinforce solidarity with people living in poverty and dedicate ourselves to strengthening policies and programmes to create inclusive, cohesive societies for all—women and men, children, young and older persons—particularly those who are vulnerable, disadvantaged and marginalized. We recognize that their special needs will require specific targeted measures to empower them to live more productive and fulfilling lives."[27]

Development and the Environment

Stimulated by the UN Conference on the Human Environment in Stockholm in 1972, concern about the environment became prominent in the latter 1970s and early 1980s. The issue became a top priority in 1983, when the General Assembly created the World Commission on Environment and Development, chaired by Gro Harlem Brundtland.

The resulting report (known as the Brundtland report) brought environmental concerns to the fore and set the agenda for the following years. Its main conclusion was that economic growth should be sustainable and should not negatively affect the opportunities of future generations to satisfy their needs.[28] A precondition for economic redistribution (social development) and ecologically sustainable development was a strong, intervening state. Sound environmental development would also require an effective international regime. In the 1980s, the prevailing ideological climate was not favorable in this regard.

Nevertheless, the UN system took up the challenge, and the World Bank joined in. The United Nations Conference on Environment and Development (UNCED; also known as the Earth Summit) held in Rio de

Janeiro in June 1992 again brought environmental issues forcefully onto the agenda. The large participation in and around the conference by governments, the UN system, and NGOs contributed to this focus. The Earth Summit adopted the Rio Declaration on Environment and Development and a comprehensive plan of action for sustainable development into the twenty-first century, Agenda 21, along with a statement of principles to establish a global consensus on the management, conservation, and sustainable development of forests. Two conventions were opened for signature at UNCED—the United Nations Framework Convention on Climatic Change and the Convention on Biological Diversity—and were signed by 154 and 156 governments, respectively.

Agenda 21 came to dominate the environmental and development agenda for the rest of the 1990s and beyond. Its preamble identified the main challenges: humanity was confronted with a worsening of poverty, hunger, ill health, and illiteracy, and the world's ecosystems were continuing to deteriorate. Agenda 21 also offered the normative answer to these challenges: integrating environmental and development concerns would lead to the fulfillment of basic needs, improved living standards for all, better-protected and better-managed ecosystems, and a safer, more prosperous future. The document stated that international cooperation should support and supplement national strategies. Of course the UN system was to play a key role in this context. Agenda 21's objectives and the 115 program areas under which it described actions would require the transfer of extensive financial resources to developing countries.[29] The average cost of implementing Agenda 21 in developing countries from 1993 to 2000 was estimated at more than $600 billion per year, including $125 billion on grant or concessional terms from the international community.[30]

Official development assistance emerged as the main source of external funding: developed countries confirmed anew the 0.7 percent target. However, a wide array of funding sources were envisaged, including the specialized agencies and other UN bodies, the multilateral development finance institutions, the Global Environment Facility, multilateral institutions, bilateral assistance programs, debt relief, and private funding. The General Assembly was to organize a regular review of implementation, while ECOSOC was to oversee the system-wide coordination and integration of the environmental and developmental aspects of UN policies and programs. It was proposed that a high-level Commission on Sustainable Development, reporting to ECOSOC, be established to ensure effective follow-up.[31]

Official development assistance was identified as an important part of the answer to the environmental and development challenge, but it was far from the most important answer: more extensive resources would have to be mobilized. The Global Environment Facility, a joint effort by the World Bank, the UNDP, and the United Nations Environment Programme (UNEP), was established in 1991 to help developing countries meet environmental challenges regarding climate change, ozone depletion, pollution of international waters, and biodiversity. UNCED recommended that the GEF be restructured to facilitate the funding of the environmental activities proposed in Agenda 21.

The environment and development agenda has never been uncontroversial, although in the discourse (prominently at UNCED), the environment and development were seen as two sides of the same coin, interrelated in a similar way as peace and development. By the late 1980s and early 1990s, the champions of both the environment and development had identified poverty as their main enemy: poverty eradication had become the prime instrument for improving the environment and facilitating social and economic development as well as an objective in its own right. Thus, fighting poverty created a link between the concern for improving the environment and development assistance, not least through the mechanism of the Global Environment Facility, which the World Bank administered. Nevertheless, "the environment" had an institutional setup of its own (UNEP) and a broader scope (including efforts to reduce ozone depletion and climactic changes) than that set for development assistance. And "environment" and "development" were competing for attention and public financial sources, including ODA.

This competition involved prioritizing between the two prime objectives. A North-South dimension was manifest, particularly in terms of financing. Developing countries tended to argue that those with the main

BOX 11.2. The Post-Rio Discourse on the Relationship between the Environment and Development

Although conceived as interlinked, the relation between "development" and "the environment" has been controversial. It hinges on the questions raised in several contexts related to development and development cooperation: what kind of development, for whom, and at what costs? Environmental "fundamentalists" see almost any kind of "development," particularly any related to western development models of the post–World War II era, as part of the problem, not part of the solution.

In the post-Rio discourse, this is illustrated in contributions by Wolfgang Sachs, Nicholas Hildyard, and Matthias Finger (see sources below). Sachs (1993: 3) argued that "the governments at Rio came around to recognizing the declining state of environment, but insisted on the relaunching of development. Indeed, most controversies arose from some party's heated defense of its 'right to development' . . . the rain dance around 'development' kept the conflicting parties together and offered a common ritual which comforted them for the one or other sacrifice made in favour of the environment. At the end, the Rio Declaration ceremoniously emphasized the sacredness of 'development' and invoked its significance throughout the document wherever possible."

Who were the winners? According to Hildyard (1993: 22), the "World Bank not only emerged with its development policies intact, but with control of an expanded Global Environment Facility (GEF), a prize that it had worked for two years to achieve. The US got the biodiversity convention it sought simply by not signing the convention on offer. The corporate sector, which throughout the UNCED process enjoyed special access to the Secretariat, also got what it wanted: the final documents not only treated TNCs with kid gloves but extolled them as a key actor in the 'battle of the planet.' Free-market environmentalism . . . has become the order of the day, uniting Southern and Northern leaders alike."

Although the issue is now firmly placed on the development agenda, perspectives differ. At one end of the spectrum are proponents of the "limits to growth" school; at the other, the technical optimists (associated with the World Bank), who argue that resource constraints could be overcome at modest cost if only the correct policies were put in place (Bhaskar and Glyn, 1995). For critical perspectives, see several contributions in Bhaskar and Glyn (eds., 1995) and Sachs (ed., 1993), Middleton et al. (1993), and Chatterjee and Finger (1994).

Sources: V. Bhaskar and Andrew Glyn, "Introduction," in *The North, the South and the Environment,* ed. Bhaskar and Glyn (Tokyo: United Nations University Press/Earthscan Publications, 1995); Pratap Chatterjee and Matthias Finger, *The Earth Brokers: Power, Politics and World Development* (London and New York: Routledge, 1994); Matthias Finger, "Politics of the UNCED Process," in *Global Ecology: A New Arena of Political Conflict,* ed. Wolfgang Sachs (London and Atlantic Heights, N.J.: Zed Books, 1993); Nicholas Hildyard, "Foxes in Charge of the Chickens," in *Global Ecology,* ed. Wolfgang Sachs; Neil Middleton, Phil O'Keefe, and Sam Moyo, *Tears of the Crocodile. From Rio to Reality in the Developing World* (London and Boulder, Colo. Pluto Press, 1993); and Wolfgang Sachs, "Global Ecology and the Shadow of 'Development,'" in *Global Ecology,* ed. Sachs.

responsibility for environmental degradation (the industrialized countries of the North) should also bear the burden of repair. They also refused to make commitments that might constrain their efforts in realizing their own goals of economic and social growth. Moreover, the resources allocated for ODA were far too modest to meet the threats to the environment: massive additional funding was necessary.

The question of how to finance activities to improve the environment invoked the principle of additionality: fresh resources had to be raised to meet environmental changes. Several governments argued that ODA budgets should be protected and some donor governments agreed, especially with regard to contributions to UNEP and the GEF. For most donor governments, however, improvement of the environment became a prime development objective in its own right, to be pursued both through aid targeted at such projects and as an integral part of all development assistance. Some governments distinguished between global environmental challenges that were to be financed by all governments (with funds raised outside ODA budgets) and solutions for national and local environmental problems that might be assisted through development cooperation programs. ODA might also be used to help developing countries fulfill their international environmental commitments.

Follow-up on implementation of the Rio Declaration and Agenda 21, coordinated by the Commission on Sustainable Development, was an issue on the agenda of the ordinary sessions of the UN General Assembly in subsequent years. In June 1997, the General Assembly held a special session in New York (called Earth Summit +5) for an overall review and appraisal of the implementation of UNCED.[32] Against the bleak background of marginal achievements in a few areas and a deteriorating global environment, the special session adopted an extensive and ambitious Programme for the Further Implementation of Agenda 21. Among the positive achievements noted were the extensive efforts governments and international organizations had made to integrate environmental, economic, and social objectives into decision making by elaborating new policies and strategies for sustainable development or by adapting existing policies and plans.[33] On the negative side, the new program observed that most developed countries had not reached their commitment to the 0.7 percent target in ODA or the 0.15 percent target for the least-developed countries; on average, ODA had actually declined.[34]

The World Summit on Sustainable Development in Johannesburg in

August–September 2002 carried out a comprehensive ten-year review of progress in implementing Agenda 21. The summit adopted a declaration and a plan of implementation that outlined priority activities, targets, and timetables aimed at stepping up the implementation of Agenda 21 and other goals that had been agreed upon in the meantime, including the MDGs. A series of partnership plenary sessions that involved governments, intergovernmental institutions, NGOs, and the private sector addressed five priority areas for action: water and sanitation, energy, health, agriculture, and biodiversity—the "WEHAB themes."[35]

In the Johannesburg Declaration on Sustainable Development, governments confirmed anew their commitment to economic and social development and environmental protection at the local, regional, and global levels. The declaration again identified poverty eradication as the overarching objective along with changes in consumption and production patterns and protection and management of the natural resource base for economic and social development. Governments further resolved to increase access to such basic requirements as clean water, sanitation, adequate shelter, energy, health care, food security, and the protection of biodiversity. The Johannesburg Plan of Implementation followed up on the declaration. In order to eradicate poverty—the greatest challenge facing the world—the plan called for the General Assembly to establish a world solidarity fund based on voluntary contributions. As in previous reviews of Agenda 21, the Johannesburg plan called for the mobilization of international resources, including increasing ODA and enhancing aid effectiveness.[36]

Action on many of the environmental challenges, especially global ones, requires an international consensus that has been hard to attain and even more so after the George W. Bush administration took over in Washington in 2001. When consensus is needed, the governments that resist reform tend to have the upper hand. Thus, although the commitments contained in the Rio Declaration and Agenda 21 served as an inspiration and remained high on the international agenda, little was achieved in practice. In the course of the 1990s, polarization on this issue built up between the United States and Europe; this division was manifest at the 2002 Johannesburg summit. The lack of consensus, despite solemn declarations to the contrary, affected what could be achieved. Since environmental issues emerged as a top priority on the international agenda in the latter 1980s, the driving forces have been the multilateral system, the

United Nations in particular, together with a host of NGO environmental and development activists.

Gender and Development

Gender has remained high on the UN development agenda, although the primary focus has changed somewhat over the years.[37] As we have seen, a specific focus on the situation of women was part of the UN strategy for DD1 and the strategies for subsequent development decades. The Commission on the Status of Women was particularly instrumental in placing the role of women in development high on the agenda. The July 1975 World Conference of the International Women's Year in Mexico City adopted the World Plan of Action, which the General Assembly set out to implement. In December 1975, the General Assembly proclaimed 1976–1985 as the United Nations Decade for Women. The themes of the decade were equality, development, and peace.[38] ECOSOC followed up this decision by the establishing the International Research and Training Institute for the Advancement of Women, while the General Assembly set up a voluntary fund and corresponding pledging conference for the UN Decade for Women. At the normative level, the Convention on the Elimination of All Forms of Discrimination against Women, adopted by the General Assembly in 1979 with entry into force in 1981, established international standards to ensure equality for men and women.[39]

Thus we see that the gender perspective has featured prominently on the human development agenda since the mid-1970s and increasingly in the 1980s. In the context of aid policy, this cross-cutting issue has been addressed, almost from the beginning, through a two-pillar strategy: supporting activities targeted specifically at women and integrating a concern for women in all development activities, with the aim of ensuring that assistance does not negatively affect development from a gender perspective.

Within the confines of the UN system, the concern for women in development continued throughout the decade, highlighted after five and ten years by well-prepared global conferences—the midterm world conference in Copenhagen in July 1980 and, in the final year of the decade, the spectacular world conference held in Nairobi in July 1985. By the late 1970s, the North-South divide, involving main issues related to the NIEO issue, had come to dominate the agenda of even more specialized world gatherings, including the Copenhagen conference.[40]

The Copenhagen conference attracted a large participation. In addition to taking stock of developments at the midpoint of the UN Decade for Women and constructing a plan of action for the second half, the conference dealt with the effects of apartheid on women in South Africa and special measures to assist them and the effects of the Israeli occupation on Palestinian women inside and outside the Occupied Territories, with a special focus on their social and economic needs and what measures could assist them. The agenda included a host of issues, several of which were highly controversial, involving both international politics and the national policies of UN member governments.[41]

The third UN world conference on women—the World Conference to Review and Appraise the Achievements of the UN Decade for Women—in Nairobi in July 1985 followed patterns established by the two previous conferences. The agenda covered broad policy fields, and most major themes on the international agenda were up for discussion.

A major advance was the first publication of the *World Survey on the Role of Women in Development,* the most important document before the Nairobi conference.[42] The survey provided an overview of the interrelations between key development issues concerning the role of women in relation to agriculture, industry, money and finance, science and technology, trade, energy and self-reliance, and the integration of women in development. The survey showed that although the contribution of women to national production activities had increased steadily since 1950 and was projected to increase further toward the year 2000, their contribution to economic development was underestimated in national and international statistics. Moreover, on average, women benefited less than men from their contributions to national production.

On this basis, the Nairobi conference reviewed the achievements of the UN Decade for Women with a view to the future, namely how to overcome the obstacles to the goals and objectives set for the decade— equality, development, and peace—by the year 2000. The Nairobi Forward-Looking Strategies for the Advancement of Women were adopted by consensus, though with reservations on specific paragraphs from several delegations. In mid-December 1985, the UN General Assembly endorsed the Nairobi strategies, affirming that implementing them "should result in the elimination of all forms of inequality between women and men and in the complete integration of women into the development process and that that should guarantee broad participation by women in efforts to strengthen peace and security in the world." It declared that the objectives of the decade remained valid.[43] The assembly also asked the Secretary-General to update the *World Survey* on a regular basis, starting in 1989.

In February–March 1990, the first five-year review and appraisal of the Nairobi forward-looking strategy took place at an extended session of the Commission on the Status of Women in Vienna. The review was based on a report by the UN Secretary-General that stated that although there had been progress in some areas, especially with regard to de jure equality, progress in achieving de facto equality had slowed down or stopped. The bleak conclusion of this report was that unless implementation was greatly improved, many of the objectives would not be attained by 2000.[44]

The regular review of the state of affairs of women in development took place almost independently of shifts in economic and political conditions during the 1980s and the constraints posed by the mainstream political ideology of the time. On the other hand, the situation of women (and children) was not unaffected by the hardships of the 1980s and 1990s, particularly those caused by the implementation of the structural adjustment policies of the Bretton Woods institutions. The UN Decade for Women was driven primarily by counterforces to the prevailing ideology; it was a broad, nongovernmental women's movement that operated on its own together with the UN system. At the intergovernmental level, the women's "cause" received ideological support from a majority of Third World governments. It also drew its strength from within the system, especially from the United Nations Development Fund for Women (UNIFEM) and special coordinators on women's affairs.

The Fourth UN World Conference on Women, held in Beijing in September 1995, was even more spectacular than its predecessors. Some 17,000 representatives of governments, NGOs, international organizations, and the media attended the conference, making it one of the largest UN conferences ever. The massive attendance was further emphasized by the parallel forum organized by NGOs in neighboring Huairou that was attended by more than 30,000 participants.[45] Never before had gender issues been brought so impressively to the fore.

The conference adopted the Beijing Declaration and the Platform for Action, both of which carried forward the objectives and strategies of the previous summits on women. These documents focused on how to accelerate implementation of the forward-looking strategies adopted in Nairobi ten years earlier. The focal points of the Platform for Action—empowering women socially, politically, and economically in both public and private life and eliminating all forms of discrimination against women—were cast in much the same mold. They stressed that plans to address societal issues must include gender in order to ensure sustainable development. The platform outlined twelve critical areas of concern: poverty, education, health, violence against women, armed conflict, economic structures, power sharing and decision making, mechanisms to promote the advancement of women, human rights, the media, the environment, and the girl child. The declaration committed the international community to the goals of advancing equity, development, and peace and implementing the Platform for Action to ensure that a gender perspective was reflected in all policies and programs.[46]

The 1995 UN women's conference set a broad agenda for gender and development, ranging from human rights to mechanisms to improve opportunities for women in the workforce and in business. The Beijing conference fit into broader UN efforts to promote human development and eradicate poverty.[47] Women are overrepresented among the poor, and the feminization of poverty has negative consequences both for societies and for families. It affects children's opportunities for development as well.

In June 2000, the first overall reviews took place, when the General Assembly held a special session entitled "Women 2000: Gender Equality, Development and Peace for the Twenty-First Century," also known as Beijing +5.[48] A new overall review of progress was made in 2005, this time at a high-level plenary meeting at the forty-ninth session of the Commission on the Status of Women. The report prepared by the UN Secretary-General made it clear that there was still a way to go.[49] The UN system continued to keep the issue high on the international agenda.

In this regard, the UN system has been ahead of the curve. The Mexico summit in 1975 brought the issue of gender forcefully onto the international agenda and sent strong impulses throughout the world. It established an institutional framework that regularly assesses how well norms have been achieved. This framework includes the Commission on the Status of Women (which was established long before the summit), UNIFEM, the Committee on the Elimination of Discrimination against Women, and coordinators for women in development. These structures integrated the UN system of organizations and programs into the work of promoting women's issues. At an early stage, NGOs (women activists in particular) were also integrated as participants in the UN process, as demonstrated with their strength in Beijing. The powerful feminist and women's movements that emerged in the late 1960s and grew in the 1970s and 1980s, both internationally and nationally, pursued their own agendas.

However, they found in the UN system an important and useful ally, and that alliance proved to be mutually reinforcing.

A parallel focus on children with a view to improving their situation was complementary to the efforts to improve the situation of women; these activities were seen as mutually reinforcing. In 1989, the Convention on the Rights of the Child was adopted by the General Assembly, entering into force on 2 September 1990.[50] Then the United Nations World Summit for Children, held in New York in late September that year, adopted the World Declaration on the Survival, Protection and Development of Children together with a Plan of Action for implementing the declaration in the 1990s. The plan was intended to guide governments, international organizations, bilateral aid agencies, and NGOs in formulating their own programs of action to ensure that the declaration was implemented.[51]

The summit for children—like previous UN world summits convened to address the development challenges confronting specific priority policy areas—looked at developments within most areas on the international agenda, from the promotion of peace to environmental issues and trade. Pressing problems within these areas as well as other problems confronting developing countries in particular (including rising external debts and stagnation in economic growth) profoundly affected the world's children as well. The Plan of Action set out detailed objectives and quantified targets for improving the situation for children during the rest of the 1990s, building foundations within this policy area that would later develop into the MDGs.

In order to attain these objectives, it was necessary that both developed and developing countries prioritize improving conditions for children and mobilize resources to this end. Governments were urged to prepare national programs of action by the end of 1991 and to encourage and assist provincial and local governments. Many developing countries, especially those of Sub-Saharan Africa and landlocked and island nations, would require additional long-term international support to complement their own national efforts in this regard.[52]

In the 1990s, other world conferences contributed to promoting the revival of the social and human dimensions of development. The 1993 World Conference on Human Rights in Vienna and the International Conference on Population and Development, held in Cairo in 1994, informed and influenced public opinion and attitudes. All these efforts, each with a specific thematic focus that mutually reinforced the others, brought the same general message home to the world: the imperative need to bring the social and human dimensions of development to the fore.

TWELVE

Evolving Priorities, Patterns, and Trends, 1982–2005

- **Overall Profile of UN Technical Cooperation: Major Patterns**
- **UNDP 1982–2005: Overall Goals and Evolving Funding and Programming Structures**
- **Bringing in Governments as Executing Agencies**
- **Coordinator of System-Wide Technical Development Cooperation?**
- **Some Concluding Observations**

The UNDP's formative years have been described and analyzed in chapter 7. This chapter will bring forward this descriptive analysis and emphasize changing trends. The analysis will focus on developments within a few policy areas that have been given particular importance by the UNDP and have become part of its identity, namely its roles as:

- Guardian of the sovereignty of member states in the asymmetrical development cooperation relationship
- Coordinator of technical assistance within the UN system
- Facilitator of the poverty orientation of aid
- Champion of the social and human dimensions of development

What changes, if any, took place within these policy areas during the two final decades of the past century? What were the main drivers of the evolving policy?

Overall Profile of UN Technical Cooperation: Major Patterns

In 1982, total operational development assistance to developing countries by the United Nations system amounted to $4.5 billion. This assistance included expenditures and disbursements from all organizations, including the IDA, IFAD, and UNEP, and assistance to refugees, humanitarian assistance, and related activities. It did not include cost-sharing or expenditures for administration and program support. Of this amount, $2.1 billion was provided as grants. The total amount accounted for about 13 percent of the total development assistance received by developing countries that year. In 1984, the amount increased to $4.8 billion, of which $2.3 billion was provided in grants (exclusive of humanitarian aid) and $2.5 billion in concessional loans.[1]

The resources the UN system spent on operational development activities continued to grow for the rest of the decade. In 1990, it spent $7.6 billion on grants and concessional lending (divided equally). The amount increased in the early 1990s, reaching $9.5 billion in 1994, again divided fairly equally between grants and loans. The UN system provided an additional $1.2 billion in humanitarian and relief aid that year. Grant expenditure by the UN system on development activities (excluding IDA and IFAD concessional loans and humanitarian assistance) amounted to $4.86 billion in 1995, reaching $6.5 billion in 2000 and $9.7 billion in 2003.[2]

The regional distribution of system-wide grant assistance is given in table 12.1. Africa has been the largest recipient of grant assistance all along, but its share has decreased somewhat since the mid-1990s. Asia and the Pacific followed as the second largest recipient until the mid-1990s, but in subsequent years, Latin America and the Arab states, at differing times, came second.

Table 12.2 shows the sectoral distribution of UN technical assistance. The distribution was influenced both by the source of funding (regular or extra-budgetary) and the organizations involved. The health sector tended to dominate regular budget-financed technical assistance, not least because of the size of the WHO's regular budget and its concentration on technical assistance. UNDP expenditures financed by indicative planning figures, in contrast, reflected developing-country priorities and tended to be concentrated in such sectors as agriculture, forestry and fisheries, natural resources, and general development issues. Social sectors other than health (including education, employment, population, and social conditions) generally absorbed a fairly large share.

During the 1980s and early 1990s, important changes took place in the composition of multilateral technical cooperation in response to changes in the international environment. The most dramatic change involved the growth in humanitarian aid from next to nothing in 1982 (0.1 percent) to

TABLE 12.1.

UN Development Grants by Region, Selected Years, 1982–2003 (by percent and in billions of U.S. dollars)[1]

	1982	1991	1995	1998	2000	2001	2002	2003
Africa	42.5	47.6	42.0	34.4	33.4	26.7	25.1	28.2
Asia and the Pacific	38.8	39.4	26.2	24.3	21.0	21.8	23.1	17.2
The Americas[2]	10.5	8.2	21.3	30.4	20.3	19.8	19.0	15.6
Arab states[3]	6.2	4.0	5.3	7.5	13.0	15.5	17.0	27.5
Europe (and the CIS)[4]	2.0	0.7	5.2	3.4	4.7	6.6	6.6	4.6
Global and interregional	0.0	0.0	0.0	0.0	7.6	9.6	9.2	6.9
TOTAL	100.0	99.9[5]	100.0	100.0	100.0	100.0	100.0	100.0
Billions of U.S. dollars[6]	2.1	4.3	4.9	5.3	6.5	7.1	7.3	9.7

Sources: Yearbook of the United Nations 1982, 626 (for 1982); Yearbook of the United Nations 1992, 556 (for 1991); Yearbook of the United Nations 1996, 766–767 (for 1995); Yearbook of the United Nations 1999, 793 (for 1998); Yearbook of the United Nations 2001, 791 (for 2000); Yearbook of the United Nations 2002, 862 (for 2001); Yearbook of the United Nations 2003, 889 (for 2002); Yearbook of the United Nations 2004, 875 (for 2003); and calculations based on this data.

1. Data provided in this table is the data available in the *Yearbook of the United Nations,* which did not provide parallel data about development grants for every year during this period.

2. Although the definition of this term changed over the period of this table, it usually referred to Latin America and the Caribbean.

3. "Western Asia" was the term used for this region from 1982 to 2000.

4. For the period of this table, Europe was sometimes combined with the Arab states (who were the main recipients) and other times with the Commonwealth of Independent States (CIS), then the main recipient. In 2000, contributions to the CIS were included among the global and interregional activities, since 2001 in Europe.

5. Percentages may not add up to exactly 100 because figures are rounded in the data on which the calculations are based.

6. Does not include concessional loans provided by the International Fund for Agricultural Development, or loans through the World Bank Group, and self-supporting programs.

TABLE 12.2.

UN Expenditures for Technical Cooperation by Sector, 1982, 1990, and 1992 (by percent and in billions of U.S. dollars)

	1982[1]	1990	1992
Health	19	24	19
Agriculture, forestry, and fisheries	18	18	11
Natural resources	10	5	6
Transport and communications	9	4	3
General development	8	7	9
Population	8	5	3
Industry	7	5	4
Employment	5	---	2
Others	5	9	4
Science and technology	4	3	2
Education	4	4	6
Culture	2	3	3
Humanitarian aid/relief	0	13	28
TOTAL	99[2]	100	100
Billions of U.S. dollars	1.4	3.8	4.6

Source: Yearbook of the United Nations 1982, 627 (for 1982); Yearbook of the United Nations 1990, 380 and Yearbook of the United Nations 1991, 367 (for 1990); and Yearbook of the United Nations 1993, 685–686 (for 1992) and calculations based on this data.

1. Total system-wide technical assistance in 1982 amounted to $2.2 billion, including the technical cooperation embodied in World Bank lending operations. Yearbook of the United Nations 1982, 626–627.

2. Percentages may not add up to exactly 100 because figures are rounded in the data on which the calculations are based.

one-quarter of total expenditures ten years later, remaining at about or beyond that level during subsequent years.[3] This reflected the crises and conflicts taking place since the 1990s and the response by the major powers, who provided emergency relief and aid to refugees.[4] Continuity is manifest in other areas: health, for example, remained a top priority from the start.[5] In 2003, almost half of total expenditures went to these two sectors. The third major sector was agriculture, forestry, and fisheries. While about one-fifth of total resources was channeled to this sector in the 1980s, the trend declined to around 10 percent of the total in 1992. Other sectors that had received a relatively large share of around 10 percent in the 1970s and early 1980s, such as industry, national resources, transport and communications, and population, showed a downward trend in the early 1990s, while the share provided for general development continued at a level of 8 to 9 percent and education at a slightly lower level of about 6 percent. Science and technology, deemed so vital to development in UN strategies, received an even lower share in the 1990s—a mere 2 percent.

During the 1980s and 1990s, the relative position of the UNDP as a funding source within the UN system was challenged by both the specialized agencies and other UN programs. The UNDP's expenditures (grants) for operational activities continued to grow, from $651 million in 1982 to $864 million in 1985, $1.1 billion in 1990, and $1.3 billion in 1995, peaking with $2.4 billion in 1999.[6] Its share of total UN expenditures these years varied somewhat, amounting to 31 percent in 1982, 34 percent in 1990, 26 percent in 1995, and 44 percent in 1999.[7] The specialized agencies expanded their operational activities during these years through their regular budgets but especially through extra-budgetary sources (direct contributions from bilateral aid agencies)—their share of system-wide grant expenditures in 1982 was 25 percent and remained about at that level.[8] The growth was especially great for the WFP and UNICEF. As we saw in earlier chapters, the UNDP and the WFP drew on somewhat different sources of funding. Through most of the 1980s, the expenditures of the two programs stayed at a similar level (with the UNDP somewhat ahead). In 1991, the WFP's share of system-wide UN expenditures was above 31 percent, reaching 34 and 31 percent respectively in 1992 and 1993, while the UNDP's share was 29, 25, and 25 percent for those years.[9] UNICEF's shares during the first years of the 1990s (1991–1993) were 14, 16, and 17 percent, respectively.[10]

During the first years of the new century (2000–2003), total UN grant expenditures for development activities increased from $6.5 billion to $9.7 billion. The combined expenditures of the specialized agencies and other UN institutions stayed at a slightly higher level than those financed by the UNDP. The WFP's expenditures on operational activities continued at a high level, constituting by far the largest share in 2003. UNICEF's expenditures on operational activities also continued at a high level.[11]

The annual pledging conferences were crucial for funding the UNDP's operational activities, and increasingly this was true for a number of other UN funds and programs as well, including the trust funds. During the 1980s and increasingly in the 1990s, however, the UNDP and other UN institutions had to look for additional funding for their operational activities (the so-called noncore funding) by establishing trust funds for special purposes, for example. Total pledges increased somewhat during the 1980s and early 1990s: from $1.1 billion in 1982 to a peak of $1.6 billion in 1990. However, from 1994, the amount pledged stayed in the range of $1.1–$1.2 billion for the rest of the decade. The UNDP's share of these commitments varied somewhat from one year to the other but stayed above 60 percent during the 1980s and above 50 percent during the 1990s.[12]

UNDP 1982–2005: Overall Goals and Evolving Funding and Programming Structures

In the 1980s, voluntary funding for operational activities provided at the annual pledging conferences stagnated; at times it even declined. UN intergovernmental bodies, including the General Assembly, expressed grave concern and appealed repeatedly to governments for more funding. When the anticipated financial resources were not forthcoming, the Governing Council was forced to readjust the budget for the third development cycle (1982–1986) and then for the fourth development cycle (1987–1991). As had happened earlier, budget constrains triggered innovative thinking about the UNDP's future role as a development agent within the UN system and how to attract new resources beyond those voluntarily provided by governments (the core funding).[13]

The Fourth Programming Cycle (1987–1991)

The fourth programming cycle followed established patterns.[14] The poverty orientation of the previous cycles continued: 80 percent of the amount available for country IPFs was allocated to countries with per capita GNP up to $750, weighted to be more advantageous for those with $375 per capita GNP and below. The remaining 20 percent was allocated to countries with per capita GNP above $750, weighted to be advantageous to those below $1,500 per capita GNP. Developing countries were expected to reimburse UNDP-financed programs and the costs of UNDP field offices, with more expected from the better-off developing countries.[15]

In a global economic situation characterized by uncertainty and the indebtedness of most developing countries, most UNDP programs stressed efficient economic management and the promotion of greater agricultural and industrial production as major objectives. However, as the UNDP administrator explained in his 1987 annual report, strategies varied within and between regions, reflecting differences in the type and degree of industrialization, the extent of food self-sufficiency, the availability of qualified human resources, the structure of external trade, and the size of external debts. Certain areas continued to receive priority in most country programs, including public-sector efficiency measures, economic reactivation through the diversification of industry exports, greater incentives for the private sector, and the use of technology in development. The budgets of many developing countries had been adapted to the demands of the IMF's structural adjustment policies, which affected social sectors negatively. This in turn affected UNDP programming, making social equality and living conditions among the rural and urban poor important considerations. Greater emphasis was also placed on incorporating women in development projects and cooperation with NGOs as partners in development.[16]

The Fifth Programming Cycle (1992–1996)

The poverty profile was further strengthened in the new programming cycle and the main objectives were more focused. The UNDP assumed an annual growth of total voluntary contributions of 8 percent, starting from $1 million in 1991.[17] The available resources were to be distributed according to a formula that was, if possible, even more detailed than that established for the fourth cycle.[18] Countries with per capita GNP of $750 or less would receive 87 percent of IPF resources. The LDCs as a whole would receive 55 percent of country IPFs. IPFs were also established for specific recipients, including national liberation movements. As with the fourth cycle, a safety clause was added to the benefit of countries with per capita GNP above $750.[19]

The focus was on building and strengthening the national capacity of developing countries within the six areas of poverty eradication and grassroots participation in development, environmental problems and natural resource management, management development, technical cooperation among developing countries, transfer and adaptation of technology for development, and women in development. The council decided that priority was to be given to programs in those areas, including intercountry indicative planning figures and that special programming resources should be used to strengthen and supplement activities funded through country indicative planning figures.[20]

However, voluntary contributions did not meet the anticipated expectations, and the UNDP was forced to put on the brake. As early as 1993, IPF commitments were reduced to 70 percent of those originally set. But in his annual report for 1995, the administrator was able to bring good tidings. Thanks to a significant increase in cost-sharing and trust funds (see table 12.3), total resources for the fifth cycle were estimated at $8.2 billion, well above both the original and revised allocations. Voluntary contributions to UNDP core resources were, however, estimated at $4.7 billion, considerably lower than the $6.3 billion originally projected in 1990.[21]

Annual contributions to UNDP core resources over the fifth programming cycle varied from $1.2 billion in 1992 to $848 million in 1996. Overall resources—core plus noncore—increased from $1.7 billion in 1992 to about $2.0 billion in 1996 if the incomes from the funds the UNDP administered are included. In the last year of the cycle, the main focus was on assisting countries to eradicate poverty and making human development sustainable.[22] A new resource distribution formula was implemented with a view to assigning more resources to the most needy countries: nearly 90 percent of core resources went to low-income countries, home of 90 percent of the world's poor. In 1996, 39 percent of core funding went to poverty eradication and livelihoods for the poor, 32 percent to governance, and 21 percent to the environment.[23]

The Changing Funding Patterns of the 1990s

The ambitions that governed both the fourth and fifth programming cycles assumed that available resources would increase. However, voluntary contributions stagnated and even declined in some years. The UNDP was looking for new sources to finance its operational activities. One of these sources was recipient governments. They were expected to contribute more than before, both to the UNDP presence in the country and to project and program costs. Another design to get more resources was to establish trust funds to obtain funding for specific purposes—such as the Special Measures Fund for the Least Developed Countries (SMF/LDCs).[24] Cost-sharing of projects and programs that involved other agencies, including bilateral donors, was another design.

This development is shown in table 12.3. Since all major policy documents now gave special priority to the least-developed countries, the table singles out contributions to the SMF/LDCs. Contributions to funds for special purposes increased in the 1990s, as did contributions to the UNDP's general fund in the form of cost-sharing by recipient governments. In the mid-1990s, third parties also increasingly contributed to such cost-sharing. The new "business" component—the management service agreements initiated in 1983—brought additional annual incomes that increased from $149 million in 1993 to $168 million three years later. Incomes were also derived from the "ordinary" trust funds administered by the UNDP. These additional incomes—about $85 million a year—are not included in table 12.3.

During the period covered by table 12.3, the income structure of the UNDP changed quite radically. In 1987, voluntary contributions—the core funding on which the organization had relied for its very existence and for its operational activities from the start—made up 86 percent of total income. Ten years later, this share had been reduced to 48 percent. Cost-sharing and trust funds provided an increasing share of UNDP funding for this period. This trend continued into the new century.[25]

The way the UNDP was funded in the latter 1990s and beyond—with noncore funding increasingly surpassing core funding—was not unproblematic, for various reasons. Reflecting on this challenge in a 1998 report to the Executive Board, UNDP administrator James Speth stressed that measures would be taken to ensure that all resources, core and noncore, would be programmed within the sustainable human development frameworks and the country cooperation frameworks approved by the board. However, maintaining the UNDP's multilateral character and the integrity of the intergovernmental process was a special challenge, given the growth of noncore resources.[26]

Policy Priorities and Structural Reforms in the Mid-1990s

The new international environment of the early 1990s had raised high hopes for a peace dividend. Such hopes were contradicted by a reality that showed a trend in the opposite direction. This applied especially to the United States, the remaining superpower, which, with the end of the Cold War, had lost an important part of its rationale for providing development assistance. This forced the UNDP to come up with fresh ideas and new initiatives. It needed to redefine its role and explore ways and means of fulfilling its vision. The international strategy for DD4 and the human development project laid much of the basis.

TABLE 12.3.

Funding Structure of the UNDP, Selected Years, 1987–1996 (in millions of U.S. dollars)

	1987	1990	1992	1994	1996
Voluntary contributions	881	1,002	1,178	928	848
Recipient government cost-sharing	118	169	294	596	701
SMF/LDCs	14	13	NA[1]	---[2]	NA
Other income[3]	12	28	97	104	202
Trust funds[4]	NA	28	51	190	NA
Total income[5]	1,025	1,240	1,620	1,818	1,751

Source: Yearbook of the United Nations 1987, 417 (for 1987); Yearbook of the United Nations 1990, 383 and Yearbook of the United Nations 1991, 368 (for 1990); Yearbook of the United Nations 1992, 557 (for 1992); Yearbook of the United Nations 1994, 792 (for 1994); Yearbook of the United Nations 1996, 783–785 (for 1996).

1. Data not available.
2. Less than $1 million (0.01).
3. Includes contributions to local UNDP offices, government cash counterpart contributions, extrabudgetary activities/income, and miscellaneous income.
4. Trust funds established by the administrator, excluding the Global Environment Fund. For 1996, no differentiation is made between these trust funds and the others administered by UNDP (included in "Other income").
5. Ordinary trust funds are not included in this overview. For 1996, however, see note 4.

In a March 1993 report on the efficiency of programming and the UNDP's comparative advantage, the administrator continued the process of defining this "new" role. He identified four broad areas as key priorities: economic management and public sector reform; social development, poverty alleviation, and community participation in development; environmental protection and sustainable natural resource management; and productive capacity, involving technology transfer and development support for the private sector. Within these areas, there was a major opportunity for the organization to develop its comparative advantage further. In 1994, Speth outlined an "agenda for change." He presented his vision of the UNDP's future role and principal goals to the Executive Board, and the board agreed: the UNDP's overall mission should be to assist program countries in their endeavor to realize sustainable human development in line with their national development programs and priorities.[27]

This demanded new financial parameters and an adjustment of the administrative structure. Reforming and adjusting an established administrative structure is a tall order for most organizations: for an international organization, the challenges involved in restructuring to adapt to new ways of working and new tasks are especially difficult. The first round of changes took place in 1994–1995, followed in the second half of the 1990s and beyond by new efforts to create a staff culture of efficiency, trust, learning, results-orientation, quality assurance, and accountability. The UNDP also needed to review and restructure operational functions to adapt to the new policy priorities and tasks. Speth initiated the second phase of change in March 1997.[28]

In order to forge partnerships, the UNDP set up several joint task forces with the FAO, the ILO, UNESCO, the WHO, the Department for Development Support and Management Services, and the regional commissions. It also reestablished the UNDP/World Bank task force to review existing relations and develop new initiatives. Several quite extensive structural changes of the UNDP were explored and implemented in order to adapt the organization to the new priorities.

But there was more basic restructuring to come. At its January and June 1995 sessions, the Executive Board considered the administrator's proposals for the next programming cycle. The programming arrangements that came out of this process involved a major restructuring that also affected resource distribution in the remaining years of the fifth cycle. Instead of the five-year programming period of previous cycles with IPFs set for the whole period for countries and regional and global programs, the board adopted a rolling three-year planning cycle. It also decided to introduce a new, more flexible three-tier target for resource assignment from the core (TRAC) scheme for allocating resources to the country level. Most important, the new programming system retained the poverty profile of its predecessors: 88 percent of all targeted resources assigned from the core would be allocated to low-income countries and 60 percent to the LDCs.[29]

In 1996, the UNDP provided preliminary TRAC figures for 1997–1999 for individual recipient countries. The revised and final figures were presented to the March 1997 session of the Executive Board.[30] Almost half of the TRAC budget lines for the three-year period was devoted to Africa (47 percent of $1.7 billion), 33 percent to Asia and the Pacific, 8 percent to the Arab states, 7 percent to Latin America and the Caribbean, and 5 percent to Europe and the Commonwealth of Independent States (CIS).[31] The poverty profile and to a large extent the geographical distribution continued into the new century.[32] In June 2002, the Executive Board changed from a three-year to a four-year program financial framework (2004–2007).

A New Design for a New Century: Toward an Upstream Development Organization

Despite the new programming system and strong appeals from UN intergovernmental bodies, including the General Assembly, for increased funding for core UNDP activities, core funding continued to decline.[33] This triggered an institutional reform process that included decentralizing and slimming UNDP headquarters and a narrowing of the focus of UNDP interventions. The Executive Board also initiated a major review of how to reverse the downward trend in contributions for UNDP core resources, resulting in the adoption of a funding strategy. However, this was only the beginning of a much more fundamental reorganization of the UNDP that involved its self-identity, major objectives, and strategy.

In 1998, the Executive Board considered a report by the administrator on ways and means to focus UNDP interventions in areas where it could achieve optimal impact in improving the lives of the world's poorest people. The guiding principles that were proposed to ensure predictability and help narrow the focus included building capacity in program countries for sustainable human development, especially poverty eradication; ensuring national ownership of development goals, strategies, policies, and programs; and promoting participation, dialogue, and choice in decision making. The report argued that helping program countries in their efforts to realize sustainable human development should remain the highest priority and UNDP assistance should be responsive and flexible, the board stressed anew.[34]

In spite of declining resources, the board again adopted an annual funding target of $1.1 billion. Stressing the need to achieve annual increases in core resources until the target was met, it decided that the UNDP should develop a multiyear funding framework (MYFF) that would integrate program objectives, resources, budget, and outcomes, with the aim of increasing core resources.[35]

At that point, the administrator presented business plans with a new vision for the UNDP. He noted that the far-reaching changes in the development arena made it necessary for the organization to embark on a major program of reform and renewal. The multiyear funding framework was a core component of this program, providing a more predictable framework of core funding. The administrator stated that the greatest demand for UNDP services was as an adviser and advocate. This indicated that the organization could maximize its output only by going upstream, concentrating efforts on policy reforms and priorities in the recipient countries rather than on supporting development projects on the ground. Policy was therefore to be realigned to make the UN Development Programme a stronger global advocate for human development, to align capacity with demand, and to make the organization more highly networked and field-based. To remain a trusted partner of program countries in developing policies and institutions, the UNDP needed to gear itself to provide services in response to demand, to assist program countries in the crafting of pro-poor policies, and to help build the institutional capacity needed to sustain and implement these policies, including in postconflict situations.[36]

The UNDP's business plans for 2000–2003 aimed at ensuring that the organization could respond effectively to the growing demand for upstream activities, complementing these activities with strong global advocacy and providing direct support to program countries through coordinating aid and mobilizing resources. A key priority would also be ensuring that the UNDP had the policy expertise, key partnerships, and internal capacity to deliver its services effectively. The point of departure should be the needs of the program countries, where the unprecedented global changes had created a tremendous demand for new kinds of support. The multiyear funding framework would meet these new demands by showing a clear trend toward upstream activities such as policy and institutional support. Those activities played to UNDP strengths. They leveraged the trust it enjoyed from program countries and built upon its role in advocacy, UN development coordination, and country-level resource mobilization. The administrator admitted that helping program countries would imply considerable change in the UNDP's operations, policies, partnerships, and culture. Programs would remain country-driven, but the UNDP would be much more effective at policy dialogue and institution-building than at directly supporting isolated poverty-alleviation projects. Project work would continue and even increase as resources grew, but it would be aligned behind policies.[37]

In a self-evaluation four years later, the administrator maintained that the internal reform initiated in the 2000–2003 business plans had transformed the UNDP. On the basis of the five pillars of policy, partnerships, people, performance, and resources and the projected outcomes of these plans, he argued that the UNDP had become a stronger global advocate for human development.[38]

The last year of the twentieth century saw the first steps of a new management system whose complexity would have to be further developed—and simplified—and adapted to the needs of other UN funds and programs. Fighting poverty was among the prime objectives, one that also was followed up in practice. The other approach to this end, the geographical distribution of resources to the LDCs and other low-income countries based on their GNP, was also followed up. In January 1999, the Executive Board reaffirmed the basic principle for resource allocation, namely that an increasing share was to go to low-income countries.[39]

Embarking on the Second Multiyear Funding Framework (2004–2007)

By 2003, the time was ripe for assessing the achievements of the 2000–2003 cycle and for setting the agenda for the next one (2004–2007). In a report on the funding of development cooperation activities of the UN system, the Secretary-General noted that the Millennium Summit and the International Conference on Financing for Development in 2002 had created a new development context with a broad consensus about a shared agenda and had given a renewed impetus to international development. In spite of reforms aimed at increasing effectiveness and efficiency—and the increase in overall funding for UN development activities from $5.61 billion in 1992 to $7.73 billion in 2001 (excluding the World Bank Group)—core (regular) resources of UN funds and programs had remained stagnant or even declined (with the exception of the WFP), although there had been a slight improvement in 2002. This long-term stagnation, when adjusted for inflation, had resulted in a decrease in the resource base in real terms.[40]

The goals established in the second MYFF reflected the Millennium Declaration and the MDGs and continued the goals of the first MYFF as they had gradually been adjusted over the years. The five core goals were 1) achieving the MDGs and reducing human poverty; 2) fostering democratic governance; 3) managing energy resources and the environment for sustainable development; 4) supporting crisis prevention and recovery; and 5) responding to HIV/AIDS. The efforts to simplify the system had to some extent been implemented: the specific areas in which the UNDP would contribute to development results at the country level were reduced to thirty within the five core goals. The strategic focus was directed toward three groups of activities:

- Building national capacities, promoting national ownership, advocating and fostering an enabling policy environment, promoting gender equity, and forging strategic partnerships

- Building UNDP organizational capacities, including initiatives to provide broad-based knowledge services and improve internal efficiency and performance

- Deepening partnerships within the UN system and community development at operational and program levels.

The Executive Board underlined that the MDGs, particularly poverty reduction, were the basis for all UNDP activities.[41]

Reducing human poverty remained the major concern during the first year of the new cycle: more than 90 percent of program countries sought support within that area. UNDP work within this area continued to be concentrated largely on local-level initiatives and monitoring and reporting, particularly around country targets related to the MDGs. Efforts had progressed from implementing scattered local poverty projects to supporting national frameworks for poverty reduction.[42]

The UNDP paid particular attention to its role in the process of producing poverty reduction strategy papers, a major instrument invented by the World Bank to direct planning in developing countries in the "right" direction. The UNDP had launched an array of global and regional programs that championed equity as an integral component of growth strategies, helping link long-term development policies to the causes of poverty and promoting a healthy national dialogue by fostering greater policy choice, especially with regard to economic policy.[43]

More than 90 percent of the program countries also sought support from the second largest thematic area, fostering democratic governance, making the UNDP the leading provider of democratic governance services worldwide. Africa remained the core region, with 85 percent of the countries reporting. The greatest concentration was in decentralization and local governance; UNDP support sustained both central government agendas toward devolution and local efforts to develop capacity.

The strategy of localizing the MDGs sought to provide service delivery through democratic participatory processes, blend the governance aspects of local capacity- and institution-building to address the HIV/ AIDS pandemic, and ensure a sustainable environment while promoting local development.[44]

In the early twenty-first century, crisis prevention and recovery emerged as a primary focus for the UNDP, particularly after 1998, when part of the responsibility for operational activities for natural disaster mitigation, prevention, and preparedness was transferred to the UNDP from the UN Office for the Coordination of Humanitarian Affairs.[45] In 2004, this was reflected in the large number of program countries seeking support within this area—75 percent of all program countries. Eighty countries sought UNDP support within this area (compared to fifty-four in 2000). Almost 90 percent of countries in Asia and the Pacific benefited from support in crisis prevention and recovery, compared to 50 to 60 percent for the other regions. This support was cast in terms of the traditional justification for development cooperation: the commitment to eradicating poverty and empowering the poorest and most vulnerable groups placed conflict prevention and recovery at the core of the UNDP development agenda. The support was clearly driven by demand: in 2004, a series of conflicts and natural disasters afflicted several countries in which the organization was working.[46]

More than 90 percent of program countries (128 countries) were engaged with the UNDP within the area of energy and environment for sustainable development. The main focus was on frameworks and strategies for sustainable development, which represented 29 percent of all reported outcomes in this area. The UNDP strengthened its focus on the linkages between energy and poverty to integrate the role of energy into national MDG frameworks and poverty reduction strategy papers. In 2004, the area was reoriented to integrate security concerns into development cooperation. Key areas included climate change, natural disaster prevention and recovery, and transboundary environmental cooperation.[47]

The demand for UNDP support regarding the response to HIV/AIDS continued to grow rapidly, nearly doubling from fifty-five countries in 2000 to ninety-seven in 2004. The response was highest in Africa, followed by Asia and the Pacific. Most of the assistance was in the form of development planning and implementation. A key feature of all country action was the heavy emphasis on forging partnerships for results, with actors ranging from governments, civil society, and the private sector to donors and the international community at large. The UNDP also worked to increase national ownership of the design and implementation of HIV/ AIDS initiatives. In 2004, there were policy advisers in all regions.[48]

Advocacy

In the early 1990s, advocacy (active promotion of its development policy) emerged as a "new" dimension of UNDP priority activities. It sprang out of the human development initiative—human development became more than just a statistical recording exercise, it became the primary objective of the organization and part of its identity as well.

The structural adjustment policies generated by the Bretton Woods institutions a decade earlier had paved the way for using development assistance as an instrument for policy reform. UNDP advocacy took advantage of this heritage, with a difference: the emergence of human development as an idea to meet the challenges of the 1990s and beyond had been nurtured by the mounting criticism against the democratic and social deficits of structural adjustment programs, particularly the conditionality involved. With the end of the Cold War, a new era was opened up for political liberalism in terms of human rights (including the right to development), good governance, and democracy, stimulated by ideas of empowerment. It was in this new international environment that the UNDP's human development policy was crafted—with a mission to make a difference. From the start, great care was taken to steer clear of any form of conditionality, in stark contrast to structural adjustment policies. Advocacy became an important part of the strategy for realizing the policy, with the Human Development Report project the main source of inspiration as well as the main instrument.

The advocacy policy had a cautious beginning for reasons already indicated: the ideological heritage—the United Nations and the UNDP in particular were there to respond to objectives and priorities generated within the recipient countries in their own political processes. This heritage made it difficult for the UNDP to pose as a political actor in its own right, actively pursuing its own development policy in words and deeds. In generating the "new" policy to be pursued by advocacy, it had to strike a balance, not least in rhetoric: this assistance was open to governments interested in policy reform in the direction of human development.

In his 1989 annual report, Administrator William Draper envisioned the UNDP's role in the 1990s in the context of rapidly changing global conditions and in consideration of the lessons learned over the past forty years. He mentioned the publication of the *Human Development Report 1990* as a major achievement that took an uncompromising look at the state of human development around the world over the past three decades, showing that, while economic growth was vital to improved living conditions, growth alone was no guarantee of human development. He also stated that the UNDP stood ready to assist governments that wanted to review options for accelerated human development. It could augment the full gamut of its multidisciplinary experience with the expertise of other relevant UN bodies in such fields as education, health, child care, nutrition, employment, industrial development, trade unions, and agriculture.[49] A program and its direction and priorities had been announced.

During the years that followed, the Human Development Reports, which were a central part of the UNDP's advocacy efforts, were published in an increasing number of languages (ten by 1998). The illustrated annual report focused on core themes and specific success stories. The strategy also included constituency-building through organized events (often in cooperation with partners) aimed at NGOs, academics, trade unions, religious groups, intergovernmental organizations, civic leaders, and grassroots organizations. Development programs increasingly incorporated advocacy and communication from the start, and information on the UNDP's role in development was provided by its network of liaison offices. More and more national Human Development Reports were also produced, usually with UNDP support. In the years after the Millennium Declaration, the UNDP increasingly integrated the Millennium Development Goals as the major points of departure in its advocacy strategy.[50]

The heavy emphasis on information and advocacy was largely a matter of policy promotion, based on the goals and priority areas of sustainable human development. It was an integral part of the greater emphasis on the "upstream" activities of the latter 1990s and beyond, hence the focus on decision-makers in developed as well as developing countries. It also went "downstream" in a broad-based effort to reach all kinds of stakeholders and social groups through a differentiated information strategy, in this way basing policy with the voters in UN countries, North and South.

During these years, UNDP funding was shrinking despite the high hopes of a peace dividend. It was more necessary than ever to present the UNDP as a dynamic development institution with fresh ideas worthy of funding. The work on the first Human Development Report offered a point of departure with its new perspective on development. The evolving strategy for development and development cooperation made advocacy come naturally, both as a survival strategy and a funding strategy and as an instrument of policy change.

The Ordinary Trust Funds

A number of small and a few large trust funds were administered by or associated with the UNDP. Some of the largest or politically most important ones were the United Nations Capital Development Fund, established in 1972; the United Nations Fund for Population Activities, established in 1967; the United Nations Volunteers program, established in 1970; the United Nations National Liberation Movement Trust Fund, established in 1973; the United Nations Revolving Fund for Natural Resource Exploration, established in 1973; and the United Nations Sahelian Office and the UN Trust Fund for Sudano-Sahelian Activities, both of which were established in the early 1970s and added to the UNDP's responsibilities in 1976. Several of these developed into independent or semi-independent programs under the UNDP administrator or the Executive Board. The UNFPA had obtained independent status in 1972.

By 1981, the UNDP was administering a total of thirteen trust funds. In addition to those mentioned, two new ones warrant special mention: the voluntary fund for the UN Decade for Women, which the Secretary-General delegated to the administrator in 1980 (which developed into UNIFEM), and the Interim Fund for Science and Technology for Development. Both of these covered policy areas that were given high priority in UN strategy papers. They are referred to as the ordinary trust funds in contrast to the new trust funds established by the administrator for specific purposes to increase the UNDP's noncore funding.[51] In 2001, a new generation of thematic trust funds was initiated to help the UNDP address the development priorities set out in the multiyear funding framework.

Our main focus here will be directed to three major trust funds that continued to develop into the new century: the UN Capital Development Fund, the UN Volunteers, and UNIFEM.

THE UNITED NATIONS CAPITAL DEVELOPMENT FUND

After its reorientation into an instrument for developing small-scale enterprises in the least-developed countries, the UNCDF became the largest of the trust funds in terms of income and expenditures in the latter 1970s, and it retained this position throughout subsequent decades. In the 1980s, like the UNDP, the UNCDF added to its core budget of voluntary pledges by seeking complementary finance from other sources, the UNDP in particular, but also through various joint-financing modalities that included bilateral donor agencies. In 1982, $28 million was made available as core funding at the pledging conference, an amount that decreased somewhat in the following years before it increased in the latter 1980s, reaching $37 million in 1989.[52]

In 1991, the fund celebrated its twenty-fifth anniversary; that became a record year also in terms of new project commitments, which reached $82 million. The following year, a new strategy based on area development emerged from an internal management review of UNCDF program development and delivery. According to the administrator, the strategy sought to take advantage of trends toward democratization and decentralization by working with governments, community groups, and NGOs to intensify participatory activities at the grassroots level. Keeping grassroots-level poverty reduction in the LDCs as its major thrust, the UNCDF continued to incorporate other themes into its programming, particularly the environment and women in development.[53]

During the following years, core funding stagnated and it began to decline in the second part of the decade. Nontraditional funding sources were actively sought, at times with some success. In 1994, the administrator stated that the UNCDF would continue to seek co-financing arrangements with multilateral organizations and tap nontraditional sources of funding. He also argued that the UNCDF should be much larger and more vital and more complementary to the UNDP as a whole. He worked with the fund to develop proposals to change its mission and objectives to make possible much greater resource mobilization and country impact. These changes emerged in a policy paper published by the UNCDF the following year. While continuing to emphasize its traditional role in providing small-scale credit and rural infrastructure in the LDCs, increased importance was to be placed on developing direct partnerships with newly empowered local governments and the community groups they served, especially the rural poor. In March 1997, the Executive Board endorsed the implementation of the new policy focus in which activities were to be concentrated on local governance, decentralization, participation, and microfinancing.[54]

A 1999 donor-led evaluation concluded that the UNCDF had responded well to the corporate change, and the Executive Board and the administrator concluded likewise.[55] Nevertheless, core resources continued to decline, remaining far below the annual target of $30 million. An impact assessment in 2004 concluded that the fund was effectively carrying out its mandate to reduce poverty in the LDCs and had adapted its portfolio to the 1995 policy shifts and responded to the recommendations of the 1999 evaluation. Nevertheless, its role within the UNDP and its future business model needed clarification.[56]

Responding to the assessment, the UNCDF management concluded that the fund would have to undergo urgent transformations to become more market oriented in its programs and financially viable as an institution while preserving and capitalizing on gains made in its support of local development and microfinance activities. A progress report in September 2004 presented two models—an ODA-based model in which the UNCDF would specialize in retail microfinance funded by voluntary contributions, and a private sector–based model, in which the fund would specialize in channeling and utilizing private capital for investments with a high social impact that supported the MDGs. Mark Malloch Brown, the UNDP administrator, recommended the private-sector model, arguing that it involved a more innovative approach and longer-term vision than the ODA-based model. The progress report also suggested that UNCDF activities and personnel dealing with local development be integrated within the UNDP Centre for Local Development, which operated primarily in the LDCs. In 2005, the Executive Board decided to maintain the UNCDF as an independent organization in order to focus on poverty and achieving the MDGs in the LDCs.[57]

THE UNITED NATIONS VOLUNTEERS

Developments within the UN Volunteers were less dramatic. The target set for the UNV program—1,000 volunteers by 1983—was attained in 1981. In stark contrast to bilateral peace corps, the UNVs were recruited internationally. The program emphasized recruiting youth from developing countries to serve in other developing countries, particularly the LDCs, leaving the national flag behind.

In 1982, $2.2 million was committed to the special fund for the UNVs, an amount that decreased during the following years. This made it necessary to get contributions from other sources, including the UNDP, to meet increasing expenditures. The number of volunteers (1,356 in 1982) continued to grow, surpassing 2,000 in 1987. In the early 1980s, most volunteers were recruited from developing countries (over 80 percent in 1983), making technical cooperation among developing countries an important feature of the program. Africa was the main recipient of UN Volunteers; in the early 1980s, the region received more than half of the total number. During the 1980s, the thrust of UNV assistance was directed to basic sectors, such as agriculture, education, and health.[58] The profile of a volunteer had changed quite fundamentally since the idea was first institutionalized: by the late 1980s, most volunteers were specialists from a wide range of disciplines.[59]

In the 1990s, the UNV program continued to grow much along the lines established in the 1980s.[60] As was the case with the UNCDF, however, the UNV had to pursue the new UNDP policy priorities of the early 1990s. In May 1992, the UNDP Governing Council asked the administrator to help formulate programs in which UNV specialists would contribute to development activities that responded to ideas from local low-income communities for building up their capacity to deal with their development needs. It welcomed the UNV's involvement in humanitarian relief and related fields, ranging from capacity-building in disaster prevention, preparedness, and mitigation to rehabilitation and reconstruction activities. The council also asked the administrator to ensure that UNV activities were consistent with the coordination exercised by the UN Department of Humanitarian Affairs. The number of volunteers continued to grow.[61]

Given the evolution of UN responsibilities and the UNDP's evolving priorities, the volunteer roles appeared particularly appropriate in the areas of peace-building and humanitarian relief. In 1994, the General Assembly asked the Secretary-General to submit a report to ECOSOC on ways to strengthen national and regional standby arrangements—including the establishment of national volunteer corps in the area of emergency humanitarian assistance—and a distinct window of the Special Voluntary Fund for channeling funds for operational purposes.[62]

In November 2000, Secretary-General Kofi Annan gave a boost to the UNV by declaring 2001 the International Year of Volunteers. In 2001, the UNV launched an extensive advocacy campaign aimed at promoting greater awareness of the role that volunteers play in social and economic development. It involved 123 national committees and a large number of local, regional, and state committees. Nevertheless, funding of volunteer activities remained problematic.

In 2004, 7,300 UNV specialists and field workers were carrying out 7,772 assignments in 139 countries. As had been the case from the very beginning, most assignments were in Africa (42 percent in 2004), followed by Asia and the Pacific (26 percent), Latin America and the Caribbean (18 percent), Europe and the Commonwealth of Independent States (8.5 percent), and the Arab states (5.5 percent). A large share of the volunteers was still being recruited from developing countries (77 percent in 2004), and these volunteers were serving in their own or another developing country, especially in the LDCs.[63]

The United Nations was not ahead of the curve when the idea of engaging idealistic youth for development was launched; if anything, it was behind the curve. When it took on the idea, however, it managed to create a "peace corps" that became a peace corps in a more real sense than most of its bilateral predecessors. It became international in a real sense and carried a distinct UN stamp. At a time when bilateral agencies had reduced or done away with their peace corps—and some of their technical expert assistance as well—the UNV was a more vibrant service than ever. The UNDP had developed it into an instrument to serve its new policy priorities—promoting and advocating human development—generously sharing its own resources with the program.

UNIFEM

The Voluntary Fund for the United Nations Decade for Women, established by the General Assembly in 1975 and delegated to the UNDP administrator in 1980, was one of the major instruments established to implement the Program of Action set for the decade. Others were the UN Centre for Social Development and Humanitarian Affairs; the International Research and Training Institute for the Advancement of Women, the focal point of the program's implementation; and, from the early 1980s, the Convention on the Elimination of All Forms of Discrimination against Women. The fund's mission was to provide financial and technical assistance to rural and poor women during the decade (1976–1985).

The fund got a modest start. In 1982, after five years of operation, almost 300 small projects had been supported that emphasized employment, human development, and planning.[64] Voluntary contributions remained at the level of $2–3 million during the following years. In 1985, it was transformed into the United Nations Development Fund for Women. UNIFEM became a separate entity in autonomous association with the

UNDP and followed in the tracks of its predecessor. Two priorities guided its use of resources: serving as a catalyst for ensuring women's involvement in mainstream development activities, preferably at the pre-investment stage; and supporting innovative and experimental projects that were directly beneficial to women in line with national and regional priorities. In 1986, its first year in operation, UNIFEM got a good start, and its income and activities continued to grow.[65]

Two ideas—broad-based cooperation within and outside the UN and sharing insights and experiences—became a trademark of UNIFEM's strategic planning and practice. An ongoing process of strategic planning was initiated in 1989, resulting in a mission statement that set out UNIFEM objectives and philosophy and a strategic plan for realizing these objectives. Taking as its point of departure the outcomes of the UN Decade for Women and inspired by policy signals emerging from the international strategy for the Fourth Development Decade, it set about pioneering new ways of promoting women's participation in national planning and innovative grassroots activities. The longer-term priorities concentrated on two sectors considered to be of strategic importance for women: 1) agriculture and food security; and 2) trade and industry. An third evolving program area was macropolicy and national planning.[66]

UNIFEM also started extensive fund-raising aimed at continued and growing funding with the support of the UNIFEM special constituency that included women in the private sector, women parliamentarians, NGOs, and women's groups. As the Beijing summit approached, UNIFEM took on a major role in facilitating the preparations of the Fourth UN World Conference on Women.

Advocacy was central to UNIFEM activities from the very beginning. The national committees for the fund constituted a network that served an important role in developing education and public awareness programs and in mobilizing resources on the fund's behalf. In January 1992, this function was institutionalized: the advocacy facility became operational, with a focus on preparing, producing, marketing, and distributing papers, training materials, books, newsletters, videos, and other women-in-development resource materials.[67]

In the mid-1990s, several major changes took place in UNIFEM's focus and orientation. Some of these were adaptations to the new international scene after the end of the Cold War, others resulted from the budgetary situation of the fund, partly because of scarcity of resources but also due to its own mismanagement at a time where incomes failed to match committed expenditures. Two evaluations also contributed to this process of change.[68] Nevertheless, the general situation was quite similar to that in which the UNDP found itself at about the same time, resulting in a shift of strategy: the decision to go "upstream" by helping governments undertake policy reform toward sustainable human development through advocacy and supplementary resources rather than by supporting projects toward this end "downstream."

By the end of 1994, UNIFEM had maneuvered itself into a financial crisis. This was only a temporary setback; however, it prevented new operational activities. UNIFEM's Consultative Committee was not afraid of taking new bold initiatives, pointing out that UNIFEM had a critical role to play in the Fourth UN World Conference on Women and in the implementation of the Platform of Action.[69]

In 1996, a strategy shift similar to that undertaken by the UNDP was under way. UNIFEM began to move from its traditional role as a broad-based grant-awarding organization to one that was providing strategic and technical know-how and support as a catalyst and mediator within the UN system. UNIFEM concentrated on economic and political empowerment. Its program on political empowerment focused on women in governance and decision making at all levels, human rights, violence against women, and peace-building and conflict resolution. The program on economic empowerment focused on globalization and economic restructuring, women and enterprise development, and natural resources management. These were not new focal points; the emphasis, however, was stronger than ever.[70]

In a report to the UNDP Executive Board, UNIFEM provided its strategy and a business plan for 1997–1999. The strategic objectives focused on increasing options for women, especially those living in poverty, through strengthening women's economic capacity, promoting the realization of women's human rights, eliminating violence against women, and engendering governance and leadership. UNIFEM would strengthen UN capacity to support women's empowerment and gender mainstreaming in its policies and programs and would strengthen partnerships with key stakeholders. The board endorsed the strategy and business plan, asking UNIFEM to support innovative and experimental activities in implementing the plan within the context of the Beijing Platform for Action. It also asked UNIFEM to further develop and strengthen its role as a catalyst with a view to reinforcing the gender perspective of development programs in recipient countries and increasing synergy with other UN agencies.[71]

The strategy and business plan for 2000–2003 was solidly anchored in its predecessor with regard to its three thematic areas and five basic objectives. The Executive Board endorsed the focus, strategy, and targets and recommended that the administrator include UNIFEM among organizations that could be given responsibility for executing UNDP projects and programs. Member states were urged to increase their contributions to UNIFEM.[72]

In 1998, funding of UNIFEM started to increase again, reaching $50.3 million in 2004, of which $23.2 million was in core resources and $25.5 million in noncore resources. One of its sub-trust funds merits special mention—the Trust Fund in Support of Actions to Eliminate Violence against Women, established in 1996. By 2003 it had awarded $8.4 million in grants to 155 projects in more than seventy countries. The General Assembly continued to highlight and express its satisfaction with the activities of UNIFEM.[73] From 1995 onward, UNIFEM increasingly became part of UNDP's overall objectives and strategies, with a special niche and a special role to play. In 2004, the first year of the 2004–2007 multiyear funding framework, the strategic results framework highlighted four key UNIFEM goals: reducing feminized poverty, ending violence against women, halting and reversing the spread of HIV/AIDS, and achieving gender equality in democratic governance and in postconflict countries.[74]

Bringing in Governments as Executing Agencies

Whenever principles governing UN development assistance have been established, UN intergovernmental bodies have taken great care to ensure the sovereignty of aid-recipient governments. In previous chapters we have seen how they have insisted that assistance be provided only at the request of the government concerned and, increasingly, that it should be integrated into the recipient country's development plans and be in accordance with the policy priorities of its government. A prominent argument for the way the delivery system was organized was that this strategy made it more effective in interacting with the recipient government.

Nevertheless, the UNDP continued to use other organizations, particularly those of the UN system, as executing agencies. In the early years of UN development assistance, the lion's share was channeled through four specialized agencies (the FAO, UNESCO, the WHO, and the ILO) and the UN Secretariat was also an executing agency (92 percent of the total for the period 1950–1965). During the 1970s, an increasing number of new institutions became executing agencies, including the UN regional commissions, the regional development banks, and the World Bank. Nevertheless, although their share decreased, the five largest executing agencies remained large: in 1980, they were executing agencies for 58 percent of UNDP resources and the UNDP was in the process of becoming a major executing agency itself (8 percent).[75] UNDP funds continued to lubricate important parts of the UN system. Recipient governments executed only 1.2 percent of the UNDP's operational development activities in 1980, increasing to 2.7 percent in 1981.

What the predominant UN norm that recipient countries should be the real masters in their own house did not achieve alone, a squeezed budgetary situation helped to put into motion. In the 1982 annual report, the development and international economic cooperation (DIEC) director-general warned of a financial crisis at hand, one that might involve sharp curtailments and even greater cutbacks in UN activities at a time when the need in developing countries was greater than ever before. To reduce costs, rationalize, and simplify procedures and enhance efficiency in program execution, further efforts were needed to promote the integration of UN operational activities with national programs and to strengthen the capacities of developing countries in the interest of self-reliance. The UNDP Governing Council agreed.[76] The General Assembly followed up by inviting UN bodies to make greater use of the capacities of developing countries in local procurement, training, and services.[77]

It was some years before the experimental period with governments as executors of UNDP assistance was implemented and evaluated. In 1988, however, a report by the administrator brought the issue some steps further. The Governing Council asked the administrator to implement the recommendations on programming responsibilities and operational issues and on accounting procedures so that governments could assume full responsibility for the custody, use, and reporting of financial outcomes of government-executed projects. It also asked him to present specific proposals and recommendations for implementing General Assembly resolution 37/226 on the operational activities to develop the UN system.[78]

In the comprehensive 1989 triennial policy review of operational activities for development of the UN system, the General Assembly set out norms and principles in resolution 44/211 that were to govern relations between the UN and recipient governments in this field, including the execution of development assistance. It recognized the need to reorient operational activities "in order to strengthen and utilize fully national capacities in all aspects of the programme and project cycle," emphasizing that "government/national execution and full utilization of national capacities would contribute to ensuring that programmes and projects are managed in an integrated manner and to promoting their longer-term sustainability and wider impact on the development project." It was necessary for the UN system "to further decentralize capacity and authority . . . to the country level in order to increase responsiveness to efficient programming and resource utilization, achieve the objectives of programmes and projects, and strengthen and utilize national capacity." It reaffirmed that recipient governments "have the sole responsibility for the co-ordination of external assistance and the principal responsibility for its design and management and that the exercise of those responsibilities is crucial to the optimal use of external assistance and to the strengthening and utilization of national capacity."[79]

Although these norms and principles were presented as new, they were well attuned to a tradition that went back to the origin of multilateral assistance through the UN system. However, over the years the actual implementation, particularly through the institutional setup, has been somewhat differently interpreted. In its 1989 triennial policy review, the General Assembly emphasized that the UN system at the country level should be structured and composed in such a way that it "corresponds to ongoing and projected co-operation programmes rather than to the institutional structure of the United Nations system." The participation of specialized agencies and technical entities of the UN system in operational activities should be redefined toward providing technical support to governments on a multisectoral and sectoral basis as well as a supportive technical role in the project cycle, "as requested by Governments." The assembly decided that the measures referred to should be accomplished within the UN system "as early as possible" and asked the director-general to submit a proposed three-year schedule for its implementation "by all organs, organizations and bodies" of the UN system and to submit annual reports on its implementation on a consolidated system-wide basis.[80]

The actual transfer of executing responsibility for UNDP funding from international and multilateral agencies and organizations to governments progressed rather slowly during the 1980s.[81] General Assembly resolution 44/211 made a difference, and in 1990, Administrator Draper followed up on the directions given. National execution, as he defined it, meant that governments were responsible for conducting all UN-financed project and program activities, including those implemented by UN specialized agencies and other organizations and institutions on their behalf, and were accountable to the administrator for implementation and financial management. He made a distinction between "execution" and "implementation": whereas responsibility for execution lay with the government, implementation involved using a broad range of national, international, and multilateral institutions to achieve development goals. The administrator proposed that after 1992, all UNDP technical cooperation activities should be nationally executed.[82] The Governing Council concurred.[83]

In 1992, the administrator continued to explore and define key concepts related to program planning and management. He also established guidelines to help governments formulate and implement national capacity-building strategies and outlined the roles of the UNDP, agencies, and governments in national execution and implementation. The Governing Council defined the concepts and terms involved accordingly. It stated that national government authorities responsible for execution and implementation needed national management staff and that the cost of managing nationally executed programs and projects should be borne by the government. UNDP assistance in the building of sustainable capacity for national execution could be financed from country IPF resources or Special Programme Resources. UNDP field office staff might provide administrative assistance to executing agents. The involvement of the Office for Project Services in national-level execution should be limited to providing nontechnical implementation services and enhancing national managerial and administrative capacities.[84]

In a report in May 1993, the administrator stated that projects approved for national execution amounted to 30 percent of all new approvals in 1991 and 37 percent in 1992, a trend he expected to accelerate in future years. Agency implementation of nationally executed projects had also increased significantly over the fourth cycle. Under the fifth cycle (1992–1996), he estimated that 40 percent of all new approvals of IPF-financed activities would be assigned for national execution. Welcoming the increased use of national execution, the Governing Council called on developing countries that received UNDP assistance to assess their national capacities for carrying out execution responsibilities before project approval. It also encouraged greater use of UN specialized agencies in the design, technical appraisal, and backstopping of nationally executed projects.[85]

This systematic approach paid off: in the annual review for 1996, the administrator reported that the continued shift toward national execution accounted for 70 percent of UNDP general fund program expenditure, compared with 60 percent in 1995 and 53 percent in 1994. National execution stayed at about that level.[86] However, national execution dropped to 66 percent in 2003, while direct execution (by the UNDP) increased to 18 percent. It dropped further to 60 percent in 2004, with the share of direct execution by UNDP increasing to 21 percent.[87]

UN intergovernmental bodies drove the process toward increased national execution, which was never considered unproblematic from a managerial point of view, particularly with regard to accountability.[88] However, the explanation for the declining trend in national execution during the first years of the twenty-first century was probably more complex. It was perhaps related to the new vision expressed in UNDP business plans for 2000–2003 aimed at ensuring that the UNDP responded effectively to demands for upstream activities. Those activities were complemented by strong advocacy and direct support to program countries through aid coordination and resource mobilization. Both the UNDP and the specialized agencies had an important role to play in implementing this policy.

Increasing national execution of UNDP development funding was accompanied by a new role for the specialized agencies and other institutions within the UN system and beyond. Their primary function would be to assist governments in capacity-building and in implementing assistance under formal government authority and responsibility toward the UNDP. As the percentages of planned national execution indicate, some UN bodies would also continue as executing agencies. In their "new" role, arrangements were made with the five major agencies (the FAO, the ILO, UNESCO, UNIDO and the UN's Department of Technical Cooperation for Development) to compensate them for their services.

Was the UNDP ahead of the curve on this issue? At the normative and ideological level, yes. The UNDP argued early and consistently that primary responsibility for all development activities belonged with the governments concerned. This perhaps influenced norms and practices of some bilateral as well as other multilateral agencies. But the UNDP did not set an example through its own practice of these norms and values: in this it was extremely slow and behind the curve, even relative to some bilateral aid agencies and some other UN organizations. The concern with building and maintaining the multilateral system—that is, a concern for its own systemic interests—conflicted with the will to implement the norms for which it argued.

Coordinator of System-Wide Technical Development Cooperation?

The UNDP has from day one been assigned an important role in the coordination of international development cooperation, with particular reference to UN technical assistance. This specific part of its mandate has constituted the core of UNDP identity.

Given the heterogeneity of the UN family, this has been a mandate difficult to fulfill. The specialized agencies, institutions, programs, and funds all have their own specific mandates to fulfill and their own governing bodies. This diversity is also reflected in their governing bodies: although their members are all appointed by member governments, they are often nominated by, instructed from, and report to their home government ministries. And then there have been separate administrations that have guarded their own specific mandates as well as their powers and associated interests—often headed by strong-willed individuals with something to prove. Add to this that the UN as a system is not characterized by an abundance of coercive powers; cooperation and coordination can be called for but not enforced.

In its pursuit of the mandate to coordinate the UN system's operational development activities, the UNDP's main strategy has been to include and involve the system's other arms. In the early 1950s, the EPTA designed this strategy, making the specialized agencies with their own development activities into executive agencies of the program. This created an institutional framework for cooperation. The additional funds provided by the EPTA made cooperation attractive because it enabled the agencies to expand their operational activities. The administrative and project support costs involved were refunded by the EPTA and later also by the Special Fund and the UNDP, making possible an extension of the staff of the executing agencies. A main instrument in fulfilling the mandate involved the system of resident representatives at the country and regional levels that the UNDP built. UN intergovernmental bodies, ultimately the General Assembly, gave consistent and firm support to these efforts and called repeatedly for greater coordination, within this framework, of development efforts involving all arms of the system.

Developments in the 1980s and 1990s made a difficult task even more challenging. Development funding, particularly core funding, stagnated or shrank, and the UNDP's position as funding agency for technical assistance was reduced both in total terms and vis-à-vis the specialized agencies, decreasing its ability to make coordination attractive. Donor governments increasingly channeled targeted resources directly through the specialized agencies or other special-purpose programs. The specialized agencies and programs increasingly established their own offices at the regional and country levels as part of acquiring projects and delivering aid.

Moving System-Wide Coordination to the UN Secretariat

The new arrangements for field representation established by the General Assembly in the late 1970s came into operation in 1980. The new system placed overall responsibility for system-wide operative development activities, including coordination, with the Secretary-General, where it had always resided. What was new was the reorganization within the Secretariat: most of its technical assistance activities ("UN as an executing agency") were placed in a Special Unit for Technical Co-operation among Developing Countries. The assembly appointed a director-general for development and international economic cooperation with overall responsibility for system-wide technical cooperation.[89]

This did not eliminate the UNDP's responsibility, as the main funding agency of technical assistance, to coordinate activities and ensure cohesion. As demonstrated in the case where resident coordinators were to take over the responsibilities of UNDP resident directors, with new authorities added (see chapter 7), the UNDP Governing Council, well aware of the challenge, turned the reform into an advantage. This dynamism also characterized its approach to the broader challenge to the organization's long-established coordinating mandate and authority. Its status as the intergovernmental body of the major funding agency for technical cooperation eased the task. Nevertheless, the new director-general came to occupy center court, making his impact felt from the very beginning.

In the new system, the resident coordinators, who were appointed by the Secretary-General, were to represent the whole UN system at the country level.[90] Overall responsibility for and coordination of operational activities at the country level became vested in one single official. The resident coordinators were expected to exercise team leadership involving all UN organizations with activities in the country concerned and were responsible for injecting a multidisciplinary dimension into sectoral development assistance programs at the country and regional levels. In conformity with long-established criteria governing such relations, the policies and priorities of the competent national authorities were to constitute the point of departure. The new arrangements were intended—and were actively used—by the Secretariat and intergovernmental bodies to provide system-wide cooperation and coordination in the field.

In its annual report for 1981–1982, the Administrative Committee on Coordination pointed out the core problem confronting these efforts: the unpredictability and erosion of resources, which made rational forward planning virtually impossible. Serious concern was expressed about the trend toward bilateral solutions rather than multilateral approaches to international economic and social issues.[91] At an early date, the ACC identified central measures to guide country-level coordination. It also underlined that the countries themselves had the sovereign right to determine their own priorities. Aside from the fact that this principle was fundamental to the UN system's role and activities, it was the most appropriate arrangement for coordinating external aid inputs and integrating them with national programs and activities. The ACC emphasized that this principle guided the measures proposed, especially measures related building competence and adjusting country programs to the specific circumstances of each country.[92]

In June 1985, the UNDP Governing Council urged developing countries to ensure the best possible coordination of all external technical assistance, establish national programs that identified priority needs, and strengthen consultative arrangements. It encouraged bilateral aid agencies and multilateral organizations to align their technical cooperation activities with these needs and invited governments to utilize the revised roundtable process to attain maximum coordination. The council urged the World Bank and regional development banks to maintain their close cooperation with the UNDP, especially in country and sectoral analysis and programming and in implementing technical cooperation. The council stated that the UNDP was ready to help developing countries strengthen their coordination capabilities, and invited governments to continue coordinating national action on operational activities for development. It reconfirmed the coordination responsibilities of the resident coordinators and urged UN organizations to cooperate with them.[93]

In his report for the triennial policy review in 1986, the DIÉC director-general moved the issue of coordination from the level of practical coordination of activities at the country level to include policy coordination as well. The focus was directed toward issues such as the fight against poverty, continuity between emergency action and development, adjustment policies, and women and development.[94]

The second triennial policy review of operational activities focused almost exclusively on ways and means of stimulating cooperation within the UN system and beyond, careful, as always, to place the responsibility for coordination at the country and local levels with the governments of the countries concerned.[95] There was also a job to be done at home in this regard. The General Assembly asked the governing bodies of the UN system's organizations "to pay particular attention to the need to rationalize" field representation and to establish new field offices "only if the required services cannot be shared with other organizations or provided in any other way." It emphasized that recipient countries should receive full information from all donors on their assistance, including information on "the cost, nature and objective of each project, concessionality, and tying status." It asked resident coordinators to help recipient governments manage information from all donors on their assistance and ensure "co-ordination and improved effectiveness of such assistance." The assembly emphasized the importance of the UNDP country program "as the framework for promoting a more coherent and co-ordinated approach to technical co-operation activities."[96]

During the years that followed, the issues this policy review referred to remained on the agenda. Year after year, ECOSOC and the General Assembly continued to stress the necessity of system-wide cooperation and coordination, pleading that all organizations engage in greater coordination through the UN country coordinator. The intergovernmental bodies extended increasing formal authority to the UN country coordinator to fulfill this function. The UNDP seldom missed an opportunity to underline the important role its extensive field organization played; thus, the administrator in his annual review of the financial situation in 1986 referred to the 112 UNDP field offices that were serving 152 countries and territories and were offering governments and other development partners numerous services that extended beyond their central responsibilities.[97]

In 1987, the DIEC director-general continued to explore issues related to the coordination of operational activities. The UNDP's Governing Council agreed fully to the suggestions involving greater system coordination at the country level. The main responsibility for defining the role of the resident coordinator rested with host governments; however, the UN system's governing bodies could take important steps toward strengthening the role of the resident coordinators by instructing their secretariats and field staff to interact with the coordinators as envisaged when the arrangement was established. The council again stressed the importance of the UNDP country program as the framework for promoting a more coherent and coordinated approach to technical cooperation activities. More harmonized and simplified procedures for the programming and delivery of technical cooperation should be more actively pursued, the council argued.[98]

In the 1989 triennial policy review, the General Assembly continued to emphasize the issue of greater coordination of UN system-wide operational activities, particularly at the country level, this time going into greater detail about how norms should be translated into structures in a setting where governments were to assume greater responsibility as executing agencies of this assistance.[99] That added a new dimension. In previous policy reviews, government authorities had consistently been identified as the partner in development; this was the case also in the 1989 review of system-wide operational activities.[100] However, the General Assembly also stressed the need for "maximum participation of populations, local communities and organizations, including national non-governmental organizations, in the development process, and encourage[d], when Governments so request, promotion of participation at the grass-roots level and of productive sectors in the operational activities of the United Nations system."[101] Again the UNDP Governing Council concurred.[102] Nevertheless, the harmonization process had a long and difficult road ahead.[103]

Country Strategy Notes as a Major Instrument for Coordination

In its 1992 triennial policy review, the General Assembly emphasized that in the administrative reform of the Secretariat and the "restructuring and revitalization" of the intergovernmental process, the mandates of the separate sectoral and specialized agencies should be respected and enhanced, taking into account their complementarities, a challenge that later system reform efforts have also had to confront. The basis for cooperation and coordination at the country level was further developed into a country strategy note. In order to achieve the objectives set, it would be necessary to strengthen the system of resident coordination. This was stressed again and again in very specific terms, revealing that there still was a long way to go.[104]

BOX 12.1. The Country Strategy Note

During most of the 1980s, successive triennial policy reviews by the General Assembly of operational activities for development within the United Nations system were introduced by an almost ritualistic confession of basic norms, stressing that:

- national plans and priorities constitute the only viable frame of reference for national programming of operational activities for development within the United Nations system;

- the fundamental characteristics of the operational activities of the United Nations system should be, *inter alia*, their universal, voluntary, and grant nature, neutrality and multilateralism, and the ability to respond to the needs of developing countries in a flexible manner, and that the operational activities of the United Nations system are carried out for the benefit of developing countries, at the request of those countries and in accordance with their own policies and priorities;

- the operational activities for development within the United Nations system have a critical role to play in enabling developing countries to take a lead role in the management of their own development process;

- in order to achieve the objectives set out above, the processes and procedures of the United Nations system should be streamlined and rationalized, especially in the interrelated areas of programming, execution, decentralization, monitoring, and evaluation, thus making the system more relevant and responsive to the national plans, priorities, and objectives of developing countries and more efficient in its delivery systems.

In 1992, the main instrument in achieving this objective was identified: "on the basis of the priorities and plans of recipient countries, and in order to ensure the effective integration of assistance provided by the United Nations system into the development process of countries, with enhanced accountability, and to facilitate the assessment and evaluation of impact and sustainability of that assistance, *a country strategy note* should be formulated by interested recipient governments, with the assistance of and in cooperation with the United Nations system, under the leadership of the resident coordinator, in all countries where the Government so chooses, taking into account the following:

a. The country strategy note should outline the contribution the operational activities for development within the United Nations system could make to respond to the requirements identified by recipient countries in their plans, strategies and priorities;

b. The contribution of the United Nations system to the country strategy note should be formulated under the leadership of the resident coordinator, in order to promote greater coordination and cooperation at the field level;

c. The country strategy note should be transmitted to the governing bodies of each funding organization as a reference for the consideration of its specific country programme;

d. The specific activities of each funding organization of the United Nations system, within the broad framework of the country strategy note, should be outlined in a specific country programme prepared by the recipient Government with the assistance of the funding organizations."

Source: "Triennial Policy Review of the Operational Activities of the United Nations Development System," General Assembly resolution 47/199, 22 December 1992 (emphasis added).

In preparing the basis for the General Assembly's 1995 triennial policy review of operational activities, the Secretary-General reported that country strategy notes had been welcomed as a promising basis for a better and more coordinated UN system. The General Assembly decided that, where it was in place, the country strategy note should serve as the common framework for UN country programs and for programming, monitoring, and evaluating UN system activities in these countries. The country strategy note should outline the UN contribution and give an indication of the level of resources needed to meet the requirements identified.[105]

However, the process of implementing the new coordination system continued to be slow. In 1998, in his report ahead of the triennial policy review, Secretary-General Kofi Annan could not reveal much progress—in all, thirty-three countries had completed country strategy notes.[106] The added value of the process had not been clearly established, and its slow introduction and adoption by a relatively small number of developing countries limited its usefulness as a standard framework for programming, he concluded. Great hopes were instead placed in the new complementary concept of the United Nations Development Assistance Framework (UNDAF) that the UN Development Group (UNDG) was preparing, the Secretary-General reported. UN organizations were also moving slowly in applying the system. A review of the decisions of executive boards that the Secretary-General presented to ECOSOC in 1997 showed that several country programs (or similar instruments) had been approved over the previous year, but there was no indication that the programs were reviewed in the context of the country strategy notes, where such were available.[107]

A further development was a request by the Executive Board that the UNDP administrator and the UNFPA executive director, together with the executive director of UNICEF, consider producing a common report on the implementation of the triennial policy review for their respective executive boards. ECOSOC requested UN funds and programs to improve coherence in its country programs by considering the possibility of joint or consecutive meetings of the executive boards on country programs and by improving the link between country programs and the country strategy notes.[108]

The process of harmonization and coordination within the UN was moving forward at a snail's pace. Intergovernmental bodies, including the General Assembly, kept stressing that the "the efficiency, effectiveness and impact of the United Nations system must be enhanced" and its "guidelines and procedures harmonized," finding it necessary to repeat such statements in almost identical terms year after year. Despite the efforts to reform and improve the resident coordinator system, much still remained to be done even there, involving relations with host countries as well.[109] Also in terms of monitoring, evaluation, and accountability, there was room for improvement, particularly involving the methodological problems of measurement and quantification; and, by 1998, no government had reported evaluation on UN operational activities.[110]

UNDP Riding High Again

In his annual report for 1995, Administrator James Speth stated that the UNDP had taken bold and imaginative steps that year to maintain its position as a leader in institutional reform within the UN system.[111] On 23 December that year, Secretary-General Boutros Boutros-Ghali designated him as special coordinator for economic and social development.[112]

In the mid-1990s, and increasingly in 1997, as part of the ongoing reform process within the Secretariat and the UNDP, the latter body gained considerable influence in coordinating system-wide operational activities, a development that a more dynamic and confident self-presentation helped to underscore.[113] In his annual report for 1996, the administrator noted that the UNDP had played a key role in developing a common understanding of the program approach within the UN system. It had continued its efforts to refine the procedures for the program approach in order to facilitate that approach in regions where it was operating. However, he added, actual application of the program approach varied greatly and was not yet widespread among the agencies.[114]

By 1997, the UNDP was in charge of coordinating system-wide operational activities.[115] In the annual report covering that year, Speth confidently noted that the UNDP had actively sought to fulfill its role as an integrating force at the country level by implementing measures to reform the United Nations, strengthen the resident coordinator system, and actively promote strategic follow-up to the major global conferences.[116] In the context of UN reform, the administrator served as the chair of the United Nations Development Group, which was established by the Secretary-General to promote greater coordination and policy coherence of the UN's development work. In the UNDG executive committee (composed of representatives of the UNDP, the UNFPA, and UNICEF, with participation from the WFP), the UNDP was leading the process to prepare a United Nations System-Wide Approach for the Eradication of Poverty. The group sought to make the right to development a central feature of UN development activities in the context of promoting poverty eradication. To stimulate that process, the UNDP had authored the paper "Integrating Human Rights with Sustainable Human Development." Furthermore, at the operational level, UNDAF was a core element in implementing UN reform at the country level. That exercise sought to accelerate the harmonization of UN policies, programs, and procedures in response to the sustainable human development needs of program countries. The members of the UNDG prepared guidelines for creating such development assistance frameworks. In 1997, designs were tried out in eighteen countries.[117]

In 1998, the General Assembly raised the level of ambition regarding development cooperation: the UN system should assist national governments "in creating an enabling environment in which the links between national Governments, the United Nations development system, civil society, national non-governmental organizations and the private sector that are involved in the development process are strengthened, with a view of seeking new and innovative solutions to development problems in accordance with national policies and priorities."[118] Reporting on UNDP involvement in this process, the administrator stated that UNDAF had accelerated the harmonization of UN system programming and responses to country needs.[119]

In May 2000, the Secretary-General reported that a new Common Country Assessment (CCA)/UNDAF system was in the process of being developed: some seventy-four country teams were at various stages of the process, based on the status of their harmonized program cycles.[120] The harmonization of programming cycles continued to present difficulties since not all UN organizations were operating on a country program basis.[121] In his report in preparation of the 2001 triennial policy review, Secretary-General Kofi Annan stated that he saw a great potential in UNDAF as a tool for inducing greater coherence and synergy in the UN's activities at the country level. However, the degree of government involvement had been uneven and the involvement of other national development partners appeared to be limited. To be relevant in development terms, UNDAF should serve not only as framework for UN system country programs but also as a broader instrument to assist program countries in achieving their own development. That required greater involvement of governments and other national partners in all stages of formulation and implementation, a better dialogue with all relevant external partners, good-quality technical work to accompany those processes, adequate monitoring, and the building of national capacities in coordination functions, he noted.[122]

In the 2001 annual report, Mark Malloch Brown stated that the UNDP had continued to build strategic partnerships with the UN system, international financial institutions, civil society organizations, foundations, and the private sector.[123] The UNDG had been restructured to mirror the new UN System Chief Executive Board that was replacing the Administrative Committee on Coordination with a view to strengthening relations between the UNDG and UN system organizations that were not members of the group. The resident coordinator system had been strengthened by increasing the pool of candidates, emphasizing female candidates and candidates from organizations other than the UNDP. By June 2001, 30 of the 115 resident coordinators were women (26 percent) and 22 were drawn from organizations other than the UNDP (19 percent). In late 2001, the UNDG decided that 50 percent of the candidates proposed by all organizations for resident coordinator assessment should be women.[124]

In addition to the UNDP administrator's other responsibilities in leading the system-wide coordination of operational activities, he also became the UN system's MDG coordinator, which placed the UNDP in the center of efforts to realize the UN Millennium Declaration and the MDGs. In 2002, the administrator reported that the UNDP had helped countries prepare their MDG reports and that the number of such reports was increasing. There was clear evidence that the work of the UNDP and its UN partners had made a real impact toward fulfilling the MDGs at the country level, he noted. In many countries, strong commitments had been made to synchronize the MDGs with poverty reduction strategy papers. The Millennium Project was launched in August 2002 to generate fresh thinking and identify options for achieving the MDGs. The UNDG, chaired by the UNDP administrator, worked intensively to shift the focus of operational work to the MDGs, including through integrated guidelines for Common Country Assessments and UNDAF and ongoing discussions with the World Bank on the relationships between the MDGs and poverty reduction strategy papers.[125] The Millennium Trust Fund was established as the principal financing mechanism for the support program (see chapter 13).

Secretary-General Kofi Annan's 2004 report on system-wide operational activities was positive about the progress that had been made in bringing cohesion to the UN system at the country level and in aligning its operations with the development agenda that was emerging from major UN conferences and summits, in particular with the Millennium Development Goals. The system had increasingly served as a catalyst for national dialogue among all stakeholders for implementing the MDGs. Partnerships for action had been built and accountability and monitoring instruments had been devised, including the MDG country reports. The evaluation of diagnostic and programming tools, including CCAs and UNDAF, had showed their potential—especially in terms of increased coherence—and highlighted the importance of a more integrated approach to national poverty reduction strategy frameworks. The UN reform processes had created strong reasons for UN agencies and programs to work together, especially involving the members of the UN Development Group. In many countries the resident coordinator system was now functioning as a vibrant instrument with a common set of goals. Clear guidelines had been issued on joint programming, and joint programs had developed in such areas as HIV/AIDS, the protection of children, and the advancement of women. The widespread adoption of results-based programming and management by organizations was helping to create a new culture of efficiency, effectiveness, and accountability.

Significant progress had also been made in integrating reconstruction, rehabilitation, and long-term development within a single strategic framework for peace-building and development, the report noted.[126]

Yet the Secretary-General was quite candid about the weaknesses of the system. Simplification and harmonization continued to be the Achilles' heel of the system: efforts to harmonize among organizations had yielded limited results, the Secretary-General stated. This had forced the UNDG to formulate a new work program to accelerate those efforts. Implementation of this program would require further institutional changes as well as funding. The system's capacity to make available relevant technical resources at the country and regional levels was constrained by the lack of real incentives to encourage the various entities to make their knowledge and expertise available to the resident coordinator system. Key requirements for progress were a deeper commitment to system-wide collaboration and the effective participation of all UN organizations, including entities with no country office. In addition, stable and predictable funding commensurate with the program priorities identified in the United Nations Development Assistance Framework was needed, noted the Secretary-General, pointing out a key constraint: efforts to improve internal coherence, simplification, and efficiency would not succeed unless member states could reform their funding practices to reduce fragmentation, inconsistency, and unnecessary competition for scarce resources. As long as funding arrangements for UN development activities remained inadequate, unstable, and unpredictable, the UN development system would not be able to fully play its role in advancing comprehensive, durable development.[127]

Since the mid-1990s, UN intergovernmental bodies, including ECOSOC and the General Assembly, have repeatedly noted that the extensive reforms within the UN development system aimed at making it more effective and relevant toward new development challenges seemed to have no payoff in terms of increased resources. In the 2004 triennial review, the General Assembly expressed "concern" that the UN development system had not benefited commensurately from recent increases in ODA despite the additional tasks entrusted to the system "in the implementation of and the follow-up to internationally agreed goals."[128]

A Common Home for the UN Family at the Country Level

Placing the many UN agencies with operational activities in developing countries under the same roof in the countries concerned was increasingly seen as a design to promote coordination and harmonization of development activities. In June 1987, the UNDP Governing Council raised the idea, urging other governing bodies to review their field representation and to consider with the UNDP the feasibility of co-location and/or common services in consultation with host governments.[129]

The General Assembly supported the idea, although indirectly.[130] In its 1989 triennial policy review, however, the response was loud and clear: at the country level, the UN system "should be structured and composed in such a way that it corresponds to ongoing and projected co-operation programmes rather than the institutional structure of the United Nations system." Among several measures to this end it decided to "request all organs, organizations and bodies of the United Nations system to make, without delay, the necessary arrangements, in co-operation with host Governments and without additional cost to developing countries, to establish common premises at the country level, and to request the Director-General to include in his annual reports on operational activities information on progress made in that area."[131] These reports, to which we return, do not stand as testimonies to the effectiveness or efficiency of the UN system in coordination and cooperation.

In 1991, the DIEC director-general described the field representation among organizations for the period 1983–1990. Available data did not permit an assessment of the cost effectiveness of existing field representation in relation to program volumes. However, the report revealed that the lack of cooperation between UN agencies was extensive. Although the governing bodies of the various organizations approved the opening of new offices and determined their functions, there were no consultations between agencies during this process, except in cases when it was a question of integrating an agency in the field mission of another. Overall, the field networks of the organizations had grown modestly but steadily since 1983. The number of UNDP offices had not changed during this period. The UNHCR was the most flexible of the agencies, adapting its field structure to crises of a natural or political character as they arose. The UNFPA had expanded because of the increased complexity of its programs. The number of UN information centers had increased by four. In 1983, a resident coordinator was heading twenty-one of these offices; by 1990, four more offices had been organized in that way. Four specialized agencies had increased their presence in developing countries—the ILO, the FAO, UNESCO, and UNIDO.[132]

The need for the UN to respond to former Soviet-bloc countries opened a new opportunity. In 1992, the Secretary-General set up seven new offices in this region on an interim basis (in Armenia, Azerbaijan, Belarus, Georgia, Kazakhstan, Ukraine, and Uzbekistan). In a statement before the Second Committee, the under-secretary-general for policy coordination and sustainable development argued that this represented an advance toward a unified cost-effective UN presence in the field. The UN representative that headed each office would function as a team leader and as the UNDP resident coordinator. The offices would not perform political functions, become a politicized new model of UN offices in the field, or be used for human rights monitoring without a mandate. They were to respond to the development needs of the countries concerned, including the coordination of humanitarian assistance, he assured the committee. UN public information activities were also part of the work of these offices.[133] The tricky issue related to the role of the UN field organization, namely the political role of the resident coordinator, continued to be explored.[134]

In October 1997, the Joint Inspection Unit reported to the General Assembly on strengthening the UN system's field representation. It concluded that despite efforts to strengthen coordination in the field, the desired results had not been achieved. In many cases, the offices of different UN organizations had continued to proliferate. Between 1985 and 1995, the number of country and regional offices had risen from 704 to 1,125, an increase of about 60 percent, and the number of field staff had increased from 11,677 to 18,728, an increase of 63 percent. During the ten-year period, costs had risen by close to 200 percent. The Joint Inspection Unit recommended that organizations refrain from establishing new offices. They should make use of existing common offices, especially through the resident coordinator, and harmonize as much as possible their offices at the regional or subregional levels. The UN resident representative should be the single UN official representing the whole UN family. Other agency representatives, who would continue to promote activities related to the mandate of their respective organizations, would be part of a team under the leadership of the resident coordinator.[135]

In 1999, the assistant administrator reported a major breakthrough on this issue: the Secretary-General had formally designated United Nations Houses in thirty-one countries, and relocation to new premises was scheduled in several other countries in the near future. In countries where UN

Houses were not an immediate prospect, separate offices were connected through a country-based intranet that facilitated the sharing of information, practices, and expertise. A survey of common services at the country level was under way and would provide a basis for a strategy for greater efficiency in the management of administrative and financial resources.[136] In May 2003, the Secretary-General reported that a total of fifty-two United Nations Houses had been established and that five more would be opened by the end of the year.[137] A basic reform was about to be realized, even though some steps still remained.

Improving Relations with the Bretton Woods Institutions

The development systems of the United Nations and the Bretton Woods institutions had always represented different worlds in the way they were structured and "owned." Accordingly, their worldviews and missions also differed. In the late 1980s, UNICEF's critique of structural adjustment policies had the most significant impact, both outside and within the Bretton Woods institutions.[138] Traditionally, the two systems represented opposed value systems—one focused on macroeconomic development (economic growth) and the other focused on social and human development. In reality, institutions within both systems found themselves somewhere between these poles.

As the Cold War ended, new countries joined the Bretton Woods institutions. This facilitated a new beginning in the relationship between the two core systems. In addition, the Bretton Woods institutions revised their policies in response to the massive critique that gradually emerged that focused on the social and human costs of structural adjustment. Over time, the relative weight of the two systems also changed. Although the UN system continued to offer more technical assistance than the World Bank in the 1980s, the World Bank offered much more assistance than the UNDP did in that decade.[139] This trend continued into the 1990s.

During the latter 1980s, the development and international economic cooperation director-general on several occasions argued that the possibilities for closer cooperation between the World Bank and regional banks and the UN agencies should be further explored. The UNDP Governing Council agreed, pointing out, however, that the two systems had different mandates.[140]

In 1995, ECOSOC decided that the high-level meeting on the operational activities segment in 1996 should focus on strengthening the collaboration between the UN development system and the Bretton Woods institutions "in the areas of social and economic development, at all levels, including the field level."[141] This gave added impetus to the process.[142]

In June 1996, Secretary-General Boutros-Ghali submitted a note to ECOSOC summarizing the current status of collaboration between UN funds and programs and the Bretton Woods institutions. The report found that the greatest need and potential for strengthening collaboration existed at the country level.[143] The ad hoc and selective approach would have to be transformed into a more structured provision of support, at the request of governments. Such cooperation needed to be sustained and should include all stages from policy formulation to project monitoring and evaluation.[144] ECOSOC concurred fully.[145] In its 1998 triennial policy review, the General Assembly strongly encouraged greater cooperation between the World Bank, regional development banks, and all UN funds and programs, "with a view to increased complementarity and better division of labour as well as enhanced coherence in their sectoral activities, building on the existing arrangements and fully in accordance with the priorities of the recipient Government."[146]

The Bretton Woods institutions responded. An IMF report argued that collaboration between the International Monetary Fund and the UN system had intensified in recent years as the IMF had increasingly integrated social concerns into the structural adjustment programs it supported and had begun to take into account the recommendations of UN global conferences on the environment, population, social development, and women.[147] In a joint report in 1998, both the UN and the Bretton Woods institutions committed themselves to closer cooperation and explored mechanisms to facilitate this. The common ground that was identified included an exchange of ideas on the linkage between human rights and development based on the joint understanding that respect for human rights was critical for economic and social development. Collaboration in promoting the 20/20 initiative and research activities that made a practical contribution to global policy formulation, specific country programs, and global knowledge networks were among other areas identified for cooperation.[148] The Bretton Woods institutions were moving in the direction of the goals and priorities set by UN global conferences, while the UN was increasingly recognizing the influence of macroeconomic factors on development opportunities.

The Millennium Declaration triggered a new awareness of the need for the main development actors to pull together to realize these goals. This was reflected in Secretary-General Kofi Annan's report that prepared the ground for the 2001 General Assembly triennial policy review.[149] The assembly repeated what it had stated three years earlier, emphasizing the importance of ensuring "greater consistency between the strategic frameworks developed by the United Nations funds, programmes and agencies and the Bretton Woods institutions, and the national poverty reduction strategies, including the poverty reduction strategy papers, where they exist."[150] In his 2003 report to ECOSOC, Secretary-General Annan took a further step: the Bretton Woods institutions, especially the World Bank, were now recasting their priorities to focus on poverty and the MDGs, he noted.[151] In the 2004 triennial policy review, the General Assembly repeated its earlier blessings and invited the UN system and the Bretton Woods institutions to explore further ways "to enhance cooperation, collaboration and coordination."[152]

At the level of declared policy, firm commitments to a closer relationship between the two major—and competing—development systems had been made.

Some Concluding Observations

No Peace Dividend

During the heyday of the Cold War, security policy and development had become interlinked, both in policy rhetoric and in international development strategies. It was believed that a development toward arms control, détente, and peace would free resources previously tied up in the arms race, redirecting them to economic and social development—not least in those areas of the world where the resources were most needed, thus turning swords into ploughshares. But nothing of the kind happened: quite the contrary. During the post–Cold War era, the high hopes of a new beginning were dashed. Instead, the UN development system, especially the UNDP, continued to be financially starved. More generally, ODA became an even more scarce resource, as evident from the overview provided in the appendix to this volume.

The two main antagonists in the Cold War contributed most to proving the peace dividend thesis wrong. The end of the Cold War turned the Soviet Union and its East European allies into nonproviders of ODA for more than a decade, and many of the new states that emerged from the Soviet empire became new recipients of ODA and official assistance. Meanwhile, the United States lost its security rationale for providing ODA. As a result, its ODA began dwindling from an already low level as a share of GNI.

The performance of other major donor countries varied during the first decade of the post–Cold War era. For some major donor countries, including the so-called frontrunners, it was more or less business as usual: a few of them increased their ODA, but other governments reduced theirs.[153]

The beginning of the new century was a fresh start, however modest. In the early years, total ODA—and the ODA of the remaining superpower—started to grow. The UN facilitated this change: the Millennium Declaration, the MDGs, and the process initiated in advocating the followup of these commitments, including in Johannesburg and Monterrey, certainly contributed to turning the tide. Nevertheless, the new growth may perhaps be even better explained by the reentry of security as a major concern of the United States. Development assistance became an instrument in the "war against terrorism" and other wars in which the Bush administration involved the United States and others, with or without the UN Security Council's blessing.

The many violent conflicts around the world in the early 1990s had prepared the ground, calling for assistance from the international community and its individual members. These so-called complex emergencies did something both to the notion of security and the role of development assistance. They affected thinking about aid and the composition of the ODA package: attention shifted from the traditional focus on economic and social development toward humanitarian aid targeted to war-torn and conflict-prone areas and assistance to help countries to recover from conflicts. Preventing conflict and promoting peace became important elements in creating an enabling environment for development.

After 9/11, the security aspect of aid has become most evident in the share of ODA channeled to Afghanistan and Iraq. The flow of ODA was only a tiny share of the total resources "invested" in these conflict areas, especially by the United States and its closest allies. These "investments" were triggered and justified by security concerns.

These developments affected the United Nations. The human misery created by the violent conflicts of the 1990s turned the WFP—as we shall see in the following chapter—into a humanitarian relief organization. At a time of scarce resources for development, voluntary contributions from donor countries became available for relief, bringing the expenditures of the WFP for operational activities beyond those of the UNDP. The same applied to UNICEF during these years: voluntary contributions to its operational activities were increasing. The UNDP followed the same track, partly in response to humanitarian concerns but with an eye as well to what kind of aid donors were willing to finance. In the latter 1990s, the UNDP increasingly recognized the "new" area of conflict prevention and peace promotion and upgraded and strengthened its organizational capacity in this area. These issues featured prominently in the UNDP's strategy for sustainable human development. Afghanistan and Iraq became targets for increased humanitarian aid.

Prioritizing Poverty Alleviation: Rhetoric and Practice

In the early days of UN development cooperation, the poverty orientation of development assistance became a question of distributing resources for development to poor countries, as measured by their GNP per capita. For a global organization composed of individual states, an approach where resources were distributed to states according to their needs may seem both natural and logical, particularly under a predominant development paradigm that saw the state as the development engine and capital as the scarce resource needed for development.

Resources to facilitate economic growth—for the UN system, mainly technical assistance on a grant basis—were from the very beginning directed to poor countries, in contrast to the capital assistance provided by the World Bank. When the IDA window was established to soften the borrowing conditions of the Bank for poor countries, a grant element also became part of the development financing that it provided. The regional development banks also established "soft windows" financed by ODA. Moreover, the World Bank expanded into technical assistance; in the mid-1980s, it even surpassed the UNDP within its own arena.

The early and mid-1970s were bristling with ideas of how development might be best brought about—ideas that focused on economic relations between rich and poor countries, directing attention toward structural constraints to development, and social and economic policy reforms within countries, such as the basic needs approach. These ideas found their way into the UN discourse on development and became manifest in its international development strategies, especially for the strategies for

DD2 and after. They may also have affected the distribution of resources across sectors—although, since the introduction of the new planning system in the early 1970s, this was true to a lesser extent for the UNDP than for sector-oriented organizations and programs. For the UNDP, the main—indeed, almost the only—mechanism for pursuing redistribution and attacking global poverty was resource distribution to countries and regions, favoring the poor and poorest. According to the norms that governed UN development cooperation, how internal resources were distributed was up to the recipient governments.

The UNDP's policy of giving priority to poor countries when it distributed its resources was further strengthened in the program for the third development cycle (1982–1986). It decided to allocate nearly 80 percent of all country indicative planning figures to countries with annual per capita income of $500 or less, with special treatment accorded to countries whose GNP per capita was below $250. As we have seen, this policy was continued during the following development cycles, with an ever-increasing share being earmarked for the poor and poorest countries and other groups of vulnerable countries (landlocked, island) or countries whose economies were severely affected by the crisis in the world economy, according to a detailed system for the distribution of IPFs. It should, however, be noted that this distribution applied to the core funding: it did not necessarily apply to noncore funding, which became increasingly important in the 1990s, with shrinking voluntary contributions.

For a global organization whose members are states, this kind of resource allocation has never been unproblematic. From the beginning, there was a tension between those who preferred distribution based on the poverty criterion and those who preferred distribution based on universality. This tension was seldom brought sharply into the open, however. Developing countries that were relatively well off compared with the LDCs also expected a share of the resources and watched to see how the proposed designs would affect their interests. The designs that emerged from the negotiating processes were careful to ensure that developing countries that were moving up the GNI ladder were not seriously affected by reductions in their IPFs. Increased stipulated incomes from one cycle to the next eased this process. Only at a late stage was it decided to phase out the assistance to the better-off developing countries.

The poverty criterion, as measured in GNP/GNI and population size, was therefore the main (almost the only) yardstick for distributing UN development assistance. The regional emphasis on Africa followed the same general logic. One implication of this distribution system should be made explicit: in principle, allocations were unrelated to the policies pursued by the recipient governments. No conditionality like the structural adjustment policies of the Bretton Woods institutions and major bilateral donors was applied. The norms that governed the policy also made little room for other political criteria to direct the resource flow. This applies, inter alia, to the kind of criteria some "progressive" European donor countries used in the 1970s, when they directed their ODA to countries whose governments pursued an active domestic welfare policy that included economic and social redistribution and did not violate human rights. Assessments of the political regime of recipients—whether a government was creating an environment conducive to economic and social development or was rent-seeking—had, in principle, almost no place in decisions related to the distribution of UNDP core funding.

A dramatic change of philosophy and strategy involving these norms took place in the early 1990s, triggered by work on the human development index and the Human Development Reports. The UNDP acquired a "new" identity as a champion and facilitator of sustainable human development. In this strategy, which evolved during the 1990s, fighting poverty became the core theme, and the mechanisms involved went far beyond the distribution of available resources according to GNI. The UNDP actively advocated this "new" gospel. Its main strategy was to provide assistance to governments that expressed a keen interest in pursuing sustainable human development through policy advice and supporting assistance—going "upstream." All along, the UNDP took care to point out that no conditionality was involved. Nevertheless, the similarity to the supplementary "positive measures" approach of second-generation aid conditionality appears striking.

Although the expressed will to give priority to the poorest countries has been strong, the ability to follow up has been more limited. The funding sought for providing extra support for the LDCs and other particularly vulnerable or exposed groups of countries was not always forthcoming, in stark contrast to policy declarations in key UN documents, such as the international strategies for successive development decades. A series of trust funds established for such purposes—involving the SMF/LDC, landlocked states, island states—serve as telling illustrations of such shortcomings: UN member governments provided virtually no core funding.

The Principle of Sovereignty and the Sustainable Human Development Policy and Advocacy of the 1990s

There are few relations between states where power is more asymmetrically distributed than in aid relations. Principles that govern relations, agreed to by the parties involved, will therefore be important, in international relations more generally as well as in aid relations. Although principles cannot be equated with practice, they establish norms that may influence practice and benchmarks against which implemented policies can be assessed and judged.

The most important principle established when the UN began providing international development assistance was the principle of the sovereignty of the recipient government: technical assistance should be provided only at the request of the recipient government and be in line with its priorities. This principle was rooted in the UN Charter. It was further developed as it applied to development assistance during the years that followed. UN assistance was to be integrated into the development plans of the recipient countries. From the very beginning, this principle has been guarded by a majority within the UN that included developing countries whose sovereignty was relatively newly won. The evolving terminology —from development assistance to development cooperation—is another expression of this principle. Both the principle and the terminology that emerged through processes in the UN system had consequences far beyond UN technical assistance; they established norms that influenced other international organizations and bilateral aid providers. This does not imply that these norms were established or followed up to the same extent by all donor agencies.

The evolving planning and programming systems designed by the UNDP have been based on this principle. Nevertheless, a principle operates within a context and may be conceived and interpreted differently over time. The difficulties involved in implementing norms are perhaps best illustrated by the long process involved in transferring real authority for implementing assistance from UN organizations to recipient governments. Indeed, four decades passed before this was seriously attended to.

A dilemma for all development cooperation is that there are at least two parties involved: the provider of assistance, whether a bilateral or multilateral agency, on the one hand, and the recipient, whether a government or a regional or global agency on the other. Both have their own expectations as to what should be the outcome of the assistance and a constituency to report to. The sovereignty principle is intended to strengthen the hand of the recipient government in negotiations. However, both the donor and the recipient need to agree not only on objectives but also on all the details. In such negotiations, a major donor—including multilateral agencies—will normally hold the upper hand, particularly vis-à-vis an aid-dependent government. A principle such as sovereignty of the recipient government may reduce this power imbalance but cannot totally remove it, even where the UN is party to the negotiations.

It may seem paradoxical, but just at the time when the UNDP was in the process of transferring executing responsibility for its development assistance from UN agencies to the governments concerned, it was also in the process of designing and pursuing its own development objectives (sustainable human development). It began providing upstream policy advice and support for governments willing to move in the direction that the UNDP strongly advocated. As a consequence, the process of transferring authority to recipient governments was halted, even reversed.

The UNDP's advocacy of particular development policies was new. However, it was not new that the UN recommended specific objectives and policies to be pursued. This had been shown in the international development strategies for successive development decades, many of which might well be subsumed under the common umbrella of human development.

The dilemma involved was made explicit when the UNDP found itself at another crossroads as it followed up on the Jackson capacity study and ironed out the 1970 consensus. In that process, the sovereignty principle was emphasized more strongly than ever, orchestrated primarily by representatives of Third World governments, India in particular. But, as one of its architects argued with the clarity of hindsight, it was never the intention that decisions about a project or program should belong to the recipient government alone. Activities should be genuinely anchored in the development policies of the recipient government, but the UNDP should show a distinct profile and be identified with certain policies and convictions. Two parties were involved, and neither should be overruled.[154] The "new" strategy that emerged in the early 1990s can therefore be interpreted as a fulfillment, more than twenty years later, of the policy aspirations of the 1970 capacity study.

This *problématique,* in a nutshell, is a core dilemma and major challenge for all development cooperation, whether it takes place within a bilateral or multilateral setting. In bilateral relations, especially those involving major powers, donor countries have traditionally held the upper hand, using aid as an instrument in their foreign policy and intervening in the domestic and foreign policies of recipients. This explains why developing countries—in tandem with architects within the UN system, inspired by what they considered to be the UN mission—anchored development assistance in the UN Charter and have keenly guarded the sovereignty principle ever since. Over time, it has been adapted and extended to new political and administrative contextual conditions.

The multilateral setting made it possible to establish clear norms within this policy field. These norms had a multiplier effect, particularly on the policy of the new bilateral donors that, in the 1960s and 1970s, were entering this policy arena. For the UN, the principle of state sovereignty becomes especially challenging when it involves issues that the UN is mandated to pursue, but where these issues are given low priority or are not seen as important at all by the governments concerned. Fighting poverty, giving priority to the most poverty-stricken social groups, including minorities, promoting human rights, and gender equality are only a few issues that illustrate the point.

These issues are prominent in the UN's sustainable human development policy. In the early 1990s, when the UNDP decided to make this policy its focal point, efforts were made to distance itself from the conditionality policies of the 1980s (and beyond). Although the UNDP argued that no conditionality was involved with its push for sustainable human development, it provided support for governments willing to pursue that path. In the literature on political conditionality involving aid, providing development assistance for policies that move development in a preferred direction is termed "positive measures"—so-called positive conditionality.[155] However, as a global organization, the UN is better placed to pursue this kind of policy than the Bretton Woods institutions, whose membership is limited, for the most part, to donor countries.

THIRTEEN

Food Aid: From Development to Humanitarian Relief

- ■ **Institutional Conflict Resolution: Behind the Curve**
- ■ **Trends since the Mid-1990s:**
  A Program for Relief, Refugees, and Development
- ■ **From Food Security to Human Security?**

The main focus of the World Food Programme was on transforming food in kind into economic and social development through projects geared toward agricultural and rural development and human resource development. However, in the 1970s, a process of change was driven by humanitarian catastrophes—first the drought catastrophe in the Sahelian belt of Africa in the early 1970s and, toward the end of the decade, the massive refugee problems caused by war and violence, especially in Afghanistan and Cambodia. By the mid-1970s, new international food aid arrangements were in place to meet emergency situations. This food aid was to be channeled through the WFP system, facilitating a process of change. The WFP aspired to become the coordinator of food aid in international emergencies.

Confronted with major humanitarian crises, it was impossible for governments—and aid agencies—to sit back and do nothing. In directing ODA (including food aid) to relief operations, governments found the WFP a convenient channel. In the early 1980s, the new drought catastrophe that hit the Sahel gave a further push to the process of change within the WFP. It could not shy away from the expectations that had been raised. The combination of new expectations and new funding from aid agencies helped loosen the "chains" of the 1960s, which had limited its activities more or less to small development projects. The efforts of the United States to involve other donor countries in burden-sharing had similar effects: actors with different interests related to food aid now became more active players.

The ideological shift in major western powers in the early 1980s affected North/South relations as well. In that decade, the United States and other major western powers used the power of the purse to regain control of the UN system. UN institutions dependent on voluntary contributions were especially vulnerable, particularly the system's operational agencies. In such a situation, leadership become crucially important. James Ingram, incoming executive director of the WFP in 1982, saw an active role for the WFP in relief assistance as a strategy to sustain its future.[1] He found that the organization needed to be better prepared for such tasks.[2] However, as noted in chapter 8, one of the parent organizations—the FAO—was a major stumbling block.[3]

This chapter will focus on major changes in the patterns described in chapter 8. Perhaps the most important change relates to the relative importance of global food aid. Food aid as share of total ODA declined particularly sharply between 1985 and 1995, as table 13.1 illustrates. In 1995, the share of food aid was only 4 percent of total ODA, down from 25 percent in 1965, when the WFP was more permanently established. This share continued to decline.[4] But by 1995, about 40 percent of all food aid was channeled through the WFP.

Institutional Conflict Resolution: Behind the Curve

Chapter 8 ended with the WFP hampered by a power struggle between its executive director and the director-general of the FAO. That conflict continued into the 1990s, sapping energy. It took the intergovernmental bodies more than fifteen years to put the house in order: in the end, the solution was to provide the WFP with a new constitution.

According to the new constitution, the WFP continued as a joint UN/FAO undertaking, but the Committee on Food Aid Policies and Programmes was given full powers to oversee the program and the WFP now had a legal status of its own. Membership in the Committee on Food Aid Policies and Programmes was increased from thirty to forty-two; twenty-seven were from developing countries and fifteen from economically more developed countries. WFP headquarters remained in Rome but not on FAO premises. Most important, the executive director was given full responsibility for administering the special trust fund and operations, including the approval of emergency assistance up to the level delegated to him by the CFA. The executive director also gained control over staff appointments. In 1991, the new general regulations were approved by ECOSOC and the FAO council and formalized by the UN

TABLE 13.1.

Global Flow of ODA and Food Aid to Developing Countries, Selected
Years, 1965–1995 (in billions of U.S. dollars and by percent)

	1965	1975	1985	1995
Total ODA (billions of U.S. dollars)	5.9	13.6	29.4	58.9
Total food aid (billions of U.S. dollars)	1.5	2.2	3.1	2.3
Food aid as a percent of ODA	25	16	11	4

Source: Edward Clay and Olav Stokke, "The Changing Role of Food Aid and Finance
for Food," in *Food Aid and Human Security,* ed. Clay and Stokke (London: Frank Cass,
2000), 28.

General Assembly and the FAO Conference.[5] They entered into force on
1 January 1992.

Power struggles between strong personalities who lead organizations
that are obliged to cooperate is of course not at all unusual.[6] Why focus on
such a trivial and "normal" conflict? It illustrates how vulnerable the UN
system can be—and dependent on the right leadership. From a systemic
perspective, it highlights the weaknesses of the political system. Although
the situation that developed from 1976 onward was well known, the intergovernmental bodies within the WFP's two "parent" organizations, the
UN and the FAO, seemed either unable or unwilling to put in order a
house in flagrant disorder. This shows how difficult it may be to reform
the UN system, which is still a top priority after the High-level Panel on
UN System-wide Coherence in the areas of development, humanitarian assistance, and the environment delivered its recommendations in
November 2006. On the other hand, it also illustrates that solutions can
be found—at long last!

How could the intergovernmental bodies allow the conflict to go on
for years? After all, the same "owners" are represented on the governing boards of the organizations. This also applies for intergovernmental
boards involved in vertical cooperation, like that between the FAO and the
WFP. Part of the explanation may be found in the compartmentalization
of politics at the national level. Government representatives in the various
intergovernmental bodies of the multilateral system may be appointed by
different ministries in the country concerned, depending on the sector.

Lack of coordination, resulting in policy incoherence, is a problem also at the national level. Thus, while representatives to UN intergovernmental institutions are traditionally nominated by and report to (and are based in) ministries or departments of foreign affairs, representatives to the FAO are traditionally nominated by and report to (and are even based in) ministries or departments of agriculture (and national FAO committees).

Toward a New Balance between Development and Humanitarian Relief

From 1975 on, both the number of WFP projects and the value of the commitments increased steeply. Between 1975 and 1980, $3.4 billion was committed to 679 development projects and relief operations. In the1980s, the number of projects and relief operations to which commitments were made stayed at this level. However, the amount granted increased, reaching $8.2 billion in the period 1981 to 1990. Between 1962 and 1990, $13.3 billion was committed to 2,688 WFP development projects and relief operations.

In the early 1990s the balance between the WFP's development activities and its humanitarian relief activities turned upside-down. This dramatic development is depicted in table 13.2. The trend is unmistakable.

A change in the original orientation of the program along the development-relief axis had been under way for some time, triggered by external events and new players with interests and priorities of their own related to funding. The outbreaks of wars and conflicts in the early 1990s created humanitarian catastrophes in many corners of the world that required relief assistance; this accelerated and strengthened the reorientation process.

Meeting the immediate needs resulting from the major disasters in the Sahel in the 1970s and 1980s demanded large amounts of food aid. The scope was a challenge to organizational skills, confronting the international relief system with pressing issues: how to bring, in time, the right kind of assistance to those hardest hit; how to move from crisis management to "normalcy," involving rehabilitation and development for those involved; and how to engineer an end to providing emergency aid. In the wider perspective, the issue was how to prevent new natural disasters from developing and, if such disasters did appear, how to be prepared to respond in time. The magnitude and complexity of these crises directed the focus toward relief management and the WFP's role in cooperation

TABLE 13.2.

World Food Programme Spending by Category, Selected Years, 1985–2003 (by percent)

	1985	1990	1995	2000	2003
Development	73.6	53.8	31.1	16.0	7.0
Relief	26.4	28.2	56.0	79.5	85.8
Special operations	0.0	0.0	0.0	2.2	2.5
Trust funds	NA[1]	17.9	12.9	1.7	2.5
Other[2]	NA	0.0	----[3]	0.6	2.2
TOTAL	100.0	99.9[4]	100.0	99.4	100.0
Millions of U.S. dollars	872.0	926.0	1,096.7	1,158.3	3,275.3

Sources: Calculations based on data in Shaw, *The UN World Food Programme and the Development of Food Aid,* tables 5.2 and 6.1 (for 1985); OECD, *The Development Effectiveness of Food Aid* (Paris: OECD, 2006), Table 1.4 (for 1990, 1995, 2000, and 2003). The data on which calculations are made for 1985 and for the remaning years may not necessarily be based on the same sources. The data for the latter are based on OECD statistics.

1. Not available.
2. Operational expenses such as general funds, insurance, and (from 2001) trust funds that cannot be apportioned by project/operation.
3. Less than 0.1 percent.
4. Percentages do not always add up to 100 due to rounding of figures in the original sources.

with the governments most directly affected and other multilateral and international organizations mandated to assist in emergencies (and other major operators, such as bilateral agencies and NGOs). The focus was on lessons to be learned, particularly with regard to the overall lack of preparedness and poor coordination. The WFP, which aspired to a role as overall coordinator of food aid, had much to learn. In the crisis of the early 1980s, it managed, to some extent, to play the role of coordinator by purchasing, transporting, and monitoring food aid for bilateral donors. One outcome of the first of these drought catastrophes was the Global Information and Early Warning System for Food and Agriculture, created by the FAO.

Humanitarian catastrophes were also caused by war and violence. In the late 1970s and early 1980s, vast numbers of refugees from Afghanistan and Cambodia were seeking safety in neighboring countries. Although cast in a humanitarian relief perspective, relief interventions in violent conflicts—more so than responses to natural disasters—have political implications; in the late 1970s and beyond, there were strong political overtones to the assistance the WFP and others provided to these refugees. In the Cold War setting, the major western powers saw refugees in Pakistan as a key instrument for ending the Soviet occupation of Afghanistan and removing the regime that had invited it. In a situation where humanitarian concerns and the security interest of one of the two superpowers coincided, there was a good possibility to obtain additional resources for those who could see and take the opportunity—and be trusted.[7]

In the early post–Cold War era, the number of intrastate conflicts compared to the number of interstate wars increased, at times involving regions. Some conflicts that had been contained under the previous system erupted, involving both social frictions and competition for power. Conflicts rooted in a nationalism that for generations had been suppressed also flared up. The civil wars in the former Yugoslavia, the Horn of Africa, southern Sudan, the Great Lakes region in Central Africa, and the Congo, among others, are illustrative of the post–Cold War security environment. These conflicts became a major threat to development, creating immense human suffering. They generated millions of refugees and internally displaced persons and were marked by systematic violence against noncombatants. They presented even greater and more complex challenges with regard to crisis management than those posed by the hunger catastrophes of the 1970s and 1980s.

The shift of resource allocations in response to the surge of intrastate conflicts is illustrated in table 13.3. If commitments to projects for refugees and displaced persons had been included, the trend would have been even more striking. This development was not entirely new, as assistance for human-made disasters had been going on for several years. The amounts provided for such assistance, however, had increased considerably in the early 1990s.

During the early 1990s, commitments of donor governments for economic and social development through the WFP decreased, especially as a share of total commitments but also as measured in dollars. WFP commitments decreased from $642 million in 1985 to $480 million in 1990; the decrease was especially steep after 1993. Traditionally, agriculture and rural development had received the largest share of WFP development assistance (78 percent in 1985, most of which was for agricultural

TABLE 13.3.

World Food Programme Commitments for Emergency Operations by Type, Selected Years, 1985–1995 (by percent and in millions of U.S. dollars)

	1985	1990	1991	1992	1993	1994	1995
Man-made disasters	65	74	62	41	95	79	86
Drought/crop failures	31	23	36	58	4	21	12
Sudden natural disasters	4	3	2	1	1	----[1]	2
Percent	100	100	100	100	100	100	100
Millions of U.S. dollars[2]	230.4	131.6	390.8	896.8	737.5	857.9	665.2

Source: D. John Shaw, *The UN World Food Programme and the Development of Food Aid* (New York: Palgrave, 2001), table 6.1, and calculations based on that source.

1. Less than 1 percent.

2. Excludes commitments for operations for protracted refugees and displaced persons from 1990 onward.

production). In the first part of the 1990s, agriculture continued to be a priority; its share of WFP assistance increased from 29 percent in 1990 to 48 percent in 1995. Human resource development, especially support for mother and child health centers and primary schools, constituted most of the rest, varying from 56 percent of total commitments in 1990 to 36 percent in 1995.[8]

Trends since the Mid-1990s: A Program for Relief, Refugees, and Development

Let us recapitulate some characteristics of food aid that came more strongly to the fore in the 1990s. Food in kind for development is an unreliable resource that depends on harvests and surpluses, both of which tend to vary. In turn, such variations influence prices—in years with no or small surpluses, prices tend to rise, and the converse. This means that a greater quantity of food can be obtained for the same amount of money in years of large food surpluses than in years when there are small surpluses or none at all.[9] The ups and downs of food aid may therefore vary according to what is measured—the market value (which the DAC uses) or the quantity (tons) of food provided as aid. In the 1990s, food aid was becoming increasingly monetized: many donors provided food aid in the form of money instead of food, enabling the program to buy food needed on the world market or in a nearby developing country. Food aid in kind was also increasingly sold (mainly in the recipient country) and the income used to buy services and promote relief or development activities.[10]

The WFP has made efforts to rid its assistance of the negative effects associated with food aid in kind but has found it especially hard because of the restrictions imposed on the monetizing of food aid. The relaxation of these strictures may to a large extent be ascribed to global trends toward trade liberalization, reinforced by structural reform of agricultural policy, particularly involving the European Union (EU) in the 1990s. Like the UNDP, the WFP sought to obtain stability in its resource availability by opting for multiyear commitments, but without much success. Its efforts to tie commitments to a certain amount of food (or funding to buy these quantities) for several years—such as the Food Aid Convention and the International Emergency Food Reserve (established in 1975)—are yet another design to establish buffers against the volatility of the basic resource involved. However, these improvements in the stability of the availability of food aid were not the result of WFP efforts: they came about thanks to successful U.S. bargaining during the Kennedy Round of GATT trade negotiations in 1964–1967 that pressured other western governments to assume responsibility for a greater share of the food aid burden.[11]

All kinds of food aid have transaction costs, not least for shipping and administration. Flexibility is greater and transaction costs less when food aid is provided in cash than when it is provided in kind. Food aid, especially when provided in kind, poses an additional administrative challenge: the WFP needs to adapt its planning and implementing capacity to an unreliable resource that may require exceptionally high capacity during a year of large surpluses and then, with scarce surpluses the next, may require much less capacity. Obviously this is not an ideal situation for any organization aiming at efficiency.

Within one important area, some changes for the better have occurred in recent years, at least for part of food aid: it has increasingly become untied from procurements and services of donor countries. However, this untying is unevenly distributed. The European Union and bilateral

European donors collectively provided over 92 percent of their food aid on an untied basis in 2005. Also, some other important donors had made progress toward untying (Japan, Australia) or had committed themselves to further acquisition of food aid in developing countries (Canada). However, since the United States has continued with almost wholly tied aid and provides 70 percent of global in-kind aid, a large share of food aid remains tied.[12]

Almost all food aid is subject to one or another form of tying—at least as to purpose. The multilateral setting has only marginally changed this state of affairs—governments have increasingly tied their contributions to the WFP to specific purposes, thereby also contributing to the "bilateralization" of WFP food aid. However, a recent OECD study that evaluated the development effectiveness of food aid found that some donors are providing more and more of their food aid in forms that reduce transaction costs.[13] Several of the most cost-effective donors (Germany, the Netherlands, Norway, Sweden, Switzerland, and the United Kingdom) have formally untied their food aid or apply the least restrictive procurement rules. In contrast, some of the main providers of food aid, including the United States, have continued to provide direct food aid, which is more costly than alternative commercial transactions.[14] The WFP fared relatively well in this scrutiny in comparison with other channels for food aid.[15]

The 1996 World Food Summit

The World Food Summit, convened by the FAO in Rome in November 1996, focused on food security. The summit adopted the Rome Declaration on World Food Security and a Plan of Action aimed at establishing the foundation for diverse paths to a common objective: food security at the individual, household, national, regional, and global levels. In these policy documents, much of the basis was laid for what became the MDGs within this field. In the declaration, governments reaffirmed the right of everyone to safe and nutritious food, the right to adequate food, and the fundamental right to freedom from hunger. They pledged to work to eradicate hunger, with an immediate view to reducing the number of undernourished people to half the current level by 2015. Seven commitments were outlined—among them, ensuring an enabling political, social, and economic environment designed to create conditions for eradicating poverty.[16] In 2002, the FAO organized the World Food Summit: Five Years Later. The summit declaration called on the international community to fulfill the 1996 pledge of halving the number of hungry people (to about 400 million) by 2015.[17]

Overall Policies, Administrative Reform, Strategic Planning, and Programming

In 1995, a new revision of the WFP's general regulations took place. The Committee on Food Aid Policies and Programmes was reconstituted as the Executive Board of the WFP, with thirty-six members elected from among the member states of the UN or from the FAO—eighteen each from ECOSOC and the FAO council.[18]

During the latter 1990s, the WFP began a process of reforming its long-term planning and programming that was to some extent parallel and similar to that initiated by the UNDP (see chapter 12). Like the UNDP's reform, the WFP process was related to the increasing scarcity of resources to fund activities financed from its regular budget. In 1994, the WFP began to develop a country-assistance program for its development activities that would replace the traditional project-by-project approach it had followed since 1963.[19]

In the early 1990s, funding for relief activities was on the rise, increasing the agency's total resources (see table 13.2). However, funding from the pledging conferences showed a downward trend, especially involving development activities. For years, the target set for the annual pledging conferences—proposed by the WFP director, endorsed by the CFA, recommended by the FAO and ECOSOC, and approved by the General Assembly—was $1.5 billion. In 1995, however, the target set for these voluntary contributions for 1997–1998 was reduced to $1.3 billion in order to adapt to reality.[20]

The target stayed at that level for the following biennium, and even that was not achieved. In 1997, it was set at $1 billion (including food and cash) for the 1999–2000 biennium. However, the targeted resources were not forthcoming and the WFP had to step up its efforts to mobilize and broaden its financial and resource base and improve the predictability and reliability of funding. In addition, there was a downward trend in nondirected multilateral donations; only 65 percent of resources for development projects were multilateral, down from 75 percent the previous year. In 1997, the WFP expressed concern about the tendency of donors to direct multilateral funds to specific countries and projects, which made it difficult to target resources to the most deserving projects. In October

2000, the Executive Board adopted a resource mobilization strategy that called for a broadened donor support base; the pledging conferences had outlived their usefulness. Instead, it recommended hiring an experienced professional fund-raiser to achieve the full potential benefits from the private sector.[21]

In practice, the WFP from its inception oriented its assistance toward poor and vulnerable segments of the population in recipient countries, even before fighting poverty became priority number one for all UN development assistance. The assistance also tended to go to vulnerable countries, most often also to poor countries. Established assistance objectives, reinforced by structural patterns and aid transmission mechanisms, have facilitated this orientation. Humanitarian assistance—to displaced persons and to other victims of human-made and natural catastrophes—is almost by definition directed toward vulnerable people, although not necessarily to the poorest countries. Much of the WFP's development assistance has also been directed to vulnerable groups, reinforced by such mechanisms as work-for-food projects and human resource development, including school meals for children. Women and girls increasingly became the main recipients of WFP assistance.[22]

WFP Resources and Their Distribution, 1995–2004

The WFP's share of global food aid increased in the 1990s. In 1993, this share amounted to 20 percent, increasing to 26 percent the following year—due mainly to a drop in total global food aid in 1994. The WFP share of global food aid deliveries in 1999 was 23 percent, rising to 36 percent in 2000, and 42 percent in 2001. In 2002, it was 39 percent, and rose further to 49 percent in 2003. In 1998, the WFP was handling nearly 70 percent of global relief food aid, up from 60 percent in 1997. Its share of global relief aid was even larger.[23]

Some major trends in the activities of the WFP since 1990 emerge from table 13.4. Annual contributions to the program, about $1.8 billion, are nevertheless stable (with an increase in 2004), but the expenditures vary somewhat from one year to the next. As measured in metric tons, however, the picture is more volatile, varying according to both demand and prices. The program's activities during these years benefitted millions of people (peaking in 2004 at 113 million) and a large number of countries.

In the latter 1990s, funding for the WFP's regular activities was not

TABLE 13.4.

Total Distribution of World Food Programme Resources, Selected Years, 1990–2004 (in millions of U.S. dollars, thousands of tons, and millions of people)

	1990[1]	1992	1996[2]	1998	2000	2002	2004
Contributions (millions of U.S. dollars)	1,750	1,750	829	1,700	1,750	1,800	2,200
Expenditures (millions of U.S. dollars)	1,000	1,690	1,200	1,348	1,490	1,600	2,000
Thousands of tons distributed	4,500	6,800	2,200	NA[3]	3,500	3,700	NA
Millions of people assisted	NA	42.5	45.3	75.0	83.0	72.0	113.0
Countries assisted	NA	NA	84	NA	83	82	80

Sources: Yearbook of the United Nations 1990, 682–683; Yearbook of the United Nations 1992, 826–827; Yearbook of the United Nations 1996, 1127–1129; Yearbook of the United Nations 1998, 1130–1133; Yearbook of the United Nations 2000, 1171; Yearbook of the United Nations 2002, 1224–1125; and Yearbook of the United Nations 2004, 1224–1226.

1. Total contributions for 1990 included contributions or pledges to the WFP's regular resources, the Food Aid Convention, and the International Emergency Food Reserve plus special contributions for the Afghanistan operation and pledges of regular resources to feed long-term refugees and displaced persons.

2. For 1996, only voluntary pledges are included in the contributions. The amount cannot be compared with total amounts given for other years.

3. Not available.

committed as the program had planned, as was the case for most other multilateral development programs and funds. The pledging conferences were eventually abolished.[24] Donors had also begun to earmark their contributions for specific purposes, especially for humanitarian relief activities. Like other multilateral programs, the WFP found it would have to seek new funding sources. In a crisis-ridden world, seeking support for humanitarian relief activities offered itself as the easiest way out.

Table 13.4 shows that WFP assistance peaked in 1992 and then again during the first years of the new century in terms of both value in U.S. dollars and the volume of food. As noted, these peaks came as responses to major catastrophes, especially violent conflicts. The intervention and war in Afghanistan and then in Iraq, first with sanctions and then with arms, can explain much of the increased relief food aid during the first years of the new century.[25] Between 2001 and 2004, more than half of WFP resources were provided by the United States.[26]

Statistics about the allocation of "development" activities and "humanitarian relief" operations will vary, depending on the basis selected—value as expressed in U.S. dollars or in tons of food. Table 13.5 gives an overview based on dollar value of food aid since 1990.

Although the percentages reported in tables 13.2 and 13.5 cannot be directly compared, the trend is clear. Since the mid-1990s, the share allocated to development has been reduced, in both relative and absolute terms.[27]

Regional Distribution of WFP Operational Activities, 1995–2004

The regional distribution of resources devoted to emerging humanitarian crises will, naturally, vary by year, reflecting the major crisis areas of the time. Development activities, in contrast, allow long-term planning and may therefore show less variation from one year to the next, reflecting the more long-term priorities of the agency.

Table 13.6 shows the regional distribution of total WFP food aid since 1992. In most years, about half of total food aid was provided to countries in Sub-Saharan Africa. Most of the remaining assistance has been channeled to Asia and the Pacific.

The regional variations in total WFP assistance from year to year reflect, in particular, shifts in the geographical location of major human-made and natural catastrophes. Typical in this context is the sudden increase of the share of food aid directed to the Middle East and North Africa in 2003 because of the war and humanitarian crisis in Iraq.

Relief and Refugees

The dramatic change in the distribution of resources in the early 1990s, as shown in table 13.2, was mainly driven by demand. In response to the human-made crises and crises due to natural causes, additional resources became available for the WFP from bilateral donors and the multilateral system.

A new working arrangement between the WFP and the UNHCR took effect in January 1992, when the WFP assumed responsibility for all

TABLE 13.5.

World Food Programme Resources for Development and Humanitarian Relief, Selected Years, 1990–2004 (by percent)

	1990	1992	1996	1998	2000	2002	2004
Development	50.6	30.8	27.0	22.0	13.5	11.8	13.9
Humanitarian relief	49.4	69.2	73.0	78.0	86.5	88.2	86.1
TOTAL	100.0	100.0	100.0	100.0	100.0	100.0	100.0

Sources: Yearbook of the United Nations 1990, 682–683; Yearbook of the United Nations 1992, 826–827; Yearbook of the United Nations 1996, 1127–1129; Yearbook of the United Nations 1998, 1130–1133; Yearbook of the United Nations 2000, 1171; Yearbook of the United Nations 2002, 1124–1125; Yearbook of the United Nations 2004, 1224–1126, and calculations based on data in these sources.

UNHCR-managed refugee-feeding operations in developing countries, involving more than 1,000 beneficiaries. In 1992, the WFP handled 60 percent of all international relief food. Its substantial deliveries of relief food to conflict-ridden areas led the WFP to strengthen its interactions with UN peacekeeping operations—as with the United Nations Protection Force (UNPROFOR) in the former Yugoslavia, the United Nations Guard Contingent in Iraq, the United Nations Operation in Somalia (UNOSOM), and peacekeeping forces in Mozambique. Relations with NGOs were also expanded. The first WFP/NGO consultation was held in November 1995, resulting in a memorandum of understanding with NGOs in which respective responsibilities were clarified. At that point, the WFP was working with more than 1,000 national and international NGOs.[28]

Food for Development

In terms of value, food resources for development started to decline in 1988. In 1992, the year when humanitarian aid peaked, food for development reached its lowest level since 1978. Resources continued to decline. In 1994, the WFP was unable to resource all projects as planned, partly because of the increased conditionality imposed by some donors on the utilization of their pledges and partly because shipments of some 120,000 tons of food had to be postponed until the following year due to donors' delays in confirming pledges.[29]

TABLE 13.6.

World Food Programme Operational Resources by Region, Selected Years, 1992–2005 (by percent)

	1992[1]	1995	1997	1999	2001	2003	2005
Sub-Saharan Africa	40	56	47	44	52	49	71
Asia and the Pacific	32	28	28	35	34	12	18
Middle East and North Africa	10	NA[2]	NA	3	2	37	3
Latin America and the Caribbean	18	12	5	8	4	2	3
Eastern Europe and the CIS[3]	NA	4	20	8	9	2	1
TOTAL	100	100	100	100	100	100	96[4]

Sources: Yearbook of the United Nations 1992, 827–28; Yearbook of the United Nations 1995, 1262; Yearbook of the United Nations 1997, 1257–1258; Yearbook of the United Nations 1999, 1152; Yearbook of the United Nations 2001, 1141; Yearbook of the United Nations 2003, 1259; and Yearbook of the United Nations 2005, 1336.

1. Data for 1992 shows the distribution of the development assistance only (humanitarian relief and emergencies are not included).

2. Not available; 1992 not given or included in other regional categories in 1995, 1997.

3. The borders for regional reporting shift from time to time. The assistance reported in 1997 was for "Mediterranean, Middle East, and CIS"; in 2004 it was reported for "Europe and CIS."

4. Percentages for 2005, as provided by the source, add up to 96 and no information is provided for the remaining 4 percent.

Nevertheless, the WFP continued with its development activities, which had become part of its identity; in fact, well into the 1990s it was *the* identity of the program. However, the resources made available to these activities declined sharply in the early 1990s and remained at that lower level—amounting to $276 million in 2004. Their relative share of WFP activities declined even more dramatically. More surprisingly, a large number of people continued to benefit from WFP development assistance; from 21 million in 1996, the number increased to 24 million in 2004.[30] This assistance followed established patterns, emphasizing agriculture and rural development and human resource development.[31]

Summing Up

From the mid-1990s, developments within the WFP followed much the same patterns as those of the UNDP. Both in its programming and its general policy, the WFP focused on poverty alleviation—reaching the poorest people and fighting poverty. In the late 1990s, added importance was given to advocacy. Such campaigns have always been an important part of food aid activities. As we saw in chapter 12, the WFP increasingly became involved in the coordination of development activities within the UNDG. This cooperation and coordination sought to construct a UN system-wide approach for eradicating poverty and implement UN reform at the country level by harmonizing policies, programs, and procedures through the United Nations Development Assistance Framework.

The violent conflicts that erupted in the early 1990s changed the basic structure of the WFP, turning it from a development to a humanitarian relief agency whose primary objective was to respond to the needs of victims of violence and wars. While resources for development activities became scarce, donors increasingly saw the WFP as a convenient agency for channeling parts of their relief assistance. During the latter 1990s, some of the major violent conflicts had ended but major natural disasters called for humanitarian emergency assistance. In the first years of the new century, conflicts and wars required massive food relief. This applied not least to the U.S.-led interventions in Afghanistan and Iraq. As the major provider of food aid in kind, the United States found the WFP a useful channel for part of its emergency food aid to these countries.[32]

From Food Security to Human Security?

Multilateral food aid has passed through several phases. In the early 1960s, the global food situation was still dominated by large U.S. agricultural surpluses where the major rationale for food aid was to get rid of the surpluses in a way that did not harm the commercial food trade. The WFP was conceived of as a complementary channel to the much larger bilateral U.S. food aid program in this regard. The major food-producing powers set framework conditions for food aid through the WFP to ensure that it would not compete with bilateral food aid programs or harm the trade in food. Its focus was to be on social and economic projects, transforming food into development. The basic identity and main orientation of the program was established during these initial years.

The next phase started in the early 1970s, triggered by the challenges emerging from the human catastrophe in the Sahel. The WFP was forced by events and bilateral aid agencies to take on a role as a provider—even a coordinator—of relief food aid. Nevertheless, food for development remained the WFP's main thrust and its basic identity. In the meantime, food had become a scarce resource globally and U.S. food policy had changed in several respects: as early as the Kennedy era, the United States considered as a tool of foreign policy. It also pressured other western donors to share the burden of meeting global food crises with food or financing for food. For these countries, the multilateral system offered itself as a convenient channel. Although the United States remained the dominant player, this process brought players with other basic interests and a different perspective on food aid more strongly onto the scene.

The late 1970s initiated the third phase, also triggered by external events: humanitarian catastrophes caused by war and violence resulting in millions of refugees. It started with the Afghan refugees in Pakistan after the Soviet invasion and Cambodian refugees from Pol Pot's terror regime who fled to Thailand. It continued, also in the 1980s, with refugees from war and violence elsewhere, particularly in Africa. These catastrophes added a political dimension to humanitarian relief, as most of them had an East-West conflict dimension. The WFP appeared as a convenient, politically neutral channel for food aid and was extensively used by the United States to sustain refugees and their host countries. These crises led the WFP to reform the administration of emergency operations. Toward the end of the 1980s, the funding for aid to protracted refugees and displaced persons was separated from the funding for aid in response to sudden disasters. The ability of the executive director to respond to sudden emergencies in their initial phases was also improved.[33] Nevertheless, although emergency food aid received increased attention and funding, "development" activities remained the first priority. Humanitarian catastrophes caused by natural disasters also remained high on the agenda.

This phase slipped into the next: the complex emergencies of the early 1990s resulting from the many intrastate and regional violent conflicts. Several of these conflicts were caused by politicians who exploited cultural differences (ethnicity) in their fight for power. These conflicts were highly political but did not fit the pattern of the previous East-West divide. The humanitarian perspective became the predominant one. Even so, food aid could not avoid playing a political role as well, exploited by the one or the other of the parties to these conflicts.

Although the traditional East-West divide was becoming history, this did not mean that the United States or other major or regional powers did not have foreign policy concerns or other vested interests. These conflicts, moreover, resulted in human misery and large numbers of refugees and internally displaced persons. In addition, new natural catastrophes called for food aid interventions. To the major donors of food aid, some of these hunger catastrophes were more politically important than others. This applied especially to the food crisis in Southern Africa, which was caused by conflict as well as drought. At that point, ensuring democracy ranked high on the political agenda of donors. These humanitarian catastrophes made countries that did not produce surplus food, especially in Europe, into major contributors of humanitarian relief assistance, including food aid. The WFP offered itself as a convenient channel for many bilateral agencies and developed into the major provider of relief aid. At the same time, however, the resources it received and allocated for development purposes were drastically reduced, both in terms of their financial value and—even more—relative to the resources for relief. During these years, U.S. contributions to the WFP were lower than in other periods.

The human-made crises of the 1990s had a security dimension beyond the traditional food security concept, in their origin as well as in the way they were approached from the outside. In addition to the actors who are usually on the scene in humanitarian crises, these complex emergencies involved military personnel engaged in conflict management and peacekeeping, even peace enforcement. These developments affected the very concept of security.[34] Whereas until the late 1980s security had been interpreted as security of territory from external aggression, as protection of national interests in foreign policy, or as global security (primarily from the threat of nuclear holocaust), increasingly, the emphasis was on an expanded concept of security: human security, as defined in the 1994 *Human Development Report*.[35]

A rights perspective on food security emerged at an early date. It was clearly reflected in the definition of food security adopted by the World Food Summit in 1995: "the right of everyone to have access to safe and nutritious food, consistent with the right to adequate food and the fundamental right of everyone to be free from hunger."[36]

In the early 1990s, the balance between the development and relief activities of the WFP turned almost upside-down, as we have seen. Other factors worked in the same direction. First of all, the argument that food aid in kind was an additional resource for promoting development had lost much of the strength it had carried in the early days. In the 1990s, its validity was largely restricted to U.S. food aid channeled through U.S. voluntary organizations and monetized before being used in their various development projects.

Food aid has been controversial from the very start, for political as well as practical reasons. Bilateral food aid has been heavily criticized for being used as a lever for obtaining political concessions, not least as regards the United States, the main supplier of this kind of assistance. Channeling food aid through the multilateral system was expected to remove the basis for these criticisms.

As we have seen, however, the United States—under Republican and Democrat administrations alike—has not been willing to respect the WFP's multilateral character, insisting on having a near-veto on norms as well as operational activities. The politics of aid has perhaps never come more clearly into the open than in food aid, including multilateral food aid.[37] Since James Ingram left as head of the WFP in 1991, the United States has insisted on filling the position of executive director of the WFP with its nominee.

Another core argument for food aid has always been that it is especially well suited for targeting the poorest people, especially women and children, through women's control of food distribution within households. The argument goes that food aid should be used in support of projects geared toward feeding undernourished people and that the selection of food aid projects should contribute to building a resource base for such beneficiaries. This has consistently been set forth as the prime objective of food aid for development.[38]

However, the effectiveness of food aid (particularly food in kind) in meeting such objectives, as organized by the WFP, came increasingly into question. As noted earlier, food is a cumbersome resource when used for development projects that seek to transform food into economic development via income from work or similar transactions. Administering this kind of aid is demanding, complicated, and expensive for donors and recipients alike. The transaction costs for this kind of assistance are relatively high, especially when compared to financial transfers.

An appraisal component was built in to WFP food aid from the start. However, such appraisals (in the WFP policy documents generally referred to as "evaluations") have usually consisted of an in-service scrutiny of the projects. In the 1980s, the evaluation unit was brought closer to those involved in project design and evaluations were extended to completed emergency operations, including external evaluations.[39] Nevertheless, there have been few major (external and independent) evaluations of the food aid system as such or the WFP's specific role in this system or in major programs run by the WFP.

In the early 1990s, however, a major evaluation took place at a critical point for the WFP. This was a tripartite evaluation initiated by the governments of Canada, the Netherlands, and Norway that focused on the performance of the WFP as a development agency. It offered several suggestions as to how the organization's development activities might be improved, with particular reference to the number and size of projects: a reduction in the number of projects and a greater concentration were the core recommendations.[40] The WFP took these recommendations on board. However, during follow-up assessment, the evaluators also indicated that the WFP's mandate should perhaps be revised from a focus on food aid as a resource to a role that combined humanitarian assistance and the alleviation of hunger.[41]

Food aid for relief operations, in contrast, has generally not been seen as politically controversial. Food aid, along with other kinds of humanitarian assistance (like medicine and shelter), has been met with general approval. However, things are not always the way they seem: in conflict situations, humanitarian aid, including food aid, may sometimes function in ways inconsistent with donor intentions, whether provided by NGOs, bilateral agencies, or multilateral organizations.[42] It may even turn into a tool of the oppressors, thereby prolonging conflicts and increasing the suffering of victims.[43]

Situations in which oppressors use food aid as a weapon, as it was in the conflict-ridden areas of the 1990s, have made humanitarian assistance increasingly controversial. The multilateral system's Achilles' heel—poorly coordinated operations, within the system and with other international and bilateral actors—is seldom more visible than during international relief operations.

The debate on food aid and its future role is bound to continue. The argument that food aid represents an additional resource beyond what would otherwise be available as development assistance remains crucial. The validity of the additionality argument has been reduced over the years and now appears to be very limited.[44] The contributions to food aid activities from most donor countries, including commitments to multilateral programs and conventions, have increasingly been financed from budgets for development assistance. This means that food aid has to compete with other bilateral and multilateral activities financed from these budgets.

The dramatic shift in the orientation of food aid from development to relief that took place in the early 1990s was driven by demand. Food aid became an important part of humanitarian relief operations. This change has also influenced thinking on the future role of this kind of assistance. Food will always constitute an important (albeit problematic) component of humanitarian relief operations. Improvements in readiness for immediate responses to catastrophes will be a challenge to the organizations involved, and here the WFP has assumed a lead role. The wider perspective, moving the focus from food security to a focus on human security, is an even greater challenge, and not just for an institution that has traditionally focused on providing food aid. The experience of dealing with the complex emergencies of the 1990s make this broader approach not only attractive but necessary. The parallel discourse on food security as a human right may facilitate a development in that direction.

A key figure in the discourse on food aid policy and development, Hans W. Singer, identified an important future role for the WFP to play, much in line with what has been argued above. We conclude this chapter by giving the floor to his perspective for the institution, condensed and conveyed in soft-spoken language:

> With its dual functions of providing development and relief assistance, WFP has been well placed to play a major role in what has come to be called the "continuum" between relief and development. From its inception, it has supported disaster prevention, preparedness and mitigation activities as well as post-disaster rehabilitation and reconstruction programmes. And its emergency assistance has been used, to the extent possible, to serve both relief and development works. There is still much to be done to create a link between relief and development. Indeed, food aid can be visualized as a means for preventing conflicts and resolving tensions before they develop into full-scale emergencies. A future task of WFP will be to stimulate the international community to remove the artificial dichotomy between emergency and development assistance in the process from crisis to recovery and development, and to broaden the humanitarian consensus from acute emergency relief to the full circle of prevention and preparedness linked to rehabilitation, reconstruction and development.[45]

True, that is a tall order, but it is also a challenge that cannot be ignored.

The problem is whether the WFP will be able to take on such a task given the way it has developed since the early 1990s. The remaining superpower has increasingly taken the wheel. The WFP has increasingly become "bilateralized," partly because of this dominance, which also led other donors to earmark their contributions more frequently than before. The problem is further exacerbated by the fact that the same superpower is the main provider of global food aid and insists on maintaining near-veto power on the WFP's operational activities. It also continues to pursue a policy of tying food aid to procurement policies at a time when most other food aid providers—even some of the major food-producing ones—have abandoned this policy or are in the process of moderating or discontinuing traditional procurement tying. As a recent OECD study found, much could be gained for "real" development if today's food aid system were freed from such constraints.[46]

Since the early 1990s, the WFP has become "bilateralized" by other major donors as well, who target their contributions for specific operations, usually humanitarian relief operations; this could be called multilaterally coordinated bilateralism.[47] Core funding has become dramatically reduced. These developments—the tight grip of the United States and the increased targeting of contributions by other donor agencies—are not unrelated. Under the circumstances, the other major donor of food aid, the European Union, has shown some reluctance to use the WFP as the main channel for its food aid.

Politics and power will always influence the outcomes of international relations, including the policy and activities of multilateral organizations. But there will be a limit to how much a single player—the most powerful one in particular—can dominate a multilateral agency without discrediting its multilateral character and making it less attractive as a joint venture for other players. Time will tell whether or not the visions of a new U.S. administration with a different approach to international and multilateral cooperation than that of the recent Republican administration will be able to break this impasse and embrace broader institutional solutions.

There is no easy way out. The challenge formulated by Hans Singer remains. If the present power imbalance within the World Food Programme is the core problem, then one possible solution may be to broaden the policy field to include neighboring policy areas for which power and resources are differently distributed and more balanced between the major actors. This is especially so if such an institutional reform could help solve other pressing problems in the UN system, such as facilitating improved cooperation and coordination among the many funds, programs, and agencies that run operational activities within the same broad area. Institutional reform will always involve dangers, but it may contribute to greater policy coherence as well.

An idea in this direction has recently been brought forward from the sidelines by another veteran within the UN system. James Ingram has suggested that the many UN organizations engaged in humanitarian relief be reorganized with WFP, UNICEF, and UNHCR relief functions providing the nucleus.[48] Although these organizations have focused primarily on humanitarian relief, they have always done so with a view to the broader framework of needs beyond the immediate relief situation, involving rehabilitation and development. Other arms of the UN system carry the main responsibility and have competence when it comes to development. There is a need for greater cooperation and coordination across the humanitarian/development divide as well.

Systemic reform within the UN system takes time, as the WFP's history testifies. The idea of a unified organization for humanitarian relief in which the main actors are included hardly tops the agenda: it was not included as a priority issue by the high-level panel on UN reform in its 2006 report.[49] Resistance to fundamental systematic reform will always be formidable and more often than not involve the leadership and staff of the fiefdoms subject to reform and their allies. Governments with vested interests in specific organizations may also present difficult hurdles.

Big is not always beautiful. Adaptation to old and new challenges by the institutions involved is the alternative to systemic reform. Given the actual institution, however—and the basic power relations involved—the question is whether it is realistic to expect that the necessary change will happen.

FOURTEEN

The Long Road toward the Millennium Development Goals

- ■ **The Millennium Declaration and Its Development Commitments**
- ■ **Making the Millennium Declaration Operational**
- ■ **Implementation, 2000–2004**
- ■ **The Recommendations of the Millennium Project**
- ■ **The Midpoint Report: Progress Achieved, but Core Goals Still Distant**
- ■ **The Global Partnership: Lagging Behind**
- ■ **Some Concluding Observations**

In 1996, the OECD Development Assistance Committee brought the conclusions arrived at in several UN global conferences together in a comprehensive, future-oriented policy document called *Shaping the 21st Century: The Contribution of Development Co-operation.*[1] At that point, DAC countries were providing almost 95 percent of global official development assistance.

The policy document established a common policy platform for DAC member countries. Although development cooperation in the form of financial and technical assistance for national capacity-building remained important, it considered the OECD's macroeconomic, trade, finance, and other policies toward developing countries to be a crucial part of an integrated approach. The policy was embedded in an ambition to attain coherence between the various, often conflicting policy areas.[2] It took the United Nations Millennium Summit to broaden the strategy and give global legitimacy to the aspirations and goals.

The Millennium Declaration and Its Development Commitments

The General Assembly designated its fifty-fifth session in 2000 as the Millennium Assembly and decided to convene a summit as part of that assembly.[3] The Millennium Summit of the United Nations, which took place in September 2000, brought together the largest-ever gathering of world leaders. Representatives of 191 nations attended, including 147 heads of state and government. The setting was special, in itself fostering special and solemn commitments. The summit was not just ceremonial; at it, world leaders adopted the United Nations Millennium Declaration.[4]

From our perspective, the summit's most important outcome was the commitment to the Millennium Development Goals. The MDGs conceptualized development and poverty eradication as integral parts of a broader perspective that included peace and security; protection of the environment; human rights; democracy and good governance; protection of the vulnerable; and particular attention to the worst off, with special reference to Africa. Improvements within such areas would also affect poverty eradication and development. Increasingly, they have been defined as development objectives in their own right as well as objectives in a development cooperation context.

Some of the particular commitments to development and poverty eradication were general but nevertheless important because they highlighted the direction of joint efforts. Others were quantified, to be achieved by a fixed date. These call for special attention. Most of the MDGs had been formulated in similar terms before as recommendations from specialized global conferences and meetings during the 1990s (and integrated into the DAC's 1996 strategy document). The Millennium Declaration gave them added authority. In brief, the summit resolved:[5]

- To halve, by the year 2015, the proportion of the world's people whose income is less than one dollar a day and the proportion of people who suffer from hunger and, by the same date, to halve the proportion of people who are unable to reach or to afford safe drinking water

- To ensure that, by the same date, children everywhere, boys and girls alike, will be able to complete a full course of primary schooling and that girls and boys will have equal access to all levels of education

- To reduce maternal mortality by three-quarters and reduce the mortality of children under five by two-thirds by 2015

- To halt and begin to reverse, the spread of HIV/AIDS, the scourge of malaria, and other major diseases that afflict humanity by 2015

- To provide special assistance to children orphaned by HIV/AIDS

- To achieve a significant improvement in the lives of at least 100 million slum dwellers by 2020

More generally, Millennium Assembly participants also resolved:[6]

- To promote gender equality and the empowerment of women as effective ways to combat poverty, hunger, and disease and to stimulate development that is truly sustainable

- To develop and implement strategies that give young people everywhere a real chance to find decent and productive work

- To encourage the pharmaceutical industry to make essential drugs more widely available and affordable by all who need them in developing countries

- To develop strong partnerships with the private sector and civil society organizations in pursuit of development and poverty eradication

- To ensure that the benefits of new technologies, especially information and communication technologies are available to all

The principles of sustainable development, including those set out in Agenda 21, were reconfirmed. The heads of state and government committed themselves to "spare no effort to promote democracy and strengthen the rule of law, as well as respect for all internationally recognized human rights and fundamental freedoms, including the right to development." The assembly resolved to combat all forms of violence against women and to implement the Convention on the Elimination of All Forms of Discrimination against Women. The participants committed themselves to "support the consolidation of democracy in Africa and assist Africans in their struggle for lasting peace, poverty eradication and sustainable development, thereby bringing Africa into the mainstream of the world economy."[7]

The declaration's themes and commitments were not entirely new. The similarities to the international strategies of the previous four development decades are striking. The form is more solemn, approaching that of the UN Charter, to which it paid tribute. In a way, it came to serve much the same function as the development strategies for earlier decades, but the form of the declaration and the way in which it was launched elevated the commitments to a higher level.

Making the Millennium Declaration Operational

In December 2000, the General Assembly asked the Secretary-General to prepare a long-term "road map" to the implementation of the Millennium Declaration within the UN system and to prepare an annual report on progress achieved on implementation.[8] In September the following year, Secretary-General Kofi Annan provided his *Road Map towards the Implementation of the United Nations Millennium Declaration,* which proposed eight Millennium Development Goals with special targets for each (in all eighteen targets) and a total of forty-eight indicators for measuring performance against the baseline year 1990.[9]

Like the declaration, the road map covered a broad field. In the introduction, the Secretary-General emphasized that the problems facing humanity were closely intertwined, with each tending to complicate the solution of others. The report focused on "cross-cutting issues, where a coordinated approach can yield much more than the sum of its parts." Kofi Annan underlined that the targets set by the declaration were not new. What was needed was not more technical or feasibility studies. "Rather, States need to demonstrate the political *will* to carry out commitments already given and to implement strategies already worked out." While the declaration emphasized goals, with almost no attention to input, the Secretary-General stressed that none of the MDGs could be reached "unless significant additional *resources* are made available." Many of these resources would have to be found within the countries where they were spent, "but a special obligation falls on the more fortunate countries to ensure that the less fortunate have a genuine opportunity to improve their lot."[10]

Here we will focus on the eight Millennium Development Goals, although they cover only part of the overall development perspective previously outlined in the international development strategies.[11]

Eradicating Extreme Poverty and Hunger

The number of people living on less than one dollar a day had decreased from 1.3 billion in 1990 to 1.2 billion in 2001; however, the decline was unevenly spread. The greatest number of poor people lived in South Asia, but the highest proportion of poor people was in Sub-Saharan

BOX 14.1. Millennium Development Goals

GOALS AND TARGETS	INDICATORS

Goal 1. Eradicate extreme poverty and hunger

Target 1. Halve, between 1990 and 2015, the proportion of people whose income is less than one dollar a day

Target 2. Halve, between 1990 and 2015, the proportion of people who suffer from hunger

1. Proportion of population living at below $1 per day
2. Poverty gap ratio (incidence x depth of poverty)
3. Share of poorest quintile in national consumption
4. Prevalence of underweight children (under five years of age)
5. Proportion of population below minimum level of dietary energy consumption

Goal 2. Achieve universal primary education

Target 3. Ensure that by 2015, children everywhere, boys and girls alike, will be able to complete a full course of primary schooling

6. Net enrollment ratio in primary education
7. Proportion of pupils starting grade 1 who reach grade 5
8. Literacy rate of 15- to 24-year-olds

Goal 3. Promote gender equality and empower women

Target 4. Eliminate gender disparity in primary and secondary education, preferably by 2005, and to all levels of education no later than 2015

9. Ratio of girls to boys in primary, secondary, and tertiary education
10. Ratio of literate females to males of 15- to 24-year-olds
11. Share of women in wage employment in the non-agricultural sector
12. Proportion of seats held by women in national parliament

Goal 4. Reduce child mortality

Target 5. Reduce by two-thirds between 1990 and 2015, the under-five mortality rate

13. Under-five mortality rate
14. Infant mortality rate
15. Proportion of 1-year-old children immunized against measles

Goal 5. Improve maternal health

Target 6. Reduce by three-quarters between 1990 and 2015, the maternal mortality ratio

16. Maternal mortality ratio
17. Proportion of births attended by skilled health personnel

Goal 6. Combat HIV/AIDS, malaria and other diseases

Target 7. Have halted by 2015 and begun to reverse the spread of HIV/AIDS

Target 8. Have halted by 2015 and begun to reverse the incidence of malaria and other major diseases

18. HIV prevalence among 15- to 24-year-old pregnant women
19. Contraceptive prevalence rate
20. Number of children orphaned by HIV/AIDS
21. Prevalence and death rates associated with malaria
22. Proportion of population in malaria risk areas using effective malaria prevention and treatment measures
23. Prevalence and death rates associated with tuberculosis
24. Proportion of tuberculosis cases detected and cured under directly observed treatment short course

Goal 7. Ensure environmental sustainability

Target 9. Integrate the principles of sustainable development into country policies and programmes and reverse the loss of environmental resources

Target 10. Halve by 2015 the proportion of people without sustainable access to safe drinking water and basic sanitation

Target 11. By 2020 to have achieved a significant improvement in the lives of at least 100 million slum dwellers

25. Proportion of land area covered by forest
26. Land area protected to maintain biological diversity
27. GDP per unit of energy use (as proxy for energy efficiency)
28. Carbon dioxide emissions (per capita) [Plus two figures of global atmospheric pollution: ozone depletion and the accumulation of global warming gases]
29. Proportion of population with sustainable access to an improved water source
30. Proportion of population with sustainable access to improved sanitation
31. Proportion of people with access to secure tenure

Goal 8. Develop a global partnership for development

Target 12. Develop further an open, rule-based, predictable, non-discriminatory trading and financial system

Target 13. Address the special needs of the least developed countries. Includes tariff- and quota-free access for least developed countries' exports; enhanced program of debt relief for HIPCs and cancellations of official bilateral debt; and more generous ODA for countries committed to poverty reduction

Target 14. Address the special needs of landlocked countries and small island developing States (through the Programme of Action for the Sustainable Development of Small Island Developing States and the outcome of the twenty-second special session of the General Assembly)

Target 15. Deal comprehensively with the debt problems of developing countries through national and international measures in order to make debt sustainable in the long term

Target 16. In cooperation with developing countries develop and implement strategies for decent and productive work for youth

Target 17. In cooperation with pharmaceutical companies provide access to affordable essential drugs in developing countries

Official development assistance

32. Net ODA as percentage of OECD/DAC donors' gross national product (target of 0.7% in total and 0.15% for LDCs)
33. Proportion of ODA to basic social services (basic education, primary health care, nutrition, safe water and sanitation)
34. Proportion of ODA that is untied
35. Proportion of ODA for environment in small island developing States
36. Proportion of ODA for transport sector in landlocked countries

Market access

37. Proportion of exports (by value and excluding arms) admitted free of duties and quotas
38. Average tariffs and quotas on agricultural products and textiles and clothing
39. Domestic and export agricultural subsidies in OECD countries
40. Proportion of ODA provided to help build trade capacity

Debt sustainability

41. Proportion of official bilateral HIPC debt cancelled
42. Debt service as a percentage of exports of goods and services
43. Proportion of ODA provided as debt relief
44. Number of countries reaching HIPC decision and completion points

Target 18. In cooperation with the private sector make available the benefits of new technologies, especially information and communications	45. Unemployment rate of 15- to 24-year-olds
	46. Proportion of population with access to affordable essential drugs on a sustainable basis
	47. Telephone lines per 1,000 people
	48. Personal computers per 1,000 people

Source: Road Map towards the Implementation of the United Nations Millennium Declaration, Report of the Secretary-General, General Assembly document A/56/326, 6 September 2001.

The road map had a tentative form: the Secretary-General proposed the goals, targets, and indicators. It was noted that some of the suggested indicators needed further development. For target 11, the road map noted that an urban/rural disaggregation of several of indicators 25–31 might be relevant for monitoring improvement in the lives of slum dwellers. It was also stated that some of the indicators for goal 8 would be monitored separately for the LDCs, Africa, landlocked countries, and small island developing states.

Nevertheless, five years later, the eight goals remained intact as first formulated in the report. Only minor revisions had been made in the formulations of the targets: after the Johannesburg summit, "and basic sanitation" was added to target 10; targets 13 and 14 were put together; and target 15 was shortened to "Deal comprehensively with developing countries' debt." United Nations, *The Millennium Development Goals Report 2006* (New York: United Nations, 2006).

Africa, where approximately 51 percent of the population lived on less than one dollar a day. The strategies prescribed for moving toward Target 1—halving the proportion of those with incomes of less than one dollar a day—included ensuring support for country-led economic and social initiatives that focused on poverty reduction, strengthening capabilities to provide basic social services, and helping build capacity for poverty assessment, monitoring, and planning.

Although the number of undernourished people fell by 40 million between 1990–1992 and 1996–1998, 826 million people in the developing world still were not getting enough food to lead normal, healthy, and active lives. Nearly 1 billion people were still denied access to clean drinking water supplies, and 2.4 million lacked access to basic sanitation.

The strategies outlined for moving forward included promoting greater investment in the water and sanitation sectors and addressing other issues related to the sustainable management of water resources at the World Summit on Sustainable Development in Johannesburg in 2002.

Achieving Universal Primary Education

In 1998, some 113 million children of school age were not enrolled in primary education. Ninety-seven percent of these children lived in developing countries, and nearly 60 percent of them were girls. Female enrollment in rural areas remained particularly low. The World Declaration on Education for All and its Framework for Action, adopted at the 1990 World Conference on Education for All, which included the UN Girls' Education Initiative, was the basis for the strategies recommended by the road map. These included urging national policymakers to accept girls' education as a strategy for achieving universal primary schooling and a goal in its own right; urging national governments, local communities, and the international community to commit significant resources for such necessities as school buildings, books, and teachers; making education systems adaptable to the needs of girl children, especially those from poor households; and supporting school meal programs and take-home rations programs that could attract girls to schools.

Reducing Maternal Mortality and the Mortality of Children under Five

At the global level, estimates of maternal mortality for 1995 indicated that 515,000 women died each year of pregnancy-related causes, 99 percent of them in developing countries. Although under-five mortality rates worldwide had decreased from 94 to 81 per 1,000 live births between 1990 and 2000, they continued at a high level: about 11 million children under five were still dying in developing countries each year, mostly from preventable diseases. The road map referred to several initiatives already at work to curb the scourge of major diseases, including the Global Alliance for Vaccines and Immunizations. Strategies included establishing (or updating) national policies, standards, and regulatory mechanisms for safe motherhood and developing systems to ensure their implementation; promoting appropriate community practices in support of safe motherhood and the reduction of under-five mortality; monitoring maternal and newborn health-care status and access to services; and supporting programs that provide immunization and vaccination, oral rehydration therapy, nutrition, and water and sanitation interventions.

Combating HIV/AIDS, Malaria, and Other Diseases

In 2000, approximately three million people died of AIDS alone and some 36 million were living with HIV/AIDS. By the end of that year, the global HIV/AIDS catastrophe had claimed 22 million lives. Eight million people developed active tuberculosis, of which nearly 2 million died annually. Over 90 percent of these deaths were in developing countries. And each year 1 million people died from malaria, the road map noted. Recommended strategies included achieving a target of $7 to $10 billion in total spending on HIV/AIDS from all sources, including affected countries; urging the international community to support the Global AIDS and Health Fund; strengthening health-care systems and addressing factors that affect the provision of HIV-related drugs, including affordable anti-retroviral drugs; and supporting and encouraging the involvement of local communities in making people aware of these diseases.

Some 13 million children had been orphaned by HIV/AIDS—over 90 percent of them in Sub-Saharan Africa—and the number was expected rise to about 40 million in that region in the first two decades of the new century. The mechanisms that caused and reinforced poverty were changing due to AIDS because the majority of those living with and dying from AIDS were in the prime of life. The strategies prescribed included mobilizing and strengthening community and family-based actions to support orphaned and vulnerable children; ensuring that governments protect children from violence, abuse, exploitation, and discrimination; ensuring that governments provide essential social services for children; ensuring that orphans and children affected by HIV/AIDS are treated on an equal basis with other children; and expanding the role of schools as community resource and care centers.

Making Drugs Available and Affordable

In May 2000, a partnership was launched between five major pharmaceutical companies and the UN to increase developing countries' access to HIV medicines, including sharp reductions in prices for anti-retroviral drugs. In May 2001, the fifty-fourth World Health Assembly called upon the international community to work together to strengthen pharmaceutical policies and practices in order to promote the development of national industries. In June 2001, the special session of the General Assembly on HIV/AIDS called for the development of and progress in implementing comprehensive care strategies, including plans for the financing and referral mechanisms required to provide access to diagnostics, affordable medicines, and the necessary technologies for care.

The road map anchored its suggested strategies in the recommendations that emerged from these sessions. These included strengthening health systems so they can provide essential medicines; increasing affordability through differential pricing and reducing or eliminating import duties, tariffs, and taxes; mobilizing sustainable financing to support the cost of expanded access to drugs in poor countries; exploring the feasibility, in collaboration with NGOs and other concerned partners, of developing and implementing systems for the voluntary monitoring and reporting of global drug prices; urging drug companies to reduce the prices of essential drugs and to improve their distribution of life-saving drugs, especially in the LDCs; utilizing nontraditional and innovative mechanisms to increase the effective distribution of drugs to those who needed them; ensuring further evaluation and assessment of international trade agreements that affect the availability of essential drugs; and stepping up research about and development of advanced medications for diseases that primarily affect developing countries.

Improving the Conditions of Slum Dwellers

The road map expected that the global urban population would double to 5 million people during the next generation, most of the increase by far taking place in developing countries. It was estimated that one-quarter of the world's population who lived in cities did not have adequate housing and often lacked access to basic social services. Strategies for meeting this challenge included ensuring support from the international community to provide basic social services such as safe water and sanitation to the urban poor; ensuring the development of integrated and participatory approaches to urban environmental planning and management; and ensuring good urban governance and planning by forging public/private partnerships.

Improving Gender Equality and the Empowerment of Women

Two-thirds of those living on less than one dollar a day were women, the road map noted. During the 1980s and 1990s, the number of rural women living in absolute poverty had risen by 50 percent, as opposed to 30 percent for men. Women would need to gain control over financial and material resources and access to opportunity through education to change this severe inequality, the road map argued. In prescribing strategies, the road map relied on the recommendations of the five-year review of the Beijing Platform for Action and the 1999 five-year review of the International Conference on Population and Development. Strategies included urging greater efforts in the areas of maternal mortality, prevention of HIV/AIDS, and gender sensitivity in education; advocating women's empowerment in employment; and supporting the inclusion of women in government and other decision-making bodies at high levels.

Giving Young People Decent and Productive Work

The population of young people was expected to reach 1.2 billion by 2010, more than half of them in Asia and the Pacific. Youth also constituted 40 percent of the unemployed, and the number of young unemployed people was increasing. Strategies prescribed in the road map included ensuring the employability of young people through increased investment in education and vocational training; ensuring equal opportunity by giving girls the same opportunities as boys; and facilitating entrepreneurship by making it easier to start and run enterprises.

Creating a Political and Financial Environment for Attaining the MDGs

The Millennium Declaration identified very specific goals, but it was vague about inputs to finance the changes it envisioned. As in all previous UN major strategy documents, the main responsibility for policies and inputs was placed at the doorsteps of the governments concerned, with more general commitments from the international community, including the UN, to assist in the process.

The road map started a process where the focus became increasingly directed toward the input side. It emphasized that developing nations needed immediate assistance in addressing issues in finance, trade, and governance. It noted that in the upcoming International Conference for Financing for Development (Monterrey, 2002), the UN planned to call upon the international community to increase its ODA and remove barriers to trade.

INCREASE IN PRIVATE CAPITAL FLOWS

The road map considered an increase in private capital flows to developing countries, especially foreign direct investment, to be a valuable supplement to the domestic resources a country could generate. Although private capital could not alleviate poverty, it could play a significant role in promoting growth, the road map stated. The strategies recommended included good governance with a strong focus on combating corruption and instituting appropriate safeguards for private investment; disciplined macroeconomic policies and fiscal policy, including clear goals for mobilizing tax and other revenues; responsible public spending on basic education and health, the rural sector, and women; and well-functioning and diverse financial systems that allocated savings to those capable of investing efficiently, including microfinance borrowers, women, and the rural sector.

INCREASE IN OFFICIAL DEVELOPMENT ASSISTANCE

The road map presented ODA as a key source of finance, especially for LDCs that lacked the infrastructure to attract private capital flows. Net ODA had declined from $58.5 billion in 1994 to $48.5 billion in 1999, at a time when a series of major UN conferences had underlined the need for increased ODA, an increasing number of developing countries had undertaken major reforms in economic and political governance, and the fiscal situation in donor countries had improved significantly. Strategies recommended included a commitment by industrial countries at the Monterrey conference to implement the target of providing ODA equal to 0.7 percent of their GNP; distinguishing between the proportion of ODA spent on development and that spent on humanitarian assistance to help prevent the erosion of development assistance in favor of humanitarian assistance; and allocation of ODA by donor nations to countries that needed it most and to countries with policies effectively directed to reducing poverty.

TRADE

The road map saw trade as an important engine of growth, not just as an important foreign exchange earner: it had multiplier effects because it generated income through employment. The upper-middle-income countries whose share increased from 8 to 11 percent of world trade in goods in the 1990s had benefited the most from eight rounds of multilateral trade negotiations, while the share of the poorest forty-eight economies had remained nearly constant at about 4 percent. The road map recommended ensuring that developed countries fully complied with the commitments made under the Uruguay Round of multilateral trade negotiations to improve market access for products from developing countries; ensuring significant improvements in market access for agricultural products from developing countries; eliminating the remaining trade barriers in manufacturing, especially for textiles and clothing; providing limited, time-bound protection of new industries in countries in the early stages of development; providing technical assistance for trade negotiations and dispute settlements; and ensuring that the next round of trade negotiations would truly be a development round.

Addressing the Special Needs of the LDCs

The road map relied on the outcome of the Third United Nations Conference on the LDCs in May 2001, which provided a framework for a global partnership to accelerate sustained economic growth and sustainable development in the LDCs. The main focus was on trade, debt relief, and increased ODA.

Duty- and quota-free access to essentially all exports from the LDCs has been on the agenda since the 1970s. In the late 1990s, the European Community announced the Everything but Arms initiative that granted duty- and quota-free access for all nonmilitary imports from the forty-nine least-developed countries starting in March 2001. The road map recommended that other developed countries follow the EU example. It emphasized strengthening efforts to integrate trade policies into national development policies to eradicate poverty; assisting the LDCs in capacity-building in trade policy and related areas, such as tariffs, customs, competition, and investment in technology; continuing to work toward the objective of access to duty-free markets for all LDC products except arms; and assisting the LDCs in upgrading their production and export capacities and capabilities.

On debt relief, the point of departure was the Heavily Indebted Poor Countries (HIPC) initiative, endorsed in 1996 by the interim development committees of the IMF and the World Bank and reviewed and modified in 1999. This would have to be extended to more debt-ridden countries and increase the tempo of the debt relief process. The road map encouraged donors to mobilize resources to finance debt relief and ensure that debt relief was additional and not an alternative to other forms of development assistance.

The report stated that official development assistance is necessary for building the infrastructure needed to attract foreign capital, direct or otherwise. In practice, however, ODA to the LDCs was far below the target of 0.15 to 0.20 percent of GNP established by the 1990 UN Conference on the Least Developed Countries: in 2000, the actual flows were only 0.06 percent. Substantially larger amounts were needed.

Small Island Developing Countries

Although small island developing countries vary considerably in terms of biophysical, sociocultural, and economic criteria, their efforts for sustainable development are constrained by such shared disadvantages as limited natural resources, fragility of the ecosystem, and vulnerability to natural hazards, the road map observed. It took the Programme of Action for Sustainable Development of Small Island Developing States adopted in 1994 and the outcomes of the twenty-second special session of the General Assembly as points of departures and recommended ensuring progress toward special and differential treatment of these countries in the spheres of finance and trade, supporting and assisting them in specific aspects of multilateral trade negotiations, and supporting any additional efforts necessary to implement the 1994 Programme of Action.

Landlocked Developing Countries

Landlocked developing countries are more negatively affected by the high cost of export and import than other developing countries. The road map recommended ensuring that landlocked and transit developing countries and the donor community work together in the Global Framework for Transit-Transport Cooperation, helping landlocked countries develop efficient and flexible transport systems, and urging donors and international financial and development agencies to promote innovative financial mechanisms to help landlocked countries meet their needs for infrastructure financing and management.

Debt Problems of Low- and Middle-Income Developing Countries

The situation of these countries was fairly complex and difficult to generalize. The road map recommended that all creditors to developing countries be urged to support measures to ensure that debt financing would become an integral part of their development efforts and not a hindrance to them. It also recommended measures to ensure better coordination between private and public creditors of debtor nations and prevent the "bunching" of debt-servicing obligations over a short period. These measures would make it possible for debt financing to play a constructive role in development finance.

Making the Benefits of New Technologies Available to All

The road map highlighted information and communications technologies as potent instruments that could accelerate broad-based growth and sustainable development and help reduce poverty. Vast regions of the world were lagging behind in connectivity and access to global information flows and knowledge and were marginalized from the emerging global knowledge-based economy. Strategies to overcome these challenges included promoting universal and affordable access to information and communications technologies, supporting the development of human resources and institutional capacity-building, and building partnerships, including with the private sector.

Implementation, 2000–2004

The opportunities of the United Nations system to pursue the MDGs were circumscribed. Its own financial muscle was utterly weak and marginal in the face of the enormous tasks to be achieved within set dates. The road map placed the main responsibility for raising these resources on the developing countries themselves, although the industrialized countries had committed to assisting in various ways to the best of their ability. The major task for UN organizations, including the intergovernmental bodies of the system and the Bretton Woods institutions, was to maintain the momentum of the Millennium Declaration by keeping the MDGs high on the international agenda and urging member states to keep their commitments.

Over the years, the chief mechanisms for maintaining momentum in important matters have become well established. Regular reviews by ECOSOC and the General Assembly are traditionally used to keep an important issue on the international agenda. The MDGs were no exception to this tradition: the Secretary-General was to report annually on progress, giving the intergovernmental bodies an opportunity to make adjustments and renewed recommendations.

Major global conferences on the general theme or on important parts of it, with major reviews after five years, is another mechanism the UN uses to bring important development issues to the fore. In 2002, two major conferences were organized—the Johannesburg summit, which focused on sustainable development and the environment; and the Monterrey conference, which focused on financing development. These gatherings attracted high-level participation from governments and huge participation on the part of multilateral and international organizations and NGOs. And probably even more important, they attracted enormous attention from the mass media.

The UNDP administrator was assigned a coordinating role within the UN system in implementing the MDGs and in mobilizing the necessary resources. In the 1990s, the UNDP had increasingly taken on an advocacy role based on the human development "project" where the main focus was on policy reform, making developing countries "put development priorities right." In the early years of the new century, the UNDP extended this advocacy to include the MDGs. It also strove to adapt poverty reduction strategy papers, the main instrument of the World Bank for ensuring conformity with what remained of the Washington consensus, toward the MDGs and the human development index. The UNDP sought to combine the two perspectives in the planning and reporting processes of developing countries.

The first two years that follow a major commitment are critically important for its momentum. In his first annual report on the progress achieved in implementing the Millennium Declaration, Secretary-General Kofi Annan concluded that the results were at best mixed. In the future, he said, progress would have to be made on a much broader front. A coordinated strategy that combined the efforts of UN member states and international institutions and agencies with the efforts of the private sector, NGOs, philanthropic foundations, academic and cultural institutions, and other parts of civil society could make the difference between progress and retreat, he argued.[12]

Nevertheless, from the broader perspective of keeping the commitments made in the declaration high on the international agenda and maintaining momentum, the achievements in 2002 were quite convincing. The two major conferences that year—in Johannesburg and Monterrey—proved this success, although they failed to meet high hopes that they would produce agreed-upon outcomes. The World Summit on Sustainable Development in August and September reviewed the implementation of Agenda 21, which had been adopted by UNCED ten years earlier, and reaffirmed the UN's commitments to the three pillars of sustainable development—economic development, social development, and environmental protection at the local, national, and international levels. Governments agreed to increase access to such basic requirements as clean water, sanitation, adequate shelter, energy, health care, and food security. They also agreed to protect the biodiversity of their nations. In addition, they recognized the need for more effective, democratic, and accountable international and multilateral institutions so that sustainable development goals could be achieved.[13]

There were high hopes for the Monterrey conference in March 2002: it was to provide the resources necessary to substantiate the MDGs.[14] The Monterrey consensus generally aspired to eradicate poverty and promote sustainable development. The first step would be to mobilize and increase the effective use of financial resources and achieve the national and international economic conditions needed to attain internationally agreed-upon development goals, including the MDGs. Achieving those goals required a new partnership between developed and developing countries. The heads of state and government, accordingly, committed themselves to mobilizing domestic resources; attracting international flows; promoting international trade; increasing international financial and technical cooperation for development, sustainable debt financing, and external debt relief; and enhancing the coherence and consistency of the international monetary, financial, and trading system. The conference expressed support for a holistic approach to the national, international, and systemic challenges of financing for development, which were interconnected.[15]

The conference emphasized creating an "enabling environment" for both the necessary domestic and international capital for development and a supportive trading system, in line with the new Bretton Woods institutions/UN consensus on development paradigms that had begun to emerge during the 1990s. The central challenge related to mobilizing international resources for development was how to create the domestic and international conditions that would facilitate direct investment flows to developing countries and countries with economies in transition. The conference combined traditional policy measures with some new measures, in particular public/private sector mechanisms for financing both debt and equity to benefit small entrepreneurs. The conference reaffirmed its commitment to trade liberalism, stressing that trade should play its full part in promoting economic growth, employment, and development for all.[16]

A substantial increase in official development assistance and other resources would be necessary if developing countries were to achieve the internationally agreed development goals and objectives, including the MDGs. The conference again urged developed countries that had not done so to make concrete steps toward meeting the internationally agreed targets—0.7 percent of GNP in ODA and 0.15 to 0.20 percent of GNP to the LDCs. Debt relief measures should be vigorously and expeditiously pursued, the conference stated; implementation of the HIPC initiative required that it be fully financed through additional resources. It recommended that the IMF and the World Bank consider making fundamental changes in the sustainability of debt caused by natural catastrophes, severe terms-of-trade shocks, or conflicts when making recommendations, including debt relief. The conference encouraged donors to ensure that resources provided for debt relief did not detract from ODA resources.[17]

The changed approach to development assistance that emerged in the late 1990s was reflected in the August 2001 report of the Secretary-General, which established the basis for the triennial comprehensive policy review of UN operational development activities. He stated that poverty eradication as a central goal of the UN system could be linked in a more structural way to the development role each organization within the system played. Poverty eradication needed to be conceived not as a remedial or compensatory initiative but as the outcome of policies and programs that promoted inclusive economic growth and overall social development.[18]

Almost immediately, the UNDP made the MDGs central to its development work. These efforts included assistance provided to countries in preparing their MDG country reports.[19] It was active in placing them at the center of the wider system as well; Mark Malloch Brown, the UNDP administrator, had been appointed coordinator of the implementation of the MDGs within the UN system. The UNDP provided assistance to developing countries as they prepared their MDG country reports. The UN Development Group, chaired by Brown, was instrumental in shifting the focus of operational activities within the system toward the MDGs. As noted in the 2002 annual report, several countries had committed themselves to synchronizing MDGs with the poverty reduction strategy papers.[20]

The most important instruments established in 2002 to enhance the realization of the MDGs were probably the launching of the Millennium Project and the establishment of the Millennium Trust Fund.[21] The Millennium Project followed the UN tradition of appointing an independent group of reputed experts to explore and offer recommendations about how complex and daring ideas could be transformed into reality. The task of the project, led by a special adviser to the Secretary-General, was to generate fresh thinking about and identify options for achieving the MDGs.[22]

At the country level, the UNDP took on an increasing role in furthering the MDG agenda through national goal-setting and building capacity for monitoring, reporting, and advocacy. The UNDP's annual report for 2003 stated that efforts had been made to build national ownership of and broader participation in the MDG campaign: the UNDP was focusing on partnering with civil society with regard to MDG monitoring, reporting, and advocacy. The UNDP Evaluation Office, however, revealed that this was no easy task and that UNDP partnerships with governments and civil society had not yet been fully realized.[23] In an assessment of the MDG reports, the UNDP Evaluation Office discovered wide variations among the reports as advocacy tools with regard to country ownership, authorship, and value added. Contrary to expectations, the reports had not yet filtered into national debates on the MDGs. There was a need for convergence and stronger links between the monitoring and reporting processes of the MDGs, poverty reduction strategy papers, and other comprehensive national development frameworks and reporting instruments like national Human Development Reports, the Common Country Assessment, and United Nations Development Assistance Framework.[24] The critical assessment and recommendations made an impact: prodded by the Executive Board, the UNDP came up with a series of responses to the several challenges that had been identified.[25]

One year later, in a report that prepared the triennial policy review of operational activities for development, Secretary-General Kofi Annan indicated that substantial progress had been achieved in bringing cohesion to the system at the country level and in aligning its operations with the development agenda emerging from major UN conferences and summits, especially the MDGs. The system increasingly served as a catalyst for national dialogue among all stakeholders for implementing the MDGs, including within the poverty reduction strategy papers, he noted.[26]

The Recommendations of the Millennium Project

In 2002, the Secretary-General initiated the UN Millennium Project in order to develop a practical plan of action to meet the MDGs. It was to serve in an independent advisory capacity under the overall direction of

Jeffery D. Sachs, special adviser to the Secretary-General on the MDGs. The analytical work was based on the work of ten thematic task forces comprised of more than 250 experts from all over the world—scientists, politicians, representatives of civil society, development practitioners, representatives of UN agencies, representatives of the Bretton Woods institutions, and members of the private sector. These task forces produced a series of reports within their respective policy areas.[27]

The MDGs Can be Realized—with Intensive Efforts by All Parties

In January 2005, the UN Millennium Project reported to the Secretary-General.[28] Its bold opening statement was that "we have the opportunity in the coming decade to cut world poverty by half. Billions more people could enjoy the fruits of the global economy. Tens of millions of lives can be saved. The practical solutions exist. The political framework is established. And for the first time, the cost is utterly affordable. . . . All that is needed is action."[29]

Progress since 1990 vis-à-vis the eight MDGs had been mixed, the report stated. It assessed this progress as measured by the MDG indicators. The report discussed the reasons for the mixed results, identifying areas where regions had fallen short.[30] The report argued that both villages and cities "can become part of global economic growth if they are empowered with the infrastructure and human capital to do so." It argued that "governments must work actively with all constituencies, particularly civil society organizations and the private sector," noting that the MDGs "create a solid framework for identifying investments that need to be made." The "key to escaping the poverty trap is to raise the economy's capital stock." Geographical vulnerabilities "can and need to be offset by targeted investments in infrastructure, agriculture, and health." And "the major policy implication for middle-income countries is to ensure that critical investments get channeled to lagging regions."[31]

The report's overall message was that attaining the MDGs was possible, provided intensive efforts were made by all parties "to improve governance, actively engage and empower civil society, promote entrepreneurship and the private sector, mobilize domestic resources, substantially increase aid to countries that need it to support MDG-based priority investments, and make suitable policy reforms at the global level, such as those in trade." If countries gave priority to these endeavors and international society provided sufficient support, the goals would be within reach even for the poorest countries.[32] More strongly than ever, the report argued that development assistance—given such an enabling environment and if targeted in accordance with the recommendations—would be able to do the trick.

Country-Level Efforts to Attain the MDGs

Attention was first directed toward country-level processes to achieve the MDGs. Practical steps to achieve the goals in each country should be planned and implemented with the proper focus and actions and combined with suitable support from the international community. Although poverty reduction was seen as the primary responsibility of developing countries themselves, "achieving the Goals in the poorest countries—those that genuinely aspire to achieve the MDG targets—will require significant increases in official development assistance to break the poverty trap."[33]

The Millennium Project came up with a core recommendation: each developing country suffering extreme poverty should start by coming up with a national development strategy ambitious enough to achieve the MDGs. The country's international development partners—including bilateral donors, UN agencies, regional development banks, and the Bretton Woods institutions—should then give all the support needed to implement the country's MDG-based poverty reduction strategy.[34] A bold approach was needed, it was argued.

The project provided a long list of areas where developing countries could bring "vital gains in well-being to millions of people and start countries on the path to the Goals" within three or fewer years. Such "quick wins" could take place within a range of areas—for example, eliminating school and uniform fees could ensure that children, especially girls, were not prevented from attending school because of their families' poverty. Similarly, providing free, long-lasting, insecticide-treated bed-nets to all children in malaria-endemic zones could decisively cut the burden of malaria. These "quick wins" would need to be embedded in the longer-term policy framework of the MDG-based poverty-reduction strategy.[35]

The project clearly identified the core challenges to realizing the MDG-based poverty reduction strategy , namely financing and implementing the interventions at scale. National upscaling to bring essential MDG-based investments and services to most or all of the population on an equitable basis by 2015 required careful planning and presupposed political leadership and a clear commitment from governments. Once that commitment was made, the next step would be to set specific objectives and plans of work; build national and local capacity in public management, human resources, and infrastructure; adopt replicable and locally appropriate delivery mechanisms; and monitor progress and allow for mid-course corrections. The project identified two other conditions: involvement and ownership of communities; and long-term, predictable donor funding and technical assistance. A distinction was made between developing countries with clearly corrupt leadership and those whose governance was weak not because of ill will of the leaders but because the state lacked the financial resources and technical capacity to manage an efficient public administration. For the first group, there was little hope for major reductions in poverty; for latter group, the picture was brighter.[36]

Support of Country-Level Processes by the International System: Ways and Means

The project then turned to analyzing how the international system could help developing countries attain the MDGs. It focused first on the development assistance system with advice about how it might be improved to meet the MDGs and how the delivery system might be made better. It then went on to analyze the role of global trade and supplementary investments in regional and global public goods. The report's main attention, however, was directed to the role of ODA in attaining the MDGs.

The report criticized the ODA system for lacking a coherent MDG-based approach to reducing poverty. The Bretton Woods institutions should do much more to help countries design and implement MDG-based poverty reduction strategies, it argued. The IMF program design had paid almost no systematic attention to the MDGs when considering a country's budget or macroeconomic framework: in the vast number of country programs supported by the IMF since 2000, there had been almost no discussion about whether the plans were consistent with achieving the MDGs. And multilateral and bilateral institutions had not encouraged the countries to take the MDGs seriously. More recently, however, the Bretton Woods institutions had directed greater attention to the MDGs in country programs they supported. Among other major shortcomings identified was the lack of coordination among multilateral agencies: frequently they were competing for donor-government funding to implement small projects instead of supporting country-scale plans and budgets, and their activities were often not well linked to the local activities of the Bretton Woods institutions and regional development banks. Public investments could not be scaled up without greatly increased ODA. The developed world, there-fore, carried the greatest responsibility for ensuring that the MDGs were achieved, the project emphasized: aid flows were not growing as fast as had been promised, and development finance of very poor quality.[37]

The report proposed a range of measures to improve these and other major shortcomings in the current aid system.[38] First of all, multilateral and bilateral development agencies needed to make the nature of their support for MDG-based poverty reduction strategies explicit. They should differentiate their support according to country-level needs and support ten-year frameworks to anchor three- to five-year strategies to address long-term development needs systematically. Bilateral and multilateral agencies should coordinate their technical support around the MDG-based poverty reduction strategies. The UN resident coordinator system "needs dramatic strengthening, both to coordinate among UN organiza-tions through the UN country team and to manage a core technical staff to support the host government in developing and implementing the MDG-based poverty reduction strategy." ODA levels should be guided by the MDG needs assessment "rather than being picked for political reasons or on the basis of incremental budgeting, as is now the case." The total cost of attaining the MDGs in low-income countries was surprisingly low and could be met, the report argued.[39] Debt sustainability should be redefined as the level of debt consistent with achieving the MDGs by 2015 without a new debt overhang, which, for many heavily indebted poor countries, would require 100 percent debt cancellation. Bilateral aid practices should be simplified to support country programs to empower national owner-ship of MDG-based strategies and to limit transaction costs. Development partners should help developing countries promote overlooked priorities such as improving maternal health, achieving gender equality, enhancing reproductive health, and addressing neglected public goods such as long-term scientific capacities, environmental management, regional integra-tion, and cross-border infrastructure. Finally, donors should measure the coherence of their own policies against the MDGs: "Donors should subject themselves to at least the same standards of transparency and coherence as they expect of developing country governments."[40]

As always, trade was seen as hugely important for the development process. However, the report took care to emphasize that it was "far from a magic bullet for achieving development," especially in the poorest coun-tries. "Trade reforms are complementary to other parts of development policy, such as infrastructure investments and social programs to develop a healthy and well educated workforce." An MDG-based international trade policy should focus on two overarching issues: improved access to markets, improved terms of trade for the poor countries, and improved supply-side competitiveness for the exports of low-income countries through increased investments in infrastructure (roads, electricity, ports) and trade facilitation.[41]

National strategies needed to link with one another and with international coordination mechanisms to provide regional and global public goods. The report emphasized that regional infrastructure and policy cooperation are critical for economic growth and poverty reduction when an economy has a small population or the country is landlocked, a small island state, or dependent on neighbors for food, water, or energy. Any strategy to meet the MDGs also required a special effort to build up scientific and technological capacities in the poorest countries, both to help drive economic development and to help find scientific solutions to challenges in those countries. Direct public financing was needed to address the most pressing scientific issues. The report also emphasized the urgent need to address climatic change, which can undo achievements in the fight against disease, hunger, poverty, and environmental degradation. It argued that an international strategy for mitigating climate change is necessary, stating that the primary responsibility rested with high-income and some of the middle-income countries.[42]

The report argued strongly that a longer-term horizon should be introduced into international development policy with a focus on overcoming short-term constraints by scaling up approaches to meeting basic needs. At the same time it underlined the need to move urgently with specific actions, recommending "a series of worldwide initiatives to kickstart progress, translating the Goals quickly from ambition to action." While bold MDG-based investment programs could not be scaled up in developing countries "with extremely poor governance," many low-income countries have strong governance and the potential for much more ambitious investment programs. A quick start was recommended for these "well governed low-income countries": they should immediately be granted "fast-track MDG status" by the international community and receive the massive increase in development assistance they needed to implement MDG-based poverty reduction strategies.[43]

In addition, the report recommended that by the end of 2005, every interested developing country should produce an MDG needs assessment and a MDG-based poverty reduction strategy and that the Secretary-

General should ask each UN country team to assist in this process. Government ownership was imperative. Furthermore, a global human resource training effort should be launched along with "quick wins" initiatives. "International agencies and bilateral donors should work with low-income countries to prepare serious strategies" to train specialists at the village level in "health, soil nutrients, irrigation, land reclamation, drinking water, sanitation, electricity, vehicle repair, road maintenance, and forest management" as well as teachers, doctors, and other professionals and specialists in information management and finance. Middle-income countries should become involved in the challenge of meeting the goals, completing the process of eradicating extreme poverty within their own countries as they joined the ranks of donor countries.[44]

Costs and Benefits of Achieving the MDGs

The report provided calculations of the overall costs of achieving the MDGs based on needs assessments (in infrastructure, human resources, and financial assistance) for five developing countries. On this basis the report concluded that to reach the goals, low-income countries needed about $80 per capita in annual public investments in 2006, upscaling to $120–130 per capita in 2015. These tentative figures related only to financial investments directly involving the MDGs, excluding other goals that were financed through official development assistance, such as technical cooperation for capacity building and emergency assistance. Developing countries would need to increase their domestic resource mobilization, significantly, including "government revenues, household contributions, and private sector investment," to finance poverty reduction strategies to meet the MDGs.[45] In poor countries, this increase in domestic resources, even though very large as a percentage of national income, would not suffice: increased ODA would be needed to fill the gap.[46]

In contrast, the report found that middle-income developing countries would be able to finance essentially all investments without resorting to external finance unless they were constrained by excessive debt burdens. However, in some cases these governments might need extra-budgetary resources, including ODA, to increase investments for the MDGs; here, special reference was made to redressing especially difficult "pockets of poverty."

The total bill for achieving the ambitious MDGs by 2015, as calculated by the project, was surprisingly low and manageable, given the resources available in the world. The cost of filling the MDG financial gap for every low-income country amounted to $73 billion in 2006, increasing to $135 billion in 2015, while middle-income countries were projected to require $10 billion. However, these amounts were restricted to MDG funding. They should not be directly related to current global ODA, which was funding a host of other purposes as well. Additional development costs at the national and international levels included the capacity-building expenditures of bilateral and multilateral agencies, expenditures on science and technology, and debt relief. The total cost of meeting the MDGs in all countries was estimated at about $121 billion in 2006, increasing to about $189 billion in 2015 (in 2003 U.S. dollars), taking into account co-financed increases at the country level. The conclusion was clear: "Our results show that several countries will 'graduate' from the need for aid to finance investments in the MDGs before 2015."[47]

The report ended on a warning note, however: although fulfilling the MDGs would dramatically reduce poverty in all its forms, this would still be only a way station on the journey of ending absolute poverty. Extreme poverty will remain a major issue requiring ongoing attention. Although upscaling high-quality development assistance would allow many countries to graduate from the need for massive external budget support, the poorest countries would still require ongoing support equal to 10 to 20 percent of their GNP to graduate from external assistance. High-income countries would therefore need to maintain support at close to 0.7 percent of their GNI until 2025. "By 2015 extreme poverty can be cut by half. By 2025 extreme poverty can be substantially eliminated," the project concluded. "Fortunately, the costs of achieving the Goals are entirely affordable and well within the promises of 0.7 percent made at Monterrey and Johannesburg." At stake was nothing less than the credibility and functioning of the international system.[48]

The Midpoint Report:
Progress Achieved, but Core Goals Still Distant

In July 2007, the United Nations published the midpoint report.[49] In the foreword, UN Secretary-General Ban Ki-moon transmitted the core message:

> The world wants no new promises. It is imperative that all stakeholders meet, in their entirety, the commitments already made in the Millennium Declaration, the 2002 Monterrey Conference on Financing for Development, and the 2005 World Summit. In particular, the lack of any significant increase in official development

assistance since 2004 makes it impossible, even for well-governed countries, to meet the MDGs. As this report makes clear, adequate resources need to be made available to countries in a predictable way for them to be able to effectively plan the scaling up of their investments. Yet, these promises remain to be fulfilled.[50]

Although results were uneven, important achievements were recorded. This applies, in particular, to Goal 1, eradicating extreme poverty and hunger. Worldwide, the number of people in developing countries living on less than one U.S. dollar a day fell from 1.25 billion in 1990 to 980 million in 2004. The proportion of people living in extreme poverty fell from 31.6 percent in 1990 to 23.4 percent in 1999 and 19.2 percent in 2004. If progress continued, the MDG target would be met, the midpoint report concluded.

However, the success was uneven, since much of the decline in global poverty was due to rapid economic growth in Asia, especially Eastern and Southeastern Asia and India. In Sub-Saharan Africa, the proportion of people living on less than one dollar a day remained very high, although it had decreased from 46.8 percent in 1990 to 45.9 percent in 1999 and 41.1 percent in 2004. In Southern Asia, the percentages for these years were 41.1, 33.4, and 29.5, respectively; in Eastern Asia 33.0, 17.8, and 9.9; in Latin America and the Caribbean 10.3, 9.6, and 8.7; and in Southeastern Asia 20.8, 8.9, and 6.8. In contrast, poverty rates in Western Asia more than doubled during this period, although remaining at a lower level: the percentages for the years referred to increased from 1.6 to 2.8 and 3.8. In most developing regions, however, the average income of those living on less than one dollar a day had increased. Between 1990 and 2004, the poverty gap ratio—which indicates the depth of poverty as well as its incidence—had decreased in all regions except Western Asia: for the developing regions put together it had gone down from 9.3 to 5.4 percent. Sub-Saharan Africa was worst off also on this criterion: the poverty gap ratio had only decreased from 19.5 to 17.5 percent.[51]

The benefits of economic growth in the developing world remained unevenly distributed both within and among countries. Between 1990 and 2004, inequality increased; the share of national consumption by the poorest fifth of the population in developing regions decreased from 4.6 to 3.9 percent. However, the proportion of children under the age of five who were underweight declined from 33 percent in 1990 to 27 percent in 2005, still a very high level. Worst off was Southern Asia, although the trend was positive: down from 53 to 46 percent. The best performance on this criterion was in Eastern Asia (mainly due to the nutritional advances of China) and Southeastern Asia: down from 19 to 7 percent and 39 to 28 percent, respectively. The report concluded that the high proportions of children who continued to go hungry in Southern Asia and Sub-Saharan Africa made it unlikely that the target of halving the proportion of people suffering from hunger between 1990 and 2015 would be achieved.[52]

Some progress, although unevenly distributed, had also been made with regard to Goal 2, achieving universal primary education. The net enrollment ratio in primary education in the developing regions increased from 80 percent in 1990 to 83 percent in 1999 and 88 percent in 2005. Several regions were close to attaining the target in 2005; others still had a long way to go, despite significant progress. In Sub-Saharan Africa, the proportion had increased from 54 percent in 1991 to 57 percent in 1999 and 70 percent in 2005. According to the report, a strong push would be needed the next years "to enroll all children in school and to fulfil their right to quality education." Despite the progress made, the actual number of children not in school in 2005 was high: 72 million children of primary school age, of which 57 million were girls.[53]

The targets set for Goal 3, promoting gender equality and empowering women, included education as well as participation in nonagricultural wage employment and in political decision making. Doors had been slowly opened for women in the labor market, with distinct regional differences. Globally, the participation of women in nonagricultural wage employment had increased from 36 percent in 1990 to 39 percent in 2005. In developed regions, women's participation had risen from 44 to 47 percent and in CIS countries from 49 to 51 percent in this period. Southern Asia, Northern Africa, and Western Asia came out weakest; Northern Africa was at a standstill. In most of Africa and in many parts of Asia and Latin America, wage employment was concentrated in urban areas; outside cities and towns, most employment was still in agriculture and mainly for family subsistence. Women in developing regions were more likely than men to work in agriculture and as contributing but unpaid family workers, the report noted.[54]

Important strides had also been made with regard to Goal 4, reducing child mortality. In developing regions, the under-five mortality rate per 1,000 live births had been reduced from 106 in 1990 to 89 in 2005, while similar data for the transition countries of Southeastern Europe and CIS Europe showed a reduction from 29 to 17 and from 27 to 17, respectively. Sub-Saharan Africa remained worst off, although some progress was recorded (down from 185 to 166), followed by Southern Asia, where progress had been greater (down from 126 to 82), CIS Asia (from 81 to 72), Oceania (from 80 to 63), and Western Asia (from 68 to 55). The regions that could show the best results were Southeastern Asia (down from 78 to 41), Northern Africa (from 88 to 35), Latin America and the Caribbean (from 54 to 31), and Eastern Asia (from 48 to 27). Nevertheless, work remained to be done, particularly in Sub-Saharan Africa, Southern Asia, and CIS countries in Asia and in Oceania to attain the target of reducing the under-five mortality rate by two-thirds. Structural differences applied here: in most countries that had made substantial reductions in child mortality during recent years, the greatest changes were observed among children living in the richest 40 percent of households or in urban areas or whose mothers had some education.[55]

Vaccinations are a major preventive mechanism, particularly with regard to measles, a leading cause of child death. Globally, deaths from measles fell by 60 percent between 2000 and 2005. Numbers may be more telling than percentages: deaths went down from 873,000 in 1999 to 345,000 in 2005. Impressive, but there is still a way to go.[56]

In several middle-income countries, rapid progress had been made in achieving Goal 5, improving maternal health. Nevertheless, maternal mortality remained high; according to the report, half a million women continued to die each year across the developing world, particularly in Sub-Saharan Africa and Southern Africa, from treatable or preventable complications of pregnancy or childbirth. Worst off was Sub-Saharan Africa, where a woman's risk of dying from such complications over the course of her lifetime was 1 in 16, compared with 1 in 3,800 in the developed world.[57]

Efforts to reduce maternal mortality needed to be tailored to local conditions, since the causes of death vary across regions and countries, the report emphasized. Preventing unplanned pregnancies alone could avert around a quarter of maternal deaths, including those resulting from unsafe abortion. An estimated 137 million women have an unmet need for family planning, and an additional 64 million were using traditional methods of contraception with high failure rates.[58]

Goal 6, combating HIV/AIDS, malaria, and other diseases, showed varying degrees of achievement. In the developing world, HIV prevalence had leveled off. However, by the end of 2006, an estimated 39.5 million people worldwide were living with HIV, up from 32.9 million in 2001, mostly in Sub-Saharan Africa. In 2006, 4.3 million people were newly infected by the virus globally, with Eastern Asia and the CIS showing the fastest rates of infection. The number of people dying from AIDS was also increasing—up from 2.2 million in 2001 to 2.9 million in 2006. In the regions hardest hit by with HIV, more than half were women. Although access to AIDS treatment had expanded, the need continued to grow. As of December 2006, 2 million people in developing regions who were living with HIV in need of treatment were receiving anti-retroviral therapy, representing 28 percent of the estimated 7.1 million people in need, even here with quite dramatic regional differences. In addition, prevention measures were failing to keep pace with the spread of HIV. And providing care for orphans is an enormous social problem that will only get worse as more parents die of AIDS, the report noted.[59]

From other areas, such as fighting malaria and tuberculosis and other major diseases, more positive results were reported. Thanks to increased attention and funding, key interventions had been made to control malaria. Although several African countries had widened coverage of insecticide-treated bed-nets, only a few countries came close to the 2005 target of 60 percent coverage set at the African Summit on Roll Back Malaria in 2000, and a strengthened commitment from all concerned was needed to reach the revised target of 80 percent use by 2010. Coverage should be more equitable, the report asserted.[60]

Performance regarding Goal 7, ensuring environmental sustainability, varied somewhat from one target to another. From 1990 to 2005, the world had lost 3 percent of its forests. Deforestation, due primarily to the conversion of forests to agricultural land in developing countries, had continued at an alarming rate—about 13 million hectares a year. Trees had been planted, degraded lands had been restored, and woodlands had been allowed to expand naturally, especially in Europe, parts of North America, and Eastern Asia. Despite increased efforts to conserve the land and seas, biodiversity continued to decline. Furthermore, increasing greenhouse gas emissions continued to outpace advances in sustainable energy technologies. The Intergovernmental Panel on Climate Change had established that human activities were responsible for climate changes that create risks to livelihood and human well-being. The primary contributor was carbon dioxide released by the burning of fossil fuels. Such emissions had reached 29 billion metric tons in 2004 and continued to rise.[61]

Nevertheless, although global energy consumption continued to expand, progress was recorded in the development and use of cleaner energy technologies. The emissions of ozone-depleting substances had also been drastically reduced—from almost 1.5 billion tons in 1989 to 89 million tons in 2005. Since the 1990s, every region had exceeded its commitments under the Montreal Protocol with regard to concentrations of ozone-depleting chlorofluorocarbons.[62]

The report placed particular focus on the target added in Johannesburg in 2002 of increasing access to basic sanitation. Although progress had been achieved in almost all regions, there was still a long way to go to attain the region-specific targets set for 2015. For developing regions as a whole, the proportion of the population using improved sanitation had increased from 35 percent in 1990 to 50 percent in 2004, while the target set for 2015 is 68 percent. The report noted that with half the developing world without basic sanitation, meeting the MDG target would require extraordinary efforts. The health, economic, and social repercussions of open defecation, poor hygiene, and lack of safe drinking water are well documented; together they contribute to about 88 percent of the deaths due to diarrhoeal diseases in children under age five (more than 1.5 million), the report noted.[63]

The rapid expansion of cities is making the goal of improving slums even more daunting, the report stated, referring to the target of improving the lives of at least 100 million slum dwellers by 2020. Nevertheless, some improvements were recorded. The proportion of urban populations living in slums conditions in developing regions had been reduced from 47 percent in 1990 to 43 percent in 2001 and 37 percent in 2005, again with quite significant regional differences. Sub-Saharan Africa came out worst, followed by Southern Asia and Eastern Asia.[64]

Goal 8, developing a global partnership for development, relates to commitments involving input. As noted, increased ODA is a central indicator in the Millennium Project. (An overview of the performance according to this indicator is provided in the appendix to this volume.) The report noted that in 2005, ODA rose to a record $106.8 billion due to large debt relief operations, particularly for Iraq and Nigeria. In 2006, however, it declined by 5.1 percent in real terms; even excluding debt relief, it declined by 1.8 percent. The rate of increase in core development programs would have to triple over the next four years for donors to deliver on their promises, the report concluded. Since 2003, aid to address the special needs of the LDCs and landlocked and small island developing countries had essentially stalled, reflecting poorly on donors who had pledged to double their aid to Africa by 2010 at the 2005 Group of 8 Summit, the report added.[65]

Progress had been modest, if there was any at all, regarding other targets. In the Millennium Declaration, governments had agreed that globalization should become a positive force for all, through the further development of an open, rule-based, predictable, nondiscriminatory trading and financial system. The report found that preferential market access for most developing countries had been stalled.[66] The debt burden, however, had been significantly reduced under two programs—the Heavily Indebted Poor Counties Initiative and the Multilateral Debt Relief Initiative, the latter proposed by the Group of 8 and launched in 2005.[67] In all regions, economies had failed to reach the target of providing full employment for their youngest people. Worldwide, youth unemployment rates had increased from 12 percent in 1996 to 14 percent in 2006, while during the same period it had decreased from 16 to 13 percent in developed regions. Worst off on this indicator was Northern Africa (from 31 to 30 percent). The number of jobless youth had risen from 74 million in 1996 to 86 million in 2006, representing almost half of the 195 million jobless people in the world.[68]

Access to information and communication technologies had increased in all regions of the world, perhaps best illustrated by the growing number of telephone subscriptions and Internet connections per 100 populations. The number of cell phone subscribers worldwide rose from 11 million in 1990 to 2.2 billion in 2005; in fixed lines, the number of subscribers increased from 520 million to 1.2 billion during the same period. Thus, by the end of 2005, a total of 130 million Africans had subscriptions to mobile telephones—15 percent of the African population, compared with 3 percent with fixed telephone lines and 4 percent using the Internet. The number of Internet users was growing throughout the world, although it was still low in most developing countries. Whereas the number of Internet users in developed regions increased from 43 percent of the population in 2002 to 53 percent in 2005, in developing regions it increased from 4 to 9 percent during the same period. Nevertheless, such increases in a matter of only three years are impressive.

The Global Partnership: Lagging Behind

The midterm report revealed that progress was mixed when it came to MDG 8, developing a global partnership for development. In 2007, Secretary-General Ban Ki-moon established the MDG Gap Task Force to look into delivery related to the global partnership, the basis for realizing the seven other MDGs. The task force's report, delivered in August 2008, presented a bleak but mixed picture of performance regarding official development assistance, access to markets, debt sustainability, access to affordable essential medicines, and access to new technologies.[69]

Progress had been slow in meeting the MDG target of developing an open, rule-based, predictable, nondiscriminatory trading and financial system and providing tariff- and quota-free access for the exports of the least-developed countries. The task force pointed to the new challenges high food prices have created and the impact of such prices on poverty and hunger. It found that important progress had been made in meeting the target of addressing the debt problem of developing countries but emphasized that additional efforts are needed to make progress sustainable. By June 2008, twenty-three of the forty-one heavily indebted countries had reached their completion point under the enhanced HIPC initiative. The MDG target aimed at providing access to affordable essential drugs in developing countries had served to mobilize resources and improve coordination to fight HIV/AIDS, malaria, and tuberculosis in many countries, but access to essential medicines in developing countries is far from adequate, the task force stated. It noted rapid progress in making available new technologies, especially information and communication technologies, that are essential for increasing productivity, sustaining economic growth, and improving service delivery in such areas as health and education.[70]

We will focus on ODA performance, although achievements within all five areas are crucial for the ability to realize the aspirations of the Millennium Declaration and the MDGs. The task force found that serious gaps existed in the delivery of aid flows and that progress in improving the quality of ODA had been slow. Current implementation gaps "are early warnings of the risk of not meeting global targets within the time frame set by the MDG agenda and reaffirmed by Member States at subsequent summits and international forums." A large gap existed in meeting commitments toward the MDG target of addressing the special need of the least-developed countries and providing more generous official development assistance for countries committed to poverty reduction. Efforts to step up ODA had suffered a setback; the only countries to reach or exceed the UN target of 0.7 percent of their GNI in 2007 were Denmark, Luxembourg, the Netherlands, Norway, and Sweden. The average effort by the twenty-two member countries of the DAC was just 0.45 percent of GNI, but weighted by the size of their economies, total net aid flow from DAC members represented only 0.28 percent of their combined national income. The financial assistance to least-developed countries also fell short of the commitments made: in addition to the five countries mentioned above, only Belgium, Ireland, and the United Kingdom had met the target of providing at least 0.15 to 0.20 percent of their GNI in aid to the LDCs. The average for all DAC countries was just 0.09 percent.[71]

Aid flows began to increase in 1997, peaking at $107 billion in 2005. This was boosted by exceptional debt relief that year. However, net ODA in constant prices dropped 4.7 percent in 2006 and another 8.4 percent in 2007. While support for core development programs, excluding debt relief and humanitarian aid, increased by more than 30 percent in constant prices since 2000, the pace of this increase had slowed dramatically since 2005, the task force reported. It observed that slow progress had been made in meeting the targets set in the 2005 Paris Declaration on Aid Effectiveness, which the task force saw as the most comprehensive effort to date to improve aid coordination and alignment with national priorities. Efforts to improve the predictability of aid and to reduce aid fragmentation and high transaction costs in the administration of aid needed to be accelerated, the task force stated. It emphasized the need for further progress in untying aid and in improving alignment of aid flows with national budgets to broaden the policy space for developing countries to define their own development priorities.[72]

The task force felt that action was urgently needed to put aid flows on track to support the achievement of MDGs 1 to 7 in developing countries. Accelerated progress required explicit action, including the following:

- Donors should increase aid flows by $18 billion (at July 2008 exchange rates) per year between 2008 and 2010 to support core development programs in order to meet the agreed targets by 2010. In 2007, total ODA fell short by over $10 billion of the amount needed to ensure a smooth path toward the agreed target.

- In order to provide a manageable path to the committed increase in the annual flow of net ODA to Africa by 2010, donors should allocate an additional $6.4 billion a year to the region at constant 2005 prices (or $7.3 billion per year at July 2008 exchange rates).

- Even if the commitments for increased net ODA to Africa are fulfilled, donors should further increase their ODA to LDCs (many of which are in Africa). The total annual flow to LDCs would have to increase on average by $8.8 billion (at July 2008 exchange rates) during the period 2008 and 2010 in order to reach the target of between 0.15 and 0.20 percent of each donor's GNI.

■ Donors, including emerging donors and recipient countries, should accelerate progress toward the alignment of aid, harmonization, management for results, and mutual account-ability of aid resources. They should also improve dialogue with non-DAC donors to adhere to these principles.[73]

Some Concluding Observations

The United Nations Millennium Assembly provided a natural meet-ing place for most world leaders to join in committing the international community to seriously address the most pressing issues confronting the world. In the early 1990s, more than forty years of threatening super-power rivalry had been brought to an end. This directed attention more strongly to threats of a different kind and of even greater complexity that had existed all along: the threats of extreme poverty in many parts of the world, the threats to the environment locally, globally, and in the bio-sphere, and threats to human security. These threats are interlinked, and so are the solutions. The Millennium Declaration captured the moment. At a high level of generalization, but with specific goals and targets to be achieved within a given time horizon, it focused attention on how the world should look by the year 2015.

Solemn commitments of a similar kind had been made before, within settings provided by the United Nations—not the least the international development strategies for the four preceding development decades. By and large, follow-up by the international community has been disap-pointing. As has been pointed out, the commitments of the Millennium Declaration were not new. In a way, the declaration was the concluding, comprehensive endpoint of the outcomes of a series of global confer-ences in the 1990s. In the process, the conclusions arrived at became more general, whereas the statements of the more "specialized" global confer-ences had been both more detailed and sharper—not least those of the Copenhagen Social Summit.

Nevertheless, both the Millennium Summit and its declaration were unique, due to the unique setting. Despite previous disappointments, expectations were created worldwide that the beginning of a new mil-lennium could bring a new start. The heads of state and government of 147 countries were present, and an additional forty-four governments were represented. Furthermore, the Bretton Woods institutions had been brought into the preparatory process, modifying but also broadening the consensus and turning it into a New York–Washington consensus.

The Millennium Declaration focused on results that were to be attained within set time horizons, involving a broad range of policies and policy reforms. The input side was, at best, vague. As with earlier major policy declarations, including the international development strategies, main responsibility for attaining the ambitious results was placed with the governments, private sectors, and civil societies of the developing world. However, the better-off countries agreed to assist developing countries in their efforts. Such assistance was considered absolutely necessary when it came to the least-developed countries. Probably because of the poor follow-up of previous commitments—particularly involving the old commitment to provide 0.7 percent of GNP in ODA—the focus on results rather than inputs was broadly greeted as an asset, seen as a new and promising start, even from the most unexpected quarters.[74]

On the basis of the declaration, the UN machinery—the intergovernmental institutions and Secretary-General Kofi Annan—set out to work in the normal way, involving the whole UN system, including the Bretton Woods institutions. As noted, the UN system's financial muscles were weak: to achieve the aspirations set out in the declaration, additional financial resources outside the system were absolutely necessary. The UN took on this mobilizing role, including advocacy and education, almost from day one. As we have seen, the UNDP was provided with coordinating responsibility for UN system activities in this field and was explicitly expected to include the Bretton Woods institutions in the process. UN offices around the world were mobilized to maintain international attention and assist developing countries in establishing policy papers and a reporting system related to the MDGs. Most important, in keeping with a long tradition, the Secretary-General operationalized the commitments made in the declaration and called on a group of ("independent") experts to provide practical recommendations as to how the commitments could be met. In that process, attention was forcefully brought back to the input side. Annual reporting on MDG-related achievements became an important instrument for keeping the MDGs high on the international development agenda.

The Millennium Project may well be open to criticism for taking too lightly the social, cultural, and political complexities involved in the development process at the local, national, and international levels. The complexity of the poverty syndrome has been addressed in the extensive multidisciplinary literature on development. The very approach—setting timed quantitative targets involving complex, multidimensional objectives such as eliminating poverty in the world—may be open to question.[75] However, it is not an invention of the new millennium; it follows a tradition of national and international planning. In the UN system, this tradition is related to the international development strategies for the development decades that set targets for both input (such as the 0.7 percent target for ODA) and the outcomes to be attained in terms of economic and social growth.

However, no magic is involved. In the past, targets have not been met, particularly the most important input target set for the well-off countries —the 0.7 target for ODA. The probability that such targets will work is lower in an international setting than in a national one, where a government may be held directly accountable. So far, no similar international regime exists to enforce international commitments that governments make. This is not to say that international commitments are of no value. The UN system's follow-up, which has revealed the achievements and shortcomings of the governments concerned, provides an accountability function. However, ultimately it is left to the voters of the nations concerned to follow up with sanctions. The only exception to this is emerging slowly—the commitments of the European Union. It has become almost an obligation of EU member states to commit to provide a certain amount of GNI in ODA for EU development activities.[76]

The strength of the Millennium Project lies in its visualization of the opportunity that exists to tackle the major challenge of our time: ridding the world of extreme poverty. The forceful argument put forward is that the resources are available if only there is the political will, in developing and more developed countries alike, to fulfill commitments made long ago.

The price tag the Millennium Project set for achieving the MDGs was stunningly low compared with the resources spent on armaments or on military operations, as in Kuwait and the Balkans recently and in Afghanistan and Iraq today. The project stressed the importance of policy reforms over a broad spectrum, including debt relief and trade, but emphasized what could be achieved if the governments of already developed countries lived up to their commitment to provide 0.7 percent of GNP in official development assistance.

The 2007 progress report recorded important achievements, particularly with regard to reductions in the number of people living in absolute poverty (those living on one dollar a day or less), but it also revealed shortcomings, albeit with significant regional differences. Although progress had been achieved within some areas, Sub-Saharan Africa came out worst on most development indicators. The most alarming message was that the countries of the developed world, with a few exceptions, had failed to deliver. This progress report covered the achievements and shortcomings on most indicators up to 2004/2005, the date when the Millennium Project presented its analysis and recommendations. It cannot, therefore, be read as the response of the international community to the calls of the Millennium Project for a more intense commitment to the fulfillment of the MDGs. However, the report made it very clear that there is still a long way to go and that a more intense commitment from all parties—developed as well as developing countries—will be necessary to meet the goals, particularly in the poorest countries and those with pockets of extreme poverty.

The UN system will continue to have an important role to play in identifying the challenges, advances, and shortcomings in attaining the MDGs. It will remain the system with the greatest capacity to prod governments and people of the world to live up to their duties. As a development operator, the UN system will also have an obligation as well as an opportunity to rid the system of the extras that act to reduce the development effects of official development assistance. Such extras are not new features associated with ODA. From the very beginning, the development effects of ODA, particularly bilateral aid, have suffered from aid tying. ODA has also been provided to serve purposes other than those that focus on fostering economic, social, cultural, and political development. This has especially been a weakness of bilateral aid pursued to meet the security and foreign policy concerns of donor countries at the expense of development concerns. The UN is well placed to exert normative influence to meet this challenge. However, there is still a job to be done at home: the UN still needs to bring its house in order, not the least in the coordination of the activities of the system's many arms. This is not a job that can be done once and for all: it demands continuous attention and vigilance.

Much ODA has been distributed to recipient countries with governments that cannot be described as development regimes. This applies to the bilateral aid of major powers for reasons already given. However, transmitting aid to the "right" recipients becomes a challenge for the United Nations as a genuinely global organization, where the universality principle has ruled. The strategy established in the 1990s—promoting sustainable human development—was a way out of this dilemma. The UN's decision to make the MDGs the focal points in its advocacy and operational activities while keeping its focus on sustainable human development may put its development policy on the right track.

FIFTEEN

The Contribution of the UN System to International Development Cooperation

- Generating and Maintaining Norms
- Development Funding
- Long-term Planning of Development Activities
- Reforms of the UN Development System
- A Convergence of Development Policy?
- Power and Policies within an Egalitarian Organization
- Real Aid
- At the End of the Road

In previous chapters we have followed the UN in its role as a generator of ideas and visions concerning development, emphasizing one of the major instruments in this regard—development cooperation. Attention has also been directed to its role as an operator in this field, emphasizing its main instrument: the United Nations Development Programme and its predecessors. The system's many other development arms have been viewed mainly from this central perspective, with the exception of another major actor, the World Food Programme. Naturally, such a centralized perspective cannot do justice to the role various other institutions have played within their more specialized policy areas in developing ideas and following them up. Several of these institutions have their own documented histories.[1] In this volume, we have sought to capture the main ideas generated and implemented within the UN system, though those specific to the Bretton Woods institutions have been included only marginally. Indeed, in our narrative the Bretton Woods institutions have been portrayed more as competitors to UN institutions than part of the extended family to which they belong.

In these previous chapters, conclusions have been drawn with regard to the UN system's policies and its achievements over almost sixty years.

This concluding chapter focuses on the specific contribution of the UN system in those areas where the system has made a difference.

During the six decades covered in this study, the world has changed more dramatically than perhaps in any previous period, involving both its more-developed and less-developed parts. Against that backdrop, it is amazing that most of the major norms that were pursued at the beginning of the road are still at the top today. The language of "development" and "aid" has remained much the same. Promoting development in the large group of LDCs is still identified as challenge number one. Objectives to be pursued—such as human rights, democracy, and participation—are conceptualized in terms that portray a commonly agreed content reality. In policy discourse, these and other key concepts in major policy documents are seldom problematized. Participation, for example, over the years has been referred to as a valuable norm in almost all major UN resolutions involving development and taken as a given (involving "all"). What does it mean, given the reality on the ground—participation for whom? The people in positions of power (people with resources) in the academic and private sectors? Democracy does not mean the same everywhere.

Generating and Maintaining Norms

The UN system's two main pillars—promoting peace and promoting development—are placed on an unequal footing. While the Security Council may be able to enforce its decisions involving peace and security (should the major powers agree), promoting development, although it is strongly emphasized in the Charter, cannot be enforced. Recognizing this is essential for analyzing and assessing the policy and performance of the United Nations and its various arms. Contributions to development are voluntary.

Naturally, this affects the approaches to obtaining the necessary resources and the ways those resources are to be used. The UN is able only to a limited extent to generate funding for its development activities on its own (although it began to do so in the 1990s). Thus, it remains almost totally dependent on contributions from outside, first and foremost from its member governments. It is necessary to persuade member governments to contribute in order to secure resources for development. Trust, therefore, becomes the sine qua non for the organization and its many development arms—and here its image as an operator becomes crucial. A good image constitutes a necessary (albeit not sufficient) precondition: member governments have to be convinced that the task is worthwhile and sufficiently important for them to contribute. This is true for both bilateral and multilateral development assistance, although the opportunities involved may be different.

When development assistance was first initiated, most of the industrialized countries were in the process of recovering from a world war, while a new conflict was developing between the major powers that emerged victorious. This was also a time when social and political movements in the colonies were demanding independence and revolutionary movements were changing the political status quo in others, China among them. Development assistance became an instrument in this global fight for power, involving ideology as well as security. For the major western governments, it became an instrument to contain the expansion of communism and to promote democracy and a market economy. At the start of the road, development assistance was driven by the East-West rivalry. In those early years, development assistance was mainly provided bilaterally by the major powers—the United States and the European colonial powers in particular.

Involving the United Nations made a dramatic difference. In power terms, the difference was not earth-shaking: the major western governments could count on a majority in the intergovernmental bodies dealing with development and aid issues. They had absolute power of the purse: during the initial years, the United States alone provided half (and often more) of the development assistance channeled through the UN system.

The dramatic change involved in moving a minute part of global development assistance from the ministries and agencies of the major powers into the multilateral system relates to the differences between the two systems in perspective and basic norms. Typically, when UN intergovernmental bodies first dealt with this almost-new policy area, they anchored the new activity in the norms and values written into the world organization's Charter. Equally important, participation was broadened: new governments came to see contributions to development in "underdeveloped" countries and regions as part of their obligations as members of the United Nation system. It also affected the vision and purpose of aid. Both for the old donors (the major western powers) and for the many newcomers, the perspective, overall objectives, norms, and principles established by the UN for development assistance had an impact beyond the tiny multilateral development programs.

In setting these norms, the UN Secretariat (and key personalities situated there) played an important role. In the intergovernmental bodies, the U.S. delegation was at the helm in formulating the key resolutions. However, representatives of independent states of the South—especially in Asia, Latin America, and the Middle East—were actively involved in the process, adding legitimacy to the outcome. In the process of moving assistance away from one set of donor institutions (the major western powers) into another set of donor institutions (multilateral agencies), a transformation took place involving the perspective, objectives, and the norms guiding distribution of aid. The national flag was removed, and economic development (growth) in recipient countries became identified as the sole rationale for assistance.

The principle of the sovereignty of recipient governments was consistently pursued as a policy norm from day one. From the very beginning it was underlined that assistance should be provided only at the request of the recipient government. This was then further developed—assistance should go to areas and projects that were prioritized by the political authorities of recipient countries and integrated in their development plans. The delivery system was gradually adapted to this norm. The UN administration was brought closer to the government administration at the recipient end through the system of resident representatives. However, all along, it was the UN system—the UNDP as a funding agency and the many arms of the system as operational agencies—that made the decisions and administered implementation. It took almost four decades before the UN development system implemented the principle of sovereignty by transferring the responsibility for implementation to recipient governments, well behind the curve and with the UNDP also lagging behind most other arms of the system.

And here we enter one of the most sensitive areas of development cooperation. Almost in whatever form, development assistance is an intervention into the recipient system. It strengthens some of the actors in the political, economic, and social system and weakens others. Traditionally, aid has been channeled through governments, meaning that the main winners will be the incumbent government and groups with the closest ties to that government.

If the principle should be fully implemented, some forms of development assistance offer themselves as more feasible than others. Budget support with no strings attached would probably come closest to the mark. From the beginning, however, the UN system gave preference to project support, which allowed for planning and control. It was within this framework that the system opted for the best possible integration of assistance with the priorities of the government of the recipient country.

This ambiguity about sovereignty has all along characterized the aid relationship, especially aid through the UN system. In actuality, the agencies that determined and implemented the aid have had a strong, even decisive, influence not only on who received the assistance but also on the purposes it served and the principles that governed its implementation. In 1970, when the General Assembly established the consensus based on the Jackson report, even Sixten Heppling (who was critical of the practice of UN agencies assuming a dominant role toward recipient governments in aid relations and had roots in Sweden's Social Democrat government, which, more strongly than any other donor government, had opted to make recipient governments the real masters in the relationship) found that the agreed text changed the relationship too radically in favor of recipients. However, the polished norm, which was repeatedly reconfirmed, continued to shine brighter than the actual practice. Nevertheless, in the 1980s and beyond, both the principle and the way it was practiced by the UN stood in stark contrast to the strategy of first-generation aid conditionality that the Bretton Woods institutions generated and pursued and most donors in the West implemented.

The ambiguity remained. In the 1990s, when the UNDP generated and promoted the sustainable human development approach, involving most of the UN development system in the process, the principle of sovereignty continued to rule its rhetoric. The UNDP was riding two horses simultaneously—on the one hand actively promoting the "new" policy of sustainable human development that gradually became its identity and on the other insisting that its resources be distributed according to the priorities of recipient governments. These two approaches did not always coincide. Shrinking resources made it necessary for the UN to set priorities, and the outcome pointed in two directions: continued strong advocacy for sustainable human development, providing governments that wanted to pursue this policy direction with advice and support; and slimming and decentralizing the delivery system, adapting it to respond to requests from the governments concerned. At the turn of the millennium, the UNDP's advocacy of sustainable human development and its provision of supportive technical assistance to governments incorporated the Millennium Development Goals. The UN system continued to ride two horses into the new century.

Development Funding

Funding is fundamental to development, although it is not the sole factor. The appendix gives an overview of global ODA as the DAC has defined it since 1960. In current U.S. dollars, the aid of the DAC countries amounted to about 52 billion in the 1960s, increasing to 130 billion in the 1970s, 339 billion in the 1980s, 558 billion in the 1990s, and 420 billion in the first six years of the new century. Given the ambitious objectives set for ODA, the amounts set aside by the "developed" world to achieve development in the "less-developed" world appear decidedly modest, in absolute and in relative terms.

Much of this assistance serves quite different primary purposes than assisting in the generation of economic and social development: indeed, it may contribute to this end only marginally. This was the case during the Cold War, not least regarding part of the ODA of the major powers, which was provided with the primary objective of ensuring support and bolstering friendly regimes for security reasons, often regimes that showed scant concern for development. This is also the case today, especially after the events of 11 September 2001 and the subsequent "war on terror." Much of what has recently been recorded as development assistance has been spent on nonmilitary support activities related to the wars in Afghanistan and Iraq.

Humanitarian relief, although it has a *problématique* of its own, has always stayed under the ODA umbrella. In the early 1990s, a large number of human-made catastrophes exploded in many corners of the world that called for immediate relief—the "complex emergencies." As ODA became the main funding source also for natural disasters, the previous balance between resources used for "development" and for "relief" changed dramatically.

Much ODA has also been invested in the recovery process after such conflicts—in reconstruction activities. Peace and development have always been closely associated. In the 1990s, promoting peace and preventing conflict became an objective in its own right for development assistance. Greater attention was also directed to such objectives as promoting democracy and human rights along with "good governance."

The appendix provides an overview of the share of global ODA made available to the multilateral system, including the UN system. The distribution of the ODA of DAC countries may illustrate the point, although they have not been alone in providing development assistance. Over the years, the multilateral share of this aid has increased, from an average of 11 percent in the 1960s to 29 percent in the 1970s, 30 percent in the 1980s, and 31 percent in the 1990s, dropping to 29 percent over the first six years of the new century. The share of this multilateral official development assistance that was channeled through the UN system varied—in 1962 it was 24 percent; in the 1970s it averaged 27 percent, in the 1980s 26 percent, and in the 1990s 25 percent, where it stayed during the first six years of the new century. Traditionally, the World Bank (the International Development Association in the first place) has been the main recipient of ODA from DAC countries, particularly involving the main powers—on average, 37 percent in the 1970s, 35 percent in the 1980s, and 29 percent in the 1990s. The first six-year period of the new century was a quite dramatic change in this regard: the World Bank group lost its position as the largest recipient of multilateral ODA. Its average share of 22 percent was surpassed both by the UN system and by the European Union, which came out on top with 33 percent.

The UN system has made every effort to increase global ODA and the share of it to be channeled through the system. The main strategy was to establish targets to be achieved within set time schedules. The first target of 1 percent of the combined national incomes of the economically advanced countries was set in the 1960s in the international strategy for the First UN Development Decade. This target was not to be restricted to ODA—the focus then was on total private and official transfers. This target was repeated in a stronger form in the international strategy for the Second Development Decade in the 1970s. *Each* economically advanced country should provide "a minimum" net amount of 1 percent of its GNP to developing countries by 1972. Since governments had little if any influence on private sector transfers, a separate target was set for official development assistance: *each* country "will progressively increase its official development assistance . . . and will exert its best efforts to reach a minimum net amount of 0.7 percent of its gross national product at market prices by the middle of the Decade." In the 1980s, the international strategy for the Third Development Decade reconfirmed the 0.7 percent target and indicated a target of 1 percent of GNP in ODA for the future.

Although decisions by UN intergovernmental bodies are not binding on member governments and cannot be enforced, this does not mean that they are without value. They set international norms for UN member states and establish expectations as to their performance. The system's main instruments are information, education, and persuasion. Providing information has been a basic activity of the UN system almost from the beginning. The UN has constantly and prominently kept development on the international agenda in big forums such as the global conferences and in a host of small committees within the system. It has constantly reviewed the commitments made, recording progress or lack of such and issuing reminders about the urgent need to follow them up.

And yet these targets have never been met—far from it. During the Cold War period, Soviet-bloc representatives in UN intergovernmental bodies supported most Third World positions on development issues. However, when it came to financial commitments, the rhetoric of that same group was that responsibility for underdevelopment in the Third World belonged to the colonial and neo-imperialist countries. Although it was some time before Soviet-bloc countries started to provide support for UN development efforts, they did provide trade and aid assistance until the end of the Cold War, albeit at a level well below the performance of most DAC countries and far below the 0.7 target.

For some small and medium-sized western countries, the strategy did work, and in several other DAC countries the target was actively used as an instrument to increase ODA. In the late 1960s and early 1970s, when the three Scandinavian governments decided to reach the target set for DD2, they did so by way of stepped-up budgetary targets aimed at reaching the 0.7 percent target by the mid-1970s. After bringing their ODA up to the 0.7 percent level, Sweden, Norway, and Denmark continued through the 1980s to increase their ODA toward the 1.0 percent target; Norway even went beyond that. The international target set for DD2 and the target hinted at in the international strategy for DD3 were taken seriously by politicians and public opinion in these countries, and the targets were instrumental for the achievements that were made. A similar development took place in the Netherlands, which also attained the 0.7 percent target and then moved its ODA toward and even beyond the 1.0 percent target during the 1970s and 1980s.

However, the example provided by the four frontrunners did not have the hoped-for catalytic effect on the aid performance of the larger economies, with the exception of France. For the United States, whose example could be expected to carry much greater weight, the effect, if any, was negative.

The Monterrey summit in 2002, therefore, cast a broader net. The funding of the MDGs within a wide variety of areas required that resources be obtained from beyond the sphere of traditional development assistance. New emphasis was given to domestic savings within the countries concerned; a more liberal trade regime for the exports of developing countries; a favorable international and domestic environment for direct financial investments; and debt relief.

Three years later, the Millennium Project followed up on the Monterrey consensus. It once again emphasized inputs, using the long-established UN norm. It asked well-off countries to set aside a tiny share of their GNI (0.7 percent) in ODA, of which about two-thirds would be used for activities to achieve the MDGs. Together with dedicated efforts from developing countries (governments and civil societies), this would do the trick. The Millennium Project also argued for "real aid."

Long-Term Planning of Development Activities

From the very beginning, the UN system emphasized planning, involving both long-term and medium-term perspectives. In the 1950s, the UN brought the necessity of development planning forcefully to the attention of recipient governments. The UN's own planning during this decade was very short term; in those early days, the development system was characterized by short-term commitments to projects, usually a one-year time horizon. In 1959, the EPTA introduced a two-year planning cycle. It also built up the resident representative system to emphasize coordination at the level of the nation-state.

Long-term development planning was dependent on a long-term funding component, especially if the recipient government was to integrate development assistance into its own development plans. It was many years before even a few countries expressed willingness to make multiyear commitments to the UNDP, although the UN system had argued for this and sympathy for this goal had been expressed in intergovernmental bodies. The UNDP tried to set an example in its own practice by establishing multiyear programming based on its anticipated income during five-year programming cycles.

The strength of the long-term planning system was that it set an international standard of multiyear planning for development. This became an instrument for facilitating a planning process in developing countries. In the strategy for DD2, developing countries strongly committed themselves to establishing or strengthening their planning mechanisms and to improving their statistical services in order to formulate and implement their national development plans. The main weakness was obvious: despite the financial frames for the five-year programming periods within the system, actual contributions often fell short of what was anticipated. This often forced the UNDP to reduce the planning figures accordingly during the final years of the cycle, causing both disappointment and disorder in planning for recipient governments affected.

The system had a multiplier effect on bilateral aid. A few donor countries picked up the idea of multiyear planning and applied it to their bilateral aid programs. From the early 1970s, the Scandinavian countries provided the governments of a group of main recipient countries with an indicative figure for the ODA they would commit for a recurrent multi-year period (three or four years). The content of the program was agreed upon between the parties for the first year of the period and was detailed through annual negotiations the following years. Other donor governments also took inspiration from the example set by the UNDP to ensure reliable, long-term development funding.

Reforms of the UN Development System

The coordination of activities and coherence of policies have been under scrutiny all along, as has the question of aid effectiveness. Criticisms of the UN's development system have been followed by demands for reform. A basic reform took place when the EPTA and the Special Fund merged into the UNDP in 1965. Another and even more basic reform followed after the review of the UNDP in the late 1960s—Jackson's capacity study—resulting in the 1970 consensus, which focused on norms to guide activities as well as structural reform of the administrative system to enhance the organization's effectiveness and efficiency.

That consensus governed activities for years. However, with the shrinking resources of the late 1980s and the 1990s came new scrutiny, this time by governments that had traditionally been among the strongest supporters of the UN development system. The critique, which was directed toward the workings of the overall UN administrative system, made the 1990s a decade of almost continuous reform. In this process the UNDP found itself at the forefront, taking initiatives to involve other major UN agencies and programs—including the World Bank—in task forces to forge a substantive partnership for work on what had been identified as priority tasks, namely sustainable human development and poverty elimination. The primary focus was on providing policy advice and support to governments requesting this kind of assistance in pursuit of sustainable human development. Previously, the main focus had been "down-stream," assisting recipient governments with projects in areas to which they gave priority. This new focus demanded a differently structured organization with regard to the skills required and placement of staff. The reorganization of the UNDP in the mid-1990s involved both decentralization and a shifting of staff from headquarters to the regions and countries, in the process trimming the total staff substantially.

As part of the reform, the UNDP administrator presented a new vision for the UNDP in his business plans, which covered four-year periods. These plans were to be followed up each year by a results-oriented report and every fourth year by an in-depth assessment. The focus came increasingly to be directed toward implementing the MDGs. The UNDP made systematic efforts to combine the sustainable human development policy approach with that of the MDGs, especially through the poverty reduction strategy papers for individual developing countries.

Overall coordination of policy and operational activities has always been a challenge for the UN system, and its achievements in this regard have been open to criticism. Structural factors within the system have contributed to this problem. The various specialized agencies, programs, funds, and other UN institutions were all established with specialized mandates of their own, institutional structures adapted to these specific mandates, and (intergovernmental) governing bodies whose members often report home to the ministry responsible for the specific policy field of the organization concerned. The identity of each organization is related to the mandate, as are the competences and primary interests involved.

In the late 1980s and beyond, the UNDP, which had been assigned a coordinating mandate in the field of operational activities, was losing its relative position as the main channel of development funding. The same (donor) governments that were expecting it to fulfill this mandate increasingly channeled their ODA directly through the specialized agencies or programs dealing with the kind of activities they wanted to prioritize rather than through the UNDP.[2]

Major operations—particularly those involving humanitarian catastrophes—have repeatedly revealed the lack of effectiveness and efficiency and the weaknesses in coordination among the many arms of the UN system. The most recent reform proposal is the report of the High-level Panel on United Nations System-wide Coherence in the areas of development, humanitarian assistance, and the environment. The panel, jointly chaired by the prime ministers of Mozambique, Norway, and Pakistan, delivered its recommendations in November 2006.[3]

The report of the panel—titled *Delivering as One*—put the MDGs up front. The UN system had played a crucial role in articulating these goals, the report stated; it now needed to take action to achieve these and the

BOX 15.1. One United Nations for Development

The High-level Panel on UN System-wide Coherence in the areas of development, humanitarian assistance, and the environment presented the following recommendations involving development in 2006:

One UN at the country level with one leader, one program, one budget and, where appropriate, one office

The role of the UNDP should be changed in order to ensure system-wide ownership of the resident coordinator system: it should focus and strengthen its operational work on policy coherence and positioning of the UN country team and should withdraw from sector-focused policy and capacity work being carried out by other UN entities. Five One UN country pilots should be established by 2007, 20 by 2009, 40 by 2010, and all other appropriate programs by 2012.

A Sustainable Development Board to be established at the headquarters level to oversee the One UN country programs

A primary task would be to provide system-wide coherence and ensure coordination and monitor the performance of global activities. The board should be responsible for endorsing the One UN country program, allocating funding and evaluating performance in terms of the objectives agreed with the program country. It should also maintain a strategic overview of the system to drive coordination and joint planning among all funds, programs, and agencies and to monitor overlaps and gaps. The Secretary-General should appoint a development coordinator (the UNDP administrator) with responsibility for the performance and accountability of UN development activities. The coordinator should report to the board and be supported by a high-level coordination group, consisting of the heads of the principal development agencies and an expert secretariat to be drawn from across the UN system. The Secretary-General should also establish an independent task force to eliminate further duplication within the UN system and consolidate UN entities where necessary.

Results-based funding, performance, and accountability

A Millennium Development Goals funding mechanism to provide multiyear funding for the One UN country programs and agencies that were performing well should be established and be governed by the Sustainable Development Board. The current UN funding patterns would have to be reformed to make the UN system able to work more coherently and effectively. Voluntary donor funding (public, private, and UN organizations) could be specified. The panel encouraged donors to contribute multiyear funding and substantially reduce earmarking. UN organizations that were committed to and demonstrated reform should receive full multiyear core funding. The board should publish internal evaluations of the UN system spending and performance as well as evaluations of the plans of individual funds, programs, and agencies. The performance of UN organizations in advancing internationally agreed-upon development goals should be measured and should inform funding decisions. The modernization and reform of business practices, to be led by the Secretary-General, should be implemented as a matter of urgent priority. Program countries and donors should be able to see and compare the true overhead costs. A UN common evaluation system should be established by 2008 on the basis of a common evaluation methodology in order to promote transparency and accountability.

Source: "Delivering as One," General Assembly document A/61/583, 20 November 2006, 11–14.

other development goals and to support governments in implementing their national plans. However, the panel noted that "without ambitious and far-reaching reforms the United Nations will be unable to deliver on its promises and maintain its legitimate position at the heart of the multilateral system."

> Despite its unique legitimacy, including the universality of its membership, the status of the United Nations as a central actor in the multilateral system is undermined by a lack of focus on results, thereby failing, more than anyone else, the poorest and most vulnerable. . . . the work of the United Nations in the areas of development and the environment is often fragmented and weak. Inefficient and ineffective governance and unpredictable funding have contributed to policy incoherence, duplication and operational ineffectiveness across the system. Cooperation between organizations has been hindered by competition for funding, mission creep and outdated business practices.[4]

This diagnosis led to a series of recommendations where the central theme was that the UN would have to overcome its fragmentation and "deliver as one through a stronger commitment to working together on the implementation of one strategy, in the pursuit of one set of goals."[5]

The main recommendations of the panel with regard to development are summarized in box 15.1. The emphasis was on creating one UN development system at headquarters and the country level and a new funding mechanism governed by a Sustainable Development Board. The panel also emphasized that coordination should be extended beyond the UN system, with special reference to the Bretton Woods institutions. It noted that the UN and Bretton Woods institutions had been established with the intention that they would work together in a complementary way. However, over the years, both World Bank and UN institutions had gradually expanded their roles, leading to increasing overlap and duplication of their work: a balance needed to be struck between healthy competition and inefficient overlap and unfilled gaps, the panel argued, recommending closer cooperation between the UN and the Bretton Woods institutions.

Reform of the UN system has a long way to go. Many institutions within the system have established interests that may run contrary to the recommendations. The leaders of these institutions will have a say and so will many others with vested interests. The Secretary-General immediately initiated a consultation process within the system. The main recommendation of the panel—the creation of a development organization with one home at headquarters and at country levels with one voice and policy, one decision-making body, and one common fund—would obviously run counter to many established interests in a landscape with a multitude of independent or semi-independent "kingdoms" ready to fight for their "sovereignty."

This recommendation, if realized, might even be challenged from the point of view of effectiveness and efficiency. Given the complexity of most development objectives, small may be beautiful, particularly when it comes to some of the "soft" development objectives. Such objectives may risk being overrun within a large centralized organization where "hard" development goals related primarily to economic growth stand a better chance of being given first priority. This may be the case especially if the principle of recipient-country ownership goes beyond rhetoric. In such a setting, the ministries of finance, governed by a macroeconomic perspective, will have a decisive say about priorities. It is interesting, and in line with priorities repeatedly stated within the UN system, that the panel singled out one of the "soft" objectives to be strengthened through consolidation and centralization, integrating women's equity and empowerment in all activities of the system.

Still, from the perspective of the principles of recipient-country ownership and sovereignty, a centralized development organization with the one development fund at its disposal might be better placed to influence policies and priorities of recipient governments in accordance with its established priorities than would a multitude of smaller, more thematically based organizations and funds. The asymmetry of power relations in aid relationships is made more intense to the degree that power is central-ized on the donor side.

The panel had a strong case in pointing out the need for greater policy coherence and cooperation among the many arms of the United Nations system. For years, the UN's central intergovernmental bodies and the Secretary General have emphasized efforts in the direction the panel rec-ommended. Within the group of operative development funds and pro-grams (including the UNDP, UNFPA, UNICEF, and the WFP), the UNDP has spearheaded such efforts—since the mid-1990s with some success, as we have seen in chapter 12.

A Convergence of Development Policy?

The 1990s opened new opportunities. With the end of the Cold War, expectations of a peace dividend were high. A lost decade was to be fol-lowed by a brighter one. The UN system radiated optimism. While by and large the UNDP had followed well-trodden paths in the 1980s, the 1990s opened up the possibility of a new vision and reform.[6] However, the 1990s failed to meet expectations. Security issues remained high on the agenda. A series of regional and intrastate conflicts and wars, some of which were characterized by extreme violence, demanded most of the attention and resources of the international community. The peace dividend did not materialize. On the contrary, the countries of the sec-ond world disappeared altogether as aid providers, becoming recipients of both official assistance and ODA. Some major western powers, par-ticularly the United States, reduced their development assistance instead of increasing it. Resources for the development efforts of the UN system were shrinking. This, naturally, was a serious constraint on the realization of the UN's visions of the early 1990s.

Although many of the ideas that were presented as new in the 1990s were in fact not new but had deep roots in the declarations and policies of the UN system, some new elements did emerge. The UNDP's firm stress on human development—reinforced by the HDR project and the "new" policy of advocacy—introduced a new dynamism. Several institu-tional reforms to realize these norms and underpin the policy of human development followed, including a decentralization of management and decision-making to the country and regional levels, efforts to improve system-wide cooperation and the coordination of operational activities, and the transfer of much of the executing responsibility to the govern-ments concerned. Nevertheless, as norms these reforms were far from new: for decades, they had been repeatedly insisted upon by the main UN intergovernmental bodies, ECOSOC and the General Assembly.

The Bretton Woods institutions ruled the ground in the 1980s, ideologically and in their impact on development policy. Structural adjustment funding was the main instrument for pursuing economic policy reform. The Bretton Woods institutions mobilized all major donors behind the policy and made almost all development assistance dependent on the recipient government agreeing to undertake reforms (first-generation conditionality). When the destructive effects of the policy became evident, particularly within the social sectors, the consequence was unavoidable: an ideologically weakened Bretton Woods system faced the 1990s.

During the latter 1990s, this changed balance was instrumental in gradually forging a closer relationship between the two systems. Originally, it was envisaged that the two systems would be complementary, but because of dissimilarities in ownership and membership structures, they came to promote different (at times conflicting) development ideologies and concerns. The bank also became increasingly "intrusive," becoming a major operator into fields originally "belonging" to the UN system in the tacit division of labor between the two such as technical assistance, although this was a technical assistance of a different kind from that originally provided by the UN system. UN institutions (and the majorities governing them) saw an opportunity to influence the policy of the Bretton Woods institutions in the direction of the worldviews, development strategies, and objectives that had emerged from the several global conferences, not least the Social Summit in Copenhagen. The Bretton Woods institutions, on the other hand, felt the need to be part of these global processes and to influence the outcomes.

Although the emphasis on the basic elements of structural adjustment policies remained intact during the 1990s, greater care was taken to avoid negative consequences for human and social development. Nevertheless, the main focus of the World Bank and the International Monetary Fund continued to be on the macroeconomic dimensions of development and the norms that facilitated such development, including good governance.

Toward the end of the 1990s and increasingly during the first years of the new century, pressure from international society was mounting for greater cooperation between the UN and the Bretton Woods institutions. The process toward the Millennium Summit and its outcome was especially instrumental in this regard.

Does this mean that an international development regime is in the making? Agreement on general aspirations, including aid objectives at a high level of generalization, is essential if such a regime is to come into existence, but is not in itself sufficient.[7] Also needed is agreement among most actors, including the major ones, on more specific objectives and how to achieve them; procedures for implementing these objectives, including mediation and conflict resolution; and institutions to set policy and monitor and enforce the rules set.

In the past, most of these other components have been absent or weakly developed within international development cooperation. How weakly is best illustrated by the lack of follow up by governments and multilateral organizations on commitments made. Only a handful of governments have yet met the target of 0.7 percent of GNP/GNI in ODA that was agreed to almost forty years ago, and even fewer have met the 1 percent target. Governments have unilaterally decided the level of their ODA.

Nevertheless, a start has been made toward an international development regime. The UN Millennium Assembly was instrumental in rallying a stronger-than-ever international consensus around some of the general but vital objectives that emerged from the global conferences of the 1990s. The multilateral system—including the Bretton Woods institutions—took an active part in the preparations for the declaration. Although international agreement on development objectives was not new, the millennium process took the international consensus on common international development goals several steps forward. Although this consensus followed the pattern of previous strategies in setting targets to be attained by a set date, it further developed and refined these patterns. The targets were both more precise and covered broader fields. They were geared not directly to economic growth but to the human development and poverty reduction that might be generated through sustainable economic growth.

In 2005, the Millennium Project produced concrete proposals for how the MDGs could be achieved within the time schedules set—involving efforts on the part of developing countries themselves and from economically better-off countries. The project stated that the costs of eliminating poverty would be covered if the economically better off countries met the 0.7 percent target for ODA. However, no serious consideration has ever been given to mechanisms that could force governments to sustain their commitments of voluntary ODA contributions. Furthermore, no mechanisms have been established within the UN system to compel governments of developing countries to do their part of the job. That would run contrary to sacred principles within the system, maintained from day one.

Nevertheless, establishing a global consensus on so many vital development goals was no small achievement. The United Nations can rightfully claim ownership of the MDGs. The World Bank, which had modified its policies somewhat in response to criticism but stayed true to its worldview, was invited to participate in the process, both in the formulation of goals and in their implementation.[8] Much of the power of its financial muscle was still intact. In the declarations and plans of action that emerged from the thematic world summits of the 1990s, especially the 1995 Copenhagen summit, commitments were cast more broadly and sharply, and with greater specification, than those of the Millennium Declaration.

A third actor, the OECD Development Assistance Committee, played an important role in creating this consensus. In a way, the process began with the 1996 policy document agreed to by this group of western developed countries, *Shaping the 21st Century: The Contribution of Development Co-operation,* which was based on the outcomes of several global UN conferences.[9] In the DAC tradition, the seven international development goals extracted from these conferences were formulated in terms that would allow measurement and assessment of performance. The seven goals contained in this policy document came to be central when the leading agencies, which had very different points of departure, were under pressure to formulate an agreed policy platform to reduce global poverty. The negotiations between the United Nations, the OECD, the International Monetary Fund, and the World Bank resulted in a compromise.[10] The negotiations over what should go into the Millennium Declaration continued over the summer of 2000, with the civil servants of the United Nations serving as the midwives.[11] The dialogue on the unresolved issues continued between the main actors when the more precise goals and the targets and indicators had to be ironed out in the Secretary-General's road map.[12] Again, the main actors on the world scene managed to agree.

Does this mean that the question posed at the beginning of this section —whether, since the mid-1990s, international agreement has emerged on development paradigms and aid policy—should be answered in the affirmative? Probably yes—if the focus is on the direction of these processes within the multilateral institutions. The Millennium Declaration and the MDG process support such a conclusion. The 1990s modifications of the Washington consensus constitute part of the convergence. A modified prototype of this consensus emerged, mellowed by a growing concern about human development. It was followed by a firm emphasis on liberal political values, human rights, and democracy, subsumed under the concept of "good governance" by the World Bank. Concern for the environment, especially the global environment and with particular reference to Agenda 21 of the 1992 UN Conference on Environment and Development, became an important part of the new consensus. This blend may well be termed the New York–Washington consensus. As we have seen, development assistance came to play an important role in all components of this ideological mix.

This new consensus is a pragmatic blend that draws on many and different development paradigms. It reflects values predominant at the center of the new world order after the transformation of the international system of the early 1990s had been consolidated. The consensus has been expressed at a high level of generalization that allows room for widely differing interpretations about operationalization and implementation. Even at the theoretical level, the mix may allow considerable variety.[13] This may strengthen its robustness. On other hand, in the face of a major crisis, the consensus may prove fragile.

All of the millennium objectives are ambitious; some are also specific. The fact that agreement has been reached on these objectives is important in its own right, setting priorities and norms for international efforts. However, experience has taught us to differentiate between lofty commitments and actual performance. National interests do not vanish into the blue. Neither do practices rooted in a range of different values and ideologies or value systems rooted in national and international traditions. When opportunity and national interests click, they may get new lives. Such interests and values will be decisive for the extent to which agreed-upon international targets are achieved and for the role development cooperation will play in this regard.

However, the power balance between the Bretton Woods institutions and the UN system has not been fundamentally affected. What can be termed "hard" political issues, involving finance and trade, have increasingly been transferred to bodies where the major industrial powers are in almost exclusive control, such as the Bretton Woods institutions and the new international trade regime, the World Trade Organization. The World Bank has expanded its operational powers even within "soft" issue areas. In contrast, the UN system has been losing ground, discredited among the major industrial powers for lack of effectiveness and efficiency. The emerging power balance is illustrated by the fate of UNCTAD. In the 1970s it was the major instrument of developing countries in their efforts to improve conditions of trade. In the 1980s and increasingly in the 1990s, UNCTAD lost much of its influence (and eventually even its main mandate) to the WTO.

Power and Policies within an Egalitarian Organization

The United Nations is an arena where its member states—and increasingly also a multitude of intergovernmental and nongovernmental organizations and institutions—can pursue their foreign policy concerns, try to influence the policies of the other actors, and forge agreements on norms and resource distribution in accordance with their interests and values. As *the* global arena, the UN is important to all governments.

However, the UN is more than just an arena for its member governments: it is a bureaucratic organization as well, in the form of the UN secretariats. They bring forward initiatives on their own, guided by the solemn commitments set out in the UN Charter or the more specialized mandates under which they operate. The leadership of these organizations therefore matters, particularly for the major and strategically important ones.

From the very beginning, the United States has been a major player, influencing and to a large extent determining major policy outcomes, more so during the first decades of the UN's development efforts than in more recent decades. The mechanisms at play have been many, interacting with each other. The fact that UN headquarters is situated in New York should not be underestimated: U.S. domestic politics—the political institutions and mass media, even academia—have set much of the political agenda for those living and working with the UN, defining the issues that really matter and how they should be solved. However, the economic and political muscle of the United States has mattered more. The United States is and has been the hegemonic power of the West. For more than four decades it was one of the two military superpowers, and since the 1990s, it has been the only one.

During the first decades, the U.S. administration could count on a majority on most development issues of importance in the intergovernmental bodies of the UN. This changed during the late 1950s and the 1960s, when a large number of new states became members of the world organization. The United States has been the largest provider of funds for UN development activities most of the time, especially during the early years.

In the 1950s, it provided more than half of the voluntary contributions and about 40 percent in the 1960s—far beyond the share of its obligatory contribution to the regular UN budget. Although the U.S. share of total voluntary contributions to UN development activities remained high, the trend has been declining.[14] In recent decades, it has been surpassed by the contributions of the group of four small Nordic countries.

Since World War II, U.S. foreign policy has been torn between two main approaches, unilateralism and multilateralism, with the isolationalism of the past lurking in the background. Both approaches have been based in a realist tradition, although multilateralism has been associated with idealism as well.[15] Throughout most of the post–World War II period, and not least during its first decades, the multilateral approach had the upper hand in Washington's foreign policy—particularly under Democratic administrations—and this strategy has served the foreign-policy interests of the superpower well.

However, variations in U.S. foreign policy have impacted Washington's relations with the UN in general, especially in the area of security policy but also involving development funding and development cooperation. The United States was the driving force behind the establishment of the first UN development assistance program, and for years it provided most of the funding. The vision of technical assistance was powerfully spelled out early in 1949, in point four of President Truman's program "for peace and freedom in four major courses of action." During the previous year, the UN had prepared the ground. A little more than ten years later, another Democratic administration initiated another major operational UN program, the World Food Programme. More than that, in September 1961, President Kennedy proposed that the 1960s be the United Nations Decade of Development, thus emphasizing the need for a long-term perspective and initiating a series of international development strategies for the 1960s and then for the next three decades. Within the United Nations, the ground had already been prepared. The push from a new dynamic U.S. administration was what was needed for them to be realized.

This was the heyday of U.S. engagement in the UN in the field of development. The two new programs established in the 1950s and the early 1960s were small, both in absolute terms and relative to the much larger U.S. bilateral programs. A major concern in the U.S. decision-making process was that similar programs organized in the UN might negatively affect the effects of Washington's own bilateral programs: care was taken to ensure that this did not happen.

Once these programs were established in the multilateral setting of the United Nations, they began a development of their own. The national flag was the first to go, as the donor country was not to be directly involved in the distribution and use of the aid. However, countries maintained indirect control through membership in governing bodies and the power of the purse.[16]

During the early years, new and more ambitious ideas were generated within the UN system. These included the idea of a UN Economic Development Administration that would combine technical assistance with financial assistance from the UN and its specialized agencies. This idea gained strong support from developing countries but was not supported enthusiastically by the United States and other major western countries. Strong resistance, especially from the United States, greeted the efforts of developing countries and the UN Secretariat to establish a UN fund for economic development (SUNFED) to provide capital assistance.

The SUNFED stalemate of the early 1950s facilitated compromises by the major western powers, involving the World Bank. This concerned first the International Finance Corporation and, at a later stage, the establishment of a soft window—the International Development Association—within the World Bank. In a situation where the United States could not command control of voting power within the UN, its de facto control of the purse was decisive. Development funding with a grant component was moved from the UN system, an arrangement that developing countries and their allies preferred, to a system where the United States was in full control for most practical purposes. The governments in control of voting power—the developing countries and their allies in the West and East—lost the case, but they gained compensation in the form of acceptance for the principle of concessionary funding for development and a multilateral institution for such funding. The World Bank had been slow in taking on this task.

The distribution of leadership positions within the UN reflects global power relations as well as the power of the purse. The highest administrative position within the UN system, the Secretary-General, has never been held by a U.S. citizen, but this does not imply that Washington does not have considerable influence on who is elected. Traditionally, the U.S. president has nominated the administrator of the UNDP, the president of the World Bank, and the chair of the OECD Development Assistance Committee. It goes without saying that leadership positions of this kind matter for the policy outcomes of these organizations.

In 1965, when the EPTA and the Special Fund merged to become the UNDP, Paul Hoffman, the managing director of the Special Fund and previously the administrator of the Marshall Plan, became the first UNDP administrator. His co-administrator was David Owen, the British development economist (in the Keynesian tradition) who, within the UN Secretariat (as deputy secretary-general) and later as the executive chairman of the EPTA, played the leading role in shaping UN development cooperation policy approaches and institutions during the first, formative years.

U.S. presidents have, in realty, decided who was to head the UNDP.[17] In consequence, several "strange birds"—picked from quite different cultural environments than that predominant in the UNDP—have been brought into the top job. In 1971, when Hoffman retired, the Republican Nixon administration picked Rudolph Peterson for the job, a U.S. banker who continued in his job as director of the California-based Bank of America while serving as administrator. In 1976, he was followed by F. Bradford Morse, who had a past as a (liberal) Republican Congressman. In 1986, Morse was followed by William H. Draper III, a U.S. businessman who came to the UNDP from the position as head of the U.S. Export-Import Bank and (according to Murphy) was nominated to the UNDP position by President Reagan "at the suggestion of Draper's old friend, Vice-President George H. W. Bush."[18] The next administrator, James Speth, was an exception to the line of Republican nominees: this Democratic environmentalist, founder of the World Resource Institute, was nominated by President Clinton and served for two periods (from 1993 to 2000).

Of course the powers of the administrator have been circumscribed from the start. He was to report to an intergovernmental governing body that was politically balanced. He was balanced also in another systemic way: the associate administrator was almost always elected from the developing world or was an individual known to represent developing-country perspectives. Nevertheless, the position as head of the organization has provided ample scope for initiatives involving policy as well as administrative restructuring and, perhaps even more importantly, a decisive hand in recruitment of senior staff to move the organization in the direction of ideological and administrative priorities, as perhaps best illustrated during the "reign" of David Owen.

During the 1980s and the 1990s, important changes took place in the international political environments that affected both North-South relations and development cooperation. In the 1970s, the major western powers under U.S. leadership had fended off demands for a new international economic order, but they continued the dialogue despite the challenges these demands posed to their interests and despite the threats the repeated oil crises had caused to their economies. The United Nations, UNCTAD in particular, served as the main arena for these demands as well as for the international dialogue on these issues. With the regime shifts in the United Kingdom and the United States in the early 1980s, patience with the call for reform of the international economic system had come to an end. In 1981, Washington effectively cut off the dialogue. This had repercussions for the UN development system: resources began drying up. More surprisingly, this decline in U.S. contributions to UN development efforts continued in the 1990s, after the Cold War had been "won" and when a Democrat was at the helm in Washington.

Whereas in the past the U.S. influence on UN development policies was sustained through extensive development funding combined with explicit or tacit signals that this funding might be made conditional, in later years, such signals were actually followed up, to the extent of actual withdrawal from the institution in question. This was the case with U.S. membership in the ILO at the end of the 1970s and with UNESCO later. In both cases, the strategy paid off. Withholding membership and funding proved effective in influencing policies in the direction that Washington wanted.

This policy came at a price. At the level of global donor cooperation, shrinking U.S. contributions—in absolute as well as relative terms—made it less natural than before that the chair of the DAC should automatically be appointed by Washington. In the 1990s, the U.S. share of total DAC aid was down to 17 percent; the United States was surpassed by Japan and was not much ahead of other members (France and Germany) or the group of small Nordic countries (see the appendix).

In the 1990s, the United States was overtaken by Japan as the main provider of multilateral aid as well. With a share of less than 15 percent, it was closely followed by Germany (14 percent) and France, and the group of Nordic countries was not far behind (above 10 percent). The lion's share of U.S. multilateral assistance was channeled through the development finance institutions (the World Bank and regional development banks), whereas other donors—including the Nordics—showed a preference for the UN system. Thus, in the 1990s, close to 30 percent of the core funding of UNDP operational activities was provided by the four Nordic countries, far beyond the share provided by the United States.

In 1999, as Speth's term as administrator came to an end, the U.S.

monopoly was challenged, in particular by major European donor governments. The UN Secretary-General nominated Mark Malloch Brown, a British political scientist who had served with the UNHCR, had founded *The Economist Development Report* and, at the time of his appointment, was head of external affairs at the World Bank. For the first time, the UNDP administrator was not a nominee of the president of the United States.

More recently, U.S. leadership has found itself challenged even within the World Bank. In 2005, President G. W. Bush nominated his deputy minister of defense, Paul Wolfowitz, from the neoconservative core of the Republican Party, as president of the Bank. In addition to his baggage as one of the main architects of the preemptive war in Iraq, Wolfowitz provoked part of the Bank ownership (member governments) and the senior leadership by bringing with him his own core leadership for change. In 2007, when Wolfowitz for quite different reasons was forced to relinquish his position, the automatic election of the candidate nominated by the U.S. president was challenged.

The perspective can be cast broader than the field of development. President Bush's unilateralism became apparent from the beginning and was further strengthened in the wake of 11 September 2001. The ideological basis for the Bush administration's policies and the modes in which it has exerted power clearly indicated a radical shift of foreign policy paradigm toward unilateralism. This had fundamental consequences for international politics, including development policy, endangering the very future of the multilateral system.

Real Aid

Development assistance has had its strong proponents during the last six decades. In this volume, the main arguments for official development assistance have been shown in terms of the visions and justifications offered when multilateral institutions for development cooperation were established, international strategies were formed, and the need of more of the same was urgently reiterated by the intergovernmental bodies of the UN system. However, most of the time, ODA has also been under fierce attack from a wide variety of perspectives—theoretical, ideological, and practical, often in combination. Some of the major criticisms have been noted here.[19] Quite naturally, a recurrent theme has been: *does aid work?* Have the visions and the less lofty objectives set for development cooperation really been achieved?

Although this crucially important issue has not been the core question to be addressed in this volume, avoiding it has been almost impossible: in the UN system, it confronts you, in one way or other, around every corner. It centers on the effectiveness of aid in terms of the objectives set and the efficiency with which aid has been used. Perspectives have varied extensively—from critical views voiced within the systems themselves, often based on evaluations, to criticism of both the aid and delivery systems from outside the system. The focus has been directed to both the macro and the microlevel. Economists exploring the effects of aid at the macrolevel—how aid has affected economic growth at the country or global levels—have at times provided the most hard-hitting criticism, arguing that effects have been almost totally absent or even negative in terms of GNP growth. Given the growth targets set in the international development strategies for the first development decades, such an approach is fully justified. Critical scrutiny has also been directed to the effectiveness of ODA with regard to objectives related to education, health, and a range of other sectors and cross-sectoral issue areas and the efficiency with which this aid has been implemented.

This is not the place for an in-depth discussion of this theme, which involves empirical as well as theoretical dimensions. Some considerations involving this perspective may, however, be warranted. First of all, expectations as to what can be achieved through development assistance, especially in terms of economic growth, have been totally unrealistic.[20]

Miracles should not be expected. Just to illustrate the point: the total ODA channeled through the whole UN system in 2000 was at about the same level as the budget of the municipality of Oslo, which served a population of only half a million people. The total ODA channeled through the multilateral system that year—primarily through the World Bank group, the UN system, the regional development banks, and the EU system—was less than four times the budget of this municipality. Such comparisons, although both incomplete and simplistic, can help illustrate the relative size of the amounts involved. Various other factors than the financial resources available will impact what can be achieved or realistically expected from a given amount of money in terms of economic growth. The conditions for achieving economic development are quite different in an environment where the economic, social, and administrative superstructures are in place and are well developed than they are in an environment where these superstructures are weakly developed and need improvement as the first step on the road.

Clearly, all aid has not been effective in promoting development for a variety of reasons related to both the aid-providing side and the recipient side. The main explanation on the recipient side is that inadequate basic structures—including the public administration through which most ODA has traditionally been channeled—are part of the poverty syndrome. This applies in particular to countries most in need of development assistance: the poorest countries found in the large group of LDCs. Governments and multilateral aid agencies that direct most of their assistance to this group of countries—and to fragile states recovering from conflict and war—will, almost by definition, be most exposed to criticism for lack of aid effectiveness and efficiency, especially if the yardstick is economic growth (increase of GNP) and if the progress is measured using indicators for other objectives set for aid.

The importance of conditions on the recipient side for the effectiveness of aid has been recognized from the early days. A concern for the absorptive capacity of the recipient country has repeatedly come to the fore—often as an excuse for the modest amount of aid provided. Since the 1980s, the need for an enabling environment has emerged as a major—perhaps the main—concern in the discourse on development and aid. In the 1980s, the focus was on the need for economic policy reform in line with the predominant neoliberal ideology of the day, with structural adjustment policies as the main instrument. In the 1990s, the major concern of the aid community moved on to the need for liberal reform involving institutions and policies (human rights, democracy, good governance), again with aid as the main instrument involving both second-generation aid conditionality and "positive measures"—assistance for institution building and other measures assumed to promote policy reform and improve capacities.

Although donors have tended to focus on weaknesses on the recipient side in explaining the lack of aid effectiveness and efficiency, much of the blame lies with the policies and practices of donor governments: not all assistance recorded as ODA by DAC can be termed "real aid" for development, whether in terms of promoting the traditional objectives of economic and social development or involving the many other objectives increasingly set for ODA during the last few decades. Donor governments have tied aid to certain purposes and double-tied it to the delivery of commodities and services from their own countries, substantially reducing the real value of the ODA to the recipient country.[21]

Aid tying has been a part of development assistance from the very start. Efforts to untie aid have focused mainly on development credits and less on technical assistance, which almost by definition has been tied. So have also some other forms of aid, including commodity aid. In recent years, efforts to untie aid from national procurement have succeeded, especially on the part of a few European countries on the initiative of the Blair government in the United Kingdom. To some extent, this has been related to the "new" forms of aid that have moved away from project aid and toward program aid.

However, even more important, sizeable portions of the assistance defined by the DAC as ODA have not been directed toward the promotion of what traditionally has been conceived of as development. This applies to much humanitarian assistance—relief aid to meet immediate needs emerging from human-made and natural catastrophes. In the 1990s, the total share of ODA of this type of aid increased as a response to many violent conflicts. Although the definition of ODA has not changed since 1972, the interpretation has been broadened to encompass new activities, including the expenses of caring for refugees during the first year of their stay in the donor country.[22]

In the mid-1980s, the Development Committee of the IMF and World Bank initiated the first major study of the effectiveness of ODA under the direction of Professor Robert Cassen of the Institute of Development Studies, Sussex. As we have noted, the report offered a balanced conclusion—"most aid does indeed work"—but it added that some aid did not. It observed that "bilateral donors often have political and commercial motives for aid, which can interfere with developmental objectives. When these motives predominate, the results can be harmful to growth and to the poor."[23]

These observations have been echoed in more recent studies, including the report of the Millennium Project, which drew a distinction between ODA and the assistance needed to achieve the MDGs: about one-third of the ODA provided in its present form did not contribute to the attainment of the MDGs, the Millennium Project argued.[24] The Reality of Aid Network, which was established in 1993 and involves NGOs from the North and South, has scrutinized various aspects of development assistance with a focus on what has been termed *real aid* in a series of reports issued every second year (*The Reality of Aid*). In the 2006 report, the network argued that since September 2001 aid allocations have been distorted to serve the foreign policy priorities of "some major powers."[25]

ActionAid may claim ownership of the concept *real aid,* by which is meant aid truly targeted at reducing poverty. In its first *Real Aid* report, published in 2005, it made a strong argument for more ODA and more targeted aid. *Real aid* was contrasted to "phantom aid."[26] According to this report, at least 61 percent of all ODA in 2003 ($69 billion) was phantom aid, with real aid accounting for only $27 billion, or a mere 0.1 percent of combined donor income.[27] It stressed that although the final figures were indicative, "our results are at the more favourable end (to donors)."[28] The next report (July 2006), which focused on technical assistance, found that the ODA provided in 2004 showed some improvements from the previous year—real aid constituted 53 percent of total ODA. However, changes in the group's research methodology may account for some of these improvements, which would also necessitate adjustments of the 2003 results.[29]

More recently, Roger C. Riddell has systematically evaluated the effectiveness of various aid policies and forms of aid. His work confirms—about two decades later—the main conclusions of the Cassen study, although in a more subtle and detailed way. However, he adds a warning note about what we know and do not know. Concerning the question of whether *most* official development aid has worked or failed, he ends up by stating that the honest answer is "we still don't know—not for lack of trying, but due to the inherent difficulties in tracing its contribution."[30]

The focus in this section on the many distortions to aid effectiveness and on the need to provide real aid for development has been directed toward official development cooperation in general and bilateral development assistance in particular. However, the general narrative of development assistance also has a bearing on multilateral aid. After all, multilateral aid—including that of the UN system—is provided by the donor governments whose aid policies and practices have been scrutinized from these perspectives. The prime function of the multilateral system may therefore be to improve the quality of development assistance by setting norms and by transforming part of global ODA into real aid through its operational programs. In a setting in which different actors are competing for scarce resources—within the UN system as well as within the multilateral system and in the global aid "market"—the UN system and its various arms cannot take this role for granted. It presupposes norms as well as leadership.

At the End of the Road

What then is the most important single contribution of the United Nations system to development and development cooperation? The answer, naturally, will depend on the perspective chosen and will be highly subjective, depending, among other things, on where the person responding is placed and on her or his storehouse of values and experience. The reader will have an idea of my own background from the foreword to this volume. After our long journey through the UN system's development policy and performance, perhaps the following condensed answer may be offered: the most important contribution has been to generate and successfully promote globally a holistic development concept, almost consistently keeping the social and human dimensions of development at the core.

The main explanation for this is simple and is related to the systemic reality of a heterogeneous and inclusive organization. Starting with the norm that assistance should be integrated in the development plans and political priorities of the recipient government (and this has been largely followed up in practice, although the norm has been interpreted somewhat differently over time), the system has responded to a wide range of economic, social, and cultural realities on the ground and to governing systems across the full spectrum of ideologies. Resources have been limited and thinly spread, unlike capital-intensive projects funded by development finance institutions and major bilateral donors.

Lessons learned from this kind of a heterogeneous, largely horizontally organized and increasingly decentralized system will, by necessity, be different from those of a closed, vertical and centralized type of organization. This has always been the weakness of the UN system. However, it has also given strength to the system, especially in conceptualizing development and forming development strategies. Lessons learned in this way have been combined with overarching development perspectives. From the very beginning, the UN system has been fortunate in attracting and involving some of the most brilliant brains and most committed individuals, and it has increasingly included NGOs and civil society institutions in these processes. Developing countries have been represented (most of the time constituting the majority) in the intergovernmental bodies of the system along with economically more well-off countries, bringing the perspectives and development challenges that confront developing countries, varying from one country and region to another, into the bodies that have the final say. The setting has therefore been conducive for forming strategies adapted to differing economic, social, and cultural environments and political systems, based on a holistic concept of development.

APPENDIX

A Bird's-Eye View of ODA to Developing Countries and Multilateral Institutions

This volume focuses on the UN and its role in generating ideas and providing assistance to promote economic and social development in developing countries. As we have seen, countries all over the world have taken part in these efforts. Oil-rich OPEC members have contributed substantially through official development assistance as well as with nonconcessional transfers, particularly in the 1970s. Nevertheless, it is the industrial countries with market economies—the members of the OECD's Development Assistance Committee—that stand out as the major providers of ODA. Since 1960, the DAC has reported the annual flow of resources to developing countries and multilateral institutions from its member states with a particular focus on ODA.

This appendix presents some basic features of global official development assistance. It focuses on the amounts given and who gave it, the relative performance of donors, and how much aid was channeled through multilateral institutions. This information will put the magnitude of UN-administered development assistance into perspective. It will also reveal trends that have affected the ability of the UN system to pursue its aspirations using the resources placed at the disposal of its many institutions.

Definitions of ODA have varied over time.[1] The ODA recorded in DAC statistics is based on reports prepared by the participating governments. However, the DAC has scrutinized these reports to see how ODA was identified and what was achieved vis-à-vis targets and norms agreed to internationally.

Since similar systematic documentation does not exist for the ODA of other groups of donor countries, the statistical overview in this appendix is based on annual reports of the DAC. The main overview tables are restricted to DAC member states. They cannot offer a picture of total ODA, not even that of DAC members before they joined the DAC. To give some idea of the ODA of non-DAC members, the magnitude of this assistance as estimated by the DAC will be indicated.

The scope of this overview makes it necessary to be selective in the choice of indicators. The first indicator is the net official development assistance. Provided in current U.S. dollars, it gives an overall picture of the flow of resources from DAC countries to developing countries and multilateral institutions over time. It also identifies who the major donor countries are and how much each of them has provided as well as how much these countries have provided together.

In the late 1940s and increasingly in the 1950s, the main focus was the need of developing countries for capital and investment from official as well as private sources. A major concern was the lack of private capital flows. The quantitative target set for the First UN Development Decade reflected this perspective: each "economically advanced country" should endeavor to provide 1 percent of its GNI at market prices annually in combined official and private annual transfers. However, the statistical overview for the 1960s presented in table A.1 does not take account of this concern—it reports the ODA as defined at a later stage. ODA was singled out for specific reporting for the first time in the DAC's 1970 review, which presented data for 1968 and 1969.[2]

The target set in the international strategy adopted for the Second Development Decade was a minimum net amount of 0.7 percent of GNP in ODA by the middle of the decade. This target was repeated in the international strategy for the Third Development Decade, which set the second half of the 1980s as the ultimate deadline for latecomers.

The second indicator in this overview—ODA as a percentage of GNP—is related to these targets and gives an indication of the willingness of governments to meet internationally agreed-upon commitments involving the social and economic development of developing countries. In addition, it provides a good picture of the relative priority the DAC governments gave to this policy area. It also reflects the actual burden-sharing among aid-providing countries.

The third indicator in this overview is the amount of assistance provided to multilateral institutions for their development efforts. This includes assistance channeled through the specialized agencies, institutions, and programs of the UN system and the development finance institutions (the World Bank and the regional development funds). Even the assistance channeled through the EU (EEC, CEC, EC) by its member governments is included. For this reason, and because the primary focus of this volume is on the UN, this indicator will be further scrutinized in terms of its major components, thus adding to the aid profiles of the various DAC donor countries.

It follows that important aspects of the country profiles will not be covered in the five major overview tables in this appendix due to the need to restrict the number of indicators. This applies also to the conditions on which ODA is provided. However, we will briefly examine the generosity of assistance, in terms of the share provided as grants or the grant element of ODA.

The 1960s: Predominance of the Big Powers and Bilateral ODA

Table A.1 shows the assistance provided during the 1960s. Ten countries were members of the DAC from its inception—Belgium, Canada, France, the Federal Republic of Germany, Italy, Japan, the Netherlands, Portugal, the United Kingdom, and the United States. In the 1960s, six new governments joined the committee—Denmark and Norway in 1961; Australia, Austria, and Sweden in 1963, and Switzerland in 1966.

Total ODA in current U.S. dollars increased only moderately during the decade, from $4.7 billion in 1960 to $6.6 billion in 1969, totaling $58 billion for the period. As a share of the GNP of DAC members, however, a declining trend was evident: from 0.52 percent in 1960 down to 0.36 percent ten years later.

As a group, the DAC countries did not meet the target set for the decade of 1 percent of GNP in official and private flows. Performance varied between 0.95 percent (1961) and 0.71 percent (1963), with a falling trend. France managed to attain the target every year, while some other DAC members met it in some years.

In the 1960s, the United States was by far the main provider of ODA, contributing 55.7 percent of the total, although with a declining trend from the middle of the decade. This decrease was reflected also in relative performance: the ODA of the United States as a share of GNP declined from 0.56 percent in 1960 to 0.32 percent in 1969. Since the GNP of the United States accounted for 51 percent of the total GNP of the DAC countries in 1969, this decline strongly affected the relative performance of the DAC as well. France, the United Kingdom, the Federal Republic of Germany, and Japan provided 14.5, 9.7, 7.5, and 4.5 percent of the total, respectively.

During the 1960s, the relative performance (ODA as a percent of GNP) was particularly high for Portugal (peaking in 1961 at 1.73 percent) and France (peaking in 1960 at 1.38 percent).[3] Australia (peaking in 1967 at 0.60

TABLE A.1.

Official Development Assistance of DAC Countries, 1960–1969 (net disbursements in millions of U.S. dollars and by percent)

	1960	1961	1962	1963	1964	1965	1966	1967	1968	1969	1960–1969	% OF TOTAL	MULTI-LATERAL ODA AS % OF TOTAL
DAC ($)[1]	4,665	5,197	5,442	5,770	5,957	5,916	6,001	6,552	6,316	6,610	58,426	100	100
% of GNP	0.52	0.53	0.52	0.51	0.49	0.44	0.41	0.42	0.38	0.36	---	100	
Multilateral aid[2]	658	811	602	411	441	452	532	736	682	1,047	6,372	100	11.0
AUSTRALIA ($)	(59)[3]	(71)	(74)	96	100	119	126	157	160	175	1,137	1.9	100
% of GNP	0.38	0.44	0.43	0.51	0.48	0.52	0.53	0.60	0.57	0.56	---	---	---
Multilateral aid				12	6	12	13	24	13	16	96	1.5	10.3
AUSTRIA ($)[1]	(---)	(3)	(7)	2	12	31	32	26	23	15	151	0.3	100
% of GNP	---	0.04	0.10	0.03	0.14	0.34	0.31	0.24	0.20	0.12	---	---	---
Multilateral aid				2	5	3	6	7	9	9	41	0.6	29.1

BELGIUM ($)	101	92	70	80	71	102	76	89	88	116	885	1.5	100
% of GNP	0.88	0.76	0.54	0.57	0.45	0.59	0.42	0.45	0.42	0.51	---	---	---
Multilateral aid	19	23	15	17	2	8	6	24	14	31	159	2.5	18.0
CANADA ($)	75	61	35	64	78	96	187	198	175	245	1,214	2.1	100
% of GNP	0.19	0.16	0.09	0.15	0.7	0.19	0.33	0.32	0.26	0.34	---	---	---
Multilateral aid	27	16	13	8	16	28	31	46	33	85	303	4.8	25.0
DENMARK ($)[1]	(5)	8	7	9	10	13	21	26	29	54	182	0.3	100
% of GNP	0.09	0.12	0.10	0.11	0.11	0.13	0.19	0.21	0.23	0.39	---	---	---
Multilateral aid		6	7	9	8	8	16	16	13	23	106	1.7	59.9
FRANCE ($)[4]	823	903	945	820	828	752	745	826	853	955	8,450	14.5	100
% of GNP	1.38	1.35	1.26	0.98	0.89	0.75	0.69	0.71	0.67	0.68	---	---	---
Multilateral aid	60	73	116	29	21	28	29	43	39	95	533	8.4	6.3
GERMANY ($)	223	366	405	389	459	456	419	509	557	579	4,362	7.5	100
% of GNP	0.31	0.44	0.45	0.41	0.44	0.40	0.34	0.41	0.41	0.38	---	---	---
Multilateral aid	101	286	102	25	10	39	36	54	100	128	881	13.8	20.2

	1960	1961	1962	1963	1964	1965	1966	1967	1968	1969	1960–1969	% OF TOTAL	MULTI-LATERAL ODA AS % OF TOTAL
ITALY ($)	77	60	80	70	48	60	78	155	146	130	904	1.5	100
% of GNP	0.22	0.15	0.18	0.14	0.09	0.10	0.12	0.22	0.19	0.16	---	---	---
Multilateral aid	27	20	32	1	-5	39	91	34	24	25	288	4.5	31.9
JAPAN ($)	105	108	85	137	116	244	283	384	356	436	2,254	3.9	100
% of GNP	0.24	0.20	0.15	0.20	0.15	0.28	0.28	0.32	0.25	0.26	---	---	---
Multilateral aid	41	11	7	12	10	17	51	45	48	96	338	5.3	15.0
NETHERLANDS ($)	35	56	65	38	49	70	94	113	123	143	786	1.3	100
% of GNP	0.31	0.45	0.48	0.26	0.28	0.36	0.45	0.49	0.49	0.51	---	---	---
Multilateral aid	22	39	44	20	15	23	42	38	24	38	305	4.8	38.8
NORWAY ($)[1]	(5)	7	7	10	9	11	14	14	27	30	134	0.2	100
% of GNP	0.11	0.14	0.14	0.17	0.15	0.16	0.18	0.17	0.29	0.30	---	---	---
Multilateral aid		8	6	18	14	8	8	11	14	61	148	2.3	114.7

PORTUGAL ($)	37	46	36	45	50	22	20	25	27	58	366	0.6	100
% of GNP	1.45	1.73	1.25	1.44	1.47	1.59	0.49	0.54	0.54	1.02	---	---	---
Multilateral aid	---	8	---	---	---	---	2	---	---	---	10	0.2	2.7
SWEDEN ($)[1]	(7)	(8)	(19)	23	33	38	57	60	71	121	437	0.7	100
% of GNP	0.05	0.06	0.12	0.14	0.18	0.19	0.26	0.25	0.28	0.43	---	---	---
Multilateral aid				16	19	21	33	39	30	66	224	3.5	55.6
SWITZERLAND ($)	(4)	(8)	(5)	(6)	(9)	(12)	13	13	24	30	124	0.2	100
% of GNP	0.04	0.08	0.05	0.05	0.07	0.08	0.08	0.08	0.14	0.16	---	---	---
Multilateral aid							-8	-3	9	12	10	0.2	12.5
UNITED KINGDOM ($)	407	457	421	414	493	472	486	485	415	431	4,481	9.7	100
% of GNP	0.56	0.59	0.52	0.48	0.53	0.47	0.46	0.44	0.40	0.39	---	---	---
Multilateral aid	95	40	41	45	46	53	56	53	62	73	564	8.9	12.6

	1960	1961	1962	1963	1964	1965	1966	1967	1968	1969	1960–1969	% OF TOTAL	MULTI-LATERAL ODA AS % OF TOTAL
UNITED STATES ($)	2,702	2,943	3,181	3,567	3,592	3,418	3,349	3,472	3,242	3,092	32,558	55.7	100
% of GNP	0.56	0.59	0.56	0.49	0.44	0.43	0.37	0.33	0.31	0.32	----	----	----
Multilateral aid	265	285	219	198	275	164	112	310	252	330	2,410	37.8	7.4

Sources: OECD, *Development Assistance, 1971 Review* (Paris: OECD DAC, 1971), table 2 (for total in U.S. dollars) and table 8 (for ODA as a percent of GNP). For contributions to multilateral institutions in U.S. dollars, see OECD, *Development Assistance Efforts and Policies in 1961 of the Members of the Development Assistance Committee* (Paris: OECD DAC, 1962), table 2 (for 1960); OECD, *Development Assistance Efforts and Policies of the Members of the Development Assistance Committee, 1964 Review* (Paris: OECD DAC, 1964), table 1 (for 1961 and 1962); OECD, *Development Assistance Efforts and Policies of the Members of the Development Assistance Committee, 1966 Review* (Paris: OECD DAC, 1966), table 5 (for 1963) and table 6 (for 1964); OECD, *Development Assistance Efforts and Policies of the Members of the Development Assistance Committee, 1967 Review* (Paris: OECD DAC, 1967), table 4 (for 1965); OECD, *Development Assistance Efforts and Policies of the Members of the Development Assistance Committee, 1968 Review* (Paris: OECD DAC, 1968), table 4 (for 1966); OECD, *Development Assistance Efforts and Policies of the Members of the Development Assistance Committee, 1969 Review* (Paris: OECD DAC, 1969), table 5 (for 1967); OECD, *Development Assistance Efforts and Policies of the Members of the Development Assistance Committee, 1970 Review* (Paris: OECD DAC, 1970), table 5 (for 1968); and OECD, *1971 Review*, table 5 (for 1969). Some discrepancies exist between the different OECD sources used.

1. The annual reports of the chairman of the DAC provided separate figures for official development assistance for the first time in OECD, *1970 Review;* the first year covered was 1968. Before that, the focus was on the flow of long-term official (and private) resources. For some countries, the flows of official resources were identical with their ODA contributions, but this was not the case for all of them, particularly not the major ones. In, OECD, *1971 Review,* the ODA for the previous decade (1960 to 1970) was calculated in two tables that gave total ODA (in U.S. dollars and as a percent of GNP)—tables 2 and 8, respectively. I decided to base table A.1 on these data, even though they were partially misleading; they included the ODA of all countries that were DAC members by 1970. The original ten members were Belgium, Canada, France, Germany, Italy, Japan, Netherlands, Portugal, the United Kingdom, and the United States. In 1961, Denmark and Norway joined, followed by Australia, Austria, and Sweden in 1963 and Switzerland in 1966. Their ODA before becoming DAC mem-

bers (given in parentheses in the table) is included in the ODA attributed to DAC for the single years and for the decade, thus increasing the DAC total by $302 million for the decade, representing 0.5 percent of the total ($80, 90, 105, 5. 9 and 12 million, respectively, the first six years). The correct ODA for DAC for the decade would, accordingly, be $58,123. However, for the single years and the period, table A.1 shows ODA in dollars and as percent of GNP for the individual countries that were DAC members in 1969 and their total ODA. My calculation of the share of total ODA provided by each country is based on these data. The contributions to multilateral institutions in table A.1 are drawn from the annual DAC reviews (which are limited, of course, to DAC countries while they were members) and, accordingly, give the correct amount for DAC. The calculations of the shares individual donor countries provided to international institutions are based on these data. A problem appeared when calculating the share provided multilaterally by the DAC and its member countries. These calculations are based on the ODA of DAC countries when they actually were DAC members, deducting the amounts given in parenthesis from the totals given (in table A.1) for the latecomers. For the DAC, this calculation is based on a DAC total of $58.123 million. The overview given in table A.1 is therefore not totally perfect for reasons given (and may even cause confusion if this explanatory note is not taken into account). Nevertheless, the picture provided captures the developments as reported by the DAC during the first decade of the organization.

2. Include grants and capital subscription payments and purchases of bonds, loans, and participation with maturities of more than one year.

3. Values in parentheses indicate ODA of a country before it joined the DAC.

4. France's ODA includes its contributions to its Départements d'Outre-Mer and Territoires d'Outre-Mer.

percent), Belgium (peaking in 1960 at 0.88 percent), the United Kingdom (peaking in 1961 at 0.59 percent), and the Netherlands (peaking in 1969 at 0.51 percent) also scored relatively high on this measure.

Only about 11 percent of total ODA in the 1960s was channeled multilaterally; this includes the contributions to all specialized agencies, organizations, and programs within the UN system and to the development finance institutions, including the World Bank. More than anything else, this small percentage indicates the preference for bilateral assistance during the 1960s. At this time, the major western powers were the main providers of development assistance. Multilateral assistance was almost an afterthought in aid programs of the 1960s.

The United States was also the main provider of multilateral ODA. However, its position here was less dominant than for total ODA: in the 1960s, it provided about 38 percent of total multilateral contributions. The trend was a downward one: from 40 percent in 1960 to 32 percent in 1969.

The $6.3 billion channeled through a variety of multilateral institutions was provided partly on a grant basis and partly as loans (see table A.2). The conditions on which official assistance was provided varied over time and from one country to another: a few countries provided all or almost all of their assistance in the form of grants, while other countries provided a mix of grants and loans, with conditions (interest rate, durations, etc.) varying from soft to hard terms. Some of the assistance was tied. The share of ODA provided on a grant basis is probably the best single indicator of the generosity of the assistance.

The 1970s: Smaller Powers Making a Difference— Growing ODA

The late 1960s brought new dynamism to development efforts. In 1969, the report of the Commission of International Development, chaired by Lester Pearson, recommended a general increase in development assistance and argued that it should be provided on more generous terms (including progressive untying of aid).[4] It also recommended that a larger share of the assistance be multilateral rather than bilateral. Probably with the major powers in mind, the report argued that "aid providers [should] increase grants and capital subscriptions for multilateral development aid programmes to a minimum of 20 per cent of the total flow of official development assistance by 1975." It emphasized

TABLE A.2.

Official Development Assistance of DAC Countries to Multilateral
Institutions in the 1960s (selected years, by percent and in millions
of U.S. dollars)

	1962	1966	1969
EEC/EDF	34.9	6.1	10.4
World Bank, including the IDA	29.3	42.9	33.0
UN agencies	24.2	42.3	29.5
Others (including the Inter-American Development Bank and the Asian Development Bank)	11.6	8.6	27.2
TOTAL[1]	100.0	99.9	100.1
Millions of U.S. dollars	601.8	532.0	1,046.9

Source: OECD, *1964 Review,* table 4; OECD, *1968 Review,* table 4, and OECD, *1972 Review,*
table 7 (for 1969), and calculations based on data in these sources.

The category of ODA contributions is comprised of grants and capital subscription payments and purchases and sales of bonds, loans, and participations with maturities of
more than one year. However, during the early years, most contributions were provided
as grants. For the years selected here, grants and capital subscriptions made up 98.6 percent (1962), 90.0 percent (1966), and 44.2 percent (1969), respectively.

1. Percentages do not always add up to exactly 100 because of rounding in the data
from which calculations were made.

the need to broaden the scope of the IDA and the regional development
banks.[5] Even more importantly, the UN system adopted this target for
official development assistance in the strategy for its Second Development
Decade—0.7 percent of GNP in ODA.

The ODA of the DAC and its member countries in the 1970s is given
in table A.3. We note that two more countries became DAC members
during this period, New Zealand (1972) and Finland (1973). Portugal was
in and out of the committee. However, only the performance of DAC
members while they were members is shown in the table. The value of
the total DAC assistance in terms of current U.S. dollars rose from $6.8
billion in 1970 to $22.4 billion in 1979. Total assistance during this decade
amounted to $129.6 billion, an impressive increase of 222 percent from
the previous decade.[6]

TABLE A.3.

Official Development Assistance of DAC Countries, 1970–1979 (net disbursements in millions of U.S. dollars and by percent)

	1970	1971	1972	1973	1974	1975	1976	1977	1978	1979	1970–1979	% OF TOTAL	MULTI-LATERAL ODA AS % OF TOTAL
DAC ($)	6,840	7,759	8,672	9,351	11,317	13,585	13,948	15,722	19,986	22,419	129,599	100	100
% of GNP	0.34	0.35	0.34	0.28	0.31	0.33	0.33	0.33	0.35	0.35	---	---	---
Multilateral aid	1,124	1,339	1,905	2,268	3,060	3,770	4,443	5,642	6,863	6,501	36,915	100	28.5
AUSTRALIA ($)	202	202	267	286	430	507	377	400	588	620	3,879	3.0	100.0
% of GNP	0.59	0.53	0.61	0.44	0.55	0.60	0.41	0.42	0.55	0.53	---	---	---
Multilateral aid	12	11	13	23	40	70	60	51	168	162	610	1.7	15.7
AUSTRIA ($)	19	12	18	40	59	64	50	108	154	127	651	0.5	100.0
% of GNP	0.07	0.07	0.09	0.14	0.17	0.17	0.12	0.22	0.27	0.19	---	---	---
Multilateral aid	6	6	14	33	39	15	20	22	41	69	265	0.7	40.7

BELGIUM ($)	120	146	193	235	271	338	340	371	536	631	3,181	2.5	100.0
% of GNP	0.46	0.50	0.55	0.51	0.50	0.59	0.59	0.46	0.55	0.57	---	---	---
Multilateral aid	27	36	63	56	64	126	111	109	226	198	1,016	2.8	31.9
CANADA ($)	346	391	492	515	713	880	887	991	1,060	1,026	7,301	5.6	100.0
% of GNP	0.42	0.42	0.47	0.42	0.48	0.55	0.46	0.50	0.52	0.48	---	---	---
Multilateral aid	79	97	154	166	217	268	358	516	442	462	2,759	7.5	37.8
DENMARK ($)	59	74	96	132	168	205	214	258	388	448	2,042	1.6	100.0
% of GNP	0.38	0.43	0.45	0.48	0.55	0.58	0.56	0.60	0.75	0.77	---	---	---
Multilateral aid	22	38	50	60	75	95	97	111	170	201	919	2.5	45.0
FINLAND ($)[1]				28	38	48	51	49	55	86	355	0.3	100.0
% of GNP				0.16	0.17	0.18	0.17	0.16	0.16	0.22	---	---	---
Multilateral aid				14	23	21	22	22	32	48	182	0.5	51.3

	1970	1971	1972	1973	1974	1975	1976	1977	1978	1979	1970–1979	% OF TOTAL	MULTILATERAL ODA AS % OF TOTAL
FRANCE ($)[2]	971	1,075	1,320	1,461	1,616	2,091	2,146	2,267	2,705	3,370	19,022	14.7	100.0
% of GNP	0.66	0.66	0.67	0.55	0.56	0.58	0.62	0.60	0.57	0.60	---	---	---
Multilateral aid	103	129	192	194	226	302	300	350	355	584	2,735	7.4	14.4
GERMANY ($)	599	734	808	1,102	1,433	1,689	1,593	1,717	2,347	3,350	15,372	11.9	100.0
% of GNP	0.32	0.34	0.31	0.28	0.34	0.36	0.36	0.33	0.37	0.45	---	---	---
Multilateral aid	133	205	207	311	418	528	549	688	787	1,189	5,015	13.6	32.6
ITALY ($)	147	183	102	192	216	182	226	198	375	273	2,094	1.6	100.0
% of GNP	0.16	0.18	0.08	0.11	0.13	0.10	0.13	0.10	0.14	0.08	---	---	---
Multilateral aid	85	46	51	74	216	124	148	163	353	251	1,511	4.1	72.2
JAPAN ($)	458	511	611	1,011	1,126	1,148	1,105	1,424	2,215	2,638	12,247	9.4	100.0
% of GNP	0.23	0.23	0.21	0.22	0.23	0.21	0.20	0.21	0.23	0.27	---	---	---

Multilateral aid	87	79	133	246	246	297	352	525	684	716	3,365	9.1	27.5
NETHERLANDS ($)	196	216	307	322	436	604	728	908	1,074	1,404	6,195	4.8	100.0
% of GNP	0.61	0.58	0.67	0.52	0.61	0.72	0.83	0.86	0.82	0.98	---	---	---
Multilateral aid	42	64	114	92	133	239	232	264	284	442	1,906	5.2	30.8
NEW ZEALAND ($)[3]			21	29	39	66	53	53	55	67	383	0.3	100.0
% of GNP			0.38	0.27	0.31	0.52	0.41	0.39	0.34	0.33	---	---	---
Multilateral aid			4	9	10	16	11	10	14	15	89	0.2	23.2
NORWAY ($)	37	42	63	87	131	184	218	295	355	429	1,841	1.4	100.0
% of GNP	0.32	0.33	0.41	0.43	0.57	0.66	0.70	0.83	0.90	0.93	---	---	---
Multilateral aid	22	24	33	46	58	82	112	130	163	181	851	2.3	46.2
PORTUGAL ($)	41	99	154								294	0.2	100.0
% of GNP	0.67	1.42	1.91								---	---	---
Multilateral aid	---	---	1								1	---	0.3

	1970	1971	1972	1973	1974	1975	1976	1977	1978	1979	1970–1979	% OF TOTAL	MULTI-LATERAL ODA AS % OF TOTAL
SWEDEN ($)	117	159	198	275	402	566	608	779	783	956	4,843	3.7	100.0
% of GNP	0.38	0.44	0.48	0.55	0.72	0.82	0.82	0.99	0.90	0.97	---	---	---
Multilateral aid	54	91	91	122	108	193	206	293	310	337	1,805	4.9	37.3
SWITZERLAND ($)	30	28	65	65	68	104	112	119	173	207	971	0.7	100.0
% of GNP	0.15	0.12	0.22	0.15	0.13	0.18	0.19	0.19	0.20	0.21	---	---	---
Multilateral aid	12	9	34	32	23	33	45	50	73	78	389	1.1	40.1
UNITED KINGDOM ($)	447	562	609	603	730	863	879	1,103	1,460	2,105	9,361	7.2	100.0
% of GNP	0.37	0.41	0.40	0.29	0.32	0.34	0.39	0.45	0.46	0.52	---	---	---
Multilateral aid	48	79	128	161	221	297	299	551	606	942	3,332	9.0	35.6
UNITED STATES ($)	3,050	3,324	3,349	2,968	3,439	4,007	4,360	4,682	5,664	4,684	39,527	30.5	100.0

% of GNP	0.31	0.32	0.29	0.21	0.22	0.24	0.26	0.25	0.27	0.20	---	---	---
Multilateral aid	393	431	625	631	882	1,066	1,552	1,785	2,190	608	10,163	27.5	25.7
EEC ($)[4]				375	598	722	501	549	805	1,257	4,807	3.7	100.0
% of GNP				---	---	---	---	---	---	---	---	---	---
Multilateral aid				46	76	108	58	71	---	---	359	1.0	7.5

Sources: OECD, *Development Co-operation, 1972 Review* (Paris: OECD DAC, 1972), table 5 (for 1970); OECD, *Development Co-operation, 1973 Review* (Paris: OECD DAC, 1973), tables 5 and 8 (for 1971); OECD, *Development Co-operation, 1974 Review* (Paris: OECD DAC, 1974), table 14 (for 1972); OECD, *Development Co-operation, 1976 Review* (Paris: OECD DAC, 1976), 11–17 (for 1973 and 1974); OECD, *Development Co-operation, 1977 Review* (Paris: OECD DAC, 1977), tables A.5 and A.9 (for 1975); OECD, *Development Co-operation, 1980 Review* (Paris: OECD DAC, 1980), tables A10–A16 (for 1976, 1977 and 1978); OECD, *Development Co-operation, 1981 Review* (Paris: OECD DAC, 1981), table 9A (for 1979). For ODA as a share of GNP: OECD, *1973 Review*, table 8 (for 1970–72; for New Zealand, OECD *1974 Review*, table 14); OECD, *1977 Review*, table A.5 (for 1973–75); and OECD, *Development Co-operation, 1982 Review* (Paris: OECD DAC, 1982), table II. A.2 (for 1976–1979). Note that figures and percentages given in DAC statistics may vary slightly from one source to another.

1. Finland joined the DAC in 1973. Calculations for Finland's ODA are based on data for 1973–1980 only.

2. France's ODA includes its contributions to its Départements d'Outre-Mer and Territoires d'Outre-Mer.

3. New Zealand joined the DAC in 1972. Calculations for New Zealand's ODA are based on data for 1972–1980 only.

4. The ODA channeled through the EEC (the European Economic Commission and the European Development Fund) is not included in the total ODA of the DAC, but in the multilateral components of the contributing EEC member states.

When this ODA is measured as percent of GNP, however, a different picture emerges: it varied between 0.28 and 0.35 percent. By contrast, in the previous decade, the share fell under the 0.4 percent level only during the two final years of the period.

Some DAC member governments did manage to attain the 0.7 percent target in the 1970s. As throughout most of the 1960s, DAC statistics reported a record high score for Portugal during the first years of the 1970s, before the country disappeared from the committee. During these years, the Salazar regime was waging war against liberation movements in its African "provinces." Sweden attained the 0.7 percent target in 1974, followed by the Netherlands in 1975, Norway in 1976, and Denmark in 1978. These four frontrunners stayed above the 0.7 percent level for the rest of the 1970s, all heading toward a target of 1 percent of GNP in ODA. The performance of other small and medium powers varied: the contributions of Australia and Belgium represented 0.5 percent of their GNP level. Canada was at 0.4 percent, while Austria, Finland, Italy, and Switzerland were generally below 0.2 percent.

The performance of the major powers varied over time. France came out on top among this group of countries. Most of the time, its ODA stayed at 0.6 percent, although it approached 0.7 percent during the first years of the decade. However, this performance represented a decline compared with its contributions in the 1960s. The performance of the United Kingdom generally remained around 0.4 percent, with a rising trend during the second half the decade that brought it to 0.5 percent in 1969. The Federal Republic of Germany more or less followed the DAC average for most years, while Japan generally stayed at the lower end of the 0.2 percent level. The sharply downward trend in U.S. performance in the 1960s continued in the 1970s: down to 0.21 and 0.22 percent in 1973 and 1974, then increasing slightly again, but ending at 0.20 percent the last year of the decade.

In the 1970s, the United States continued as the largest donor by far, providing almost one-third of total ODA among DAC countries. However, its share fell dramatically, from 55.7 percent of total DAC assistance in the 1960s to 30.5 percent in the 1970s. France (14.7 percent) followed next, staying at about the same relative level as in the previous decade. Then came the Federal Republic of Germany (11.9 percent, up from 7.5 percent the previous decade), and Japan (9.4 percent, up from 3.9 percent). The performance of the United Kingdom declined somewhat (7.2 percent, down from 9.7 percent), while Canada (5.6 percent, up from 2.1 percent), the Netherlands (4.8 percent, up from 1.3 percent), and Sweden (3.5 percent, up from 0.7 percent) appeared as new major donor countries in the 1970s on this indicator.

In the 1970s, the share of total ODA channeled by DAC countries through multilateral institutions almost tripled: 29 percent, up from 11 percent in the 1960s. It grew from $6 billion in the 1960s to $37 billion. The United States continued as the largest contributor to multilateral institutions in the 1970s, although with a downward trend (28 percent of total DAC contributions as against 38 percent in the previous decade).

The relative priority of multilateral institutions among DAC countries is best expressed as the share of total ODA they channeled through these institutions. Here we see that priorities varied extensively among DAC countries. Italy came out on the top (with 72 percent channeled through multilateral institutions), followed by Finland (51 percent), Norway (46 percent), Denmark (45 percent), Austria (41 percent), Switzerland (40 percent), Canada (38 percent), and Sweden (37 percent). Among the major powers, the United Kingdom (36, up from 13 in the 1960s) and the Federal Republic of Germany (33, up from 20) came out on the top, followed by Japan (28, up from 15) and the United States (26, a considerable increase from 7), while France channeled only 14 percent of its ODA through multilateral institutions in the 1970s. As in the 1960s, Portugal (which rejoined DAC after the revolution and resultant independence of its colonies) made only a negligible contribution to multilateral institutions.

It appears that over the course of the 1970s, DAC countries as a group gave greater priority to the World Bank system (in particular to its soft window, the International Development Association) than to the many institutions of the United Nations system. During the 1970s, DAC countries channeled $13.5 billion through the World Bank system, as against $9.9 billion through the UN system (table A.4). The obligatory contributions of EEC members to the aid programs of the community made up a large part of their multilateral development assistance and may be part of the explanation for the relatively high level of their multilateral aid.

Table A.5 offers a more detailed picture of total ODA to developing countries and multilateral agencies in the 1970s. Among the Council for Mutual Economic Assistance (CMEA) countries, the Soviet Union was by far the largest provider of development assistance. Its total net disbursements, according to DAC estimates, amounted to $745 million in 1970

TABLE A.4.

Official Development Assistance of DAC Countries to Multilateral Institutions, 1970–1979 (by percent and in millions of U.S. dollars)[1]

	1970	1971	1972	1973	1974	1975	1976	1977	1978	1979	1970–79
UN Agencies	32.7	32.4	33.4	29.0	27.3	31.8	27.7	23.0	23.2	26.1	26.9
IBRD and IDA	26.0	28.2	32.2	29.1	37.8	31.7	33.3	41.6	50.4	32.1	37.0
EEC	11.5	13.5	9.7	12.3	17.6	17.8	15.0	12.7	7.9	18.7	13.9
Others[2]	29.9	26.0	24.7	29.7	17.6	18.7	24.0	22.8	19.3	23.1	22.3
Total ($)	1,124	1,339	1,905	2,253	3,047	3,770	4,161	5,665	6,817	6,501	36,581

Sources: OECD, *1974 Review*, table 33 (for 1970–1973); OECD, *1977 Review*, table A.17 (for 1974–1976), and OECD, *1981 Review*, table 17 (for 1977–1979), and calculations based on these sources.

1. Data provided in different DAC sources may differ from each other. Both table A.3 and table A.4 are based on overview data provided in the annual DAC reports. For some years, the figures given for contributions to multilateral institutions differ, as may be detected when comparing the figures given (in U.S. dollars) in table A.3 and table A.4 for the years 1973, 1974, 1976, 1977, and 1978. This affects the totals for the 1970s as well; the total on table A.3 is $36.9 billion and the total for table A.4 is $36.6 billion. Note also that figures given in DAC reports for subcomponents do not always add up to the figures given for the total flow of resources to multilateral institutions in table A.4 (see, in particular, the data given for 1974 and 1978). Nevertheless, I decided to use the figures given in the sources. This explains why percentages in some columns do not add up to 100 (see in particular 1974 and 1978). However, these inaccuracies in the sources do not affect the general picture given in table A.4.

2. Including contributions to regional development banks and concessional lending.

TABLE A.5.

Total Official Development Assistance Receipts of Developing Countries from All Sources, 1970–1979 (in billions of U.S. dollars)

	1970	1971	1972	1973	1974	1975	1976	1977	1978	1979	TOTAL	PERCENT
Bilateral:												
DAC countries	5.66	6.33	6.63	7.09	8.23	9.81	9.50	10.08	13.12	15.91	92.36	55.9
OPEC countries	0.36	0.37	0.48	1.22	3.02	4.92	4.54	3.94	3.25	4.93	27.03	16.3
CMEA countries	0.96	1.26	1.38	1.35	1.26	0.73	1.05	1.09	1.28	1.75	12.11	7.3
Other countries	NA	NA	NA	NA	NA	0.03	0.06	0.08	0.10	0.12	0.39	0.2
Subtotal bilateral	6.98	7.96	8.49	9.66	12.51	15.49	15.15	15.19	17.75	22.71	131.89	79.8
Multilateral	1.07	1.33	1.39	1.96	2.82	3.84	3.87	4.97	6.00	6.20	33.45	20.2
Total ODA	8.05	9.29	9.88	11.62	15.33	19.33	19.02	20.16	23.75	28.91	165.34	100

Source: OECD, *1981 Review,* table A.1 and calculations based on data in this source.

and increased to $1,403 million in 1979, totaling $9.6 billion for the period, slightly more than the ODA of the United Kingdom in the same period. During this period, its assistance as a percent of GNP varied between 0.20 percent and 0.07 percent.[7]

Special mention should be made of the impressive performance of OPEC countries during the 1970s, in absolute and relative terms: this was an Arab adventure in the history of ODA that had not happened before and has not been repeated since by any government. In absolute terms, Saudi Arabia was the largest donor by far, providing more than all the other OPEC member countries put together. Its contribution in relative terms was also impressive: above 5 percent of GNP for every year of the 1970s, peaking at 14.80 percent in 1973. The generosity of Saudi Arabia on this criterion was matched, for some years in the period, only by its small neighboring states. They all peaked in 1973: Qatar with 15.62, the United Arab Emirates with 12.67, and Kuwait with 8.62 percent of their respective GNPs.

As table A.6 shows, an overwhelming share of the total concessional assistance of OPEC countries in the 1970s came from these four Gulf states alone: a full 84 percent. However, other Arab states, not least Iraq and Libya, were also major donors in both absolute and relative terms. Iraq peaked with 3.98 percent of its GNP in 1974 and Libya with 3.33 percent in 1973, while Algeria surpassed the 0.7 percent target in 1979 (with 0.89 percent of GNP). Iran alone provided three-fourths of the total contributed by the non-Arab OPEC members ($2,290), concentrating much of its aid during the years 1974–78. It met the 0.7 percent target from 1974 to 1976—with 0.87, 1.13, and 1.16 percent of its GNP, respectively.[8]

The financial conditions of ODA differed both for the total assistance provided by the main groups of countries and from one country to another within the groups—and also from one year to another. By the end of the decade (1979), 76 percent of total DAC assistance was provided as grants, as against 59 percent for total OPEC assistance and 29 percent of total CMEA assistance.[9]

The 1980s: Stagnation in ODA Flows

Over the course of the 1970s—after two oil shocks, stagflation in most DAC donor countries and a mounting debt crisis in most developing countries—the developmental optimism that had characterized the late 1960s, as reflected in the Pearson report and the international strategy

TABLE A.6.

Concessional Assistance of OPEC Countries in 1970–1979, Selected Years (in millions of U.S. dollars and by percent)

	1970		1973		1975		1977		1979		% OF TOTAL[1]	TOTAL ODA 1970–1979
	$	%	$	%	$	%	$	%	$	%		$
Kuwait	148	6.21	356	8.62	946	7.40	1,309	8.20	477	1.79	13.2	5,651
Qatar	NA	NA	94	15.62	338	15.59	194	7.76	280	6.03	3.2	1,395
Saudi Arabia	173	5.60	1,118	14.80	2,756	7.76	3,138	5.33	4,674	6.12	53.9	23,132
United Arab Emirates	NA	NA	289	12.67	1,046	11.69	1,060	7.27	967	5.09	13.7	5,905
Other Arab states[2]	72	1.10	251	1.21	515	1.31	221	0.39	1,224	1.40	8.8	3,794
Non-Arab states[3]	5	0.02	25	0.04	638	0.55	341	0.21	164	0.08	7.1	3,070
Totals	398	1.18	2,133	2.25	6,239	2.92	6,263	2.03	7,786	1.88	100	42,950

Source: OECD, *1982 Review*, tables II.F.1 and 2 and calculations based on data in this source.

1. Percentages do not add up to 100 because of rounding in the data on which calculations are based.
2. Algeria, Iraq, and Libya.
3. Iran, Nigeria, and Venezuela.

for the Second Development Decade, had faded away. The demands for a new international economic order had not been silenced, but they had been effectively fended off by the major western powers. Toward the end of the 1970s, the prospects for its success had been further weakened by the regime shifts in the United Kingdom and the United States bringing stalemate into the North-South dialogue. Although the promptings to channel more ODA through international institutions had been followed up, only a handful of DAC member countries succeeded in achieving the international target set for the Second Development Decade—0.7 percent of GNP in ODA; on average, they got halfway. Nevertheless, the strategy for the Third UN Development Decade moved the ODA target further upwards—retaining the 0.7 percent target, but opting for 1 percent of GNP in ODA as soon as possible after the mid-1980s.

In current prices, ODA rose from $130 billion in the 1970s to $339 billion in the 1980s—an increase of 262 percent.[10] Even as a percentage of GNP, a slight rise may be detected: with only one exception (1989), it stayed on the level of 0.35 percent or higher. Still, actual performance remained far from the 0.7 percent target—not to mention the new long-term target of 1 percent.

Although Japan ousted the United States as the largest provider of ODA in the final year of the decade, the latter remained the largest contributor of ODA also in the 1980s. However, its share of total DAC assistance continued to decline, albeit less dramatically than in the 1970s: 24.7 percent, as against 30.5 percent the previous decade. Then followed Japan (15.5 percent, up from 9.4 percent), France (14.7 percent), the Federal Republic of Germany (10.8 percent), the United Kingdom (5.7 percent, down from 7.2 percent), Italy (5.0 percent), Canada and the Netherlands (4.8 percent each), and Sweden (3.2 percent).

Contributions of total ODA of DAC member countries to multilateral institutions grew from $29 billion in the 1970s to $101 billion in the 1980s; there was also a slight increase when measured as a percentage of total ODA—from 28.5 percent to 29.7 percent. The largest share in absolute terms (U.S. dollars) was again provided by the United States (21.5 percent, but this was down from 27.5 percent in the 1970s).

On share of ODA channeled through multilateral institutions, the DAC newcomer Ireland came out on top in the 1980s, with 59 percent, followed by Denmark (47 percent), the United Kingdom (43 percent), Norway (42 percent), Italy and Finland (39 percent each), Belgium (37 percent), Canada (35 percent), the Federal Republic of Germany and Sweden (32 percent each), Japan (31 percent), the Netherlands (30 percent), Australia (29 percent), Switzerland (27 percent), the United States (26 percent), and New Zealand (20 percent). France (18 percent) found itself at the bottom on this criterion, as it had in the 1970s.

The distribution of multilateral assistance to the major multilateral institutions is shown in table A.8. The DAC countries as a group continued to show a clear preference for the World Bank system (mainly to the soft window of that system, the IDA). Of the $101 billion that went to multilateral institutions from DAC countries in the 1980s, $35 billion went to the World Bank (IDA) and $26 billion to the UN system. Much of the multilateral assistance of EEC member states was channeled through that organization—$18 billion.

The share of ODA from non-DAC donors peaked in 1975 at 40 percent of total ODA when OPEC (Arab) countries were at the top as aid donors. ODA from non-DAC countries showed a downward trend in the last part of the 1970s. This trend continued in the first half of the 1980s, due not least to reduced contributions from OPEC countries. In 1980, non-DAC countries provided about 32 percent of global ODA; in 1985 this share had fallen to about 21 percent. During this period, the share of OPEC countries declined from 24 to 10 percent of global ODA, while that of CMEA countries had increased from 7 to 10 percent. The share of other donors remained at about 1 percent of global ODA.[11]

Nevertheless, the golden age of Arab donors was not over. Both in absolute and relative terms, their ODA remained on a high level. This applied in particular to the Arab countries that continued to provide the brunt of the burden—the four Gulf states, among which Saudi Arabia and Kuwait were the main donors. The most important trend during the first half of the 1980s was that the combined share of Saudi Arabia and Kuwait increased from 70 percent of OPEC's total ODA in 1980 to 96 percent in 1985, making it less meaningful to talk about "OPEC ODA." The contribution of Arab countries (in reality mainly Saudi Arabia and Kuwait) continued at a high but declining level in the second part of the 1980s. Saudi Arabian ODA was well above 1 percent of GNP for the whole period.[12]

During the 1980s, a large and growing share of total CMEA aid was provided by the Soviet Union. By 1985, its assistance (resulting from a substantial expansion of oil and other commodity assistance) was estimated at $3 billion (0.28 percent of GNP). This represented about 85 percent of

TABLE A.7.

Official Development Assistance of DAC Countries, 1980–1989
(net disbursements in millions of U.S. dollars and by percent)

	1980	1981	1982	1983	1984	1985
DAC ($)[1]	27,267	25,540	27,731	27,592	28,742	29,429
% of GNP	0.38	0.35	0.38	0.36	0.36	0.35
Multilateral aid[1]	9,157	7,345	9,297	8,963	9,048	7,512
AUSTRALIA ($)	667	650	882	753	777	749
% of GNP	0.48	0.41	0.56	0.49	0.45	0.48
Multilateral aid	180	102	318	219	169	214
AUSTRIA ($)	178	220	236	158	181	248
% of GNP	0.23	0.33	0.35	0.24	0.28	0.38
Multilateral aid	27	59	71	31	44	74
BELGIUM ($)	595	575	499	479	446	440
% of GNP	0.52	0.50	0.59	0.59	0.58	0.55
Multilateral aid	139	206	206	181	183	165
CANADA ($)	1,075	1,189	1,197	1,429	1,625	1,631
% of GNP	0.43	0.43	0.41	0.45	0.50	0.49
Multilateral aid	418	443	370	580	586	634
DENMARK ($)	481	403	415	395	449	440
% of GNP	0.74	0.73	0.76	0.73	0.85	0.80
Multilateral aid	215	201	200	158	226	211
FINLAND ($)	111	135	144	153	178	211
% of GNP	0.22	0.28	0.30	0.32	0.35	0.40
Multilateral aid	45	56	58	61	70	83

1986	1987	1988	1989	1980–1989	% OF TOTAL	MULTI-LATERAL ODA AS % OF TOTAL
36,663	41,595	48,114	46,712	339,385	100.0	100.0
0.35	0.35	0.36	0.33	----	----	----
10,448	11,580	14,958	12,484	100,792	100.0	29.7
752	627	1,101	1,020	7,978	2.4	100.0
0.47	0.34	0.46	0.38	----	----	----
239	92	479	314	2,326	2.3	29.2
198	201	301	282	2,203	0.6	100.0
0.21	0.17	0.24	0.23	----	----	----
56	44	139	82	627	0.6	28.5
547	687	601	703	5,572	1.6	100.0
0.48	0.48	0.39	0.46	----	----	----
187	259	185	347	2,058	2.0	36.9
1,695	1,885	2,347	2,320	16,393	4.8	100.0
0.48	0.47	0.50	0.44	----	----	----
641	626	763	739	5,800	5.8	35.4
695	859	922	937	5,996	1.8	100.0
0.89	0.88	0.89	0.93	----	----	----
333	400	444	415	2,803	2.8	46.7
313	433	608	706	2,992	0.9	100.0
0.45	0.49	0.59	0.63	----	----	----
125	170	228	271	1,167	1.2	39.0

	1980	1981	1982	1983	1984	1985
FRANCE ($)[2]	4,162	4,177	4,034	3,815	3,788	3,995
% of GNP	0.64	0.73	0.75	0.74	0.77	0.78
Multilateral aid	701	632	722	670	618	733
GERMANY ($)	3,567	3,181	3,152	3,176	2,782	2,942
% of GNP	0.44	0.47	0.48	0.48	0.45	0.47
Multilateral aid	1,243	937	886	1,075	914	962
IRELAND ($)[3]			47	33	35	39
% of GNP			0.27	0.20	0.22	0.24
Multilateral aid			34	19	20	22
ITALY ($)	683	666	811	834	1,133	1,098
% of GNP	0.17	0.19	0.24	0.20	0.28	0.26
Multilateral aid	600	493	502	385	508	317
JAPAN ($)	3,353	3,171	3,023	3,761	4,319	3,797
% of GNP	0.32	0.28	0.28	0.32	0.34	0.29
Multilateral aid	1,343	910	656	1,336	1,891	1,240
NETHERLANDS ($)	1,630	1,510	1,472	1,195	1,268	1,136
% of GNP	1.03	1.08	1.08	0.91	1.02	0.91
Multilateral aid	403	367	408	383	389	374
NEW ZEALAND ($)	72	68	65	61	55	54
% of GNP	0.33	0.29	0.28	0.28	0.25	0.25
Multilateral aid	20	17	16	14	11	11

1986	1987	1988	1989	1980–1989	% OF TOTAL	MULTI-LATERAL ODA AS % OF TOTAL
5,105	6,525	6,865	7,450	49,916	14.7	100.0
0.70	0.74	0.72	0.77	----	----	----
943	1,199	1,265	1,315	8,798	8.7	17.6
3,832	4,391	4,731	4,948	36,702	10.8	100.0
0.43	0.39	0.39	0.41	----	----	----
1,189	1,300	1,559	1,773	11,838	11.7	32.3
62	51	57	49	373	0.1	100.0
0.28	0.19	0.20	0.17	----	----	----
37	24	35	30	221	0.2	59.2
2,403	2,615	3,193	3,613	17,049	5.0	100.0
0.40	0.35	0.39	0.42	----	----	----
917	737	785	1,424	6,668	6.6	39.1
5,634	7,342	9,134	8,965	52,499	15.5	100.0
0.29	0.31	0.32	0.31	----	----	----
1,788	2,207	2,712	2,186	16,269	16.1	31.0
1,740	2,094	2,231	2,094	16,370	4.8	100.0
1.01	0.98	0.98	0.94	----	----	----
560	676	679	582	4,821	4.8	29.5
75	87	104	87	728	0.2	100.0
0.30	0.26	0.27	0.22	----	----	----
14	20	10	11	144	0.1	19.8

	1980	1981	1982	1983	1984	1985
NORWAY ($)	486	467	559	584	540	574
% of GNP	0.85	0.82	0.99	1.10	1.03	1.01
Multilateral aid	202	202	233	251	236	246
SWEDEN ($)	962	919	987	754	741	840
% of GNP	0.79	0.83	1.02	0.84	0.80	0.86
Multilateral aid	247	316	401	228	215	260
SWITZERLAND ($)	253	237	252	320	286	303
% of GNP	0.24	0.24	0.25	0.31	0.30	0.31
Multilateral aid	76	74	68	102	67	75
UNITED KINGDOM ($)	1,854	2,192	1,800	1,610	1,430	1,530
% of GNP	0.35	0.43	0.37	0.35	0.33	0.33
Multilateral aid	526	865	842	751	646	670
UNITED STATES ($)	7,138	5,782	8,202	8,081	8,711	9,403
% of GNP	0.27	0.20	0.27	0.24	0.24	0.24
Multilateral aid	2,772	1,465	3,341	2,518	2,254	1,221
EEC ($)[4]	1,294	1,676	1,339	1,386	1,476	1,510
% of GNP	----	----	----	----	----	----
Multilateral aid	233	237	196	171	188	103

Sources: OECD, *Development Co-operation, 1984 Review* (Paris: OECD DAC, 1984), tables II.I.3–9 (for 1980–1982); OECD, *Development Co-operation, 1987 Report* (Paris: OECD DAC, 1987), tables 37–44 (for 1983–1985); OECD, *Development Co-operation, 1990 Report* (Paris: OECD DAC, 1990), tables 53–60 (for 1986–1988); and OECD, *Development Co-operation, 1991 Report* (Paris: OECD DAC, 1991), tables 49–56 (for 1989), and calculations based on these data.

1. Some minor discrepancies exist between the sum given for the total contributions of DAC countries and the data given for the individual countries as added for the period

1986	1987	1988	1989	1980–1989	% OF TOTAL	MULTI-LATERAL ODA AS % OF TOTAL
798	890	985	917	6,800	2.0	100.0
1.17	1.09	1.13	1.05	----	----	----
319	363	413	363	2,828	2.8	41.6
1,090	1,375	1,534	1,799	11,001	3.2	100.0
0.85	0.88	0.86	0.96	----	----	----
313	479	500	524	3,483	3.5	31.7
422	547	617	558	3,795	1.1	100.0
0.30	0.31	0.32	0.30	----	----	----
98	158	172	134	1,024	1.0	27.0
1,737	1,871	2,645	2,587	19,256	5.7	100.0
0.31	0.28	0.32	0.31	----	----	----
726	863	1,215	1,124	8,228	8.2	42.7
9,564	9,115	10,141	7,676	83,813	24.7	100.0
0.23	0.20	0.21	0.15	----	----	----
1,962	1,961	3,376	850	21,720	21.5	25.9
1,899	1,951	2,879	2,690	18,100	5.3	100.0
----	----	----	----	----	----	----
240	204	328	217	2,117	2.1	11.7

($31 million). This slightly affects the percentages (share of total DAC contributions to multilateral institutions).

2. France's ODA includes its contributions to its Départements d'Outre-Mer and Territoires d'Outre-Mer.

3. Ireland joined the DAC in 1982.

4. The ODA provided by the EEC is not included in the figures given for "Total DAC countries" as recorded for each member country.

total CMEA assistance, up from 82 percent in 1980. This trend continued during the second part of the 1980s: the USSR's share of total ODA from Central and Eastern Europe from 1986 through 1989 was 89.3 percent.[13]

A few OECD countries were not members of the DAC, so their official development assistance was not included in DAC figures for ODA. However, their ODA was small in both absolute and relative terms.[14] Many developing countries contributed ODA, particularly through UN development programs. China and India were the main contributors subsumed under the category "Other (LDC) donors" in table A.9.

From the data presented in tables A.7 and A.9, we see that estimated total ODA provided in the 1980s amounted to about $431.4 billion. In that decade, the share provided by DAC member countries constituted 78.7 percent of global ODA, that of OPEC member countries (mainly its Arab members) 11.2 percent, that of the CMEA member states (mainly the USSR) 8.5 percent, that of non-OPEC developing countries 1.0 percent, and that of non-DAC OECD members 0.6 percent. Toward the end of the decade, the position of the DAC as the major donor became even more prominent: by 1989, its share of global ODA had increased to 88.6 percent.

In 1978, a separate norm of 90 percent was recommended for the grant element of ODA commitments to all least-developed countries. In 1989, the ODA from the DAC met this norm—the grant element of aid to the LDCs was 95.0 percent. In fact, the grant element of twelve DAC member countries (Australia, Belgium, Canada, Denmark, Finland, Germany, Ireland, Netherlands, New Zealand, Sweden, Switzerland, and the United Kingdom) was 100 percent. Four other countries also met the 90 percent norm—Norway (98.5), the United States (98.1), Austria (95.8), and Japan (91.7)—while France (89.0) and Italy (88.5) came close to it.[15]

The 1990s: No Peace Dividend

The late 1980s and early 1990s saw the most dramatic international system transformation since the late 1940s, when the World War II allies created a bipolar world order. The political disintegration of the Second World and its hegemonic power brought to an end more than forty years of cold war. According to Cold War rhetoric, a peace dividend was to be expected.

The official development assistance of the 1990s seems a reasonably relevant test of the validity of this claim. Table A.10 gives the answer as far as the DAC member countries are concerned. In the course of the 1990s, DAC membership rose to twenty-two. In 1990, Portugal joined again and Luxembourg and Spain became new members; Greece joined in 1996. As table A.10 shows, annual transfers in current prices continued to grow during the first years of the 1990s. The total amount of ODA from DAC countries in the 1990s was greater than the total in the 1980s—$557.7 billion as against $339.4 billion. Measured as a percentage of GNP, however, a quite dramatic declining curve emerged from 1991 onward, from 0.35 percent in 1990 down to 0.22 percent in 1997, rising to 0.24 percent in 1999. The 0.7 percent target seemed more remote than ever.

The ODA performance of a few major powers was primarily responsible for the negative curve, particularly the United States. From an already low level in 1990 of 0.21 percent of GNP (well below the DAC average of 0.35 percent), the ODA of the United States fell to 0.15 percent of GNP in 1993, 0.10 percent in 1995, and then to a record low of 0.09 percent in 1997, remaining at 0.10 percent for the two last years of the decade. The "peace dividend" was a negative one; the end of the Cold War had removed much of the security rationale of the United States for providing development assistance. Because of its sizeable GNP—close to 40 percent of total DAC GNP in 1999—the steep downward trend in the U.S. performance had a negative effect on average DAC performance as well.

The ODA performance of most other major powers showed a negative trend as well, although it was less pronounced than that of the United States (under Republican as well as Democratic administrations). The ODA of France fell from a relatively high level in 1994 (0.64 percent of GNP) to 0.39 percent the last year of the decade. Germany's performance also declined, from 0.42 percent of GNP in 1990 to 0.26 percent in the last two years of the decade. The same was true for Italy during the second half of the decade, whose ODA declined from 0.31 percent of GNP in 1990 to 0.15 percent in 1999. Among the major powers, Japan and the United Kingdom were the exceptions. Japan started at 0.31 percent of GNP the first year of the decade and ended up with 0.34 percent of GNP in 1999, though its performance dropped in some of the intervening years. The ODA performance of the United Kingdom increased somewhat during the first years of the 1990s and stayed at or above about the 1990 level throughout most of the 1990s.

In previous decades, the United States had been the by far largest provider of ODA in absolute terms, albeit with a downward trend. In the

TABLE A.8.

Official Development Assistance by DAC Countries to Multilateral Institutions, 1980–1989 (by percent and in millions of U.S. dollars)

	1980	1981	1982	1983	1984	1985	1986	1987[1]	1988	1989	1980–1989
UN agencies	23.7	30.3	24.4	24.9	25.4	31.1	25.7	25.9	23.2	27.3	25.9
IBRD and IDA	35.4	34.5	39.6	37.8	37.6	28.0	37.3	36.3	35.4	26.1	34.7
EEC	17.2	21.2	15.6	15.2	16.3	18.9	16.1	16.1	17.2	21.1	17.5
Other[2]	23.7	13.9	20.5	22.0	20.6	22.0	20.8	21.7	24.2	25.5	21.9
Total[3]	100.0	99.9	100.1	99.9	99.9	100.0	99.9	100.0	100.0	100.0	100.0
Millions of U.S. dollars	9,157	7,345	9,297	8,930	9,048	7,512	10,450	11,580	14,958	12,484	100,761

Sources: OECD, *1984 Review*, table II.I.8 (for 1980–1983); OECD, *1987 Report*, table 43 (for 1984–1986); OECD, *1991 Report*, table 55 (for 1987–1989); and calculations based on data in these sources.

1. In 1987, the DAC stopped including data about capital subscriptions. I have calculated these amounts and included them in the "Other" category of the table for the last three years of the decade.

2. The "Other" category is comprised of other grants, capital subscription payments, and concessional lending. Almost all contributions recorded in the "Other" category were made to the regional development banks. I have included capital subscriptions to the World Bank since 1987 (excluding contributions to the IDA) in this category.

3. Percentages do not always add up to exactly 100 because of rounding in the data on which calculations are based.

TABLE A.9.

Official Development Assistance of Non-DAC Countries, 1980–1989
(net disbursements in billions of U.S. dollars and ODA as a percent of GNP)

	1980	1981	1982	1983	1984	1985	1986	1987	1988	1989	1980–1989	% of Total Non-DAC
Total, non-DAC	12.98	12.16	9.65	8.63	8.16	7.53	9.99	9.08	7.78	6.03	92.01	100.0
OPEC[1]	9.64	8.34	5.78	5.02	4.49	3.53	4.50	3.29	2.26	1.49	48.34	52.5
ODA as % of GNP	1.84	1.46	0.99	0.87	0.83	0.65	1.81	1.24	0.85	0.54	NA	NA
CMEA[2]	2.73	3.18	3.23	3.22	3.24	3.52	4.54	4.97	4.74	3.34	36.71	39.9
ODA as % of GNP	0.18	0.22	0.22	0.21	0.23	0.23	NA	NA	NA	NA	NA	NA
OECD, non-DAC ($)	0.17	0.25	0.24	0.08	0.15	0.18	0.27	0.29	0.37	0.70	2.70	2.9
ODA as % of GNP	0.06	NA	NA	NA	NA	NA	0.09	0.08	0.08	0.14	NA	NA
Other (LDC) donors ($)	0.44	0.39	0.40	0.31	0.28	0.32	0.68	0.54	0.42	0.50	4.28	4.7
ODA as % of GNP	0.10	NA	NA	NA	NA	NA	0.08	0.06	0.04	0.04	NA	NA

Sources: OECD, *Development Co-operation, 1986 Report* (Paris: OECD DAC, 1987), table V-1 (for 1980–1985); and OECD, *1991 Report*, table VIII-1 (for 1980 and 1986–1989), and calculations based on data in these sources.

1. Up to 1986, OPEC countries were presented as a group, although the Arab members were contributing almost all of the ODA. From 1986, however, only the Arab states are included here; non-Arab OPEC members, including Venezuela (which provided $0.22 billion in ODA in the years 1986 through 1989) are included among "Other LDC donors." With the exception of Venezuela, however, the ODA of non-Arab OPEC members was negligible (sometimes even negative because of repayments).

2. Estimates by the DAC secretariat up to 1988; data for 1989 provided by Soviet officials.

TABLE A.10.

Official Development Assistance of DAC Countries, 1960–1969
(net disbursements in millions of U.S. dollars and by percent)

	1990	1991	1992	1993	1994	1995
DAC ($)[1]	52,961	56,678	60,850	56,486	59,152	58,926
% of GNP[2]	0.35	0.33	0.33	0.30	0.30	0.27
Multilateral aid	15,802	15,425	19,601	17,127	17,852	18,299
AUSTRALIA ($)	955	1,050	1,015	953	1,091	1,194
% of GNP	0.34	0.38	0.37	0.35	0.34	0.36
Multilateral aid	202	326	276	239	267	267
AUSTRIA ($)	394	547	556	544	655	767
% of GNP	0.25	0.34	0.30	0.30	0.33	0.33
Multilateral aid	94	114	136	133	120	207
BELGIUM ($)	889	831	870	810	727	1,034
% of GNP	0.46	0.41	0.39	0.39	0.32	0.38
Multilateral aid	342	336	321	342	291	520
CANADA ($)	2,470	2,604	2,515	2,400	2,250	2,067
% of GNP	0.44	0.45	0.46	0.45	0.43	0.38
Multilateral aid	780	815	809	778	827	682
DENMARK ($)	1,171	1,200	1,392	1,340	1,446	1,623
% of GNP	0.94	0.96	1.02	1.03	1.03	0.96
Multilateral aid	476	514	635	585	643	728
FINLAND ($)	846	930	644	355	290	388
% of GNP	0.65	0.80	0.64	0.45	0.31	0.32
Multilateral aid	348	345	223	113	76	168

1996	1997	1998	1999	1990–1999	% OF TOTAL[1]	MULTI-LATERAL ODA AS % OF TOTAL
55,622	48,497	52,084	56,428	557,684	100	100
0.25	0.22	0.23	0.24	----	----	----
16,503	16,068	16,880	18,551	172,108	100	30.9
1,074	1,061	960	982	10,335	1.9	100
0.28	0.28	0.27	0.26	----	----	----
222	285	209	252	2,545	1.5	24.6
557	527	456	527	5,530	1.0	100
0.24	0.26	0.22	0.26	----	----	----
145	221	164	183	1,517	0.9	27.4
913	764	883	760	8,481	1.5	100
0.34	0.31	0.35	0.30	----	----	----
384	326	346	323	3,531	2.1	41.6
1,795	2,045	1,707	1,706	21,559	3.9	100
0.32	0.34	0.30	0.28	----	----	----
439	781	484	534	6,929	4.0	32.1
1,772	1,637	1,704	1,733	15,018	2.7	100
1.04	0.97	0.99	1.01	----	----	----
715	627	690	708	6,321	3.7	42.1
408	379	396	416	5,052	0.9	100
0.34	0.33	0.32	0.33	----	----	----
194	179	187	176	2,009	1.2	39.8

	1990	1991	1992	1993	1994	1995
FRANCE ($)	7,163	7,386	8,270	7,915	8,466	8,443
% of GNP	0.60	0.62	0.63	0.63	0.64	0.55
Multilateral aid	1,551	1,614	1,968	1,761	1,885	2,015
GERMANY ($)	6,320	6,890	7,583	6,954	6,818	7,524
% of GNP	0.42	0.40	0.39	0.36	0.34	0.31
Multilateral aid	1,841	2,315	2,341	2,437	2,674	2,709
GREECE ($)[3]						
% of GNP						
Multilateral aid						
IRELAND ($)	57	72	70	81	109	153
% of GNP	0.16	0.19	0.16	0.20	0.25	0.29
Multilateral aid	34	43	42	41	53	65
ITALY ($)	3,395	3,347	4,122	3,043	2,705	1,623
% of GNP	0.31	0.30	0.34	0.31	0.27	0.15
Multilateral aid	1,283	1,102	1,691	1,113	870	817
JAPAN ($)	9,069	10,952	11,151	11,259	13,239	14,489
% of GNP	0.31	0.32	0.30	0.27	0.29	0.28
Multilateral aid	2,282	2,092	2,766	3,215	3,681	4,071
LUXEMBOURG ($)[3]	25	42	38	50	59	65
% of GNP	0.21	0.33	0.26	0.35	0.40	0.36
Multilateral aid	11	16	16	18	19	22

1996	1997	1998	1999	1990–1999	% OF TOTAL[1]	MULTI-LATERAL ODA AS % OF TOTAL
7,451	6,307	5,742	5,639	72,782	13.1	100
0.48	0.45	0.40	0.39	----	----	----
1,697	1,530	1,557	1,512	17,060	9.9	23.4
7,601	5,857	5,581	5,515	66,643	11.9	100
0.32	0.28	0.26	0.26	----	----	----
3,066	2,218	2,090	2,238	23,929	13.9	35.9
184	173	179	194	730	0.1	100
0.15	0.14	0.15	0.15	----	----	----
156	136	116	115	523	0.3	71.6
179	187	199	245	1,352	0.2	100
0.31	0.31	0.30	0.31	----	----	----
65	67	75	97	582	0.3	43.0
2,416	1,266	2,278	1,806	26,001	4.7	100
0.20	0.11	0.20	0.15	----	----	----
1,604	812	1,581	1,355	12,228	7.1	47.0
9,439	9,358	10,640	15,323	114,919	20.6	100
0.20	0.22	0.28	0.34	----	----	----
1,232	2,806	2,087	4,848	29,080	16.9	25.3
82	95	112	119	687	0.1	100
0.44	0.55	0.65	0.66	----	----	----
26	28	35	30	221	0.1	32.2

	1990	1991	1992	1993	1994	1995
NETHERLANDS ($)	2,538	2,517	2,753	2,525	2,517	3,226
% of GNP	0.92	0.88	0.86	0.82	0.76	0.81
Multilateral aid	705	761	873	749	816	981
NEW ZEALAND ($)	95	100	97	98	110	123
% of GNP	0.23	0.25	0.26	0.25	0.24	0.23
Multilateral aid	14	19	23	24	25	26
NORWAY ($)	1,205	1,178	1,273	1,014	1,137	1,244
% of GNP	1.17	1.13	1.16	1.01	1.05	0.87
Multilateral aid	449	443	462	356	309	337
PORTUGAL ($)[3]	148	213	302	235	303	258
% of GNP	0.25	0.31	0.36	0.28	0.34	0.25
Multilateral aid	39	47	60	57	93	92
SPAIN ($)[3]	965	1,262	1,518	1,304	1,305	1,348
% of GNP	0.20	0.24	0.27	0.28	0.28	0.24
Multilateral aid	332	501	419	367	450	532
SWEDEN ($)	2,007	2,116	2,460	1,769	1,819	1,704
% of GNP	0.91	0.90	1.03	0.99	0.96	0.77
Multilateral aid	628	640	683	437	446	515
SWITZERLAND ($)	750	863	1,139	793	982	1,084
% of GNP	0.32	0.36	0.45	0.33	0.36	0.34
Multilateral aid	199	136	462	158	258	304

1996	1997	1998	1999	1990–1999	% OF TOTAL[1]	MULTI-LATERAL ODA AS % OF TOTAL
3,246	2,947	3,042	3,134	28,445	5.1	100
0.81	0.81	0.80	0.79	----	----	----
971	813	909	972	8,550	5.0	30.0
122	154	130	134	1,163	0.2	100
0.21	0.26	0.27	0.27	----	----	----
20	41	32	33	257	0.1	22.1
1,311	1,306	1,321	1,370	12,359	2.2	100
0.85	0.86	0.91	0.90	----	----	----
367	390	371	363	3,847	2.2	31.1
218	250	259	276	2,462	0.4	100
0.21	0.25	0.24	0.26	----	----	----
61	87	82	69	687	0.4	27.9
1,251	1,234	1,376	1,363	12,926	2.3	100
0.22	0.24	0.24	0.23	----	----	----
364	469	538	534	4,506	2.6	34.9
1,999	1,731	1,573	1,630	18,808	3.4	100
0.84	0.79	0.72	0.70	----	----	----
604	522	532	484	5,491	3.2	29.2
1,026	911	898	984	9,430	1.7	100
0.34	0.34	0.32	0.35	----	----	----
304	335	265	252	2,673	1.6	28.3

	1990	1991	1992	1993	1994	1995
UNITED KINGDOM ($)	2,638	3,201	3,243	2,920	3,197	3,202
% of GNP	0.27	0.32	0.31	0.31	0.31	0.29
Multilateral aid	1,164	1,382	1,544	1,397	1,435	1,487
UNITED STATES ($)	11,394	11,262	11,709	10,123	9,927	7,367
% of GNP	0.21	0.20	0.20	0.15	0.14	0.10
Multilateral aid	3,027	1,866	3,850	2,806	2,643	1,753
CEC ($)[4]	2,862	3,818	4,462	3,966	4,825	5,398
% of GNP	----	----	----	----	----	----
Multilateral aid	244	224	306	329	494	675

Sources: OECD, *Development Co-operation, 1994 Report* (Paris: OECD DAC, 1995), tables 13–21 (for 1990–1992); OECD, *Development Co-operation, 1997 Report* (Paris: OECD DAC, 1998), tables 14–22 (for 1993–1995); OECD, *The DAC Journal Development Co-operation, 2000 Report,* 2, no.1 (2001) (Paris: OECD DAC, 2001), table 14 (for 1996–1998); and OECD, *The DAC Journal Development Co-operation, 2001 Report* 3, no.1 (2002), table 14 (for 1999), and calculations based on these sources.

1. A discrepancy exists during this period between the sum of total ODA reported for DAC and the sum of the ODA reported for individual DAC countries (the latter sum is $562,975 million, $5,291 million larger than the former). This explains why the calculated percentages of the shares of individual countries do not add up to 100.

2. From 1999, ODA as a percent of GNI for the DAC and DAC members.

3. In 1990, Luxembourg, Portugal (again), and Spain became DAC members, followed in 1996 by Greece. The ODA of Greece before joining is not reported or included in the ODA of the DAC.

4. The ODA reported for the CEC/EC is not included in the DAC total. It is included in the ODA of EC members.

1990s, Japan emerged as the single largest contributor: 20.6 percent of the DAC's total ODA, up from 15.5 percent the previous decade. The United States came second (17.2 percent, down from 24.7 percent).

Member states of the European Community contributed the most ODA through multilateral institutions. Part of the explanation may be the

1996	1997	1998	1999	1990–1999	% OF TOTAL[1]	MULTI-LATERAL ODA AS % OF TOTAL
3,199	3,433	3,864	3,426	32,323	5.8	100
0.27	0.26	0.27	0.24	----	----	----
1,409	1,454	1,732	1,178	14,182	8.2	44.1
9,377	6,878	8,786	9,145	95,968	17.2	100
0.12	0.09	0.10	0.10	----	----	----
2,460	1,939	2,798	2,297	25,439	14.8	26.5
5,455	5,261	5,140	4,937	46,124	8.3	100
----	----	----	----	----	----	----
193	105	16	26	2,612	1.5	5.7

fact that they contributed to programs run by the CEC in addition to contributing to components common to all DAC members (the UN system, the World Bank, and regional development banks). The CEC component was almost obligatory for these countries, which therefore gave it priority. This tended to increase their multilateral component even further, especially countries whose ODA was low as a percent of GNP.

The multilateral component for the decade, which totaled $171 billion, was distributed among a number of aid agencies and institutions for development finance (see table A.11). For the decade as a whole, the UN system of organizations received around the 25 percent level with a slightly declining trend. This trend may also be traced over decades: 26.9 percent in the 1970s, 25.9 percent in the 1980s, and 24.5 percent in the 1990s. The table shows the shares of two major UN programs in focus in this volume—the UNDP and the WFP—for all years of the 1990s, while the shares of UNICEF and the UNHCR are specified for only the last years of the decade. The UNDP's overall share amounted to 5.3 percent, with a distinct downward trend across the decade. The share of the WFP amounted to 3.9 percent; its share also declined during the second half of the 1990s.

TABLE A.11.

Official Development Assistance from DAC Countries to Multilateral Aid
Agencies and Development Finance Institutions, 1990–1999 (by percent)

	1990	1991	1992	1993	1994
UN agencies	*25.8*	*28.3*	*24.2*	*23.6*	*24.1*
UNDP	6.9	6.7	5.4	5.2	5.4
WFP	4.5	5.1	4.0	4.2	4.5
UNICEF	NA	NA	NA	NA	NA
UNHCR	NA	NA	NA	NA	NA
World Bank	*30.8*	*31.1*	*35.9*	*31.2*	*28.0*
IDA	27.5	29.1	32.4	29.2	25.8
Regional development banks	*14.4*	*6.7*	*11.0*	*12.9*	*13.3*
European Commission/ Commission of the European Communities	*19.4*	*28.4*	*21.9*	*24.0*	*26.4*
Other	*9.6*	*5.5*	*6.8*	*7.7*	*8.3*
IFAD	NA	NA	NA	NA	NA
IMF	NA	NA	NA	NA	NA
Total (percent)[1]	*100.0*	*100.0*	*99.8*	*99.4*	*100.1*
Total (millions of U.S. dollars)	*15,372*	*15,410*	*19,531*	*17,031*	*17,864*

Source: OECD, *1991 Report,* table 26; OECD, *Development Co-operation, 1992 Report* (Paris: OECD DAC, 1992), table 26; OECD, *Development Co-operation, 1993 Report* (Paris: OECD DAC, 1994), table 22; OECD, *1994 Report,* table 22; OECD, *Development Co-operation, 1995 Report* (Paris: OECD DAC, 1996), table 23; OECD, *Development Co-operation, 1996 Report* (Paris: OECD DAC, 1997), table 23; OECD, *1997 Report,* table 23; OECD, *Development Co-operation, 1998 Report* (Paris: OECD DAC, 1999), table 15; OECD, *The DAC Journal Development Co-operation, 1999 Report* (Paris: OECD, 2000), table 15; OECD, *2001 Report,* table 15; and calculations based on these sources.

1995	1996	1997	1998	1999	1990–1999	MILLIONS OF U.S. DOLLARS
23.4	26.7	24.5	25.3	19.7	24.5	41,837
5.0	5.5	4.9	4.5	3.9	5.3	9,053
4.5	3.3	3.8	3.5	1.5	3.9	6,613
NA	NA	2.3	2.2	1.9	NA	NA
NA	NA	2.7	3.3	1.8	NA	NA
32.9	26.6	27.5	25.8	15.7	28.6	48,851
29.7	24.4	25.4	24.8	15.3	26.3	45,043
6.5	8.0	9.9	11.2	27.0	12.2	20,943
29.5	28.1	29.6	29.2	26.9	26.3	45,020
8.1	10.5	8.4	8.5	10.6	8.4	14,368
NA	NA	0.7	0.4	0.3	NA	NA
NA	NA	2.0	3.2	2.8	NA	NA
100.4	99.9	99.9	100.0	99.9	100.0	
18,229	16,347	15,989	16,764	18,517	171,054	171,054

Amounts given in the sources for the categories listed do not always add up to the amounts given for total ODA distributed among multilateral agencies, especially for 1993 and 1995. This naturally affects the percentages for these years and for the period. The amounts (and accordingly the calculated percentages) given for the single years (and accordingly for the decade) in table A.10 and A.11 deviate somewhat from each other: they are based on different OECD DAC sources. This does not, however, seriously affect the trends indicated.

1. Percentages do not always add up to exactly 100 because of rounding in the data from which calculations were made.

The largest share in the 1990s, as in previous decades, went to the World Bank, particularly the IDA. But this share was declining, more strongly than was the case for the UN system: its share in the 1990s was 29 percent, as against 37 percent in the 1970s and 35 percent in the 1980s. In the 1990s, the European Commission emerged as a major provider of multilateral ODA, at the same level as the IDA and at a higher level than the UN system. About 26 percent of total ODA channeled multilaterally by DAC countries was administered by the Commission of the European Communities—up from 14 percent in the 1970s and 18 percent in the 1980s. In the 1990s, the share of the regional development banks—the IDB, the Asian Development Bank, and the African Development Fund (and Bank)—totaled 12 percent. The emergence of the IMF toward the end of the decade as a major recipient of ODA from these countries—at levels equal to and greater than the assistance channeled to the WFP, UNICEF, and the UNHCR—is an interesting new development.

The ODA of DAC countries made up a large and growing share of global ODA. This trend became increasingly manifest in the 1990s, when the Soviet Union and Eastern Europe almost disappeared as ODA providers. These countries now became recipients of official assistance, a development that negatively affected the amount of resources the main political players of the West made available for ODA. The Federal Republic of Germany, which took over and integrated the former German Democratic Republic during this decade, took on a particularly heavy burden. Several former Soviet states that had relied on transfers of resources from the center for their development were now recognized as developing countries according to DAC criteria and became recipients of official development assistance—thus increasing the number of states that were to share a stagnating volume of ODA.

The DAC countries were not the only providers of ODA, as can be seen from table A.12. The Arab Gulf states—Kuwait, Saudi Arabia, and the United Arab Emirates—continued as major ODA donors in the 1990s, although their combined ODA fell steeply in 1991 and again in 1992 and continued this downward trend throughout the rest of the decade. All the same, their combined ODA made up more than three-quarters of the total ODA by non-DAC countries in the 1990s.

DAC member countries were the dominant donors of ODA in the 1990s. They provided $557.7 billion of the global total of $576.9 billion—96.7 percent of total ODA. Moreover, this percentage increased across the decade: their share grew from 89.8 percent of global ODA in 1990 to 98.2 percent by 1999.

The First Years of the New Century: Toward the Millennium Goals?

In September 2000, representatives of 191 governments, along with the largest-ever gathering of heads of state and government (147), signed the United Nations Millennium Declaration. The single most important outcome, from the perspective of this volume, was the formation of the Millennium Development Goals.

ODA was an integral part of the MDGs. In relation to MDG 8 —developing a global partnership for development—the established international ODA targets (0.7 percent of DAC donors' GNI in total ODA and 0.15 percent for LDCs) were brought in as indicators. After the Millennium Declaration, several governments committed themselves to increasing their ODA, some of them with a set target to be achieved by a set date.[16]

Actual performance in the early years of the new millennium is shown in table A.13, which covers the years 2000 through 2006. After a slow start during the first three years, the ODA of DAC countries moved up from the low level of 0.22–0.23 percent of GNI to reach 0.25 percent of GNI in 2003, moving further up to 0.26 percent the following year and reaching 0.33 percent of GNI by 2005 (0.31 percent in 2006). This growth becomes even more impressive if measured in current U.S. dollars: DAC ODA almost doubled, from 54 billion in 2000 to 107 billion in 2005 (104 billion in 2006).

In the wake of 11 September 2001, the major powers contributed to this growth. This applied especially to the United States; its ODA more than doubled as a share of GNI, from 0.10 percent in 2000 (the low level at which it had remained since 1995) to 0.22 percent in 2005 before declining again in 2006 to 0.18 percent. In current U.S. dollars, ODA more than doubled, from 10 billion in 2000 to 24 billion in 2006. The United Kingdom followed suit: its ODA as a share of GNI increased from 0.31 to 0.32 percent during the years 2000 through 2002, reaching 0.51 percent in 2006. In absolute terms, it almost tripled, moving up from $4.5 billion in 2000 to $12.5 billion in 2006. France showed the same pattern: its ODA as a percent of GNI moved up from 0.32 percent in 2000 and 2001 to reach 0.47 percent in 2005 and 2006; in absolute terms it increased from $4 billion in 2000 and 2001 to $10.6 billion in 2006.

TABLE A.12.

Official Development Assistance Contributions of Non-DAC Donors, 1990–1999 (in millions of U.S. dollars and by percent)[1]

	1990	1991	1992	1993	1994	1995	1996	1997	1998	1999	1990–1999 $	1990–1999 %
OECD non-DAC countries[2]	**5**	**155**	**322**	**489**	**359**	**223**	**247**	**263**	**287**	**479**	**2,829**	**14.7**
Korea[3]	(65)	(73)	77	112	140	116	159	186	183	317	1,290	6.7
Turkey	3	104	185	260	66	107	88	77	69	120	1,076	5.6
Arab countries	**5,835**	**2,652**	**1,158**	**1,183**	**972**	**641**	**772**	**739**	**629**	**424**	**15,005**	**77.9**
Kuwait	1,295	390	203	395	555	384	414	373	278	147	4,434	23.0
Saudi Arabia	3,652	1,704	783	549	317	192	327	251	288	185	8,248	41.4
United Arab Emirates	888	558	172	239	100	65	31	115	63	92	2,323	12.1
Other donors[4]	**198**	**279**	**192**	**86**	**107**	**92**	**88**	**154**	**114**	**114**	**1,424**	**7.4**
Chinese Taipei	25	125	106	61	79	92	88	65	27	NA	668	3.5
Total[5]	**6,038**	**3,086**	**1,672**	**1,758**	**1,438**	**956**	**1,107**	**1,157**	**1,030**	**1,018**	**19,258**	**100.0**

Germany moved slowly in the same direction. Its ODA as a percentage of GNI remained at 0.27–0.28 percent until 2005, when it increased to 0.36 percent, where it remained in 2006. Japan's ODA as a percent of GNI fell from 0.28 percent in 2000 to 0.19 percent in 2004 before reaching 0.28 percent again in 2005, then declining to 0.25 percent in 2006. Italy's ODA as a percent of GNI remained at a low level for most of the period, varying between 0.13 and 0.15 percent most of the years before rising to 0.29 percent in 2005, then declining to 0.20 percent in 2006.

The four frontrunners—Denmark, the Netherlands, Norway, and Sweden—continued to meet the internationally agreed-upon 0.7 percent target. In 2000 they were joined by Luxembourg. They showed different trends, however. Denmark, which led the group in the second part of the 1990s through 2002 with ODA as a percent of GNP above the 1 percent level most of the years, showed a decline to 0.80 percent in 2006, the result of a change in government. The Netherlands generally stayed above 0.8 percent, while Luxembourg moved upward to reach 0.8 percent. Sweden also moved up, taking the lead position of 1.02 percent in 2006; it was followed by Luxembourg and Norway at 0.89 percent each.

The increase of ODA in the last years of the period under review was clearly related to the wars in Afghanistan and Iraq. In 2005, Iraq ranked first among the top ten recipients of DAC ODA with $13 billion, far above the next countries on the list (Nigeria, China, Afghanistan, and Indonesia, at

---

Source: OECD, *1995 Report,* table VI-1 (for 1990–1991); OECD, *1996 Report,* table 43 (for 1992–1994); OECD, *2000 Report,* table 35 (for 1995); OECD, *2001 Report,* table 33 (for 1996–1999); and calculations based on data in these sources.

1. Data provided from different OECD sources may differ considerably. For example, total net disbursement for non-DAC donors for 1991 amounted to $3,086 million, according to OECD, *1995 Report,* table VI-I, and $1,672 million in OECD, *1996 Report,* table 43. Nevertheless, although exact data are not provided throughout, the general trends on table A.12 are clear.

2. Includes the Czech Republic (since 1993), Greece (since 1991), Korea (since 1992), Poland (since 1998), and the Slovak Republic (since 1999).

3. The parentheses around data in 1990 and 1991 for Korea indicate that its ODA was included in the category "Other donors" for those years in OECD sources.

4. In addition to Chinese Taipei, includes the Czech Republic (1992), India (1990–1994), and Israel (1997–1999). However, DAC statistics do not include the aid of some major non-DAC donors, such as China and India, because their aid has not been disclosed.

5. Percentages do not always add up to exactly 100 because of rounding in the data from which calculations were made.

TABLE A.13.

Official Development Assistance of DAC Countries, 2000–2006 (net disbursements in millions of U.S. dollars and by percent)

	2000	2001	2002	2003	2004	2005	2006	2000–2006	% of total	Multilateral ODA as % of total
DAC ($)	53,749	52,435	58,292	69,029	79,410	106,777	104,421	524,113	100.0	100.0
% of GNI	0.22	0.22	0.23	0.25	0.26	0.33	0.31	---	---	---
Multilateral aid	18,364	17,685	17,311	17,540	25,127	24,644	27,461	148,132	100.0	28.3
AUSTRALIA ($)	987	873	989	1,219	1,460	1,680	2,123	9,331	1.8	100.0
% of GNI	0.27	0.25	0.26	0.25	0.25	0.25	0.30	---	---	---
Multilateral aid	229	212	215	244	270	231	327	1,728	1.2	18.5
AUSTRIA ($)	440	633	520	505	678	1,573	1,498	5,847	1.1	100.0
% of GNI	0.23	0.34	0.26	0.20	0.23	0.52	0.47	---	---	---
Multilateral aid	167	191	156	276	325	341	407	1,863	1.3	31.9
BELGIUM ($)	820	867	1,072	1,853	1,463	1,963	1,978	10,016	1.9	100.0
% of GNI	0.36	0.37	0.43	0.60	0.41	0.53	0.50	---	---	---

Multilateral aid	343	365	360	385	561	655	620	3,289	2.2	32.8
CANADA ($)	1,744	1,533	2,004	2,031	2,599	3,756	3,684	17,351	3.3	100.0
% of GNI	0.25	0.22	0.28	0.24	0.27	0.34	0.29	---	---	---
Multilateral aid	583	333	503	683	608	923	1,153	4,786	3.2	27.6
DENMARK ($)	1,664	1,634	1,643	1,748	2,037	2,109	2,236	13,071	2.5	100.0
% of GNI	1.06	1.03	0.96	0.84	0.85	0.81	0.80	---	---	---
Multilateral aid	641	600	605	717	835	751	772	4,921	3.3	37.6
FINLAND ($)	371	389	462	558	680	902	834	4,196	0.8	100.0
% of GNI	0.31	0.32	0.35	0.35	0.37	0.46	0.40	---	---	---
Multilateral aid	154	165	211	250	278	305	380	1,743	1.2	41.5
FRANCE ($)	4,105	4,198	5,486	7,253	8,473	10,026	10,601	50,142	9.6	100.0
% of GNI	0.32	0.32	0.38	0.41	0.41	0.47	0.47	---	---	---
Multilateral aid	1,276	1,602	1,871	2,040	2,906	2,787	2,681	15,163	10.2	30.2

	2000	2001	2002	2003	2004	2005	2006	2000–2006	% of total	Multilateral ODA as % of total
GERMANY ($)	5,030	4,990	5,324	6,784	7,534	10,082	10,435	50,179	9.6	100.0
% of GNI	0.27	0.27	0.27	0.28	0.28	0.36	0.36	---	---	---
Multilateral aid	2,343	2,136	1,997	2,724	3,712	2,635	3,401	18,948	12.8	37.8
GREECE ($)	226	202	276	362	321	384	424	2,195	0.4	100.0
% of GNI	0.20	0.17	0.21	0.21	0.16	0.17	0.17	---	---	---
Multilateral aid	127	119	169	134	160	178	235	1,122	0.8	50.1
IRELAND ($)	234	287	398	504	607	719	1,022	3,771	0.7	100.0
% of GNI	0.29	0.33	0.40	0.39	0.39	0.42	0.54	---	---	---
Multilateral aid	80	102	131	152	198	237	389	1,289	0.9	34.2
ITALY ($)	1,376	1,627	2,332	2,433	2,462	5,091	3,641	18,962	3.6	100.0
% of GNI	0.13	0.15	0.20	0.17	0.15	0.29	0.20	---	---	---
Multilateral aid	999	1,185	1,326	1,372	1,759	2,821	1,640	11,102	7.5	58.5

JAPAN ($)	13,508	9,847	9,283	8,880	8,922	13,147	11,187	74,774	14.3	100.0
% of GNI	0.28	0.23	0.23	0.20	0.19	0.28	0.25	---	---	---
Multilateral aid	3,740	2,389	2,591	2,545	3,005	2,740	3,874	20,884	14.1	27.9
LUXEMBOURG ($)	123	139	147	194	236	256	291	1,386	0.3	100.0
% of GNI	0.71	0.76	0.77	0.81	0.83	0.82	0.89	---	---	---
Multilateral aid	24	32	31	44	64	69	86	350	0.2	25.3
NETHERLANDS ($)	3,135	3,172	3,338	3,981	4,204	5,115	5,452	28,397	5.4	100.0
% of GNI	0.84	0.82	0.81	0.80	0.73	0.82	0.81	---	---	---
Multilateral aid	892	948	889	1,030	1,534	1,432	1,169	7,894	5.3	27.8
NEW ZEALAND ($)	113	112	122	165	212	274	259	1,257	0.2	100.0
% of GNI	0.25	0.25	0.22	0.23	0.23	0.27	0.27	---	---	---
Multilateral aid	28	27	30	36	53	50	56	280	0.2	22.3

	2000	2001	2002	2003	2004	2005	2006	2000–2006	% of total	Multilateral ODA as % of total
NORWAY ($)	1,264	1,346	1,696	2,042	2,199	2,786	2,954	15,551	3.0	100.0
% of GNI	0.76	0.80	0.89	0.92	0.87	0.94	0.89	---	---	---
Multilateral aid	330	406	551	580	662	754	756	4,039	2.7	26.0
PORTUGAL ($)	271	268	323	320	1,031	377	396	2,986	0.6	100.0
% of GNI	0.26	0.25	0.27	0.22	0.63	0.21	0.21	---	---	---
Multilateral aid	92	85	137	137	158	159	185	816	0.6	27.3
SPAIN ($)	1,195	1,737	1,712	1,961	2,437	3,018	3,814	15,874	3.0	100.0
% of GNI	0.22	0.30	0.26	0.23	0.24	0.27	0.32	---	---	---
Multilateral aid	475	588	714	810	1,037	1,155	1,722	6,501	4.4	41.0
SWEDEN ($)	1,799	1,666	2,012	2,400	2,722	3,362	3,955	17,916	3.4	100.0
% of GNI	0.80	0.77	0.84	0.79	0.78	0.94	1.02	---	---	---
Multilateral aid	557	461	741	621	646	1,106	1,103	5,235	3.5	29.2
SWITZERLAND ($)	890	908	939	1,299	1,545	1,767	1,646	8,994	1.7	100.0

% of GNI	0.34	0.34	0.32	0.39	0.41	0.44	0.39	----	----	----
Multilateral aid	263	263	174	355	359	367	392	2,173	1.5	24.2
UNITED KINGDOM ($)	4,501	4,579	4,924	6,282	7,883	10,767	12,459	51,395	9.8	100.0
% of GNI	0.32	0.32	0.31	0.34	0.36	0.47	0.51	----	----	----
Multilateral aid	1,792	1,957	1,419	2,421	2,544	2,603	3,741	16,477	11.1	32.1
UNITED STATES ($)	9,955	11,429	13,290	16,254	19,705	27,622	23,532	121,787	23.2	100.0
% of GNI	0.10	0.11	0.13	0.15	0.17	0.22	0.18	----	----	----
Multilateral aid	2,550	3,145	2,720	1,661	3,455	2,343	2,370	18,244	12.3	15.0
EU ($)	4,912	5,961	5,448	7,173	8,704	9,390	10,245	51,833	9.9	100.0
% of GNI	----	----	----	----	----	----	----	----	----	----
Multilateral aid	498	444	298	728	636	703	756	4,063	2.7	7.8

Sources: OECD, *The DAC Journal Development Co-operation, 2004 Report* (Paris: OECD DAC, 2005), table 14 (for 2000–2003); OECD, *OECD Journal Development, Development Co-operation, Report 2006* (Paris: OECD, 2007), table 14 (for 2004 and 2005); OECD, *OECD Journal on Development, Development Co-operation Report 2007* (Paris: OECD, 2008), tables 13 and 14 (for 2007), and calculations based on these data.

The amounts provided in the three sources may deviate from each other, influencing the total amounts provided for the period and calculations made on that basis. Note also that the amounts provided for the EU are not included in the totals because they are reported by the individual members of the EU. Percentages for the totals of individual countries do not add up to 100 (100.2).

TABLE A.14.

Official Development Assistance from DAC Countries to Multilateral Aid Agencies and Development Finance Institutions, 2000–2006
(by percent and in millions of U.S. dollars)

	2000	2001	2002	2003	2004	2005	2006	2000–2006 %	2000–2006 $
UN agencies	*29.3*	*30.2*	*26.5*	*24.5*	*19.6*	*22.1*	*19.0*	*23.8*	*35,390*
UNDP	3.8	4.2	4.7	4.5	3.9	4.4	3.7	4.2	6,185
WFP	5.1	5.3	2.1	1.9	1.4	1.4	0.9	2.4	3,508
UNICEF	2.4	2.7	2.9	2.8	2.6	2.9	2.4	3.6	5,333
UNHCR	2.9	3.3	3.7	2.9	1.3	1.6	1.1	2.2	3,307
World Bank Group	*21.4*	*22.7*	*21.3*	*18.4*	*25.3*	*21.2*	*26.2*	*22.6*	*33,734*
IDA	20.8	20.5	18.5	15.8	22.7	19.6	24.7	20.7	30,793
Regional development banks	*12.3*	*8.5*	*10.3*	*9.0*	*9.0*	*8.5*	*8.9*	*9.4*	*13,980*
African Development Bank	5.7	4.1	4.1	4.3	3.5	4.4	5.1	4.5	6,644
Asian Development Bank	4.8	3.4	4.8	3.4	4.6	3.3	3.2	3.9	5,756
Inter-American Development Bank	1.4	0.7	0.4	0.4	0.3	0.3	0.2	0.5	701

European Community	28.0	28.5	32.5	35.6	35.5	37.4	36.0	33.8	50,419
Others	9.1	10.0	9.5	12.6	10.7	10.9	9.8	10.4	15,473
IFAD[1]	0.3	0.5	0.6	0.7	0.7	(0.4)	(0.6)	(0.6)	(858)
IMF	1.3	2.0	1.1	0.7	0.4	0.3	-1.3	0.5	732
TOTAL[2]	100.0	100.0	100.0	100.0	100.0	100.0	100.0	100.0	100.0
TOTAL (millions of U.S. dollars)	17,694	17,314	17,540	19,217	25,126	24,644	27,461	148,995	148,995

Sources: OECD, *2001 Report*, table 15 (for 2000); OECD, *The DAC Journal Development Co-operation Report 2002* 4, no. 1 (2003): table 15 (for 2001); OECD, *The DAC Journal Development Co-operation Report 2003* 5, no. 1 (2004): table 15 (for 2002); OECD, *Report 2004*, table 15 (for 2003); OECD, *Development Co-operation Report 2005* (Paris: OECD DAC, 2006), table 15 (for 2004); OECD, *Report 2006*, table 15 (for 2005); OECD, *Report 2007*, table 15 (for 2006), and calculations based on these sources.

1. For 2005 and 2006, data for IFAD in the OECD source is included among UN agencies, not among "Other."

2. Percentages do not necessarily add up to 100 because of rounding off. This also explains other minor discrepancies.

$3.2, 2.7, 1.9, and 1.9 billion, respectively). A similar picture emerged the following year.[17] This trend was particularly prominent with regard to aid from the United States: in 2005, Iraq received $6.9 billion, increasing to $8.0 billion in 2006. It was followed by Afghanistan ($1.1 billion in 2005, $1.4 billion in 2006), far above Washington's traditional politically motivated assistance to Egypt, which came in third with $0.75 billion in 2005 and fifth with $0.5 billion the following year.[18] For the remaining superpower, security concerns were again the main driver of increased aid. Security concerns and humanitarian concerns (related to misery caused by war and conflict but also suffering caused by natural catastrophes) also motivated the increase in ODA in many other donor countries.

The share of total aid channeled through multilateral institutions decreased during the early years of the new century. In current prices, multilateral ODA remained at about the same level as in the 1990s, although its dollar value was higher in the period 2004 to 2006. For the years 2000 through 2006, it totaled $148 billion. This accounted for 28.3 percent of total ODA for these years, as compared with 30.9 percent in the 1990s.

Normally, the priority given to multilateral aid is reflected in the share of total ODA that is provided through multilateral institutions. However, this does not necessarily apply to all the member states of the European Union, particularly members whose ODA represents only a small share of their GNI. As noted, EU countries are obliged to contribute to the development cooperation administered by the European Community according to their GNI. For member states that provide a small share of their GNI in ODA (such as, for most years, Austria, Greece, Italy, and Portugal—and even Spain), a sizeable proportion of their total ODA has to be channeled to the European Community, which leaves less for bilateral aid and for aid channeled through other multilateral institutions. Not least for this reason, EU countries emerge as those who channel the largest share of their aid through multilateral institutions, including the EC.

In the period 2000 to 2006, assistance channeled through the European Community increased, in terms of both actual volume and relative position. This development had started in the 1990s: more than 26 percent of total DAC multilateral assistance during that decade was channeled through the EC. In the first years of the new century, the share continued to grow, amounting to 33.8 percent for the seven-year period. This made the European Community the largest multilateral aid agency, far larger than the UN system and the World Bank group. The balance between the UN system and the World Bank group also changed. For decades, the greatest share of multilateral ODA had been channeled through the World Bank group, particularly the IDA. But in the first seven years of the new century, the UN system received a slightly larger share (23.8 percent, against the World Bank group's 22.6 percent). The proportion channeled through the regional development banks also decreased, from 12.2 percent in the 1990s to 9.4 percent in the first seven years of the new century.

Within the UN system, the relative position of the UNDP weakened during the 1990s, declining from 6.9 percent of total multilateral aid in the first year of the decade to 3.9 percent in the last. The downward trend was halted in the early years of the new century: its share amounted to 4.2 percent for the seven-year period. During this period, the proportion channeled through UNICEF and the UNCHR grew significantly. In contrast, the proportion channeled through the WFP varied extensively; in 2000 and 2001 it was the UN agency through which the DAC countries channeled most ODA.

Over the course of the 1990s, the DAC countries emerged as the main providers of ODA. By 1999, their contributions amounted to 98.2 percent of global ODA. They maintained this dominant position in the first seven years of the new century. Nevertheless, a few non-DAC countries continued to provide ODA as they had in the 1990s. Some of them increased their contributions, particularly after 2002. For some of these countries, their desire to join the European Union—with its expectation that member states would share in its development efforts—might have triggered this change. This was probably the case with Turkey and certain former Soviet-bloc Eastern European countries that are now non-DAC members of the OECD (the Czech Republic, Hungary, Poland, and the Slovak Republic). Some of the Arab states, Saudi Arabia in particular, continued to provide significant development assistance, although not of the same magnitude as in the heyday of the 1970s and early 1980s.

The performance of the non-DAC countries is shown in table A.15. Their ODA was on the rise from 2002, when Saudi Arabia increased its contributions substantially, as did South Korea. During the seven-year period, non-DAC countries together provided more than $22 billion in ODA, about 4.1 percent of total global development assistance as registered by the DAC. The largest share came from Arab states (2.4 percent of global ODA), followed by the group of OECD countries that were not DAC members (1.2 percent). It follows that for the years 2000–2006, DAC

TABLE A.15.

Official Development Assistance from Selected Non-DAC Donors, 2000–2005 (in millions of U.S. dollars and by percent)

	2000	2001	2002	2003	2004	2005	2006	TOTAL 2000–2006	PERCENT TOTAL FOR 2000–2006
OECD non-DAC countries	*354*	*409*	*431*	*605*	*1,107*	*1,876*	*1,872*	*6,654*	*30.1*
Czech Republic	16	26	45	91	108	135	161	582	2.6
Hungary	NA	NA	NA	21	70	100	149	340	1.5
Iceland	9	10	13	18	21	27	41	139	0.6
Korea	212	265	279	366	423	752	455	2,752	12.4
Poland	29	36	14	27	118	205	297	726	3.3
Slovak Republic	6	8	7	15	28	56	55	175	0.8
Turkey	82	64	73	67	339	601	714	1,940	8.8
Arab countries	*610*	*690*	*2,654*	*2,717*	*2,124*	*1,693*	*2,502*	*12,990*	*58.7*
Kuwait	165	73	20	138	209	547	158	1,310	5.9
Saudi Arabia	295	490	2,478	2,391	1,734	1,005	2,095	10,488	47.4
UAE	150	127	156	188	181	141	249	1,192	5.4

Others	165	95	134	116	527	665	798	2,500	11.3
Chinese Taipei	NA	NA	NA	NA	421	483	513	1,417	6.4
Israel[1]	164	93	131	112	84	95	90	769	3.5
Other	1	2	3	4	22	87	195	314	1.4
Total[2]	**1,128**	**1,194**	**3,218**	**3,436**	**3,759**	**4,236**	**5,172**	**22,143**	**100.1**

Source: OECD, *Report 2005*, table 33 (for 2000); OECD, *Report 2006*, table 33 (for 2001–2005); OECD, *Report 2007*, table 33 (for Saudi Arabia 2005 and for all categories 2006); and calculations based on data in these sources.

This overview is not complete; it does not include aid provided by several major emerging non-OECD countries because data about their aid has not been disclosed. Such countries include, among others, China, India, and Russia. See OECD, *Report 2005*, 103; OECD, *Report 2007*, 221.

1. Israel's ODA includes expenses for first-year sustenance for persons arriving in Israel for various humanitarian reasons (refugees, etc.). During the six-year period, these expenses made up more than half of Israel's ODA ($416.1 million, or 54.1 percent). See OECD, *Report 2005*, 243; OECD, *Report 2006*, 217; and OECD, *Report 2007*, 221.

2. The figures given for individual countries do not always add up to amounts given in the total because of rounding in the data provided in the sources. Percentages do not always add up to exactly 100 for the same reason.

countries provided 95.9 percent of global ODA and the member countries of the OECD provided 97.1 percent of total development assistance.

Most of the ODA of the DAC countries was provided as grants: the grant share of total ODA for the years 2005 and 2006 was 89.4 percent. Seven DAC countries (Austria, Canada, Greece, Ireland, Luxembourg, the Netherlands, and New Zealand) provided all of their ODA as grants during these years. While the grant element of total DAC assistance (excluding debt reorganization) was 91.8 percent in 1995–1996, it rose to 97.5 percent for the years 2005–2006. During the last year of the period covered by table A.13, seventeen of the twenty-two DAC countries had a grant element of 100 percent (the norm set was 86 percent). These seventeen were Australia, Austria, Canada, Denmark, Finland, Greece, Ireland, Italy, Luxembourg, the Netherlands, New Zealand, Norway, Portugal, Sweden, Switzerland, the United Kingdom, and the United States. The ODA of two other countries had a grant element above 95 percent (Belgium 99.4 and Germany 95.7) and two others were close to that mark (France 94.7 and Spain 94.5). The grant element of Japanese ODA was 89.6 percent.[19]

In 2006, all DAC countries met another target that had been set, namely that the grant element of bilateral ODA commitments (except debt reorganization) to all the LDCs should be 90 percent. For nineteen of the DAC countries, the grant element of this assistance was 100 percent and for the three others the grant element was above 97 percent.[20]

ODA showed a significant upward trend during the first years of the new century, particularly during the four final years of the period under review. While the UN Millennium Declaration placed the main focus on the results to be attained with little focus on the input side (including ODA), several governments committed themselves to raising their ODA with a view to sustaining the process toward the MDGs. The Monterrey consensus reinforced these efforts. In 2005, the Millennium Project emphasized the crucial role ODA would play in attaining the MDGs, reviving the long-established 0.7 percent target.

These efforts have clearly led many countries to increase their ODA during the period under review. However, the tempo has been far too slow to sustain the MDGs within the time targets that have been set. And the main rationale for the increases in ODA, particularly when it comes to the remaining superpower, has been more in the area of security than development. This in turn has influenced the utilization of resources for humanitarian (and relief) assistance rather than for social and economic development.

NOTES

FOREWORD

1. Craig N. Murphy, *The United Nations Development Programme: A Better Way?* (Cambridge: Cambridge University Press, 2006).

2. D. John Shaw, *The UN World Food Programme and the Development of Food Aid* (New York: Palgrave, 2001).

3. Maggie Black, *The Children and the Nations* (New York: UNICEF, 1986); and *Children First: The Story of UNICEF* (Oxford: Oxford University Press, 1996).

4. For details on the forty books in the Global Institutions Series, edited by Thomas G. Weiss and Rorden Wilkinson, see http://www.routledgepolitics.com/books/series/Global_Institutions.

5. Thomas G. Weiss and Sam Daws, eds., *The Oxford Handbook on the United Nations* (Oxford: Oxford University Press, 2007).

6. United Nations Intellectual History Project, *The Complete Oral History Transcripts from UN Voices* (New York: Ralph Bunche Institute for International Studies, 2007).

7. Paul Collier, *The Bottom Billion: Why the Poorest Countries Are Failing and What Can Be Done about It* (Oxford: Oxford University Press, 2007).

8. Richard Jolly, Louis Emmerij, Dharam Ghai, and Frédéric Lapeyre, *UN Contributions to Development Thinking and Practice* (Bloomington: Indiana University Press, 2004). See also Richard Jolly, Louis Emmerij, and Thomas G. Weiss, *The Power of UN Ideas: Lessons from the First 60 Years* (New York: United Nations Intellectual History Project, 2005).

9. See Thomas G. Weiss, Tatiana Carayannis, and Richard Jolly, "The 'Third' United Nations," *Global Governance* 15 (2009):123–142.

10. Louis Emmerij, Richard Jolly, and Thomas G. Weiss, *Ahead of the Curve? UN Ideas and Global Challenges* (Bloomington: Indiana University Press, 2001), xi.

PREFACE AND ACKNOWLEDGMENTS

1. Craig N. Murphy, *The United Nations Development Programme, A Better Way?* (Cambridge: Cambridge University Press, 2006); D. John Shaw, *The UN World Food Programme and the Development of Food Aid* (New York: Palgrave, 2001).

2. Sixten Heppling, *UNDP: From Agency Shares to Country Programmes, 1949–1975* (Stockholm: Ministry for Foreign Affairs, 1995), 84.

3. See Edward Clay and Olav Stokke, eds., *Food Aid Reconsidered: Assessing the Impact on Third World Countries* (London: Frank Cass, 1991; 2nd ed. 1995); Olav Stokke, ed., *Evaluating Development Assistance: Policies and Performance* (London: Frank Cass, 1991); Lodewijk Berlage and Olav Stokke, eds., *Evaluating Development Assistance: Approaches and Methods* (London: Frank Cass, 1992); Olav Stokke, ed., *Aid and Political Conditionality* (London: Frank Cass, 1995); Olav Stokke, ed., *Foreign Aid Towards the Year 2000: Experiences and Challenges* (London: Frank Cass, 1996); Jacques Forster and Olav Stokke, eds., *Policy Coherence in Development Co-operation* (London: Frank Cass, 1999); Edward Clay and Olav Stokke, eds., *Food Aid and Human Security* (London: Frank Cass, 2000); and Paul Hoebink and Olav Stokke, eds., *Perspectives on European Development*

Co-operation, Policy and Performance of Individual Donor Countries and the EU (London: Routledge, 2005).

INTRODUCTION

1. For a condensed overview, see Olav Stokke, "The Changing International and Conceptual Environments of Development Co-operation," in *Perspectives on European Development Co-operation,* ed. Paul Hoebink and Olav Stokke (London: Routledge, 2005), 32–112.

2. The original members of this group (which was set up on 13 January 1960) were Belgium, Canada, France, the Federal Republic of Germany, Italy, Portugal, the United Kingdom, the United States, and the Commission of the European Economic Community. Japan was invited to join (and accepted the invitation), and the Netherlands joined the group six months later.

3. Resolution adopted by the DAG on 29 March 1961. See Helmut Führer, *The Story of Official Development Assistance: A History of the Development Assistance Committee and the Development Co-operation Directorate in Dates, Names and Figures* (Paris: OECD, 1994), 14. See also the appendix in this volume.

4. For the principal targets, see box 5.1 in this volume.

5. Prominent among the critics was John Toye. See his *Dilemmas of Development: Reflections on the Counter-Revolution in Development Theory and Policy* (Oxford: Basil Blackwell, 1987).

6. Giovanni Andrea Cornia, Richard Jolly, and Frances Stewart, eds., *Adjustment with a Human Face,* vol. 1 *Protecting the Vulnerable and Promoting Growth* (Oxford: Oxford University Press, 1987).

7. World Commission on Environment and Development, *Our Common Future* (Oxford: Oxford University Press, 1987).

8. See contributions in Olav Stokke, ed., *Aid and Political Conditionality* (London: Frank Cass, 1995), particularly Stokke, "Aid and Political Conditionality: Core Issues and State of the Art," 1–87; and Adrian P. Hewitt and Tony Killick, "Bilateral Aid Conditionality and Policy Leverage," in *Foreign Aid Towards the Year 2000: Experiences and Challenges,* ed. Olav Stokke (London: Frank Cass, 1996), 130–167.

9. See contributions in Jacques Forster and Olav Stokke, eds., *Policy Coherence in Developing Co-operation* (London: Frank Cass, 1999), particularly Forster and Stokke, "Coherence of Policies Towards Developing Countries: Approaching the Problematique," 16–57.

10. "United Nations Millennium Declaration," General Assembly resolution 55/2, 8 September 2000.

11. OECD, *Shaping the 21st Century: The Contribution of Development Co-operation* (Paris: OECD DAC, 1996).

12. UNDP, *Investing in Development: A Practical Plan to Achieve the Millennium Development Goals: Overview* (New York: UNDP, Millennium Project, 2005).

13. The roots of the realist school in international relations can be traced back to Machiavelli in the sixteenth century. The classic work in this field is Hans Morgenthau's seminal *Politics among Nations* (New York: Knopf, 1948). Important later contributions include Kenneth Waltz, *Man, the State, and War* (New York: Columbia University Press, 1959); Kenneth Waltz, *Theory of International Politics* (Reading, Mass.: Addison-Wesley, 1979); and Robert O. Keohane, *After Hegemony: Cooperation and Discord in the World Political Economy* (Princeton, N.J.: Princeton University Press, 1984). The realist school emphasizes security interests, but economic interests also rank high in the national inter-

est concept. It is not limited to material concerns; the predominant ideology and basic norms of a government are part of the extended concept. Within realist paradigms, ideology may even stand out as the prime national interest in its own right and for its potential to steer the actions of those under its sway. Over the years, the paradigm has been developed from Morgenthau's classic core via the neorealism of Waltz. It remains central in the study of international relations, attracting the interest of new generations of students, as is evident in Michael C. Williams, ed., *Realism Reconsidered: The Legacy of Hans Morgenthau in International Relations* (Oxford: Oxford University Press, 2007).

14. It is up to the government concerned to define the content of the core concept (the national interest). In a complex society, interests may compete and conflict. Whereas in the past (but still in the post–World War II era) foreign policy was the almost exclusive domain of a country's ministry of foreign affairs, other sector ministries have increasingly become actors in the international arena on issues for which they have responsibility, leaving ministries of foreign affairs with a coordinating role. In this way, domestic actors interacting with the sector ministries became involved in foreign policy decision making, broadening the policy field and rendering it more complex. The private sector and NGOs have also become increasingly involved in the decision-making process and even as direct foreign policy actors. Add to this the competing concept of the "nation" and its cultural (ethnic) connotations, which may appear as a formal or informal structure within the state or may even transcend state borders.

15. Several observers have argued that the aid policy of the United States was from the outset driven by security concerns. See, inter alia, Keith Griffin, "Foreign Aid and the Cold War," *Development and Change* 22, no. 4 (1991): 645–685; Carol Lancaster, "Governance and Development: The Views from Washington," *IDS Bulletin* 24, no. 1 (1993): 9–15; and Carol Lancaster, *Transforming Foreign Aid, United States Assistance in the 21st Century* (Washington, D.C.: Institute for International Economics, 2000). A parallel may be drawn to the economic assistance provided to Europe after World War II. According to Robert Wood, two major U.S. objectives may be highlighted: containing communist influence and reintegrating national economies into an open international economic system. See Wood, *From the Marshall Plan to Debt Crisis: Foreign Aid and Development Choices in the World Economy* (Berkeley: University of California Press, 1986).

16. See contributions in Cranford Pratt, ed., *Internationalism under Strain* (Toronto: Toronto University Press, 1989); Cranford Pratt, ed., *Middle Power Internationalism: The North-South Dimension* (Kingston: McGill-Queen's University Press, 1990); and Olav Stokke, ed., *Western Middle Powers and Global Poverty: The Determinants of the Aid Policies of Canada, Denmark, the Netherlands, Norway and Sweden* (Uppsala: Scandinavian Institute of African Studies, 1989).

17. For a condensed discussion of humane internationalism, see Olav Stokke, "Foreign Aid: What Now?" in Stokke, *Foreign Aid Towards the Year 2000,* 20–25. Within the context of North-South relations, humane internationalism implies responsiveness to the needs of the South with regard to social and economic development. However, it does not stop there: civil and political rights are also considered to be universal values. Within humane internationalism, such ethical considerations are combined with deeply held values associated with the common good such as stability, peace, equality, and social justice.

18. Ibid. For another contribution that emphasizes the role of values in international relations, with particular reference to foreign aid, see David Halloran Lumsdaine, *Moral Vision in International Politics: The Foreign Aid Regime, 1949–1989* (Princeton, N.J.: Princeton University Press, 1993), chapter 1.

19. Stokke, "Foreign Aid: What Now?" 30ff.

20. Walt Rostow was one of the most influential economists to shape the worldview of foreign policy actors concerned with development issues in those days. See his *The Stages of Economic Growth: A Non-Communist Manifesto* (Cambridge: Cambridge University Press, 1960). Rostow characterized development as an endogenous process in which developing societies passed through five stages, starting with "traditional" society. The ethnocentrism of this model is obvious: western consumer society was the ultimate objective.

21. Regime theory identifies factors of critical importance in this regard. For a mainstream definition, see Stephen D. Krasner, "Structural Cause and Regime Consequences: Regimes as Intervening Variables," *International Organization* 36, no. 2 (1982): 185. According to Robert O. Keohane, "regimes can be identified by the existence of explicit rules that are referred to in an affirmative manner by governments, even if they are not necessarily scrupulously observed"; see "Analysis of International Regimes: Towards an European–American Research Programme," in *Regimes in International Relations,* ed. Volker Rittberger (Oxford: Clarendon Press, 1993), 28.

22. M. D. Cohen, J. G. March, and J. P. Olsen, "A Garbage Can Model of Organizational Choice," *Administrative Science Quarterly* 17, no. 1 (1972): 1–25.

23. R. G. A. Jackson, *A Study of the Capacity of the United Nations Development System* (Geneva: UN, 1969).

PART 1 INTRODUCTION

1. The predominant term used in UN documents during the late 1940s and most of the 1950s was "underdeveloped" countries and regions (the adjective "backward" was also used). This terminology referred in particular to the level of economic or industrial development, although this distinction was seldom made explicit. In Part 1 we will by and large use the term "less-developed," which appeared toward the end of the 1950s. These connotations, in turn, differed from those of the concept that came into common use later on—"developing countries." Another descriptive term might have been "poor countries," as suggested by the UN group of experts ("countries in which per capita real income is low when compared with the per capita real incomes of the United States of America, Canada, Australasia and Western Europe"). See United Nations, *Measures for the Economic Development of Underdeveloped Countries: Report by a Group of Experts Appointed by the Secretary-General of the United Nations* (New York: United Nations, Department of Economic Affairs, May 1951), 3.

1. PRE-AID TRADITIONS AND IDEAS AND THE INSTITUTIONAL HERITAGE

1. The literature on colonialism and the decolonization processes is extensive; any short list will be arbitrary and may omit important aspects as well as outstanding authors. For some good overviews, see Frank Heinlein, *British Government Policy and Decolonisation 1945–1963, Scrutinising the Official Mind* (London: Frank Cass, 2002); John Springhall, *Decolonization since 1945* (New York: Palgrave, 2001); Phillip Darby, *Three Faces of Imperialism: British and American Approaches to Asia and Africa, 1870–1970* (New Haven, Conn.: Yale University Press, 1987); John Kent, *The Internationalization of Colonialism: Britain, France, and Black Africa, 1939–1956* (Oxford: Clarendon Press, 1992); Bernard Waites, *Europe and the Third World: From Colonisation to Decolonisation, c. 1500–1998* (London: Macmillan, 1999); M. E. Chamberlain, *Decolonization,* 2nd ed. (Oxford:

Blackwell, 1999); Stephen Howe, *Anticolonialism in British Politics: The Left and the End of Empire, 1918–1964* (Oxford: Clarendon, 1993); and David Ryan and Victor Pungong, eds., *The United States and Decolonization: Power and Freedom* (Basingstoke: Macmillan, 2000).

2. The humanitarian efforts to rescue the populations of Russia and Ukraine in 1921–1923 illustrate the complexity of relief operations as well as the politics involved. The region was hit by a drought that had catastrophic consequences for millions of people who were just emerging from a world war, a revolution, and a civil war. More than 20 million were starving, many had left their homes in search of food, and epidemic illnesses were widespread. It is estimated that several million lost their lives. The organization first on the spot was the American Relief Administration under the leadership of Herbert Hoover. It had been established two years earlier to help rebuild Europe after World War I. The American Relief Administration had a free hand in its relief operations without interference from the Soviet government. By contrast, the agreement that Norway's Fridtjof Nansen negotiated with the authorities on behalf of a relief conference organized in Geneva by several European voluntary organizations gave the host government considerable influence over how relief activities were to be organized and implemented through a Moscow-based cooperative body with one representative from the Geneva-based committee and one from the host government. Nevertheless, the agreement negotiated by Nansen opened doors for other humanitarian organizations. See Merle Curti, *American Philanthropy Abroad: A History* (New Brunswick, N.J.: Rutgers University Press, 1963), 174ff.; Roland Huntford, *Fridtjof Nansen* (Oslo: Aschehoug, 1996), 507ff.; and Carl Emil Vogt, *"Et ikke ubetydelig bidrag": Fridtjof Nansens hjelpearbeid i Russland og Ukraina, 1921–1923* (Oslo: Norwegian Institute for Defence Studies, 2002), 35ff.

3. The history of the first fifty years of the ICRC has been told by Pierre Boissier, *De Solférino à Tsoushima* (Paris: Plon, 1963). For later years, see André Durand, *History of the International Committee of the Red Cross from Sarajevo to Hiroshima* (Geneva: Henry Dunant Institute, ICRC, 1978). (Both Boissier and Durand were insiders.) See also Francois Bugnion, *Le Comité International de la Croix-Rouge et la Protection des Victimes de la Guerre* (Genève: Comité international de la Croix-Rouge, 1994); John F. Hutchinson, *Champions of Charity: War and the Rise of the Red Cross* (Boulder, Colo.: Westview, 1996); and Caroline Moorehead, *Dunant's Dream: War, Switzerland and the History of the Red Cross* (London: HarperCollins, 1998).

4. Relief operations through the American Relief Administration were driven by strategic as well as humanitarian concerns; see Curti, *American Philanthropy Abroad.* This has been characteristic of relief operations closer to our time as well. Even with the best of intentions, humanitarian relief organizations may be (mis)used by the parties to a conflict, as shown in recent conflicts in the Horn of Africa and Africa's Great Lakes region; see Alex de Waal, *Famine Crimes: Politics & the Disaster Relief Industry in Africa* (London: Africa Rights & the International African Institute in association with James Currey and Indiana University Press, 1997); Milton J. Esman, *Can Foreign Aid Moderate Ethnic Conflict?* (Washington, D.C.: United States Institute of Peace, 1997); NAR, *Development Cooperation between War and Peace* (The Hague: National Advisory Council for Development Cooperation, 1996); and John Prendergast, *Frontline Diplomacy: Humanitarian Aid and Conflict in Africa* (Boulder, Colo.: Lynne Rienner, 1996). See also Thomas G. Weiss and Cindy Collins, eds., *Humanitarian Challenges and Intervention: World Politics and the Dilemma of Help* (Boulder, Colo.: Westview Press, 1996).

5. The literature on this topic is overwhelming, and any brief selection will, of necessity, omit important contributions, even the "obligatory" classics, and run the risk of being biased. Among the contributions to be noted is a series on solidarity (in English

and French) edited by Jacques Métadier in the early 1940s with the stated purpose of establishing a "platform for all those who can help to plan a better world"; Jacques Métadier, ed., *Solidarity*, vols. 1, 2, and 3 (London: George G. Harrap, 1942–1943); and vols. 4 and 5 (London: MacDonald, 1943 and 1944). See also Lewis L. Lorwin, *The International Labor Movement: History, Policies, Outlook* (New York: Harper & Brothers, 1953); Charles Levinson, *International Trade Unionism* (London: George Allen & Unwin, 1972); Jackie Smith, Charles Chatfield, and Ron Pagnucco, eds., *Transnational Social Movements and Global Politics: Solidarity beyond the State* (Syracuse, N.Y.: Syracuse University Press, 1997); and Willie Thompson, *The Left in History: Revolution and Reform in Twentieth-Century Politics* (London: Pluto Press, 1997). For a broader historical overview, see John Huddleston, *The Search for a Just Society* (Oxford: George Ronald, 1989).

6. See Adrian Hastings, *The Church in Africa 1450–1950* (Oxford: Clarendon Press, 1994).

7. The literature on the emergence and codification of human rights is extensive and growing. For an introduction and overview, see Henry J. Steiner and Philip Alston Steiner, *International Human Rights in Context, Law, Politics, Morals* (Oxford: Clarendon Press, 1996). For a discussion of the controversial issue of the universality of human rights, see Eva Brems, *Human Rights: Universality and Diversity* (The Hague: Martinus Nijhoff, 2001). For a historical perspective, see James Avery Joyce, *The New Politics of Human Rights* (New York: St. Martin's Press, 1978). See also Karel Vasak, ed. with Philip Alston, *The International Dimensions of Human Rights,* vols. 1 and 2 (Westport, Conn.: Greenwood Press with UNESCO, 1982).

8. Björn Hettne, *Development Theory and the Three Worlds* (1990; repr., London: Longman Scientific & Technical, 1995).

9. In the Harrod-Domar model, growth was seen as continuous progress toward higher stages of development: each increase in output would provide the basis for further growth as part of the surplus was reinvested. The ability to save (invest) would increase with the level of income. Once the process was started, therefore, economic growth would be self-sustaining.

10. The modernization paradigm includes broader approaches than those associated with development economics. Other social sciences set their stamp on the theory. See, for example, Hettne, *Development Theory and the Three Worlds,* 50–51. For critical reappraisals see David E. Apter, *Rethinking Development: Modernization, Dependency and Postmodern Politics* (Newbury Park, Calif.: Sage, 1987); and Colin Leys, *The Rise & Fall of Development Theory* (London, Bloomington, and Nairobi: James Currey, Indiana University Press, and East African Educational Publishers, 1996).

11. Walt Rostow, *The Stages of Economic Growth: A Non-Communist Manifesto* (Cambridge: Cambridge University Press, 1960). Other development economists who strongly influenced development thinking during these formative years include Gunnar Myrdal, *Economic Theory and Underdeveloped Regions* (London: Duckworth, 1957); Albert O. Hirschman, *The Strategy of Economic Development* (New Haven, Conn.: Yale University Press, 1958); and Raúl Prebisch, "The Economic Development of Latin America and Its Principal Problems," *Economic Bulletin for Latin America* 7, no. 1 (February 1962): 1–22.

In the period 1955–1965, the modernization paradigm had a hegemonic position in the West; it also influenced development thinking and practice beyond that period. For an interesting retrospective on major contributions, written by the pioneers of development economics themselves, see Gerald M. Meier and Dudley Seers, eds., *Pioneers in Development* (New York: Oxford University Press, IBRD, 1984), especially Gerald M. Meier, "The Formative Period," in Meier and Seers, *Pioneers in Development.*

12. The report of the Bruce Committee recommended that an agency be established to supervise the economic and social work of the League of Nations and coordinate the activities of the different international administrative agencies. It proposed that a Central Committee for Economic and Social Questions be established to meet at least once annually. The committee was to decide its own agenda, elect its own president and civil servants, appoint members of the major standing committees and, if found necessary, establish other committees. All issues were to be decided by the majority of those members who were present. The similarity to Chapters IX and X of the UN Charter is evident.

13. In the Preamble, the founding nations stated: "We the peoples of the United Nations determined . . . to promote social progress and better standards of life in larger freedom" and "to employ international machinery for the promotion of economic and social advancement of all peoples."

Chapter IX, Article 55 of the Charter states:

> With a view to the creation of conditions of stability and well-being which are necessary for peaceful and friendly relations among nations based on respect for the principle of equal rights and self-determination of peoples, the United Nations shall promote:
>
> a. higher standards of living, full employment, and conditions of economic and social progress and development;
> b. solutions of international economic, social, health, and related problems; and international cultural and educational co-operation; and
> c. universal respect for, and observance of, human rights and fundamental freedoms for all without distinction as to race, sex, language, or religion.

14. Currency is expressed in U.S. dollars in this volume unless otherwise specified.

15. See Edward Clay, "Conditionality and Programme Food Aid: From the Marshall Plan to Structural Adjustment," in *Aid and Political Conditionality,* ed. Olav Stokke (London: Frank Cass, 1995), 336–359; Mitchel B. Wallerstein, *Food for War—Food for Peace: United States Food Aid in a Global Context* (Cambridge, Mass.: MIT Press, 1980); and Robert Wood, *From the Marshall Plan to Debt Crisis: Foreign Aid and Development Choices in the World Economy* (Berkeley: University of California Press, 1986).

2. THE EXPANDED PROGRAMME OF TECHNICAL ASSISTANCE

1. "Provision of Expert Advice by the United Nations to Member States," General Assembly resolution 52 (I), 14 December 1946.

2. See, in particular, "Reports of the Specialized Agencies," ECOSOC resolution 167 (VII), 19, 24, 26, 27, and 28 August 1948; and "Economic Development of Under-Developed Countries," General Assembly resolution 198 (III), 4 December 1948.

3. See Sixten Heppling, *UNDP: From Agency Shares to Country Programmes, 1949–1975* (Stockholm: Ministry of Foreign Affairs, 1995), 11.

In describing the creation of the EPTA and its operation during the first decade, I have relied on various sources, particularly the official records of several UN bodies (reports, debates, and resolutions). When it comes to observations and assessments of events during these early years, I am particularly indebted to the insights and judgments of Sixten Heppling, a Swedish "participant observer," who provided in two soft-spoken and unpretentious volumes, the one referred to above, the other written in Swedish:

Sixten Heppling, *FN och de fattiga länderna* (The UN and the Poor Countries) (1967; Stockholm: Prisma, 1970).

Heppling served as executive secretary of the Central Committee for Swedish Technical Assistance to Less Developed Areas from 1952 to 1961. He moved on to the UN system, serving as resident representative of the EPTA and director of Special Fund operations in Afghanistan from 1962 to 1965. In subsequent years he served in a range of leading positions within the Swedish aid administration (SIDA) and UNDP—in the UNDP both as an international civil servant (as resident representative in Turkey and head of the administration division at headquarters) and as representative of the Swedish government in UN intergovernmental bodies dealing with development assistance, especially technical assistance.

4. "Conditions Relating to Technical Assistance," ECOSOC resolution 27 (IV), 28 March 1947.

5. "Expert Assistance to Member Governments," ECOSOC resolution 51 (IV), 28 March 1947.

6. "Economic Development of Under-Developed Countries," General Assembly resolution 198 (III), 4 December 1948.

7. Ibid.

8. "Technical Assistance for Economic Development," General Assembly resolution 200 (III), 4 December 1948.

9. Behind the scenes, David Owen played an important role in preparing the ground for resolution 200 (III) and as midwife to the EPTA. Owen served as deputy secretary-general and head of the Economic Department of the UN Secretariat during the initial phase and became the chairman of the Technical Assistance Board of the EPTA. According to Heppling, Owen succeeded in persuading four developing countries to present the resolution as their own. See Heppling, *FN och de fattiga länderna,* 16.

10. Quoted in Dennis Merill, ed., *Documentary History of the Truman Presidency,* vol. 27, *The Point Four Program: Reaching Out to Help the Less Developed Countries* (Bethesda, Md.: University Publications of America, 1999), 4. Truman's "Point Four" was Washington's first attempt to aid nonwestern countries. Although the initiative "evolved partly from a long American tradition of humanitarianism, it cannot be fully understood outside the international political economy of the early postwar era. By 1949 cold war lines had begun to harden in Europe" (xxxix).

11. Heppling, *UNDP,* 23.

12. "Technical Assistance for Economic Development," ECOSOC resolution 180 (VIII), 4 March 1949.

13. In addition to the heads of these organizations, the Secretary-General entered into direct consultations with the heads of the IBRD, the IMF, and the International Refugee Organization.

14. United Nations, *Technical Assistance for Economic Development. Plan for an Expanded Co-operative Programme through the United Nations and the Specialized Agencies* (Lake Success, N.Y.: United Nations, May 1949).

15. See statement by Mr. Katz-Suchy (Poland), *ESCOR,* 9th Session, 309th Meeting, 26 July 1949, 381, 383; and statement by Mr. Arutiunian (USSR), *ESCOR,* 9th Session, 310th Meeting, 26 July 1949, 397, 408–409.

16. *ESCOR,* 9th Session, 307th Meeting, 25 July 1949, 324–332; *ESCOR,* 9th Session, 311th Meeting, 27 July 1949, 422–425.

17. *ESCOR,* 9th Session, 312th Meeting, 27 July 1949, 433–435. During the discussion that preceded this decision, the social dimension of development was brought to the fore at the UN at an early stage.

18. *ESCOR,* 9th Session, 340th Meeting, 14 August 1949, 848; and *Report of the Economic Committee,* ECOSOC document E/1526 and Annex A and B, 13 August 1949.

19. "Economic Development of Under-Developed Countries," ECOSOC resolution 222A and B (IX), Annex I and II, 14 and 15 August 1949; and "Expanded Programme of Technical Assistance for Economic Development of Under-Developed Countries," General Assembly resolution 304 (IV), 16 November 1949.

20. The representatives of the Soviet Union and Poland contributed to the final wording of the objective by broadening the perspective to include the industrial development of the countries concerned and by promoting political and economic independence with a fairly direct reference to imperialism and economic exploitation. For this reason, France abstained. See *ESCOR,* 9th Session, 343rd Meeting, 15 August 1949, 914ff.

21. "Economic Development of Under-Developed Countries," ECOSOC resolution 222 (IX), Annex I, 14 and 15 August.

22. Ibid. Other prescriptions followed: experts should be given adequate preparation that was "designed to give understanding of the broad objectives of the common effort and to encourage open-mindedness and adaptability." They "should not engage in political, commercial, or any activities other than those for which they are sent," and the scope of their duty should be strictly defined in each case "by agreement between the country requesting assistance and the organizations providing assistance."

23. Ibid.

24. Ibid.

25. United Nations, *Technical Assistance for Economic Development.*

26. "Economic Development of Under-Developed Countries," ECOSOC resolution 222 (IX), Annex I, 14 and 15 August.

27. Statement by Mr. Van Tichelen (Belgium), *ESCOR,* 9th Session, 342nd Meeting, 15 August 1949, 889–890. Van Tichelen observed that the specialized agencies, "with their extensive powers and great responsibilities, were directed by strong personalities who naturally tried to win acceptance for their own views and to override all others. That tendency has been particularly in evidence during the Secretary-General's report on technical assistance." However, providing the central authority with strong powers would not suffice: "The imposition of a central authority without the active participation of the specialized agencies would necessarily involve friction which might lead to administrative disorder and open the way to individualistic tendencies to the detriment of unified action." These agencies should therefore "be asked for their prior approval, and allowed to express their views freely. By that means, they would be induced to co-operate voluntarily in the centralization of the programme."

28. Statement by Mr. Walker (Australia), *ESCOR,* 9th Session, 340th Meeting, 14 August 1949, 852–854. France took the opposite position: "The best way of encouraging Governments to join in the scheme and national constitutional bodies to vote the funds would be to give them an opportunity of contributing to specific projects rather than to an anonymous fund" (854–855).

29. *ESCOR,* 9th Session, 343rd Meeting, 15 August 1949, 909–911; Heppling, *UNDP,* 38.

30. *Report of the Economic Committee,* ECOSOC document E/1526/Add. 1, 13 August 1949.

31. "Economic Development of Under-Developed Countries"; "Expanded Programme of Technical Assistance for Economic Development of Under-Developed Countries."

32. *Report of the Economic Committee,* ECOSOC document E/1526/Add. 1, 13 August 1949.

33. See Technical Assistance Committee, *Annual Report of the Technical Assistance Board for 1956*, ECOSOC document E/2965, E/TAC/REP/97, May 1957, 9, 12; Technical Assistance Committee, *Annual Report of the Technical Assistance Board for 1957*, ECOSOC document E/3080, E/TAC/REP/120, 1958, 13; Technical Assistance Committee, *Annual Report of the Technical Assistance Board for 1959*, ECOSOC document E/3337, E/TAC/REP/166, June 1960, 17; and Technical Assistance Committee, *Annual Report of the Technical Assistance Board for 1964, Final Report on the Implementation of the 1963–1964 Programme*, ECOSOC document E/4021/Rev.1, E/TAC/REP/276, 1965, 16 (Table 11).

34. See Technical Assistance Committee, *Fifth Report of the Technical Assistance Board*, ECOSOC document E/2433, 1 June 1953, 6, 19. In 1952, the EPTA had resident representatives in twenty-eight countries: ten in Latin America, fourteen in Asia and the Middle East, two in Africa, and two in Europe.

35. "A Forward Look, Report of the Technical Assistance Board (with the Comments Thereon of the Administrative Committee on Co-ordination)," *ESCOR*, 22nd Session, 11 May 1956, Annexes E/2885 (incorporating Corr.1), 22–37.

36. Ibid., 36. The TAB report challenged the UN system and its member governments. It stated that the possibility to provide the necessary expert personnel was there and no organizational or administrative considerations would impede a substantial expansion of the work; financial resources were what was lacking.

37. In August 1951, the TAC decided to set up a working party to study "ways and means whereby the activities . . . might be more effectively co-ordinated and the programme more effectively administrated." See Technical Assistance Committee, *Fifth Report of the Technical Assistance Board*, ECOSOC document E/2433, 1 June 1953, 18.

38. This decision was also triggered by a need to ensure greater stability of the program in the face of variations in pledges from one year to another and slow payments by governments. Two years later, that particular problem was tackled through the establishment of a Working Capital and Reserve Fund from the annual contributions. Its financial framework was $12 million, the size to be determined from time to time. See "Expanded Programme of Technical Assistance," ECOSOC resolution 521 (XVII), 5 April 1954.

39. Through his formal position at the EPTA, David Owen put his stamp on the program. According to Heppling, however, "most of his authority derived from his continued ability to maintain relative harmony among the members of the Board" (which included the heads of the specialized agencies or their representatives). Heppling offered the stability in distribution patterns as the main cause of this harmony. Heppling, *UNDP*, 45.

40. Such concerns followed the EPTA right up to its end. In an evaluation of the programming for the period 1963–1964, some resident representatives referred to shortcomings in the process of formulating projects. In some cases, one or two participating organizations had "persuasively" suggested to government departments projects that would have absorbed almost the entire amount of the EPTA country target. In other cases, projects had been suggested and accepted on the basis of their theoretical desirability without adequate consideration of the difficulties involved in their implementation. These critics felt that "each project should be analyzed according to agreed criteria such as, for instance, the amount of support offered by the Government to it, and the project's importance to the economic and social development of the country and its possible contribution to such development." See TAC, *Annual Report of the Technical Assistance Board for 1964*, 83–84.

41. United Nations, *Measures for the Economic Development of Underdeveloped*

Countries (New York: United Nations, Department of Economic Affairs, 1951), 446–447; and *Fourth Report by the Secretary-General on Activities under the General Assembly Resolution 200 (III)*, ECOSOC document E/1700,5 June 1950, 13–14.

42. In 1950, the TAB began to experiment with placing resident representatives in Afghanistan, Colombia, Haiti, Indonesia, and Pakistan. For vivid descriptions of the early years, see Margaret J. Anstee, "The Field Office and How It Grew," in *Generation— Portrait of the UNDP*, ed. UNDP (New York: UNDP, 1985); and the Oral History Interview of Margaret J. Anstee, 14 December 2000, in the Oral History Collection of the United Nations Intellectual History Project, The Graduate Center, The City University of New York.

43. The Colombo Plan for Co-operative Economic Development in South and South-East Asia was conceived at a meeting of the (British) Commonwealth foreign ministers held in Colombo, Sri Lanka, in January 1950. Although it was started by Commonwealth countries, it opened up its membership to other countries both within and outside the region, including the United States and members of the Economic Commission for Asia and the Far East. The model involved development cooperation not only between industrial countries and developing countries but also between countries within the region, especially involving technical assistance. HMSO, *The Colombo Plan*, Central Office of Information Reference Pamphlet 58 (London: Her Majesty's Stationery Office, 1964).

44. Technical Assistance Committee, *Seventh Report of the Technical Assistance Board*, ECOSOC document E/2714, E/TAC/REP/35, 4 April 1955, 6.

45. See statement by Mr. Saksena (India), *ESCOR*, 17th Session, 760th Meeting, 2 April 1952, 26.

46. "Expanded Programme of Technical Assistance," ECOSOC resolution 521 (XVII), 5 April 1954. The resolution was supported by the delegations of Argentina, Australia, Cuba, Norway, Pakistan, Turkey, and Yugoslavia. It suggested four alternatives to the existing system and invited the TAC to formulate a proposal that ECOSOC could consider at its next session.

47. Heppling, *UNDP*, 49–50.

48. This statement was given in the introduction of "Technical Assistance," ECOSOC resolution 542 B II (XVIII), 29 July 1954, reaffirming a principle established five years earlier.

49. Ibid. The French delegation had formulated the resolution. In the final debate, the French spokesman summarized the main concerns: "The French delegation had constantly borne in mind three fundamental principles: first, recipient governments must be given a chance to state freely and fully the nature of their needs; second, the specialized agencies must be given the necessary financial and administrative stability to enable them to carry out successfully the tasks assigned to them; and third, the main direction and implementation of the Programme as a whole must be left to TAB"; Mr. Abelin, *ESCOR*, 18th Session, 820th Meeting, 29 July 1953, 196. See also "Programmes of Technical Assistance," General Assembly resolution 831 (IX), 26 November 1954.

50. According to the TAB's annual report for 1956, the first year of operation after the reform was fully implemented, the constitutional position of the resident representatives had been consolidated: "Their working relations with Governments and Participating Organizations was strengthened by the new country programming procedures; and the number of field offices of the Board increased by the early 1957 to thirty, serving forty-nine countries." Recipient governments saw the importance of having a TAB resident representative in their capital city. According to the report, governments

pressed the executive chairman to set up such offices. They offered office space, local staff, and transportation facilities, making it "possible to open offices which would otherwise have had to be deferred." See TAC, *Annual Report of the Technical Assistance Board for 1956*, 3.

51. Technical Assistance Committee, "Annual Report of the Technical Assistance Board for 1960," *ESCOR*, 32nd Session, Supplement no. 5, 1961, 49.

52. "Co-ordination of Technical Assistance Activities," ECOSOC resolution 851 (XXXII), 4 August 1961.

53. "Report of the Ad Hoc Committee of Eight Established under Economic and Social Council Resolution 851 (XXXII)," ECOSOC resolution 900B (XXXIV), 2 August 1962.

54. See Technical Assistance Committee, *Annual Report of the Technical Assistance Board for 1963, Interim Report on the Implementation of the 1963–1964 Programme*, ECOSOC document E/3871/Rev.1, E/TAC/REO/265,1964, 2, 18. Resident representatives came to wear many different hats, in addition to the "ordinary" ones of the TAB and the Special Fund. Almost everywhere they were also the "technical assistance mission chiefs" for the UN programs and in many places they acted on request as country representative for one or more of the other participating organizations. In a few countries they also directed the UN Information Center.

55. TAC, *Annual Report of the Technical Assistance Board for 1964*, 76.

56. "General Review of the Development, Co-ordination and Concentration of the Economic, Social and Human Rights Programmes and Activities of the United Nations, the Specialized Agencies and the International Atomic Energy Agency as a Whole," ECOSOC resolution 1090B (XXXIX), 31 July 1965.

57. However, principles and guidelines do not operate in a vacuum. As reported by a resident representative in a Latin American country, "the disappointing low level of achievement has been basically due to the presentation of unsound requests by the Government, though contributory factors, such as financial difficulties and poor administration, have also played their part in the operational stage." The principal lesson to be learned, he urged, was that "requests should not be accepted at their face value, but should be analysed in detail to ascertain whether they really respond to a felt need and a firm determination on the part of the Government, or merely to the passing whim of an individual." This might not be as easy as it sounded "because projects of the latter type are often those pressed most forcefully for political or other reasons." TAC, *Annual Report of the Technical Assistance Board for 1959*, 67.

58. TAC, *Annual Report of the Technical Assistance Board for 1964*, 82. The report argued that participating organizations were primarily interested in their own projects, resulting in a relatively small number of joint ventures that could enhance the quality and efficiency of individual projects.

59. TAC, *Annual Report of the Technical Assistance Board for 1959*, 5.

60. Ibid., 3.

61. "Country Programming Procedures: Project Programming," ECOSOC resolution 854 (XXXII), 4 August 1961.

62. The TAB concluded that the recipient governments continued to view the EPTA as a flexible source of diverse assistance to be drawn upon as required rather than as a basic resource for long-term development planning. In their evaluation of the 1963–1964 program, the resident representatives provided additional insights: in countries that enjoyed considerable technical and capital assistance from bilateral sources, the EPTA's resources "tended to be used to fill the gaps in bilateral programmes, rather than

be deployed in a concentrated and co-ordinated manner in fields of activities with high-est priority for economic and social development." TAC, *Annual Report of the Technical Assistance Board for 1964*, 3, 83.

63. TAC, *Annual Report of the Technical Assistance Board for 1957*, 3, 65–92.

64. For the 1963–1964 evaluation, see TAC, *Annual Report of the Technical Assistance Board for 1964*, 79–96.

65. UNESCO hired experts to prepare a report on the subject. The report appeared in 1955 and was later revised in the light of comments by UN officials, specialists in the social sciences, and experts working in the field. The core publication appeared in 1959. See TAC, *Annual Report of the Technical Assistance Board for 1957*, 67–68; and Samuel Hayes, *Measuring the Results of Development Projects* (Paris: UNESCO, 1959). Shortly afterward, most international agencies active in the field published their own evaluation manuals. The early and pioneering role of UNESCO in this field should be empha-sized. See also Enno W. Hommes, "Aid Evaluation in the Netherlands," in *Evaluating Development Assistance: Policies and Performance,* ed. Olav Stokke (London: Frank Cass, 1991), 149–150, which argued that most bilateral actors were latecomers in the field of evaluation, including even a frontrunner such as the Netherlands.

66. "Evaluation of Programmes," ECOSOC resolution 908 (XXXIV), 2 August 1962.

67. TAC, *Annual Report of the Technical Assistance Board for 1964*, 94–95. The resi-dent representatives did not say much about the methodology used except that the most frequent form of evaluation carried out by individual ministries was a review of projects in connection with parliamentary debates or the biennial programming exercises. They found it difficult to express an opinion on the quality of these reviews.

68. See "Evaluation of Programmes," ECOSOC resolution 1042 (XXXVII), 15 August 1964; and "Evaluation of Programmes," ECOSOC resolution 1092 (XXXXIX), 31 July 1965.

69. An interesting trend was that three Scandinavian countries (Denmark, Sweden, Norway) increasingly were major contributors to multilateral technical assistance: their combined share of total pledges to the EPTA for 1965 was 11.5 percent.

70. Already during the first year and a half (1950–1951), the experts who were recruited represented sixty-one nationalities; in 1964, this figure had increased to eighty-seven, of which thirteen were from Africa and twenty-two from Latin America (calcula-tions based on TAB statistics).

71. The data presented in this subsection are based on TAC, *Fifth Report of the Technical Assistance Board,* Annex III; TAC, *Annual Report of the Technical Assistance Board for 1956,* Annex XIII; TAC, *Report of the Technical Assistance Board for 1960,* Annex VIII; TAC, *Annual Report of the Technical Assistance Board for 1964,* Annex VIII; UNDP, *15 Years and 150,000 Skills, An Anniversary Review of the United Nations Expanded Programme of Technical Assistance, Prepared by the Technical Assistance Board* (New York: United Nations, 1965), Annex V; and *Yearbook of the United Nations 1965* (New York: United Nations, Office of Public Information, 1967), 296–300.

72. Part of the explanation may be the low level of UN salaries at that time com-pared with U.S. salaries.

73. Intergovernmental bodies repeatedly stated that their goal was to keep administrative costs at a minimum in order to get a maximum level of "development" from available resources. In 1961, ECOSOC decided that, for the 1963–1964 bien-nium, the implementing agencies were to receive a lump sum of 12 percent of their respective shares in the approved program. Similar arrangements were determined in

1963 for the program for 1965–1966. In 1965, this percentage was raised to 13 percent of one-half of an organization's share of the approved field program for the previous biennium, and in 1966, the share was increased to 14 percent of such costs with upward flexibility for organizations that executed a smaller share of projects. See "Allocation of Administrative and Operational Services Costs between Regular and Expanded Programme Budgets," ECOSOC resolution 855 (XXXII), 4 August 1961; "Allocation of Administrative and Operational Services Costs between Regular and Expanded Programme Budgets," ECOSOC resolution 950 (XXXVI), 5 July 1963; and "Administrative and Operational Services Costs," ECOSOC resolution 1060 (XXXIX), 13 July 1965.

74. Calculations based on data in *Yearbook of the United Nations 1959* (New York: United Nations, Office of Public Information, 1960), 115–116; and *Yearbook of the United Nations 1965*, 285.

3. A UN FUND FOR ECONOMIC DEVELOPMENT

1. For an overview of the history of development thought, see Richard Jolly, Louis Emmerij, Dharam Ghai, and Frédéric Lapeyre, *UN Contributions to Development Thinking and Practice* (Bloomington: Indiana University Press, 2004), chapters 2 and 3.

2. The interesting history of the role development economists played during this period is best told by the economists themselves. See Gerald M. Meier and Dudley Seers, eds., *Pioneers in Development* (New York: Oxford University Press, IBRD, 1984). One of the most ardent opponents of development economics from a neoclassical perspective was Peter Bauer, who based his theoretical work on empirical studies of economic activities in developing countries. See Peter T. Bauer, *Dissent on Development* (London: Weidenfeld and Nicolson, 1971); and Lord [Peter T.] Bauer, "Remembrance of Studies Past: Retracing First Steps," in Meier and Seers, *Pioneers in Development*, 27–43. For a fascinating description and assessment of the role the handful of development economists in the UN Secretariat played ("almost all radicals of some shape or form"), see John Toye and Richard Toye, *The UN and Global Political Economy* (Bloomington: Indiana University Press, 2004).

3. See *Report on the First Session, 17 November–16 December, of the Sub-Commission on Economic Development of the Economic and Employment Commission of ECOSOC,* ECOSOC document E/CN.1/47, 18 December 1947. In its second report, the commission reiterated "its view that industrialization forms the decisive element in economic development. The Sub-Commission, therefore, suggests that the primary objective of the Secretariat studies relating to economic development should be to analyse the various obstacles to economic development, taking into particular account the problems and obstacles to industrialization in the under-developed countries, including Trust and Non-Self-Governing Territories." See *Report of the Second Session of the Sub-Commission on Economic Development*, ECOSOC document E/CN.1/61, 1 July 1948, 3. The subcommission insisted that UN action "must be governed by the principle of primary reliance on the national resources of the under-developed countries themselves, on the one hand, and the principle of international co-operation, on the other." The subcommission referred to obligations regarding international cooperation set out in the UN Charter (Article 56) and emphasized that "such co-operation must be based on a foundation of mutual respect, equality among countries, the sovereignty of countries and their national interests." Combining these principles, the subcommission declared that "the responsibility for economic development 'rests with the governments and peoples of the

countries or areas concerned who may seek assistance from whatever source they deem expedient'" (both quotes in *Report of the Second Session*, 5).

4. See, in particular, United Nations, *Relative Prices of Exports and Imports of Under-Developed Countries* (New York: United Nations, 1949); and United Nations, *Relative Prices of Primary Products and Manufactures in International Trade* (New York: United Nations, 1953). Hans W. Singer, who at that time worked in the UN Department of Economic Affairs, was the main author of the first of these reports, which exerted considerable influence on current thinking. Investments by industrialized countries in less-developed countries to enable them to specialize in production of food and other raw materials for export to industrial countries were unfortunate for the less-developed countries, Singer argued; they lost most of the secondary and cumulative effects of the investments and the investment was diverted into types of activities that offered less scope for technical progress. In addition, the terms of trade were disadvantageous for this kind of export specialization. See Hans W. Singer, "The Distribution of Gains between Investing and Borrowing Countries," *American Economic Review, Papers and Proceedings*, 11, no. 2 (May 1950), reprinted in Hans W. Singer, *International Development: Growth and Change* (New York: McGraw-Hill, 1964).

5. United Nations, *Measures for the Economic Development of Underdeveloped Countries: Report by a Group of Experts Appointed by the Secretary-General of the United Nations* (New York: United Nations, Department of Economic Affairs, May 1951), 9. The Secretary-General appointed the group of experts at the request of ECOSOC to prepare a report on employment and underemployment. Members included Alberto Baltra Cortez (Chile), D. R. Gadil (India), Georg Hakim (Lebanon), Arthur W. Lewis (UK/West Indies), and T. W. Schultz (United States). Two of these (Lewis and Schultz) later became Nobel laureates in economics. The group's report emphasized economic development rather than unemployment and underemployment; it saw development as a prerequisite for new employment.

6. In his preface to the report, Secretary-General Trygve Lie put the report in the broader context of the development of a Twenty-Year Programme for Achieving Peace through the United Nations. Ibid., iii.

7. See United Nations, *The Economic Development of Latin America and Its Principal Problems* (Lake Success, N.Y.: United Nations, Department of Economic Affairs, Economic Commission for Latin America, 1950), reprinted as Raúl Prebisch, "The Economic Development of Latin America and Its Principal Problems," *Economic Bulletin for Latin America* 7, no. 1, (February 1962): 1–22. See also United Nations, *Economic Survey of Latin America 1951–1952* (New York: United Nations, Department of Economic Affairs, ECLA, 1954).

8. United Nations, *The Economic Development of Latin America and Its Principal Problems*, 1.

9. A clear and penetrating analysis of the core concept of the *dependencia* school, the center/periphery paradigm, is given in Johan Galtung, "A Structural Theory of Imperialism," *Journal of Peace Research* 8, no. 2 (1971): 81–117.

10. The debate at the UN in the mid-1950s, as in the mid-1970s, focused on concessions from industrialized countries in the field of trade, mechanisms to stabilize export prices of primary commodities and raw materials, and forms of compensatory finance. See United Nations, *Commodity Trade and Economic Development* (New York: United Nations, 1954). On the notion of "just" prices, see "Financing of Economic Development through the Establishment of Fair and Equitable International Prices for Primary Commodities and through the Execution of National Programmes of

Integrated Economic Development," General Assembly resolution 623 (VII), 21 December 1952.

11. For an early analysis of the lack of capital for development in underdeveloped countries and ways out of this problem, with particular reference to domestic savings, see United Nations, *Methods of Financing Economic Development in Under-Developed Countries* (Lake Success, N.Y.: United Nations, Department of Economic Affairs, 1949). In its 1951 report, the UN group of experts calculated the total annual savings of these countries to be about $5.2 billion, while the annual capital requirement needed to expand their agricultural production and to industrialize was found to be almost four times larger ($19.1 billion) if these countries were to raise their national income per capita by 2 percent annually. See United Nations, *Measures for the Economic Development of Underdeveloped Countries,* Table 2.

12. United Nations, *The International Flow of Private Capital 1946–1952* (New York: United Nations, Department of Economic Affairs, 1954). This study concluded that the prevailing international disequilibrium, which was reflected in the nonconvertibility of currencies and in exchange controls, tended to reduce the volume of private capital exported for investment purposes. Foreign private investments were operating in a less favorable climate than before because of government regulations and insecurity regarding the framework conditions. The report concluded that "in most under-developed countries . . . the domestic market is still too small, or other conditions for large-scale manufacturing most suitable for foreign investment are lacking. Moreover, the balance of payments of these countries generally permits the development of manufacturing through a continued inflow of foreign capital only if primary production for export is expanding" (59–61).

13. See United Nations, *Relative Prices of Exports and Imports of Under-Developed Countries.*

14. In its third report, the Sub-Commission on Economic Development considered the role of domestic finance in economic development as "the prerequisite for enabling countries to implement the social, political and economic policies which they consider most suitable for the improvement of their standards of living. The role of foreign finance in economic development can therefore only be of a subordinate character; at the same time the Sub-Commission recognizes that there is an important place for foreign capital in the financing of economic development, particularly in enabling under-developed countries to get foreign equipment and technique, and in accelerating the pace of their development. The Sub-Commission would emphasize, however, that the introduction of foreign capital should not be inconsistent with the basic objectives of economic development and it should not, therefore, be made in a manner or on conditions which are detrimental to the national interest and sovereignty of the under-developed countries, nor should it be linked with any political or economic privileges for the capital-exporting countries, the establishment of military bases, etc." *Report of the Third Session of the Sub-Commission on Economic Development,* ECOSOC document E/CN.1/65, 12 April 1949, 6.

15. See Odd-Helge Fjeldstad and Joseph Semboja, "Dilemmas of Fiscal Decentralisation: A Study of Local Government Taxation in Tanzania," *Forum for Development Studies* 27, no. 1 (2000): 7–41; Mick Moore, "Taxation and the Political Agenda, North and South," *Forum for Development Studies,* 31, no. 1 (2004): 7–32; and Deborah Brautigam, Odd-Helge Fjeldstad, and Mick Moore, eds., *Taxation and State-Building in Developing Countries: Capacity and Consent* (Cambridge: Cambridge University Press, 2007).

16. *Report on the First Session, 17 November–16 December, of the Sub-Commission on Economic Development.*

17. United Nations, *Measures for the Economic Development of Underdeveloped Countries,* 82–84, 95.

18. "Financing of Economic Development of Under-Developed Countries," General Assembly resolution 400 (V), 20 November 1950.

19. United Nations, *Measures for the Economic Development of Underdeveloped Countries,* 84ff., 95. The amount was to increase rapidly to almost $3 billion a year, a sum "equivalent to rather less than 1 per cent of the national incomes of Western Europe, Australasia, the United States and Canada."

20. See Singer, "The Distribution of Gains between Investing and Borrowing Countries"; "The Economic Development of Latin America and Its Principal Problems," ECOSOC document E/CN.12/89/Rev.1, 27 April 1950; "Economic Development of Under-Developed Countries," ECOSOC resolution 416 (XIV), 23 June 1952; and United Nations, *United Nations Fund for Economic Development, Report of the Committee of Experts* (New York: United Nations, 1955).

21. United Nations, *Measures for the Economic Development of Underdeveloped Countries,* 15 (points 33–35).

22. Ibid., 15–16 (points 36 and 37).

23. Ibid., 16 (point 38).

24. See "Reports of the Specialized Agencies," ECOSOC resolution167 (VII), 19, 24, 26, 27, and 28 August 1948; and "Economic Development of Under-Developed Countries," General Assembly resolution 198 (III), 4 December 1948.

25. In its eighth session, ECOSOC adopted a resolution proposed by Chile, requesting the Secretary-General to prepare a report "setting forth methods of financing economic development of under-developed countries, including methods of stimulating the international flow of capital for this purpose, paying due attention to questions of a social nature which directly condition international development"; "Economic Development of Under-Developed Countries," ECOSOC resolution 179 (VIII), 4 March 1949. The report of the Secretary-General (United Nations, *Methods of Financing Economic Development in Under-Developed Countries*) triggered new debate in the ninth session of ECOSOC.

26. "Economic Development of Under-Developed Countries," ECOSOC resolution 222A and B (IX), Annex I and II, 14 and 15 August 1949. In the debate, heated exchanges took place. Mr. Arutiunian (USSR) and Mr. Katz-Suchy (Poland) argued that the "sole purpose [of development finance] was to provide special guarantees for foreign capital, and that it failed to make provision for the special needs of receiving countries in the matters of credit conditions, rates of interest, periods of redemption, etc." Mr. Santa Cruz (Chile) and Mr. Campos (Brazil) rejected these interpretations as being totally unfounded. The draft resolution, as amended, was adopted by 14 votes to 3, with 1 abstention. *ESCOR,* 9th Session, 341st Meeting, 14 August 1949, 872–877.

27. *Report of the Economic Committee,* ECOSOC document E/1526/Add.1, 13 August 1949.

28. This subcommission had one representative each from the United States and the Soviet Union, four representatives of (major) less-developed countries (Brazil, China, India, and Mexico), and one from Czechoslovakia. *ESCOR,* 9th Session, 336th Meeting, 11 August 1949, 796–805, and 337th Meeting, 12 August 1949, 811–816.

29. "Suggestions for Creation of New International Agency for Financing of Basic Economic Development," in United Nations, *Methods of Financing Economic Development*

in Under-Developed Countries, 129–132. According to Shaw, it was Singer who saw to it that the proposal appeared as an annex in this report of the Secretary-General; D. John Shaw, *Sir Hans Singer, The Life and Work of a Development Economist* (Basingstoke: Palgrave, 2002), 74. Singer had drafted the report; D. John Shaw, "Introduction," in *International Development Co-operation. Selected Essays by H. W. Singer on Aid and the United Nations System,* ed. D. John Shaw (Basingstoke: Palgrave, 2001), 11.

The U.S. representative on the subcommission disagreed with the proposal, arguing that the U.S. government should look primarily to American private enterprise and should rely fundamentally on the IBRD for financing or collaborating in financing development projects not readily suited for implementation by purely private financing. Since no unanimous support could be achieved in the subcommission, Mr. Rao submitted it as his own proposal (in his capacity as chairman of the subcommission) appended to the report. The World Bank also reacted negatively to the proposal, indicating that the functions proposed for the UNEDA either came within the IBRD's terms of reference or did not need to be performed anyway. Shaw, "Introduction," 11–12.

30. The Economic and Employment Commission "felt that there was no need for the creation of a new international agency in the field of international finance," although "certain members of the Commission were also of the opinion that the proposal of a member of the Sub-Commission . . . deserved further and detailed consideration." *Report of the Fourth Session of the Economic and Employment Commission,* ECOSOC document E/1356, 1949.

31. The historians of the World Bank have observed that the idea of the United Nations Economic Development Administration "resurfaced as an International Development Authority, as a Special United Nations Fund for Economic Development (SUNFED), and under other aliases before achieving any real-life identity. The desire of the less-developed countries for access to capital on easier terms than those of the World Bank began to take on the proportions of a campaign at the Economic and Social Council in 1950. From 1950 until at least 1960, 'financing of economic development' was the most passionately debated economic issue in the United Nations. The less developed countries, led primarily by Chile, India, and Yugoslavia, showed extraordinary ingenuity in keeping the issue alive and inching forward towards their goal. Their campaign splashed over from the United Nations channels into other channels and back again. . . . The developed countries, led by an increasingly isolated United States, at first opposed, then postponed, and eventually deflected the campaign. The World Bank, a major beneficiary of the diversionary tactic, gradually shifted its position on soft loans 180 degrees." Edward S. Mason and Robert E. Asher, *The World Bank since Bretton Woods: The Origins, Policies, Operations, and Impact of the International Bank for Reconstruction and Development and the Other Members of the World Bank Group: The International Finance Corporation, the International Development Association, the International Centre for Settlement of Investment Disputes* (Washington, D.C.: Brookings Institution), 383.

32. United Nations, *Measures for the Economic Development of Underdeveloped Countries,* 95.

33. See "Methods of Financing Economic Development of Under-Developed Countries," ECOSOC resolution 368 (XIII), 22 August 1951. The Soviet-bloc countries abstained because they found that the measures recommended were not geared to extend effective aid to underdeveloped countries but would instead protect foreign capitalists. See statements by Mr. Katz-Suchy (Poland), Mr. Arkadiev (USSR), and Mr. Tauber (Czechoslovakia) in *ESCOR,* 13th Session, 514th Meeting, 22 August 1951, 316–320.

34. "Financing of Economic Development of Under-Developed Countries,"

General Assembly resolution 520, 12 January 1952. This resolution was adopted by 30 votes (mostly from less-developed countries) against 16 (mostly from the West), with 11 abstentions (by the Soviet bloc and a few less-developed countries, including Brazil and Thailand). See *GAOR*, 6th Session, 360th Plenary Meeting, 12 January 1952, 331–338.

35. United Nations, *Methods of Financing Economic Development*.

36. See United Nations, *Report on a Special United Nations Fund for Economic Development* (New York: United Nations, Department of Economic Affairs, 1953), 1–60. The committee recommended that the fund should not be established "until the equivalent of at least $250 million has been pledged by at least thirty contributing governments." Savings "due to disarmament . . . should be regarded as an additional factor . . . as justification for more substantial contributions in future" (13, 15).

37. See the debate in ECOSOC (*ESCOR*, 16th Session, 15–18 July 1953, 137–183).

38. President Eisenhower's vision was introduced in United Nations. According to Mr. Baker, the U.S. Congress had authorized "over half a thousand million dollars for technical and financial assistance to under-developed countries during the current fiscal year," mostly on a grant basis. The U.S. president had, however, held out a bolder vision of the future, outlining ways how international distrust could be dissipated and the burden of armament reduced and appealed to the world to face its greatest task, the defeat of poverty, hunger, and ignorance. "His Government was ready to ask its people to join with all nations in devoting a substantial percentage of the savings which would be achieved by such disarmament to a fund for world aid and reconstruction." The peace aimed at "should not be a *pax romana,* nor a peace imposed by any single nation, but a *pax mundi,* peace through the United Nations" (ibid., 139–140).

39. According to the U.S. spokesman, the precise form that such a fund might take could not be foreseen. It might serve as an instrument for making loans and grants or it might be largely concerned with technical assistance. It might be used to promote social as well as economic progress and might even develop novel procedures for associating private and public initiatives.

In ECOSOC, the U.S. draft resolution was welcomed by many delegations. However, several representatives, including those of Argentina, Egypt, India, and Yugoslavia, argued that expansion of financial aid to underdeveloped countries should not be entirely contingent upon disarmament. The Philippines pointed out that General Assembly resolution 520 (VI) had envisaged disarmament as providing an additional source of funds but had not implied that establishing an international fund depended upon disarmament. See *Yearbook of the United Nations 1953* (New York: United Nations, Office of Public Information, 1954), 296–297.

40. "Economic Development of Under-Developed Countries," General Assembly resolution 724 A (VIII), 7 December 1953, contained the following declaration: "We, the governments of the States Members of the United Nations, in order to promote higher standards of living and conditions of economic and social progress and development, stand ready to ask our peoples, when sufficient progress has been made in internationally supervised world-wide disarmament, to devote a portion of the savings achieved through such disarmament to an international fund, within the framework of the United Nations, to assist development and reconstruction in under-developed countries." It was adopted by 44 votes to 0, with 6 abstentions.

In the debate in the Second Committee of the General Assembly, arguments put forward in ECOSOC were by and large repeated. The main position of the more-developed, capital-exporting western countries was that they had no additional financial resources available for the proposed fund and that current efforts should concentrate on making existing programs and sources of financing more effective. The Soviet group of countries pointed to industrialization as the key to development. The best way to help underdeveloped countries obtain funds was to develop nondiscriminatory international trade relations, they argued. Developing countries argued that the fund should not depend on disarmament and that savings from disarmament should be viewed only as an additional source of finance. They turned the main argument around, arguing that the speeding up of economic development, which would be accomplished by such a fund, would help secure world peace and put an end to the internal threats and political unrest that endangered that peace. The acceleration of economic development must not be postponed indefinitely nor put off pending worldwide disarmament, they argued. See *Yearbook of the United Nations 1953,* 298.

41. "Economic Development of Under-Developed Countries," General Assembly resolution 724B (VIII), 7 December 1953. The General Assembly asked the president of ECOSOC, Mr. Raymond Scheyven (Belgium), to examine the comments of the governments and consult with them and report to ECOSOC and the General Assembly. It directed him to facilitate the establishment of such a fund as soon as possible.

42. United Nations, *Special United Nations Fund for Economic Development, Final Report by Raymond Scheyven* (New York: United Nations). For a summary of the positions taken, see *Yearbook of the United Nations 1955* (New York: United Nations, Department of Public Information, 1956), 91–98.

43. In retrospect, it is interesting to note that three NATO member governments—Denmark, the Netherlands, and Norway—disassociated themselves from the disarmament condition and argued strongly in favor of establishing SUNFED. Their rationale was that the Cold War between East and West and stalemates in the field of security policy should not block the creation of mechanisms aimed at promoting development in less-developed countries. Later, these governments—together with that of Sweden—became frontrunners as aid providers. Twenty years later, they constituted the core of the so-called group of likeminded (industrial) countries that promoted NIEO demands among the more reluctant industrial powers of the West.

44. In 1954, the General Assembly requested a new report from Mr. Scheyven (assisted by an ad hoc group of experts) that would provide a full picture of the form, functions, and responsibilities that might be given to SUNFED. See "Question of the Establishment of a Special United Nations Fund for Economic Development," General Assembly resolution 822 (IX), 11 December 1954. In 1955, it followed up on this report by calling for a new ad hoc committee, this time of government representatives, to analyze the responses of governments to a questionnaire formed to extract their views on the form, functions, and financial frame of the proposed fund. See "Question of the Establishment of a Special United Nations Fund for Economic Development," General Assembly resolution 923 (X), 9 December 1955. This committee reported the written views of the governments the following year. See General Assembly, "Final Report of the *Ad Hoc* Committee on the Question of the Establishment of a Special United Nations Fund for Economic Development Prepared in Accordance with General Assembly resolution 923(X)," *GAOR,* 12th Session, Annexes A/3579 and ADD.1, 16 May 1957.

45. See Jolly, Emmerij, Ghai, and Lapeyre, *UN Contributions to Development Thinking and Practice,* 82–83.

46. "Question of the Establishment of a Special United Nations Fund for Economic Development," General Assembly resolution 1030 (XI), 26 February 1957.

47. General Assembly, "Final Report of the *Ad Hoc* Committee on the Question of the Establishment of a Special United Nations Fund for Economic Development"; and

General Assembly, "Supplementary Report of the *Ad Hoc* Committee on the Question of the Establishment of a Special United Nations Fund for Economic Development," *GAOR,* 12th Session, Annexes, 27 May 1957.

48. In ECOSOC, the U.S. and UK spokesmen insisted on linking disarmament and development, arguing that immense sums would become available if a certain percentage of resources allocated to defense could be devoted to economic development. The UK spokesman, Sir Alec Randall, "could not think of any United Nations programme for which a prime necessity had not been the support of the chief contributing government of the United Nations—namely that of the United States of America. That was a fact of international life and there was nothing regrettable or sinister about it." See *ESCOR,* 24th Session, 992nd Meeting, 30 July 1957, 188–189, 192. The U.S. spokesman, Mr. Jacoby, argued that the prospect was "that the assets of SUNFED would consist of a few million dollars in a heterogeneous assortment of currencies and possibly some contributions in goods and services, and he wondered if it were reasonable for a new international financing agency entrusted with far-reaching objectives to be established with such pitifully meager resources. In view of all that was being done by private investors, by international leading agencies, and by the United States of America and other countries through bilateral programmes to direct thousands of millions of dollars into economic development, it could hardly be maintained that the establishment of a Lilliputian SUNFED was the nostrum which would obliterate poverty among millions of people in large parts of the world. . . . Indeed, action to establish SUNFED forthwith without United States would more probably deter than promote subsequent participation. If SUNFED were established under those conditions, it could only lead to deep disappointment and disillusionment in the under-developed countries, who would be encouraged by the establishment to entertain hopes which could not possibly be fulfilled. Far from strengthening the authority of the United Nations and maintaining its moral credit, it would only discredit the United Nations in the eyes of the world" (ibid., 192).

49. For the debate and the vote in ECOSOC, see *ESCOR,* 24th Session, 26–31 July 1957, 171–204. Some delegations argued strongly for the establishment of a fund even if it was not adopted unanimously. See the spokesman of the Netherlands, introducing a draft resolution co-sponsored by Argentina, Egypt, Greece, Indonesia, Mexico, and Yugoslavia; ibid., 172–175. Mr. J. Kaufmann, councilor at the Netherlands' Permanent Mission to the UN, acted as the rapporteur of the ad hoc committee, underscoring the prominent role played by the Netherlands in this issue. Behind the scenes, Professor Jan Tinbergen was among the advisers in the delegation of the Netherlands.

50. "Financing of Economic Development," ECOSOC resolution 662 (XXIV) B, 31 July 1957.

51. See also statements by the representatives of Poland (Mr. Michalowski) and the Soviet Union (Mr. Chernyshev); *ESCOR,* 24 Session, 991st Meeting, 29 July 1957, 182.

52. After finalizing his Ph.D. in economics at Cambridge under Keynes, V. K. R. V. Rao eventually became one of India's leading economists, founder and director of the New Delhi Institute of Economic Growth, vice-chancellor of the Delhi University, and a founder of the Economic and Social Research Institute in Bangalore. He also became a minister in India's federal government. See Shaw, *Sir Hans Singer,* 17.

53. Hans W. Singer started his studies in economics in Bonn under Joseph Schumpeter before a scholarship brought him to King's College, Cambridge University. Here he finalized his Ph.D. at a time when Keynes was working on his general theory of employment, interest, and money. V. K. R. V. Rao was a fellow Ph.D. student, and the

two men established a lifelong friendship. They had the same supervisor (Colin Clark) and their dissertations were approved on the same day, making them the third and fourth candidates to be awarded a Ph.D. in economics from Cambridge. Singer's record at the UN in a range of capacities is portrayed in Shaw, *Sir Hans Singer*. In 1947, he joined the Economic Affairs Department of the UN Secretariat, serving in a small development section of only three people, reflecting the priority given to the problems of developing countries at that point. By the time Singer left the UN, twenty-two years later, the number of people dealing with the problems of developing countries had increased to around 3,000.

54. Reflecting on these early years some forty years later, Hans W. Singer captured the prevailing consensus that was carried throughout the UN system: "There was a strong feeling that the same principles of planning, macroeconomic management of the economy by governments and mobilization of latent resources based on Keynesian principles, were also applicable to the problems of developing countries. . . . For many in the West, it seemed natural to expand the principles of the welfare state from the national to the international sphere, and the idea of international income transfers, including large-scale multilateral transfers centred in the UN, began to take shape." Singer, "Lessons of Post-War Development Experience, 1945–88," 34.

55. According to Jonas Haralz, the idea of promoting private investment was being articulated even before the Bretton Woods conference. The U.S. State Department had proposed that the World Bank be permitted to lend without guarantee from the host government. However, the more cautious view of the U.S. Treasury Department prevailed. Jonas Haralz, "The International Finance Corporation," in Devesh Kapur, John P. Lewis, and Richard Webb, *The World Bank: Its First Half Century,* vol. 1, *History* (Washington, D.C.: Brookings Institution Press, 1997), 807.

56. "Economic Development of Under-Developed Countries," ECOSOC resolution 416 C (XIV), 23 June 1952; and "Financing of Economic Development of Under-Developed Countries," General Assembly resolution 622B (VII), 21 December 1952.

57. Haralz is quite clear about the parentage: the idea "dedicated to furthering economic development through the growth of productive private enterprise, was formed into concrete proposal in the World Bank and would never have become reality without the Bank's perseverance." Haralz, "The International Finance Corporation," 805–806. However, other actors were involved. In a report to President Truman in March 1951, the International Development Advisory Board (chaired by Nelson A. Rockefeller) recommended that an International Finance Corporation be established as an affiliate of the World Bank. This proposal had a long journey before it was accepted by the U.S. administration in November 1954 and finally by the U.S. Congress in May 1955. The opposition had primarily come from U.S. business organizations and the Treasury Department, while the State Department was in favor. Ibid., 808–812.

58. "Economic Development of Under-Developed Countries," General Assembly resolution 724C (VIII), 7 December 1953. The positions of countries and groupings of countries toward private financing in developing countries and the role of the IFC in this context varied extensively. In the Second Committee, most developing countries argued in favor of the establishment of the IFC, stressing the importance of increasing the flow of private foreign capital. The representatives of Canada and India argued that many of the fears of underdeveloped countries with regard to private financing were not justified in all cases but were based on unfortunate incidents. Representatives of Belgium and Cuba stated that private capital would feel more secure with an international finance corporation and that the fears of both private creditors and underdeveloped countries

might thus be allayed. Saudi Arabia proposed that an international code to govern relations be drafted between government borrowers and their private creditors, a suggestion that the spokesmen of China and the United States supported. See *Yearbook of the United Nations 1953,* 301ff.

59. Eugene R. Black, president of the IBRD during these formative years, did not consider developing countries to be creditworthy enough to help build a loan portfolio that would support the World Bank's own creditworthiness. When the group of prominent experts appointed by the Secretary-General visited Black in early 1951, expecting that the Bank would move rapidly to an annual lending rate of at least $1 billion to these countries, Black responded that an amount of $400 million would be quite enough for some time. According to World Bank historians, "Black seemed [at the time] to have little sympathy for the demands then mounting for additional flows of multilateral resources to the poorer countries *at concessional*—that is, less than market (less than IBRD)—terms." But as the 1950s proceeded, two things changed. First, the Bank in general, and Black in particular, became concerned about the way creditworthiness considerations were inhibiting the bank's outreach to would-be borrowers. This was notably the case in the institution's dealings with its most populous clients, India and Pakistan. Second, from the end of the 1940s, proposals were being pressed on a multilateral concessional assistance program under the auspices of a new agency to be established under the authority of ECOSOC. "Eugene Black and his colleagues thought that, whatever its intrinsic merits, if there were to be such a program, it might be better run by the World Bank." Kapur, Lewis, and Webb, *The World Bank: Its First Half Century,* 1120–1121, 1126–1127; quotes on 1121.

60. Ibid., 1124.

61. Ibid., 384.

62. Ibid., 1125. From the beginning of the new regime, there was a division that eventually would enlist the U.S. executive branch in the pro-IBRD/IDA camp. However, the "thoroughly conservative, isolationist, antigovernmental wing of the Republican Party, represented within the administration by Secretary of the Treasury George Humphrey, had little or no use for pro-development governmental interventions, therefore little for foreign aid, and none at all for multilateral assistance" (ibid.).

63. Ibid., 1125–1126. According to Kapur, Lewis, and Webb, this alliance drew leaders from both parties "as well as from the corporate, trade union, academic, and journalistic world" (ibid.).

64. Ibid., 1127. The experiences of the United States with its bilateral food program triggered Monroney's engagement. He wanted to learn how to make use of the resources for real aid that were locked in local currencies resulting from sales of U.S. food aid and, since 1957, from repayments of loans from the U.S. Development Loan Fund. Mason and Asher remarked that "Monroney's grasp of international economics was not profound, but he was a humanitarian and a skillful politician"; Edward S. Mason and Robert E. Asher, *The World Bank since Bretton Woods* (Washington, D.C.: The Brookings Institution, 1973), 386–389, 392–393; quote on 387. According to Kapur, Lewis, and Webb, Monroney played a crucial role in the U.S. decision process on the IDA; they found it "somewhat bizarre, although it underscored how separate governmental powers are in the United States." The idea that triggered Monroney's initiative, namely to use the IDA to activate U.S.-owned holdings of local, inconvertible currencies, however, never got off the ground, even though Monroney had generated support for it. Kapur, Lewis, and Webb, *The World Bank: Its First Half Century,* 1127–1129; quote on 1127.

65. Kapur, Lewis, and Webb, *The World Bank: Its First Half Century,* 1129. Before

the end of January 1960, the board of the IBRD distributed articles of agreement to members for ratification, specifying that the fund needed at least $650 million in subscriptions. This level was reached on 24 September 1960. IDA operations began with the inaugural meeting of its board on 8 November 1960; the board of the IBRD acted as the board of the IDA. The proposed guidelines prescribed, inter alia, that the purpose of the IDA was to promote the development of less-developed members whose needs could not be met by the IBRD by financing high-priority projects.

66. According to Shaw, Singer and some of his colleagues "were under no illusion that if and when it came to a matter of choice, any new soft-financing facility would go to the World Bank, not the United Nations. . . . He recognized, with an element of pathos, that 'it fell to us in the UN secretariat to play the role of the "radical," "politically naïve," "amateurish," "inexperienced," "utopians" (all adjectives used throughout the SUNFED saga)' but in the event the cause of SUNFED was kept alive 'until it became acceptable, when it was time for the "responsible," "pragmatic," "experienced," "professional," "well-tried" institution [the World Bank] to take over'"; Shaw, *Sir Hans Singer,* 89. See also James H. Weaver, *The International Development Association: A New Approach to Foreign Aid* (New York: Praeger, 1965), 28.

67. Kapur, Lewis, and Webb, *The World Bank: Its First Half Century,* 1119.

68. Paul G. Hoffman, "Blueprint for Foreign Aid," *New York Times Magazine,* 17 February 1957. See also Jolly, Emmerij, Ghai, and Lapeyre, *UN Contributions to Development Thinking and Practice,* 79.

69. "Financing of Economic Development," General Assembly resolution 1219, 14 December 1957.

70. "Economic Development of Under-Developed Countries (and Annex: Draft Resolution Recommended for Adoption by the General Assembly)," ECOSOC resolution 692 (XXVI), 31 July 1958.

71. "Establishment of the Special Fund," General Assembly resolution 1240 (XIII), 14 October 1958. The resolution stated that the Special Fund would:

> (a) Be a separate fund; (b) Provide systematic and sustained assistance in fields essential to the integrated technical, economic and social development of the less developed countries; (c) In view of the resources prospectively available at this time, which are not likely to exceed $100 million annually, direct its operations towards enlarging the scope of the United Nations programmes of technical assistance so as to include special projects in certain basic fields as outlined hereunder.
>
> The Special Fund is thus envisaged as a constructive advance in United Nations assistance to the less developed countries which should be of immediate significance in accelerating their economic development by facilitating new capital investments of all types by creating conditions which would make such investments either feasible or more effective.

72. Ibid.

73. Ibid. It also stated that "due consideration shall be given to a wide geographical distribution in allowances over a period of years." Upper and lower financial limits for projects were established: to be considered, projects were not to cost more than $5 million and not less than $500,000. However, as activities of the fund proceeded, the lower limit was reduced to $250,000.

74. In 1963, the General Assembly expanded the Governing Council by six mem-

bers; "Enlargement of the Governing Council of the Special Fund," General Assembly resolution 1945 (XVIII), 11 December 1963.

75. Representatives of the specialized agencies (and the IAEA) were to be invited to the meetings of this board when projects that fell mainly within their fields came up for consideration. The managing director of the fund was to have a small staff and was expected to rely on the existing facilities of the UN, the specialized agencies, the IAEA, and the TAB. To facilitate coordination in the field between the EPTA and the fund, the managing director of the fund was expected to enter into agreement with the executive chairman of the TAB concerning the role of the resident representatives in the work of the fund. The projects were to be executed by the UN, its special agencies, or the IAEA.

76. As noted above, Paul G. Hoffman was instrumental in creating the UN Special Fund when serving as the U.S. representative on the Second Committee of the General Assembly. He became the first and only managing director of the fund; he was appointed for a four-year period that began on 1 January 1959 and was reappointed on 5 December 1962 for a new four-year term. In 1965, when the Special Fund and the EPTA merged to become the UNDP, Hoffman was appointed the first administrator of the new organization. Before joining the UN, Hoffman had served as the administrator of the Marshall Plan. For the rest of the century, the United States retained a monopoly when it came to appointments of the head of the UNDP.

77. *Yearbook of the United Nations 1959* (New York: United Nations, Office of Public Information, 1960), 112.

78. Ibid. A few developing countries (Afghanistan, Guinea, and Pakistan), however, warned against too rigid an application of the principle that the assistance should lead to early investments: they argued that this might bar projects of social significance and might result in too little emphasis on the improvement of the economic infrastructure. The representatives of Canada and the United States also emphasized the importance of the social aspects of economic development. Other delegations (Czechoslovakia, Morocco, Peru, and Portugal) argued that increasing attention should be given to industrial development.

79. *Yearbook of the United Nations 1962* (New York: United Nations, Office of Public Information, 1964), 197. In a statement to the Second Committee of the General Assembly in 1962, the Special Fund's managing director stressed the flexibility of the fund's responses to the needs of governments requesting assistance. The fund sought to assist developing countries through developing sound plans and informed planners; through studies and surveys to enable these countries to know their resources, both physical and human; through applied research and support of local institutions of advanced technical education and training to enable them to make the best use of their resources; and through supplementing its efforts to demonstrate the feasibility of investments in projects assisted by the fund and, when requested by the recipient governments, advisors to assist in arranging financing from sources of their choice (200–201).

80. See *Yearbook of the United Nations 1961* (New York: United Nations, Office of Public Information, 1963), 197–198; *Yearbook of the United Nations 1962*, 200; *Yearbook of the United Nations 1963* (New York: United Nations, Office of Public Information, 1965), 183–184; *Yearbook of the United Nations 1964* (New York: United Nations, Office of Public Information, 1966), 239; and *Yearbook of the United Nations 1965* (New York: United Nations, Office of Public Information, 1967), 280. The Centre for Industrial Development was governed by the Committee for Industrial Development and ultimately by ECOSOC.

81. *Yearbook of the United Nations 1963*, 183–184. In 1964, several representatives of

the South in ECOSOC (Argentina, India, and Indonesia) asked the Special Fund to bear in mind the recommendations of UNCTAD with regard to projects that would help increase the exports of developing countries. UNCTAD recommended that the Special Fund be gradually transformed so that it would also provide capital investment assistance, a proposal that India and Tanzania supported but the United Kingdom opposed on the grounds that such a transformation would inevitably have an adverse effect on pre-investment activities, a field in which the fund was irreplaceable. See *Yearbook of the United Nations 1964*, 240.

82. In 1961, the General Assembly responded by (unanimously) expressing the hope that the fund would give "prompt and sympathetic" consideration to the establishment of economic development and planning institutes as requested by the governments concerned and acting through the regional economic commissions. "Planning for Economic Development," General Assembly resolution 1708 (XVI), 19 December 1961.

83. *Yearbook of the United Nations 1962*, 197–198; *Yearbook of the United Nations 1963*, 180; and *Yearbook of the United Nations 1964*, 236.

84. See "World Campaign for Universal Literacy," General Assembly resolution 1937 (XVIII), 11 December 1963, which asked the fund to collaborate with the Secretary-General in exploring ways and means in supporting national efforts for the eradication of illiteracy; "Community Action," General Assembly resolution 1915 (XVIII), 5 December 1963, which asked the fund to assist governments in preparing community development programs; "Housing, Building and Planning," General Assembly resolution 1917 (XVIII), 5 December 1963, which asked the fund to consider the feasibility of including pilot projects in housing, building, and planning among its pre-investment activities; and "Participation of Women in National, Social and Economic Development," General Assembly resolution 1920 (XVIII), 5 December 1965, which asked the fund to cooperate with the Secretary-General in a study on the possibilities of the participation of women of developing countries in economic and social development. In 1964, the Governing Council agreed to a report by the managing director to meet the need for published information, advisory services, training programs, and information for capital-supplying countries. *Yearbook of the United Nations 1964*, 239.

85. The managing director, quite naturally, emphasized the multiplier value of the support provided by the fund. In 1962, he pointed out to the Second Committee of the General Assembly that the four fund-assisted projects that had been completed so far, which had cost less than $2 million, had attracted extensive external investments. Such investments committed to only one of these projects amounted to more than $300 million and hundreds of million dollars more were possible for this and the other projects. *Yearbook of the United Nations 1962*, 201.

86. One of these projects, which was completed in 1961, may illustrate the point in more specific terms. The government of Nigeria asked the Special Fund to assist in determining suitable dam sites for the multipurpose development of the Niger River. The cost of the survey was $2.4 million, which was split between the fund ($735,000) and the government (the equivalent of $1,690,000). The IBRD was the executing agency. The survey resulted in a $208 million investment program for the dam that was recommended by the study. This project, which was considered of crucial importance in Nigeria's six-year national development plan, was financed by a loan from the IBRD ($82 million); by separate loans from Italy, the Netherlands, the United Kingdom, and the United States ($58.5 million); and by domestic sources ($67.5 million). *Yearbook of the United Nations 1964*, 237.

87. In 1964, the Governing Council revised the financial regulations of the fund and expanded the mandate of the managing director to allocate funds. In 1965, it increased the frame of the administrative budget to $6.2 million. *Yearbook of the United Nations 1963*, 180; *Yearbook of the United Nations 1964*, 239; and *Yearbook of the United Nations 1965*, 279–280.

88. ECOSOC and, in turn, the General Assembly repeatedly appealed to member states and specialized agencies to do their utmost to increase their contributions to the Special Fund and the EPTA in order to obtain $150 million in annual contributions to these two organizations. See "Contributions to the Special Fund and to the Expanded Programme of Technical Assistance," General Assembly resolution 1529 (XV), 15 December 1960; "United Nations Development Decade: A Programme for International Economic Co-operation (II)," General Assembly resolution 1715 (XVI), 19 December 1961; and "Progress and Operations of the Special Fund; United Nations Programmes of Technical Co-operation," General Assembly resolution 1833 (XVII), 18 December 1962.

89. *Yearbook of the United Nations 1965*, 276.

90. At the pledging conferences, the U.S. committed itself to a fixed amount in U.S. dollars for the EPTA and the Special Fund, provided that the amount did not constitute more than 40 percent of the total contributions by all governments.

91. Interestingly, this approach was contested in the Second Committee of the General Assembly when it first discussed the operation of the fund. Representatives of some leading countries of the South and the East (Afghanistan, Byelorussian SSR, Chile, India, Pakistan, the USSR) pointed out the possibility of using national agencies as executing agencies, provided they were capable and competent. Similar arguments were raised, the following year, when ECOSOC considered the recommendation of the report of the fund's Governing Council that greater use should be made of national agencies of recipient countries in the execution of the projects. This point was raised again the following year by the Soviet Union: agencies of the recipient governments should themselves be entrusted with the execution of projects. See *Yearbook of the United Nations 1959*, 112; *Yearbook of the United Nations 1960* (New York: United Nations, Office of Public Information, 1961), 238; and *Yearbook of the United Nations 1962*, 200.

92. By the end of the first year of operation, requests for assistance had been received for 164 projects at a cost of $159 million.

93. Heppling notes that "in part it was no doubt due to the strong personal conviction held by Paul Hoffman [executive director of the Special Fund] himself that keeping the organizations of the United Nations system alive and active and allowing them to grow stronger was of the utmost importance. Support for all parts of the multilateral system was the duty of each component of it." Sixten Heppling, *UNDP: From Agency Shares to Country Programmes, 1949–1975* (Stockholm: Ministry of Foreign Affairs, 1995), 62.

94. Ibid.

95. *Yearbook of the United Nations 1965*, 276ff. As noted, the primary objective of the fund was to assist developing countries in expanding their productive resource basis through projects in strategically important areas. The primary purpose was to facilitate capital investments by others (the recipient governments themselves assisted by foreign aid or private domestic or foreign investors) by preparing the ground. Pre-investment studies became the main instrument.

The 522 projects approved by the Governing Council during its seven years of operation show a great variety of activities:

- 223 projects were surveys and feasibility studies providing eighty-seven countries with economic and technical information on their soils, mineral deposits, forest, and water resources and on their power, transport, and communication possibilities;

- 186 projects provided assistance to centers for advanced education and technical training, assisting seventy-four countries in making effective use of their human and other wealth-producing resources;

- 104 supported applied research institutes, assisting thirty-nine countries in adapting scientific and technological techniques to their development needs; and

- nine assisted more than sixty governments through advisory and training institutes by developing and disseminating key techniques for national and regional economic planning.

96. Ibid., 278.
97. Ibid., 276.

4. FIRST STEPS DOWN THE ROAD

1. For early descriptions and analyses of the bilateral aid policies of European countries, see contributions in Olav Stokke, ed., *European Development Assistance,* vol. 1, *Policies and Performance* (Tilburg: EADI, 1984). The colonial heritage of the former imperial powers was seen as the most important tradition from which their development cooperation emerged, and the lion's share of their early development assistance went to their former colonies; see Olav Stokke, "European Aid Policies: Some Emerging Trends," in Stokke, *European Development Assistance,* 10ff.

2. There were exceptions to this conclusion, illustrated by the Andean Indian Programme in Bolivia, Peru, and Ecuador. According to Dame Margaret Anstee, who served as EPTA resident representative in Bolivia, the program sought to integrate the Andean Indian people, who before the 1952 Bolivian revolution had been serfs, into all economic, social, cultural, and political aspects of national life. Education was emphasized: every child was to be entitled to schooling. There were no explicit references to human rights, but the whole process worked to this end (Anstee, personal communication). Many development projects supported by the EPTA and the Special Fund that were geared toward economic and social development had similar indirect effects on the human rights situation of vulnerable groups—minorities, children, and women in particular—without being cast in a human rights perspective.

3. Carol Lancaster underlines that security concerns have been the principal pillar of the U.S. aid program for forty-five years, noting that "from the very beginning, US foreign aid has rested heavily on the need to respond to external threats to US and world security emanating from the Soviet Union. Indeed, it seems likely that without such threats, an insular American public and a sceptical Congress would have never acquiesced to a sizeable foreign aid programme in the years following the Second World War." See Lancaster, "Governance and Development: The Views from Washington," *IDS Bulletin* 24, no. 1 (1993): 13. For the connection of Soviet development policy to security concerns, see Crawford Young, "Democratization and Structural Adjustment: A Political Overview," in *Democratization and Structural Adjustment in Africa in the 1990s,* ed. Lulal Deng, Markus Kostner, and Crawford Young (Madison: University of Wisconsin–Madison, Africa Studies Program, 1991), 15.

4. Crawford Young argues that the "competitive pursuit of strategic clients in the superpower cold war competition led both sides in the conflict to help sustain regimes supplying geopolitical services whose damage to policy and economy is now universally acknowledged (Mobuto Sese Seko for the Americans, Mengistu Haile Mariam for the Soviets). The possibility of relying on external protection to preserve power removed whatever shreds of accountability might exist in various patrimonial autocracies." Young, "Democratization and Structural Adjustment: A Political Overview," in *Democratization and Structural Adjustment in Africa in the 1990s,* ed. Lulal Deng, Markus Kostner, and Crawford Young (Madison: University of Wisconsin-Madison, Africa Studies Program, 1991), 15.

5. See Sixten Heppling, *FN och de fattiga länderna* (Stockholm: Prisma, 1970), 121–122.

6. When the UN was established in 1945, thirty-three of the fifty-one countries that signed the Charter came from the South. Five years later, this group of countries had increased to forty. By 1960, this group had increased to sixty-seven states, which was two-thirds of the UN membership.

7. United Nations, *Measures for the Economic Development of Underdeveloped Countries* (New York: United Nations, Department of Economic Affairs, May 1951).

PART 2 INTRODUCTION

1. See, for example, United Nations, *The Economic Development of Latin America and Its Principal Problems* (Lake Success, N.Y.: United Nations, Department of Economic Affairs/Economic Commission for Latin America, 1950); Hans W. Singer, "The Distribution of Gains between Investing and Borrowing Countries," *American Economic Review, Papers and Proceedings* 11, no. 2 (1950): 473–485; and Raúl Prebisch, "The Economic Development of Latin America and Its Principal Problems," *Economic Bulletin for Latin America,* 7, no. 1 (1962): 1–22.

2. André Gunder Frank, *Capitalism and Underdevelopment in Latin America: Historic Studies of Chile and Brazil* (London: Monthly Review Press, 1967).

3. Johan Galtung, "A Structural Theory of Imperialism," *Journal of Peace Research* 8, no. 2 (1971): 81–117.

4. In the spring of 1974, the United Nations 6th Extraordinary General Assembly (which was devoted to commodities and development issues) adopted both the "Declaration on the Establishment of a New International Order" (General Assembly resolution 3201 [S-VI], 1 May 1974) and the "Programme of Action on the Establishment of a New International Economic Order" (General Assembly resolution 3202 [S-VI], 1 May 1974). The General Assembly adopted the Charter of Economic Rights and Duties of States in the autumn of 1974 at its ordinary session. The 7th Extraordinary General Assembly adopted the resolution on development and international economic cooperation in 1975; "Development and International Economic Co-operation," General Assembly resolution 3362 (S-VII), 16 September 1975.

5. Some governments of the North, particularly those of the Netherlands and the Scandinavian countries, made efforts to combine the two concerns when promoting the NIEO policy; see Olav Stokke, "European Aid Policies: Some Emerging Trends," in *European Development Assistance,* vol. 1, *Policies and Performance,* ed. Olav Stokke (Tilburg: EADI, 1984), 9–64.

6. Hollis Chenery, Montek S. Ahluwalia, C. L. G. Bell, John H. Duloy, and Richard Jolly, *Redistribution with Growth: Policies to Improve Income Distribution in Developing Countries in the Context of Economic Growth* (London: Oxford University Press, 1974).

7. "Basic needs" was defined in various ways. Some defined basic needs as what would be required for mere survival, such as access to food, shelter, and health. Others broadened the concept to include facilities that would allow the individual to take command of his or her fate, such as access to education and the exercise of civil and political human rights. Johan Galtung has distinguished between four categories of basic human needs—safety, welfare, liberty, and identity—arguing that they should not be ranked but should be addressed simultaneously: material needs should not be given priority except in situations calling for relief operations. Interview in *Mazingira* 8 (1978): 7, 30–35.

8. In the mid-1970s, many reports, declarations, and action programs dealing with the general problem area associated with the basic needs approach appeared, providing ideas for those willing to pick them up. Important contributions include "Cocoyoc Declaration" [Mexico, 1974], in *Pugwash on Self-Reliance,* ed. W. K. Chagula et al. (New Delhi: Pugwash, 1977); and the 1975 Dag Hammarskjöld Report on Development and International Cooperation, *What Now—Another Development* (Uppsala: Dag Hammarskjöld Foundation, 1975). For institutions that adapted such ideas to their particular settings, see ILO, *Employment, Growth and Basic Needs: A One World Problem* (New York: Praeger, 1976); V. Djukanovic and E. P. Mach, eds., *Alternative Approaches to Meeting Basic Needs in Developing Countries* (Geneva: WHO, 1975), a joint study by the WHO and UNICEF; and UNICEF, *A Strategy for Basic Services* (New York: UNICEF, 1977).

9. A series of publications from a group around the Uppsala-based Hammarskjöld Foundation and the Swiss-based International Foundation for Development Alternatives (IFDA) managed to synthesize the family of utopian ideas that were floating around into an "another development" paradigm. This was elaborated in several issues of *Development Dialogue* and in a series of IFDA dossiers. See, in particular, IFDA, *A United Nations Development Strategy for the 80s and Beyond: Participation of the "Third System" in Its Elaboration and Implementation: A Project Description* (Nyon, Switzerland: IFDA, 1978); and Marc Nerfin, ed., *Another Development: Approaches and Strategies* (Uppsala: Hammarskjöld Foundation, 1977). From the very beginning, environmental concerns constituted the core perspective. Development should be needs-oriented, geared to meeting material and nonmaterial human needs. It should be endogenous: each society should define its values and visions for the future. Development should be self-reliant: each society should rely primarily on its own strengths and resources. It should be ecologically sound. And it should be based on structural transformations in social relations, economic activities and their spatial distribution, and the power structure in order to realize self-management and participating in decision-making by those affected by the decisions. These five basic elements were seen as being organically interlinked: in isolation they would not produce the desired results.

10. Björn Hettne, *Development Theory and the Three Worlds* (1990; repr., London: Longman, 1995).

11. R. G. A. Jackson, *A Study of the Capacity of the United Nations Development System,* 2 vols. (Geneva: United Nations, 1969).

12. Lester Pearson, *Partners in Development: Report of the Commission on International Development* (New York: Praeger, 1969).

5. THE FIRST DEVELOPMENT DECADE

1. *GAOR,* 16th Session, 1013th Meeting, 25 September 1961, 55–59. President Kennedy's main concern, however, was security, the focus of the first half of the speech. Before again turning to security policy—threats to peace emanating from so-called wars

of liberation in Southeast Asia and the Berlin crisis—he devoted two paragraphs (72 and 73) to development. He said, "Political sovereignty is but a mockery, without the means of meeting poverty, illiteracy and disease. Self-determination is but a slogan if the future holds no hope. That is why my nation—which has freely shared its capital and its technology to help others help themselves—now proposes officially designating this decade of the 1960's as the 'United Nations Decade of Development'" (ibid., 58).

2. "United Nations Development Decade, A Programme for International Economic Co-operation (I)," General Assembly resolution 1710 (XVI), 19 December 1961.

3. Ibid.

4. "United Nations Development Decade, A Programme for International Economic Co-operation (II)," General Assembly resolution 1715 (XVI), 19 December 1961.

5. "Accelerated Flow of Capital and Technical Assistance to the Developing Countries," General Assembly resolution 1522 (XV), 15 December 1960. Resolution 1715 (XVI) also set separate targets for national expenditures on health (in the range of 10 to 20 percent of general government consumption spending), education (a target of 4 percent domestic spending on education by the end of the decade that would be supplemented by substantial external assistance), and scientific research. Later international policy visions and programs have drawn inspiration from this strategy without much acknowledgement.

6. Secretary-General U Thant was very clear about these limitations: "In international society no one is ultimately responsible. There is no government to take the final praise or blame." Although there was a growing awareness of interdependence, he said, even the most powerful player was only "one part player." "There is no conductor," he continued. "There is no score. Nor can there be a question of central guidance at this stage." "The United Nations Development Decade at Mid-Point: An Appraisal by the Secretary General," *ESCOR*, 39th Session, Annexes (E/4071), 11 June 1965, 104 (paragraph 24).

7. See "Interim Report of the Secretary-General," *ESCOR*, 41st Session, Annexes (E/4196 and ADD.3), 5 May 1966. My ambition here is to see how the *idea* of the DD1 developed, focusing on the thinking during the process rather than on the results achieved. I found the 1966 interim report more useful as the prime source than the midterm report (E/4071) submitted in June 1965. The latter leaned on the more detailed (traditional) progress report submitted to ECOSOC less than one month earlier; see "Progress Report Submitted by the Secretary-General in Accordance with Council Resolution 984 I (XXXVI)," *ESCOR*, 39th Session, Annexes (E/4033), 14 May 1965. The 1966 interim report combined a description of the achievements to date with a concern for ways and means (and plans) for the years ahead.

8. "Interim Report of the Secretary-General," 3. Similar observations were made in the Secretary-General's midterm report. In the early 1960s, many of the poorest economies had continued to grow most slowly, the report stated. Moreover, the "gap between the *per capita* incomes of developing countries and those of the developed countries has also widened during the 1960s." "The United Nations Development Decade at Mid-Point," 101–102.

9. "Interim Report of the Secretary-General," 3–4.

10. U Thant identified the basic idea behind the development decade: "It tries to dramatize the stark fact that the gap in resources between the fully modernized nations and their still developing neighbours is tending to widen, leaving some two-thirds of

humanity below the poverty line, turning the developed societies, whether or not they realize it, into a privileged elite." "The United Nations Development Decade at Mid-Point," 101.

11. United Nations, *The United Nations Development Decade: Proposals for Action* (New York: United Nations, 1962); "United Nations Development Decade," ECOSOC resolution 916 (XXXIV), 3 August 1962.

12. "United Nations Development Decade," General Assembly resolution 2084 (XX), 20 December 1965; and "Interim Report of the Secretary-General," 3–10.

13. "Interim Report of the Secretary-General," 5.

14. Ibid. According to the Secretary-General, "almost all the organizations in the United Nations System contribute in some way to the spread of development planning, by helping to develop and introduce new planning methods, by assisting Governments in the setting of realistic targets and by trying to ensure that overall plans take account of the needs of various sectors and problem areas. The United Nations Secretariat has been steadily expanding its activities in development planning" (ibid., 12–13).

15. Ibid., 5.

16. Ibid., 7.

17. Ibid., 8.

18. Since 1952, the UN *Report on the World Social Situation* had undertaken periodic reviews of the social trends, in cooperation with the ILO, the FAO, UNESCO, and the WHO. This report was supplemented in 1963 with a *Compendium of Social Statistics* that provided trend data on a range of social factors during 1950–1960. For years, the ILO had reported on trends concerning employment, labor conditions, and human resource development (*International Labour Review; Yearbook of International Labour Statistics*). And so had the FAO (with the annual publication of *The State of Food and Agriculture*) and UNESCO and the WHO (through a series of overview studies and publications).

19. "Interim Report of the Secretary-General," 11.

20. Ibid., 15–16. The Secretary-General observed that in many developing countries "the administrative system cannot carry out the policies of a Government which has to be the prime mover of economic and social development. Some countries still do not have facilities for training administrative personnel, or effective methods of operation, or condition of service sufficiently good to retain technical staff, or forms of local government and administration that are conducive to local development." There was more to it: "the means for bringing about social change are often lacking or inadequate; the existing institutions and social structures may be out of date, and oriented towards the past. For example, the land tenure system in many countries still stands in the way of efforts to develop agriculture and modernize farming communities. The tax system is often regressive and fails to contribute to increasing productivity or to spreading the benefits of any increased production that is obtained. Women frequently continue to be isolated from modern influences and prevented from actively contributing to national life."

21. Ibid., 16. U Thant stated: "While improving the status of women raises questions of human rights and social justice, it may play a critical role in economic and social development. The emancipation of women can help to break down traditions, attitudes and practices that impede development and thus facilitate economic and technological change."

22. U Thant said: "The United Nations and the agencies concerned are increasingly able to assist Governments in these matters. However, they face a problem in that organizational change, like land reform and tax reform, often has political overtones. If

nothing is done, organizational and structural obstacles may defeat efforts to promote rapid economic and social growth, but if international organizations attempt to bring about reforms, it may be claimed that their role is no longer technical, but political." Laconically, he added: "This problem should be recognized, but not exaggerated." Ibid.

23. See "Development and Utilization of Human Resources," General Assembly resolution 2083 (XX), 20 December 1965; and "Development and Utilization of Human Resources," ECOSOC resolution 1090A (XXXIX), 31 July 1965.

24. "Interim Report of the Secretary-General," 16.

25. "Youth and National Development," ECOSOC resolution 1086J (XXXIX), 30 July 1965.

26. In the late 1940s and the 1950s, the transfer of science and technology to developing countries was considered the key to modernization. The major UN development programs were oriented to facilitate such transfers. Gradually, the emphasis changed from transferring science and technology to *developing* science and technology, especially through access to higher education and new research, an area where the gap between most developing countries and the industrialized world was wider than in most other fields and the costs involved in bridging the gap was greater than in most other areas. However, this strong belief in science and technology as the primary key to development was blind. In his midterm report, Secretary-General U Thant observed that the position of developing countries confronted with a huge influx of modern technology "is not all gain." He warned that much of the technology being transferred had been designed for other societies in other times and contexts. It was not appropriate to the current needs of emergent states and might even involve them in contradictions that more-developed societies had avoided. He cited the examples of "the tendency of modern health measures to bring about a very marked increase in population before any other factor in the community—food production, educational development, savings, industrial development—has become really dynamic"; productive technology that had been geared to the needs of societies in which labor tends to be scarce and capital abundant, in stark contrast to the situation prevailing in developing countries; and the lack of capital flows to increase the competitiveness of the primary resources developing countries produced in the context of a developed world that had already found substitutes for such commodities. "The United Nations Development Decade at Mid-Point," chapter 5.

27. "Interim Report of the Secretary-General," *ESCOR,* 41st Session, Annexes (E/4196 and ADD.3), 5 May 1966. For a similar analysis and conclusion, see "The United Nations Development Decade at Mid-Point," where U Thant criticized UN development programs for lack of dedication to the decade's goals: "The words are spoken, the gestures are made, but the sense of clear commitment seems elusive. The richer nations of the West, a little bemused by the quick, easy success of the Marshall Plan among a group of essentially already developed nations, have tended to approach the whole problem with an unrealistic time-scale. Put in the aid, mobilize the resources and, within a decade, the young economies should be well on their way to self-sustaining growth" (111).

28. "Interim Report of the Secretary-General," 26.

29. Ibid., 26ff. In "The United Nations Development Decade at Mid-Point," U Thant referred to the priority accorded to agriculture: "Unless production on the farms—on which the great bulk of the people still live—begins to increase, there is no surplus for saving, no surplus to feed the towns, no surplus to keep pace with rising population and keep down costly imports of food, no agricultural raw materials to feed into industry, above all, no rise in farm income to provide an expanding market for the

nascent industrial system. There is no conflict between the priorities of farming and industry, and the need to re-emphasize farming springs not from any desire to 'keep developing economies dependent' but simply to counteract the glamour of factory chimneys, which may all too often be smoking above products that no one in the community can afford to buy" (113).

30. "Interim Report of the Secretary-General," 30–31.

31. Ibid., 31.

32. Ibid., 32. U Thant noted that "private firms control a large part of the expertise, 'know-how' and financial resources required for setting up industries, and the mobilization of these resources through public action when needed is a delicate operation. The same is true at the other end in the developing countries themselves. It is not easy to organize public international support for private firms in developing countries, even at the request of Governments."

33. Ibid., 32

34. Ibid., 34. The report stated: "Between 1960 and 1970 the world's population can be expected to increase by some 600 million people, and about 85 per cent of this growth will occur in the developing countries. Many of the major cities in these countries are gaining population at two and three times the national growth rates. It is not surprising, then, that uncontrolled acceleration of population increase and rural-urban migration are now considered major deterrents to real economic progress in many countries."

35. Ibid., 34–35.

36. "Development of Non-Agricultural Resources: Report of the Secretary-General," *ESCOR*, 40th Session, Annexes (E/4132), 18 January 1966.

37. "Interim report of the Secretary-General," 38.

38. Ibid., 38–40.

39. "Travel, Transport, and Communications," ECOSOC resolution 1082A (XXXIX), 30 July 1965.

40. See "Progress Report Submitted by the Secretary-General in Accordance with Council Resolution 984 I (XXXVI)," *ESCOR*, 39th Session, Annexes (E/4033), 14 May 1965, 88ff.; and "Interim Report of the Secretary-General," 40–41.

41. In its first mimeographed form, the chapter (Chapter IV) was published separately as ECOSOC document E/4196/Add.3. For the 1965 report, see "Progress Report Submitted by the Secretary-General in Accordance with Council Resolution 984 I (XXXVI)," 95–97.

42. "Measures to Accelerate the Promotion of Respect for Human Rights and Fundamental Freedoms," General Assembly resolution 2027 (XX), 18 November 1965.

43. "Interim Report of the Secretary-General," 44–54.

44. "International Year for Human Rights," General Assembly resolution 2081 (XX), 20 December 1965.

45. For the discourse on second-generation aid conditionality, see Olav Stokke, "Aid and Political Conditionality: Core Issues and State of the Art," in *Aid and Political Conditionality*, ed. Olav Stokke (London: Frank Cass, 1995), 1–87.

46. John Toye and Richard Toye, *The UN and Global Political Economy* (Bloomington: Indiana University Press, 2004), 3.

47. "The United Nations Development Decade at Mid-Point," 114. A greater emphasis on multilateral agencies might "permit the vital task [development assistance] to go forward in an atmosphere less charged with political tension."

48. As early as 1966, ECOSOC had asked the Secretary-General to start planning, in consultation with interested organizations of the UN family, for concerted international action for the period after the decade and to determine how this planning could be best coordinated with national development programs; see "United Nations Development Decade," ECOSOC resolution 1152 (XLI), 4 August 1966. Later that year, the General Assembly asked the Secretary-General to submit (through ECOSOC) a preliminary framework of an international development strategy for the 1970s; see "United Nations Development Decade," General Assembly resolution 2218 (XXI), 19 December 1966.

49. ECOSOC did discuss the UN's development experiences during the decade. In its mid-1968 session, the council examined the process, problems, and policies of economic growth on the basis of the experience of developing countries during the period 1955–1965. For a brief summary of the conclusions, see *Yearbook of the United Nations 1968* (New York: United Nations, Office of Public Information, 1971), 326–327. The Secretariat produced another comprehensive study that focused on the methodological problems involved in measuring progress in developing countries in 1971. This study constituted an important basis for the review and appraisal system established for DD2. See United Nations, *World Economic Survey, 1969–1790, The Developing Countries in the 1960s: The Problem of Appraising Progress* (New York: United Nations, Department of Economic and Social Affairs, 1971).

50. *Yearbook of the United Nations 1968,* 328–329. The Commission for Social Development concluded that, by and large, the decade had failed to achieve its goals. One of the main reasons for the failure was that its overall targets were expressed in global and universal terms and did not reflect the varying conditions in different regions and subregions of the world and that the targets had been too simplistic and too few. Moreover, the decade had failed to indicate clearly and in any detail the means for achieving its specified ends. See *Yearbook of the United Nations 1969* (New York: United Nations, Office of Public Information, 1972), 439.

6. THE SECOND DEVELOPMENT DECADE

1. See "Declaration on the Occasion of the Twenty-fifth Anniversary of the United Nations," General Assembly resolution 2627 (XXV), 24 October 1970, paragraph 9, which emphasizes that the proclaimed Second Development Decade "coincides with and is linked to the Disarmament Decade." The resolution urged governments to give their full support to the International Development Strategy to ensure the "most complete and effective implementation in order to realize the fundamental objectives of the Charter." The decade was proclaimed and the international development strategy for the decade adopted on the same day. "International Development Strategy for the Second United Nations Development Decade," General Assembly resolution 2626 (XXV), 24 October 1970.

2. The Economic Committee of ECOSOC came to play a particularly important role in the preparatory work at the intergovernmental level. In 1968, ECOSOC doubled the membership of the committee from twenty-seven to fifty-four state members. This did not take place in a political vacuum: it was a carefully balanced compromise between delegations that favored UNCTAD and those that favored ECOSOC as the forum for government participation in the preparatory work on DD2.

Another conflict concerned whether to include state members of the UN and other UN bodies and specialized agencies. The Soviet bloc wanted to limit membership to UN members and argued strongly against including the Federal Republic of Germany (which at the time was not a member state). After a proposal to this effect was rejected, committee members from the East abstained from taking part in the preparatory work. A proposal late in 1969 by the East to include the German Democratic Republic in the committee prompted the representatives of France, the United Kingdom, and the United States to respond that only "the freely and lawfully elected" government of the Federal Republic of Germany was entitled to speak in the name of the German people in international affairs, leading to new protests from the Soviet bloc. See *Yearbook of the United Nations 1968* (New York: United Nations, Office of Public Information, 1971), 334–335, 1073–1074; *Yearbook of the United Nations 1969* (New York: United Nations, Office of Public Information, 1972), 284–285; and *Yearbook of the United Nations 1970* (New York: United Nations, Office of Public Information, 1972), 306. The chilly winds of the Cold War were indeed blowing as the UN prepared for the Second Development Decade.

3. "Mobilization of Public Opinion in Developed and Developing Countries Regarding the United Nations Development Decade," ECOSOC resolution 1357 (XLV), 2 August 1968.

4. "Second United Nations Development Decade," ECOSOC resolution 1556A (XLIX), 31 July 1970.

5. "International Development Strategy for the Second United Nations Development Decade," 1. It was added, however, that the success of international development activities would depend on improvements in the international situation, "particularly on concrete progress towards general and complete disarmament under effective international control, on the elimination of colonialism, radical discrimination, *apartheid* and occupation of territories of any State and on the promotion of equal political, economic, social and cultural rights for all members of society. Progress towards general and complete disarmament should release substantial additional resources which could be utilized for the purpose of economic and social development, in particular that of developing countries" (5). There should therefore be a close link between the Second Development Decade and the Disarmament Decade, the General Assembly argued.

6. Ibid., paragraphs 7, 11, and 12.

7. Ibid., paragraph 19.

8. Ibid., paragraph 28.

9. Ibid., paragraph 29

10. Ibid., paragraph 38.

11. Ibid., paragraph 39.

12. Ibid., paragraph 40.

13. Ibid., paragraph 41.

14. Ibid., paragraph 42.

15. Ibid., paragraph 43. During the process, these commitments were weakened and made more flexible. The Committee for Development Planning proposed 1972 as the date for meeting the 1 percent target. The preparatory committee proposed (but did not agree on) an annual contribution of 0.75 percent of GNP in ODA, and this target was supported by many speakers at the July 1970 session of ECOSOC.

In the Second Committee, several countries, including Canada and New Zealand, had reservations about the time limits set for implementing the financial resource transfers. Australia, Austria, and Italy stated that they were unable to commit themselves to meeting either the quantitative targets or target dates. Japan and the United Kingdom did not accept any targets with regard to ODA, and France found the quantitative target for ODA too high. *Yearbook of the United Nations 1970,* 305ff.

16. Reservations were made, however. The resolution stated that "while it may not be possible to untie assistance in all cases, developed countries will rapidly and progressively take what measures they can in this respect both to reduce the extent of tying of assistance and to mitigate harmful effects. Where loans are tied essentially to particular sources, developed countries will make, to the greatest extent possible, such loans available for utilization by the recipient countries for the purchase of goods and services from other developing countries." "International Development Strategy for the Second United Nations Development Decade," paragraphs 44–45, quote in paragraph 45.

17. Ibid., paragraphs 46–47, quote in paragraph 46.

18. Ibid., paragraph 49.

19. Ibid., paragraph 48.

20. Ibid., paragraph 50.

21. Ibid., paragraph 53.

22. Ibid., paragraphs 54–55.

23. Ibid., paragraphs 56–57, quote in paragraph 56. Particular attention would "be paid to overcoming their problem of scarcity of indigenous technical and managerial cadres, to building the economic and social infrastructure, to the exploitation by these countries of their natural resources and to assisting them in the task of formulating and implementing national development plans" (paragraph 57).

24. Ibid., paragraph 58. "In the field of manufactures and semi-manufactures, measures in favour of developing countries will so be devised as to allow the least developed of developed countries to be in a position to derive equitable benefits from such measures. Particular consideration will be given to the question of including in the general system of preferences products of export interest to these countries." These countries, in cooperation with other developing countries, "will intensify their efforts for subregional and regional co-operation, and the developed countries will facilitate their task through technical assistance and favourable financial and trade policy measures."

25. Ibid., paragraph 59.

26. Ibid., paragraphs 60–64, quotes in paragraph 61. The strategy went on to state that particular attention would be devoted to technologies suitable to these countries. The resolution stated that developing countries were to concentrate research efforts "in relation to selected problems the solutions to which can have a catalytic effect in accelerating development. Assistance will also be provided for building up and, as appropriate, for expanding and improving research institutions in developing countries, especially on a regional and subregional basis. Efforts will be made to promote close co-operation between the scientific work and staff of the research centres in developing countries and between those in developed and developing countries" (paragraph 62).

27. Ibid., paragraph 63. The Preparatory Committee had proposed a target for aid to developing countries of 0.05 percent of GNP for science and technology development and a target of 5 percent of total research and development expenditure for work that specifically related to developing countries; *Yearbook of the United Nations 1970,* 312. In the strategy adopted, the decision on such targets was postponed.

28. "International Development Strategy for the Second United Nations Development Decade," paragraph 64. Such a program would review the international conventions on patents and identify and reduce obstacles to the transfer of technology to developing countries.

29. Ibid., paragraph 65.

30. Ibid., paragraph 67.

31. Ibid., paragraph 68.

32. Ibid., paragraphs 69–72.

33. Ibid., paragraph 74.

34. Ibid., paragraph 75.

35. Ibid., paragraph 76.

36. In 1967, the Committee for Development Planning observed that while many countries had drawn up plans, few had been successful in implementing them. The committee emphasized that it was not meaningful to talk of the implementation of development plans if the policies necessary to ensure social change, such as land reform and income redistribution, or the measures necessary for social discipline, including fiscal and financial restraints, were avoided. *Yearbook of the United Nations 1967* (New York: United Nations, Office of Public Information, 1969), 390–391.

37. "International Development Strategy for the Second United Nations Development Decade," paragraph 78.

38. Ibid., paragraphs 79–83.

39. Ibid., paragraph 84.

40. On 16 October 1970, the same day that the Second Committee adopted the strategy without a vote, several groups submitted joint formal statements to the General Assembly and member states submitted another forty statements. Eighty-eight developing countries stated that although the development strategy was not an adequate expression of their aspirations, it was the best reflection of the current stage of humankind's collective conscience in one of the most crucial areas of the organization concerning human society. They stressed the importance of definite target dates for implementing the policy measures. A group of ten landlocked countries expressed general agreement with the strategy (they were signatories of the statement of the 88-country group as well) but found that it did not meet their needs: they would have little chance to participate in development unless provided with adequate guarantees for their right of free access to the sea and adequate financial and technical assistance. A statement by France, submitted on behalf of the EEC, disagreed with price policies and the practice of liberating trade with commodities. A statement by five Latin American states expressed approval of the strategy and stressed the necessity of establishing time limits for transferring resources from developed to developing countries. The eight Eastern European countries filed an extensive statement, expressing support, in principle, of UN measures that could contribute to the elimination of the difficult social and economic conditions of hundreds of millions of people. *Yearbook of the United Nations 1970*, 312ff.

41. Ibid., 314. Among those voicing reservations were countries that in the past had been the main contributors to international development assistance, including through the multilateral system (France, the United Kingdom, and the United States). The U.S. statement is particularly noteworthy: the United States had been reexamining its aid policy and was unable to accept the time limit and target for official aid. It could not give assurance that the 1 percent target for total financial assistance would be met, although it felt that the flow of private resources would respond to mutually beneficial investment policies in developing countries.

42. See "Mid-Term Review and Appraisal of Progress in the Implementation of the International Development Strategy for the Second United Nations Development Decade," General Assembly resolution 3517 (XXX), 15 December 1975; "Declaration

on the Establishment of a New International Order," General Assembly resolution 3201 (S-VI), 1 May 1974; and "Programme of Action on the Establishment of a New International Economic Order," General Assembly resolution 3202 (S-VI), 1 May 1974.

43. *Yearbook of the United Nations 1975* (New York: United Nations, Office of Public Information, 1978), 366.

44. Ibid.

45. Ibid., 366–367. The Second Committee of the General Assembly, in turn, approved a draft resolution that was adopted by the General Assembly by 123 votes to 0, with 8 abstentions; General Assembly resolution 3517 (XXX), 15 December 1975.

46. General Assembly resolution 3517 (XXX), 15 December 1975, paragraphs 3–4, 5–10, and 12, and tables 1–4 and 6.

47. Ibid., paragraph 25.

48. Ibid., paragraph 26 and table 5. According to the review, debt-service payments had "grown from an annual average of 9.6 percent during the 1960s to about 16.5 percent during the period 1970–72. . . . The ratio of debt-service payments to export earnings for a number of developing countries exceeded 10 percent in 1974 and in some cases passed the 20 percent level" (ibid., paragraph 27).

49. Ibid., paragraph 28.

50. The General Assembly passed a resolution sponsored by developing countries on implementing the charter by a vote of 114 to 3, with 11 abstentions; "Implementation of the Charter of Economic Rights and Duties of States," General Assembly resolution 3486 (XXX), 12 December 1975. Although it gained support from a vast majority, the resolution encountered strong objections from major western powers; *Yearbook of the United Nations 1975*, 389.

51. "Resolution Adopted by the General Assembly at Its 107th Plenary Meeting," General Assembly resolution 32/174, 19 December 1977.

52. "Global Negotiations Relating to International Economic Co-operation for Development," General Assembly resolution 34/138, 14 December 1979.

53. *Yearbook of the United Nations 1980* (New York: United Nations, Office of Public Information, 1983), 489.

54. Ibid., 487, 491.

55. Ibid., 492.

56. *Yearbook of the United Nations 1980,* 492ff.

57. Ibid., 492ff. Jordan compared the assistance from Arab oil-producing countries (more that 5 percent of their annual GNP) to that of developed world, meaning the OECD countries (one-third of 1 percent). The United Arab Emirates stated that its contribution was more than 16 percent of its GNP, while Qatar claimed that Arab oil producers had exceeded the target by figures ranging from six to twenty-two times. Kuwait stated that it was offering soft terms and long grace periods in its financial operations with developing countries (494).

58. Ibid., 494–495.

59. Ibid., 494.

60. Ibid., 495ff. Representatives of Soviet-bloc countries denied that aid from the Soviet bloc was small compared with that provided by western countries. A substantial part of the aid from the West was merely compensation for colonial exploitation, for which the socialist states had no responsibility, they argued.

61. "Global Negotiations Relating to International Economic Co-operation for Development"; and "International Development Strategy for the Third United Nations Development Decade," General Assembly resolution 35/56, 5 December 1980.

Individual governments and political groupings expressed reservations to particular items in the strategy when explaining their vote, both in the ad hoc committee and in the plenary session of the special assembly and later in the Second Committee and the plenary of the General Assembly.

62. "International Development Strategy for the Third United Nations Development Decade," Annex, paragraph 1.

63. Ibid., Annex, paragraphs 2–3.

64. Ibid., paragraph 7.

65. Ibid., paragraph 8. The resolution reiterated fundamental norms: "Full respect for the independence, sovereignty and territorial integrity of every country, abstention from the threat or use of force against any State, non-interference in the internal affairs of other States and the settlement by peaceful means of disputes among States are of the utmost importance for the success of the International Development Strategy." It stated that all members of the international community should take urgent action "to end without delay colonialism, imperialism, neo-colonialism, interference in internal affairs, *apartheid,* racial discrimination, hegemony, expansionism, and all forms of foreign aggression and occupation, which constitute major obstacles to the economic emancipation and development of developing countries" (paragraphs 12–13).

66. Ibid., paragraph 20. Other economic growth targets set for developing countries as a whole included an annual 4.5 percent increase in GDP/capita; an annual increase of at least 4 percent in agriculture; and an annual increase of 9 percent in manufacturing. The resolution stated that gross investments should reach 28 percent of GDP in 1990 and that exports and imports of goods and services should expand at an annual rate of not less than 7.5 percent (exports) and 8 percent (imports) (paragraphs 21–23, 29).

67. Ibid., especially paragraphs 19 and 52–80.

68. Burden-sharing was one topic in this debate—an item that came to remain on the agenda for years to come. Luxembourg, speaking on behalf of the EEC, argued that ODA should be shared in a more equitable way among developed countries, regardless of their economic and social systems, an opinion shared by Norway and the United States.

69. "International Development Strategy for the Third United Nations Development Decade," General Assembly resolution 35/56, 5 December 1980, especially paragraphs 19 and 52–80. "A rapid and substantial increase will be made in official development assistance by all developed countries, with a view to reaching and where possible surpassing the agreed international target of 0.7 percent of the gross national product of developed countries. To this end, developed countries which have not yet reached the target should make their best efforts to reach it by 1985, and in any case not later than in the second half of the Decade. The target of 1 percent should be reached as soon as possible thereafter. The efforts of developed countries should be greater, the lower their relative performance. Developing countries in a position to do so should also continue to provide assistance to other developing countries."

Several countries did not accept the target. For example, the United States argued that ODA was not necessarily the most appropriate remedy for the problems of special-category countries. Belgium and Luxembourg stated that the 1 percent target was unrealistic, given the difficult budgetary situation they were experiencing. The Federal Republic of Germany could not accept the higher target in view of the uncertain world economic development. France and Ireland stated that the target could not be seen as an agreed international target, while Italy stated that it should only be considered as a future indicator. Also Japan had reservations, both with regard to the time frame set and for the 1 percent target itself.

The strongest reservations came from the Eastern European socialist states: they found it unjustified that they should have to take on the demands and criteria addressed to developed capitalist countries.

A few countries welcomed and fully accepted the target. These included Denmark, the Netherlands, and Sweden. Norway would have preferred that the target be more ambitious with regard to time frames. Austria and New Zealand accepted the ODA target as an indicative one but under the current economic circumstances saw little likelihood of being able to expand their ODA in the near future. *Yearbook of the United Nations 1980,* 500–502.

70. "International Development Strategy for the Third United Nations Development Decade," Annex, paragraph 99. The commitment included multiyear pledges to UN development assistance programs. The resolution encouraged all donors to pay special attention to "timely and substantial increases in the soft resources through multilateral institutions." The "average rate of concessionality" of ODA should be increased and ODA to the LDCs should be provided as grants. ODA should "as a general rule" be untied, and the share of "programme assistance and local and recurrent cost financing" in ODA should be increased substantially.

71. Ibid., paragraphs 103, 106, 110. Mixed credit was an instrument a government could use to support its national firms to win international bidding contracts. Grant aid (ODA) was provided to reduce the costs involved (the bid), thus skewing the competition. In essence, it was an instrument to promote exports. If the grant element was 25 percent or more, it was recorded as ODA.

72. Ibid., paragraphs 18 and 24; see also paragraphs 136–146. The United States did not consider ODA to be the most appropriate way to deal with the problems of these countries. Also, the members of the EEC found it inopportune to fix subtargets for ODA, since this could lead to inappropriate rigidities in the distribution of ODA. See *Yearbook of the United Nations 1980,* 500.

73. "International Development Strategy for the Third United Nations Development Decade," Annex, paragraphs 147–155.

74. Ibid., paragraphs 28 and 81–95. The resolution viewed food aid in the context of agricultural and rural development pursued in developing countries through their development plans and efforts. Developing countries, "firmly supported" by the international community, would "take all necessary measures to accelerate food and agricultural production in order to improve national and collective self-sufficiency in food as early as possible." The resolution urged them to give adequate consideration to agrarian reforms "as one of the important factors for increasing agricultural production."

75. Ibid., paragraphs 30, 36, 92–80. The United Nations Industrial Development Fund was the main operational arm of UNIDO. It was governed by the Industrial Development Board. Like the UNDP, it was dependent on voluntary contributions.

76. Ibid., paragraphs 46–48.

77. Ibid., paragraphs 162–167, quote paragraph 162.

78. Ibid., paragraph 110.

79. Ibid.

80. Ibid., paragraph 115. In paragraph 26, the strategy stated that in stipulating the conditions attached to the use of its resources, the IMF would "pay due regard to the social and political domestic objectives of member countries, to their economic priorities and circumstances."

With hindsight it is interesting to note that the core of the harsh critique of the adjustment policy pursued by the Bretton Woods Institutions during the 1980s was that in actual practice it went contrary to this prescription for the 1980s. The most hard-hitting critique came from a prominent insider; see Joseph E. Stiglitz, *Globalization and its Discontents* (London: Penguin Allen Lane, 2002).

81. Ibid., Annex, paragraph 116.

82. Ibid., paragraphs 117–125. The strategy stated that "access to and mastery of modern scientific and technological knowledge are essential for the economic and social progress of developing countries." Transfer of technology was of "utmost importance." All countries should take steps for the early finalization of an international code of conduct on the transfer of technology. Developed countries should "increase substantially the proportion of their research and development expenditure and efforts to be devoted to the solution of jointly identified specific problems of prime importance to developing countries with the active participation of researchers and institutions of developing countries." They should also "intensify their support of developing countries' efforts towards greater self-reliance in the field of technological development." Developing countries would, with the necessary support of developed countries and international financial institutions, "intensify their efforts to strengthen their scientific and technological infrastructure and develop their endogenous technological and inventive capacities, in order to enhance their capacity to design and generate new technologies as well as to select and acquire, apply and adapt existing technology." And "substantial resources" should be mobilized for the UN Financing System for Science and Technology for Development established in 1979 by the General Assembly.

83. Ibid., paragraphs 6, 32, 34–35, and 126–127. In interpretive statements, representatives of industrialized countries (Australia, Canada, the EEC members, and the United States) stated that such rights must be exercised in accordance with the principles of international law.

84. Ibid., paragraphs 128–133.

85. Ibid., paragraph 41.

86. World Commission on Environment and Development, *Our Common Future* (Oxford: Oxford University Press, 1987).

87. "International Development Strategy for the Third United Nations Development Decade," Annex, paragraph 40.

88. *Yearbook of the United Nations 1979* (New York: United Nations, Office of Public Information, 1983), 462ff.; *Yearbook of the United Nations 1980,* 485ff.

89. *Yearbook of the United Nations 1980,* 485ff. India presented working papers to the committee on behalf of the G-77, and Italy presented statements on behalf of the EEC, Japan, Norway, Switzerland, and the United States. Several other delegations provided written statements on their positions (488).

90. *Yearbook of the United Nations 1980,* 521. The frustration of developing countries was manifest in India's statement of position at the end of the June/July 1980 session of the Committee on the Whole on behalf of the G-77 countries. Developed countries were using stalling tactics, India said. When formulations were arrived at in the negotiating group, developed countries invariably suggested changes to weaken the text. The vague proposals of the western industrialized countries seemed to suggest that they were trying to halt or reverse the transfer of resources. The statement concluded that industrialized countries seemed determined to keep current institutional arrangements and decision-making processes intact.

91. Ibid., 522. The responsibility for lack of agreement lay with states at the helm

of the world economy, Stoltenberg argued. He deplored the lack of mutual confidence shown and added that although some developed countries had suggested flexible and helpful proposals, it was the developing countries that were ready to make considerable concessions.

92. Ibid., 524–525. The proposal suggested that the General Assembly convene a UN conference with universal participation at a high international level to serve as the forum for coordinating and conducting global negotiations with a view to ensuring a simultaneous, coherent, and integrated approach to the issues negotiated and to result in a package agreement. In the Ad Hoc Committee, the United States asserted that it could not accept the proposal because it did not resolve the conceptual differences regarding the division of responsibility between the proposed conference and the specialized agencies and might permit the conference to renegotiate agreements reached in the agencies. Since no consensus existed, the United States could not accept the proposal. The Federal Republic of Germany and the United Kingdom associated themselves with this view.

93. Ibid., 519.

94. Ibid.

95. At the end of the ordinary sessions of the General Assembly, the president reported that no agreement had been reached in the consultations and moved that the issue be placed on the agenda of its next session "to allow further informal, but intensive, consultations." *Yearbook of the United Nations 1981* (New York: United Nations, Office of Public Information, 1985), 378–380; *Yearbook of the United Nations 1982* (New York: United Nations, Office of Public Information, 1986), 595–597; *Yearbook of the United Nations 1983* (New York: United Nations, Office of Public Information, 1987), 405–406; *Yearbook of the United Nations 1984* (New York: United Nations, Office of Public Information, 1988), 390–391; *Yearbook of the United Nations 1985* (New York: United Nations, Office of Public Information/Martinus Nijhoff Publishers, 1989), 417–418; *Yearbook of the United Nations 1986* (New York: United Nations, Office of Public Information/Martinus Nijhoff Publishers, 1990), 394; *Yearbook of the United Nations 1987* (New York: United Nations, Office of Public Information/Martinus Nijhoff Publishers, 1992), 378.

7. THE UNITED NATIONS DEVELOPMENT PROGRAMME, 1966–1981

1. "Consolidation of the Special Fund and the Expanded Programme of Technical Assistance in a United Nations Development Programme," General Assembly resolution 2029 (XX), 22 November 1965, adopted by 98 votes to 0, with 9 abstentions.

2. *Report of the Secretary-General under Resolution 900A (XXXIV): Part I. Expanded Programme of Technical Assistance and Special Fund,* ECOSOC document E/3850, 9 January 1964; *Report of the Secretary-General under Council Resolution 900A (XXXIV): Part II. Regular Technical Assistance Programmes of the United Nations, the Specialized Agencies and the International Atomic Energy Agency,* ECOSOC document E/3851, 31 January 1964.

3. The General Assembly asked the Secretary-General to prepare a study that outlined the practical steps needed to transform the Special Fund into a capital development fund; "Establishment of a United Nations Development Fund," General Assembly resolution 1936 (XVIII), 11 December 1963. The roots of the idea of a UN capital investment program had went back to the struggle for SUNFED. Several members of ECOSOC and its Coordination Committee, especially those representing the Soviet Union, Czechoslovakia, and the United Arab Republic, feared that the merger

might tip the balance toward converting the Special Fund into a capital development fund. *Yearbook of the United Nations 1964* (New York: United Nations, Office of Public Information, 1966), 232.

4. Principles to guide the composition of the Governing Council were set out in an Annex called "Consolidation of the Special Fund and the Expanded Programme of Technical Assistance in a United Nations Development Programme." Nineteen seats were to be filled by developing countries (distributed geographically: seven African countries, six Asian countries, and six Latin American countries) and seventeen seats by economically more developed countries (fourteen by Western European and other countries and three by Eastern European countries). The remaining seat was to rotate between the groups identified according to a preset order within a nine-year cycle.

5. "United Nations Development Decade: A Programme for International Economic Co-operation (II)," General Assembly resolution 1715 (XVI), 19 December 1961; "United Nations Development Programme," General Assembly resolution 2093 (XX), 20 December 1965.

6. *Yearbook of the United Nations 1968* (New York: United Nations, Office of Public Information, 1971), 347–348. Other criteria applied as well. At its fourth session (June 1967), the Governing Council asked the administrator to take into account such factors as the degree of a country's development, per capita income, population size, extent of other aid, and the capacity of a country to absorb technical assistance when preparing country targets. *Yearbook of the United Nations 1967* (New York: United Nations, Office of Public Information, 1969), 307.

7. *Yearbook of the United Nations 1968,* 348.

8. "Co-ordination at the Country Level," ECOSOC resolution 1262 (XLIII), 3 August 1967. The following year, ECOSOC emphasized once again the central role of resident representatives in coordinating technical cooperation and pre-investment programs of the UN and its related organizations in the field. "Co-ordination at the Country Level: The Role of the Resident Representatives of the United Nations Development Programme," ECOSOC resolution 1453 (XLVII).

9. *Yearbook of the United Nations 1967, 306.* At its third session (January 1967), the Governing Council empowered the administrator to accept donations from nongovernmental sources for purposes consistent with those of the UNDP and on the condition that no limitation be set on the use of such donations. The administrator was also allowed to accept and administer trust funds, subject to prior approval in each case.

10. In 1968, the UNDP administrator participated in five trust funds at the request of the Secretary-General: the Special Industrial Services Trust Fund (together with UNIDO, involving $8 million in the years 1965–1968), the Fund of the UN for the Development of West Irian (which the administrator became responsible for in February 1967 and which totaled $30 million at the end of 1968), the Fund-in-Trust Programme for the Democratic Republic of the Congo (under UNDP administration since 1966, since then involving almost $12 million), and the UN Korean Reconstruction Agency Residual Assets.

In comparison, the total (voluntary) pledges by governments for ordinary UNDP activities in 1968 amounted to $183.5 million: $118.9 million for the Special Fund component and $64.6 million for the technical assistance component. In addition, contributions from recipient governments for assessed local costs amounted to $10.7 million. *Yearbook of the United Nations 1968, 344–345.*

11. "Technical Assistance in Trade and Related Fields," General Assembly resolution 2401 (XXXIII), 13 December 1968.

12. "Evaluation Programmes of Technical Co-operation," ECOSOC resolution 1151 (XLI), 4 August 1966.

13. "Evaluation of Programmes of Technical Assistance," ECOSOC resolution 1263 (XLIII), 3 August 1967.

14. "Evaluation of Programmes of Technical Co-operation," ECOSOC resolution 1364 (XLV), 2 August 1968. ECOSOC emphasized that "evaluation activities should at all times be related to the practical purpose of ensuring that the principles of good management are exercised at all stages of technical co-operation projects."

15. "United Nations Capital Development Fund," General Assembly resolution 2321 (XXII), 15 December 1967.

16. "Report on the United Nations Capital Development Fund," ECOSOC resolution 1350 (XLV), 2 August 1968; "United Nations Capital Development Fund," General Assembly resolution 2410 (XXIII), 17 December 1968.

17. *Yearbook of the United Nations 1966* (New York: United Nations, Office of Public Information, 1968), 227; *Yearbook of the United Nations 1968*, 348–349; *Yearbook of the United Nations 1969* (New York: United Nations, Office of Public Information, 1972), 301; *Yearbook of the United Nations 1970* (New York: United Nations, Office of Public Information, 1972), 348.

18. "Long-Term Policies and Programmes for Youth in National Development," ECOSOC resolution 1407 (XLVI), 5 June 1969.

19. "Utilization of Volunteers in United Nations Development Projects," ECOSOC resolution 1444 (XLVII), 31 July 1969. ECOSOC asked the Secretary-General to study the constitutional, administrative, and financial arrangements for an international corps of volunteers based on the following principles:

a. A volunteer should be a person who gives his services without regard to financial benefits and with the purpose of contributing to the development of the recipient country;

b. A volunteer scheme should consist of persons recruited on as wide a geographical basis as possible;

c. Where possible the composition of teams should be on a multilateral basis;

d. No volunteer shall be sent to a country without the explicit request and approval of the receiving country.

20. "Feasibility of Creating an International Corps of Volunteers for Development," ECOSOC resolution 1539 (XLIX), 28 July 1970; "United Nations Volunteers," General Assembly resolution 2659 (XXV), 7 December 1970. The guidelines followed ECOSOC's advice.

21. "The Role of the Regional Economic Commissions in the Field of Development Planning during the Second United Nations Development Decade," General Assembly resolution 2563 (XXIV), 13 December 1969.

22. "Development Planning Advisory Services," ECOSOC resolution 1552 (XLIX), 30 July 1960.

23. By 30 April 1970, 126 governments had pledged $225.4 million for the 1970 program; *Yearbook of the United Nations 1970*, 299.

24. Calculations based on data in *Yearbook of the United Nations 1965*, 281–282, 289; and *Yearbook of the United Nations 1970*, 299–300.

25. "Procedures for Implementation of New Arrangements for Regional and Interregional Projects under the Technical Assistance Component of the United Nations

Development Programme," ECOSOC resolution 1432 (XLVII), 25 July 1969; "Procedures for Implementation of New Arrangements for Regional and Interregional Projects under the Technical Assistance Component of the United Nations Development Programme," General Assembly resolution 2513 (XXIV), 21 November 1969.

26. Sixten Heppling, *UNDP: From Agency Shares to Country Programmes, 1949–1975* (Stockholm: Ministry of Foreign Affairs, 1995), 76.

27. Robert Jackson selected a staff of six to assist him on a full-time basis. In addition, a consultant firm was chosen to develop a specific aspect of the study. A few individuals in leading positions and to a large extent from developing countries were asked to form a reference group.

The staff consisted of experienced people: Margaret Joan Anstee, who had held posts as resident representative; Leonce Bloch, who had been resident representative in Francophone Africa; Sixten Heppling, a top administrator in the Swedish aid administration and, from 1953, delegate to several TAC and Governing Council meetings; Karl Kraczkiewics, a retired assistant administrator for administration at UNDP headquarters; and Marc Nerfin, a Swiss citizen who in the mid-1970s played a central role in elaborating the "another development" paradigm. The consulting firm made a full-time staff member, Bruce Rohrbacher, available to carry out a special study on an improved information system. The commissioner, Robert G. A. Jackson, was designated to succeed Paul Hoffmann as administrator of the UNDP.

For a vivid description of the evolving terms of reference for the capacity study as the issue moved from one body of the system to the next, see R. G. A. Jackson, *A Study of the Capacity of the United Nations Development System,* 2 vols. (Geneva: United Nations, 1969), 2:423–430.

28. Jackson, *A Study of the Capacity of the United Nations Development System.*

29. Ibid., 1:12. The capacity of current operations was overextended in certain critical areas. In the words of the commissioner, the major constraints were as follows:

- The inability, as yet, to develop fully effective techniques for transferring knowledge and experience.
- The slow application of science and technology to major problems.
- The difficulty of attracting manpower of the quality and experience demanded by the operations.
- The absence of an effective system for the control of the resources entrusted to it.
- The lack of an organization specifically designed to cooperate with the developing countries.
- The diffusion of responsibility throughout the system.
- The general reluctance of the agencies (with one or two significant exceptions) to contract outside the system.

Jackson added another constraint, perhaps the most serious one: "For many years, I have been looking for 'the brain' which guides the policies and operations of the UN development system. The search has been in vain. Here and there throughout the system there are offices and units collecting the information available, but there is no group (or Brains Trust) that is constantly monitoring the present operations, learning from experience, grasping at all that science and technology has to offer, launching new ideas and methods, challenging established practices, and provoking thought inside and outside the system. Deprived of such a vital stimulus, it is obvious that the best use cannot be made of the resources available to the operation." Ibid., 1:13.

30. Ibid., 1:25–26.

31. Ibid., 1:32–34.

32. Ibid., 1:8–10. Jackson's critique of past practice was quite candid: the performance of the principal executing agencies (the UN, the ILO, the FAO, and UNESCO were responsible for 80 percent of the Special Fund component of UNDP activities—the pre-investment studies) had become slower with increased allocations. It could take up to three or four years (and even longer) from the time a project was first considered until operations were started, and more delays occurred during the implementation period. Reports on completed projects were also generated much too slowly. The critique was equally harsh on the qualitative side: the nature of technical assistance had changed very little over the years. Activities had a "donor basis": the initiative would come from an agency and not from the country itself. The agencies had showed "a failure to recognize the need for a comprehensive approach to development problems."

33. As Heppling observed, the development plans were expected to reflect the priorities of the people and government of a given recipient country. "Assistance projects which contravened national priorities and value systems stood little chance of being effective." This did not mean, however, that multilateral development assistance programs should not have certain priorities of their own and firm criteria for the projects approved. The country programs would thus be the result of a process of negotiation. Heppling, *UNDP*, 82.

34. Jackson, *A Study of the Capacity of the United Nations Development System*, 1:12.

35. Ibid., 1:41. During the 1960s, the UN system's intergovernmental bodies repeatedly emphasized the core role of the resident representatives. Jackson argued that they should be recruited into a new career UN development service (including a staff college to train such personnel) and be "given real authority."

36. Ibid., 1:44. In view of existing practice, the idea of an indicative planning figure was quite "revolutionary" because of its potential to facilitate long-term development planning that also included development assistance. In the capacity study, the idea was underplayed, probably to avoid scaring away governments with an aversion to long-term planning and commitments. The commissioner cautioned: "This would *not* be a country target, nor would it constitute a financial commitment, but would serve as a guide for planning purposes only. Global and country 'orders of magnitude' and global allocation ceilings would be annually projected one year further ahead, and programmes will be adjusted accordingly. Governments will note that the proposed procedures are similar in nature to the new policies recently approved by the Governing Council for the TA component."

Resistance to the idea of long-term planning might also be anticipated from the administrative level. One of the architects of the new programming system observed that the administrator, the main architect of the old Special Fund way of operating, "showed little enthusiasm, if any at all" when presented with the proposed system: "He and his staff preferred a situation where they exercised all the judgement that was required on the merits or demerits of each project application"; Heppling, *UNDP*, 91.

37. Jackson, *A Study of the Capacity of the United Nations Development System*, 1:27, 34, 36. The UNDP administrator, not the agencies, was to be responsible for the operation as a whole and for the funds to finance it. Agencies that were clearly overburdened would be given "a breathing space": less resources to administer, allowing them "a better balance between their operational and constitutional functions." Separate

representation of the agencies at the country level should be restricted "to cases where their non-UNDP activities are large enough to require it, and should be financed entirely from the Agency's regular budget." As Heppling summarized, "There could no more be any fixed shares or percentage limitations in the transfers of resources from one sector of the programme to another, when country programmes were planned. It would no longer be possible for an Agency during the planning period to invoke its 'rightful place' in the programme, as sometimes happened in earlier days." Heppling, *UNDP*, 82.

38. In 1969, the UNDP received almost $200 million in pledges. According to Heppling, the starting point for the capacity study was the assumption that annual contributions would reach $500 million by 1975; Heppling, *UNDP*, 79.

39. Jackson, *A Study of the Capacity of the United Nations Development System*, 1:43ff.

40. Ibid., 2:215–278.

41. The Governing Council considered the study during its ninth and tenth sessions (January and June) and at a special session in March. ECOSOC approved the recommendations of the Governing Council by consensus ("The Capacity of the United Nations Development System," ECOSOC resolution 1530 [XLIX], 22 July 1970) and so did the General Assembly ("The Capacity of the United Nations Development System," General Assembly resolution 2688 [XXV], 11 December 1970).

42. For an interesting discussion of this point, which has been crucial in the discourse on development cooperation since the early 1950s, see Heppling, *UNDP*, 85ff. Heppling noted that it was important for those participating in the capacity study that the UNDP "could show a distinct profile and was identified with certain policies and convictions. Certainly we did not want UNDP in a position where it would have to accept project requests against its own better judgement and comprehensive experiences. That made it very important that programmes grew out of a proper problem inventory and analysis, evaluation of past performance and experience on the part of all concerned. They therefore had to result from negotiations, in which both recipients and donors played an active role. None of the parties would try to dictate the contents of a programme to the other." However, this position encountered strong opposition in both the working party of the Governing Council and later in the plenary: developing-country representatives "wanted the total responsibility for the content of a UNDP country programme of development assistance placed with the requesting country and wished it expressed in the most categorical terms, leaving the UNDP with virtually no say in the matter." Ibid., 86–87.

43. "The Capacity of the United Nations Development System," General Assembly resolution 2688 (XXV), 11 December 1970, Annex.

44. Ibid., paragraphs 30 and 53.

45. Ibid., Annex. The 1970 consensus resolution followed the administrative design that the capacity study had proposed: at headquarters, regional bureaus would be established to facilitate a direct link between the administrator and the resident representatives in all matters concerning field activities. A small staff for long-term planning would be established to analyze the main trends of the program's evolution in order to give it new direction and to explore new possibilities for making it more effective. At the country level, the resident representatives would become UNDP resident directors and would be appointed by the administrator.

46. Ibid. The resolution stated: "When necessary to ensure the maximum effectiveness of Programme assistance or to increase its capacity, and with due regard to the cost factor, increased use may appropriately be made of suitable services obtained

from governmental and non-governmental institutions and firms, in agreement with the recipient Government concerned and in accordance with the principles of international competitive bidding." It also stated that "maximum use should be made of national institutions and firms, if available, within the recipient countries." And in cases "where expertise or services are required which are not adequately available in kind, quantity and quality within the United Nations system, the Administrator will, in agreement with the Government concerned, exercise his authority to obtain them, while inviting, in appropriate cases, the relevant United Nations organization to provide complementary support." Every executing agent would be accountable to the administrator for implementing program assistance.

47. Heppling put it this way: "The same thing happened to the Consensus as had happened to the UN Charter: its balances and checks have proved so delicately designed that nobody has dared to insist on any far-reaching changes. As long as I attended meetings of the Governing Council of the UNDP, ie a few years into the 1980's, ideas of amendments in the fabric of relationships between the UNDP, the participating organizations and governments would always founder on this simple obstacle: the proposed reform might require some modifications of the Consensus text. And that could amount to opening the Pandora's box full of problems and difficult conflicts. So, it always seemed better not to touch the Consensus. Incidentally, to my knowledge it is the only Consensus in the United Nations system that is spelled with a capital C." Heppling, *UNDP,* 90.

48. "Charter of Economic Rights and Duties of States," General Assembly resolution 3281 (XXIX), 12 December 1974. Within the UN system, UNCTAD drove the issue. Outside the UN framework, it was driven, in particular, by meetings of the non-aligned states in 1972 and 1973. The resolution was adopted by a roll-call vote of 120 to 6 (Belgium, Denmark, Germany, Luxembourg, the United Kingdom, and the United States), with 10 abstentions. India welcomed the charter as one more step toward a more orderly and just economic order in the world. Not only did it redress the imbalance of rights and duties of the underprivileged nations but, in India's view, it took due account of the interests of the more affluent states as well. The United States, in contrast, argued that the provisions of the charter would tend to discourage capital flow for vital development. An agreed charter would be preferable to one that was meaningless without the agreement of countries that might be small in number but whose significance in international economic relations and development could hardly be ignored. For a summary of the debate, see *Yearbook of the United Nations 1974* (New York: United Nations, Office of Public Information, 1977), 386ff.

49. "Declaration on the Establishment of a New International Order," General Assembly resolution 3201(S-VI), 1 May 1974; "Programme of Action on the Establishment of a New International Economic Order," General Assembly resolution 3202 (S-VI), 1 May 1974.

50. Peterson indicated that emphasis should be placed on building and strengthening institutions in developing countries as a way of promoting self-reliance. He argued that governments and institutions should be given more responsibility for formulating, implementing, and carrying out projects and that the UNDP should use more flexibility when integrating technical cooperation and capital assistance so it could fund more high-risk projects. In addition, he wanted to develop a more results-oriented approach to future projects. He also felt that resident representatives should be given a more central role. He presented these new dimensions in technical cooperation as an effort to

overcome some of the constraints that had hampered operations in the past. *Yearbook of the United Nations 1975* (New York: United Nations, Office of Public Information, 1978), 411–412.

51. ECOSOC and the General Assembly endorsed the new guidelines; see "Reports of the Governing Council of the United Nations Development Programme," ECOSOC resolution 116 (LIX), 30 July 1975; and "New Dimensions in Technical Assistance," General Assembly resolution 3405 (XXX), 28 November 1975. The General Assembly also asked the UNDP and specialized agencies to intensify efforts to "achieve full utilization" of national institutions in developing countries and build up new capacities in these countries as it promoted technical cooperation among them; "Technical Co-operation among Developing Countries," General Assembly resolution 3461 (XXX), 11 December 1975.

52. *Yearbook of the United Nations 1971* (New York: United Nations, Office of Public Information, 1974), 248–249.

53. *Yearbook of the United Nations 1974*, 415.

54. *Yearbook of the United Nations 1975*, 411.

55. "Financial Contributions to the United Nations Development Programme," ECOSOC resolution 1615 (LI), 26 July 1971. This resolution was adopted by a roll-call vote of 17 to 4, with 6 abstentions. Those in favor were all developing countries.

56. "Financial Contributions to the United Nations Development Programme," General Assembly resolution 2811 (XXVI), 14 December 1971. The resolution was proposed and adopted by representatives of developing countries. Almost all industrial countries abstained. Five western countries, including the United States, voted against it.

57. The UNDP introduced new procedures regarding the selection, recruitment, and training of UNDP staff: it worked to increase the recruitment of younger people, often at colleges and universities, and to improve the geographical balance of staff. Almost one-third of new staff members in 1972 came from developing countries. See *Yearbook of the United Nations 1972* (New York: United Nations, Office of Public Information, 1975), 247.

58. *Yearbook of the United Nations 1972*, 247; *Yearbook of the United Nations 1973* (New York: United Nations, Office of Public Information, 1976), 326; *Yearbook of the United Nations 1974*, 408; *Yearbook of the United Nations 1975*, 405.

59. *Yearbook of the United Nations 1972*, 254. In addition, various supplementary criteria were recommended.

60. Ibid., 254; *Yearbook of the United Nations 1974*, 408. Looking back, Heppling noted that the Governing Council agreed to the basic criteria on which the indicative planning figures for each country were to be decided (per capita income, population, degree of development, special needs and circumstances, and so forth) but that a "special problem was created by countries, which could not be said to qualify as poor or backward or low in resources, but which all the same demanded a share in UNDP funds for development projects. They did so in the name of the principle of universality, which was the foundation on which the United Nations and its family of organizations rested." Sixten Heppling, *UNDP*, 92ff., quote at 93.

61. *Yearbook of the United Nations 1976* (New York: United Nations, Office of Public Information, 1979), 367.

62. Ibid.

63. Ibid., 370, and calculations based on these data.

64. *Yearbook of the United Nations 1977* (New York: United Nations, Office of Public Information, 1980), 447–448; *Yearbook of the United Nations 1978* (New York: United Nations, Office of Public Information, 1981), 460.

65. "Restructuring the Economic and Social Sectors of the United Nations System," General Assembly resolution 32/197, 20 December 1977.

66. "Comprehensive Policy Review of Operational Activities," General Assembly resolution 33/201, 29 January 1979. The Nordic countries and the Netherlands sponsored the resolution, an indication of the special responsibility that this group of countries had already assumed for improving the effectiveness of the UN development system (and not just in terms of funding).

67. "Programme Budget for the Biennium 1978–1979," General Assembly resolution 3405 (XXX), Annex, 29 January 1979.

68. *Yearbook of the United Nations 1977*, 448; *Yearbook of the United Nations 1978*, 461; *Yearbook of the United Nations 1979* (New York: United Nations, Office of Public Information, 1982), 532, 534. Other indicators of relevance: the number of experts from developing countries serving on UNDP-financed projects rose to 2,506, a 28 percent increase from 1978; the dollar value of subcontracts awarded to institutions in developing countries rose by 61 percent (27.5 percent of the value of new subcontracts awarded); the number of training fellowships provided by developing-country institutions increased by 27 percent; and developing-country institutions hosted 31.2 percent of the training fellowships awarded.

69. *Yearbook of the United Nations 1979*, 534. In August 1979, revised instructions were promulgated that sought to broaden the scope for using nationals in project implementation. The first step was the appointment of national project coordinators.

70. Ibid., 537.

71. The share amounted to less than 3 percent. However, the same reality can be reported in different ways. The poor performance in this account was also reported as a stunning increase: "expenditures on projects directly executed by Governments increased by 32 per cent in 1981 over the 1980 level, to an amount of $10.3 million, signalling a continuing increase." *Yearbook of the United Nations 1981* (New York: United Nations, Office of Public Information, 1985), 446.

72. *Yearbook of the United Nations 1981*, 446.

73. Ibid.

74. *Role of Qualified National Personnel in the Social and Economic Development of the Developing Countries: Report of the Administrator*, UNDP document 443, 21 March 1980.

75. *Yearbook of the United Nations 1980*, 591. The report suggested that governments should plan and monitor human resource development in the context of a comprehensive manpower management system and that they should take special care to provide equal opportunities for women and men. It suggested a range of approaches to improving general, technical and vocational training and reversing the brain drain from developing countries.

76. "Role of Qualified National Personnel in the Social and Economic Development of Developing Countries," General Assembly resolution 35/80, 5 December 1980.

77. "Restructuring of Economic and Social Sectors of the United Nations System," General Assembly resolution 33/202, 29 January 1979.

78. "Implementation of Section IV of the Annex to General Assembly Resolution 32/197 on the Restructuring of the Economic and Social Sectors of the United Nations System," General Assembly resolution 34/206, 19 December 1979.

79. *Yearbook of the United Nations 1979*, 541.

80. Ibid., 541–542. The ACC noted the desirability of joint interagency advisory groups and periodic reviews of current and planned activities to assist the coordinator in planning, programming, reviewing, and evaluating operational activities and in achieving an effective dialogue with government authorities.

81. "Implementation of Section V of the Annex to General Assembly Resolution 32/197 on the Restructuring of the Economic and Social Sectors of the United Nations System," General Assembly resolution 34/213, 19 December 1979. The UNDP resident representative was normally to be designated resident coordinator.

82. *Yearbook of the United Nations 1980* (New York: United Nations, Office of Public Information, 1983), 613–614.

83. "Report of the Governing Council of the United Nations Development Programme," ECOSOC resolution 1981/59, 22 July 1981. In the Second Committee, Australia and Bangladesh found that the resident coordinators played an important role in avoiding waste, duplication, and competition among organizations. Argentina, Ecuador, and Zambia argued that agencies should discontinue the establishment of regional offices with functions similar to those of the coordinators; see *Yearbook of the United Nations 1981*, 430–431.

84. Such extra-budgetary activities included supplying operational, executive, and administrative personnel to serve as officials of recipient governments that requested this service and of a (growing) number of trust funds. *Yearbook of the United Nations 1979*, 532–533.

85. In 1973, agency overhead costs were $34.1 million and UNDP administrative and program support costs $36.4 million—together 20.2 percent of total expenditures (overhead costs included). For the following years these costs were (in millions of U.S. dollars) 42.8 and 43.8—together 23.4 percent (1974); 56.3 and 52.4—together 21.0 percent (1975); 55.3 and 57.2—together 23.5 percent (1976); 45.3 and 59.0—together 23.9 percent (1977); 58.0 and 63.6—together 21.9 percent (1978) (government cash counterpart was included in the total expenditures in this and the following years, slightly reducing the percentage of administrative and program support expenses); 75.3 and 76.1—together 21.7 percent (1979). Agency support costs increased from $87.9 million in 1980 to $94.3 million in 1981—12.9 percent of the field program. In 1981, the UNDP's own administrative costs were even higher, $104.6 million (13.9 percent), and were projected to increase to 14.5 percent for 1982–1983. The reason given was that although decreasing contributions to the UNDP forced reductions in program delivery, the administrative services for this delivery had to be maintained. *Yearbook of the United Nations 1973*, 329; *Yearbook of the United Nations 1974*, 413; *Yearbook of the United Nations 1975*, 409; *Yearbook of the United Nations 1976*, 370; *Yearbook of the United Nations 1977*, 451; *Yearbook of the United Nations 1978*, 464; *Yearbook of the United Nations 1979*, 535; *Yearbook of the United Nations 1981*, 447, 449, and calculations based on these sources.

86. "Measures to Strengthen the Executing Agencies of the United Nations Development Programme," General Assembly resolution 2975 (XXVII), 14 December 1972. The general survey of activities in 1974 referred to the many activities performed by the UNDP's 104 field offices as a consequence of the decentralization of functions and activities that accompanied country programming. Many of these were not related to projects. These services, which were financed through administrative support and agency overhead costs, included providing development planning advice at national and sector levels; offering technical advice; problem-solving at the request of the sector ministry concerned; providing advice and services related to follow-up investments; acting as a focal point in the event of emergencies; assisting in the formulation, management, and evaluation of country programs; and participating in the coordination of other external assistance. *Yearbook of the United Nations 1974*, 409.

87. *Yearbook of the United Nations 1980*, 592–593. ECOSOC endorsed this decision "Report of the Governing Council of the United Nations Development Programme," ECOSOC resolution 1980/65, 25 July 1980.

88. "Questions Relating to the Programme Budget for the Biennium 1980–1981," General Assembly resolution 35/217, section V, 17 December 1980.

89. Some executing agencies would continue to be granted flexibility in the form of a higher reimbursement rate, but the UNDP administrator was to review those arrangements and recommend guidelines, including eligibility ceilings. As a safeguard applicable through 1986, no agency would receive less reimbursement in U.S. dollar terms than it received in 1981, with the exception that the reimbursement would never increase to above 14 percent. Where actual support costs could be identified, they would establish the upper limit for reimbursement. Hardship cases due to fluctuations in currency exchange rates would be dealt with on an ad hoc basis under guidelines to be recommended by the administrator. The World Bank would continue to be reimbursed at a rate of 11 percent. Each agency was requested to present details of what it had spent to support UNDP projects during the previous year. *Yearbook of the United Nations 1980,* 580, 592.

90. "United Nations Development Programme," General Assembly resolution (36/200), 17 December 1981.

91. "Operational Activities for Development," General Assembly resolution 36/199, 17 December 1981. In the Second Committee, positions had been divided. Several states expressed the need for cuts in administrative costs, but others warned against excessive reductions in administrative expenses. The Netherlands argued that the field network should be reduced only as a last resort. *Yearbook of the United Nations 1981,* 428–429.

92. *Yearbook of the United Nations 1979,* 533; *Yearbook of the United Nations 1980,* 581.

93. *Yearbook of the United Nations 1981,* 445.

94. *Yearbook of the United Nations 1980,* 584.

95. The costs of carrying out thematic evaluations for 1980–1981 amounted to about $400,000, an indication of the relatively low emphasis given to this exercise. *Yearbook of the United Nations 1981,* 445–446.

96. *Yearbook of the United Nations 1980,* 580, 582.

97. Ibid. The regional distribution was as follows: Africa, $283.4 million (38.8 percent); Asia and the Pacific, $296.1 million (40.6 percent); Latin America, $76.5 million (10.5 percent); Arab States, $57.8 million (7.9 percent); and Europe, $16.2 million (2.2 percent).

98. *Yearbook of the United Nations 1981,* 442.

99. Ibid., 442–443.

100. Ibid., 443.

101. Ibid., 444.

102. "United Nations Development Programme," General Assembly resolution 36/200, 17 December 1981. In the Second Committee, the prospect of scarce resources triggered a debate about the poverty profile. Argentina, observing that the impact of the reduction of available funds seemed to fall almost entirely on Latin America, objected to any distinction between developing countries that led to a reduction in resources for those considered "most developed." *Yearbook of the United Nations 1981,* 445.

103. In 1980, ECOSOC adopted a resolution sponsored by Denmark, Finland, the Netherlands, Norway, and Sweden; see "Operational Activities for Development," ECOSOC resolution 1980/66, 25 July 1980. However, in the process, some of the main recommendations contained in the original draft resolution were watered down, if not outright killed. In the original draft, a list of seven issues was suggested for priority consideration by the General Assembly: increasing the flow of resources on a continuous and assured basis; strengthening operational capacities in areas of critical importance for

a balanced international economy; improving links between research and analysis functions; helping developing countries plan for external aid by informing them in advance of what resources they were likely to get from the UN system; strengthening links between technical cooperation and investment; making it easier for governments to progressively assume responsibility for executing projects supported by the UN; and intensifying efforts to enhance efficiency, harmonize procedures, and evaluate activities. The paragraph containing this list was omitted from the resolution: France and the United Kingdom had questioned some of the items on the list. For an example, see *Yearbook of the United Nations 1980*, 609.

104. *Yearbook of the United Nations 1981*, 426.

105. "Comprehensive Policy Review of Operational Activities for Development," General Assembly resolution 35/81, 5 December 1980. The original draft resolution was submitted by Venezuela on behalf of the UN member states that belonged to the G-77, but it had been amended on its way through the UN's intergovernmental bodies. It was adopted without a vote. *Yearbook of the United Nations 1980*, 610–611.

106. Ibid., 432–433.

107. *Yearbook of the United Nations 1977*, 453.

108. "Role and Activities of the United Nations Development Programme," ECOSOC resolution 2110 (LXIII), 3 August 1977, Annex.

109. Ibid.; and "United Nations Development Programme," General Assembly resolution 32/114, 15 December 1977. The issue stayed on the Governing Council's agenda. At the June–July 1978 session, it considered a report by the administrator on the UNDP's role and activities that emphasized the progress that had been made to develop a system of planning appraisal and program evaluation and the steps taken to combat poverty and integrate women into the development process. The council asked the administrator to continue discussions with the executing agencies on how best to use the country programming process as a frame of reference for operational activities. It also asked him to strengthen program evaluation and involve developing countries more closely in a flexible technical cooperation program. *Yearbook of the United Nations 1978*, 471.

110. Total expenditures by the UN system on operational activities for development and nondevelopment assistance in 1981 amounted to $6.7 billion when expenditures on refugee, humanitarian, and disaster relief assistance ($648 million) are included. *Yearbook of the United Nations 1981*, 420–421.

111. Ibid., 419. The net transfer of concessional loans distributed by the IDA in 1981 amounted to $1.6 billion; IFAD provided $75 million. The net transfer of nonconcessional assistance provided by the World Bank amounted to $1.8 billion; the IFC provided $327 million.

112. Calculations based on data in *Yearbook of the United Nations 1981*, 419.

113. Total technical cooperation expenditures in 1981 amounted to $2 billion, of which the UNDP contributed $732 million (35.8 percent). The World Bank and the IDA were approaching the level of the UNDP even within this area, contributing $519 million, followed by the WHO ($275 million), the FAO ($134 million), the ILO ($51 million), and UNESCO ($48 million). *Yearbook of the United Nations 1981*, 431, and calculations on data therein.

114. "Report of the Governing Council of the United Nations Development Programme," ECOSOC resolution 1981/59, 22 July 1981.

115. *Yearbook of the United Nations 1972*, 247; *Yearbook of the United Nations 1973*, 329; *Yearbook of the United Nations 1974*, 413; *Yearbook of the United Nations 1975*, 409; *Yearbook of the United Nations 1976*, 370.

116. *Yearbook of the United Nations 1977*, 451.

117. "Special Measures in Favour of the Least Developed among the Developing Countries," ECOSOC resolution 1754 (LIV), 16 May 1973; "Special Measures in Favour of the Least Developed Countries," General Assembly resolution 3174 (XXVIII), 17 December 1973; *Yearbook of the United Nations 1972*, 247, 250; *Yearbook of the United Nations 1973*, 326, 332–333.

118. However, money does not always follow in the wake of strong commitments. In 1978, the General Assembly decided to suspend the UN Special Fund's activities for countries most seriously affected by the international economic crisis due to lack of contributions. *Yearbook of the United Nations 1981*, 417.

119. In 1979, UNCTAD endorsed a Comprehensive New Programme of Action for the Least Developed Countries in two phases, an Immediate Action Programme (1979–1981) and a Substantial New Programme of Action for the 1980. This prodded the UN system to begin preparing for a major conference with a focus on the special problems of the LDCs and ways and means of solving them.

120. "United Nations Conference on the Least Developed Countries," General Assembly resolution 36/194, 17 December 1981.

121. "United Nations Special Fund for Land-Locked Developing Countries," General Assembly resolution 36/195, 17 December 1981.

122. "Co-operation among Developing Countries in the United Nations Technical Co-operation Programmes and Increased Efficiency of the Capacity of the United Nations Development System," General Assembly resolution 2974 (XXVII), 14 December 1972.

123. "Technical Co-operation Among Developing Countries," General Assembly resolution 3251 (XXXIX), 4 December 1974.

124. In 1977, the Governing Council invited developing countries to avail themselves of the services provided by the UN development system in order to pool, coordinate, streamline, and possibly twin their consultancy services. *Yearbook of the United Nations 1977*, 454. The General Assembly agreed and called for action to assist developing countries in designing projects that would promote their technical cooperation. "Technical Co-operation among Developing Countries," General Assembly resolution 32/182, 19 December 1977.

125. *Yearbook of the United Nations 1976*, 370–371, 375–376. More than eighty-five countries submitted conference reports on their policies, activities, and approaches to technical cooperation among developing countries. In 1977, the UNDP issued its first *Directory of Services for Technical Co-operation among Developing Countries*, which covered 900 institutions in sixty-seven developing countries. *Yearbook of the United Nations 1977*, 448.

126. "United Nations Conference on Technical Co-operation among Developing Countries," General Assembly resolution 31/179, 21 December 1976. Representatives of 138 states took part in the conference. In addition, the special agencies and UN bodies and programs were represented, as were intergovernmental organizations and institutions and forty-nine NGOs. Some national liberation movements were also represented. *Yearbook of the United Nations 1978*, 467.

127. United Nations, *Report of the United Nations Conference on Technical Co-operation among Developing Countries, Buenos Aires, 30 August to 12 September 1978* (New York: United Nations, 1978), chapter 1.

128. "United Nations Conference on Technical Co-operation among Developing Countries," General Assembly resolution 33/134, 19 December 1978.

129. "Technical Co-operation among Developing Countries," General Assembly resolution 34/117, 14 December 1979. However, warnings came from the Soviet bloc. Bulgaria spoke on behalf of the Eastern European countries and stated that they considered the paragraph that urged developed states to comply with provisions of the Buenos Aires Plan of Action regarding increased financial support to be beyond the scope of the Vienna conference action. *Yearbook of the United Nations 1979*, 540–541.

130. *Yearbook of the United Nations 1980*, 590.

131. "Technical Co-operation among Developing Countries," General Assembly resolution 36/44, 19 November 1981.

132. Several speakers, including those from Argentina, Gambia, and Guinea, urged developed countries to support technical cooperation among developing countries. India stated that it was unfortunate that developed countries paid only lip service to technical cooperation among developing countries and felt threatened by it. Romania's representative found it unsatisfactory that most activities relative to technical cooperation among developing countries were financed by the developing countries themselves and argued that developed countries, development banks, and the UN system should raise their contributions substantially. *Yearbook of the United Nations 1981*, 463–464.

133. *Yearbook of the United Nations 1978*, 461; *Yearbook of the United Nations 1979*, 534.

134. *Yearbook of the United Nations 1972*, 247. A summary of reported investment commitments to UNDP-supported projects at the end of 1973 made a distinction between investments that resulted directly from UNDP projects ($3.1 billion in 1973) and investments that were related to UNDP projects ($843 million). Of the total amount, more than half (52.2 percent) came from domestic financial sources of the country concerned, almost all from public sources (48 percent of the total). Multilateral sources provided 30.5 percent of the total, mainly the IBRD/IDA, while bilateral sources provided the remaining 17.2 percent, again mainly with public sources. The contributions of the private sector both inside and outside the country concerned were almost marginal. *Yearbook of the United Nations 1973*, 327, and calculations based on these data.

135. *Yearbook of the United Nations 1980*, 581; *Yearbook of the United Nations 1981*, 444.

136. *Yearbook of the United Nations 1979*, 533; *Yearbook of the United Nations 1981*, 443.

137. The Governing Council defined pre-investment projects as those that clearly sought to collect, analyze, and present economic, financial, technical, institutional, and social data in any development sector in a form that would facilitate decision making about the feasibility of committing capital to create physical assets, produce goods and services, or develop human and natural resources. These were distinguished from investment-oriented projects such as natural resources surveys, sector studies, master plans, regional plans, research, and pilot schemes. *Yearbook of the United Nations 1981*, 443.

138. A few examples from 1980 may illustrate the point. In West Africa, the UNDP helped finance an action plan for the development of the Gambia River that would be submitted to a multilateral donors' conference in 1981. When Zimbabwe attained independence in April 1980, the UNDP helped the government organize a meeting of UN organizations in May to prepare projects for financing by the IBRD and the African Development Bank. It also proposed a donors' conference in Salisbury in 1981. Also in 1980, the UNDP financed the main management training services for an Indonesian program to resettle 2.5 million people. *Yearbook of the United Nations 1980*, 581.

139. *Yearbook of the United Nations 1981*, 444.

140. These experts combined their jobs with training nationals to take over from

them as quickly as possible. In 1980, the UNDP financed 131 operational experts in forty developing countries. *Yearbook of the United Nations 1980, 583.*

141. The Trust Fund for the UN Korean Reconstruction Agency was formally terminated in 1960; in 1979, unallocated funds were transferred to the UN. The Fund of the UN for the Development of West Irian (Irian Jaya) was in the process of being terminated in 1979. The trust fund for Lesotho, established in 1967 by an agreement between Sweden and the UN, was to finance operational and administrative posts that covered a range of fields, from industrial development and educational programming to road transportation and tourism. Sweden was the sole contributor, providing $1.2 million in 1980 and pledging $1.4 million for activities in 1981. This applied also to the trust fund for Swaziland, which was established in 1969 following an agreement with Sweden: the amounts contributed and pledged by Sweden in 1980 and 1981 were somewhat smaller—$0.4 and $0.3 million, respectively. *Yearbook of the United Nations 1979, 539; Yearbook of the United Nations 1980, 586.*

142. The United Nations Special Fund for Land-Locked Developing Countries was established in 1975 to help nineteen landlocked developing countries overcome their transport and communications problem. However, it had a slow start with few resources: during its first year of full-scale operation in 1979, its resources were still very modest. Its total income in 1979 was $124,780; expenditures amounted to $39,000. By the end of the year, its balance was $685,055, of which $489,001 was unspent. Its income in 1980—nearly $200,000, including contributions from seven countries—did not make much of a difference to this general picture. *Yearbook of the United Nations 1979, 538, 585; Yearbook of the United Nations 1980, 585.*

143. During its first year, the Interim Fund for Science and Technology for Development received more than 800 project proposals from eighty governments. It approved an initial nineteen projects with another twenty-four under preparation. The project components that were to be covered by the fund amounted to $16 million. At the pledging conference on 27 March 1980, thirty-five governments pledged $25.8 million for 1980–1981; that amount rose to about $50 million by the end of the year. However, this was only one-fifth of the target of $250 million for the biennium initially agreed at the UN Conference on Science and Technology for Development in 1979. *Yearbook of the United Nations 1980, 585.*

144. The issue of women in development was set prominently on the international agenda by the Mexico City conference in 1975. In 1977, the UNDP followed up on the integration of women in development by issuing detailed guidelines aimed at helping women participate in and benefit from UNDP-supported projects and providing information and training materials designed to help planners expand and upgrade the role of women in the development process. *Yearbook of the United Nations 1977, 448.* The UNDP made this a prominent issue at the institutional level by establishing a special coordinator for women in development.

145. A special energy account was established and the administrator addressed a letter to major donors inviting contributions. Before the November 1980 pledging conference, he made a special appeal to all governments. However, response was weak. Only two countries responded, paying $2.8 million in 1981 and pledging $1.0 million for 1982. *Yearbook of the United Nations 1980, 583, 586; Yearbook of the United Nations 1981, 274.*

146. Every year, the UNDP network of country offices was called on to assist in

emergency or disaster relief operations on behalf of the UN system. It often coordi-
nated UN responses on behalf of the United Nations Disaster Relief Organization.
During 1980, it assisted in emergency situations in Algeria, Djibouti, the Caribbean,
Ethiopia, Nepal, Nicaragua, Uganda, and Vietnam and provided aid to Kampucheans.
Yearbook of the United Nations 1980, 586.

147. For a description of such activities in 1980, see *Yearbook of the United Nations
1980*, Chapter XXII.

148. *Yearbook of the United Nations 1973*, 328; *Yearbook of the United Nations 1974*, 411.

149. *Yearbook of the United Nations 1978*, 464; *Yearbook of the United Nations 1979*, 537;
Yearbook of the United Nations 1980, 584, 606; *Yearbook of the United Nations 1981*, 468.

150. *Yearbook of the United Nations 1981*, 468.

151. "United Nations Capital Development Fund," General Assembly resolution
36/196, 17 December 1981.

152. "United Nations Fund for Population Activities," General Assembly resolution
3019 (XXXII), 18 December 1972; *Yearbook of the United Nations 1972*, 374.

153. The Secretary-General's report on the population situation in 1981 indicated
that toward the end of the century the annual increase in the population of developing countries might well reach 84 million, or 93 percent of the projected total annual
growth in world population. It also indicated that mortality had regained world attention as a serious demographic problem, particularly in Sub-Saharan Africa. *Yearbook of
the United Nations 1981*, 779.

154. In addition to organizing conferences that put the population issue high on
the international agenda (the director-general of the UNFPA was responsible for preparing the 1974 World Population Conference), meetings of experts, and the like, the
UN placed great emphasis on issuing publications surveying this field, including regular
reports and report series. It published, inter alia, the *Demographic Yearbook*, and the
Population Commission revitalized the *Population Bulletin of the United Nations*. In 1975,
volumes 1 and 2 of *The Population Debate: Dimensions and Perspectives* were issued. The
previous year, the Sub-Committee on Population of the ACC had published the *Concise
Report on the World Population Situation in 1970–75 and Its Long-Range Implications*.

155. "United Nations Fund for Population Activities," ECOSOC resolution
2025 (LXI), 4 August 1976; "United Nations Fund for Population Activities," General
Assembly resolution 31/170, 21 December 1976.

156. *Yearbook of the United Nations 1981*, 781–782.

157. By the end of 1972, the UNFPA had distributed some $50 million in alloca-
tions and grants. The number of donors had reached fifty-six, and total pledges since
the fund's inception in 1967 amounted to almost $80 million. The activities funded
included collecting and analyzing demographic data; providing demographic research
and training facilities; providing demonstration programs in family planning connected
with maternal and child welfare services; providing courses on a wide range of population subjects; providing fellowships in the fields of population statistics, census-taking,
demography, health education, human reproduction, communications evaluation, and
public administration; providing contraceptive supplies and manufacturing materials; and formulating population policies and measures to be taken in accordance with
national development objectives. *Yearbook of the United Nations 1972*, 249.

158. *Yearbook of the United Nations 1973*, 329.

159. Allocations reached $68.4 million in 1974, $85.7 million in 1975, $81 million in
1976 and 1977, $110 million in 1978, and $149 million in 1979 before they stagnated in
1980 and declined in 1981 ($151 million and $131 million, respectively). *Yearbook of the*

United Nations 1974, 563; *Yearbook of the United Nations 1975*, 547; *Yearbook of the United Nations 1976*, 542; *Yearbook of the United Nations 1977*, 580; *Yearbook of the United Nations 1978*, 608; *Yearbook of the United Nations 1979*, 788; *Yearbook of the United Nations 1980*, 793; *Yearbook of the United Nations 1981*, 782, 784.

160. *Yearbook of the United Nations 1974*, 563; *Yearbook of the United Nations 1977*, 580; *Yearbook of the United Nations 1978*, 608; *Yearbook of the United Nations 1979*, 788–789; *Yearbook of the United Nations 1980*, 793; *Yearbook of the United Nations 1981*, 781–784, and calculations based on data in these sources.

161. "United Nations Volunteers Programme," ECOSOC resolution 1618 (LI), 27 July, 1971; "United Nations Volunteers Programme," General Assembly resolution 2810 (XXVI), 14 December 1971. In its June 1973 session, the Governing Council agreed to a joint proposal by the Secretary-General and the administrator to expand the program by sending teams of volunteers to selected countries, focusing on the LDCs (70 percent of the volunteers were to be assigned to this group of countries). It also agreed to increase the proportion of volunteers from developing countries. These guidelines were endorsed by the General Assembly. "Special Measures in Favour of the Least Developed Countries," General Assembly resolution 3174 (XXVIII), 17 December 1973.

162. "United Nations Volunteers Programme," General Assembly resolution 31/131, 16 December 1976.

163. Ibid.

164. *Yearbook of the United Nations 1975*, 413–414; *Yearbook of the United Nations 1976*, 371–372, 377; *Yearbook of the United Nations 1978*, 472.

165. By the end of 1972, about 100 volunteers, more than half of them from developing countries, had been recruited to serve in nineteen countries in a range of professional fields. By the end of 1976, 285 UN volunteers were working in fifty-two developing countries, 65 percent of them in the LDCs. There was also a growth in the number recruited from developing countries to more than half of the total. By the end of 1980, the total volunteers had increased to 863. This group represented seventy-nine nationalities and were in service in eighty-seven developing countries. By the end of 1981, ninety-one countries were receiving assistance from the program. *Yearbook of the United Nations 1972*, 249–250; *Yearbook of the United Nations 1976*, 371; *Yearbook of the United Nations 1980*, 584, 592; *Yearbook of the United Nations 1981*, 460.

166. "Documents Relating to Operational Activities for Development," UN General Assembly document A/DEC/34/429, 14 December 1979.

167. Pledges to the Special Voluntary Fund were modest from the start: $300,000 by the end of 1972; $563,595 in 1973. In 1980, contributions from fourteen governments amounted to $1 million (with Belgium, Sweden, Germany, Switzerland, and the Netherlands as the major donors). In addition $500,000 was allocated from the UNDP revenue reserves. In 1981, payments dropped to less than $600,000, and pledges for 1982 amounted to less than $500,000. *Yearbook of the United Nations 1972*, 249–250; *Yearbook of the United Nations 1973*, 329; *Yearbook of the United Nations 1980*, 584, 592; *Yearbook of the United Nations 1981*, 461–462.

168. "United Nations Volunteers Programme," General Assembly resolution 36/198, 17 December 1981. Titles matter, both for institutions and their officials. In 1980, the Governing Council asked the administrator, after consulting delegations, to recommend that the General Assembly change the title of the coordinator of the UNV. The General Assembly responded on 5 December with the new title of Executive Co-ordinator.

169. Activities included offering various educational programs; initiating

agricultural projects aimed at improving food production capacity and making the national liberation movements fairly self-sufficient in basic food requirements; and providing administrative support. The assistance provided to transitional governments included financing for programs and project formulation, providing short-term emergency supplies, and a host of small-scale projects in Mozambique, Cape Verde, and Angola. *Yearbook of the United Nations 1974,* 411.

170. These liberation movements included the Mouvement de libération de Djibouti, the Front de libération de la Côte des Somalis, the African National Council (Zimbabwe), the Movimento de Liberatacão de São Tomé e Principe, the Partido Africano de Independência da Guiné e Cabo Verde, the South West Africa People's Organization, and the transitional governments of Cape Verde and Angola.

171. *Yearbook of the United Nations 1975,* 408, 414; *Yearbook of the United Nations 1976,* 372, 377; *Yearbook of the United Nations 1977,* 450; *Yearbook of the United Nations 1978,* 463, 472; *Yearbook of the United Nations 1979,* 539.

172. "United Nations Revolving Fund for Natural Resources Exploration," General Assembly resolution 3167 (XXXVIII), 17 December 1973.

173. In 1980, expenditures amounted to $4.8 million; by the end of the year, the fund had a balance of $20.5 million. *Yearbook of the United Nations 1975,* 409, 411; *Yearbook of the United Nations 1980,* 584.

174. *Yearbook of the United Nations 1978,* 464; *Yearbook of the United Nations 1979,* 538; *Yearbook of the United Nations 1980,* 585–586.

175. Calculations based on data in *Yearbook of the United Nations 1970,* 343–344; *Yearbook of the United Nations 1971,* 247–248; *Yearbook of the United Nations 1972,* 251; *Yearbook of the United Nations 1973,* 330–331; *Yearbook of the United Nations 1974,* 413–414; *Yearbook of the United Nations 1975,* 410–411; *Yearbook of the United Nations 1976,* 373–374; *Yearbook of the United Nations 1977,* 452; *Yearbook of the United Nations 1978,* 465; *Yearbook of the United Nations 1979,* 555–556; *Yearbook of the United Nations 1981,* 453–455; *Yearbook of the United Nations 1982,* 651–653.

176. The percentages based on IPFs for the second (1977–1981) and third (1982–1986) development cycles are as follows (third-cycle figures in parentheses): Asia and the Pacific, 29.2 percent (31.7), Africa 29.0 percent (30.2), Latin America 12.8 percent (7.8), Arab states 9.6 percent (5.9), and Europe 3.2 percent (1.6). Regional projects were allocated 12.7 percent (14.6), global projects 2.0 percent (2.3), and interregional projects 1.4 percent (1.5). *Yearbook of the United Nations 1981,* 437–444, and calculations based on data in this source. Percentages do not add up to 100 because of the "other and undefined" category.

177. "United Nations Development Programme: Projects in the Field of Industrial Development," ECOSOC resolution 1617 (LI), 27 July 1971.

178. "Report of the Special International Conference of the United Nations Industrial Development Organization," General Assembly resolution 2823 (XXVI), 16 December 1971.

179. "Co-operation between the United Nations Development Programme and the United Nations Industrial Development Organization," General Assembly resolution 2953 (XXVII), 11 December 1972.

180. *Yearbook of the United Nations 1980,* 580.

181. *Yearbook of the United Nations 1981,* 418.

182. Total income in 1981, including trust funds, amounted to $890.7 million, a slight decline from the $897.5 million of the previous year. The income of the central

account was $804.3 million, a decrease from the $821.4 million of the previous year. In 1981, expenditures exceeded income by $153.2 million. *Yearbook of the United Nations 1980*, 587; *Yearbook of the United Nations 1981*, 418, 446–447.

183. "Operational Activities for Development," General Assembly resolution 36/199, 17 December 1981.

184. *Yearbook of the United Nations 1981*, 425–426.

8. THE WORLD FOOD PROGRAMME, 1961–1981

1. D. John Shaw, *The UN World Food Programme and the Development of Food Aid* (Basingstoke: Palgrave, 2001), 1.

2. The WHO was the first specialized agency that was clearly mandated to undertake operational tasks to assist member countries. In 1949 it was provided with a budget line to enable it to fulfill this obligation. According to Heppling, this was because between the founding of other major agencies such as the FAO and UNESCO at the end of World War II and the establishment of the WHO in 1949, "a great number of new nations had arisen out [of] the decolonization process, some of them very large in population and area." Sixten Heppling, *UNDP: From Agency Shares to Country Programmes, 1949–1975* (Stockholm: Ministry of Foreign Affairs, 1995), 14–15.

3. Gove Hambidge, *The Story of FAO* (New York: D. Van Nostrand, 1955), 52–53.

4. FAO, *Proposals for a World Food Board* (Washington, D.C.: FAO, 1946).

5. FAO, *Disposal of Agricultural Surpluses: Principles Recommended by the FAO* (Rome: FAO, 1954). Mounting U.S. surpluses were the immediate background for adopting these guidelines. Although they were not legally binding, they carried strong influence. For the evolving norms established since 1953, see FAO, *Principles of Surplus Disposal and Consultative Obligations of Member Nations* (1972; Rome: FAO, 1980).

6. FAO, *Uses of Agricultural Surpluses to Finance Economic Development in Under-Developed Countries: A Pilot Study in India* (Rome: FAO, 1955).

7. FAO, *Report of Group of Experts on the Establishment of an Emergency Famine Reserve* (Rome: FAO, 1953); FAO, *Functions of a World Food Reserve: Scope and Limitations* (Rome: FAO, 1956); FAO, *National Food Reserve Policies in Underdeveloped Countries* (Rome: FAO, 1958).

8. FAO, *Index, FAO Conference and Council Decisions 1945–1972* (Rome: FAO, 1973).

9. According to Mitchel B. Wallerstein, it was ultimately the support of the U.S. agricultural community—"as embodied by its principal lobbying group, the American Farm Bureau Federation (AFBF)—that assured the eventual passage of PL 480." PL 480 institutionalized the first formal U.S. food aid program on a permanent basis in 1954. See *Food for War—Food for Peace: United States Food Aid in a Global Context* (Cambridge, Mass.: MIT Press, 1980), 34ff.

10. For a brief account of the historical antecedents of U.S. food aid, with particular reference to the role of Herbert Hoover before and after serving as president of the United States, see Wallerstein, *Food for War—Food for Peace*, 26–30. One characteristic was common to these initiatives through the end of World War II: "The food was conceptualized and packaged as an ad hoc, limited-duration response to sudden and acute crisis situations. Moreover, there was generally little or no attempt made to institutionalize the assistance as a regular government function. But, with the advent of the European Recovery Program [the Marshall Plan] at the close of the war . . . all this changed" (31–32).

11. Under the Lend-Lease Act (1941), about $6 billion in food aid was provided to European allies. The Surplus Property Act (1944) and the Agricultural Act (1949) authorized the Commodity Credit Corporation to sell stockpiled surpluses in the international market at below the market price. Surpluses were also used for disaster relief under special legislation—in India (1951) and Pakistan (1953), making possible the sale of such surpluses for local currencies. In 1951, the Mutual Security Act (PL 82-165) contained a new budgetary provision under which food aid was provided. Shaw, *The UN World Food Programme and the Development of Food Aid*, 29–30.

12. Ibid., 30.

13. Ibid., 32.

14. "Provision of Food Surpluses to Food-Deficit People through the United Nations System," General Assembly resolution 1496 (XV), 27 October 1960. The resolution was initiated by the (Republican) Eisenhower administration.

15. Ibid.

16. FAO, "Expanded Program of Surplus Food Utilization," Report by the Expert Group to the Director-General of FAO, in *Development through Food: A Strategy for Surplus Utilization* (Rome: FAO, 1961). For Hans W. Singer's prominent role in preparing for a multilateral food aid agency, see D. John Shaw, *Sir Hans Singer: The Life and Work of a Development Economist* (Basingstoke: Palgrave, 2002), 98–102; and D. John Shaw, ed., *International Development Co-operation. Selected Essays by H. W. Singer on Aid and the United Nations System* (Basingstoke: Palgrave, 2001), chapter 10.

The group of experts held that food surpluses used for economic development would eventually enable hungry people to produce their food or other products to buy food. This perspective was dominant when the WFP came into being.

17. "Joint Proposal by the United Nations and the Food and Agriculture Organization of the United Nations (FAO) Regarding Procedures and Arrangements for Multilateral Utilization of Surplus Food," General Assembly document A/4907, 6 October 1961, Annex IV.

18. "World Food Programme," General Assembly resolution 1714 (XVI), 19 December 1961.

19. Ibid.

20. Ibid.

21. Ibid.

22. *First Report of the United Nations/FAO Intergovernmental Committee of the World Food Programme to the Economic and Social Council and to the Council of the Food and Agriculture Organization of the United Nations*, ECOSOC document E/3791, 19 June 1963; *Second Annual Report of the United Nations/FAO Intergovernmental Committee on the World Food Programme*, ECOSOC document E/3949, 17 July 1964; *Third Annual Report of the United Nations/FAO Intergovernmental Committee on the World Food Programme*, ECOSOC document E/4054, 28 May 1965.

23. *Second Annual Report of the United Nations/FAO Intergovernmental Committee on the World Food Programme; Third Annual Report of the United Nations/FAO Intergovernmental Committee on the World Food Programme.*

24. "World Food Programme," General Assembly resolution 1714 (XVI), 19 December 1961, Annex I.

25. Ibid.

26. Ibid.

27. "World Food Programme," General Assembly resolution 1825 (XVII), 18 December 1962.

28. By 17 May 1963, new pledges had been made, bringing the number of donor countries to fifty (half of which were developing countries) and the amount pledged to $89.8 million, of which $65.9 million was in commodities, $5.8 million in services (shipping and insurance), and $18.1 million in cash; see *First Report of the United Nations/FAO Intergovernmental Committee of the World Food Programme*, 2. By 30 June 1964, the amount pledged had increased slightly (to $91.1 million) with seventeen new donor countries. By then, two-thirds of the donors were developing countries, contributing about 3.9 percent of the total; see *Second Annual Report of the United Nations/FAO Intergovernmental Committee on World Food Programme*, 2. In its third and last annual report during the experimental period, the Intergovernmental Committee reported that by 14 April 1965, the total resources of the program had reached $94,229,100; sixty-eight countries had pledged $93.7 million Of this total, 17 percent had been earmarked for emergency operations and 75 percent for economic and social development projects. Four percent had been budgeted for administrative costs; *Third Annual Report of the United Nations/ FAO Intergovernmental Committee of the World Food Programme*, 65.

In its second session, the Intergovernmental Committee allowed the executive director to consult and correspond with NGOs that had consultative status with the UN and/or FAO and with nongovernmental bodies with the consent of the government concerned. Interestingly, he was also authorized to accept cash contributions from NGOs and private individuals. See *Second Annual Report of the United Nations/FAO Intergovernmental Committee on World Food Programme*, 3.

29. *First Report of the United Nations/FAO Intergovernmental Committee of the World Food Programme*, 5–6; *Second Annual Report of the United Nations/FAO Intergovernmental Committee on World Food Programme*, Annex I.

30. *Third Annual Report of the United Nations/FAO Intergovernmental Committee of the World Food Programme*, 5.

31. *First Report of the United Nations/FAO Intergovernmental Committee of the World Food Programme*, 5.

32. In the foreword to the report, the executive director stated that its purpose was "to put forward the case for a renewal and extension of the Programme's mandate." He wrote that "the Programme has succeeded in lighting a lamp in many lands where because of poverty, malnutrition or even hunger, food aid is a necessity in the preservation of human life and a means through which a better and fuller existence can be achieved. . . . A window has been opened to a better world. It is from such glimpses that hope rises anew, and mankind receives the encouragement to strive for better things. The challenge of the future is far greater than any Programme has yet faced, but I am confident that this greater task can also be accomplished." *Report on the Food Programme by the Executive Director*, ECOSOC document E/4043, 14 May 1965.

33. *Report of the Secretary-General of the United Nations and the Director-General of the Food and Agriculture Organization of the United Nations*, ECOSOC document E/4015, 30 March 1965, 2–3.

34. The study (by P. N. Rosenstein-Rodan and S. Chakravarty, professors at the Center for International Studies, Massachusetts Institute of Technology) maintained that food aid provided to a developing country in a given period should be related to its total nonaid supplies of food (domestic production plus imports minus exports).

Thus linked, the food aid would not prove a disincentive to domestic production or to normal commercial imports. The two professors agreed that the role of planning was crucial. They argued that the scope for food aid might be (and should be) more limited in countries that lacked adequate development plans. *Report on the Food Programme by the Executive Director,* ECOSOC document E/4043, 14 May 1965, 39.

35. Ibid., 41.

36. The author of the study was J. Dessau, professor at the Institut de Science économique appliquée, Paris.

37. *Report on the Food Programme by the Executive Director,* ECOSOC document E/4043, 14 May 1965, 40, 42.

38. The executive director found this state of affairs "unsatisfactory as far as the recipient country is concerned" and noted that it "arises from the fact that the supplying country attaches lower priority to aid needs than to commercial markets, so that supplies available for aid are always residual and therefore subject to substantial variation." He expressed the hope that, as the performance of such projects became evident, "donor governments will give higher priorities to fulfilling commitments to food-aid programmes and projects, notwithstanding other claims on existing supplies." Ibid., 50–51.

39. Ibid., 49, 52, 54.

40. Ibid., 44, 46–48.

41. Ibid., 48–56.

42. Only a tiny share of the food aid was channeled multilaterally. The WFP share was about 2 percent, and even after the proposed expansion it would still handle only about 10 percent of the noncommercial food distribution. "Bearing in mind the preference shown by some countries for multilateral channels for aid, and the fact that the multilateral approach has some distinct advantages in increasing the range of foods available for distribution and in allowing for a broad approach which could take due account of the variety of international experience, an increase in the share of multilateral food aid in total food aid seems justified." *Report of the Secretary-General of the United Nations and the Director-General of the Food and Agriculture Organization of the United Nations,* ECOSOC document E/4015, 30 March 1965, 3.

43. Local public work schemes would be a valuable contribution to economic and social development, the Secretary-General and the FAO director-general argued. However, "the well-being of the rural population depends on the progress of the economy as a whole, including its most advanced sectors. Industrialization involves construction work, labour-intensive processes, work canteens, and industrial estates, all of which provide opportunities for the utilization of food aid, as does also the expansion of mining. Urbanization opens up new needs for public works, low-cost housing, community facilities and general neighbourhood improvement, which also can be facilitated by direct use of food." Ibid., 7.

44. "Continuation of the World Food Programme," FAO Conference resolution 4/65, 6 December 1965; "Continuation of the World Food Programme," General Assembly resolution 2095 (XX), 20 December 1965.

45. This arrangement made the FAO director-general (not the executive director of the WFP) the custodian of the special trust fund: he would determine the bank(s) in which the fund was (were) to be placed, decide on how to invest available funding that had not been put into active use, establish and maintain a reserve fund, and prepare the regular statements of WFP accounts and similar reports to the Intergovernmental Committee of the WFP. The annual accounts were to be submitted to the external auditors of the FAO. Initially, the WFP had no independent legal status and had to consult with its two parent organizations, the FAO and the UN.

The program had to cooperate closely with other UN agencies, bilateral donor agencies, and NGOs in activities it pursued. Staff in these organizations (particularly in the FAO and the UN but also in the ILO, UNESCO, and the WHO) were appointed to liaise with the WFP. The same applied to the representatives in the recipient countries; staff at the office of the resident representatives were appointed to serve as WFP resident representatives in addition to their other tasks.

46. For a discussion and analysis of the concept, see Jacques Forster and Olav Stokke, "Coherence of Policies towards Developing Countries: Approaching the Problematique," in *Policy Coherence in Developing Co-operation,* ed. Forster and Stokke (London: Frank Cass, 1999), 16–57.

47. According to Shaw, to become WFP representatives, WFP staff members would have had to resign their positions in the WFP to become staff members of the UNDP. He notes that "few made that transition." *The UN World Food Programme and the Development of Food Aid,* 209.

48. For a critical assessment from the outside, with particular reference to the early years of the program, see Wallerstein, *Food for War—Food for Peace,* 107–109. Three interactive sets of issues accounted for "the WFP's partially deserved reputation for management mediocrity: ad hocism in management practices and policies; the politics of the program's governing council; and the nature of the multilateral aid mechanism itself" (107).

Wallerstein repeats the critique on a more fundamental basis, related to the core norm on which activities of the WFP (and other UN operational agencies) has been based: the responsibility for delivering food aid commodities was transferred to the host government as soon as it reached the port of entry. While Wallerstein admits that this self-administration might in the long run build an increased LDC capacity for dealing with indigenous food distribution bottlenecks, he argues that in the short term it was more likely to take the form of unacceptably high levels of food spoilage, diversion, and waste, particularly in countries suffering from substantial infrastructural and / or managerial deficiencies. Ibid., 235–236.

James Ingram, who headed the WFP for ten years (1982–1991), has sharply criticized the model and the way it was practiced during his period of tenure. He argues that the chief executive was responsible "to manage effectively all aspects of operations, though required to use the services of other organizations (mainly FAO) irrespective of considerations of cost, timeliness and quality." James Ingram, *Bread and Stones: Leadership and the Struggle to Reform the United Nations World Food Programme* (Charleston, S.C.: BookSurge, 2007), 273–274.

49. Shaw, *The UN World Food Programme and the Development of Food Aid,* 210ff. According to one observer, Saouma was perceived as "self-perpetuating by whatever means, preoccupied with personal prestige, and egocentric towards authority." According to another, he established an unrivaled position that created enemies in the donor countries but support in the developing world. Shaw added that this strategy "was to serve him well in his re-election campaigns, which led to an unprecedented 18 years as the executive head of FAO (1976–93)" (211–212).

The story of the Saouma regime in the FAO and its effects for the WFP, told by an insider, is fascinating reading because it reveals how vulnerable and person-dependent a system can be. It also demonstrates the inertia of the system. Although the problems were evident and well known to the main actors involved, both within the UN system and at intergovernmental levels, they were allowed to continue for years, despite the many (and regular) opportunities to correct the situation.

50. The techniques used included "keeping senior WFP appointees on an interim

basis for varying lengths of time, and . . . making it clear to them that they owed their appointment directly to him and, therefore, [he] expected their full allegiance in return." According to Shaw, "in 1982, Saouma had already established a style of management by which he considered that he had *de facto* control of the organization. On the abrupt resignation of Brito, he summoned WFP's senior staff to his office and told them in no uncertain terms that he considered WFP to be 'part of FAO'" (ibid., 212).

51. For the UN Secretary-General, the WFP was one institution among many and there were more important ones needing his attention. Usually he appointed deputies to represent the UN Secretariat at WFP sessions in Rome. The FAO director-general, in contrast, was often present in person at these sessions (and was always around). This "access" to the WFP was developed further after Saouma was elected to this office; he insisted on seeing all policy papers and the draft reports of the WFP before they were forwarded to the Committee on Food Aid Policies and Programmes for adoption (for the policy papers, rightly so; see the following note). According to Shaw, he "used selected developing country representatives on the WFP's governing body as surrogates or channels to present his views. The reward could be appointment to a senior FAO post. Failure to comply could lead to a request to the government of the country concerned to withdraw their representative from Rome" (ibid., 213).

52. The mandate for emergency food aid ultimately belonged to the FAO director-general and during the experimental period was delegated to the executive director of the WFP, providing emergency food aid was identified as a major task for the WFP. As director-general of the FAO, Saouma insisted on exercising this authority (ibid., 214).

53. "Reconstitution of the United Nations/FAO Intergovernmental Committee of the World Food Programme as a Committee on Food Aid Policies and Programmes," General Assembly resolution 3404 (XXX), 28 November 1975.

54. The WFP secretariat was split on this issue. One view was that a special unit should be established to service the CFA in its handling of its wider functions; another view was that the reputation of the WFP as an effective operational program might be at stake if the secretariat did not succeed in carrying out the new functions that had been proposed in a satisfactory way. The less daring view prevailed. However, a small unit (a senior economist with a secretary) was established in the office of the executive director to prepare policy papers for presentation to the CFA, in cooperation with the FAO. Shaw, *The UN World Food Programme and the Development of Food Aid,* 210–211.

55. The dilemma Ingram faced was that "policy, emergencies approvals, public information, levels, numbers, assignments and choice of staff were under FAO's tight control. Saouma and his predecessors saw WFP as a ward of FAO that existed for its greater glory, period. . . . Attempts to break out of the FAO embrace without a 'power struggle' were simply not open to me. . . . if WFP was not to stagnate it had to break that stranglehold. . . . WFP was in a much better shape at the end of my tenure than the organisation I found and . . . was held in high esteem by donor and recipient . . . If I had been unwilling to resist the bear's embrace almost certainly that would not have been the case. The fact is that despite all the obstacles, WFP prospered under my leadership. In 1992 we transported, bought, and delivered to almost as many beneficiaries as WFP ever subsequently did, with a fraction of the staff and much lower overhead costs." Personal communication, 4 April 2008. See also Ingram, *Bread and Stones,* 75ff., and 307ff.

56. Shaw, *The UN World Food Programme and the Development of Food Aid,* 222. Years afterward, Ingram reflected on the struggle in which he had been involved, broadening the perspective to the need for UN reform: "FAO's initial reactions to my actions, though characteristic of the brutally aggressive style of the organization at the time,

was not substantially at odds with the basic culture of the UN system, a consortium of competing entities dependent on continued funding by governments. They, like the United States, pursued separate strategies formulated without a coherent overarching policy in relation to the system as a whole, or when such a policy nominally existed, without the institutional mechanisms to produce consistency." *Bread and Stones,* 313.

57. For 1969–1970, the target was $200 million, increasing to $340 million for 1973–1974 and $750 million for 1977–1978, reaching $1 billion for 1981–1982. "Review of the World Food Programme," General Assembly resolution 2290 (XXII), 8 December 1967; "Pledging Target for the World Food Programme for the Period 1973–1974," General Assembly resolution 2805 (XXVI), 14 December 1971; "Target for World Food Programme Pledges for the Period 1977–1978," General Assembly resolution 3407 (XXX), 28 November 1975; and "Target for World Food Programme Pledges for the Period 1981–1982," General Assembly resolution 34/108, 14 December 1979.

In 1975, when the executive director recommended a big leap, from $440 million for 1975–1976 to $750 million for 1977–1978, the Intergovernmental Committee first felt that it was not in a position to make a recommendation; some representatives argued that the matter required a review of the ability of various donors to reach the figure. Nevertheless, at its September–October session, it unanimously agreed to recommend the target, and so did ECOSOC. The General Assembly decided accordingly. *Yearbook of the United Nations 1975* (New York: United Nations, Office of Public Information, 1978), 428.

58. "Multilateral Food Aid," General Assembly resolution 2682 (XXV), 11 December 1970; *Yearbook of the United Nations 1970* (New York: United Nations, Office of Public Information, 1972), 370.

59. By and large, the United States complied with the request that it provide one-third of its contributions in the form of cash and services. For statistics for the 1970s, see volumes of *Yearbook of the United Nations* for that decade.

60. *Yearbook of the United Nations 1976* (New York: United Nations, Office of Public Information, 1979), 390; *Yearbook of the United Nations 1977,* 267, 470; *Yearbook of the United Nations 1978* (New York: United Nations, Office of Public Information, 1981), 483, 486; *Yearbook of the United Nations 1979,* 669–670; *Yearbook of the United Nations 1980* (New York: United Nations, Office of Public Information, 1983), 701; *Yearbook of the United Nations 1981* (New York: United Nations, Office of Public Information, 1985), 732.

61. *Yearbook of the United Nations 1981,* 698.

62. *Report of the Seventh Session of the United Nations/FAO Committee of Food Aid Policies and Programmes,* WFP/CFA 7/21, June 1979, Annex IV; *Yearbook of the United Nations 1978,* 483–484; *Yearbook of the United Nations 1979,* 666.

63. Almost 40 percent of the WFP's new resources were allocated to countries where the greatest need existed (Bangladesh, India, Pakistan, and Sri Lanka). Increased emphasis was placed on feeding vulnerable groups, in accordance with the recommendations of the World Food Conference. *Yearbook of the United Nations 1975,* 427.

64. *Yearbook of the United Nations 1978,* 483; *Yearbook of the United Nations 1979,* 665; *Yearbook of the United Nations 1981,* 727.

65. Calculations based on Shaw, *The UN World Food Programme and the Development of Food Aid,* Statistical Annex 2.

66. WFP projects encompassed a great variety of development activities, "ranging from development of human resources by feeding of vulnerable groups to the improvement of irrigation schemes; they included feeding of mothers and young children, nutritional education, feeding of students in primary and secondary schools and of university

students, vocational training, youth camps, literary campaigns, feeding of hospital patients and hospital development, livestock improvement, dairy development, oil conservation, land reclamation and settlement, reforestation, construction of dikes, dams, roads and railroads, self-help housing, and construction of community facilities through mutual-help schemes." *Yearbook of the United Nations 1969*, 320.

67. *Yearbook of the United Nations 1980*, 696–697.

68. The executive director of the WFP acted on behalf of the director-general of the FAO in emergency issues, although the director-general had the final say. For details of emergency projects in the 1970s, see *Yearbook of the United Nations 1969*, 320; *Yearbook of the United Nations 1970*, 369; *Yearbook of the United Nations 1971*, 266; *Yearbook of the United Nations 1973* (New York: United Nations, Office of Public Information, 1976), 342; and *Yearbook of the United Nations 1974*, 427.

69. *Yearbook of the United Nations 1972* (New York: United Nations, Office of Public Information, 1975), 271; *Yearbook of the United Nations 1973*, 342; *Yearbook of the United Nations 1974*, 427.

70. *Yearbook of the United Nations 1974*, 427.

71. Ibid.

72. *Yearbook of the United Nations 1976*, 390; *Yearbook of the United Nations 1977*, 267.

73. *Yearbook of the United Nations 1979*, 666; *Yearbook of the United Nations 1980*, 697–698, 701; *Yearbook of the United Nations 1981*, 727, 731.

74. Shaw, *The UN World Food Programme and the Development of Food Aid*, Table 6.1, and calculations based on this data.

75. Just to indicate its relative magnitude: during the initial period (1964–1966) multilateral food aid amounted to 1.0 percent of bilateral food aid, increasing to 7.6 percent in 1969, 13.7 percent in 1971, 24.7 percent in 1973, and 26.5 percent in 1977. Wallerstein, *Food for War—Food for Peace*, Table 11.2.

76. So far, we have taken the notion of "food aid" at face value to refer to the resources made available by the WFP. However, it is not quite that simple. Definitions of food aid vary, and these variations impact international food aid statistics. How food aid is defined has important policy implications, involving both objectives and results. Responsibility for food aid statistics has been split. The WFP's International Food Aid Information System and the FAO have the main international responsibility for reporting food aid flows in physical terms (tons of food). The OECD Development Assistance Committee reports food aid in financial terms.

77. See Robert Wood, *From the Marshall Plan to Debt Crisis: Foreign Aid and Development Choices in the World Economy* (Berkeley: University of California Press, 1986). On U.S. food aid to Bangladesh, see Mosharaff Hossein, "Aid Conditionality: Some Comments," in *European Development Assistance*, vol. II, *Third World Perspectives on Policies and Performance*, ed. Olav Stokke (Tilburg: EADI, 1984). For more recent developments such as the system transformation under way in Eastern Europe, see Charlotte Benson and Edward J. Clay, "Additionality or Diversion? Food Aid to Eastern Europe and the Former Soviet Republics and the Implications for Developing Countries," *World Development* 26, no. 1 (1998): 31–44.

For a systematic analysis of food aid used as an instrument in U.S. foreign policy for the period 1961–1976, see Wallerstein, *Food for War—Food for Peace*, 119–146. He distinguishes between using food aid as a carrot and using it as a stick in pursuit of U.S. foreign policy, security policy, and trade objectives. Wallerstein argues that "in fact, that food is *not* superior in any respect to other forms of assistance; it is simply more available" (130).

78. For in-depth analysis of the problems with food aid, see Edward Clay and Olav Stokke, eds., *Food Aid Reconsidered: Assessing the Impact on Third World Countries* (1991; repr., London: Frank Cass, 1995); and Clay and Stokke, eds., *Food Aid and Human Security*. Several of the problematic aspects of food aid were identified at an early stage in the critical studies that were commissioned before the WFP was established on a more permanent basis. Most of them are still core issues in the current discourse. Some of the more problematic aspects have been accentuated since the mid-1990s; see OECD, *The Development Effectiveness of Food Aid: Does Tying Matter?* (Paris: OECD, 2006), 28–48, 87–121.

79. An extensive literature exists on the negative effects of food aid. At an early stage, Nobel laureate Theodore Schultz gave voice to the idea that food aid could harm the poor; see Theodore W. Schultz, "Value of US Farm Surpluses to Underdeveloped Countries," *Journal of Farm Economics* 42, no. 5 (1960): 1019–1030. Perhaps the most devastating negative effect attributed to food aid (and other forms of aid provided in such a way, especially commodity aid) is that it becomes a disincentive to local production and development. See Simon Maxwell, "The Disincentive Effects of Food Aid: A Programmatic Approach," in Clay and Stokke, *Food Aid Reconsidered*, 66–90. Such criticisms came forward even before the WFP was established, directed particularly toward the counterproductive effects of U.S. bulk food aid. This may be part of the explanation of why project aid became the preferred form of WFP aid for development. See R. G. Smethurst, "Direct Commodity Aid: A Multilateral Experiment," *Journal of Development Studies* 5, no. 3 (1969): 205–219.

However, the case for food aid has also been forcefully argued. See World Bank and WFP, *Food Aid in Africa: An Agenda for the 1990s*, a Joint Study by the World Bank and the World Food Programme (Washington, D.C., and Rome: World Bank and WFP, 1991): "To cite just one indicator, the net value of food aid to Africa in 1985–90 averaged $1 billion a year, about the same as the net transfers to the region by the World Bank and the International Development Association" (iii).

80. In a statement to the fifth session of the CFA, FAO director-general Edouard Saouma made the point that "aid should be given in a form which corresponds to people's food habits. But what is one to do, for example, in a case of emergency in rice-consuming developing regions, when the stocks of this commodity are at their lowest and the funds available for food aid extremely limited? . . . The solution undoubtedly lies in buying rice from other developing countries with surpluses. But once again it is a question of resources."

He insisted that food aid in itself was not sufficient: it was necessary that aid be made available in time and where most needed. "It must therefore be accompanied by logistic assistance for unloading the ships, and for storage, transport and distribution of food. Aid in the form of agricultural inputs is equally essential for preparation of the future harvests. For all these needs, again, the financial resources are often lacking." *Report of the Fifth Session of the United Nations/FAO Committee of Food Aid Policies and Programmes, Rome, 10–21 April 1978*, WFP/CFA 5/18, May 1978, Annex III.

81. The WFP was the major organizer of triangular transactions. For a study of the WFP's experiences with such transactions during the first years, commissioned by the WFP and directed by Edward Clay, see RDI, *A Study of Triangular Transactions and Local Purchases in Food Aid*, WFP Occasional Papers no. 11 (London: Relief and Development Institute, 1987).

82. "Report of the Secretary-General," *ESCOR*, 41st Session, document E/4210, 6 June 1966, 2.

83. As Wallerstein observed in *Food for War—Food for Peace,* although Europe has historically been an aggregate food importer, since the late 1960s, the agricultural policies of the EEC have produced surpluses, particularly in dairy products. The main rationale for the EEC food aid policy during this early period became to get rid of surplus agricultural production. Thus, "EEC food assistance policy—like that of the United States—has been developed more in response to the needs of its own agricultural producers than in order to meet the particular *food* needs of recipients" (83–84).

84. See, inter alia, Christopher B. Barrett and Daniel G. Maxwell, *Food Aid after Fifty Years* (London and New York: Routledge, 2005); Edward Clay and Olav Stokke, "Food and Human Security: Retrospective and an Agenda for Change," in Clay and Stokke, *Food Aid and Human Security;* C. E. Hanrahan, "The Food Security Commodity Reserve: The Replenishment Issue," *CRS Report for Congress 98-398* (Washington, D.C.: Congressional Research Service, Library of Congress, 1998); C. E. Hanrahan and I. Leach, "PL480 Food Aid: History and Legislation, Programs and Policy Issues," *CRS Report for Congress 94-3035* (Washington, D.C.: Congressional Research Service, Library of Congress, 1994); V. W. Ruttan, *Why Food Aid?* (Baltimore, Md.: Johns Hopkins University Press, 1993); V. W. Ruttan, *United States Development Assistance Policy. The Domestic Politics of Foreign Economic Aid* (Baltimore, Md.: Johns Hopkins University Press, 1996); and Wallerstein, *Food for War—Food for Peace.*

85. Shaw, *The UN World Food Programme and the Development of Food Aid,* 12–15.

86. Although the traditional justification of removing agricultural surpluses remained predominant, the incoming administration also saw this as an opportunity to boost a new and dynamic image for itself and the United States, turning its food aid into a foreign policy instrument. During the 1960 presidential campaign, Vice-President Nixon was the first to make the proposal. This served the dual purpose of creating a positive international image for the United States and circumventing charges of Canada and Australia that U.S. policy was motivated by a desire to dispose of surpluses by co-opting them into a joint undertaking. Nixon also wanted to "out-innovate" his rival, who was calling for new U.S food aid initiatives. The Eisenhower administration followed this up in the UN. According to Wallerstein, President Kennedy's multilateral food aid policy was marked by a dual set of concerns: a unilateral interest in redistributing the international responsibility for food aid while retaining the capacity to dispose of U.S. agricultural surpluses and a broader interest in building an international institutional capacity to allocate food aid for economic and social development. He wanted to shift thinking at the operational level from a philosophy of surplus disposal to recognition of the political and economic value of food aid. See Wallerstein, *Food for War—Food for Peace,* 167–170, 181ff.

87. The FAO-driven Freedom from Hunger Campaign, which was launched in 1960 and was instrumental in creating the WFP, may illustrate the point. The campaign included several publications by the FAO and other UN organizations, including a world food survey. See FAO, *Third World Food Survey* (Rome: FAO, 1963) and a series of other studies that covered specific aspects of the basic problems involved. These included FAO, *Nutrition and Working Efficiency* (Rome: FAO, 1962); FAO, *Education and Training in Nutrition* (Rome: FAO, 1962); United Nations, *Population and Food Supplies* (New York: United Nations, 1962); United Nations, *Aspects of Economic Development—The Background to Freedom from Hunger* (New York: United Nations, 1962); FAO, *Possibilities for Increasing World Food Production* (Rome: FAO, 1963); WHO, *Malnutrition and Disease. A Major Problem of the Human Race* (Geneva: World Health Organization, 1963); ILO, *Hunger and Social Policy* (Geneva: ILO, 1963); and UNESCO, *Education and Agricultural Development*

(Paris: UNESCO, 1963). The WFP made important contributions in this policy field through many studies and reports that were prepared by the program itself or commissioned by the program or its parent organizations and other arms of the multilateral system.

88. By the late 1970s, the United States was no longer able to dominate the multilateral arena through the sheer weight of its resource contribution. It found "its proposals outvoted—and its wishes ignored—within the WFP governing council, the CFA, although this situation is also a function of the polarized international political environment as well." The United States "attempted to compensate to some degree for the loss of direct leverage by regulating the size of their multilateral food contributions. The strategy here is to apply indirect pressure on the WFP to accede to the donor's wishes or face the possible reduction—or outright withdrawal—of pledged resources. Donors have occasionally been forced to resort to this strategy in self-defence against what they considered the tyranny of the voting by the Group of 77"; Wallerstein, *Food for War— Food for Peace*, 222, 234–235.

89. United Nations, *Inter-Agency Study on Multilateral Food Aid* (New York: United Nations, 1968).

9. THE 1960s AND 1970s

1. United Nations, *Measures for the Economic Development of Underdeveloped Countries: Report by a Group of Experts appointed by the Secretary-General of the United Nations* (New York: United Nations, Department of Economic Affairs, May 1951), 84ff., 95. The amount was to increase rapidly toward $3 billion a year. The Group of Experts pointed out that this sum "would be equivalent to rather less than 1 per cent of the national incomes of Western Europe, Australasia, the United States and Canada" (84).

2. The Pearson report traces the idea back to 1958, when the World Council of Churches adopted a statement that was circulated to all UN delegations that suggested that if contributing countries could divert at least 1 percent of their national income to grants and concessional loans, the international picture would be much more hopeful. The idea was agreed to by the General Assembly in 1960 and further developed by UNCTAD at its first meeting and endorsed by the OECD's DAC. The Pearson report added that it was "ironic to note that total resource flows actually did exceed 1 per cent of combined national income in the five years preceding the adaptation of the target by DAC. Since then, the target has never been met." See Lester B. Pearson, *Partners in Development. Report of the Commission on International Development* (New York: Praeger Publishers, 1969), 144.

3. According to Hans Singer, the idea originated in a group of economic advisers to President Kennedy when he assumed power in 1961. It had a counterpart target of a 5 percent growth rate for the national income of the "less-developed" countries themselves. See "That One Per Cent Aid Target (Some Reflections on the Arithmetic of International Targetry)," *IDS Bulletin* 37, no. 4 (2006): 8–11. The article was originally published in 2, no. 2 (1969) of *IDS Bulletin*.

4. The Soviet bloc followed a more or less consistent line when the issue of financial or other international commitments of the kind came up: they abstained or voted for resolutions but explained that the commitments did not apply to their governments, which had no responsibility for the situation in developing countries. That responsibility, they argued, rested with the past and present imperialist and neocolonial policies of the major western powers.

5. The report of the chairman of the DAC for 1961 begins with the following statement: "There are few issues of such fundamental importance for world peace and prosperity as that of aid to the less-developed countries. The very existence of the Development Assistance Committee is a demonstration of the increasing significance which the developed, capital-exporting countries attach to their aid policies and to the working-out, as far as possible, of a common approach to aid questions." OECD, *Development Assistance Efforts and Policies in 1961 of the Members of the Development Assistance Committee* (Paris: OECD, September 1962), 7. The purpose and objectives of the DAC were set out in a resolution adopted by its member governments in March 1961 on common aid efforts, recommending that members "agree to expand the flow of resources to the less-developed countries, . . . improve the effectiveness of development assistance, and . . . provide for increased assistance in the form of grants or loans on favourable terms." The report stated that "all the Member Governments have accepted this common aid objective" (9).

6. Ibid., 9–10. The main instrument was an annual aid review that would enable members "to exchange experience in giving bilateral aid with a view to improving their aid efforts and to adapting it better to the needs of the recipient countries." The 1961 report was the first of its kind; it established a system of annual scrutiny of the aid policies and performance of DAC member countries. It was based on the responses by member governments to a list of written questions prepared by the DAC secretariat and scrutinized by the DAC. The report stated that "although this was the first exercise of its kind in the field of development assistance, the O.E.C.D. has used the technique of confrontation and collective review of national policies with a great deal of success in other aspects of its work, namely economic and financial policies, agricultural and educational policies."

7. Ibid., 13. "By far the largest part of the official contributions of several D.A.C. Members is already [in 1961] in the form of grants or loans on very lenient terms, e.g. Belgium, Canada, France, the Netherlands and the Development Fund of the E.E.C. Since 1961 the United States has been making some loans through the Agency for International Development at ¾ of one per cent for period of up to 40 years. This is part of the explicit United States policy of making loans repayable in dollars at favourable terms, rather than grants and loans repayable in recipients' currencies."

8. "Recommendation on Financial Terms and Conditions Adopted by the Development Assistance Committee at its 58th Session on 22nd and 23rd July, 1965," in OECD, *Development Assistance Efforts and Policies, 1965 Review* (Paris: OECD, 1965).

9. OECD, *Development Assistance, 1970 Review* (Paris: OECD, December 1970). Previous reports had focused on the flow of long-term official (and private) resources. For some countries, the flow of official resources was more or less identical with their ODA contributions; for others (particularly the major ones), it was not.

10. The report found that "the real economic burden of foreign aid to wealthy countries" was exaggerated. It stated that although the total flow of resources to developing countries was often referred to as something that the rich countries "give" to the poor, "nothing could be further from the truth, or more misleading. . . . Only Official Development Assistance [referring to DAC categories of flows] should be designated as 'aid.' The flow of private capital and official credits (Other Official Flows) undertaken for commercial reasons have no more the character of 'aid' when they flow to developing countries than when they flow between industrialized countries." The report furthermore observed that the share of grants in ODA had declined from 87 percent in 1961 to 63 percent in 1968 and that official lending generated "considerable reverse flow

to the developed countries" in the form of interest payments. The report found that calculating the grant element of loans (a numerical approximation of the degree to which a loan is concessional) was useful mainly for comparing the relative terms of different loans. It also noted that "much of the aid is still directed to military purposes and only secondary to long-term development." Although there is "no satisfactory way to translate the real burden of aid into a precise figure, it clearly runs far below the dollar value of all resources transferred. This fact deserves to be widely known," the report emphasized. Pearson, *Partners in Development*, 139–141.

11. Ibid., 147–149. The commission found that it was "warranted to seek agreement on a target for official aid which is simple, attainable, and adequate without, however, limiting other forms of aid within the 1 per cent target figure. *We therefore recommend that each aid-giver increase commitments of official development assistance to the level necessary for net disbursements to reach 0.70 per cent of its gross national product by 1975 or shortly thereafter, but in no case later than 1980*" (148–149; emphasis in original).

12. "International Development Strategy for the Second Development Decade," General Assembly resolution 2626 (XXV), 24 October 1970, 41 and 42. The strategy also highlighted qualitative aspects such as softening and harmonizing the terms and conditions of the assistance and untying financial assistance, as UNCTAD II recommended (44 and 45). Foreign private capital had a place in the strategy, but it was not embraced with the enthusiasm of previous years. It was limited: foreign private investment in developing countries should be undertaken in a manner consistent with the development objectives and priorities established in their national plans. Foreign private investors should provide resources to increase the local share of management and administration, for employment and training of local labor, for participation of local capital, and for reinvestment of profits (50).

13. In the strategy for DD3 (the 1980s), the 0.7 percent target was set anew, to be attained by 1985 by those countries that had not yet reached it. An ODA target for the future, with no date set, was added: 1 percent as soon as possible. "International Development Strategy for the Third United Nations Development Decade," General Assembly resolution 35/56, 5 December 1980, paragraphs 24 and 98.

14. Olav Stokke, ed., *Western Middle Powers and Global Poverty: The Determinants of the Aid Policies of Canada, Denmark, the Netherlands, Norway and Sweden* (Uppsala, Sweden: The Scandinavian Institute of African Studies, 1989).

15. The first UNCTAD conference was convened in Geneva in 1964 and established as a permanent organ under the General Assembly with a Trade and Development Board and a secretariat because of pressure from Third World governments. UNCTAD (and the General Assembly) became the most important forums for the work of these governments to make an impact on the international development agenda.

16. This change of perspective involved developing technical cooperation and bridging the science and technology gap between developed and developing countries. See "International Development Strategy for the Third United Nations Development Decade."

17. Gunnar Myrdal, *Asian Drama: An Enquiry into the Poverty of Nations* (New York: Twentieth Century Fund and Pantheon, 1968).

18. See Robert H. Jackson and Carl G. Rosberg, "Sovereignty and Underdevelopment: Juridical Statehood in the African Crisis," *Journal of Modern African Studies* 24, no. 1 (1986): 1–31; and Georg Sørensen, "Conditionality, Democracy and Development," in *Aid and Political Conditionality*, ed. Olav Stokke (London: Frank Cass, 1995), 392–409.

19. In 1972, aid-financed agricultural exports amounted to $1.1 billion and commercial food exports amounted to $6.9 billion. In 1975, aid-financed agricultural exports remained at $1.1 billion, while commercial food exports had quadrupled to $21.8 billion. As a result, in the midst of the world food crisis period, available supplies of food were not sufficient to meet aggregate demands. Mitchel B. Wallerstein, *Food for War—Food for Peace: United States Food Aid in a Global Context* (Cambridge, Mass.: MIT Press, 1980), 46–47.

20. Ibid., 111ff. The specific provisions were finalized at the International Wheat Conference during the summer of 1967 and included in a Wheat Trade Convention and a Food Aid Convention. The FAC committed the United States and eleven other better-off countries to provide 4.5 million tons of grain annually in the form of bilateral food aid on grant terms. Japan and the food-importing countries of Europe (including the United Kingdom) and the EEC were strongly against the arrangement they had to accept as a part of a package deal.

PART 3 INTRODUCTION

1. Olav Stokke, "Foreign Aid: What Now?" in *Foreign Aid Towards the Year 2000: Experiences and Challenges,* ed. Stokke (London: Frank Cass, 1996), 16–129.

2. South Commission, *The Challenge to the South: The Report of the South Commission* (Oxford: Oxford University Press, 1990).

3. The term was coined by John Toye in *Dilemmas of Development: Reflections on the Counter-Revolution in Development Theory and Policy* (Oxford: Basil Blackwell, 1987).

4. The UN consensus was that for many developing countries, "the 1980s have been viewed as a decade lost for development. Living conditions in Africa and Latin America and the Caribbean and in parts of Asia, deteriorated, and economic and social infrastructure eroded, impairing stability and prospects for growth and development. Other developing countries were able to achieve economic and social progress." "Declaration on International Co-operation, in Particular the Revitalization of Economic Growth and Development of the Developing Countries," General Assembly resolution S-18/3, 1 May 1990, Annex.

5. Georg Sørensen has defined neopatrimonialism as government based on personal loyalty especially to the leading figure of the regime. Important political, bureaucratic, military, and police positions in the state are filled by loyal followers, such as relatives, friends, kinsmen, and tribesmen. Political decisions are for sale, and the capacity of the bureaucracy is destroyed because of its participation in the spoils system. The weakest point is the political elite itself. "Very little in terms of *statecraft* seriously promoting economic development can be expected to emerge in this situation." See "Democracy, Authoritarianism and State Strength," *European Journal of Development Research* 5, no. 1 (1993): 15–17. For other important contributions, see Robert H. Jackson and Carl G. Rosberg, "Sovereignty and Underdevelopment: Juridical Statehood in the African Crisis," *Journal of Modern African Studies* 24, no. 1 (1986): 1–31; Larry Diamond, "Introduction: Roots of Failure, Seeds of Hope," in *Democracy in Developing Countries,* ed. Larry Diamond, Juan J. Linz, and Seymour Martin Lipset (Boulder, Colo.: Lynne Rienner, 1988); and Georg Sørensen, *Democracy and Democratization* (Boulder, Colo.: Westview, 1993).

6. Olav Stokke, "Aid and Political Conditionality: Core Issues and State of the Art," in *Aid and Political Conditionality,* ed. Stokke (London: Frank Cass, 1995), 1–87; Adrian Hewitt and Tony Killick, "Bilateral Aid Conditionality and Policy Leverage," in

Foreign Aid Towards the Year 2000: Experiences and Challenges, ed. Olav Stokke (London: Frank Cass, 1996), 130–167.

7. Giovanni Andrea Cornia, Richard Jolly, and Frances Stewart, eds., *Adjustment with a Human Face,* vol. 1, *Protecting the Vulnerable and Promoting Growth* (Oxford: Oxford University Press, 1987).

8. Joseph E. Stiglitz, *Globalization and Its Discontents* (London: Penguin Allen Lane, 2002).

9. The Monrovia strategy of 1979, as operationalized in the Lagos Plan of Action adopted by the Lagos Economic Summit in 1980 is a case in point. See OAU, *Lagos Plan of Action for the Economic Development of Africa 1980–2000* (Geneva: International Institute for Labour Studies, 1981). Within a year, however, the World Bank came up with an alternative; see World Bank, *Accelerated Development in Sub-Saharan Africa: An Agenda for Action* (Washington, D.C.: World Bank, 1981). According to Adebayo Adedeji, the World Bank's development program was in many ways an antithesis of the Lagos Plan: "Where the [Lagos] plan emphasized self-reliance and self-sustaining development based on integrated and dynamic national, subregional, and regional markets, the Bank put the emphasis on the external market and the continuation of the colonial export-oriented economic structures inherited at independence. While the Bank identified agricultural export as the motor for African development, the Lagos Plan of Action recognized that the motor in each country will depend on the content and nature of its natural resource endowment." "The ECA: Forging a Future for Africa," in *Unity and Diversity in Development Ideas: Perspectives from the UN Regional Commissions,* ed. Yves Berthelot (Bloomington: Indiana University Press, 2004), 266.

10. Brandt Commission, *North-South: A Programme for Survival* (Cambridge, Mass.: MIT Press, 1980); World Commission on Environment and Development, *Our Common Future* (Oxford and New York: Oxford University Press, 1987).

11. Robert Cassen and Associates, *Does Aid Work?* (Oxford: Clarendon Press, 1986), 11. Professor R. H. Cassen of the Institute of Development Studies, University of Sussex, directed the study. The report was based on a series of commissioned country studies and studies of various forms of aid (technical cooperation, project aid, comparisons of multilateral and bilateral aid agencies, etc.).

12. The new focus affected perceptions of the concept of peace. As Dieter Senghaas has observed, the main point "is to find and institutionalize lasting forms of constructive and nonviolent conflict management" in order to design mechanisms for securing internal peace in the face of an always latent civil war. He distinguished between traditional and modern concepts of peace, which are related to entirely different types of societies: "the one non-politicized/elitist, the other broadly politicized on a mass basis." See Senghaas, "Assessing War, Violence and Peace Today," *Security Dialogue* 26, no. 2 (1995): 307, 316.

13. Olav Stokke, "Violent Conflict Prevention and Development Co-operation: Coherent or Conflicting Perspectives?" *Forum for Development Studies* 24, no. 2 (1997): 196.

14. UNDP, *Human Development Report 1994* (New York, N.Y.: Oxford University Press, 1994).

15. Cornia, Jolly, and Stewart, *Adjustment with a Human Face.*

16. Diamond argued for a definition of democracy that separates the political system from the economic and social system to which it is attached. He insists that economic and social democracy should be separated from the question of governing structure. See Diamond, "Introduction: Roots of Failure, Seeds of Hope," xvi.

17. Samir Amin, "The Challenge of Globalization: Delinking," in *Facing the*

Challenge: Responses to the Report of the South Commission, ed. The South Centre (London: Zed Books/South Centre, 1993); Barry Gills, Joel Rocamora, and Richard Wilson, eds., *Low Intensity Democracy* (London: Pluto Press, 1993).

18. Sørensen, *Democracy and Democratization;* John Healey, Richard Ketley, and Mark Robinson, "Will Political Reform Bring about Improved Management in Sub-Saharan Africa?" *IDS Bulletin* 24, no. 1 (1993): 31–38; Adrian Leftwich, "Bringing Politics Back In: Towards a Model for the Developmental State," *Journal of Development Studies* 31, no. 3 (1995): 400–427; Gordon White, "Towards a Democratic Developmental State," *IDS Bulletin* 26, no. 2 (1995): 27–36.

19. Stokke, "Aid and Political Conditionality."

20. In 1975, the U.S. Congress passed legislation that established such a link; see Joan M. Nelson with Stephanie J. Eglinton, *Encouraging Democracy: What Role for Aid?* (Washington, D.C.: Overseas Development Council, 1992), 26–27. The following year, the Norwegian Parliament determined that it would select as new partner countries only governments that contributed to the economic, social, and civil rights incorporated in the UN declaration and conventions on human rights, and the Netherlands made compliance with human rights one criterion for the selection of its main partner countries for bilateral aid. See Olav Stokke, ed., *European Development Assistance,* vol. 1, *Policies and Performance* (Tilburg: EADI, 1984).

21. World Bank, *Governance and Development* (Washington, D.C.: World Bank, 1992), 1.

22. Although the World Bank definition was criticized from different perspectives, during the early period, the defining initiative within this policy area remained with the World Bank. A fundamental criticism came from Adrian Leftwich; see "Governance, the State and the Politics of Development," *Development and Change* 25, no. 2 (1994): 372, 381. He found its prescriptions for good governance naïve because they failed to recognize that good governance was a function of state character and capacity, which in turn were functions of politics: "Neither sophisticated institutional innovations nor the best-trained or best-motivated public service will be able to withstand the withering effects of corruption or resist the developmentally-enervating pulls of special or favoured interests if the politics and authority of the state do not sustain and protect them" (381).

23. OECD, *DAC and OECD Public Policy Statements on Participatory Development/Good Governance* (Paris: DAC, 1992); OECD, *DAC Orientations on Participatory Development and Good Governance* (Paris: OECD, 1993); OECD, *Participatory Development and Good Governance* (Paris: DAC, 1993); OECD, *Ad Hoc Working Group on Participatory Development and Good Governance* (Paris: OECD, 1995).

24. The World Bank can claim ownership of the concept of good governance and made major efforts to explore and define it. The Bank needed an explanation for the limited success of its structural adjustment programs, particularly in Africa, and had, in the late 1980s, come to the conclusion that in order to work, economic policy reforms had to be bolstered by reform of the governing system of the countries concerned. See World Bank, *Sub-Saharan Africa: From Crisis to Sustainable Growth* (Washington, D.C.: World Bank, 1989); and Carol Lancaster, "Governance and Development: The Views from Washington," *IDS Bulletin* 24, no. 1 (1993): 9–15.

25. For a comprehensive analysis of U.S. policy in promoting democracy abroad, see Thomas Carothers, *Aiding Democracy Abroad: The Learning Curve* (Washington, D.C.: Carnegie Endowment for International Peace, 1999). For an analysis of EU efforts in this field, see Carlos Santiso, "Sisyphus in the Castle: Improving European Union

Strategies for Democracy Promotion and Governance Conditionality," *European Journal of Development Research* 15, no. 1 (2003): 1–26.

26. OECD, *DAC Orientations on Participatory Development and Good Governance,* 14.

27. Gelase Mutahaba, "Foreign Assistance and Local Capacity-Building: The Case of Swedish Aid to Tanzania's Rural Water Supply," *European Journal of Development Research* 1, no. 1 (1990): 108–123.

28. Martin Doornbos, "The African State in Academic Debate: Retrospect and Prospect," *Journal of Modern African Studies* 28, no. 2 (1990): 179–198; Martin Doornbos, "State Formation Processes under External Supervision: Reflections on 'Good Governance,'" in Stokke, *Aid and Political Conditionality,* 377–389.

29. Amartya Sen, *Development as Freedom* (Oxford: Oxford University Press, 1999).

10. VISIONS AND PRIORITIES FOR THE 1990s

1. The preparatory work on the strategy followed established patterns. It was initiated by the General Assembly in 1987; see "Preparation of the New International Development Strategy for the Fourth United Nations Development Decade," General Assembly resolution 42/193, 11 December 1987. The assembly continued this initiative one year later, when it invited the Committee for Development Planning, UNCTAD, "the regional commissions, and other organizations and specialized agencies" of the UN to include their contributions to the preparations on their agendas for 1989; see "Preparation of an International Development Strategy for the Fourth United Nations Development Decade," General Assembly resolution 43/182, 20 December 1988.

2. "Launching of Global Negotiations on International Economic Co-operation for Development," General Assembly decision 43/457, 22 December 1988.

3. The General Assembly stressed the need to continue to improve the quality of ODA, expressed concern about the stagnation of aid at a level significantly below the level of the 0.7 percent target, and stressed the importance of achieving the target of 0.15 percent of GNP of donor countries in ODA for the LDCs; "Fulfilment of the Target for Official Development Assistance," General Assembly resolution 43/197, 20 December 1988. In a recorded vote on this resolution (148 to 0, with 1 abstention), the United States abstained.

4. "Preparations for the Special Session of the General Assembly Devoted to International Economic Co-operation, in Particular to the Revitalization of Economic Growth and Development of the Developing Countries," General Assembly decision 44/444, 22 December 1989, Annex. In a recorded vote on this decision (123 to 1), the United States voted against.

5. In response to the "Charter of Economic Rights and Duties of States" (General Assembly resolution 40/182, 17 December 1985), the Secretary-General submitted a report on the implementation of the charter that concluded that although the charter had not been implemented, the easing of international tensions was cause for cautious optimism. However, as reflected in the recorded voting on the resolution that emerged from the report, previous patterns remained. The United States voted against, and all the other western governments abstained. It was adopted by 131 votes to 1 with 23 abstentions. See "Charter of Economic Rights and Duties," General Assembly resolution 44/170, 19 December 1989.

6. "Preparations for the Special Session of the General Assembly Devoted to International Economic Co-operation, in Particular to the Revitalization of Economic

Growth and Development of the Developing Countries," General Assembly decision 44/444, 22 December 1989, Annex.

7. "International Co-operation for the Eradication of Poverty in Developing Countries," General Assembly resolution 44/212, 22 December 1989.

8. "Declaration on International Economic Co-operation, in Particular the Revitalization of Economic Growth and Development of the Developing Countries," General Assembly resolution S-18/3, 1 May 1990, Annex. The introduction reflected optimism at the end of the Cold War: "We, the State Members of the United Nations, solemnly proclaim our strong commitment to a global consensus to promote urgently international economic co-operation for sustained growth of the world economy and, in particular, to the revitalization of economic growth and development of the developing countries so as to realize the basic right of all human beings to a life free from hunger, poverty, ignorance, disease and fear. . . . This is a time of positive transformation in international relations. The reduction in international political tensions, the increasing integration of the world economy and the broad movement towards economic and political reform will create an opportunity for strengthening international economic co-operation based on the need to provide just and equal opportunities to all peoples to enable them to develop their full potential." The resolution was adopted without a vote.

9. "International Development Strategy for the Fourth United Nations Development Decade," General Assembly resolution 45/199, 21 December 1990, Annex.

10. Ibid., quotes at paragraphs 6 and 7.

11. Ibid., quotes at paragraph 13.

12. Ibid., quotes at paragraph 16.

13. Ibid., paragraph 13. Six interrelated goals had to be met in order to achieve these fundamental aims: "(a) A surge in the pace of economic growth in the developing countries; (b) A development process that is responsive to social needs, seeks a significant reduction in extreme poverty, promotes the development and utilization of human resources and skills and is environmentally sound and sustainable; (c) An improvement of the international systems of money, finance and trade so as to support the development process; (d) A setting of strength and stability in the world economy and sound macro-economic management, nationally and internationally; (e) A decisive strengthening of international development co-operation; (f) A special effort to deal with the problems of the least developed countries, the weakest among the developing countries" (paragraph 13).

14. Ibid., quotes at paragraph 17.

15. Ibid., quotes at paragraph 37.

16. Ibid., paragraphs 40–44, quote at 40. The resources of these institutions had been falling behind the growth of the world economy and especially behind that of capital markets. As the strategy states: "The net lending of the World Bank and regional development banks was, by the late 1980s, negligible or negative for a large number of developing countries" (paragraph 44). Their resources, therefore, would have to be considerably expanded in the 1990s. The strategy argued that institutions should be enabled to serve the role of intermediary between developing countries and capital markets, for which they had been designed, adding that the conditionality associated with the use of resources "should be realistic and in accordance with the need to ensure effective utilization by recipient countries" (ibid.).

17. Ibid., paragraphs 52–61, quote at paragraph 56.

18. Ibid., paragraphs 62–63.

19. Ibid., paragraph 66.

20. Ibid., paragraphs 67–68, quote at paragraph 67. The strategy added that industrialization should be enhanced through cooperation among developing countries (paragraph 69).

21. Ibid., paragraphs 70–77, quotes at 72 and 73, respectively.

22. Ibid., paragraph 78.

23. Ibid.

24. Ibid., paragraph 80.

25. Ibid., paragraphs 81–86, quote at paragraph 86.

26. Ibid., paragraphs 98–102.

27. Ibid., paragraph 95. The strategy stated that "assistance to developing countries in the area of population should be substantially increased in the 1990s. Developing countries should also intensify their efforts to allocate adequate resources to population programmes" (ibid.).

28. Ibid., paragraph 96.

29. Ibid., paragraphs 98–102.

30. Ibid., paragraphs 103–107. "The [UN] system has played a unique role in bringing the development issue to the attention of the international community. Through its studies on the several aspects of the development problem, both national and international, through the international conferences it has convened on major issues, through the understandings, conventions and agreements it has helped to negotiate—some of them of a legal or quasi-legal character—and not least through the technical assistance it has provided to developing countries, it has made an invaluable contribution to ideas, policies and actions in the realm of development" (paragraph 103).

31. *Yearbook of the United Nations 1996* (New York: United Nations, Office of Public Information, 1998), 729. The report concluded that since the adoption of the strategy, a growing convergence of opinion as to what constituted an "appropriate" economic development strategy had appeared. For example, in pursuing reform, a distinction had to be drawn between the attainment of macroeconomic stability and achieving structural reform. More important, it had become increasingly evident that to be successful in the longer run, policies needed to focus not just on growth but on improving the lot of the population at large as well. In a moment of modesty, the report also stated that in reality very little was conclusively known about the determinants of economic growth.

32. *Yearbook of the United Nations 2000* (New York: United Nations, Office of Public Information, 2002), 786.

33. In 1999, the General Assembly asked the Secretary-General, in collaboration with all concerned organizations of the UN system, to draft a new international development strategy for the first decade of the new millennium; "Implementation of the Commitments and Policies Agreed upon in the Declaration on International Economic Cooperation, in Particular the Revitalization of Economic Growth and Development of the Developing Countries, and implementation of the International Development Strategy for the Fourth United Nations Development Decade," General Assembly resolution 54/206, 22 December 1999. The Secretary-General submitted a report to ECOSOC that contained a draft strategy for the new decade that focused on goals and desirable policy measures and actions, retaining the quantifiable goals set by several major UN conferences for the year 2015; *Yearbook of the United Nations 2000,* 787. However, the General Assembly, having reaffirmed the UN Millennium Declaration, in particular the targets and commitments relating to development and poverty eradication, referred to a series of development-oriented meetings to be convened under UN auspices over the following

years and decided to postpone the further development of a new international develop-ment strategy; "Implementation of the Commitments and Policies Agreed upon in the Declaration on International Economic Cooperation, in Particular the Revitalization of Economic Growth and Development of the Developing Countries, and Implementation of the International Development Strategy for the Fourth United Nations Development Decade," General Assembly resolution 55/190, 20 December 2000.

11. THE REVIVAL OF THE SOCIAL AND HUMAN DIMENSIONS OF DEVELOPMENT

1. Giovanni Andrea Cornia, Richard Jolly, and Frances Stewart, eds., *Adjustment with a Human Face,* vol. 1, *Protecting the Vulnerable and Promoting Growth* (Oxford: Oxford University Press, 1987).

2. World Bank, *World Development Report 1989* (Washington, D.C.: World Bank, 1989).

3. World Bank, *World Development Report 1990* (Washington, D.C.: World Bank, 1990).

4. See World Bank, *Assistance to Strategies to Reduce Poverty* (Washington, D.C.: World Bank, 1991); World Bank, *Poverty Reduction Handbook* (Washington, D.C.: World Bank, 1992); World Bank, *Poverty Reduction and the World Bank, Progress in Fiscal 1993* (Washington, D.C.: World Bank, 1994); and World Bank, *The World Bank and the Poorest Countries: Support for Development in the 1990s* (Washington, D.C.: World Bank, 1994). However, rhetoric and policy implementation do not always coincide: see Louis Emmerij, "A Critical Review of the World Bank Approach to Social Sector Lending and Poverty Alleviation," in *International Monetary and Financial Issues for the 1990s: Research Papers for the Group of Twenty-four,* vol. 5 (New York and Geneva: UNCTAD, 1995).

5. UNDP, *Human Development Report 1990* (New York/Oxford: Oxford University Press, 1990).

6. Mahbub ul Haq, for years situated at the center of power both in his home country (as minister of finance in Pakistan) and internationally (in the World Bank and the UN system), was the main architect of this silent revolution in the perception of development. His reflections on human development are developed in Mahbub ul Haq, *Reflections on Human Development* (New York: Oxford University Press, 1995). The human development idea was developed further by Amartya Sen, particularly through his entitlement approach; see Amartya Sen, *Development as Freedom* (Oxford: Oxford University Press, 1999); and Amartya Sen, *On Ethics and Economics* (Oxford and New York: Blackwell, 1987).

7. UNDP, *Human Development Report 1990,* 9–10.

8. For UNRISD's previous work to construct indicators of the social development performance of countries, see Donald V. McGranahan et al., *Content and Measurement of Socioeconomic Development: An Empirical Enquiry* (Geneva: United Nations Research Institute for Social Development, 1970); and Donald V. McGranahan, Eduardo Pizarro, and Claud Richard, *Measurement and Analysis of Socioeconomic Development: An Enquiry into International Indicators of Development and Quantitative Interrelations of Social and Economic Components of Development* (Geneva: United Nations Research Institute for Social Development, 1985).

9. The indicators chosen when the HDI was constructed are discussed in UNDP, *Human Development Report 1990,* 13, 104ff., especially Box 1.4 and the technical notes. See also Sudhir Anand and Amartya K. Sen, *Human Development Index: Methodology and Measurement* (New York: UNDP, 1994); and Sudhir Anand and Amartya K. Sen,

Sustainable Human Development: Concepts and Priorities (New York: UNDP). The HDI did not include indicators for political freedom, such as respect for human rights and democracy, or indicators for inequality. These issues were extensively dealt with in several of the annual HDRs, including those for 2000, 2002, and 2004, which focused on human rights and human development, deepening democracy in a fragmented world, and cultural liberty, respectively.

During the years that followed the first report, efforts were also made elsewhere, in particular within the OECD, to find and refine relevant indicators for social and human development beyond the traditional ones. See Bjørn K. Wold, "A Social Statistics System for the Millennium Development Goals?" *Forum for Development Studies*, 32, no. 1 (2005): 219–242. See also Michael Ward, *Quantifying the World: UN Ideas and Statistics* (Bloomington: Indiana University Press, 2004).

10. According to Murphy, ul Haq wrote out the first report by hand "at a table in a 'little room at the UNDP where the supply stuff was kept.' His immediate collaborators were his wife (unofficially), a secretary, and Inge Kaul. . . . In addition . . . there was a small group of notable 'core consultants'—Amartya Sen, Paul Streeten, Francis Stewart, Gus Ranis and Meghnad Desai." Craig N. Murphy, *The United Nations Development Programme, A Better Way?* (Cambridge: Cambridge University Press, 2006), 246–247.

11. UNDP, *Human Development Report 1995* (New York/Oxford: Oxford University Press, 1995), 72ff.

12. The Arab 2002 and 2003 reports, both published by the UNDP in cooperation with the Arab Fund for Economic and Social Development, may serve as good illustrations; see UNDP, *Arab Human Development Report 2002: Creating Opportunities for Future Generations* (New York: UNDP, Regional Bureau for Arab States, 2002); UNDP, *Arab Human Development Report 2003, Building a Knowledge Society* (New York: UNDP, Regional Bureau for Arab States, 2003). See likewise the 2003 South Africa report; UNDP, *South Africa Human Development Report 2003: The Challenge of Sustainable Development in South Africa: Unlocking People's Creativity* (Cape Town: Oxford University Press Southern Africa, 2003).

According to Murphy, more than 500 separate reports have been published over the years, covering the vast majority of developing countries and former Soviet-bloc countries. The New York office has provided a network of training workshops, and the regional offices have often provided financial support for these activities. However, the reports were "designed and executed by networks of local scholars, often among the most distinguished social scientists in that part of the world." *The United Nations Development Programme*, 250.

13. As Richard Jolly, Louis Emmerij, Dharam Ghai, and Frédéric Lapeyre have dryly observed, the HDIs, although widely distributed, "apparently did not penetrate the bastions of international financial power"; see *UN Contributions to Development Thinking and Practice* (Bloomington: Indiana University Press, 2004), 180. This was a reference to a statement by Jacques Pollak, who had spent a lifetime with the IMF. He said that the report "is not put on the agenda of the Executive Board of the IMF. I doubt many people in this building have even looked at it. I don't think it is generally distributed even." Interview of 15 March 2000, in the Oral History Collection, UNIHP, 41.

14. Robert S. McNamara, *Address to the Board of Governors, Nairobi, 24 September 1973* (Washington, D.C.: World Bank, 1973).

15. World Bank, *World Development Report 1990*.

16. World Bank, *World Development Report 2000/2001: Attacking Poverty* (New York: Oxford University Press and the World Bank, 2001).

17. World Bank, *World Development Report 2003: Sustainable Development in a*

Dynamic World (New York: Oxford University Press and the World Bank, 2003), chapter 1.

18. *Yearbook of the United Nations 1995,* 1114ff.

19. Ibid., 1114–1115.

20. Ibid., 1115–1116.

21. Ibid., 1116–1117.

22. Ibid., 1117.

23. Ibid., 1118. Later that year, ECOSOC assumed responsibility for facilitating this follow-up; "Social Development," ECOSOC resolution 1995/60, 28 July 1995. So did the General Assembly, which fully endorsed the main recommendations of the summit; "Implementation of the Outcome of the Fourth World Summit for Social Development," General Assembly resolution 50/161, 1 March 1996.

24. "First United Nations Decade for the Eradication of Poverty," General Assembly resolution 51/178, 11 February 1997.

25. ECOSOC decided "in view of the traditional importance of non-governmental organizations in the promotion of social development" that NGOs should be encouraged "to participate in the work of the Commission and in the monitoring and implementation process related to the Summit to the maximum extent possible to implement the recommendations of the summit." The practice of inviting experts "to contribute to the effective follow-up to the Summit" was continued. "Follow-Up to the World Summit for Social Development and the Future Role of the Commission for Social Development," ECOSOC resolution 1996/7, 22 July 1996.

26. "Further Initiatives for Social Development," General Assembly resolution S-24/2, 1 July 2000, Annex I.

27. Ibid.

28. World Commission on Environment and Development, *Our Common Future* (Oxford and New York: Oxford University Press, 1987), 43.

29. *Yearbook of the United Nations 1992* (New York: United Nations, Office of Public Information, 1993), 672.

30. Ibid., 72–74.

31. Ibid., 675. The intergovernmental commission was appointed by ECOSOC in 1992. It has been in operation since 1993.

32. The huge participation—which included fifty-five heads of state or government, 178 ministers, and a large number of international organizations and institutions as well as representatives of a great many NGOs—indicates the importance given to the nineteenth special session of the General Assembly. *Yearbook of the United Nations 1997* (New York: United Nations, Office of Public Information, 2000), 790.

33. One hundred and fifty countries responded to the commitments established at UNCED through national-level commissions or coordinating mechanisms designed to develop an integrated approach to sustainable development; "Programme for the Further Implementation of Agenda 21," General Assembly resolution S-19/2, 28 June 1997, Annex, quote at paragraph 11.

34. Ibid.

35. *Yearbook of the United Nations 2002* (New York: United Nations, Office of Public Information, 2004), 821ff.

36. Ibid., 821–824. Later that year, the Johannesburg Declaration and Plan of Implementation was endorsed by the General Assembly; "World Summit on Sustainable Development," General Assembly resolution 57/253, 20 December 2002.

37. For an excellent overview and analysis, see Devaki Jain, *Women, Development and the UN: A Sixty-Year Quest for Equality and Justice* (Bloomington: Indiana University Press, 2005). For an exploration of future opportunities, see Devaki Jain and Shubha Chacko, "Unfolding Women's Engagement with Development and the UN: Pointers for the Future," *Forum for Development Studies* 35, no. 1 (2008): 5–36.

38. "Implementation of the World Plan of Action Adopted by the World Conference of the International Women's Year," General Assembly resolution 3490 (XXX), 12 December 1975. The General Assembly approved the program for the UN Decade for Women, which focused especially on the first part of the decade (1976–1980). Its objectives were formulating and implementing international and national standards to eliminate discrimination against women, integrating women in development, and increasing the involvement of women in political life, international cooperation, and the maintenance of peace; see "United Nations Decade for Women," General Assembly resolution 31/136, 16 December 1976.

39. "Convention on the Elimination of All Forms of Discrimination against Women," General Assembly resolution 34/80, 18 December 1979. The convention is annexed to the resolution. The Committee on the Elimination of Discrimination against Women, established in 1982, monitors compliance with the convention.

40. Devaki Jain emphasizes the cooperation of women of developing countries under the ideological umbrella of the Non-Aligned Movement (NAM). "The NAM was a strong and supportive presence, though physically invisible, in the UN conferences on women," she notes, with particular reference to the NAM conference in Baghdad on the role of women in 1979 and the Sixth Conference of NAM in Havana later that year, both of which were held prior to the Copenhagen world conference the following year. The NAM "saw women's role in development as an international and political issue, in contrast to its earlier conceptualization of issues relating to women's status as social or cultural phenomena." The movement understood that for the majority of women, development had meant little more than stagnation or increased misery, greater vulnerability to exploitation, and sometimes even a decline in opportunities and status in certain sectors. Jain, *Women, Development and the UN,* 80ff., quote on 81.

41. The conference adopted a program of action for the second half of the decade. Its aim was to promote equality, development, and peace, with particular emphasis on employment, health, and education. It set out practical measures for advancing the status of women and strengthening strategies to remove obstacles to women's full and equal participation in development, including action to solve the problems of underdevelopment and socioeconomic structures that placed women in an inferior position. However, conflicts over particular issues prevented a consensus program. The Nairobi Programme of Action was adopted as a whole by a roll-call vote of 94 to 4, with 22 abstentions. Australia, Canada, Israel, and United States voted against, while most governments of Western Europe abstained. *Yearbook of the United Nations 1980* (New York: United Nations, Office of Public Information, 1983), 888–891.

42. United Nations, *World Survey on the Role of Women in Development* (New York: United Nations, Department of International Economic and Social Affairs, 1986). The Nairobi World Conference on the Role of Women in Development took note of the survey and passed it on to the General Assembly. The assembly asked the UN system, especially the Commission on the Status of Women and the Secretary-General, to take the findings of the survey into account when making recommendations and formulating plans. It also asked the Secretary-General to update the survey and submit

a progress report on that update. "Effective Mobilization and Integration of Women in Development," General Assembly resolution 40/204, 17 December 1985.

43. "Implementation of the Nairobi Forward-Looking Strategies for the Advancement of Women," General Assembly resolution 40/108, 13 December 1985, paragraphs 2–4, quote at paragraph 3.

44. *Yearbook of the United Nations 1990* (New York: United Nations, Office of Public Information, 1999), 772–773. The commission presented twenty-two recommendations about equality, development, and peace. It identified the priority themes for the period 1993–1996: in the pursuit of development, the first priority should be women in extreme poverty; women in urban areas; promoting literacy, education, and training, including technological skills; and child and dependent care, including sharing of work and family responsibilities.

45. *Yearbook of the United Nations 1995* (New York: United Nations, Office of Public Information, 1997), 1167.

46. Ibid., 1169–1170. Endorsing the Beijing Declaration and Platform for Action, the General Assembly emphasized that governments should develop comprehensive implementation strategies or plans of action, including time-bound targets and benchmarks for monitoring no later than 1996; "Follow-Up on the Fourth World Conference on Women and Full Implementation of the Beijing Declaration and Platform for Action," General Assembly resolution 50/203, 22 December 1995.

47. As noted, the *Human Development Report 1995* focused on the situation of women in development and served as a background for the conference.

48. The twenty-third special session of the General Assembly adopted a policy declaration and an extensive "outcome document" that assessed performance, confirmed the Beijing Declaration and Platform for Action, came up with further actions and initiatives to overcome constraints in realizing these objectives, and reaffirmed the importance of gender mainstreaming in all areas and at all levels and the complementarity between mainstreaming and special activities targeting women. See "Political Declaration," General Assembly resolution S-23/2, 10 June 2000; and "Further Actions and Initiatives to Implement the Beijing Declaration and Platform for Action," General Assembly resolution S-23/3, 10 June 2000.

49. The Secretary-General recommended that the General Assembly continue to call for gender equality and ensure gender mainstreaming in the implementation and follow-up to major international conferences and summits, especially in the review, scheduled for 2005, of the implementation of the 2000 UN Millennium Declaration. See *Yearbook of the United Nations 2004* (New York: United Nations, Office of Public Information, 2006), 1144–1145.

50. "Convention on the Rights of the Child," General Assembly resolution 44/25, 20 November 1989.

51. The summit attracted representatives from 159 countries who represented 99 percent of the world's population, including seventy-one heads of state or government and eighty-eight senior ministers and ambassadors; *Yearbook of the United Nations 1990,* 797.

52. Ibid., 799–800. The General Assembly welcomed the declaration and plan of action; "World Summit for Children," General Assembly resolution 45/217, 21 December 1990. UNICEF actively participated in preparing for the summit and drafting the outcome that emerged from the summit.

12. EVOLVING PRIORITIES, PATTERNS, AND TRENDS, 1982–2005

1. *Yearbook of the United Nations 1982* (New York: United Nations, Office of Public Information, 1986), 623, 626; *Yearbook of the United Nations 1984* (New York: United Nations, Office of Public Information, 1988), 426.

2. *Yearbook of the United Nations 1990* (New York: United Nations, Office of Public Information, 1999), 380; *Yearbook of the United Nations 1994* (New York: United Nations, Office of Public Information, 1995), 787, 790–791; *Yearbook of the United Nations 1996* (New York: United Nations, Office of Public Information, 1998), 766–767; *Yearbook of the United Nations 2001* (New York: United Nations, Office of Public Information, 2003), 791; *Yearbook of the United Nations 2004* (New York: United Nations, Office of Public Information, 2006), 875.

3. In 1993, its share was 24 percent; by 2000, it was 26 percent. In 2003, humanitarian assistance almost doubled from the previous year—increasing from $ 1.5 billion to $2.9 billion, more than 30 percent of total expenditures. *Yearbook of the United Nations 1994*, 791; *Yearbook of the United Nations 2001*, 791; *Yearbook of the United Nations 2004*, 875, and calculations based on data in these sources.

4. The three countries that received the most development assistance in 2002 were Afghanistan ($355 million), Brazil ($344 million), and Iraq ($340 million), which together was about 14 percent of total technical assistance. *Yearbook of the United Nations 2003* (New York: United Nations, Office of Public Information, 2005), 889, and calculations based on this source. Nevertheless, for conflict-torn Afghanistan and Iraq, humanitarian aid was only a small percentage of the cost of the military and political interventions in these countries.

5. In 1993, its share was 24 percent, decreasing to 21 percent in 2000 and 18 percent in 2003. *Yearbook of the United Nations 1994*, 791; *Yearbook of the United Nations 2001*, 791; *Yearbook of the United Nations 2004*, 875, and calculations based on data in these sources.

6. Expenditures include UNDP core funding and funds under its administration but do not include expenditures financed from cost-sharing and from cash-counterpart contributions. Amounts given are in current U.S. dollars. See *Yearbook of the United Nations 1982*, 626–627, 632–633 (for 1982); *Yearbook of the United Nations 1985*, 456, 261–462 (for 1985); *Yearbook of the United Nations 1990*, 380, and *Yearbook of the United Nations 1991*, 367–368 (for 1990); *Yearbook of the United Nations 1995*, 879, 886–887, 896–896 (for 1995); and *Yearbook of the United Nations 2000*, 822 (for 1999).

7. Ibid. Calculations based on these sources.

8. Ibid. Their share was 28 percent in 1985, 24 percent in 1990, 29 percent in 1995, and 26 percent in 1999.

9. *Yearbook of the United Nations 1991*, 362, 366–367, 378–379 (for 1990 and 1991); *Yearbook of the United Nations 1992*, 550, 556–557, 566 (for 1991 and 1992); *Yearbook of the United Nations 1993*, 683, 685–687, 697–698 (for 1992 and 1993); and *Yearbook of the United Nations 1994*, 787, 790–791, 802 (for 1993), and calculations based on these sources.

10. Ibid.

11. The combined share of the specialized agencies during 2001–2003 was 29, 31, and 26 percent, respectively, compared with 29, 29, and 25 percent, respectively, for the UNDP. The WFP's share continued at a high level for these years: 25, 22, and 34 percent, respectively. UNICEF's shares were 14 percent for 2001 and 2002 and 13 percent for 2003. See *Yearbook of the United Nations 2001*, 791 (for 2000); *Yearbook of the United Nations 2002*, 862 (for 2001); *Yearbook of the United Nations 2003*, 889 (for 2002); *Yearbook of the United Nations 2004*, 875 (for 2003), and calculations based on these sources.

12. See *Yearbook of the United Nations 1982,* 633 (for 1982); *Yearbook of the United Nations 1983,* 452 (for 1983); *Yearbook of the United Nations 1984,* 433 (for 1984); *Yearbook of the United Nations 1985,* 463 (for 1985); *Yearbook of the United Nations 1986,* 416 (for 1986 and 1987); *Yearbook of the United Nations 1987,* 406 (for 1988); *Yearbook of the United Nations 1988,* 337; *Yearbook of the United Nations 1989,* 307 (for 1989); *Yearbook of the United Nations 1990,* 381 (for 1990); *Yearbook of the United Nations 1991,* 367 (for 1991); *Yearbook of the United Nations 1992,* 557 (for 1992); *Yearbook of the United Nations 1993,* 686 (for 1993); *Yearbook of the United Nations 1994,* 791 (for 1994); *Yearbook of the United Nations 1995,* 887 (for 1995); *Yearbook of the United Nations 1996,* 767 (for 1995); *Yearbook of the United Nations 1996,* 767 (for 1996); *Yearbook of the United Nations 1997,* 857 (for 1997); *Yearbook of the United Nations 1998,* 808 (for 1998); *Yearbook of the United Nations 1999,* 793 (for 1999), and calculations based on these sources.

13. The development decades and their strategies have been the main organizers of the chapters of this volume. However, in the early 1970s, UNDP and UN programming began to follow five-year cycles. As in chapter 7, description of the UNDP's operational activities in this chapter is based on the aspirations, programming, and outcomes of these cycles.

14. For forward planning purposes, an assumed annual growth of voluntary contributions of at least 8 percent was set, taking the $700 million target anticipated for 1986 as the point of departure. Of the total resources allocated for IPFs, 19 percent was to go to intercountry IPFs (79.5 percent for regional programs, 8 percent for interregional programs, and 12.5 percent for the global program) and 81 percent to country IPFs. *Yearbook of the United Nations 1985* (New York: United Nations, Office of Public Information, 1989), 471.

15. Ibid., 471, 473–474. The detailed, technical, and specific rules laid down also ensured special treatment for countries with specific geographical and economic disadvantages, including those whose terms of trade had declined by more than 15 percent and particularly debt-ridden countries.

16. *Yearbook of the United Nations 1987* (New York: United Nations, Office of Public Information, 1992), 407.

17. The Governing Council emphasized again that the recipient government was exclusively responsible for formulating its national development plan, priorities, and objectives. It stated that integrating UN system operational activities with national plans and objectives would enhance the impact and relevance of those activities: national plans and priorities were the only viable frame of reference for the national programming of UN operational activities. It also emphasized that the UNDP should promote human development so developing countries could become self-reliant through national capacity-building. *Yearbook of the United Nations 1990,* 391.

18. Ibid., 391–392. The field program would be divided as follows: 77 percent for country IPFs, 16 percent for intercountry IPFs (12 percent to regional IPFs, 1.5 percent for interregional IPFs, and 2.5 percent for the global IPF), and 7 percent for Special Programme Resources that would cover thematic activities.

19. *Yearbook of the United Nations 1989* (New York: United Nations, Office of Public Information, 1997), 317–318; *Yearbook of the United Nations 1990,* 391–392.

20. *Yearbook of the United Nations 1990,* 391. In this report, UNDP administrator William Draper found reason to believe that the thawing of the Cold War in the 1990s would produce a shift from ideological conflict toward a global effort to bring about peace, social justice, and a sustainable world ecology (382).

21. *Yearbook of the United Nations 1993* (New York: United Nations, Office of Public

Information, 1994), 685, 696–697; *Yearbook of the United Nations 1995* (New York: United Nations, Office of Public Information, 1997), 887.

22. In March 1996, the Poverty Strategies Initiative was launched to support country implementation of the commitments in the declaration of the 1995 Social Summit held in Copenhagen. Efforts under this initiative included formulating national poverty eradication plans and strategies and elaborating national definitions, measurements, criteria, and indicators of absolute poverty. During the first year, initiatives were under way in seventy countries. *Yearbook of the United Nations 1996,* 778.

23. Ibid., 767–768.

24. In 1994, the administrator established fifteen new trust funds on behalf of the UNDP that involved a wide variety of purposes and donors. *Yearbook of the United Nations 1993,* 804.

25. This share would have been even lower if the calculation had been based on total income that included the "ordinary" trust funds, the Global Environment Facility, and the "business" component. In 1996, 62 percent of noncore resources were provided by program-country governments and 38 percent by traditional donors. By 1999, the UNDP's regular resource base represented only 28 percent of total UNDP resources. This development was not unique to the UNDP. In a June 2003 report on the funding of development cooperation activities, the Secretary-General pointed out that over 95 percent of the core funding of the UNDP, the UNFPA, UNICEF, and the WFP was provided by DAC members and that efforts to broaden that donor base had not succeeded. UNDP core funding had declined from $1.2 billion in 1992 to $634 million in 2001, while noncore contributions had increased fourfold, from $408 million in 1992 to $1.6 billion in 2001. *Yearbook of the United Nations 1998* (New York: United Nations, Office of Public Information, 2001), 823; *Yearbook of the United Nations 2000* (New York: United Nations, Office of Public Information, 2002), 833; *Yearbook of the United Nations 2003,* 887–888.

26. *Yearbook of the United Nations 1998,* 823–824.

27. *Yearbook of the United Nations 1993,* 694; *Yearbook of the United Nations 1994,* 792, 798–799; *Yearbook of the United Nations 1995,* 894.

28. The process resulted in a dramatic restructuring that moved staff from headquarters to assignments at regional and country levels and substantially reduced the number of staff. Craig Murphy, *The United Nations Development Programme, A Better Way?* (Cambridge: Cambridge University Press, 2006), 303ff. The process was initiated by "reprofiling" all the jobs within the organization, first at headquarters in New York, then in the country offices, with the aim of cutting the number of people in New York by 25 percent, sending some to the country offices, and then cutting the core budget of each field office by 15 percent, which meant eliminating all "unnecessary" tasks.

The operation also offered an opportunity to bring the organization's operational arms in line with UN norms. Brian Gleeson, justifying the slimming operation of which he was in charge, said that he had found parts of the organization in a mess and in need of reform, estimating that "fifty per cent of the country offices that I visited had a dysfunctional leadership team . . . the Res Rep in charge, or the deputy . . . not being in sync with staff. Sad to see. International staff in these countries disempowering national staff with cultural bias, lack of cultural sensitivity, harassment, violence. . . . Many of these people had never seen anyone from headquarters. . . . All the real stories came out." Quoted in Murphy, *The United Nations Development Programme,* 303–304. The UNDP provided severance packages for more than 1,000 of those it let go, and a large group received training.

29. *Yearbook of the United Nations 1994,* 798–799; *Yearbook of the United Nations 1995,*

895–896. Under the rolling three-year planning concept, the financial period was rolled forward at the end of the year: a new year was added and the first year was dropped and additional resources were released.

30. As the Executive Board decided in 1995, these figures were based on GNP per capita and population, with a bonus for the LDCs. The 1994 per capita GNP estimates for forty-five countries had been revised downward, resulting in higher TRAC earmark-ings for fourteen countries; for the remaining thirty-one countries (all middle-income countries), the change did not result in higher earmarkings, since their GNP was higher than the established floor. In 1995, the board established an unallocated reserve of $25 million for the three-year period to finance upward revisions of the 1994 basic data. *Yearbook of the United Nations 1997* (New York: United Nations, Office of Public Information, 2000), 874–875.

31. Ibid., 875.

32. The revised and final TRAC earmarking for 2001–2003 (TRAC lines 1 and 2) allocated 88 percent of the total of $1.8 billion to low-income countries with GNP per capita of $375 or less and 12 percent for middle-income countries. Africa would receive 48 percent, Asia and the Pacific 31 percent, Arab states 8 percent, Europe and the CIS 8 percent, and Latin America and the Caribbean 5 percent. *Yearbook of the United Nations 2000*, 833–834.

33. In his 1998 annual report, the administrator stated that the year had been marked by crisis after crisis—war, genocide, refugee movements, financial volatility, environmental degradation, and growing social pressures stemming from increasing inequalities—that had increased the demand for UNDP support at the global, regional, and country levels. Despite that demand, UNDP core resources stood at just over $750 million, under two-thirds of the $1.1 billion annual level agreed on in 1995. However, noncore resources had increased to $1.2 billion in 1998. *Yearbook of the United Nations 1998*, 809.

34. Ibid., 821–822. The six other points were as follows: build on UNDP compara-tive advantages while complementing the work of other providers of development services; support aid coordination; support the mobilization of additional resources for development; use the program approach to the maximum extent possible; build on lessons learned and on best practices; and ensure that the program design was result-oriented and allowed for measurement and evaluation of impact.

35. Ibid., 825–826.

36. *Yearbook of the United Nations 1999* (New York: United Nations, Office of Public Information, 2001), 794.

37. Ibid., 802–803.

38. *Yearbook of the United Nations 2003*, 890–891. The 2003 annual report noted that the UNDP had worked to operationalize the UN strategy for implementing the MDGs, linking global and country-level campaigning for the MDGs with research and the insti-tutional and financial reforms needed to achieve them. It added that the UNDP's advo-cacy work related to the Human Development Report was complemented by regional and national HDRs. The UNDP had withdrawn its program and technical capacity in nonpriority areas and refined a niche in areas such as HIV/AIDS and crisis prevention and recovery.

39. *Yearbook of the United Nations 1999*, 807–808.

40. *Yearbook of the United Nations 2003*, 887.

41. Ibid., 901. In the 2004 triennial policy review, the General Assembly empha-sized this core area, reiterating "the importance of the development of national

capacities to eradicate poverty and pursue sustained economic growth and sustainable development as a central goal of the development cooperation of the United Nations system" and confirming the other goals, principles, and strategic approaches contained in the second MYFF; "Triennial Comprehensive Policy Review of Operational Activities for Development of the United Nations System," General Assembly resolution 59/250, 17 August 2005, 2.

42. *Yearbook of the United Nations 2004,* 876, 879–880. The 1999 results-oriented annual report had revealed that the bulk of UNDP support for poverty reduction was targeted at the community level, with "downstream" expenditures twice as high as "upstream" expenditures. By 2003, that had changed and UNDP support for national poverty strategies was focused on poverty monitoring and participation, but the 2003 report stated that more needed to be done to strengthen government capacity to develop pro-poor policies and budgets. *Yearbook of the United Nations 2003,* 893.

43. *Yearbook of the United Nations 2004,* 880.

44. Ibid., 876, 880–881. One of the specific activities noted was the report *Democracy in Latin America: Towards a Citizen's Democracy,* which was launched in partnership with the European Union. It offered a comprehensive analysis of the state of democracy in eighteen Latin American countries and proposals for guiding the debate on democratic governance in the region. It recognized the UNDP as one of the key providers of technical cooperation to support elections and parliaments; it supported one out of every three parliaments and, on average, one election of every two somewhere in the world. A main challenge for democratic governance practice was building on ongoing efforts and increasing the emphasis on gender equality.

45. The new UNDP Disaster Management Programme was established to protect development gains by helping build national capacity for disaster mitigation, prevention, and preparedness. In February 2001, the Executive Board recognized that crisis prevention and disaster mitigation should be integral parts of sustainable human development strategies. *Yearbook of the United Nations 1998,* 819; *Yearbook of the United Nations 2001,* 801–802.

46. *Yearbook of the United Nations 2004,* 876, 881.

47. Ibid., 876, 881–882. In forty-seven countries, support for biodiversity initiatives resulted in specific progress in integrating biodiversity into one or more of their sector strategies in agriculture, forestry, rangeland and grazing, coastal management, fisheries, and wildlife. Sixty-six countries had made progress in adjusting their legal frameworks to incorporate biodiversity, the report claimed. Cross-practice initiatives had also been initiated with a view to improving gender equality.

48. Ibid., 876, 882–883. Fifty percent of the policy advisers were women, and 54 percent of 132 registered practitioners at the end of the year were women.

49. *Yearbook of the United Nations 1989,* 308–309.

50. *Yearbook of the United Nations 1998,* 822–823; *Yearbook of the United Nations 1999,* 804–805; *Yearbook of the United Nations 2000,* 822–823; *Yearbook of the United Nations 2003,* 890–891.

51. In the 1990s, the administrator established a large number of new trust funds in order to increase UNDP's noncore funding. Also sub-trust funds were established to increase the financial strength of trust funds beyond their regular funding through the pledging conferences. In 1992, contributions to the seventy-five trust funds and sub-trust funds in operation totaled $118.3 million (expenditures amounted to $42.7 million). Two years later, contributions to the eighty-one trust funds and sub-trust funds then in operation had increased: $265.6 million (expenditures $131.2 million). *Yearbook of the*

United Nations 1992 (New York: United Nations, Office of Public Information, 1993), 568; *Yearbook of the United Nations 1994*, 804.

52. *Yearbook of the United Nations 1982*, 633; *Yearbook of the United Nations 1989*, 333.

53. *Yearbook of the United Nations 1991* (New York: United Nations, Office of Public Information, 1992), 393; *Yearbook of the United Nations 1992*, 574.

54. *Yearbook of the United Nations 1994*, 787, 810–811; *Yearbook of the United Nations 1995*, 903; *Yearbook of the United Nations 1996*, 793; *Yearbook of the United Nations 1997*, 894–895; *Yearbook of the United Nations 1998*, 837; and *Yearbook of the United Nations 2004*, 898. Voluntary contributions to the United Nations Capital Development Fund amounted to $33 million in 1994. Pledges had decreased from a record level of $41.8 million in 1991 to $31.3 million in 1994. In 1998 they fell to $31 million and were further reduced to $17 million in 2005.

55. *Yearbook of the United Nations 1999*, 821–822; *Yearbook of the United Nations 2002* (New York: United Nations, Office of Public Information, 2004), 884.

56. According to the impact assessment, the fund had contributed to significant results in poverty reduction, policy impact, and replication of its projects by donors. However, its financial viability after 2004 was questionable because of the mismatch between the UNCDF's niche and international donor funding trends, its governance structure, and the need for clarification of its role in the UNDP group. *Yearbook of the United Nations 2004*, 898–899.

57. Ibid., 899–900; *Yearbook of the United Nations, 2005* (New York: United Nations, Office of Public Information, 2008), 986.

58. *Yearbook of the United Nations 1982*, 633; *Yearbook of the United Nations 1983*, 452, 481; *Yearbook of the United Nations 1984*, 433, 456; *Yearbook of the United Nations 1985*, 463, 486; *Yearbook of the United Nations 1986* (New York: United Nations, Office of Public Information, 1990), 435–436; *Yearbook of the United Nations 1987*, 426–427; *Yearbook of the United Nations 1988*, 357. To boost the activity, the General Assembly established 5 December as the International Volunteer Day for Economic and Social Development; "International Volunteer Day for Economic and Social Development," General Assembly resolution 40/212, 17 December 1985.

59. The administrator stated in his biennial report on the UNV program for 1988–1989 that the typical volunteer was in his or her thirties and had several years of professional experience as well as solid academic training: the average program participant was thirty-eight years old, had ten years of professional experience, and held a master's degree. This profile deviated dramatically from the popular image of inexperienced, relatively young, dedicated and enthusiastic individuals who had relatively few technical skills to offer. The typical annual cost of a volunteer assignment was about one-fifth that of regular technical cooperation personnel. In 1989, about 85 percent of UNV specialists served in projects funded from IPFs and about half served in projects by UN specialized agencies. *Yearbook of the United Nations 1989*, 332–333.

60. In his 1990–1991 report, the administrator observed that the number of UNV specialists and domestic development service field workers had increased from 1,801 at the end of 1989 to an estimated 2,080 by the end of 1991. Nearly three-quarters of all UNV assignments were in LDCs or in landlocked and small island states. About half were in Africa and about 30 percent were in Asia and the Pacific. The Special Voluntary Fund paid for part of the external costs of volunteers and field workers, but it accounted for less than one-third of the total external costs; the rest came from project budgets. *Yearbook of the United Nations 1991*, 387–388.

61. The number of UNV specialists and field workers increased after UNV head-

quarters was moved from Geneva to Bonn in 1996, reaching 3,620 in 1997 and 7,772 in 2004. The German authorities provided extra resources. *Yearbook of the United Nations 1993*, 705; *Yearbook of the United Nations 1997*, 886; *Yearbook of the United Nations 2000*, 843; *Yearbook of the United Nations 2001*, 814; *Yearbook of the United Nations 2002*, 880; *Yearbook of the United Nations 2003*, 910; *Yearbook of the United Nations 2004*, 896–897.

62. "Strengthening the Coordination of Emergency Humanitarian Assistance of the United Nations," General Assembly resolution 49/139 B, 20 December 1994.

63. *Yearbook of the United Nations 2004*, 896–897. Women accounted for 35 percent of all volunteers in 2004. The share of volunteers recruited from developing countries varied somewhat; in 2001, it was 66 percent and, for the subsequent three years, 70, 72, and 77 percent, respectively. See also *Yearbook of the United Nations 2001*, 814; *Yearbook of the United Nations 2002*, 880; *Yearbook of the United Nations 2003*, 910.

64. During the first five years, 294 projects had received support from the fund, of which seventy-five projects were completed. In 1982, voluntary payments to the fund amounted to $1.8 million, contributed by forty-two countries; three countries contributed 65 percent of the total (Italy 15 percent, the Netherlands 12 percent, and Norway 38 percent). *Yearbook of the United Nations 1982*, 1147; *Yearbook of the United Nations 1983* (New York: United Nations, Office of Public Information, 1987), 911.

65. The priorities were set in "Arrangements for the Future Management of the Voluntary Fund for the United Nations Decade for Women," General Assembly resolution 39/125, 14 December 1984. According a report by the administrator on 1986 activities, UNIFEM started out with 260 ongoing activities, of which two-thirds were executed by national executing agencies, either governments or NGOs. Total income was $4.9 million ($3.9 million in pledges from forty-nine member states and $0.7 million in joint financing), and expenditures were $5.2 million. By the end of the year, the fund's balance was $12.2 million, $8.2 million of which were unspent allocations. The administrator had established two sub-trust funds for UNIFEM in 1986. *Yearbook of the United Nations 1986*, 795–796; *Yearbook of the United Nations 1987*, 841; *Yearbook of the United Nations 1988*, 629; *Yearbook of the United Nations 1989*, 659; *Yearbook of the United Nations 1990*, 789.

66. *Yearbook of the United Nations 1989*, 659; *Yearbook of the United Nations 1990*, 789; *Yearbook of the United Nations 1994*, 1187.

67. "United Nations Development Fund for Women," General Assembly resolution 44/74, 8 December 1989; *Yearbook of the United Nations 1992*, 873.

68. A UNDP evaluation of UNIFEM's performance as a recipient of UNDP special program resources concluded that there was a need for clearer program guidelines, greater emphasis on gender in development rather than on women in development, and improved communication between the gender-in-development program and the regional bureaus, and integrating UNIFEM activities more strongly into the UNDP fold. In contrast, an evaluation of UNIFEM activities from 1990 to 1995 conducted by an external consulting firm recommended that UNIFEM should continue as an autonomous and separate organization in the UN system. *Yearbook of the United Nations 1996*, 1077.

69. In 1995, the committee also pointed out that when post-Beijing institutional arrangements and mandates were discussed, the role of UNIFEM in Eastern Europe should be considered (its original mandate limited its activities to developing countries). The committee highlighted the importance of the role UNIFEM played. *Yearbook of the United Nations 1994*, 1187; *Yearbook of the United Nations 1995*, 1180; *Yearbook of the United Nations 1996*, 1078.

70. In 1996, UNIFEM increased its coordination and collaboration with other UN

and international agencies. Its operational activities revolved around five strategies aimed at empowering women economically and politically through building the capacity and leadership of women's organizations to advocate for gender-sensitive development; undertaking advocacy activities to leverage political and financial support for women; facilitating effective partnerships between women's organizations, governments, the UN system, and the private sector; undertaking pilot and demonstration projects for main-streaming to the benefit of women; and documenting and disseminating information on best practices and lessons learned, *Yearbook of the United Nations 1996*, 1077.

71. *Yearbook of the United Nations 1997*, 1206. The General Assembly approved the strategy, endorsing "the role of the Fund in strengthening women's economic capac-ity, encouraging women to become key economic players in combating the feminiza-tion of poverty and strengthening women's leadership and political empowerment so as to increase their participation on decision-making processes." "United Nations Development Fund for Women," General Assembly resolution 52/94, 12 December 1997, 2.

72. *Yearbook of the United Nations 2000*, 1127.

73. *Yearbook of the United Nations 2002*, 1165; *Yearbook of the United Nations 2003*, 1194; *Yearbook of the United Nations 2004*, 1172. For General Assembly support, see "United Nations Development Fund for Women," General Assembly resolution 52/94, 12 December 1997; and "United Nations Development Fund for Women," General Assembly resolution 56/130, 19 December 2001.

74. In 2004, UNIFEM contributed to strengthening policies and laws to enhance the empowerment and rights of women in forty-one instances; it contributed to strengthening the capacity of key institutions to deliver on commitments to gender equality in seventy-seven instances; it expanded the capacity of governmental and non-governmental organizations and networks to advocate for gender equality in sixty-four instances; and it contributed to reversing harmful practices that discriminated against women and girls in sixteen instances. UNIFEM provided support for programs in forty-three countries and technical advice and/or catalytic funding in forty other countries; coordinated gender-themed groups in eleven countries; and provided input for the MDG processes in twenty countries. *Yearbook of the United Nations 2004*, 1172.

75. At this point, the FAO was the largest single recipient (25 percent) and the UN second (12 percent), while the position of the WHO had declined (3 percent). Other agencies that were major executors of UNDP funds included UNIDO (8 percent), the ICAO (5 percent), and the IBRD and the ITU (4 percent each).

76. *Yearbook of the United Nations 1982*, 623, 643, 646.

77. "Operational Activities for Development of the United Nations System," General Assembly resolution 37/226, 20 December 1982. In its first comprehensive pol-icy review of operational activities for development, the General Assembly welcomed the Governing Council's decision to promote government execution of UNDP-funded projects; "Comprehensive Policy Review of Operational Activities for Development," General Assembly resolution 38/171, 19 December 1983.

78. *Yearbook of the United Nations 1988*, 345.

79. "Comprehensive Triennial Policy Review of Operational Activities for Development of the United Nations System," General Assembly resolution 44/211, 22 December 1989.

80. Ibid.

81. In 1982, the share of government-executed UNDP technical assistance was a mere 2.5 percent, but it increased in the next three years to 2.6, 3.5, and 4.3 percent,

respectively. *Yearbook of the United Nations 1982*, 643; *Yearbook of the United Nations 1983*, 447; *Yearbook of the United Nations 1984*, 431; *Yearbook of the United Nations 1985*. In 1990, twenty-four UN agencies were executing 70 percent of the UNDP-funded programs. By then, the share executed by governments had reached 12 percent. *Yearbook of the United Nations 1991*, 367.

82. *Yearbook of the United Nations 1990*, 394. The administrator stressed the ideological justification for the reform: the concept of national execution was a reaffirmation of the fundamental principle that development was a national process.

83. Ibid., 394–395.

84. *Yearbook of the United Nations 1992*, 562–563.

85. *Yearbook of the United Nations 1993*, 694.

86. *Yearbook of the United Nations 1996*, 784; *Yearbook of the United Nations 1997*, 880.

87. *Yearbook of the United Nations 2003*, 903; *Yearbook of the United Nations 2004*, 888.

88. In a report on the implementation of General Assembly resolution 53/192, the Secretary-General observed that while funds and programs reported progress in national execution, evaluations of the system indicated a possible tension between accountability and the capacity-building aspects of national execution. Strengthening the monitoring and evaluation functions was seen as the answer to that challenge. *Yearbook of the United Nations 1999*, 788.

89. "Restructuring the Economic and Social Sectors within the United Nations System," General Assembly resolution 32/197, 20 December 1977.

90. Resident coordinators were to be appointed by the Secretary-General after an extensive consultation process that included most institutions of the system that had operational activities for development and the government concerned.

91. *Yearbook of the United Nations 1982*, 634.

92. Among the measures suggested were continued assistance for developing countries to enhance their planning and programming capacity and to strengthen their central and sectoral planning units and related mechanisms for external inputs, programming, and coordination. *Yearbook of the United Nations 1983*, 441–442.

93. *Yearbook of the United Nations 1985*, 472.

94. *Yearbook of the United Nations 1986*, 411.

95. "Policy Review of Operational Activities for Development," ECOSOC resolution 1986/74, 23 July 1986.

96. "Operational Activities for Development," General Assembly resolution 41/171, 5 December 1986, quotes at paragraphs 17–19 and 21. The resolution also invited UN organizations "to continue to pursue measures to enhance the involvement of non-governmental organizations and enterprises in operational activities, in accordance with the objectives and priorities of each developing country." It urged them "to integrate economic and technical co-operation among developing countries into operational activities, *inter alia*, by orienting their programmes and projects towards strengthening such co-operation in accordance with the priorities defined by the developing countries themselves" (paragraphs 27 and 29).

97. He offered three examples: efforts of UNDP-assisted projects to mobilize resources and generate parallel financing; assistance in delivering non-UNDP expenditures that were supported by the UNDP's field infrastructure; and assistance to recipients of World Bank loans by placing at their disposal the UNDP field-based delivery system to aid in implementing bank-financed technical cooperation projects. *Yearbook of the United Nations 1986*, 428.

98. *Yearbook of the United Nations 1987*, 399–400.

99. "Comprehensive Triennial Policy Review of Operational Activities for Development of the United Nations System," General Assembly resolution 44/211, 22 December 1989. The resolution called for "a more integrated and co-ordinated" programming of UN system cooperation, in which "programming processes would be based on an overall national programme framework for operational activities for development to be prepared by the recipient Government, with a view of submitting it to the organizations of the United Nations system for their support and funding, whose response would be co-ordinated by the resident co-ordinator" (paragraph 17). The assembly stated that introducing budgetary cycles on a rolling basis should be considered. Generally, the assembly invited organizations to increase their efforts toward integrated programming under the leadership of governments. The recommendation about programming cycles was repeated three years later. "Triennial Policy Review of Operational Activities for Development within the United Nations System," General Assembly resolution 47/199, 22 December 1992.

100. While the General Assembly reaffirmed that recipient governments had sole responsibility for coordinating external assistance in 1989 (see "Comprehensive Triennial Policy Review of Operational Activities for Development of the United Nations System," General Assembly resolution 44/211, 22 December 1989), nine years later, the assembly stated that governments had "the primary responsibility" for coordinating external assistance (see "Triennial Policy Review of Operational Activities for Development of the United Nations System," General Assembly resolution 53/192, 15 December 1998).

101. "Comprehensive Triennial Policy Review of Operational Activities for Development of the United Nations System," General Assembly resolution 44/211, 22 December 1989, quote at paragraph 6.

102. *Yearbook of the United Nations 1988*, 333–334. The Governing Council stated that the system's capacity for analytical work should be strengthened by ensuring that representatives of the specialized agencies had technical functions and capacities within their sectoral areas and by strengthening the resident coordinators' capacity to draw on that expertise in support of government programs. Collaboration with the international financial institutions should take into account the special character, mandates, and policies of the institutions involved and should respect their differences.

In June 1989, the Governing Council decided that the UNDP's main coordination task was to work to strengthen the capacity of developing countries to coordinate external assistance in keeping with their priorities and requirements. In May 1992, the council stressed that the program approach should be applied on a country-specific basis and that the UNDP should ensure the smooth implementation of country programs. See *Yearbook of the United Nations 1989*, 312; *Yearbook of the United Nations 1992*, 563.

103. In 1993, the Secretary-General reported that the Joint Consultative Group on Policy (comprised of the UNDP, UNICEF, the UNFPA, IFAD, and the WFP) had established several targets: to achieve, by 1996, 80 percent harmonization of countries with programming cycles of the UNDP, the UNFPA, and UNICEF and to relate them to WFP projects; to adapt UNDP, UNFPA, and UNICEF programming cycles to the national plans of countries that had such plans; and to harmonize programming cycles among themselves in countries that did not have a formal plan. Based on these targets, in 1993, the Joint Consultative Group issued, a joint UNDP/UNFPA/UNICEF letter to resident coordinators, country directors, and field representatives that contained guiding principles on how to proceed with harmonizing country program cycles; *Yearbook of the United Nations 1993*, 684. By May 1994, some 33 percent of these program cycles

had been harmonized. Progress was also reported in establishing field-level coordination mechanisms as called for in General Assembly resolution 47/199: of the 128 countries with resident coordinators, seventy-four had established such mechanisms; *Yearbook of the United Nations 1994*, 787–788.

Nevertheless, the process went slowly. In his 1997 annual report, the UNDP administrator reported that by June of that year, program cycles had been harmonized in twenty-seven countries and that they were expected to be harmonized in another fifty-four countries by 1999, followed later by another twenty-six countries. *Yearbook of the United Nations 1997,* 846. This time, expectations were more than fulfilled. In 1999, the Secretary-General reported that harmonization had been achieved in eighty-six countries and that the UNDG was working on an overall action plan to increase that number to ninety-nine by 2003; *Yearbook of the United Nations 1999*, 787.

104. "Triennial Policy Review of the Operational Activities of the United Nations Development System," General Assembly resolution 47/199, 22 December 1992. The General Assembly said that at the country level, the UN system should be tailored to the specific needs of the country in such a way as to correspond to ongoing and projected cooperation programs rather than to the institutional structure of the UN.

105. "Triennial Policy Review of Operational Activities for Development of the United Nations System," General Assembly resolution 50/120, 20 December 1995.

106. The UNDP administrator reported that by May 1998, country strategy notes had been prepared in twenty-seven countries and drafts had been prepared in nineteen others. A total of ninety-two countries had expressed interest in the system. *Yearbook of the United Nations 1998*, 806.

107. *Yearbook of the United Nations 1997*, 845; *Yearbook of the United Nations 1998*, 801.

108. "Operational Activities of the United Nations for International Development Cooperation Segment," ECOSOC resolution 1995/50, 28 July 1995. The executive boards of UNDP/UNFPA and UNICEF followed up on the recommendation. In 1999, the first meeting of executive boards of these funds and the bureaus of ECOSOC held joint sessions; *Yearbook of the United Nations 1999*, 792.

109. In 1998, the Secretary-General observed that the relationship with the host country needed more attention regarding issues such as the flow of information, the existence of government focal points, and the need in some countries for greater government interest and support. There was also room to increase the participation of all relevant UN partners in the resident coordinator system at the country level, including agencies without field representation. The Secretary-General concluded that greater simplification and harmonization of procedures and more delegated authority at the country level would strengthen the system considerably. *Yearbook of the United Nations 1998*, 801.

110. Ibid.

111. *Yearbook of the United Nations 1995*, 887.

112. In his capacity as special coordinator, the administrator assumed the lead role at the UN in enhancing the coordination of development activities; promoting an integrated follow-up of recent global conferences and related Administrative Committee on Coordination agreements and arrangements; and supporting the Secretary-General in his role as chair of the Administrative Committee on Coordination. These responsibilities were distinct from his role as the UNDP administrator.

113. The UNDP's more dynamic presentation of its policies, activities, and achievements was probably not unconnected with the expansion of its information and advocacy functions in the early and mid-1990s.

114. *Yearbook of the United Nations 1997*, 846. The *Operational Activities Reference*

Manual was published in 1996 by the Consultative Committee on Programme and Operational Questions of the Administrative Committee on Coordination and prepared in cooperation with the UNDP. It was part of efforts to create a common understanding of the program approach.

115. The Secretary-General had decided that the UNDP should continue as the manager and funder of the resident coordinator system with appropriate staff support. The resident coordinator was responsible to coordinate UN activities at the country level and would report to the Secretary-General through the administrator. UNDP regional bureaus would be responsible for the UNDP program but not for the resident coordinator per se; they would support the operational activities of the resident coordinator as co-owners of the resident coordinator system. Operational and system-wide activities would include preparing and monitoring the country strategy note, paying increased attention to common country assessments, and supporting the roundtable and consultative group meetings. In May 1997, the Executive Board welcomed UNDP measures to improve its capacity to support the resident coordinator system and asked the UNDP to continue consultations with other funds and programs about their roles in that regard. Ibid., 855, 858, 872–873.

116. Ibid., 857–858. The year had been an important one on many fronts, the administrator stated. The UNDP had strengthened its identity in policy dialogue and program activities based on its mission to help to eradicate poverty through sustainable human development and had provided support for good governance, a key part of the enabling environment for poverty eradication. The UNDP had implemented organizational changes designed to make it a more efficient and more effective organization that included greater accountability, a culture of cost-consciousness, and a sharper focus on country operations. The country offices had been strengthened, as had the organization's commitment to the resident coordinator system. The focus of UNDP work had been narrowed, giving priority to gender issues and countries in special circumstances, and management actions had been implemented to accelerate change and improve the organization's governance.

117. Ibid.

118. "Triennial Policy Review of Operational Activities for Development of the United Nations System," General Assembly resolution 53/192, 25 February 1999.

119. *Yearbook of the United Nations 1998,* 806.

120. However, according to the Secretary-General, several challenges remained, including rationalizing and simplifying relevant programming procedures, monitoring the UNDAF timeline and synchronizing it with individual country programs and projects derived from UNDAF; using the common country assessment, which was originally conceived as a development tool, in crises and postconflict countries; collaborating further with the Bretton Woods institutions; and actively involving civil society and the private sector in policy debates generated by the common country assessment and UNDAF processes. *Yearbook of the United Nations 2000,* 816.

121. Ibid.

122. *Yearbook of the United Nations 2001,* 783. The review repeated the concern about the multiplicity of country-level coordination frameworks and the burden they placed on program countries, UN system staff, and other multilateral and bilateral institutions, resulting in higher transaction costs.

123. Ibid., 792. Among the achievements reported was the compact agreed between the Department of Economic and Social Affairs and the UNDP for mutually reinforcing their distinct but complementary roles, particularly in pursuing the MDGs. The UNDP

had also worked with the World Bank on poverty reduction strategies and had worked to develop policy-based partnership with civil society organizations from both the South and North; the latter was important for building UNDP's profile as a policy and advocacy organization.

124. Ibid., 798.

125. *Yearbook of the United Nations 2002,* 862–863. In the 2003 report, the administrator noted that UNDP had played a leading role in discussions with other development actors about ways to strengthen linkages between the MDGs and the PRSPs that had resulted in a joint UNDG/World Bank/IMF statement on the relationships between the two instruments and their respective roles. *Yearbook of the United Nations 2003,* 890.

126. *Yearbook of the United Nations 2004,* 866.

127. Ibid., 866–867.

128. "Triennial Comprehensive Policy Review of Operational Activities for Development of the United Nations System," General Assembly resolution 59/250, 22 December 2004.

129. *Yearbook of the United Nations 1987,* 400.

130. The assembly asked the DIEC director-general, in consultation with the UNDP administrator and the executive heads of other organizations of the UN system, to assess the constraints on using the UNDP's country program and programming process as a frame of reference for the operational activities of the UN system. "Operational Activities for Development," General Assembly resolution 42/196, 11 December 1987.

131. "Comprehensive Triennial Policy Review of the Operational Activities for Development of the United Nations System," General Assembly resolution 44/211, 22 December 1989.

132. *Yearbook of the United Nations 1991,* 367–368. The DIEC director-general noted that changes in location and closures of offices were few, and when such changes happened it was often in response to compelling local events, such as civil strife. The UNHCR was an exception because it closed offices whenever a specific refugee situation was resolved. More recently, there had been a sharp drop in long-term internationally recruited project staff due to a sizeable increase in short-term consultants and nationally recruited staff.

133. *Yearbook of the United Nations 1993,* 686. Later that year, the General Assembly authorized these establishments; see "Operational Activities for Development: Field Offices of the United Nations Development System," General Assembly resolution 48/209, 21 December 1993.

134. In 1994, a Joint Inspection Unit report presented proposals for rationalizing and unifying the field organization of the UN organizations. It suggested a "political" solution as one of the options for redefining the resident coordinator's role to be 1) the Secretary-General's representative and spokesperson in the country on all UN matters; the representative of the UN High Commissioner for Refugees and the UN Department of Humanitarian Affairs; 2) the director of the UN information center; and 3) a coordinator for development assistance and for early warning (mainly in the area of refugee flows and political, humanitarian, or environmental emergencies) and for political reporting. A long-term option proposed establishing a single UN office that would cover all UN system needs and activities that would be headed by a UN representative with an enhanced political profile. The Administrative Committee on Coordination supported strengthening the functions of the resident coordinator but warned that the combination of responsibility for political, humanitarian, and human rights issues with development issues might be taken by some developing countries to mean that conditionality

was brought into the development dialogue. The committee recommended that the major focus of the resident coordinator should remain on development. *Yearbook of the United Nations 1994,* 791–792.

135. *Yearbook of the United Nations 1997,* 855. By 1997, these recommendations were not new ideas. In March 1998, the administrator submitted the UNDP's comments to the report, fully supporting the recommendations about unifying representation and harmonizing geographical representation, strengthening thematic groups headed by a lead agency at the country level, and accelerating the establishment or enhancement of common premises. The UNDP had responded to the recommendation that coordination at the country level be more institutionalized, especially between the UN system and other actors. It had already taken steps to do this in its activities to develop capacity for coordinating and managing aid, the report stated. It added that the recommendation that the Secretary-General designate a single high official at the Secretariat to be in charge of the resident coordinator system had been superseded by his recommendation on UN reform (designating the UNDP and its administrator to fill these functions). *Yearbook of the United Nations 1998,* 807.

136. *Yearbook of the United Nations 1999,* 793.

137. *Yearbook of the United Nations 2003,* 882.

138. Giovanni Andrea Cornia, Richard Jolly, and Frances Stewart, eds., *Adjustment with a Human Face,* vol. 1, *Protecting the Vulnerable and Promoting Growth* (Oxford: Oxford University Press, 1987).

139. In 1985, World Bank expenditures (World Bank loans and IDA credits for training and consultants) were $947 million and UNDP-financed technical assistance expenditures were $564 million. The UN system spent $1.4 billion on technical assistance that year. See *Yearbook of the United Nations 1985,* 461–462.

140. *Yearbook of the United Nations 1987,* 400.

141. "Operational Activities of the United Nations for International Development Cooperation Segment," ECOSOC resolution 1995/50, 28 July 1995.

142. In his report to the General Assembly, the Secretary-General emphasized that enhanced cooperation with the Bretton Woods institutions was "imperative"; *Yearbook of the United Nations 1995,* 882. The General Assembly agreed with the ECOSOC decision; "Triennial Policy Review of Operational Activities for Development of the United Nations System," General Assembly resolution 50/120, 20 December 1995.

143. The report stated that the record of cooperation between the Bretton Woods institutions and the UN system was extensive, involving several major joint initiatives. They had forged close links around specific themes such as social development, environment, population and reproductive health, and HIV/AIDS. At the country level, the report noted several areas where collaboration was taking place, including poverty reduction, capacity-building, human development, complementing and mitigating the effects of structural adjustment programs, the Joint and Co-sponsored United Nations Programme on HIV/AIDS, policy dialogue, the country strategy note and policy framework papers process, the resident coordinator system, aid coordination, country missions, connectivity at the country level, and the program approach. *Yearbook of the United Nations 1996,* 764–765.

144. Ibid., 765.

145. "Strengthening Collaboration between the United Nations Development System and the Bretton Woods Institutions," ECOSOC resolution 1996/43, 26 July 1996.

146. "Triennial Policy Review of Operational Activities for Development of the United Nations System," General Assembly resolution 53/192, 15 December 1998.

147. According to the IMF report, collaboration with the UN entailed increased participation by IMF staff in meetings and initiatives organized by intergovernmental and interagency committees and commissions, exchange of information, and collaboration in generating statistical data and in postconflict situations. Country-level collaboration took place mainly between IMF missions and/or resident representatives and the UN resident coordinators and representatives of special agencies. The report argued that cooperation with the UN had helped the IMF integrate social and environmental concerns into its policy advice and the design of adjustment programs. The IMF also had something to offer: there might be a need to more clearly define specific areas of collaboration in selected countries, including building capacity to manage public resources transparently through joint technical assistance programs to prepare for comprehensive macroeconomic and structural adjustment reforms. The country strategy notes were sometimes overly donor-driven, with insufficient participation of governments: this had hampered consistency and complementarity with other government policy papers, the IMF argued. The country strategy notes had not always benefited from comments from IMF staff. *Yearbook of the United Nations 1997*, 853–854.

148. *Yearbook of the United Nations 1998*, 807–808.

149. The Secretary-General argued that considerable scope existed for tripartite collaboration involving the UN development system, the Bretton Woods institutions, and regional development banks; *Yearbook of the United Nations 2001*, 783.

150. "Triennial Policy Review of Operational Activities for Development of the United Nations System," General Assembly resolution 56/201, 21 December 2001.

151. *Yearbook of the United Nations 2003*, 882.

152. "Triennial Comprehensive Policy Review of Operational Activities for Development of the United Nations System," General Assembly resolution 59/250, 17 August 2005.

153. See the introduction and chapters on the development cooperation policies of fifteen European donor countries and the European Union in Paul Hoebink and Olav Stokke, eds., *Perspectives on European Development Co-operation* (London: Routledge, 2005).

154. Sixten Heppling, *UNDP: From Agency Shares to Country Programmes, 1949–1975* (Stockholm: Ministry of Foreign Affairs, 1995), 86–87.

155. See Olav Stokke, "Aid and Political Conditionality: Core Issues and State of the Art," in *Aid and Political Conditionality*, ed. Olav Stokke (London: Frank Cass, 1995), 1–87.

13. FOOD AID

1. James Ingram, *Bread and Stones: Leadership and the Struggle to Reform the United Nations World Food Programme* (Charleston, S.C.: BookSurge, 2007), 129, 200, 206.

2. Ibid., 70, 73–74. Although the shift to emergency aid had begun with the Sahelian drought of 1973–1975, Ingram found when he began his assignment with the WFP in 1982 that emergency work was not properly staffed: "It was seen as second-best, reflecting the now entrenched 'development' culture in WFP. Overcoming that bias became another of my priorities." It was "urgent to strengthen our ability to deal with emergencies and our general administration which was starved of qualified personnel."

3. According to Ingram, Saouma, then the director-general of the FAO, "several times told me, he saw WFP exclusively as a logistic agency to deliver food to FAO-designed development projects and FAO-approved emergency operations." Ingram, *Bread and Stones*, 309.

4. In 2005, when total ODA amounted to $60.6 billion, total food aid amounted

to $3.9 billion, 3.4 percent of total ODA. However, the major donor countries contributed food aid at unequal levels. The United States provided 57 percent of global food aid. This was 8 percent of that country's total ODA and 8.7 percent of its bilateral ODA. The countries that came closest using the variable of food aid as a percentage of total ODA were Ireland (4.2), Canada (4.0), Australia (3.9), Norway (3.9), and New Zealand (3.5). For major donor countries such as France, Germany, Japan, and the United Kingdom, the share was only 1 percent or less. Edward Clay, "Food Aid, Tying and Trade Distortion: A Proportionate Response," paper for the international conference Food Aid: Exploring the Challenges, Berlin, 3–5 May 2007. For the United States, the share of food aid of total ODA was highly volatile: in the years between 1995 and 2003, it varied between 10 and 17 percent of its foreign assistance. OECD, *The Development Effectiveness of Food Aid: Does Tying Matter?* (Paris: OECD, 2006), 30.

5. "Revision of the General Regulations of the World Food Programme and Enlargement of the Committee on Food Aid Policies and Programmes of the World Food Programme," General Assembly resolution 46/22, 5 December 1991.

6. Ingram argues that although no other UN agency faced the same combination of factors, the WFP's experience was not atypical. "The role of personalities, the power and ambitions of agency heads, the political division within governments and governing bodies, the ultra-bureaucratic culture of secretariats, are all characteristics of system agencies . . . Moreover the structure of the system is antithetical to strong leadership." Ingram, *Bread and Stones,* 322.

7. As the WFP's executive director observed during these years, the "WFP was good at matching the known foreign policy interest of donors, the foods that they could provide and the dietary patterns of recipients. Indeed, our skill in this respect was one reason why donors often used WFP as their preferred disaster response vehicle." Ibid., 301–302.

8. D. John Shaw, *The UN World Food Programme and the Development of Food Aid* (New York: Palgrave, 2001), table 5.3 and calculations based on this source.

9. An OECD study concluded that "need appears to have little influence on the overall availability of food aid"; OECD, *The Development Effectiveness of Food Aid,* 31–32.

10. For a discussion of these and other characteristics of food aid, see several contributions in Edward Clay and Olav Stokke, eds., *Food Aid Reconsidered: Assessing the Impact on Third World Countries* (London: Frank Cass, 1991); and Edward Clay and Olav Stokke, eds., *Food Aid and Human Security* (London: Frank Cass, 2000).

11. As stocks of food dwindled and competing pressures on the use of food as an aid resource increased, the administration of President Lyndon Johnson began to insist on a larger degree of international burden-sharing. According to Wallerstein, during the Kennedy Round of trade negotiations (1967), the food-importing developed countries were not given much of a choice but to accept an obligation to provide a certain amount of food in quantitative terms rather than by currency value (sharing 4.5 tons of grain). This aid was provided bilaterally on grant terms, with each donor choosing the individual recipients for its assistance: "It is more accurate to state that the United States did not *seek* wider food aid burden-sharing through the GATT negotiations, but *demanded* it as the price of its participation and of its specific commodity concessions." Its own contribution was aid that it would have provided anyway. Mitchel B. Wallerstein, *Food for War—Food for Peace. United States Food Aid in a Global Context* (Cambridge, Mass.: MIT Press, 1980), 67, 111–115, quote at 112.

12. Clay, "Food Aid, Tying and Trade Distortion," 5.

13. OECD, *The Development Effectiveness of Food Aid.*

14. Ibid., 61–64. The least cost-effective food aid according to this parameter was provided by Australia, Belgium, Canada, and the United States. In the United States and Canada, the status of tying is unambiguous, regulated by legislation (the United States) or regulations governing food aid operations (Canada). The United States requires that 50 percent of commodities be processed and packed (value added) before shipment and that 75 percent of the food aid provided by the U.S. Agency for International Development and 50 percent of the food aid managed by the U.S. Department of Agriculture be transported by vessels registered in the United States (ibid., 51).

15. Ibid., 65.

16. *Yearbook of the United Nations 1996* (New York: United Nations, Office of Public Information, 1998), 1129–1130.

17. *Yearbook of the United Nations 2002* (New York: United Nations, Office of Public Information, 2004), 1225.

18. "Further Measures for Restructuring and Revitalization of the United Nations in the Economic, Social and Related Fields," General Assembly resolution 50/227, 24 May 1996.

19. *Yearbook of the United Nations 1994* (New York: United Nations, Office of Public Information, 1995), 1134.

20. "Target for World Food Programme Pledges for the Period 1997–1998," General Assembly resolution 50/127, 20 December 1995.

21. *Yearbook of the United Nations 2000* (New York: United Nations, Office of Public Information, 2002), 1171. The following year, contributions increased to $1.9 billion, including a $1.2 billion contribution from the United States, the largest-ever contribution from a single donor. *Yearbook of the United Nations 2001* (New York: United Nations, Office of Public Information, 2003), 1141.

22. In 1990, low-income food-deficit countries received 86 percent of the WFP's development assistance commitments, 85 percent of its emergency aid, and 90 percent of its assistance for protracted refugee operations. The LDCs received 76 percent of the development assistance. In 1994, slightly less than one-third of all new commitments for development went to the LDCs and 93 percent went to low-income, food-deficient countries. In 1997, 60 percent of the WFP's total operational expenditures took place in the LDCs. In 2004, 94 percent of the 24 million beneficiaries of WFP development assistance were in low-income, food-deficit countries. *Yearbook of the United Nations 1990, 683; Yearbook of the United Nations 1994, 1134; Yearbook of the United Nations 1997* (New York: United Nations, Office of Public Information, 2000), 1257; *Yearbook of the United Nations 2004* (New York: United Nations, Office of Public Information, 2006), 1225.

In 1998, women and girls accounted for nearly half of the 75 million people who received food assistance from the WFP. In 2004, 113 million people were assisted by the WFP; 89 million were women and children, including 8.7 million boys and 7.9 million girls assisted through school feeding programs. *Yearbook of the United Nations 1998* (New York: United Nations, Office of Public Information, 2001), 1131; *Yearbook of the United Nations 2004, 1225.*

23. *Yearbook of the United Nations 1994,* 1133; *Yearbook of the United Nations 1998,* 1131; *Yearbook of the United Nations 1999* (New York: United Nations, Office of Public Information, 2001), 1152; *Yearbook of the United Nations 2000,* 1171; *Yearbook of the United Nations 2001,* 1141; *Yearbook of the United Nations 2002,* 1225; and *Yearbook of the United Nations 2003* (New York: United Nations, Office of Public Information, 2005), 1259.

24. The pledging conference for the WFP held in New York on 6 November 2002 was attended by representatives of only six member states (Algeria, Bhutan, Djibouti, El

Salvador, India, and Nicaragua) and the Holy See. Total pledges amounted to $27,500 in cash and $1.9 million in goods. *Yearbook of the United Nations 2002,* 1225.

25. In 2003, Iraq alone received more than one-third of the total food aid channeled through the WFP (2.1 million tons out of 6.0 million tons in this peak year for the program). This was 20.6 percent of global food aid for that year. *Yearbook of the United Nations 2003,* 1259, and calculations based on data in this source.

26. In 2001, the United States contributed $1.2 billion to the WFP, more than 63 percent of the total contributions that year. The United States was also the major contributor to the WFP in 2002 ($930 million; 52 percent of the total), in the peak year of 2003 ($1.4 billion; 54 percent of the total), and in 2004 ($1 billion; 45 percent of the total). *Yearbook of the United Nations 2001,* 1141; *Yearbook of the United Nations 2002,* 1225; *Yearbook of the United Nations 2003,* 1260; *Yearbook of the United Nations 2004,* 1225, and calculations based on data in these sources.

27. In current U.S. dollars, the amount allocated to development (in millions of dollars) was 499.5 in 1989, 398.4 in 1993, 254.3 in 1998, 185.0 in 2000, and 228.7 in 2003; OECD, *The Development Effectiveness of Food Aid,* table 1.4.

28. *Yearbook of the United Nations 1992* (New York: United Nations, Office of Public Information, 1993), 827; *Yearbook of the United Nations 1993* (New York: United Nations, Office of Public Information, 1994), 25; *Yearbook of the United Nations 1994,* 1134; *Yearbook of the United Nations 1995,* 1262.

29. *Yearbook of the United Nations 1992,* 25; *Yearbook of the United Nations 1994,* 1134.

30. *Yearbook of the United Nations 1996,* 1127–1129; *Yearbook of the United Nations 2004,* 1224–1226.

31. In 1996, 58 percent of the resources went to agriculture and rural development and 42 percent to human resource development. In 1997, 14 million people benefited from agriculture and rural development projects and 9.8 million from human resource development projects. *Yearbook of the United Nations 1996,* 1128; *Yearbook of the United Nations 1997,* 1257.

32. There is nothing new about U.S. food aid following in the trail of U.S. military interventions. Between 1968 and 1973, South Vietnam alone received twenty times the value of food aid that the five African countries most seriously affected by drought (the Sahelian region) received in the same period. Wallerstein observed that by 1973, "almost half of all US food assistance was flowing to South Vietnam and Cambodia, as the Nixon administration attempted to circumvent the increasingly stringent congressional limitations on US assistance to the war effort in Southeast Asia." Wallerstein, *Food for War—Food for Peace,* 46.

33. James Ingram referred to the change in funding for placing refugees and displaced persons as "a whole new era of cooperation with UNHCR and a better deal for the displaced." He felt that this was one of his important innovations. Personal communication, 4 April 2008; see also Ingram, *Bread and Stones,* 307ff.

34. See Dieter Senghaas, "Assessing War, Violence and Peace Today," *Security Dialogue* 26, no. 2 (1995): 307, 316.

35. The concept of human security has two aspects: safety from chronic threats such as hunger, disease, and repression and protection from sudden and hurtful disruptions in the pattern of daily life. The absence of such security undermines the processes of development and may lead to social disintegration and humanitarian catastrophe. See UNDP, *Human Development Report 2004: Cultural Liberty in Today's Diverse World* (New York: Oxford University Press, 2004); and S. Neil MacFarlane and Yuen Fong Khong, *Human Security and the UN: A Critical History* (Bloomington: Indiana University Press,

2006). For a history of the UN system and food security, see D. John Shaw, *World Food Security: A History since 1945* (Basingstoke: Palgrave, 2007). Shaw concludes on a pessimistic note: the history of attempts to achieve world food security and eliminate hunger and poverty since World War II "is a history of good intentions, as can be seen in the graveyard of noble aspirations, depicting a civilization that now seems able to live with the ignominy and shame of knowing that the large number of its citizens continue to live in hunger and poverty, while the knowledge, resources and repeated commitments to end this scourge exist, and obesity in some parts of the world is becoming a major killer" (Shaw, *World Food Security,* 461).

36. FAO, "Food Security and Food Assistance," in *Technical Background Documents,* no. 13 (Rome: FAO, 1996). A growing amount of literature on the topic includes Wenche Barth Eide and Uwe Kracht, eds., *Food and Human Rights in Development,* vol. 1, Legal and Institutional Dimensions and Selected Topics (Antwerp: Intersentia, 2005); and vol. 2, *Evolving Issues and Emerging Applications* (Mortsel, Belgium: Intersentia, 2007).

37. James Ingram recalls that "politics was always a factor in our [humanitarian relief] operations. The political interests of the US were the driving force, then as now, as to who was helped." He added that "it became quickly evident that politics, rather than need, plays a role in the distribution of [development] aid as between different claimants. It was always a tussle to ensure that countries like Vietnam, Cuba, Nicaragua and Ethiopia, unpopular with the United States, were not discriminated against." James Ingram, "Reforming the United Nations? An Iconoclastic View from Inside," unpublished paper, Lowy Institute, 8 August 2007. For a detailed account with reference to Vietnam and Cuba, see Ingram, *Bread and Stones,* 61–64. The United States made a distinction between support for development projects and support for humanitarian assistance.

38. WFP, *Tackling Hunger in a World Full of Food: Tasks Ahead for Food Aid* (Rome: World Food Programme, Public Affairs Division, WFP, 1996); WFP, *Time for Change: Food Aid and Development* (Rome: World Food Programme, 1999).

39. One such evaluation merits special mention—the evaluation of the UN Border Relief Operation (for which the WFP was the lead agency) by Oxford University's Refugee Studies Programme. According to Ingram, the evaluation "revealed a shocking abuse of human rights." In the context of a complex situation in which the responsibility for the operation involved several UN organizations and the Secretariat, the WFP decided to withdraw from its lead role. *Bread and Stones,* 198–199.

40. CMI, *Evaluation of the World Food Programme: Final Report* (Bergen, Norway: Chr. Michelsen Institute, 1993); Governments of Canada, the Netherlands, and Norway, *Evaluation of the World Food Programme: Main Report* (Ottawa: Canadian International Development Agency, 1994).

41. Just Faaland, Diana McLean, and Ole David Koht Norbye, "The World Food Programme (WFP) and International Food Aid," in Clay and Stokke, *Food Aid and Human Security,* 221–225.

42. Clay and Stokke, "Food and Human Security: Retrospective and an Agenda for Change," in Clay and Stokke, *Food Aid and Human Security.*

43. Such (unintended) effects of humanitarian relief operations have been well documented in Sudan and in the Great Lakes region of Central Africa. See Alex de Waal, *Famine, Crimes, Politics & the Disaster Relief Industry in Africa* (London: Africa Rights & the International African Institute in association with James Currey and Indiana University Press, 1997); Milton J. Esman, *Can Foreign Aid Moderate Ethnic Conflict?* (Washington, D.C.: United States Institute of Peace, 1997); John Prendergast, *Frontline Diplomacy: Humanitarian Aid and Conflict in Africa* (Boulder, Colo.: Lynne Rienner,

1996); and Olav Stokke, "Violent Conflict Prevention and Development Co-operation: Coherent or Conflicting Perspectives?" *Forum for Development Studies* 24, no. 2 (1997): 195–250. Alex de Waal's critique is fundamental and goes to the core justification for humanitarian relief aid. The way international humanism operates is an obstacle rather than an aid to conquering famine in Africa, he claims. "Sending relief is a weapon of first resort: popular at home, usually unobjectable abroad, and an excuse for not looking more deeply into underlying political problems. At worst, supporting humanitarianism is a smokescreen for political inaction." De Waal, *Famine, Crimes, Politics & the Disaster Relief Industry in Africa,* 134

44. See Clay and Stokke, "Food and Human Security: Retrospective and an Agenda for Change." The OECD's evaluation of 2006 revisited the issue and recommended further investigation. OECD, *The Development Effectiveness of Food Aid,* 36–37, 83.

45. Hans W. Singer, "Foreword," in D. John Shaw, *The UN World Food Programme and the Development of Food Aid* (Basingstoke: Palgrave, 2001), xi.

46. OECD, *The Development Effectiveness of Food Aid: Does Tying Matter?*

47. Wallerstein, *Food for War—Food for Peace,* 247.

48. "A single global operational UN agency would facilitate a more effective UN system response. Hopefully, it would be better able to coordinate activities of the scores of NGOs who quickly become involved in natural and man-made disasters than is currently the case"; Ingram, "Reforming the United Nations?" 6. See also Ingram, *Bread and Stones,* 325.

49. *Delivering as One: Report of the High-level Panel on United Nations System-Wide Coherence in the Areas of Development, Humanitarian Assistance and the Environment,* General Assembly document A/61/583, 20 November 2006.

14. THE LONG ROAD TOWARD THE MILLENNIUM DEVELOPMENT GOALS

1. OECD, *Shaping the 21st Century: The Contribution of Development Co-operation* (Paris: OECD DAC, 1996).

2. For a description and discussion, see Jacques Forster and Olav Stokke, "Coherence of Policies towards Developing Countries: Approaching the Problematique," in *Policy Coherence in Development Co-operation,* ed. Forster and Stokke (London: Frank Cass, 1999), 16–57.

3. "The Millennium Assembly of the United Nations," General Assembly resolution 53/202, 17 December 1998.

4. "United Nations Millennium Declaration," General Assembly resolution 55/2, 8 September 2000.

5. United Nations, *United Nations Millennium Declaration* (New York: United Nations Department of Public Information, 2000), point 19.

6. Ibid., point 20.

7. Ibid., points 21–28.

8. "Follow-Up to the Outcome of the Millennium Summit," General Assembly resolution 55/162, 18 December 2000.

9. See *Road Map towards the Implementation of the United Nations Millennium Declaration, Report of the Secretary-General,* General Assembly document A/56/326, 6 September 2001; and "Follow-Up to the Outcome of the Millennium Summit," General Assembly resolution 56/95, 14 December 2001. The General Assembly recommended that the UN system consider the road map "as a useful guide in the implementation of the Millennium Declaration" and invited member states as well as the

Bretton Woods institutions, the World Trade Organization, and other interested parties to consider the road map when formulating plans for implementing goals related to the declaration.

10. *Road Map towards the Implementation of the United Nations Millennium Declaration,* points 7 and 9, italics in original.

11. This "routine" follow-up generated research and evaluation both with regard to the results that had been achieved (or not) and the actual performance of the major involved actors. ECOSOC and the General Assembly also scrutinized the strategies and mechanisms used to attain these results and the very basis on which they rested. It also provided the secretariats of the UN system and the intergovernmental bodies, especially the UN Secretariat and the General Assembly but also the specialized agencies and major programs, with an opportunity to scrutinize and make new recommendations and renewed appeals.

12. *Yearbook of the United Nations 2002* (New York: United Nations, Office of Public Information, 2004), 1355–1356. The Secretary-General transmitted the Joint Inspection Unit's report on the implementation of the MDGs to the General Assembly. The critical report pointed out that no strategic framework had been accepted by all actors working toward the MDGs and that no process had been established to organize better coordination of actors. The report recommended new instruments and a new process that could enable the UN system to adopt a meaningful, realistic approach and provide member states with other important tools for monitoring progress toward implementation of the MDGs.

13. Ibid., 821–822.

14. The conference followed many of the patterns established for these summits, involving high-level governmental representation and intergovernmental and NGOs in great numbers. A high-level official segment was held on 18 March, a ministerial segment on 18–20 March, and a summit segment on 21–22 March. It was preceded by a NGO forum 14–16 March and a parliamentarians' forum (in Mexico City) on 14 March.

15. *Yearbook of the United Nations 2002,* 953–954.

16. Ibid., 954–955.

17. Ibid. The Monterrey consensus was endorsed by the General Assembly; see "International Conference on Financing for Development," General Assembly resolution 56/210B, 9 July 2002. ECOSOC, along with the Bretton Woods institutions and the World Trade Organization, was given a special role in implementation and agreed to take on the coordination. Reporting on the immediate implementation of the consensus, the Secretary-General was able to bring some good news: during the period March–June 2002, the European Union heads of state and government had committed themselves to increase their ODA from the current level of 0.33 percent to an average of 0.39 percent of their GNP by 2006, involving an extra $7 billion per year in 2006 and $20 billion over the period 2002–2006. In addition, the EU had agreed on various other measures, including immediate implementation of the DAC recommendation on untying aid to the LDCs. Even the United States was moving: on 14 March, President George W. Bush had proposed a new compact for global development, which would link greater contributions by developed countries to greater responsibility by developing countries. As part of the new compact, the United States pledged a 50 percent increase in its core assistance to developing countries over the next three years to a running rate of $15 billion per year by 2006. A few other countries had also committed to increase their ODA. Ibid., 958–959.

18. *Yearbook of the United Nations 2001* (New York: United Nations, Office of Public Information, 2003), 783.

19. *Yearbook of the United Nations 2002*, 862–863. An increasing number of MDG country reports were produced during 2002. By the end of the year, sixteen reports had been published and another fifty were being prepared in a process led by resident coordinators and country teams. Furthermore, a regional MDG report for Africa had been issued in June. Some thirty-six country offices in Africa, the Arab states, Asia and the Pacific, Europe and the Commonwealth of Independent States, and Latin America and the Caribbean had received funding to initiate or expand advocacy and activities to raise awareness of the MDGs in collaboration with UN country teams.

20. Ibid.

21. Ibid. Almost two-third of the planned expenditures of the fund for 2002–2003, including for the Millennium Project, had been funded by the end of 2002.

22. Ibid., 863.

23. The UNDP found that only a few poverty reduction strategy papers had benefited from an analysis of the MDGs. Most countries had simply adopted the MDGs rather than adapting them through a national consultative process to make them country specific. It also stated that the strategy papers had made no clear link between poverty diagnosis and poverty reduction policies; rather, these policies tended to be an "add-on" to a general growth strategy. The evaluation report found that the institutional arrangements for monitoring poverty in order to ensure implementation of PRSPs were inadequate. *Yearbook of the United Nations 2003* (New York: United Nations, Office of Public Information, 2005), 893–894.

24. Ibid., 899–900.

25. In May 2004, the UNDP reported on steps taken. Closer collaboration had been established between the monitoring and campaign units; the United Nations Development Group had published *Indicators for Monitoring the Millennium Development Goals: Definitions, Rationale, Concepts and Sources* to promote a better understanding of the MDG indicators; and the United Nations Development Group was focusing more closely on statistical capacity. *Yearbook of the United Nations 2004* (New York: United Nations, Office of Public Information, 2006), 880, 885–886.

26. Ibid., 866.

27. The main outcome—the overview report—was co-authored by the twenty-five coordinators of the twelve task forces and the project director. See UNDP, *Investing in Development: A Practical Plan to Achieve the Millennium Development Goals,* Overview, Report to the UN Secretary-General (New York: UNDP, Millennium Project, 2005).

28. In September 2004, the Millennium Project posted its draft *Global Plan to Achieve the Millennium Development Goals,* together with background research, on its Web site for public comment. That year, the project initiated country-level advisory work in several developing countries (Cambodia, the Dominican Republic, Ethiopia, Ghana, Kenya, Senegal, Tajikistan, and Yemen). By the end of September that year, eighty-four MDG country reports had been produced. *Yearbook of the United Nations 2004*, 877.

29. UNDP, *Investing in Development,* 1. The reward for attaining the MDGs in 2015 would be high: "More than 500 million people will be lifted out of extreme poverty. More than 300 million will no longer suffer from hunger. There will also be dramatic progress in child health. Rather than die before reaching their fifth birthdays, 30 million children will be saved. So will the lives of more than 2 million mothers. . . . 350 million fewer people [would] live without the benefits of basic sanitation . . . Hundreds of millions more women and girls will go school, access to economic and political opportunity, and have greater security and safety."

30. Ibid., 15–23. Emphasizing that there were no one-size-fits-all explanations, the

report identified four shortfalls in achieving the MDGs: governance failures, poverty traps, pockets of poverty, and areas of specific policy neglect.

31. Ibid.

32. Ibid., 22. The report struck an optimistic chord even with regard to Sub-Saharan Africa, which lagged behind on almost all development indicators. It found Africa's vulnerability to be very high but not insurmountable. However, targeted investments would be needed in infrastructure, agriculture, and health. Such investments would be too costly for the poorest countries to bear on their own: much more help from the donor countries would be required.

33. Ibid., 23. "We urge all low-income countries to increase their own resource mobilization for the Goals by devoting budget revenues to priority investments. And in all countries where governance is adequate but domestic resources are not, we call on donors to follow through on their long-standing commitments to increase aid significantly. In short, we call for co-financing the scale up of MDG-based investments. The rich countries must no longer delay on their side of the bargain."

34. Ibid., 24. The report emphasized that official development assistance, in particular, should be generous enough to fill the financial needs, assuming that governance limitations were not the binding constraint and that recipient countries were making their own reasonable efforts to increase domestic resource mobilization.

35. Ibid., 25–31.

36. Ibid., 31–36. The key in cases where governance was weak because of lack of resources would be to invest in improving governance, emphasizing the promotion of the rule of law, political and social rights, accountable and efficient public administration, sound economic policies, and support for civil society.

37. Ibid., 36–40. The overview argued that development programs were systematically overlooking major MDG priorities, such as investing in regional integration, managing the environment, upgrading technology, and promoting gender equality. Programs were even failing to make investments in such core areas as roads, electricity, adequate shelter, disease control, soil nutrients, and sexual and reproductive health. The overview added that policy incoherence was pervasive and was a core problem for many developed countries.

The overview also noted that too often bilateral aid was highly unpredictable and was targeted toward technical assistance and emergency aid rather than investments, long-term capacity, and institutional support. It was often tied to contractors from donor countries and was driven by separate donor objectives rather than coordinated to support a national plan. Too often it was directed toward poorly governed countries for geopolitical reasons, and it was almost never documented systematically or evaluated for results. "Low-quality official development assistance has fostered the serious misperception that aid does not work and has thereby threatened long-term public support for development assistance," the report held. It maintained that aid works "and promotes economic growth as well as advances in specific sectors, when it is directed to real investments on the ground in countries with reasonable governance." The problem was not aid, "it is how and when aid has been delivered, to which countries, and in what amounts." The project had calculated that only 24 percent of bilateral ODA to low-income countries in 2002 was actually financing MDG investments on the ground. Ibid., 39–42.

38. Ibid., table 4.

39. Ibid., 45. The report noted that the UN Millennium Project had done the first "bottom-up needs assessment of the country-level investments required to achieve the Goals." Although these estimates "need to be refined through the real country-level

processes," the report estimated the total cost to be on the order of $70–80 per capita per year in 2006, increasing to $120–160 per capita per year in 2015. While middle-income countries "will generally be able to afford these investments on their own," the low-income countries "even after they initiate a major increase in their resource mobilization, will require $40–$50 per capita in external finance in 2006, rising to $70–$100 in 2015."

40. Ibid., 40–46.

41. Ibid., 46–47. The main proposal that emerged from the project in this regard was that global political leaders should first agree to a conveniently distant long-term target (for example 2025) for the total removal of barriers to merchandise trade, a substantial and across-the-board liberalization of trade in services, and universal enforcement of the principle of reciprocity and nondiscrimination.

42. Ibid., 47–49.

43. Ibid., 50–53. The criteria for selecting these fast-track countries were a combination of recently established criteria for "deserving" governments under the HIPC Initiative. These included governments that had acceded to the African Peer Review Mechanism of the New Partnership for African Development and governments with favorable reviews through World Bank–IMF assessments of poverty reduction strategy papers. The project presented an overview of sixty-three potential candidates for MDG fast-tracking based on these criteria, of which a large number met the criteria set by only one or several of these institutions. The single criterion most frequently met was the existence of a poverty reduction strategy paper; as of 20 December 2004, forty-two countries had met this requirement. See ibid., box 10.

44. Ibid., 53–55, quote on 53.

45. Ibid., 55. The increasing government expenditures (up to 4 percent of GDP through 2015) "will likely need to be raised through a broad-based revenue source such as a value-added tax, as well as by rechanneling current low-priority spending into higher priority MDG investments."

46. Ibid., 55. In a typical low-income country with an average per capita income of $300 in 2005, external financing of public interventions would be required in the order of 10–20 percent of GNP. For these countries, the cost of achieving the MDGs would need to be split roughly evenly between domestic finance and ODA, according to the report.

47. Ibid., 55–56. The adjusted calculations indicated that for DAC countries to meet the MDGs, the overall ODA required was $135 billion in 2006, increasing to $195 billion in 2015, equivalent to 0.44 and 0.54 percent of the anticipated donor GNP. These calculations suggested that donors should prepare to double their ODA-to-GNP ratios during 2006–2015, increasing to 0.5 percent of GNP or above. Since the calculations omitted certain categories of aid (such as major infrastructure projects, increased spending on adjustments to climate change, postconflict reconstruction, and other high-profile geopolitical priorities), the project settled on a recommendation that donors should commit themselves to reaching the long-standing target of 0.7 percent of GNP by 2015. Of this, roughly three-quarters was to be directed to the MDGs and the rest to other ODA needs. Ibid., 56–59.

48. Ibid., 60–65.

49. United Nations, *The Millennium Development Goals Report 2007* (New York: United Nations, Department of Economic and Social Affairs DESA, June 2007).

50. Ibid., 3.

51. Ibid., 6–7.

52. Ibid., 8.

53. Ibid., 10–11. However, the report pointed out several weaknesses associated with the statistical basis on which the overview was based. Many children who were

enrolled were not actually attending school. Moreover, neither enrollment nor attendance figures reflect the number of children who do not attend school regularly. Official data are not usually available from countries in conflict or postconflict situations. The children most likely to drop out of school or to not attend at all "are those from poorer households or living in rural areas," the report added, noting a structural problem: "Nearly a third of children of primary school age in rural areas of the developing world are out of school, compared with 18 per cent of children in the same age group living in cities."

54. Ibid., 12–13.

55. Ibid., 14–15.

56. Ibid., 15. Immunization programs stagnated between 1990 and 1999. Since then immunization has rapidly gained ground. For developing regions, the percentage of children twelve to twenty-three months of age that received at least one dose of measles vaccine increased from 71 percent in 1990 to 75 percent in 2005.

57. Ibid., 16.

58. Ibid., 17.

59. Ibid., 18–20.

60. Ibid., 20–21. In Sub-Saharan Africa, only 5 percent of children under five slept under insecticide-treated bednets. In rural areas of countries where malaria is endemic, the burden of malaria was often highest and the availability of bednets the lowest.

61. Ibid., 24. In developed regions, emissions of carbon dioxide had increased from 9.7 billion metric tons in 1990 to 12.5 in 2004; in developing regions from 6.9 to 12.4 during the same period. The regional distribution was uneven: in several regions, carbon dioxide emissions had doubled (in Eastern Asia from 2.9 to 5.6, in Southern Asia from 1.0 to 2.0, in Northern Africa from 0.2 to 0.5); in other regions, emissions remained at a low relative level or were even reduced (Oceania less than 0.1, CIS countries down from 3.2 to 2.4). In Sub-Saharan Africa, it increased from 0.5 to 0.7 and in Latin America and the Caribbean it increased from 1.1 to 1.4. Eastern Asia contributed most to the increase recorded for the developing regions. However, the countries of the developed regions were the main polluters on a per capita basis. While developed regions accounted for about 12 tons per person on average, Western Asia, the highest per capita emitter among developing regions, produced less than half that amount, and Sub-Saharan Africa produced less than one tenth of that amount.

62. Ibid., 24–25.

63. Ibid., 25–26. Regional differences were also significant for this indicator. Sub-Saharan Africa came out worst—the proportion with basic sanitation had increased from 32 percent in 1990 to 37 percent in 2004, far from the target of 66 percent in 2015 established for the region. Next followed Southern and Eastern Asia, where progress had been much greater—up from 20 to 38 percent and from 24 to 45 percent, respectively.

64. Ibid., 26–27.

65. Ibid., 28–29.

66. Ibid., 30.

67. Ibid.

68. Ibid., 29–31.

69. United Nations, *Delivering on the Global Partnership for Achieving the Millennium Development Goals,* MDG Gap Task Force Report 2008 (New York: United Nations, 2008).

70. Ibid., ix–xiii.

71. Ibid., vii–viii, 57; quote at viii.

72. Ibid. The task force observed that in recent years, non-DAC donors, developing-country donors, and private funds had increased the availability of financial

resources for development. Total ODA from non-DAC had increased from $1.5 billion in 2000 to $5.1 billion in 2006, according to estimates. The report concluded that it was necessary to improve dialogue and coordination with these new stakeholders to avoid fragmenting further aid and increasing the transaction costs among recipient countries.

73. Ibid., viii.

74. See Jan Pronk, "Collateral Damage or Calculated Default? The Millennium Development Goals and the Politics of Globalisation," Inaugural Address as Professor of the Theory and Practice of International Development delivered on 11 December 2003 at the Institute of Social Studies, The Hague, the Netherlands (mimeo).

75. For critical scrutiny at an early point, see several contributions in Richard Black and Howard White, eds., *Targeting Development: Critical Perspectives on the Millennium Development Goals* (London: Routledge, 2004), especially Howard White and Richard Black, "Millennium Development Goals: A Drop in the Ocean?," 1–24; and Howard White, "Using Development Goals and Targets for Donor Agency Performance Measurement," 47–76.

76. For a discussion, see Paul Hoebink and Olav Stokke, "Introduction: European Development Co-operation at the Beginning of the New Millennium," in *Perspectives on European Development Co-operation,* ed. Paul Hoebink and Olav Stokke (London: Routledge, 2005), 1–31. See also Sven Grimm, *European Development Co-operation to 2020—The EU as an Answer to Global Challenges?* Briefing Paper No. 1 (Bonn: European Development Cooperation to 2020 Project, 2008).

15. THE CONTRIBUTION OF THE UN SYSTEM TO INTERNATIONAL DEVELOPMENT COOPERATION

1. For the FAO, see Gove Hambidge, *The Story of FAO* (New York: D. Van Nostrand Company, Inc., 1955); for the WFP, see D. John Shaw, *The UN World Food Programme and the Development of Food Aid* (Basingstoke: Palgrave, 2001); for UNICEF, see Maggie Black, *Children First, The Story of UNICEF, Past and Present* (Oxford: Oxford University Press for UNICEF, 1996) and Judith M. Spiegelman and UNICEF, *We Are the Children: A Celebration of UNICEF's First Forty Years* (Boston: The Atlantic Monthly Press, 1986); for the UNDP, see Craig N. Murphy, *The United Nations Development Programme, A Better Way?* (Cambridge: Cambridge University Press, 2006). For the World Bank see, inter alia, Edward S. Mason and Robert E. Asher, *The World Bank since Bretton Woods: The Origins, Policies, Operations, and Impact of the International Bank for Reconstruction and Development and the Other Members of the World Bank Group: The International Finance Corporation, The International Development Association, The International Centre for Settlement of Investment Disputes* (Washington, D.C.: The Brookings Institution, 1973); and Devesh Kapur, John P. Lewis, and Richard Webb, *The World Bank: Its First Half Century,* vol. 1, *History* (Washington, D.C.: Brookings Institution Press,1997).

2. In 1989, the UNDP observed that at the time of the consensus, its share of the UN's technical cooperation funding was 75 percent. Despite acceptance of the UNDP's central funding role in the consensus, its share in the late 1980s was only 30 percent if the resources of UNICEF and WFP were included. UNDP, "UNDP and World Development by the Year 2000," Report of the Administrator to the Governing Council of the UNDP, June 1989, dated 8 May 1989 (mimeo, unedited version), 28.

3. "Follow-Up to the Outcome of the Millennium Summit," General Assembly document A/61/583, 20 November 2006.

4. Ibid., 9–10.

5. Ibid., 10.

6. The annual report for 1993 discussed the changes in the international community's thinking about and approaches to development. The UNDP's contribution was based on a concept of sustainable human development that included alleviating poverty, generating employment, empowering disadvantaged groups in society, fostering equity, and regenerating the environment. The administrator said that the UNDP had been promoting the concept and reorienting its cooperation at all levels to support national efforts to achieve and sustain human development in economic, sociocultural, environmental, political, and other terms. *Yearbook of the United Nations 1993* (New York: United Nations, Office of Public Information, 1994), 687.

7. Stephen D. Krasner defines international regimes as "principles, norms, rules and decision-making procedures around which actor expectations converge in a given issue-area." See Krasner, "Structural Causes and Regime Consequences: Regimes as Intervening Variables," *International Organization* 36, no. 2 (1982): 185.

8. The efforts of the World Bank during the 1990s to design and promote new directions in development thinking are systemized in the 1999/2000 *World Development Report.* The key themes have been macroeconomic policy and trade (1991, 1997); government, regulation, and corruption (1996, 1997); social safety nets (1990, 1995); health (1993); education (1998/1999); infrastructure (1994); the environment (1992, 1998/1999); rural strategy (1990); private-sector strategy (1996, 1997); and gender (1990, 1993, 1998/1999). See World Bank, *World Development Report 1999/2000: Entering the 21st Century* (New York: Oxford University Press and the World Bank, 2000).

9. OECD, *Shaping the 21st Century: The Contribution of Development Co-operation* (Paris: OECD, 1996).

10. See IMF, OECD, United Nations, World Bank, *2000: A Better World for All* (Washington, D.C.: IMF and World Bank; New York: United Nations). This document was signed in June 2000 by the heads of these leading organizations: Kofi A. Annan (the UN), Donald J. Johnston (OECD), Horst Köhler (IMF), and James D. Wolfensohn (World Bank Group). In this negotiating process, the position of the United Nations regarding the issues involved was contained in Kofi Annan, *We the Peoples: The Role of the United Nations in the Twenty First Century* (New York: United Nations, 2000).

11. For an interesting analysis of the process, see David Hulme, *The Making of the Millennium Development Goals: Human Development Meets Results-Based Management In an Imperfect World* (Manchester: Brooks World Poverty Institute, 2007). Hulme pays a particular tribute to the role played by Claire Short, the secretary of state for international development of the United Kingdom during this period, and her three fellow development ministers in the so-called Utstein group, all of whom were women. In the power vacuum at that time created by the lack of U.S. leadership in this policy field, Short used the 1996 OECD international development goals to convince her cabinet colleagues and sway UK public opinion. Then "Short hawked them [the seven OECD international development goals] around the world" and sold them to African and Asian heads of state and ministers (8).

12. Ibid., 12–19. In March 2001, the World Bank convened a meeting to reconcile the positions. The meeting was attended by more than 200 delegates from the multilateral agencies, bilateral donors, and several developing countries. The main issue to be resolved was whether to continue with a twin-track process in which the OECD and the UN both got their own way or to reconcile the goals, which would mean that Kofi Annan would have to modify the agreement reached at the Millennium Conference and the OECD would have to change the international development goals that had been agreed to in 1996 and that the UN, the World Bank, and the IMF had agreed to in June 2000. Again a compromise was reached: there should be a division of labor between

the approach of the international finance institutions (the PRSPs) and the approach of the United Nations (the MDGs). A task force was set up with members from the Development Assistance Committee (OECD), the World Bank, the IMF, and the UNDP to reach concordance between the two sides. This task force finalized the Millennium Development Goals.

13. Some ideas of the past do not seem to thrive within the confines of the new consensus, especially the "utopian" development paradigms of the mid-1970s. See Dag Hammarskjöld Foundation, *What Now—Another Development* (Uppsala: Dag Hammarskjöld Foundation, 1975); International Federation for Development Alternatives, *A United Nations Development Strategy for the 80s and Beyond: Participation of the "Third System" in Its Elaboration and Implementation* (Nyon: International Federation for Development Alternatives, 1978); Marc Nerfin, ed., *Another Development: Approaches and Strategies* (Uppsala: Hammarskjöld Foundation, 1977). Such ideas are still around, waiting to be picked up when the time becomes ripe. In the first years of the new millennium, they are perhaps most strongly represented in movements protesting globalization.

14. Until 1974, the dues for the UN's regular activities from the United States were 33 percent of the total expenses. In 1972, the United States requested and obtained a reduced share of 25 percent. This agreement had implications for voluntary U.S. contributions to the UN programs and funds, including to the UNDP, which also were not to exceed 25 percent.

15. Unilateralism seeks to attain foreign policy objectives as defined within a domestic framework by means of its own national instruments, using bilateral diplomacy as well as economic and military power. However, multilateral solutions are not a priori excluded from a unilateral approach if the primary objectives are not compromised; rather, they are circumstantial and are not sought on a permanent or committing basis. Multilateralism, in contrast, seeks to realize foreign policy objectives through international cooperation in combination with national foreign-policy instruments. This strategy can involve ad hoc solutions but will have a preference for long-term collective commitments and international regimes associated with international law.

16. For the major provider of multilateral ODA, this "indirect" control might at times be more than merely indirect. Craig Murphy notes that the UNDP's pursuit of policies that conflicted with major U.S. foreign policy interests was no cakewalk. "To win over donors, administrators have had to be unusually creative. Moreover, because successive administrators have (out of loyalty as much as out of necessity) engaged the most conservative wing of the US Republican Party—a group consistently opposed to the UN visions of international relations and of development—these executive heads have honed their 'sailor's skills' on the roughest of seas." Murphy, *The United Nations Development Programme,* 21.

17. Craig Murphy notes that until 1999, "the man nominated by the US President became UNDP's Administrator. It was a matter of coincidence that when the post became vacant, the President, who always nominated someone from his own party, was on most occasions a Republican"; Murphy, *The United Nations Development Programme,* 21.

18. Ibid., 234.

19. The best and most balanced discussion that I have found of the case for development assistance and the main arguments against is Roger C. Riddell, *Foreign Aid Reconsidered* (Baltimore, Md.: Johns Hopkins University Press, 1987).

20. Large amounts have been provided over the years in ODA, and NGOs have increasingly emerged as major donors of aid. Global ODA since 1960 by the members

of OECD Development Assistance Committee increased from a modest $58 billion in the 1960s to reach $130 billion in the 1970s, $339 billion in the 1980s, $558 billion in the 1990s, and $420 billion in the six-year period 2000 to 2005 (see appendix).

Roger C. Riddell has reminded us that NGOs and civil society organizations have increasingly emerged as major donors of aid, along with organizations that provide humanitarian and relief aid. These actors have not operated solely as channels for ODA provided by governments. According to Riddell, in 2003 the amount of money NGOs raised through private donations to finance their own development and humanitarian aid activities topped $10 billion for the first time and amounted to almost $15 billion if in-kind contributions were added to the total. "More than two dozen of the largest NGOs, such as ActionAid and Caritas, have annual budgets in excess of US$100 mil-lion; some, such as Save the Children, Oxfam and the Red Cross, double or triple that amount; and the giants, the Cooperative for Assistance and Relief Everywhere (CARE) and the Catholic Relief Services, have annual budgets in excess of half a billion dollars." Roger C. Riddell, *Does Foreign Aid Really Work?* (London: Oxford University Press, 2007), 8–9.

21. According to the calculations by C. J. Jepma, procurement tying reduces the real value of aid in financial terms by 15 to 30 percent. In addition, administering tied aid may be complicated and costly for the recipient country. A classic case from Kenya in the 1980s, where a water development program received eighteen different types of pumps supplied by different donors who had tied their aid, may illustrate the point: it is easy to imagine the problems involved in running such a program when service and spare parts are required. See C. J. Jepma, *The Tying of Aid* (Paris: OECD, 1991); and C. J. Jepma, *Inter-Nation Policy Co-ordination and Untying of Aid* (Aldershot: Avebury, 1994).

22. This practice was controversial when introduced in the early 1990s. When Canada first reported a figure for in-Canada refugee support in 1993, it amounted to 8 percent of total Canadian ODA. Previously (from 1979), administrative costs had been reported as ODA. OECD, *OECD Journal on Development, Development Co-operation Report 2006* (Paris: OECD DAC, 2007), 231.

23. Robert Cassen and Associates, *Does Aid Work?* (Oxford: Clarendon Press, 1986), 11.

24. UNDP, *Investing in Development: A Practical Plan to Achieve the Millennium Development Goals: Overview* (New York: UNDP, Millennium Project, 2005).

25. Ibon Foundation, *The Reality of Aid 2006* (London: Zed Books Ltd., 2006), 8. See also Nagaire Woods, "The Shifting Politics of Foreign Aid," *International Affairs* 81, no. 2 (2005): 393–409.

26. Phantom aid has been defined as aid that is:

- not targeted for poverty reduction
- double-counted as debt relief
- overpriced and ineffective Technical Assistance
- tied to goods and services from the donor country
- poorly coordinated and with high transaction costs
- too unpredictable to be useful to the recipient
- spent on immigration-related costs in the donor country
- spent on excess administration costs

In 2003, aid that fell in these categories totaled about $42 billion. ActionAid, *Real Aid, An Agenda for Making Aid Work,* vol. 2 (Johannesburg: ActionAid International, 2005), 17.

27. Ibid. ActionAid broke down its findings to reveal the scale of the gap between official and actual aid:

- For G7 countries, official ODA was US$50 billion in 2003, or 0.21% of their combined GNI. Yet real aid was less than a third of this sum at US$16 billion, or 0.07% of GNI. In other words, when phantom aid is taken out, the G7 countries are only 10% of the way to the 0.7% target.

- Eighty-six cents in every dollar in American aid is phantom aid, largely because it is so heavily tied to the purchase of US goods and services, and because it is so badly targeted at poor countries.

- Just 11% of French aid is real aid. France spends nearly US$2 billion of its aid budget each year on Technical Assistance, and US$0.5 billion on refugee and immigration expenditures in France. Forty per cent of French aid is provided as debt relief, much of which is an accounting exercise rather than a real resource transfer.

ActionAid continued, "In real terms, the Norwegians are nearly 40 times more generous per person than the Americans, and 4 times more generous than the average Briton" (ibid.).

28. Ibid.

29. ActionAid, *Real Aid, Making Technical Aid Work* (Johannesburg: ActionAid International, 2006), 9–13. ActionAid defined much of the technical assistance as phantom aid that is overpriced and ineffective and argued that like a relic from an earlier age, technical assistance has been largely insulated from donors' efforts to improve the quality of their aid (3). Needless to say, such assessments met with protests from aid agencies.

30. Riddell, *Does Foreign Aid Really Work?,* 254.

APPENDIX

1. In the early period, colonial powers tended to include assistance to their dependencies in the reported transfers. French ODA may illustrate the point: France attained the target set for the Second Development Decade (0.7 percent of GNP) in 1981. However, this figure included its assistance to its dependencies and colonies, Départements d'Outre-Mer and Territoires d'Outre-Mer. If the assistance to the dependencies and colonies had been excluded, the performance would have been reduced to 0.46 percent of GNP that year. Olav Stokke, "European Aid Policies: Some Emerging Trends," in *European Development Assistance,* vol. 1, *Policies and Performance,* ed. Stokke (Tilburg: EADI, 1984), 22.

2. OECD, *Development Assistance, 1970 Review* (Paris: OECD DAC, 1970).

3. Portugal was a special case; the ODA and official transfers reported were almost exclusively transfers to Portuguese colonies (at that time claimed to be "part" of Portugal).

4. Lester Pearson, *Partners in Development: Report of the Commission on International Development* (New York: Praeger, 1969), 148–149.

5. Ibid., 215; quote on 229.

6. When deflated by the DAC Secretariat's ODA deflator (1979=100), the perfor-

mance becomes less impressive. See OECD, *Development Co-operation, 1981 Review* (Paris: OECD DAC, 1981), table A.8.

7. Much of this assistance went to political allies, particularly to Cuba, Korea PDR, and Vietnam; $2 billion (about one-fifth of the total assistance provided in the 1970s) was left for the remaining developing countries and multilateral agencies when the "political" assistance to these allies and to three other allies (Afghanistan, Kampuchea, and Laos) is deducted. A similar picture appears for the East European countries. OECD, *Development Co-operation, 1981 Review,* Annex I, tables 1 and 2, and calculations based on data in this source.

8. Ibid., tables II.F.1. and 2 and calculations based on data in this source.

9. Ibid., tables VI-3; B.2, IX-1, and IX-7.

10. As calculated at 1988 prices and exchange rates, total DAC contributions had increased from $38.3 billion in 1980 to $47.3 billion in 1989: a real growth in ODA had taken place.

11. OECD, *Development Co-operation, 1986 Review* (Paris: OECD DAC, 1986), table V-1.

12. Ibid., 78.

13. Ibid., 81–83; OECD, *Development Co-operation, 1991 Review* (Paris: OECD DAC, 1991), table VIII-1, and calculations based on data in this source.

14. Non-DAC members of the OECD included Iceland, Luxembourg, Spain, and Portugal.

15. OECD, *Development Co-operation, 1991 Review,* table 31.

16. Before the Monterrey conference in Mexico in 2002, the European Councils (in Gothenburg in June and in Laeken in December 2001) adopted resolutions to substantially increase European ODA for "the fight against poverty." Later on, the EU committed its member states to provide 0.39 percent of their GNI as ODA by 2006, a decision that also applied to new members. Following this decision, EU countries that had been lagging behind made commitments to improve their performance: Austria, Germany, Greece, Italy, Portugal, and Spain committed to reach 0.33 percent of GNI by 2006. Paul Hoebink and Olav Stokke, "Introduction: European Development Co-operation at the Beginning of a New Millennium," in *Perspectives on European Development Co-operation,* ed. Hoebink and Stokke (London: Routledge, 2005), 26–28.

17. OECD, *OECD Journal on Development, Development Co-operation Report 2006* (Paris: OECD DAC, 2007), 70; OECD, *OECD Journal on Development, Development Co-operation Report 2007* (Paris: OECD DAC, 2008), 71. In 2006, Iraq ($15.2 billion) was followed by Nigeria ($8.7 billion), China ($2.5 billion), Indonesia ($2.4 billion), and Afghanistan ($2.3 billion).

18. In both 2005 and 2006, Iraq was the main recipient of ODA from several other DAC countries, including Austria, Canada, Finland, Italy, Japan, and Switzerland. Interestingly, however, Iraq was not among the top ten recipients of ODA from Denmark, Greece, Ireland, Luxembourg, New Zealand, and Norway during these years or from the European Union. OECD, *OECD Journal on Development, Development Co-operation Report 2006,* 70–77, 79, 82–86, 88–90, 92–95, and 97; OECD, *Report 2007,* 72–99.

19. OECD, *OECD Journal on Development, Development Co-operation Report 2007,* tables 20 and 21.

20. Ibid., table 21.

INDEX

Page numbers in italics refer to tables.

ABOUT THE AUTHOR

Olav Stokke is Senior Researcher at the Norwegian Institute of International Affairs, where he served for several years as Research Director, Deputy Director, and head of the Department of Development Studies. For twenty-four years, he served as the convener of the working group on aid policy and performance of the European Association of Development Research and Training Institutes. He has been the editor of the Nordic journal *Forum for Development Studies* since 1974. His latest books are *Perspectives on European Development Co-operation* (with Paul Hoebink); *Food Aid and Human Security* (with Edward Clay); and *Policy Coherence in Development Co-operation* (with Jacques Forster).

ABOUT THE UNITED NATIONS INTELLECTUAL HISTORY PROJECT

Ideas and concepts are a main driving force in human progress, and they are arguably the most important contribution of the United Nations. Yet there has been little historical study of the origins and evolution of the history of economic and social ideas cultivated within the world organization and their impact on wider thinking and international action. The United Nations Intellectual History Project (UNIHP) is filling this knowledge gap about the UN by tracing the origin and analyzing the evolution of key ideas and concepts about international economic and social development that were born or have been nurtured under UN auspices. UNIHP began operations in mid-1999 when the secretariat, the hub of a worldwide network of specialists on the UN, was established at the Ralph Bunche Institute for International Studies of The CUNY Graduate Center.

UNIHP has two main components, oral history interviews and a series of books on specific topics. The seventy-nine in-depth oral history interviews with leading contributors to crucial ideas and concepts within the UN system provide the raw material for this volume and other volumes. In addition, complete and indexed transcripts are available to researchers and the general public in an electronic book format on CD-Rom distributed by the secretariat.

The project has commissioned fifteen studies about the major economic and social ideas or concepts that are central to UN activity, which are being published by Indiana University Press.

- *Ahead of the Curve? UN Ideas and Global Challenges,* by Louis Emmerij, Richard Jolly, and Thomas G. Weiss (2001)

- *Unity and Diversity in Development Ideas: Perspectives from the UN Regional Commissions,* edited by Yves Berthelot with contributions from Adebayo Adedeji, Yves Berthelot, Leelananda de Silva, Paul Rayment, Gert Rosenthal, and Blandine Destremeau (2003)

- *Quantifying the World: UN Contributions to Statistics,* by Michael Ward (2004)

- *UN Contributions to Development Thinking and Practice,* by Richard Jolly, Louis Emmerij, Dharam Ghai, and Frédéric Lapeyre (2004)

- *The UN and Global Political Economy: Trade, Finance, and Development,* by John Toye and Richard Toye (2004)

- *UN Voices: The Struggle for Development and Social Justice,* by Thomas G. Weiss, Tatiana Carayannis, Louis Emmerij, and Richard Jolly (2005)

- *Women, Development, and the United Nations: A Sixty-Year Quest for Equality and Justice,* by Devaki Jain (2005)

- *Human Security and the UN: A Critical History,* by S. Neil MacFarlane and Yuen Foong Khong (2006)

- *Human Rights at the UN: The Political History of Universal Justice,* Roger Normand and Sarah Zaidi (2007)

- *Preventive Diplomacy at the UN,* by Bertrand G. Ramcharan (2008)

- *The UN and Transnational Corporations: From Code of Conduct to Global Compact,* by Tagi Sagafi-nejad in collaboration with John H. Dunning (2008)

- *The UN and Development: From Aid to Cooperation,* by Olav Stokke (2009)

Forthcoming Titles:

- *UN Ideas That Changed the World,* by Richard Jolly, Louis Emmerij, and Thomas G. Weiss

- *The UN and Global Governance: An Unfinished History,* by Thomas G. Weiss and Ramesh Thakur

- *The UN and the Global Commons: Development without Destruction,* by Nico Schrijver

The project also collaborated on *The Oxford Handbook on the United Nations,* edited by Thomas G. Weiss and Sam Daws, published by Oxford University Press in 2007.

For further information, the interested reader should contact:

UN Intellectual History Project
The CUNY Graduate Center
365 Fifth Avenue, Suite 5203
New York, New York 10016-4309
212-817-1920 Tel
212-817-1565 Fax
UNHistory@gc.cuny.edu
www.unhistory.org